펼쳐 보면 느껴집니다

단 한 줄도 배움의 공백이 생기지 않도록
문장 한 줄마다 20년이 넘는
해커스의 영어교육 노하우를 담았음을

덮고 나면 확신합니다

수많은 선생님의 목소리와
정확한 출제 데이터 분석으로 꽉 찬
교재 한 권이면 충분함을

해커스북 중·고등
HackersBook.com

해커스 중학영어듣기 모의고사 24회가 특별한 이유!

최신 경향과 출제 패턴을 반영한 문제로 실전 대비!

1

최신 출제경향을 그대로 반영한

양질의 실전 모의고사

2

듣기 능력을 한 단계 업그레이드해주는

만점 도전 고난도 모의고사

3

시험에 매번 나오는 기출 유형을 익히는

14개 대표 기출문제

해커스 중학영어듣기 모의고사 24회

Level 1 Level 2 Level 3

다양한 버전의 음성으로 편리한 학습!

4

수준별로 속도를
선택해서 듣는

**기본 속도/1.2배속/
1.5배속 MP3**

5

복습이 간편해지는

**딕테이션 MP3/
문항별 MP3**

6

모든 음성 버전을
한 손에 쏙!

**문제 음성 듣기
QR코드**

해커스 중학영어듣기 모의고사 시리즈를 검토해주신 선생님들

경기
김하윤 프라임EM보습학원
이미림 다능학원
장윤진 골든클래스아카데미
조은혜 이든영수학원
최유리 제이엠학원
최희정 SJ클쌤영어

광주
박지수 JC에듀영어수학학원
조성영 이지스터디학원

대전
신주희 파써블영어학원

부산
정호경 A+단과학원

서울
이계윤 씨앤씨(목동) 학원
이지안 제임스영어
편영우 자이언학원

전북
김효성 연세입시학원

충남
성승민 SDH어학원 불당캠퍼스

해커스 어학연구소 자문위원단 3기

강원
박정선 잉글리쉬클럽
최현주 최샘영어

경기
강민정 YLP김진성열정어학원
강상훈 평촌RTS학원
강지인 강지인영어학원
권계미 A&T+ 영어
김미아 김쌤영어학원
김설화 업라이트잉글리쉬
김성재 스윗스터디학원
김세훈 모두의학원
김수아 더스터디(The STUDY)
김영아 백송고등학교
김유경 벨트어학원
김유경 포시즌스어학원
김유동 이스턴영어학원
김지숙 위디벨럽학원
김지현 이지프레임영어학원
김해빈 해빛영어학원
김현지 지앤비영어학원
박가영 한민고등학교
박영서 스윗스터디학원
박은별 더킹영수학원
박재홍 록키어학원
성승민 SDH어학원 불당캠퍼스
신소연 Ashley English
오귀연 루나영어학원
유신애 에듀포커스학원
윤소정 ILP이화어학원
이동진 이룸학원
이상미 버밍엄영어교습소
이연경 명품M비욘드수학영어학원
이은수 광주세종학원
이지혜 리케이온
이진희 이엠원영수학원
이충기 영어나무
이효명 갈매리드앤톡영어독서학원
임한글 Apsun앞선영어학원
장광명 엠케이영어학원
전상호 평촌이지어학원
정선영 코어플러스영어학원
정준 고양외국어고등학교
조연아 카이트학원
채기림 고려대학교EIE영어학원
최지영 다른영어학원
최한나 석사영수전문
최희정 SJ클쌤영어학원
현지환 모두의학원
홍태경 공감국어영어전문학원

경남
강다훤 더(the)오르다영어학원
라승희 아이작잉글리쉬
박주언 유니크학원
배송현 두잇영어교습소
안윤서 어썸영어학원
임진희 어썸영어학원

경북
권현민 삼성영어석적우방교실
김으뜸 EIE영어학원 옥계캠퍼스
배세왕 비케이영수전문고등관학원
유영선 아이비티어학원

광주
김유희 김유희영어학원
서희연 SDL영어수학학원
오진우 SLT어학원수학원
정영철 정영철영어전문학원
최경옥 봉선중학교

대구
권익재 제이슨영어
김명일 독학인학원
김보곤 베스트영어
김연정 달서고등학교
김혜란 김혜란영어학원
문애주 프렌즈입시학원
박정근 공부의힘pnk학원
박희숙 열공열강영어수학학원
신동기 신통외국어학원
위영선 위영선영어학원
윤창원 공터영어학원 상인센터
이승현 학문당입시학원
이주현 이주현영어학원
이헌욱 이헌욱영어학원
장준현 장쌤독해종결영어학원
최윤정 최강영어학원

대전
곽선영 위드유학원
김지운 더포스둔산학원
박미현 라시움영어대동학원
박세리 EM101학원

부산
김건희 레지나잉글리쉬 영어학원
김미나 위드중고등영어학원
박수진 정모클영어국어학원
박수진 지니잉글리쉬
박인숙 리더스영어전문학원
옥지윤 더센텀영어학원
윤진희 위니드영어전문교습소
이종혁 진수학원
정혜인 엠티엠영어학원
조정래 알파카의영어농장
주태양 솔라영어학원

서울
Erica Sull 하버드브레인영어학원
강고은 케이앤학원
강신아 교우학원
공현미 이은재어학원
권영진 경동고등학교
김나영 프라임클래스영어학원
김달수 대일외국어고등학교
김대니 채움학원
김문영 창문여자고등학교
김정은 강북뉴스터디학원
김혜경 대동세무고등학교
남혜원 함영원입시전문학원
노시은 케이앤학원
박선정 강북세일학원
박수진 이은재어학원
박지수 이플러스영수학원
서승희 함영원입시전문학원
양세희 양세희수능영어학원
우정용 제임스영어앤드학원
이박원 이박원어학원
이승혜 스텔라영어
이정욱 이은재어학원
이지연 중계케이트영어학원
임예찬 학습컨설턴트
장지희 고려대학교사범대학부속고등학교
정미라 미라정영어학원
조민규 조민규영어
채가희 대성세그루영수학원

울산
김기태 그라티아어학원
이민주 로이아카데미
홍영민 더이안영어전문학원

인천
강재민 스터디위드제이쌤
고현순 정상학원
권효진 Genie's English
김솔 전문과외
김정아 밀턴영어학원
서상천 최정서학원
이윤주 트리플원
최예영 영웅아카데미

전남
강희진 강희진영어학원
김두환 해남맨체스터영수학원
송승연 송승연영수학원
윤세광 비상구영어학원

전북
김길자 맨투맨학원
김미영 링크영어학원
김효성 연세입시학원
노빈나 노빈나영어전문학원
라성남 하포드어학원
박재훈 위니드수학지앤비영어학원
박향숙 STA영어전문학원
서종원 서종원영어학원
이상훈 나는학원
장지원 링컨더글라스학원
지근영 한솔영어수학학원
최성령 연세입시학원
최혜영 이든영어수학학원

제주
김랑 KLS어학원
박자은 KLS어학원

충남
김예지 더배움프라임영수학원
김철홍 청경학원
노태겸 최상위학원

충북
라은경 이화윤스영어교습소
신유정 비타민영어클리닉학원

영어듣기 만점을 위한 완벽한 실전 대비서

해커스 중학영어듣기 모의고사 24회

LEVEL 2

해커스 어학연구소

기출 유형 분석

실전 모의고사

고난도 모의고사

책의 구성과 특징

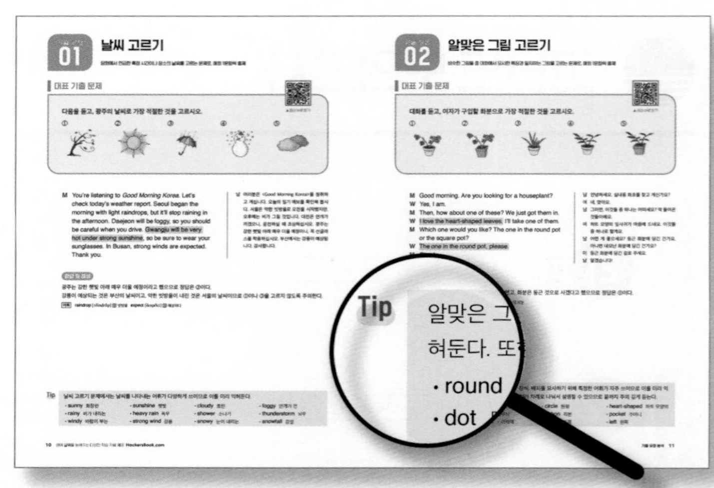

기출 유형 분석

<전국 16개 시·도교육청 공동 주관 영어듣기능력평가>에 꼭 나오는 문제 유형을 철저히 분석했습니다. 14개 대표 기출 문제를 풀어보며 듣기 시험 전략을 적용해볼 수 있습니다.

유형별 빈출 오답 포인트나 자주 출제되는 단어, 표현 등 유용한 정보를 **Tip**에서 추가로 익힐 수 있습니다.

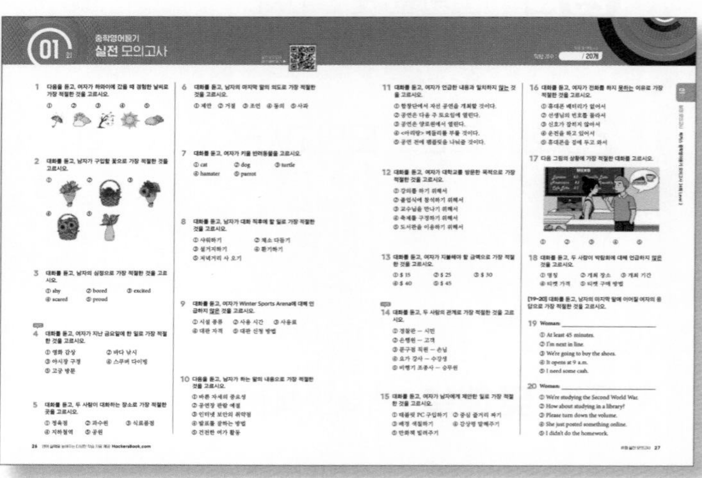

실전 모의고사 20회

실제 시험과 유형 및 출제 순서, 난이도가 동일한 20회분의 실전 모의고사 문제를 풀어보며 문제 풀이 능력을 향상시키고 듣기 실력을 쌓을 수 있습니다.

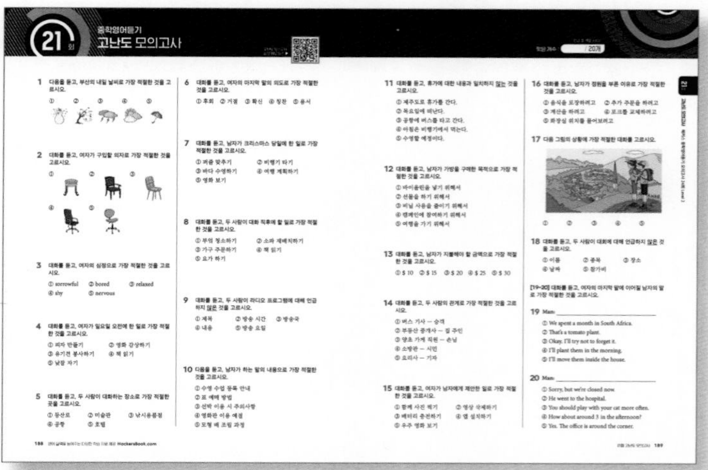

고난도 모의고사 4회

실제 시험보다 길이가 더 길고 어려운 표현이 쓰인 4회분의 고난도 모의고사를 풀어보며 실제 시험에서 어려운 문제가 나와도 흔들리지 않고 고득점을 받을 수 있도록 완벽히 대비할 수 있습니다.

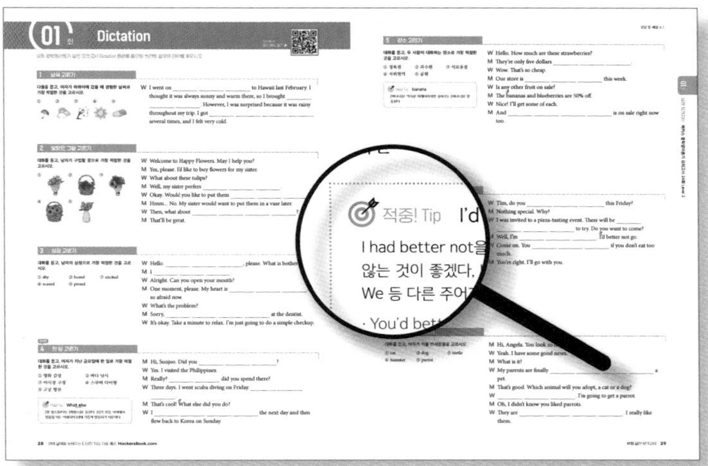

Dictation

매회 문제 풀이 후 Dictation을 하며 정답 단서를 스스로 확인하고, 잘 못 들었던 부분도 다시 들으며 복습할 수 있습니다.
연음 등 잘 들리지 않는 발음과 빈출 표현을 **적중! Tip**에서 짚어보며 듣기 기본기를 확실히 다질 수 있습니다.

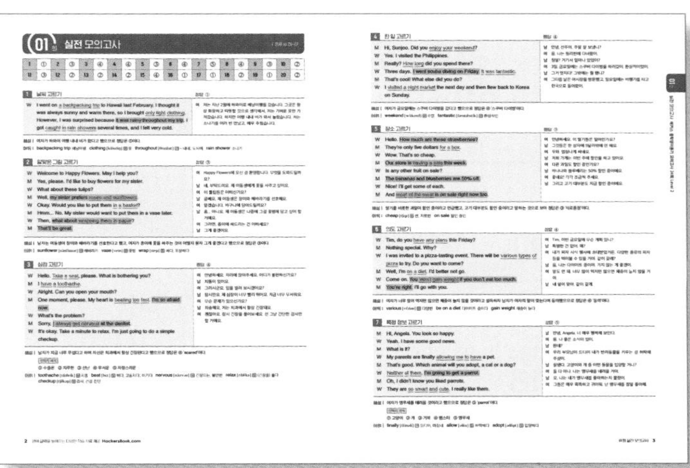

정답 및 해설

정답을 결정하는 단서와 자세한 해설을 통해 스스로 오답의 이유를 찾으며 다시 틀리지 않도록 확실하게 복습할 수 있습니다.

다양한 버전의 MP3

다양한 버전의 MP3를 이용해 학습 목적과 수준에 맞게 효과적으로 학습할 수 있습니다.

- 기출과 동일한 속도의 **기본 속도 MP3**
- 듣기 실력 향상을 위한 **1.2배속 / 1.5배속 MP3**
- 틀린 문제만 골라 다시 들으며 복습하는 **문항별 MP3**
- 대화문만 들으며 Dictation 하는 **딕테이션 MP3**

MP3 스트리밍 QR코드

매회 모의고사와 Dictation에 있는 QR코드로 간편하게 음성을 이용할 수 있습니다.
HackersBook.com에서 MP3 파일 다운로드도 가능합니다.

시험 소개

<전국 16개 시·도교육청 공동 주관 영어듣기능력평가>란?

<전국 16개 시·도교육청 공동 주관 영어듣기능력평가>는 **매년 4월과 9월**, **총 두 차례**에 걸쳐 전국 16개 시·도교육청 주관 하에 시행되는 시험입니다.

학교에 따라 영어 내신 수행평가 점수에 5%~20%까지 반영되므로 실제 시험과 비슷한 모의고사를 풀어보면서 대비해두는 것이 좋습니다.

문제 출제 패턴

매회 **총 20문제가 출제**되며, 시험에 나오는 문제 유형이 정해져 있고, 출제 순서도 매회 크게 달라지지 않는답니다. 최근에는 각 문제 유형이 아래와 같은 순서로 자주 출제되고 있습니다.

제1회 전국 16개 시·도교육청 공동 주관 영어듣기능력평가(중2)

1.	날씨 고르기	
2.	알맞은 그림 고르기	
3.	심정 고르기	출제율 60%
	언급하지 않은 내용 고르기	출제율 20%
	의도 고르기	출제율 20%
4.	한 일 고르기	출제율 90%
	특정 정보 고르기	출제율 10%
5.	장소 고르기	
6.	의도 고르기	출제율 80%
	일치하지 않는 내용 고르기	출제율 20%
7.	특정 정보 고르기	출제율 80%
	할 일 고르기	출제율 10%
	한 일 고르기	출제율 10%
8.	할 일 고르기	
9.	언급하지 않은 내용 고르기	
10.	주제 고르기	
11.	일치하지 않는 내용 고르기	
12.	목적 고르기	
13.	금액정보 고르기	출제율 70%
	시간 정보 고르기	출제율 30%
14.	관계 고르기	
15.	부탁·요청한 일 고르기	출제율 80%
	제안한 일 고르기	출제율 20%
16.	이유 고르기	
17.	그림 상황에 적절한 대화 고르기	
18.	언급하지 않은 내용 고르기	
19.	적절한 응답 고르기	
20.	적절한 응답 고르기	

듣기 문제 풀이 Tip

듣기 문제를 풀 때에 어떤 문제 유형이든 빠짐없이 적용할 수 있는 두 가지 Tip이 있습니다. 어려운 문제도 수월하게 풀 수 있는 방법이니 기억해두고, 듣기 문제를 풀 때 꼭 실천하세요.

1 문제와 보기를 꼼꼼히 읽습니다.

음성이 나오기 전에 문제와 보기를 꼼꼼히 읽어두면 어떤 내용이 나올지 미리 파악할 수 있고, 대화에서 여자와 남자 중 어떤 사람의 말을 더 주의 깊게 들어야 할지 확인할 수 있습니다. 문제 음성이 끝나면 문제를 푸는 시간이 주어지므로, 음성이 끝나면 바로 정답을 체크하고, 남은 시간 동안 다음 문제와 보기를 확인해두면 좋습니다.

[문제지]

9 **대화를 듣고, 여자가 대화 직후에 할 일로 가장 적절한 것을 고르시오.**

① 기념품 사러 가기 ② 범퍼카 타러 가기
③ 퍼레이드 구경하기 ④ 핫도그 먹으러 가기
⑤ 안내데스크 방문하기

이 대화를 마치고 나서 여자가 할 일에 대해 언급하겠구나. 보기에 나온 단어를 말하는지 잘 들어보자.

2 음성은 끝까지 주의 깊게 듣습니다.

음성에서 여러 가지 선택지를 언급하다가 마지막 부분에서야 결정적인 정답 단서가 나오는 경우도 있으니 음성이 끝날 때까지 잘 듣고 정답을 고릅니다. 대화의 앞부분이나 일부 단어만 듣고 섣불리 정답을 판단하는 것은 좋지 않습니다.

[음성]

M Wow! The bumper cars were really fun.
W Yeah. It was so exciting.
M Where do you want to go next?
W Well... I feel a little hungry now.
M **Then why don't we have some hotdogs?**
W **Sounds good.** Let's go get some.

남자가 핫도그를 먹자고
제안했는데 여자가 좋다고 했으니
④번이 정답!
'범퍼카'에 속을 뻔 했지만
끝까지 잘 들었어!

기출 유형 분석

날씨 고르기

담화에서 언급한 특정 시간이나 장소의 날씨를 고르는 문제로, 매회 1문항씩 출제

대표 기출 문제

▲음성 바로 듣기

다음을 듣고, 광주의 날씨로 가장 적절한 것을 고르시오.

① 
② 
③ 
④ 
⑤ 

M You're listening to *Good Morning Korea*. Let's check today's weather report. Seoul began the morning with light raindrops, but it'll stop raining in the afternoon. Daejeon will be foggy, so you should be careful when you drive. Gwangju will be very hot under strong sunshine, so be sure to wear your sunglasses. In Busan, strong winds are expected. Thank you.

남 여러분은 <Good Morning Korea>를 청취하고 계십니다. 오늘의 일기 예보를 확인해 봅시다. 서울은 약한 빗방울로 오전을 시작했지만, 오후에는 비가 그칠 것입니다. 대전은 안개가 끼겠으니, 운전하실 때 조심하십시오. 광주는 강한 햇빛 아래 매우 더울 예정이니, 꼭 선글라스를 착용하십시오. 부산에서는 강풍이 예상됩니다. 감사합니다.

정답 및 해설

광주는 강한 햇빛 아래 매우 더울 예정이라고 했으므로 정답은 ②이다.
강풍이 예상되는 것은 부산의 날씨이고, 약한 빗방울이 내린 것은 서울의 날씨이므로 ①이나 ③을 고르지 않도록 주의한다.

어휘 raindrop [réindràp] 명 빗방울 expect [ikspékt] 동 예상하다

Tip 날씨 고르기 문제에서는 날씨를 나타내는 어휘가 다양하게 쓰이므로 이를 미리 익혀둔다.

• sunny 화창한	• sunshine 햇빛	• cloudy 흐린	• foggy 안개가 낀
• rainy 비가 내리는	• heavy rain 폭우	• shower 소나기	• thunderstorm 뇌우
• windy 바람이 부는	• strong wind 강풍	• snowy 눈이 내리는	• snowfall 강설

알맞은 그림 고르기

비슷한 그림들 중 대화에서 묘사한 특징과 일치하는 그림을 고르는 문제로, 매회 1문항씩 출제

대표 기출 문제

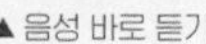

대화를 듣고, 여자가 구입할 화분으로 가장 적절한 것을 고르시오.

▲ 음성 바로 듣기

① ② ③ ④ ⑤

M Good morning. Are you looking for a houseplant?
W Yes, I am.
M Then, how about one of these? We just got them in.
W I love the heart-shaped leaves. I'll take one of them.
M Which one would you like? The one in the round pot or the square pot?
W The one in the round pot, please.
M Okay!

남 안녕하세요. 실내용 화초를 찾고 계신가요?
여 네, 맞아요.
남 그러면, 이것들 중 하나는 어떠세요? 막 들여온 것들이에요.
여 하트 모양의 잎사귀가 마음에 드네요. 이것들 중 하나로 할게요.
남 어떤 게 좋으세요? 둥근 화분에 담긴 건가요, 아니면 네모난 화분에 담긴 건가요?
여 둥근 화분에 담긴 걸로 주세요.
남 알겠습니다!

정답 및 해설

여자가 하트 모양의 잎사귀가 마음에 든다고 했고, 화분은 둥근 것으로 사겠다고 했으므로 정답은 ①이다.

어휘 houseplant [háusplænt] 명 실내용 화초 pot [pat] 명 화분

Tip 알맞은 그림 고르기 문제에서는 사물의 모양, 무늬, 장식, 배치를 묘사하기 위해 특정한 어휘가 자주 쓰이므로 이를 미리 익혀둔다. 또한 각각의 특징을 한 번에 묘사하지 않고 여러 차례로 나눠서 설명할 수 있으므로 끝까지 주의 깊게 듣는다.

- round 둥근
- square 네모난, 사각형
- circle 원형
- heart-shaped 하트 모양의
- dot 물방울무늬
- stripe 줄무늬
- ribbon 리본
- pocket 주머니
- handle 손잡이
- under ~ 아래에
- right 오른쪽
- left 왼쪽

심정 고르기

대화 속 화자의 심정을 고르는 문제로, 매회 0~1문항씩 출제

대표 기출 문제

▲ 음성 바로 듣기

대화를 듣고, 여자의 심정으로 가장 적절한 것을 고르시오.

① excited ② scared ③ angry
④ bored ⑤ shy

W Mike, I have surprising news.
M Surprising news? What is it?
W My favorite singer is having a concert in our town.
M Oh, really? You mean Alice is coming to our town?
W Yes. And my mom bought me a ticket.
M Good for you! You've waited so long for this.
W You're right. I can't wait to see her.

여 Mike, 놀랄만한 소식이 있어.
남 놀랄만한 소식? 그게 뭔데?
여 내가 가장 좋아하는 가수가 우리 동네에서 콘서트를 열 거야.
남 오, 정말? 네 말은 Alice가 우리 동네에 올 거라는 거지?
여 응. 그리고 우리 엄마가 내게 티켓을 사주셨어.
남 잘됐다! 넌 이걸 정말 오랫동안 기다려왔잖아.
여 맞아. 난 그녀를 보는 게 너무 기대돼.

정답 및 해설

여자가 자신이 좋아하는 가수의 공연 소식을 듣고 그것을 기대하고 있으므로 정답은 ①이다.

선택지 해석 ① 신난 ② 무서운 ③ 화난 ④ 지루한 ⑤ 수줍은

어휘 surprising [sərpráiziŋ] 형 놀랄, 놀라운

Tip 심정 고르기 문제에서는 사람의 감정을 나타내는 어휘가 자주 쓰이므로 이를 미리 익혀둔다.

- excited 신난
- thankful 고마운
- scared 무서운
- can't wait 기대되다
- proud 자랑스러운
- afraid 두려운, 걱정하는
- cheerful 쾌활한
- satisfied 만족한
- nervous 초조한
- pleased 기쁜
- peaceful 평화로운
- disappointed 실망한

한 일/할 일 고르기

대화 속 화자가 특정 시간에 한 일 또는 할 일을 고르는 문제로,
한 일은 매회 0~2문항씩, 할 일은 매회 1~2문항씩 출제

대표 기출 문제

▲음성 바로 듣기

대화를 듣고, 여자가 어제 한 일로 가장 적절한 것을 고르시오.

① 놀이공원 가기
② 여행 계획하기
③ 시계 수리하기
④ 고궁 방문하기
⑤ 강아지 산책시키기

W Adam, what did you do yesterday?
M I walked my dog at the park. What about you, Gracie?
W I went to Gyeongbokgung Palace with my family.
M Sounds like fun. How was it?
W We had a great time. We wore Hanbok and took a lot of pictures.
M Can you show me some of them?
W Sure. Look at this!

여 Adam, 어제 너 뭐 했니?
남 공원에서 개를 산책시켰어. 너는 뭐 했니, Gracie?
여 나는 가족들과 함께 경복궁에 갔어.
남 재미있었을 것 같아. 어땠어?
여 정말 좋은 시간을 보냈어. 우리는 한복을 입고 사진을 많이 찍었어.
남 사진 좀 보여줄 수 있어?
여 물론이지. 이걸 봐!

정답 및 해설

여자가 가족들과 함께 경복궁에 갔다고 했으므로 정답은 ④이다.
개를 산책시킨 것은 남자가 어제 한 일이므로 ⑤를 고르지 않도록 주의한다.

어휘 take a picture 사진을 찍다

Tip 한 일 고르기 문제에서는 주로 대화 초반에 남자가 한 일과 여자가 한 일이 모두 언급된다. 그러므로 문제에서 어떤 화자가 한 일/할 일을 묻고 있는지 확인한 후 듣는다.

의도 고르기

대화 속 화자가 마지막에 한 말의 의도를 고르는 문제로, 매회 1문항씩 출제

대표 기출 문제

▲음성 바로 듣기

대화를 듣고, 남자의 마지막 말의 의도로 가장 적절한 것을 고르시오.

① 비난　② 조언　③ 동의
④ 거절　⑤ 용서

W Let's go out for lunch together. I'm very hungry.
M Me too. What do you want to eat?
W There is a new Mexican restaurant on Rose Street. It's popular.
M Well, I don't like Mexican food. It is too spicy for me.
W Then, what about Italian food like pizza or pasta?
M That's a great idea. I like it.

여 점심 먹으러 같이 나가자. 나 너무 배고파.
남 나도 그래. 뭐 먹고 싶니?
여 로즈 가에 새로 생긴 멕시코 음식점이 있어. 거기 인기 있어.
남 음, 나는 멕시코 음식을 안 좋아해. 내게는 너무 맵거든.
여 그러면, 피자나 파스타 같은 이탈리아 음식은 어때?
남 정말 좋은 생각이야. 좋아.

정답 및 해설

이탈리아 음식을 제안하는 여자의 말에 정말 좋은 생각이라고 대답했으므로 정답은 ③이다.

어휘 popular [pápjulər] 형 인기 있는 spicy [spáisi] 형 매운

Tip 의도 고르기 문제에서는 선택지가 격려, 허락, 조언, 제안 등으로 출제되는 경우가 많으므로 상황별 관련 표현을 미리 익혀 둔다.

- I'm sure you will do better next time. 다음에는 분명 더 잘 할 수 있을 거야. (격려)
- Sure! You can take a lot of pictures. 물론이지! 사진 많이 찍어도 돼. (허락)
- You should make eye contact during the speech. 연설하는 동안에는 눈을 마주쳐야 해. (조언)
- Why don't we make the coupons after school? 우리 방과 후에 쿠폰을 만드는 건 어때? (제안)

특정 정보 고르기

문제에서 물어본 특정 정보를 대화 속에서 파악하여 고르는 문제로, 매회 0~2문항씩 출제

대표 기출 문제

▲음성 바로 듣기

대화를 듣고, 여자가 가져올 물건으로 가장 적절한 것을 고르시오.

① 교과서 ② 계산기 ③ 텀블러
④ 필기도구 ⑤ 수학 잡지

M Let's start our math project. Why don't we go to a study room?
W Sounds good. What do we need to bring?
M I have a math textbook and a tablet PC. Do we need anything else?
W I think we need math magazines to look for information.
M I agree, but I don't have any.
W I have some math magazines at home. I'll bring them.
M Okay. See you later.

남 우리 수학 수행평가를 시작하자. 스터디룸에 가는 게 어때?
여 좋아. 뭘 가져가야 할까?
남 내가 수학 교과서와 태블릿 PC를 가지고 있어. 또 필요한 게 있을까?
여 정보를 찾으려면 수학 잡지도 필요한 것 같아.
남 동감이지만, 나는 가지고 있지 않아.
여 집에 수학 잡지가 좀 있어. 내가 가져갈게.
남 알겠어. 이따 보자.

정답 및 해설

마지막에 여자가 수학 잡지를 가져가겠다고 했으므로 정답은 ⑤이다.
초반에 남자가 언급한 수학 교과서는 남자가 가져올 물건이므로 ①을 고르지 않도록 주의한다.

어휘 project [prádʒekt] 명 과제; 계획 textbook [tékstbuk] 명 교과서 look for 찾다

Tip 특정 정보 고르기 문제에서 물어보는 것은 가져올·빌릴·교환할 물건, 가입할 동아리, 연주할 악기 등과 같이 다양하므로, 문제를 읽고 대화 속에서 파악해야 하는 정보가 무엇인지 확인한다.

언급하지 않은 내용 고르기

담화나 대화에서 언급하지 않은 내용이나, 대화 속 설명과 일치하지 않는 내용을 고르는 문제로,
미언급은 매회 2~3문항씩, 불일치는 1~2문항씩 출제

대표 기출 문제

▲음성 바로 듣기

대화를 듣고, 두 사람이 만화책에 대해 언급하지 않은 것을 고르시오.

① 작가 ② 출간일 ③ 제목
④ 장르 ⑤ 판매 부수

W Isaac, what are you reading?
M It's a new comic book by my favorite author, Paul David.
W Oh, I saw it on the news. It came out on March 1st. What was the title?
M It's *New Planet*. It's about human life on a new planet.
W That sounds like science fiction.
M Yes, it is. I like science fiction very much.

여 Isaac, 무엇을 읽고 있니?
남 이건 내가 가장 좋아하는 작가인 Paul David의 새 만화책이야.
여 오, 나 그거 뉴스에서 봤었어. 3월 1일에 출간됐지. 제목이 뭐더라?
남 <New Planet>이야. 새로운 행성에서의 인간의 삶에 관한 거야.
여 공상 과학 소설인 것같네.
남 응, 맞아. 난 공상 과학 소설을 정말 많이 좋아하거든.

정답 및 해설

① 작가(Paul David), ② 출간일(3월 1일), ③ 제목(<New Planet>), ④ 장르(공상 과학 소설)에 대해 순서대로 언급한 반면, 판매 부수에 대해서는 언급하지 않았으므로 정답은 ⑤이다.

어휘 author [ɔ́:θər] 명 작가 planet [plǽnit] 명 행성 science fiction 공상 과학 소설

Tip 언급하지 않은 내용 고르기 문제에서는 일반적으로 선택지의 순서대로 내용을 언급하므로, ①부터 차례대로 언급되었는지 확인하며 듣는다.

주제 고르기

담화의 주제를 고르는 문제로, 매회 각 1문항씩 출제

대표 기출 문제

▲음성 바로 듣기

다음을 듣고, 남자가 하는 말의 내용으로 가장 적절한 것을 고르시오.

① 급식실 공사
② 소화기 사용법
③ 시험 주의사항
④ 학급 회장 선거
⑤ 동아리 가입 방법

M Good morning, everyone. Your final exams start today. Please, listen to the directions carefully. First, clear your desk. You shouldn't have any books on your desk. Second, you cannot talk to your friends during the exam. Third, raise your hand quietly if you have a question. Lastly, finish the exam on time. Is everything clear? *[Pause]* Good luck and do your best.

남 좋은 아침입니다, 여러분. 여러분의 기말고사가 오늘 시작됩니다. 지시 사항들을 주의 깊게 들어주세요. 먼저, 책상을 정리하세요. 책상 위에 어떤 책도 있어서는 안 됩니다. 둘째, 시험을 보는 동안 친구들과 대화를 할 수 없습니다. 셋째, 질문이 있다면 조용히 손을 드세요. 마지막으로, 제때 시험을 끝내세요. 모두 이해되었나요? *[잠시 멈춤]* 행운을 빌며 최선을 다하세요.

정답 및 해설

오늘 시작되는 기말고사의 지시 사항들을 들어달라고 하면서, 네 가지 주의사항을 설명하고 있으므로 정답은 ③이다.

어휘 final exam 기말고사 directions [dirékʃənz] 명 지시 사항 direction [dirékʃən] 명 방향 on time 제때

Tip 주제 고르기 문제에서는 주로 담화 초반에 주제를 직접적으로 언급한다. 특히 주제가 주의사항이나 수칙일 경우 directions (지시 사항), rules(규칙)가 언급되는 경우가 많고, 주제가 방법일 경우 how to(~하는 방법)가 언급되는 경우가 많다.

- Please follow these **rules** while you're using the roller coaster. 롤러코스터 이용 시 이 규칙들을 따라주세요.
- I'd like to explain **how to** make better study plans. 더 나은 공부 계획을 세우는 방법을 설명하고 싶습니다.
- Let me tell you **how to** use your cell phone wisely. 휴대폰을 현명하게 사용하는 방법을 말씀해드리겠습니다.

목적/이유 고르기

대화 속 화자의 행동에 대한 목적이나 이유를 고르는 문제로, 매회 각 1문항씩 출제

대표 기출 문제

▲음성 바로 듣기

대화를 듣고, 남자가 전화를 건 목적으로 가장 적절한 것을 고르시오.

① 신용카드를 찾기 위해서
② 저녁 약속을 잡기 위해서
③ 귀가 시간을 알려주기 위해서
④ 연극을 함께 보러 가기 위해서
⑤ 컴퓨터 사용 방법을 물어보기 위해서

[Cellphone rings.]
W Hi, Dad.
M Hey, Grace. Are you home?
W Yes. Why?
M Do you see my credit card there?
W Oh, you mean the blue one?
M Yes. I can't find it in my wallet. Can you look for it?
W *[Pause]* Oh, here's your credit card! You left it on the kitchen table.
M Whew... I thought I lost it. Thanks.
W No problem. Bye, Dad.

[휴대폰이 울린다.]
여 안녕하세요, 아빠.
남 안녕, Grace. 집이니?
여 네. 왜요?
남 거기 내 신용카드가 보이니?
여 오, 파란색 카드를 말씀하시는 거예요?
남 그래. 지갑에서 찾을 수가 없어서 말이야. 그것 좀 찾아주겠니?
여 *[잠시 멈춤]* 오, 아빠 신용카드가 여기 있어요! 부엌 식탁 위에 두고 가셨네요.
남 휴... 잃어버린 줄 알았단다. 고맙구나.
여 천만에요. 끊을게요, 아빠.

정답 및 해설

남자가 여자에게 집에서 자신의 신용카드를 찾아달라고 했으므로 정답은 ①이다.

어휘 credit card 신용카드 wallet [wálit] 명 지갑

Tip 목적 고르기 문제에서는 전화를 건 목적 외에도 매장을 방문한 목적 등 특정 장소를 방문한 목적을 물어볼 수 있다.

금액/시간 정보 고르기

문제에서 물어본 금액이나 시간을 대화 속에서 파악하여 고르는 문제로, 둘 중 한 유형으로 매회 1문항씩 출제

대표 기출 문제

▲음성 바로 듣기

대화를 듣고, 여자가 지불해야 할 금액으로 가장 적절한 것을 고르시오.

① $ 10　② $ 12　③ $ 20
④ $ 24　⑤ $ 30

M Hi, welcome to Central Aquarium. How may I help you?
W Hi, I'd like to buy two tickets, please.
M No problem. It's 12 dollars for each person.
W Do you have any discounts for students?
M Yes, we do. There's a 2-dollar discount.
W Then, it's 10 dollars each, right?
M Yes. Your total will be 20 dollars.
W Here you are. Thanks.

남 안녕하세요, 센트럴 수족관에 오신 걸 환영합니다. 어떻게 도와드릴까요?
여 안녕하세요, 표 두 장을 사고 싶어요.
남 알겠습니다. 한 사람당 12달러입니다.
여 학생 할인이 있나요?
남 네, 있어요. 2달러 할인이 있습니다.
여 그러면, 한 명당 10달러죠, 맞나요?
남 네. 총 20달러 되겠습니다.
여 여기 있습니다. 감사합니다.

정답 및 해설

수족관 표는 한 장에 12달러로 표 2장을 샀고, 한 사람당 학생 할인으로 2달러씩 할인받아서 총 20달러라고 했으므로 정답은 ③이다.

어휘 discount [dískaunt] 명 할인

Tip 금액 정보 고르기 문제에서는 in total 또는 your total 등을 이용하여 지불해야 하는 총액을 말해주므로, 해당 표현이 나오면 주의 깊게 듣는다. 또한 지불해야 할 금액 외에도 받은 거스름돈을 물어볼 수 있다. 문제에서 거스름돈을 물어볼 때는 간단한 숫자 계산이 필요할 수 있으므로 숫자 정보를 메모하며 듣는다.

- It's eight dollars **in total**. 총 8달러입니다.
- **The total** comes to 20 dollars. 총 20달러 되겠습니다.

관계/장소 고르기

대화 속 화자의 관계나, 대화가 이루어지는 장소를 고르는 문제로, 매회 각 1문항씩 출제

대표 기출 문제

▲음성 바로 듣기

대화를 듣고, 두 사람의 관계로 가장 적절한 것을 고르시오.

① 꽃가게 점원 — 손님
② 축구선수 — 코치
③ 안과의사 — 환자
④ 은행원 — 고객
⑤ 교사 — 학생

W Good afternoon. What can I do for you?
M Good afternoon. I want to order a flower basket for my wife.
W If you choose the flowers, I can make it for you.
M Okay. My wife likes roses and tulips.
W That's a good choice.
M Can you deliver it to her office?
W Sure. The total will be 35 dollars.

여 안녕하세요. 무엇을 도와드릴까요?
남 안녕하세요. 제 아내를 위해 꽃바구니를 주문하고 싶어요.
여 꽃을 골라주시면, 제가 만들어 드릴게요.
남 네. 제 아내는 장미와 튤립을 좋아해요.
여 좋은 선택이네요.
남 아내의 사무실로 배달해주실 수 있나요?
여 물론이죠. 총 35달러 되겠습니다.

정답 및 해설

초반에 남자가 아내를 위해 꽃바구니를 주문하고 싶다고 하는 것으로 보아 정답은 ①이다.

어휘 deliver [dilívər] 통 배달하다

Tip 관계 고르기 문제에서는 일반적으로 대화 초반에 두 사람의 관계를 알 수 있게 해주는 내용이 나온다. 특히 직원과 손님의 대화일 경우, 손님의 방문 목적을 듣고 관계를 파악할 수 있다.

- I'd like to order a cake for my mom's birthday. 어머니의 생일 케이크를 주문하고 싶어요. (제빵사 — 손님)
- I'm looking for a new smart TV. 새로운 스마트 TV를 찾고 있어요. (전자 제품 판매원 — 손님)
- When I drive, my car makes a strange sound. 운전할 때, 차에서 이상한 소리가 나요. (자동차 정비사 — 고객)

부탁·요청/제안한 일 고르기

대화 속 화자가 부탁·요청한 일이나, 제안한 것을 고르는 문제로, 둘 중 한 유형으로 매회 1문항씩 출제

대표 기출 문제

▲음성 바로 듣기

대화를 듣고, 여자가 남자에게 부탁한 일로 가장 적절한 것을 고르시오.

① 설탕 사오기 ② 에어컨 켜기
③ 얼음 꺼내주기 ④ 형광등 교체하기
⑤ 화장실 청소하기

M Mom, I feel like eating ice cream. Do we have any?
W No, we don't. But we can make it at home.
M Really? Let's make chocolate ice cream.
W Okay. We just need milk, sugar, and chocolate.
M Let me check. *[Rustling sound]* We only have milk and chocolate.
W Then, can you go and buy some sugar now? I'll give you money.
M Sure.

남 엄마, 저 아이스크림이 먹고 싶어요. 있나요?
여 아니, 없단다. 하지만 집에서 만들 수 있어.
남 정말요? 초콜릿 아이스크림을 만들어요.
여 그래. 우유, 설탕, 그리고 초콜릿만 있으면 돼.
남 제가 확인해볼게요. *[달그락거리는 소리]* 우유랑 초콜릿만 있어요.
여 그러면, 지금 가서 설탕 좀 사오겠니? 돈을 주마.
남 물론이죠.

정답 및 해설

마지막에 여자가 남자에게 설탕을 사와 달라고 부탁했으므로 정답은 ①이다.

어휘 sugar [ʃúgər] 명 설탕

Tip 부탁·요청한 일 고르기 문제에서는 대화 마지막에 조동사 can이나 could를 써서 부탁하거나 요청하는 경우가 많으므로, 해당 표현이 나오면 주의 깊게 듣는다.

- **Can** you tell me the website address? 웹사이트 주소를 내게 알려줄래?
- **Can** you carry my bag to the classroom? 내 가방을 교실로 옮겨줄래?
- **Could** you book a ticket for me? 날 위해 표를 예매해줄래?
- **Could** you buy me some new batteries? 내게 새 건전지 좀 사다 줄래?

그림 상황에 적절한 대화 고르기

주어진 그림 속 상황에 적절한 대화를 고르는 문제로, 매회 1문항씩 출제

대표 기출 문제

▲음성 바로 듣기

다음 그림의 상황에 가장 적절한 대화를 고르시오.

① ② ③ ④ ⑤

① **M** When was it painted?
W It was painted back in 1887.
② **M** Watch out! The cup is very hot.
W Oh, I didn't know that. Thank you.
③ **M** Wake up! You're late for school!
W Just five more minutes, Dad.
④ **M** This badminton game is really exciting.
W Yes. Look at that player!
⑤ **M** How may I help you?
W I want to buy earphones.

① **남** 이건 언제 그려진 건가요?
여 1887년에 그려졌습니다.
② **남** 조심하세요! 컵이 매우 뜨거워요.
여 오, 몰랐어요. 감사합니다.
③ **남** 일어나렴! 학교에 늦었단다!
여 딱 5분만 더요, 아빠.
④ **남** 이 배드민턴 경기는 정말 흥미진진해.
여 응. 저 선수 좀 봐!
⑤ **남** 무엇을 도와드릴까요?
여 이어폰을 사고 싶은데요.

정답 및 해설

미술관에서 큐레이터와 관람객이 사진을 두고 대화를 하고 있는 상황이므로 정답은 ①이다.

어휘 player [pléiər] 명 선수

Tip 그림 상황에 적절한 대화 고르기 문제에서 그림에 팻말이나 말풍선이 있을 경우, 이는 대화의 장소나 상황을 빠르게 파악하도록 돕는 단서가 된다. 또, 선택지가 짧은 대화로 이루어져 있으므로 대화를 놓치지 않도록 집중하며 듣는다.

적절한 응답 고르기

대화의 흐름상 마지막 말에 이어질 가장 적절한 응답을 고르는 문제로, 매회 2문항씩 출제

대표 기출 문제

▲음성 바로 듣기

대화를 듣고, 남자의 마지막 말에 이어질 여자의 말로 가장 적절한 것을 고르시오.

Woman: ______________________________

① Turn right, please.

② He doesn't have to.

③ Where are you from?

④ How can I get there?

⑤ Jogging could be good.

M Can you believe it? We have no school next week!
W Yeah. It's already summer vacation.
M Time goes by so fast!
W Right. Do you have any special plans for the vacation?
M Well, I plan to exercise at least three times a week.
W Awesome! What kind of exercise are you going to do?
M I didn't decide yet. Can you recommend something?
W ______________________________

남 믿어지니? 다음 주면 학교 수업이 없어!
여 그러게. 벌써 여름 방학이네.
남 시간이 정말 빨리 흘러!
여 맞아. 너는 특별한 방학 계획이 있니?
남 글쎄, 일주일에 적어도 세 번은 운동할 계획이야.
여 멋진걸! 어떤 종류의 운동을 할 거니?
남 아직 결정 못했어. 네가 뭔가 추천해줄 수 있을까?
여 ______________________________

정답 및 해설

마지막에 여자가 어떤 종류의 운동을 할 것인지를 묻자, 남자가 여자에게 운동을 추천해주길 부탁했으므로 정답은 ⑤이다.

선택지 해석
① 우회전해 줘.
② 그는 그럴 필요가 없어.
③ 어디에서 왔니?
④ 거기 어떻게 갈 수 있을까?
⑤ 조깅이 좋을 수도 있어.

어휘 decide [disáid] 동 결정하다 recommend [rèkəménd] 동 추천하다

Tip 적절한 응답 고르기 문제에서는 대화의 마지막 말을 놓치지 않도록 끝까지 집중하며 듣는다. 특히 마지막 말이 의문사가 없는 의문문일 경우, 마지막 말 외에도 대화의 전체적인 상황까지 고려하여 질문에 적절한 응답을 고른다.

해커스북 중·고등

www.HackersBook.com

실전 모의고사

01~20회 실전 모의고사

01회 중학영어듣기 실전 모의고사

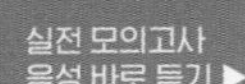

1 다음을 듣고, 여자가 하와이에 갔을 때 경험한 날씨로 가장 적절한 것을 고르시오.

①  ②   ③  ④   ⑤ 

2 대화를 듣고, 남자가 구입할 꽃으로 가장 적절한 것을 고르시오.

①  ②  ③ 
④  ⑤ 

3 대화를 듣고, 남자의 심정으로 가장 적절한 것을 고르시오.

① shy ② bored ③ excited
④ scared ⑤ proud

고난도

4 대화를 듣고, 여자가 지난 금요일에 한 일로 가장 적절한 것을 고르시오.

① 영화 감상 ② 바다 낚시
③ 야시장 구경 ④ 스쿠버 다이빙
⑤ 고궁 방문

5 대화를 듣고, 두 사람이 대화하는 장소로 가장 적절한 곳을 고르시오.

① 정육점 ② 과수원 ③ 식료품점
④ 지하철역 ⑤ 공원

6 대화를 듣고, 남자의 마지막 말의 의도로 가장 적절한 것을 고르시오.

① 제안 ② 거절 ③ 조언 ④ 동의 ⑤ 사과

7 대화를 듣고, 여자가 키울 반려동물을 고르시오.

① cat ② dog ③ turtle
④ hamster ⑤ parrot

8 대화를 듣고, 남자가 대화 직후에 할 일로 가장 적절한 것을 고르시오.

① 샤워하기 ② 채소 다듬기
③ 설거지하기 ④ 환기하기
⑤ 저녁거리 사 오기

9 다음을 듣고, 여자가 Winter Sports Arena에 대해 언급하지 않은 것을 고르시오.

① 시설 종류 ② 사용 시간 ③ 사용료
④ 대관 자격 ⑤ 대관 신청 방법

10 다음을 듣고, 남자가 하는 말의 내용으로 가장 적절한 것을 고르시오.

① 바른 자세의 중요성
② 공연장 관람 예절
③ 인터넷 보안의 취약점
④ 발표를 잘하는 방법
⑤ 건전한 여가 활동

11 대화를 듣고, 여자가 언급한 내용과 일치하지 <u>않는</u> 것을 고르시오.

① 합창단에서 자선 공연을 개최할 것이다.
② 공연은 다음 주 토요일에 열린다.
③ 공연은 양로원에서 열린다.
④ <아리랑> 메들리를 부를 것이다.
⑤ 공연 전에 팸플릿을 나눠줄 것이다.

12 대화를 듣고, 여자가 대학교를 방문한 목적으로 가장 적절한 것을 고르시오.

① 강의를 하기 위해서
② 졸업식에 참석하기 위해서
③ 교수님을 만나기 위해서
④ 축제를 구경하기 위해서
⑤ 도서관을 이용하기 위해서

13 대화를 듣고, 여자가 지불해야 할 금액으로 가장 적절한 것을 고르시오.

① $ 15 ② $ 25 ③ $ 30
④ $ 40 ⑤ $ 45

고난도
14 대화를 듣고, 두 사람의 관계로 가장 적절한 것을 고르시오.

① 경찰관 — 시민
② 은행원 — 고객
③ 문구점 직원 — 손님
④ 요가 강사 — 수강생
⑤ 비행기 조종사 — 승무원

15 대화를 듣고, 여자가 남자에게 제안한 일로 가장 적절한 것을 고르시오.

① 태블릿 PC 구입하기 ② 중심 줄거리 짜기
③ 배경 색칠하기 ④ 감상평 말해주기
⑤ 만화책 빌려주기

16 대화를 듣고, 여자가 전화를 하지 <u>못하는</u> 이유로 가장 적절한 것을 고르시오.

① 휴대폰 배터리가 없어서
② 선생님의 번호를 몰라서
③ 신호가 잡히지 않아서
④ 운전을 하고 있어서
⑤ 휴대폰을 집에 두고 와서

17 다음 그림의 상황에 가장 적절한 대화를 고르시오.

MENU
Espresso 4.0
Americano 4.5
Cafe Latte 5.0
Vanilla Latte
Smoothie

① ② ③ ④ ⑤

18 대화를 듣고, 두 사람이 박람회에 대해 언급하지 <u>않은</u> 것을 고르시오.

① 명칭 ② 개최 장소 ③ 개최 기간
④ 티켓 가격 ⑤ 티켓 구매 방법

[19-20] 대화를 듣고, 남자의 마지막 말에 이어질 여자의 응답으로 가장 적절한 것을 고르시오.

19 **Woman:** ______________________

① At least 45 minutes.
② I'm next in line.
③ We're going to buy the shoes.
④ It opens at 9 a.m.
⑤ I need some cash.

20 **Woman:** ______________________

① We're studying the Second World War.
② How about studying in a library?
③ Please turn down the volume.
④ She just posted something online.
⑤ I didn't do the homework.

01회 Dictation

Dictation 음성 바로 듣기 ▶

01회 중학영어듣기 실전 모의고사 Dictation 음성을 들으며 빈칸에 알맞은 단어를 채우시오.

1 | 날씨 고르기

다음을 듣고, 여자가 하와이에 갔을 때 경험한 날씨로 가장 적절한 것을 고르시오.

① ② ③ ④ ⑤

W I went on _____ _____ _____ to Hawaii last February. I thought it was always sunny and warm there, so I brought _____ _____ _____. However, I was surprised because it was rainy throughout my trip. I got _____ _____ _____ _____ several times, and I felt very cold.

2 | 알맞은 그림 고르기

대화를 듣고, 남자가 구입할 꽃으로 가장 적절한 것을 고르시오.

① ② ③ ④ ⑤

W Welcome to Happy Flowers. May I help you?

M Yes, please. I'd like to buy flowers for my sister.

W What about these tulips?

M Well, my sister prefers _____ _____ _____.

W Okay. Would you like to put them _____ _____ _____?

M Hmm... No. My sister would want to put them in a vase later.

W Then, what about _____ _____ _____ _____?

M That'll be great.

3 | 심정 고르기

대화를 듣고, 남자의 심정으로 가장 적절한 것을 고르시오.

① shy ② bored ③ excited
④ scared ⑤ proud

W Hello. _____ _____ _____, please. What is bothering you?

M I _____ _____ _____.

W Alright. Can you open your mouth?

M One moment, please. My heart is _____ _____ _____. I'm so afraid now.

W What's the problem?

M Sorry, _____ _____ _____ _____ at the dentist.

W It's okay. Take a minute to relax. I'm just going to do a simple checkup.

고난도

4 | 한 일 고르기

대화를 듣고, 여자가 지난 금요일에 한 일로 가장 적절한 것을 고르시오.

① 영화 감상 ② 바다 낚시
③ 야시장 구경 ④ 스쿠버 다이빙
⑤ 고궁 방문

> 적중! Tip What else
>
> [왓 앨스]보다는 [와랠스]로 들린다. [t]가 모음 사이에서 발음될 때는 약화되어 [r]에 가깝게 발음되기 때문이다.

M Hi, Sunjoo. Did you _____ _____ _____?

W Yes. I visited the Philippines.

M Really? _____ _____ did you spend there?

W Three days. I went scuba diving on Friday. _____ _____ _____.

M That's cool! What else did you do?

W I _____ _____ _____ _____ the next day and then flew back to Korea on Sunday.

5 | 장소 고르기

대화를 듣고, 두 사람이 대화하는 장소로 가장 적절한 곳을 고르시오.

① 정육점 ② 과수원 ③ 식료품점
④ 지하철역 ⑤ 공원

적중! Tip banana
[바나나]로 익숙한 외래어이지만 실제로는 [버내나]로 발음된다.

W Hello. How much are these strawberries?
M They're only five dollars ________ ________ ________.
W Wow. That's so cheap.
M Our store is ________ ________ ________ this week.
W Is any other fruit on sale?
M The bananas and blueberries are 50% off.
W Nice! I'll get some of each.
M And ________ ________ ________ ________ is on sale right now too.

6 | 의도 고르기

대화를 듣고, 남자의 마지막 말의 의도로 가장 적절한 것을 고르시오.

① 제안 ② 거절 ③ 조언 ④ 동의 ⑤ 사과

적중! Tip I'd better not ~.
I had better not을 축약해서 간단히 말한 것으로, '~하지 않는 것이 좋겠다, 낫겠다'라는 의미이다. I 자리에는 You, We 등 다른 주어가 올 수 있다.
· You'd better not put your bag there.
너는 그곳에 네 가방을 두지 않는 것이 낫겠어.

W Tim, do you ________ ________ ________ this Friday?
M Nothing special. Why?
W I was invited to a pizza-tasting event. There will be ________ ________ ________ ________ to try. Do you want to come?
M Well, I'm ________ ________ ________. I'd better not go.
W Come on. You ________ ________ ________ if you don't eat too much.
M You're right. I'll go with you.

7 | 특정 정보 고르기

대화를 듣고, 여자가 키울 반려동물을 고르시오.

① cat ② dog ③ turtle
④ hamster ⑤ parrot

M Hi, Angela. You look so happy.
W Yeah. I have some good news.
M What is it?
W My parents are finally ________ ________ ________ ________ a pet.
M That's good. Which animal will you adopt, a cat or a dog?
W ________ ________ ________. I'm going to get a parrot.
M Oh, I didn't know you liked parrots.
W They are ________ ________ ________ ________. I really like them.

8 할 일 고르기

대화를 듣고, 남자가 대화 직후에 할 일로 가장 적절한 것을 고르시오.

① 샤워하기 ② 채소 다듬기
③ 설거지하기 ④ 환기하기
⑤ 저녁거리 사 오기

적중! Tip air in
[에얼 인]보다는 [에어린]으로 들린다. 앞에 나온 단어의 끝 자음과 뒤에 나온 단어의 첫 모음이 연음되기 때문이다.

M Mom, I ________ ________ ________ in the kitchen.
W Oh, no! I forgot to turn off the gas stove.
M Let me check. *[Pause]* The pot was burned.
W I guess I'll need to ________ ________ ________.
M Can I help you?
W Sure. But we need to ________ ________ ________ the smell of the burned food first.
M Alright. I'll ________ ________ ________ to let some fresh air in.

9 언급하지 않은 내용 고르기

다음을 듣고, 여자가 Winter Sports Arena에 대해 언급하지 않은 것을 고르시오.

① 시설 종류 ② 사용 시간 ③ 사용료
④ 대관 자격 ⑤ 대관 신청 방법

W Welcome to the Winter Sports Arena. We have several ice rinks for skating, ice hockey, and curling. The general public can use them for ________ ________ ________ ________ a day. Only professional athletes can rent our ice rinks for a full day or longer. If you are ________ ________ ________ one of our rinks, please ________ ________ ________ ________ by e-mail. Thank you. Have a nice day.

10 주제 고르기

다음을 듣고, 남자가 하는 말의 내용으로 가장 적절한 것을 고르시오.

① 바른 자세의 중요성
② 공연장 관람 예절
③ 인터넷 보안의 취약점
④ 발표를 잘하는 방법
⑤ 건전한 여가 활동

M Hello, visitors. Please ________ ________ ________ so that everyone can enjoy the ballet. First, please get to your seat 10 minutes ________ ________ ________ ________. Second, you should not talk loudly or move around during the show. Lastly, make sure to turn off or ________ ________ ________ before the performance begins. Thank you.

11 일치하지 않는 내용 고르기

대화를 듣고, 여자가 언급한 내용과 일치하지 않는 것을 고르시오.

① 합창단에서 자선 공연을 개최할 것이다.
② 공연은 다음 주 토요일에 열린다.
③ 공연은 양로원에서 열린다.
④ <아리랑> 메들리를 부를 것이다.
⑤ 공연 전에 팸플릿을 나눠줄 것이다.

W Jinsu, do you ________ ________ ________ for next weekend?
M No, I don't. Why?
W My school choir will have a charity concert on Saturday. Can you come and ________ ________ ________ ________?
M Where will it be held?
W At Green Hospital. We're going to sing the *Arirang* medley.
M That sounds great! I'd love to help. What can I do for you?
W I want you to ________ ________ ________ ________ before the concert begins.
M My pleasure.

12 목적 고르기

대화를 듣고, 여자가 대학교를 방문한 목적으로 가장 적절한 것을 고르시오.

① 강의를 하기 위해서
② 졸업식에 참석하기 위해서
③ 교수님을 만나기 위해서
④ 축제를 구경하기 위해서
⑤ 도서관을 이용하기 위해서

적중! Tip It's nice to see you again.
상대방을 오랜만에 만났을 때 사용되는 표현으로 '다시 만나서 반가워'라는 의미이다.

M Hey, Miranda. Long time no see.
W Hi, Jeff. It's nice to see you again.
M You too. I teach physics at this university. ________ ________ ________ ________?
W I'm here to attend the graduation ceremony.
M Oh, ________ ________ ________ this year?
W My little brother. He ________ ________ ________ ________.
M Good for him. Please give him my congratulations.

13 금액 정보 고르기

대화를 듣고, 여자가 지불해야 할 금액으로 가장 적절한 것을 고르시오.

① $ 15 ② $ 25 ③ $ 30
④ $ 40 ⑤ $ 45

W Excuse me. I'd like to ________ ________ ________ ________ for four people.
M How long will you rent it?
W Two hours. ________ ________ ________ ________ ________?
M It costs 15 dollars ________ ________.
W Okay. We'll take it.
M If you are ________ ________, you can get a five-dollar discount.
W Great. We're all locals.
M Then, your total will be 25 dollars.

고난도

14 관계 고르기

대화를 듣고, 두 사람의 관계로 가장 적절한 것을 고르시오.

① 경찰관 — 시민
② 은행원 — 고객
③ 문구점 직원 — 손님
④ 요가 강사 — 수강생
⑤ 비행기 조종사 — 승무원

W Hi. How can I help you today, sir?
M Hello. I'd like to ________ ________ ________.
W What type of money do you need?
M I want some British pounds, please. I have 500,000 won here.
W Alright. Can I ________ ________ ________ for you?
M Actually, I also need a new credit card. Mine doesn't work sometimes.
W No problem. I'll ________ ________ ________ ________ right away.

15 | 제안한 일 고르기

대화를 듣고, 여자가 남자에게 제안한 일로 가장 적절한 것을 고르시오.

① 태블릿 PC 구입하기 ② 중심 줄거리 짜기
③ 배경 색칠하기 ④ 감상평 말해주기
⑤ 만화책 빌려주기

W Ian, _____ _____ _____ _____?
M I'm making a webtoon on my tablet PC.
W Wow. That's amazing. Did you do it _____ _____ _____ _____?
M No. My friend Joe wrote the main story.
W And you did all _____ _____ _____ _____, right?
M Yes, I did. I want to hear other people's opinions about it though.
W I can take a look and give you mine.
M I'd love that.

16 | 이유 고르기

대화를 듣고, 여자가 전화를 하지 못하는 이유로 가장 적절한 것을 고르시오.

① 휴대폰 배터리가 없어서
② 선생님의 번호를 몰라서
③ 신호가 잡히지 않아서
④ 운전을 하고 있어서
⑤ 휴대폰을 집에 두고 와서

적중! Tip academy
[아카데미]가 한 음절씩 들리기보다는 [카]가 가장 강하게 들리고 나머지 발음은 흘러가듯 약하게 들리니 주의한다.

M Lisa, it'll take another hour _____ _____ _____ for our school's art festival.
W But I have a piano lesson soon.
M _____ _____ _____ _____ your instructor and tell him you'll be late?
W Okay. *[Pause]* My phone isn't working.
M What happened?
W It _____ _____ _____ _____. Can I borrow yours?
M Of course. Do you know your instructor's cellphone number?
W It's on the academy's website.

17 | 그림 상황에 적절한 대화 고르기

다음 그림의 상황에 가장 적절한 대화를 고르시오.

① ② ③ ④ ⑤

① **W** What would you like to order, sir?
M I'd like a coffee and _____ _____ _____ _____, please.
② **W** What are you doing today?
M I'm baking cookies for my class.
③ **W** I have _____ _____ _____ and a headache.
M I will get you a cup of warm water.
④ **W** Do you see my phone? I can't find it.
M It's here! It was _____ _____ _____ _____.
⑤ **W** What is that smell? It's so nice.
M It's _____ _____ _____.

18 | 언급하지 않은 내용 고르기

대화를 듣고, 두 사람이 박람회에 대해 언급하지 않은 것을 고르시오.

① 명칭 ② 개최 장소 ③ 개최 기간
④ 티켓 가격 ⑤ 티켓 구매 방법

적중! Tip Do you know how to ~?
뭔가를 하는 방법을 아냐고 물을 때 사용되는 표현으로, how to 다음에는 동사원형이 온다.
· Do you know how to solve the problem?
너는 어떻게 이 문제를 푸는지 아니?

W Minsu, did you know the Golden Comic Convention is coming up?
M No. When will it be held?
W ________ ________ ________ 15th to 20th. Do you want to go together?
M Sure. How much ________ ________ ________?
W They are 10 dollars each.
M Do you know how to buy them?
W Yes. ________ ________ ________ ________ from the convention's website.
M Okay. When do you want to go?
W How about March 17th?
M Alright. It should be fun.

19 | 적절한 응답 고르기

대화를 듣고, 남자의 마지막 말에 이어질 여자의 응답으로 가장 적절한 것을 고르시오.

Woman: ______________________________

① At least 45 minutes.
② I'm next in line.
③ We're going to buy the shoes.
④ It opens at 9 a.m.
⑤ I need some cash.

M Excuse me. ________ ________ ________ ________ for?
W This is the line for ________ ________ ________ ________.
M Oh, really? The line is so long.
W Yes. They are very popular.
M Will the store still have any of the sneakers tomorrow?
W I don't think so. They will ________ ________ ________ ________.
M I see. How long will I need to ________ ________ ________ then?

20 | 적절한 응답 고르기

대화를 듣고, 남자의 마지막 말에 이어질 여자의 응답으로 가장 적절한 것을 고르시오.

Woman: ______________________________

① We're studying the Second World War.
② How about studying in a library?
③ Please turn down the volume.
④ She just posted something online.
⑤ I didn't do the homework.

M What are you doing, Eunji?
W I'm ________ ________ ________ for the history test, but I'll take a break soon.
M You're already ________ ________ ________ ________. I admire you!
W Are you having trouble studying?
M Yes. I can't focus on the textbook ________ ________ ________ ________.
W Well, you listen to music while studying. You should ________ ________ ________.
M I've tried that, but it didn't change anything. What else can I do?

02회 중학영어듣기 실전 모의고사

실전 모의고사 음성 바로 듣기 ▶

1 다음을 듣고, 창원의 내일 날씨로 가장 적절한 것을 고르시오.

① ② ③ ④ ⑤

2 대화를 듣고, 여자가 구입할 거울로 가장 적절한 것을 고르시오.

①

②

③

④

⑤

3 대화를 듣고, 여자의 심정으로 가장 적절한 것을 고르시오.

① shy ② scared ③ pleased
④ worried ⑤ bored

4 대화를 듣고, 남자가 지난 주말에 한 일로 가장 적절한 것을 고르시오.

① 목도리 뜨기 ② 그림 그리기
③ 안경 구매하기 ④ 전시회 관람하기
⑤ 수영장 가기

5 대화를 듣고, 두 사람이 대화하는 장소로 가장 적절한 곳을 고르시오.

① 분실물 센터 ② 버스 터미널
③ 경찰서 ④ 서점
⑤ 축구 경기장

6 대화를 듣고, 남자의 마지막 말의 의도로 가장 적절한 것을 고르시오.

① 사과 ② 동의 ③ 조언 ④ 칭찬 ⑤ 용서

7 대화를 듣고, 여자가 Eco Festival에서 한 일을 고르시오.

① 비누 제작하기 ② 나무 심기
③ 대나무 칫솔 만들기 ④ 에코백 꾸미기
⑤ 환경 포스터 만들기

8 대화를 듣고, 남자가 대화 직후에 할 일로 가장 적절한 것을 고르시오.

① 파티 열어주기 ② 케이크 만들기
③ 제과점 방문하기 ④ 카페 검색하기
⑤ 형에게 전화하기

9 대화를 듣고, 두 사람이 뮤지컬에 대해 언급하지 않은 것을 고르시오.

① 제목 ② 내용
③ 주연 배우 ④ 관객 수
⑤ 수상 후보 여부

10 다음을 듣고, 여자가 하는 말의 내용으로 가장 적절한 것을 고르시오.

① 봉사 활동 신청 ② 도난 사고 주의
③ 동아리 안내 ④ 당선 포부
⑤ 취미 생활 소개

고난도
11 대화를 듣고, Miracle Science Museum에 대한 내용과 일치하지 않는 것을 고르시오.

① 학교와 가까이에 있다.
② 초록색 건물에 있다.
③ 작년에 개관했다.
④ 학생 할인을 제공한다.
⑤ 오전 11시에 문을 연다.

12 대화를 듣고, 남자가 전화를 건 목적으로 가장 적절한 것을 고르시오.

① 촬영용 카메라를 빌리기 위해서
② 약속을 취소하기 위해서
③ 이사 차량을 알아보기 위해서
④ 관광 명소를 물어보기 위해서
⑤ 지역 축제에 가기 위해서

고난도
13 대화를 듣고, 여자가 받은 거스름돈으로 가장 적절한 것을 고르시오.

① $ 1 ② $ 2 ③ $ 3
④ $ 4 ⑤ $ 5

14 대화를 듣고, 두 사람의 관계로 가장 적절한 것을 고르시오.

① 의사 — 환자
② 옷가게 점원 — 손님
③ 노트북 수리기사 — 고객
④ 컴퓨터 학원 직원 — 학생
⑤ 목수 — 가구 제작자

15 대화를 듣고, 남자가 여자에게 제안한 일로 가장 적절한 것을 고르시오.

① 선반 조립하기
② 온라인 주문하기
③ 결혼식 참석하기
④ 해외 택배 보내기
⑤ 다른 가게 방문하기

16 대화를 듣고, 남자가 걸어온 이유로 가장 적절한 것을 고르시오.

① 지각을 피하려고 ② 운동을 하려고
③ 자전거가 고장 나서 ④ 버스를 놓쳐서
⑤ 친구를 만나려고

17 다음 그림의 상황에 가장 적절한 대화를 고르시오.

① ② ③ ④ ⑤

18 대화를 듣고, 두 사람이 앱에 관해 언급하지 않은 것을 고르시오.

① 이름 ② 기능
③ 가격 ④ 평점
⑤ 다운로드 횟수

[19-20] 대화를 듣고, 남자의 마지막 말에 이어질 여자의 응답으로 가장 적절한 것을 고르시오.

19 **Woman:** ______________________

① Can we change the schedule?
② Yes. That sounds good.
③ Try not to be late.
④ My favorite sports is swimming.
⑤ Glad you could come.

20 **Woman:** ______________________

① This shopping mall is huge.
② Sorry, but I can't walk anymore.
③ The price is so cheap.
④ The toilet is downstairs.
⑤ Okay. I'll go there.

02회 Dictation

Dictation 음성 바로 듣기 ▶

02회 중학영어듣기 실전 모의고사 Dictation 음성을 들으며 빈칸에 알맞은 단어를 채우시오.

1 날씨 고르기

다음을 듣고, 창원의 내일 날씨로 가장 적절한 것을 고르시오.

① ② ③ ④ ⑤

M Good morning. Here's the weather report. Tomorrow, Seoul and Daejeon will be cloudy. In Chuncheon, there will be ________ ________ ________ ________, so try to ________ ________ ________. And in Changwon, strong wind is expected, so ________ ________ ________. Thank you for listening.

2 알맞은 그림 고르기

대화를 듣고, 여자가 구입할 거울로 가장 적절한 것을 고르시오.

① ② ③ ④ ⑤

M Hello. How can I help you?
W I'm ________ ________ ________ ________.
M Okay. How about these round ones?
W They look nice. I'll ________ ________ ________ ________.
M Good. Do you prefer the mirror with the smiley face or the heart?
W The one ________ ________ ________, please.
M Great choice!

3 심정 고르기

대화를 듣고, 여자의 심정으로 가장 적절한 것을 고르시오.

① shy ② scared ③ pleased
④ worried ⑤ bored

[Cellphone rings.]
W Ben, why are you so late?
M I'm sorry. I left my wallet at home, and I had to go back to get it.
W But ________ ________ ________ in 15 minutes. Where are you now?
M I just reached the subway station.
W I'm afraid you'll ________ ________ ________ of the movie.
M I will run to the theater ________ ________ ________ I can!

4 한 일 고르기

대화를 듣고, 남자가 지난 주말에 한 일로 가장 적절한 것을 고르시오.

① 목도리 뜨기 ② 그림 그리기
③ 안경 구매하기 ④ 전시회 관람하기
⑤ 수영장 가기

적중! Tip **k**nit
[닛]으로 발음된다. -n 앞에 오면서 단어의 맨 처음에 쓰인 [k]는 묵음이다.
· **k**nife [나이프] · **k**now [노우]

M Claire, what did you do last weekend?
W I went to ________ ________ ________. What about you, Connor?
M I knitted a muffler.
W How did you learn to knit?
M My sister ________ ________ ________ ________. It's her hobby.
W Wow. I want to learn, but I'm not good with my hands.
M ________ ________ ________! I can help you if you want.

5 | 장소 고르기

대화를 듣고, 두 사람이 대화하는 장소로 가장 적절한 곳을 고르시오.

① 분실물 센터 ② 버스 터미널
③ 경찰서 ④ 서점
⑤ 축구 경기장

적중! Tip **I'll**
[아일]보다는 [아올]로 들린다. 조동사 will의 축약형은 앞에 나오는 주어와 연결해서 약하게 발음되기 때문이다.

M Hello. Do you need any help?
W That would be great. I want to buy a book.
M Alright. _________ _________ _________ _________ do you want?
W I'm going to be on an airplane _________ _________ _________ _________. So, I want an exciting story.
M What about *The Game*? It's a novel about a _________ _________ _________ _________.
W That sounds interesting. I'll buy it.

6 | 의도 고르기

대화를 듣고, 남자의 마지막 말의 의도로 가장 적절한 것을 고르시오.

① 사과 ② 동의 ③ 조언 ④ 칭찬 ⑤ 용서

W Do you have a minute, Mr. Jones?
M Of course. What can I do for you, Mary?
W I'm a little _________ _________ _________ _________ you asked me to write.
M What's wrong?
W I can't choose a topic.
M I _________ _________ _________ in yesterday's class.
W Yes. But none of them are interesting to me.
M You should make _________ _________ _________ _________ _________. Then, pick the one that is most appealing.

7 | 한 일 고르기

대화를 듣고, 여자가 Eco Festival에서 한 일을 고르시오.

① 비누 제작하기 ② 나무 심기
③ 대나무 칫솔 만들기 ④ 에코백 꾸미기
⑤ 환경 포스터 만들기

W Carter, do you know about the Eco Festival?
M No, I don't. What is it?
W It's a festival to encourage people to _________ _________ _________.
M Have you been there?
W Yes. I did a lot of fun things there last year.
M _________ _________ _________ _________?
W I learned _________ _________ _________ less plastic. I even made a bamboo toothbrush.
M Wow! That's great.

8 | 할 일 고르기

대화를 듣고, 남자가 대화 직후에 할 일로 가장 적절한 것을 고르시오.

① 파티 열어주기 ② 케이크 만들기
③ 제과점 방문하기 ④ 카페 검색하기
⑤ 형에게 전화하기

M Your brother came in first in the speech contest.
W I know, Dad. He has talked about it all day.
M I'm very proud of him. It is an impressive achievement.
W Why don't we ________ ________ ________ for him?
M That's what I was thinking. How about going to a bakery ________ ________ ________ ________ now?
W Okay. Can we also get some lemonade? It'll go well with the cake.
M Sure. I'll ________ ________ ________ ________ online now.

9 | 언급하지 않은 내용 고르기

대화를 듣고, 두 사람이 뮤지컬에 대해 언급하지 않은 것을 고르시오.

① 제목 ② 내용
③ 주연 배우 ④ 관객 수
⑤ 수상 후보 여부

M Hello. We have musical director Jess Hwang on our show today.
W I'm ________ ________ ________ ________.
M Our pleasure. So, tell us about your new musical, *LA to New York*.
W It's about a rock band ________ ________ ________ ________.
M Who plays the main character?
W Paul Klein. His acting and singing are unbelievable.
M I also heard the news that *LA to New York* was nominated for a musical award. ________!
W Thank you so much.

10 | 주제 고르기

다음을 듣고, 여자가 하는 말의 내용으로 가장 적절한 것을 고르시오.

① 봉사 활동 신청 ② 도난 사고 주의
③ 동아리 안내 ④ 당선 포부
⑤ 취미 생활 소개

W Hello, fellow students. My name is Jimin. As your new student leader, I will make our school ________ ________ ________. To do so, I will ________ ________ ________ in the hallway and install more security cameras. I will also make new clubs. ________ ________ ________ ________ for me in the last student election. I promise to ________ ________ ________.

고난도

11 | 일치하지 않는 내용 고르기

대화를 듣고, Miracle Science Museum에 대한 내용과 일치하지 않는 것을 고르시오.

① 학교와 가까이에 있다.
② 초록색 건물에 있다.
③ 작년에 개관했다.
④ 학생 할인을 제공한다.
⑤ 오전 11시에 문을 연다.

적중! Tip **Have you ever been to ~?**
어떤 장소에 가본 경험을 물을 때 사용되는 표현으로 '~에 가봤니?, 가본 적이 있니?'라는 의미이다. 이때 to 다음에는 장소명이 온다.
· Have you ever been to Africa?
너는 아프리카에 가봤니?

W Sam, have you ever been to the Miracle Science Museum?
M Where is it?
W It's the big green building ________ ________ ________ from our school.
M Oh, I know the one you mean. ________ ________ ________ ________, right?
W That's the one. So, have you ever visited it?
M No. I'd like to someday.
W Why don't we go on Saturday? It ________ ________ ________ for students.
M Okay. It opens at 10, so let's meet there at 11 a.m.
W Perfect.

12 | 목적 고르기

대화를 듣고, 남자가 전화를 건 목적으로 가장 적절한 것을 고르시오.

① 촬영용 카메라를 빌리기 위해서
② 약속을 취소하기 위해서
③ 이사 차량을 알아보기 위해서
④ 관광 명소를 물어보기 위해서
⑤ 지역 축제에 가기 위해서

[Cellphone rings.]
M Hey, Gracie.
W Hi, Brad. What's up?
M Didn't you say that ________ ________ ________ Jeonju?
W Right. I've been there twice.
M I'm traveling there next week. Can you ________ ________ ________ some good places to visit?
W Sure. You should visit the Hanok Village and Nambu Market.
M Thanks! I'll definitely go there and ________ ________.
W I hope you have a great time. ________ ________ ________ ________ later.

고난도

13 | 금액 정보 고르기

대화를 듣고, 여자가 받은 거스름돈으로 가장 적절한 것을 고르시오.

① $ 1 ② $ 2 ③ $ 3
④ $ 4 ⑤ $ 5

적중! Tip right away
[롸이트 어웨이]보다는 [롸이러웨이]로 들린다. [t]가 모음 사이에서 발음될 때는 약화되어 [r]에 가깝게 발음되기 때문이다.

M Good afternoon. What would you ________ ________ ________?
W Yes. I'd like to have one hamburger set and one sandwich set.
M Which size would you like, regular or large?
W Both regular, please. How much are they?
M They're 18 dollars ________ ________.
W Here's 20 dollars.
M ________ ________ ________. I'll get the hamburger and sandwich sets right away.
W Thanks a lot.

14 | 관계 고르기

대화를 듣고, 두 사람의 관계로 가장 적절한 것을 고르시오.

① 의사 — 환자
② 옷가게 점원 — 손님
③ 노트북 수리기사 — 고객
④ 컴퓨터 학원 직원 — 학생
⑤ 목수 — 가구 제작자

W Hello. Can I help you with anything?
M Yes. I would like to ________ ________ ________ a programming class.
W Okay. Have you learned anything related to programming before?
M No. This is my first time.
W I ________ ________ ________ ________ then. It starts at 1 p.m. Does that work for you?
M Sure. What do you teach on the first day of the class?
W You will learn ________ ________ ________.

15 | 제안한 일 고르기

대화를 듣고, 남자가 여자에게 제안한 일로 가장 적절한 것을 고르시오.

① 선반 조립하기
② 온라인 주문하기
③ 결혼식 참석하기
④ 해외 택배 보내기
⑤ 다른 가게 방문하기

M Good afternoon. How may I help you?
W Could you check if you have these shoes in a size 250?
M There should be some on the shelves in the ________ ________ ________.
W I looked there, but I couldn't find them.
M Hmm... ________ ________ ________. *[Typing sound]* Sorry, they are all sold out.
W I need them by Saturday for a wedding. Do you have any suggestions?
M If you order the shoes on our website today, you can get them ________ ________ ________ ________ by then.
W Great. Thanks.

16 | 이유 고르기

대화를 듣고, 남자가 걸어온 이유로 가장 적절한 것을 고르시오.

① 지각을 피하려고　② 운동을 하려고
③ 자전거가 고장 나서　④ 버스를 놓쳐서
⑤ 친구를 만나려고

M Mom, I'm home.
W Hi, Jonghyun. Why are you so sweaty?
M I walked ________ ________ ________ ________ after school.
W Why? Were you trying to get some exercise?
M No. ________ ________ ________ ________ ________ fell off.
W Oh, no. You must be exhausted from pushing your bike home.
M I am. Now I have to ________ ________ ________ ________.
W I can help you with that.

17 | 그림 상황에 적절한 대화 고르기

다음 그림의 상황에 가장 적절한 대화를 고르시오.

beauty salon

① ② ③ ④ ⑤

① **M** Was ________ ________ ________ ________?
W Yes. It's raining outside.
② **M** Is that your favorite player?
W Yes. ________ ________ ________ on the team.
③ **M** What do you usually do on Saturdays?
W I go to my favorite café.
④ **M** ________ ________ ________ ________.
W Yeah. It's snowing a lot.
⑤ **M** Where are the kids?
W They're playing on the playground with a ball.

18 | 언급하지 않은 내용 고르기

대화를 듣고, 두 사람이 앱에 관해 언급하지 않은 것을 고르시오.

① 이름　② 기능
③ 가격　④ 평점
⑤ 다운로드 횟수

적중! Tip　mobile
미국식으로는 [모블]로 발음되고, 영국식으로는 [모우바일]로 발음된다.

W Hi, Michael. What's the matter?
M Hey, Janet. My phone is ________ ________ ________.
W Have you tried Safe Cleaner?
M What is it?
W It's an app to ________ ________ ________ ________ from a mobile phone.
M I'll install it now. *[Pause]* Wow, more than one million people ________ ________ ________ ________.
W Yeah. And it has a high rating from users. It almost has five stars.
M Thanks for ________ ________ ________ about this.
W You're welcome.

19 | 적절한 응답 고르기

대화를 듣고, 남자의 마지막 말에 이어질 여자의 응답으로 가장 적절한 것을 고르시오.

Woman: ______________________________

① Can we change the schedule?
② Yes. That sounds good.
③ Try not to be late.
④ My favorite sports is swimming.
⑤ Glad you could come.

적중! Tip　What are the options?
어떤 선택지가 있는지 물을 때 사용되는 표현으로, 이 표현 다음에 여러 선택지에 대한 세부 사항(수업 종류, 시간) 등이 나올 수 있다.

M Hello. Welcome to Central Gym. ________ ________ ________ ________ ________?
W I want to sign up for a class.
M Okay. ________ ________ ________ ________ do you want to register for?
W What are the options?
M Well, there are kickboxing and swimming classes in the mornings.
W Oh, ________ ________ ________ at night.
M No problem. There's a popular golf class in the evening. ________ ________ ________?

20 | 적절한 응답 고르기

대화를 듣고, 남자의 마지막 말에 이어질 여자의 응답으로 가장 적절한 것을 고르시오.

Woman: ______________________________

① This shopping mall is huge.
② Sorry, but I can't walk anymore.
③ The price is so cheap.
④ The toilet is downstairs.
⑤ Okay. I'll go there.

[Cellphone rings.]
M Hey, Martha. What are you doing?
W I just ________ ________ ________ ________.
M Then, are you in the department store now?
W Yes. I'm ________ ________ ________ ________.
M Who are you shopping with?
W I'm ________ ________. Why do you ask that?
M I need to buy a new backpack. ________ ________ ________ ________?
W Of course you can.
M Good. I'm really close to the store. Let's meet on the first floor.

중학영어듣기 실전 모의고사 03회

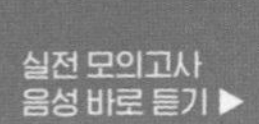

1 다음을 듣고, 수요일의 날씨로 가장 적절한 것을 고르시오.

①  ②  ③  ④ ⑤

고난도

2 대화를 듣고, 여자가 구입할 컵으로 가장 적절한 것을 고르시오.

①  ② ③ 

④ 

⑤ 

3 대화를 듣고, 남자의 심정으로 가장 적절한 것을 고르시오.

① happy ② proud ③ shy
④ bored ⑤ disappointed

4 대화를 듣고, 남자가 어제 한 일로 가장 적절한 것을 고르시오.

① 쿠키 굽기 ② 줄넘기하기
③ 요리법 알려주기 ④ 여동생 돌보기
⑤ 친구 방문하기

5 대화를 듣고, 두 사람이 대화하는 장소로 가장 적절한 곳을 고르시오.

① 카페 ② 아쿠아리움 ③ 동물원
④ 영화관 ⑤ 도서관

고난도

6 대화를 듣고, 여자의 마지막 말의 의도로 가장 적절한 것을 고르시오.

① 사과 ② 불평 ③ 승낙 ④ 충고 ⑤ 비난

7 대화를 듣고, 여자가 주문하지 <u>않은</u> 음식으로 가장 적절한 것을 고르시오.

① 수프 ② 샐러드 ③ 감자튀김
④ 주스 ⑤ 케이크

8 대화를 듣고, 남자가 대화 직후에 할 일로 가장 적절한 것을 고르시오.

① 전화하기 ② 문자 보내기
③ 사다리 주문하기 ④ 창고 확인하기
⑤ 전구 교체하기

9 대화를 듣고, 두 사람이 식당에 대해 언급하지 <u>않은</u> 것을 고르시오.

① 위치 ② 이름 ③ 개업 연도
④ 개점 시간 ⑤ 배달 요금

10 다음을 듣고, 여자가 하는 말의 내용으로 가장 적절한 것을 고르시오.

① 수영 대회 준비 ② 바닥 청소 방법
③ 수영장 안전 수칙 ④ 수업 수강 방법
⑤ 수영장 공사 일정

11 대화를 듣고, 농구 경기에 대한 내용과 일치하지 않는 것을 고르시오.

① 이번 주 토요일에 열린다.
② 오후에 시작한다.
③ 경기 시작 전 연습 시간이 있다.
④ 티켓이 이미 매진이다.
⑤ 가족은 경기 입장료가 무료이다.

12 대화를 듣고, 남자가 병원을 방문한 목적으로 가장 적절한 것을 고르시오.

① 진료를 받기 위해서
② 처방전을 받기 위해서
③ 병문안을 가기 위해서
④ 예방 접종을 받기 위해서
⑤ 봉사 활동을 하기 위해서

13 대화를 듣고, 남자의 현재 키를 고르시오.

① 165cm ② 170cm ③ 175cm
④ 180cm ⑤ 185cm

14 대화를 듣고, 두 사람의 관계로 가장 적절한 것을 고르시오.

① 감독 — 야구 선수 ② 학부모 — 교사
③ 역사 교사 — 학생 ④ 서점 직원 — 손님
⑤ 심리 상담사 — 고객

15 대화를 듣고, 여자가 남자에게 부탁한 일로 가장 적절한 것을 고르시오.

① 잡채 만들기 ② 식탁 차리기
③ 음료 따르기 ④ 당근 사 오기
⑤ 설거지하기

16 대화를 듣고, 남자가 도서관에 가는 이유로 가장 적절한 것을 고르시오.

① 책을 빌리기 위해서
② 공부를 하기 위해서
③ 행사에 참석하기 위해서
④ 친구를 만나기 위해서
⑤ 자료를 조사하기 위해서

17 다음 그림의 상황에 가장 적절한 대화를 고르시오.

① ② ③ ④ ⑤

18 다음을 듣고, 여자가 핫도그 먹기 대회에 대해 언급하지 않은 것을 고르시오.

① 개최 장소 ② 시작 연도 ③ 상품
④ 최고 기록 ⑤ 우승자 이름

[19-20] 대화를 듣고, 남자의 마지막 말에 이어질 여자의 말로 가장 적절한 것을 고르시오.

19 **Woman:** ______________________

① Their new album was just released.
② I want to get a refund.
③ She likes the red car.
④ The smaller one is perfect.
⑤ I wasn't invited to the party.

20 **Woman:** ______________________

① This candle smells good.
② I like to do yoga.
③ No. I want vanilla ice cream.
④ I prefer strawberry.
⑤ I have to relieve stress.

03회 Dictation

Dictation 음성 바로 듣기 ▶ 

03회 중학영어듣기 실전 모의고사 Dictation 음성을 들으며 빈칸에 알맞은 단어를 채우시오.

1 | 날씨 고르기

다음을 듣고, 수요일의 날씨로 가장 적절한 것을 고르시오.

① ② ③ ④ ⑤

W Good evening, everyone. Here's the weekly weather report. On Monday and Tuesday, _________ _________ _________, so bring your umbrella. On Wednesday, however, it'll be sunny all day. The weather will be _________ _________ _________ _________. Starting Thursday, it'll be cloudy, and it will rain _________ _________ _________.

고난도

2 | 알맞은 그림 고르기

대화를 듣고, 여자가 구입할 컵으로 가장 적절한 것을 고르시오.

① ② ③ ④ ⑤

M May I help you?
W I'm _________ _________ _________ _________ for my friend.
M Okay. This cup with the tail-shaped handle is our best seller.
W It looks _________ _________ _________.
M How about these ones with letters on them? They just came in yesterday.
W Actually, my friend's name is Karen, so I think the one with the letter *K* is perfect.
M Do you want the one without a handle?
W No. I'll take the one _________ _________ _________.

3 | 심정 고르기

대화를 듣고, 남자의 심정으로 가장 적절한 것을 고르시오.

① happy ② proud ③ shy ④ bored ⑤ disappointed

적중! Tip was so
[워즈 쏘]보다는 [워쏘]로 들린다. 비슷하게 발음되는 자음이 나란히 나오면 앞 단어의 끝 자음이 탈락되기 때문이다.

[Cellphone rings.]
W Hi, Jake.
M Hello, Cathy. I'm _________ _________ _________ you about our camping trip this weekend.
W We have a problem.
M _________ _________?
W The weather forecast said that it's going to rain all weekend.
M Oh, no! I was so excited to go!
W I know. Sorry, but I think we need to _________ _________ _________.
M I can't believe this!

4 | 한 일 고르기

대화를 듣고, 남자가 어제 한 일로 가장 적절한 것을 고르시오.

① 쿠키 굽기 ② 줄넘기하기
③ 요리법 알려주기 ④ 여동생 돌보기
⑤ 친구 방문하기

M Janet, this is my present for you.
W Thanks, Tim. What's in the box?
M They are _________ _________ _________ _________ with my younger sister yesterday.
W They smell delicious. _________ _________ _________ _________ in the cookies?
M Chocolate chips and nuts.
W I want to learn _________ _________ _________ too.
M You should come to my house next weekend. I'll show you how to bake them.

5 | 장소 고르기

대화를 듣고, 두 사람이 대화하는 장소로 가장 적절한 곳을 고르시오.

① 카페 ② 아쿠아리움 ③ 동물원
④ 영화관 ⑤ 도서관

W Which animal do you want to see first, Will?
M I don't know. Let's ________ ________ ________ ________.
W It says that ________ ________ ________ ________ here. We could go there.
M The lions are also nearby.
W Oh, I really want to ________ ________ ________. Can we go there first?
M Sure. After that, we can see the elephants and have lunch.
W That sounds like ________ ________ ________.

고난도

6 | 의도 고르기

대화를 듣고, 여자의 마지막 말의 의도로 가장 적절한 것을 고르시오.

① 사과 ② 불평 ③ 승낙 ④ 충고 ⑤ 비난

W Ron, can I talk to you for a minute?
M Yes, Ms. Robinson.
W ________ ________ ________ your math quiz score?
M I think I didn't really understand the equations. They were so confusing.
W That's too bad.
M Can I ________ ________ ________ about that part now?
W Of course! I'm always ________ ________ ________.

7 | 특정 정보 고르기

대화를 듣고, 여자가 주문하지 않은 음식으로 가장 적절한 것을 고르시오.

① 수프 ② 샐러드 ③ 감자튀김
④ 주스 ⑤ 케이크

> 적중! Tip Are you ready to ~?
> 상대방에게 무언가를 할 준비가 되었는지 확인할 때 사용되는 표현으로, to 다음에는 동사원형이 온다.
> · Are you ready to go out?
> 너는 외출할 준비가 되었니?

M Are you ready to place your order?
W Yes. I'll ________ ________ ________, please.
M Okay. Would you like soup or salad with that?
W Soup. I would also like some French fries.
M Of course. I'll add that ________ ________ ________. Do you want something to drink?
W An orange juice would be nice. Oh, one more thing. Do you sell cheesecake?
M We do. It's the chef's specialty.
W Wonderful. I'll have that ________ ________.

8 | 할 일 고르기

대화를 듣고, 남자가 대화 직후에 할 일로 가장 적절한 것을 고르시오.

① 전화하기 ② 문자 보내기
③ 사다리 주문하기 ④ 창고 확인하기
⑤ 전구 교체하기

적중! Tip ladder
[래덜]보다는 [래럴]로 들린다. [d]가 모음 사이에서 발음될 때는 약화되어 [r]에 가깝게 발음되기 때문이다.

W Matt, do you have a ladder?
M No. Why?
W I need to change the light bulb in the living room, but _________ _________ _________.
M Why don't you buy a new one?
W I ordered one, but _________ _________ _________ until next week.
M Hmm... You should ask James _________ _________ _________ _________.
W That's a good idea. But I don't know his phone number.
M I'll _________ _________ _________ _________.

9 | 언급하지 않은 내용 고르기

대화를 듣고, 두 사람이 식당에 대해 언급하지 않은 것을 고르시오.

① 위치 ② 이름 ③ 개업 연도
④ 개점 시간 ⑤ 배달 요금

W Michael, have you tried the pizza place in Itaewon?
M You mean Louise's Pizzeria, right?
W Yeah. I _________ _________ _________ yet.
M Really? The chef came to Korea _________ _________ _________ _________ a few years ago.
W I heard that they sell _________ _________ _________ in the city.
M They open at 5 p.m., so we can get their pizza for dinner now.
W Or, we can _________ _________ _________. It only costs 2 dollars for the delivery service.
M That's cheap.

10 | 주제 고르기

다음을 듣고, 여자가 하는 말의 내용으로 가장 적절한 것을 고르시오.

① 수영 대회 준비 ② 바닥 청소 방법
③ 수영장 안전 수칙 ④ 수업 수강 방법
⑤ 수영장 공사 일정

W Hello, everyone. Today, I'll talk _________ _________ _________ _________ at the Madison Swimming Center. First, do not run in the pool area. The floor is wet, so you might _________ _________ _________ _________. Second, do not dive. The water is not deep, so diving may cause a head injury. Finally, food and drinks _________ _________ _________ in the pool area.

11 | 일치하지 않는 내용 고르기

대화를 듣고, 농구 경기에 대한 내용과 일치하지 않는 것을 고르시오.

① 이번 주 토요일에 열린다.
② 오후에 시작한다.
③ 경기 시작 전 연습 시간이 있다.
④ 티켓이 이미 매진이다.
⑤ 가족은 경기 입장료가 무료이다.

W Mr. Benson, when is our next basketball game?
M It's this Saturday.
W I have _________ _________ _________ on Saturday at 11 a.m.
M That's fine. The game starts at 3 p.m.
W What about the practice?
M You'll _________ _________ _________ _________, but that won't be a problem.
W Okay. By the way, my parents _________ _________ _________ _________ for the game. Are they sold out?
M No, they aren't. And the tickets are _________ _________ _________ _________.

12 목적 고르기

대화를 듣고, 남자가 병원을 방문한 목적으로 가장 적절한 것을 고르시오.

① 진료를 받기 위해서
② 처방전을 받기 위해서
③ 병문안을 가기 위해서
④ 예방 접종을 받기 위해서
⑤ 봉사 활동을 하기 위해서

적중! Tip I hope ~.
희망이나 기대감을 나타낼 때 사용되는 표현으로 '~하기를 바랄게요, ~하면 좋겠어요'라는 의미이다.
· I hope he likes the gift.
그가 그 선물을 좋아하기를 바랄게요.

W May I help you?
M __________ __________ __________ a patient. She's in Room 405.
W Take the stairs on the right. That room's on the fourth floor.
M Okay.
W Are you __________ __________ __________?
M No. My sister was in a car accident yesterday.
W Oh, no. I hope __________ __________ __________ __________.
M I hope so too.

13 숫자 정보 고르기

대화를 듣고, 남자의 현재 키를 고르시오.

① 165cm ② 170cm ③ 175cm
④ 180cm ⑤ 185cm

W Hi, Jason. I didn't recognize you! When did you get so tall?
M Hey, Amanda. I grew 10 centimeters this year.
W How tall are you?
M I was 175 centimeters tall when you __________ __________ __________ __________.
W Then, you are now 185 centimeters tall?
M Yeah. Now, I am __________ __________ __________ __________.
W Wow. You should really __________ __________ __________ the volleyball team.
M Maybe I will.

14 관계 고르기

대화를 듣고, 두 사람의 관계로 가장 적절한 것을 고르시오.

① 감독 — 야구 선수 ② 학부모 — 교사
③ 역사 교사 — 학생 ④ 서점 직원 — 손님
⑤ 심리 상담사 — 고객

M Hi, Ms. Simmons.
W Hey, Richard. Did you __________ __________ __________ for your history project?
M I want to do my presentation on the Joseon Dynasty.
W That's __________ __________ __________. Why did you pick the Joseon Dynasty?
M I want to learn more about King Sejo.
W Okay. I can __________ __________ __________ to read for your project.
M I'd like that.
W Remember, you also have to __________ __________ __________ __________ on Friday.

15 | 부탁·요청한 일 고르기

대화를 듣고, 여자가 남자에게 부탁한 일로 가장 적절한 것을 고르시오.

① 잡채 만들기 ② 식탁 차리기
③ 음료 따르기 ④ 당근 사 오기
⑤ 설거지하기

M Honey, what is ________ ________ ________?
W I'm making gimbab and egg soup for dinner.
M Great. I'll set the table. Uh, what are ________ ________ ________?
W Oh, I forgot. I was going to use them to make japchae, but we didn't ________ ________ ________.
M Do you want me to get those now?
W Yes, please. Can you go buy two carrots?
M Sure.

16 | 이유 고르기

대화를 듣고, 남자가 도서관에 가는 이유로 가장 적절한 것을 고르시오.

① 책을 빌리기 위해서
② 공부를 하기 위해서
③ 행사에 참석하기 위해서
④ 친구를 만나기 위해서
⑤ 자료를 조사하기 위해서

적중! Tip Why not?
상대방의 의견이나 제안에 동의할 때 쓰는 표현이다. '왜 안 되겠어?'라는 뉘앙스로 즉, '당연하지'라는 의미이다.

M Hi, Tara!
W Hey, Paul! Where are you going?
M I'm going to the library.
W Oh, are you going to ________ ________ ________ for the science report?
M No. I already bought the books I need from the bookstore.
W Then, ________ ________ ________ to the library?
M ________ ________ ________ is coming to the library. He is going to read a chapter of his new book for his fans.
W That's cool. Can I ________ ________ ________?
M Why not?

17 | 그림 상황에 적절한 대화 고르기

다음 그림의 상황에 가장 적절한 대화를 고르시오.

① ② ③ ④ ⑤

① **M** I ________ ________ ________. Your trip looked amazing.
W Yes. I didn't want to come back.
② **M** What should we eat tonight?
W I'll order a chicken.
③ **M** How can I help you?
W I need to ________ ________ ________.
④ **M** Let me help you carry those boxes. They look heavy.
W Thank you ________ ________ ________.
⑤ **M** What do you want for your birthday present?
W I'd like ________ ________ ________.

18 | 언급하지 않은 내용 고르기

다음을 듣고, 여자가 핫도그 먹기 대회에 대해 언급하지 않은 것을 고르시오.

① 개최 장소 ② 시작 연도 ③ 상품
④ 최고 기록 ⑤ 우승자 이름

W Did you know that ________ ________ ________ ________ ________ is held on Coney Island? This event ________ ________ ________ every year since 1972. The winner of this event is awarded a yellow belt. In 2021, a man ________ ________ ________ ________ by eating 76 hotdogs in 10 minutes.

19 | 적절한 응답 고르기

대화를 듣고, 남자의 마지막 말에 이어질 여자의 말로 가장 적절한 것을 고르시오.

Woman: ____________________

① Their new album was just released.
② I want to get a refund.
③ She likes the red car.
④ The smaller one is perfect.
⑤ I wasn't invited to the party.

M Hello. Do you need help ________ ________ ________ ________?
W Yes. I'm looking for a poster of my favorite band.
M Okay. What is your favorite band?
W I am ________ ________ ________ ________ Red Punk.
M Oh, they're very popular. Here are two of their posters.
W I love the one with them in the car.
M Okay. Do you want ________ ________ ________ ________ poster?

20 | 적절한 응답 고르기

대화를 듣고, 남자의 마지막 말에 이어질 여자의 말로 가장 적절한 것을 고르시오.

Woman: ____________________

① This candle smells good.
② I like to do yoga.
③ No. I want vanilla ice cream.
④ I prefer strawberry.
⑤ I have to relieve stress.

적중! Tip need to

[니드 투]보다는 [니투]로 들린다. [d]와 [t]처럼 발음할 때 혀의 위치가 비슷한 자음이 나란히 나오면 앞 단어의 끝 자음이 탈락되기 때문이다.

· spend time [스펜타임] · front desk [프론데스크]

M It smells so good in here. What is that scent?
W It's ________ ________ ________ that I bought. It has a coffee smell.
M That's one of ________ ________ ________. I love vanilla candles too.
W I don't really like vanilla, but I like the smell of lavender a lot. It helps me relax.
M I need to ________ ________ ________. What else do you do to relax?

04회 중학영어듣기 실전 모의고사

실전 모의고사 음성 바로 듣기 ▶

1 다음을 듣고, 런던의 날씨로 가장 적절한 것을 고르시오.

① ② ③ ④ ⑤

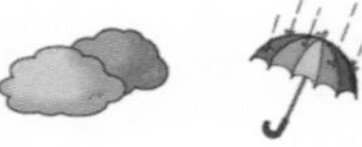

고난도

2 대화를 듣고, 여자가 만든 머리핀으로 가장 적절한 것을 고르시오.

① ② ③

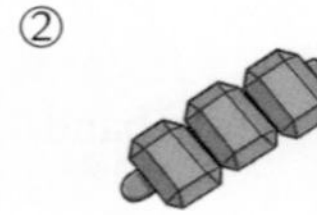

④ ⑤

3 대화를 듣고, 남자의 마지막 말의 의도로 가장 적절한 것을 고르시오.

① 거절 ② 감사 ③ 부탁 ④ 축하 ⑤ 동의

4 대화를 듣고, 남자가 스승의 날에 한 일로 가장 적절한 것을 고르시오.

① 노래하기 ② 편지 쓰기
③ 카네이션 접기 ④ 소풍 가기
⑤ 단체 사진 찍기

5 대화를 듣고, 두 사람이 대화하는 장소로 가장 적절한 곳을 고르시오.

① 놀이공원 ② 공항 ③ 옷가게
④ 농구 경기장 ⑤ 애완용품점

6 대화를 듣고, 새로운 도서관에 대한 내용으로 일치하지 않는 것을 고르시오.

① 건축가 Nicole Williams가 지었다.
② 다음 주에 개관한다.
③ 시내에 위치하고 있다.
④ 큰 아동 도서 코너가 있다.
⑤ 한 달에 한 번 행사를 한다.

7 대화를 듣고, 남자가 이탈리아어를 배우기 위해 할 일을 고르시오.

① 서점에 가기 ② 라디오 듣기
③ 이탈리아 영화 보기 ④ 인터넷 강의 듣기
⑤ 이탈리아 친구 사귀기

8 대화를 듣고, 남자가 대화 직후에 할 일로 가장 적절한 것을 고르시오.

① 운동화 검색하기 ② 동영상 보기
③ 신발 가게 가기 ④ 육상부 가입하기
⑤ 응원 용품 사기

9 대화를 듣고, 여자가 체험 학습에 대해 언급하지 않은 것을 고르시오.

① 체험 장소 ② 교통편 ③ 준비물
④ 체험 내용 ⑤ 종료 시간

고난도

10 다음을 듣고, 남자가 하는 말의 내용으로 가장 적절한 것을 고르시오.

① 티켓 예매 방법 ② 과학실 이용 예절
③ 재난 대피 요령 ④ 태풍 체험전 안전 수칙
⑤ 실험 도구 사용 안내

11 대화를 듣고, 음악 연주회에 대한 내용과 일치하지 않는 것을 고르시오.

① 오페라 하우스에서 열린다.
② 이번 주 일요일에 열린다.
③ 티켓 가격은 무료이다.
④ 유명한 가수가 공연한다.
⑤ 오후 5시 30분에 시작한다.

고난도
12 대화를 듣고, 여자가 백화점에 가는 목적으로 가장 적절한 것을 고르시오.

① 밥을 먹기 위해서
② 친구 선물을 사기 위해서
③ 장화를 사기 위해서
④ 전시를 보기 위해서
⑤ 목걸이를 수리하기 위해서

13 대화를 듣고, 여자가 지불해야 할 금액으로 가장 적절한 것을 고르시오.

① $ 2 ② $ 3 ③ $ 10
④ $ 13 ⑤ $ 15

14 대화를 듣고, 두 사람의 관계로 가장 적절한 것을 고르시오.

① 승무원 — 탑승객
② 바리스타 — 손님
③ 교사 — 학생
④ 여행 가이드 — 여행객
⑤ 만화 작가 — 독자

15 대화를 듣고, 여자가 남자에게 요청한 일로 가장 적절한 것을 고르시오.

① 가방 맡기기 ② 이어폰 빌려주기
③ 개 산책시키기 ④ 공원에 함께 가기
⑤ 음악 찾아보기

16 대화를 듣고, 여자가 남자에게 마카롱을 준 이유로 가장 적절한 것을 고르시오.

① 가게를 홍보하고 싶어서
② 가정 실습 후 나눠먹기 위해서
③ 생일을 축하하고 싶어서
④ 응원하는 마음을 전하기 위해서
⑤ 다른 친구의 부탁을 받아서

17 다음 그림의 상황에 가장 적절한 대화를 고르시오.

① ② ③ ④ ⑤

18 다음을 듣고, 여자가 TV 프로그램에 대해 언급하지 않은 것을 고르시오.

① 방영 채널 ② 방영 요일 ③ 진행자
④ 방송 주제 ⑤ 방송 시간

[19-20] 대화를 듣고, 여자의 마지막 말에 이어질 남자의 말로 가장 적절한 것을 고르시오.

19 **Man:** ______________________

① I don't know the answer.
② I failed the science quiz.
③ She won the game.
④ Those are the rules.
⑤ Sure. I'll install it right away.

20 **Man:** ______________________

① Okay, I'll see you then.
② It's very scary.
③ Popcorn, please.
④ That's her favorite movie.
⑤ The tickets are sold out.

04회 Dictation

Dictation
음성 바로 듣기 ▶

04회 중학영어듣기 실전 모의고사 Dictation 음성을 들으며 빈칸에 알맞은 단어를 채우시오.

1 날씨 고르기

다음을 듣고, 런던의 날씨로 가장 적절한 것을 고르시오.

① ② ③ ④ ⑤

M Good morning! Here is today's ________ ________. In Seoul, there will be ________ ________ ________ ________ and strong wind. London will have heavy rain, and there is ________ ________ ________ ________. In San Francisco, however, it's going to be sunny and the sky will be clear. Thank you.

고난도

2 알맞은 그림 고르기

대화를 듣고, 여자가 만든 머리핀으로 가장 적절한 것 고르시오.

① ② ③ ④ ⑤

M Melinda, how was your day?

W It was great. I ________ ________ ________ ________ for Mom.

M Is this it? I like the diamond-shaped jewel ________ ________ ________ ________. Where did you get that jewel?

W I bought it at a Seoul Market yesterday. I also bought a shell-shaped jewel.

M Oh, why didn't you put it ________ ________ ________?

W I didn't think Mom would like it.

3 의도 고르기

대화를 듣고, 남자의 마지막 말의 의도로 가장 적절한 것을 고르시오.

① 거절 ② 감사 ③ 부탁 ④ 축하 ⑤ 동의

W Good morning, Dad. You ________ ________ ________ ________ today.

M Yes. I'm going on a business trip to Pyeongchang today.

W I heard that it's going to snow a lot there this week. Please be careful ________ ________ ________ on the highway.

M Alright, I'll be careful. ________ ________ ________, and have some cereal.

W Okay, Dad. Can you ________ ________ ________ ________ to school today?

M I'm sorry, but could you take the bus?

4 한 일 고르기

대화를 듣고, 남자가 스승의 날에 한 일로 가장 적절한 것을 고르시오.

① 노래하기 ② 편지 쓰기
③ 카네이션 접기 ④ 소풍 가기
⑤ 단체 사진 찍기

W Andy, what are you watching on your cellphone?

M ________ ________ ________ ________ that I took on Teachers' Day, Grandma.

W Oh, who is the girl singing in front of the class?

M That's Christine, and she also played the guitar.

W ________ ________ ________ ________. Did you give your teacher something for Teachers' Day?

M Yes. My classmates and I ________ ________ ________ on a big piece of paper.

W That is ________ ________ ________ ________.

5 | 장소 고르기

대화를 듣고, 두 사람이 대화하는 장소로 가장 적절한 곳을 고르시오.

① 놀이공원 ② 공항 ③ 옷가게
④ 농구 경기장 ⑤ 애완용품점

적중! Tip gift shop
[기프트 샵]보다는 [깁샵]으로 들린다. 자음 3개가 연속해서 나오면 중간 자음은 발음되지 않기 때문이다.

M I __________ __________ __________ __________ this basketball game.
W Me too. It's going to be so exciting!
M Do you want to __________ __________ __________?
W Yes. And I want to buy a T-shirt at the gift shop.
M Okay. Let's go there first.
W We have so much to do. Hurry!
M Relax. We still __________ __________ __________ before the game starts.

6 | 일치하지 않는 내용 고르기

대화를 듣고, 새로운 도서관에 대한 내용으로 일치하지 않는 것을 고르시오.

① 건축가 Nicole Williams가 지었다.
② 다음 주에 개관한다.
③ 시내에 위치하고 있다.
④ 큰 아동 도서 코너가 있다.
⑤ 한 달에 한 번 행사를 한다.

W Kevin, what are you reading?
M I'm reading an article about the new library __________ __________ __________ __________.
W I heard it opens next week, doesn't it?
M Right. And it was built __________ __________ __________ __________, Nicole Williams.
W Oh, really?
M Yeah! And there will be a huge children's section.
W Wow, I __________ __________ __________.
M They'll also __________ __________ at the library every week.
W I really want to visit soon.

7 | 할 일 고르기

대화를 듣고, 남자가 이탈리아어를 배우기 위해 할 일을 고르시오.

① 서점에 가기 ② 라디오 듣기
③ 이탈리아 영화 보기 ④ 인터넷 강의 듣기
⑤ 이탈리아 친구 사귀기

적중! Tip bored these days
[보얼드 디즈 데이즈]보다는 [보얼디즈데이즈]로 들린다. 비슷하게 발음되는 자음이 나란히 오면 앞 단어의 끝 자음이 탈락되기 때문이다.

W Hey, Paul. How are you doing?
M To be honest, I'm really bored these days.
W Then, why don't you __________ __________ __________?
M That's not a bad idea. Learning Italian could be fun.
W How are you going to study it?
M I'll __________ __________ __________ __________ for kids and learn some basic words first.
W That sounds like a good way __________ __________ __________ __________ __________.

8 할 일 고르기

대화를 듣고, 남자가 대화 직후에 할 일로 가장 적절한 것을 고르시오.

① 운동화 검색하기 ② 동영상 보기
③ 신발 가게 가기 ④ 육상부 가입하기
⑤ 응원 용품 사기

적중! Tip That's why ~.

어떤 일에 대한 이유를 나타낼 때 사용되는 표현으로 '그래서 ~하다, 그것이 ~한 이유이다'라는 의미이다.

· That's why she looked sad.
그래서 그녀가 슬퍼 보였던 거예요.

M Brenda, _____ _____ _____ _____ _____?
W I'm going to the running track now.
M That's why you're _____ _____ _____.
W Yes. I love these shoes. They are so light that I can run fast.
M That's exactly _____ _____ _____. Where did you buy those?
W The shoe shop on 3rd Street. These shoes are on sale now.
M Then, I'll go there right now.

9 언급하지 않은 내용 고르기

대화를 듣고, 여자가 체험 학습에 대해 언급하지 않은 것을 고르시오.

① 체험 장소 ② 교통편 ③ 준비물
④ 체험 내용 ⑤ 종료 시간

W Tomorrow, our class will go on _____ _____ _____ to a farm.
M Ms. Green, how will we get there?
W We'll take a bus _____ _____ _____.
M Is there anything we should bring?
W Good question! You need to _____ _____ _____ _____.
M Why do we need gloves?
W We will plant potatoes at the farm, so you'll need them _____ _____ _____ _____.
M Okay.

고난도

10 주제 고르기

다음을 듣고, 남자가 하는 말의 내용으로 가장 적절한 것을 고르시오.

① 티켓 예매 방법 ② 과학실 이용 예절
③ 재난 대피 요령 ④ 태풍 체험전 안전 수칙
⑤ 실험 도구 사용 안내

M Welcome to the National Science Museum. Please _____ _____ _____ _____ in the Typhoon Experience Exhibit. First of all, _____ _____ _____ will blow, so hold on to the rail in front of you. Also, do not _____ _____ _____ _____. Lastly, keep your raincoat on. If you take it off, your clothes will get wet.

11 일치하지 않는 내용 고르기

대화를 듣고, 음악 연주회에 대한 내용과 일치하지 않는 것을 고르시오.

① 오페라 하우스에서 열린다.
② 이번 주 일요일에 열린다.
③ 티켓 가격은 무료이다.
④ 유명한 가수가 공연한다.
⑤ 오후 5시 30분에 시작한다.

W Harry, do you want to go to _____ _____ _____ _____ held at the Opera House?
M Sure. When is it?
W It's going to _____ _____ _____ _____.
M I've never been there before. _____ _____ _____?
W No. They are free. I also heard that a famous singer will perform that day.
M It _____ _____ _____. I think we should get there early.
W It begins at 6, so let's meet at 5.
M Perfect!

고난도

12 | 목적 고르기

대화를 듣고, 여자가 백화점에 가는 목적으로 가장 적절한 것을 고르시오.

① 밥을 먹기 위해서
② 친구 선물을 사기 위해서
③ 장화를 사기 위해서
④ 전시를 보기 위해서
⑤ 목걸이를 수리하기 위해서

M Hi, Kate. Where are you going?
W _________ _________ _________ a department store.
M The one next to the police station?
W Yes. I need to buy a birthday gift for my friend.
M Have you decided _________ _________ _________?
W Yes. I searched for shirts on the Internet, but I want to see them in person.
M Yeah. Sometimes products _________ _________ online.
W Do you want to come with me?
M Okay. I'm free now.

13 | 금액 정보 고르기

대화를 듣고, 여자가 지불해야 할 금액으로 가장 적절한 것을 고르시오.

① $ 2 ② $ 3 ③ $ 10
④ $ 13 ⑤ $ 15

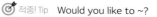

 적중! Tip Would you like to ~?
'~하고 싶으신가요?, ~하시겠어요?'라는 의미이며, 특히 가게에서 점원이 손님에게 의향을 물어볼 때 많이 사용된다.
· Would you like to drink a cup of tea?
차 한 잔 드시겠어요?

M Good morning. _________ _________ _________ _________ _________?
W I'd like to order a bulgogi hamburger set.
M Okay. It's 10 dollars.
W Could I have a large drink _________ _________ _________ _________ _________?
M Sure, but it will cost two dollars more. Would you like to change your French fries to a large size too?
W Yes. _________ _________ _________ _________ in total?
M It's 13 dollars.
W Here you are.
M Thank you. _________ _________ _________ _________.

14 | 관계 고르기

대화를 듣고, 두 사람의 관계로 가장 적절한 것을 고르시오.

① 승무원 — 탑승객
② 바리스타 — 손님
③ 교사 — 학생
④ 여행 가이드 — 여행객
⑤ 만화 작가 — 독자

W Hi. I'm sorry, but there is a mistake.
M What's wrong?
W I ordered an iced coffee, but I _________ _________ _________ _________.
M Oh, I see. Can I see your receipt, please?
W Sure. Here you go.
M You are right. _________ _________ _________ _________ an iced coffee right away.
W Thank you so much!
M Please take this cookie too. We _________ _________ _________ _________.

15 | 부탁·요청한 일 고르기

대화를 듣고, 여자가 남자에게 요청한 일로 가장 적절한 것을 고르시오.

① 가방 맡기기 ② 이어폰 빌려주기
③ 개 산책시키기 ④ 공원에 함께 가기
⑤ 음악 찾아보기

M Olivia, can I borrow your earphones?
W Sure. They're in my bag. *[Pause]* Oh, no!
M What's wrong?
W I think ________ ________ ________ on a bench in the park.
M What did you do there?
W I sat down on a bench ________ ________ ________ ________. Can you go to the park with me to find my earphones?
M Of course.
W Thank you so much. I hope ________ ________ ________ ________.

16 | 이유 고르기

대화를 듣고, 여자가 남자에게 마카롱을 준 이유로 가장 적절한 것을 고르시오.

① 가게를 홍보하고 싶어서
② 가정 실습 후 나눠먹기 위해서
③ 생일을 축하하고 싶어서
④ 응원하는 마음을 전하기 위해서
⑤ 다른 친구의 부탁을 받아서

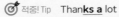

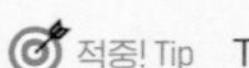
적중! Tip Than**ks a** lot
[땡크스 어 랏]보다는 [땡써랏]으로 들린다. 자음 3개가 연속해서 나오면 중간 자음은 발음되지 않고, 앞에 나온 단어의 끝 자음과 뒤에 나온 단어의 첫 모음이 연음되기 때문이다.

M Hey, Yura. What is this box?
W It's ________ ________ ________ ________. Open it up.
M Really? Thanks a lot. *[Pause]* Wow, there are macarons in the box!
W You're welcome.
M Why are you giving these to me? It's not my birthday today.
W I know. I just want to ________ ________ ________. You seem exhausted recently.
M You're so kind.
W I'm ________ ________ ________ ________.

17 | 그림 상황에 적절한 대화 고르기

다음 그림의 상황에 가장 적절한 대화를 고르시오.

① ② ③ ④ ⑤

① **M** Would you like ________ ________ ________?
W Yes. I'd like a glass of apple juice, please.
② **M** ________ ________ ________ ________ with my dog?
W Actually, he is a bit overweight for his age.
③ **M** Your rabbit is so cute!
W Thanks. Her name is Bella.
④ **M** What's your favorite animal?
W ________ ________ ________ ________.
⑤ **M** Can I borrow your pen?
W Yes. Here you go.

18 | 언급하지 않은 내용 고르기

다음을 듣고, 여자가 TV 프로그램에 대해 언급하지 않은 것을 고르시오.

① 방영 채널 ② 방영 요일 ③ 진행자
④ 방송 주제 ⑤ 방송 시간

W Hello, everyone. ________ ________ ________ ________ our new TV program *History Mystery Show*. This amazing new show ________ ________ ________ on Channel 4 tonight. Jisoo, a popular celebrity in Korea, will be the host. Don't miss the first episode on ________ ________ ________ ________ ________. Tune in tonight at 7 p.m.

19 | 적절한 응답 고르기

대화를 듣고, 여자의 마지막 말에 이어질 남자의 말로 가장 적절한 것을 고르시오.

Man: ____________________

① I don't know the answer.
② I failed the science quiz.
③ She won the game.
④ Those are the rules.
⑤ Sure. I'll install it right away.

M What are you playing on your phone, Olivia?
W It's *Quiz Mania*. It's a new game I bought.
M What are the quizzes about?
W You can ________ ________ ________ ________ including science, culture, and history.
M Is it difficult?
W Yeah. But it's also fun. Are you ________ ________ ________ ________ too?
M Yes. I think I'll download it now.
W Then, I can invite you to this game. What about ________ ________ ________ now?

20 | 적절한 응답 고르기

대화를 듣고, 여자의 마지막 말에 이어질 남자의 말로 가장 적절한 것을 고르시오.

Man: ____________________

① Okay, I'll see you then.
② It's very scary.
③ Popcorn, please.
④ That's her favorite movie.
⑤ The tickets are sold out.

적중! Tip Absolu**tely**

[앱솔루틀리]보다는 [앱솔룻올리]로 들린다. [t]와 [l]처럼 발음할 때 혀의 위치가 비슷한 자음이 나란히 나오면 앞 발음이 탈락되기 때문이다.

· la**tel**y [레잇올리] · shor**tl**y [숄올리]

W What should we do at your house tonight, Blake?
M Why don't we ________ ________ ________?
W Okay. What kind of movies do you prefer?
M ________ ________ ________ ________.
W Me too! What about the new zombie movie?
M That's perfect. Should we also ________ ________ ________?
W Absolutely! I can bring nachos or popcorn. ________ ________ ________ ________ ________?

05회 중학영어듣기 실전 모의고사

실전 모의고사 음성 바로 듣기 ▶

1 다음을 듣고, 일요일 오전의 날씨로 가장 적절한 것을 고르시오.

①  ②  ③  ④ ⑤ 

2 대화를 듣고, 여자가 구입할 모자로 가장 적절한 것을 고르시오.

①   ②   ③ 

④  ⑤ 

3 대화를 듣고, 남자의 마지막 말의 의도로 가장 적절한 것을 고르시오.

① 조언 ② 부탁 ③ 거절 ④ 격려 ⑤ 동의

4 대화를 듣고, 남자가 여름방학에 한 일로 가장 적절한 것을 고르시오.

① 사촌 만나기
② 여행 가기
③ 놀이공원 가기
④ 수영 배우기
⑤ 맛집 탐방하기

5 대화를 듣고, 두 사람이 대화하는 장소로 가장 적절한 곳을 고르시오.

① 기차역
② 도서관
③ 세탁소
④ 병원
⑤ 박물관

고난도

6 대화를 듣고, 요리 강좌에 대한 내용과 일치하지 않는 것을 고르시오.

① 채식 요리를 배운다.
② 다음 일요일에 열린다.
③ 유료 강좌이다.
④ 활동 시간은 2시간이다.
⑤ 앞치마를 가져가야 한다.

7 대화를 듣고, 여자가 좋아하는 운동으로 가장 적절한 것을 고르시오.

① 축구
② 농구
③ 테니스
④ 스키 점프
⑤ 스피드 스케이팅

8 대화를 듣고, 남자가 대화 직후에 할 일로 가장 적절한 것을 고르시오.

① 물건 구입하기
② 환불 처리하기
③ 창고 확인하기
④ 재고 정리하기
⑤ 매니저 부르기

고난도

9 대화를 듣고, 두 사람이 Hamilton Park에 대해 언급하지 않은 것을 고르시오.

① 공원 입장료
② 지도 가격
③ 공원 크기
④ 공원 시설
⑤ 시설 예약 방법

10 다음을 듣고, 남자가 하는 말의 내용으로 가장 적절한 것을 고르시오.

① 컴퓨터 사용법
② 성적을 향상하는 법
③ 시험 응시 신청 방법
④ 인터넷 강의 종류
⑤ 적절한 휴식의 필요성

고난도

11 대화를 듣고, Griffith Marathon 행사에 대한 내용과 일치하지 않는 것을 고르시오.

① 다음 주 토요일에 열린다.
② 야생동물 보호를 위한 모금 행사이다.
③ 5km 마라톤의 참가비는 50달러이다.
④ 오전 7시 45분에 줄을 서야 한다.
⑤ 참가자가 물을 준비해야 한다.

12 대화를 듣고, 여자가 전화를 건 목적으로 가장 적절한 것을 고르시오.

① 분실물을 찾기 위해서
② 배달을 요청하기 위해서
③ 메뉴를 선주문하기 위해서
④ 예약을 변경하기 위해서
⑤ 식당 정보를 얻기 위해서

13 대화를 듣고, 두 사람이 만날 시각을 고르시오.

① 2:30 p.m. ② 3:00 p.m. ③ 3:30 p.m.
④ 4:00 p.m. ⑤ 4:30 p.m.

14 대화를 듣고, 두 사람의 관계로 가장 적절한 것을 고르시오.

① 소설가 — 독자 ② 디자이너 — 모델
③ 꽃집 직원 — 손님 ④ 기자 — 화가
⑤ 과학 교사 — 학생

15 대화를 듣고, 여자가 남자에게 부탁한 일로 가장 적절한 것을 고르시오.

① 빨래하기 ② 설거지하기
③ 식탁 차리기 ④ 떡볶이 만들기
⑤ 청소기 돌리기

16 대화를 듣고, 여자가 비행기를 놓친 이유로 가장 적절한 것을 고르시오.

① 차가 고장 나서
② 늦게 일어나서
③ 친구가 늦게 와서
④ 여권을 두고 와서
⑤ 공항에서 길을 잃어서

17 다음 그림의 상황에 가장 적절한 대화를 고르시오.

① ② ③ ④ ⑤

18 다음을 듣고, 여자가 Fremont Art Festival에 대해 언급하지 않은 것을 고르시오.

① 행사 목적 ② 행사 날짜 ③ 참가비
④ 전시 품목 ⑤ 공연 장소

[19-20] 대화를 듣고, 남자의 마지막 말에 이어질 여자의 말로 가장 적절한 것을 고르시오.

19 **Woman:** ______________________

① She's working out hard.
② No. I don't know the way there.
③ The water is so blue!
④ It's about 500 meters away.
⑤ Two cokes, please.

20 **Woman:** ______________________

① He won a prize.
② It's a poetry contest.
③ The competition will begin soon.
④ You can begin writing.
⑤ I need a vacation.

05회 Dictation

Dictation 음성 바로 듣기 ▶ 

05회 중학영어듣기 실전 모의고사 Dictation 음성을 들으며 빈칸에 알맞은 단어를 채우시오.

1 | 날씨 고르기

다음을 듣고, 일요일 오전의 날씨로 가장 적절한 것을 고르시오.

① ② ③ ④ ⑤

W It's time for the weekend weather forecast. On Saturday morning, you'll _________ _________ _________ and clear skies. In the afternoon, however, it'll be cloudy and gray. On Sunday, it's going to _________ _________ until noon. The snow will stop in the evening, and then the sky will clear. It'll be perfect for _________ _________ _________ in the snow.

2 | 알맞은 그림 고르기

대화를 듣고, 여자가 구입할 모자로 가장 적절한 것을 고르시오.

① ② ③ ④ ⑤

W Hi. I'm _________ _________ _________ _________ for my nephew.
M Welcome to our store. We have a variety of children's hats.
W Wow, they all look cute.
M What about this cap with a little duck on it?
W I _________ _________ _________ in animal shapes.
M Okay. We have one with rabbit ears. And this one has frog eyes instead of ears. Which one do you like better?
W I'll take the _________ _________ _________ _________.

3 | 의도 고르기

대화를 듣고, 남자의 마지막 말의 의도로 가장 적절한 것을 고르시오.

① 조언 ② 부탁 ③ 거절 ④ 격려 ⑤ 동의

M Hey, Minji. Have you _________ _________ _________ Nara?
W No, not yet.
M What's wrong? Why didn't you tell her you're sorry?
W Well, she also hurt my feelings.
M Listen. The fight was your fault. You told her a lie.
W But I didn't _________ _________ _________ _________.
M I know you didn't. But that's not an excuse. _________ _________ _________.

4 | 한 일 고르기

대화를 듣고, 남자가 여름방학에 한 일로 가장 적절한 것을 고르시오.

① 사촌 만나기 ② 여행 가기
③ 놀이공원 가기 ④ 수영 배우기
⑤ 맛집 탐방하기

적중! Tip glad to
[글래드 투]보다는 [글래투]로 들린다. [d]와 [t]처럼 발음할 때 혀의 위치가 비슷한 자음이 나란히 나오면 앞 단어의 끝 자음이 탈락되기 때문이다.

W Suho, long time no see.
M Hi, Jihyun. It's nice to see you. _________ _________ _________ _________ _________?
W I had a great time. I visited my cousin in Hong Kong.
M That _________ _________! What did you like the most?
W My favorite was going to a theme park. I also had a lot of _________ _________. What about you?
M I finally learned _________ _________ _________.
W I'm glad to hear that!

5 장소 고르기

대화를 듣고, 두 사람이 대화하는 장소로 가장 적절한 곳을 고르시오.

① 기차역 ② 도서관 ③ 세탁소
④ 병원 ⑤ 박물관

 적중! Tip look at

[룩 앳]보다는 [루깻]으로 들린다. 앞에 나온 단어의 끝 자음과 뒤에 나온 단어의 첫 모음이 연음되고, 이때 강세가 없는 [k]는 된소리로 발음되기 때문이다.

· pick up [피컵] · talk about [토꺼바웃]

W What should we look at first, Jinsu?
M I would like to see ________ ________ ________ ________. I find them interesting.
W Me too. This museum has ________ ________ ________ ________ dinosaur bones in our country.
M I didn't know that. That's amazing.
W Let's go there now.
M ________ ________ ________ that the collection is on the third floor.
W Okay. I can't wait!

고난도

6 일치하지 않는 내용 고르기

대화를 듣고, 요리 강좌에 대한 내용과 일치하지 않는 것을 고르시오.

① 채식 요리를 배운다.
② 다음 일요일에 열린다.
③ 유료 강좌이다.
④ 활동 시간은 2시간이다.
⑤ 앞치마를 가져가야 한다.

M Stacy, look at this poster. There's a Vegetarians for Beginners Workshop next Friday.
W Are you interested?
M Yes. Let's sign up for it. We can learn how to cook delicious meals ________ ________ ________.
W Is it a free class?
M No. But it ________ ________ ________ ________. The event starts at 9 a.m.
W It ends before 12 p.m., right?
M Yes. It ________ ________ ________ ________.
W I'll see you then.
M Don't forget to bring an apron.

7 특정 정보 고르기

대화를 듣고, 여자가 좋아하는 운동으로 가장 적절한 것을 고르시오.

① 축구 ② 농구
③ 테니스 ④ 스키 점프
⑤ 스피드 스케이팅

W Who is that in the picture, Aaron?
M This is Harry Kane, an English soccer player.
W I think I ________ ________ ________ in a magazine.
M He's famous, so you can find many interviews. Who's ________ ________ ________?
W I like Lee Sanghwa. She was a Korean speed skater.
M I know her. She won a gold medal at the Olympics, right?
W Yeah. Speed skating became my favorite sport ________ ________ ________ ________.

8 | 할 일 고르기

대화를 듣고, 남자가 대화 직후에 할 일로 가장 적절한 것을 고르시오.

① 물건 구입하기 ② 환불 처리하기
③ 창고 확인하기 ④ 재고 정리하기
⑤ 매니저 부르기

M Good afternoon. What can I do for you?
W Hi, I ________ ________ ________ ________.
M Okay. One jacket, two shirts, and a pair of socks. Will that be all?
W Yes. I don't need anything else.
M Did you check the sizes of ________ ________ ________?
W Uh, wait. This isn't medium. Do you have this jacket in medium?
M Just a minute. ________ ________ ________ in storage.

고난도

9 | 언급하지 않은 내용 고르기

대화를 듣고, 두 사람이 Hamilton Park에 대해 언급하지 않은 것을 고르시오.

① 공원 입장료 ② 지도 가격
③ 공원 크기 ④ 공원 시설
⑤ 시설 예약 방법

W Welcome to the Hamilton Park Information Center. How can I help you today?
M Hi. I was wondering if I could ________ ________ ________ of the park.
W It's two dollars. Here you go. ________ ________?
M How big is the park?
W It's the size of 70 soccer fields.
M Wow, that's really big. ________ ________ ________ ________?
W It has a rose garden, four tennis courts, and a restaurant.
M Do I need a reservation to use the tennis court?
W Yes. You can ________ ________ ________ on our website.

10 | 주제 고르기

다음을 듣고, 남자가 하는 말의 내용으로 가장 적절한 것을 고르시오.

① 컴퓨터 사용법
② 성적을 향상하는 법
③ 시험 응시 신청 방법
④ 인터넷 강의 종류
⑤ 적절한 휴식의 필요성

M Hello, everyone. Today, I'm going to tell you how to ________ ________ ________. First, you should pay attention in class. Listening to your teacher during class is the best way to ________ ________ ________. Second, get enough sleep. If you are tired, it's ________ ________ ________ in class. Lastly, don't start studying right before the test. You should study a little every day.

고난도

11 | 일치하지 않는 내용 고르기

대화를 듣고, Griffith Marathon 행사에 대한 내용과 일치하지 않는 것을 고르시오.

① 다음 주 토요일에 열린다.
② 야생동물 보호를 위한 모금 행사이다.
③ 5km 마라톤의 참가비는 50달러이다.
④ 오전 7시 45분에 줄을 서야 한다.
⑤ 참가자가 물을 준비해야 한다.

> 적중! Tip drin**k**s
> [드링크스]보다는 [드링쓰]로 들린다. 자음 3개가 연속해서 나오면 중간 자음은 발음되지 않기 때문이다.
> · mon**th**s [먼쓰] · gran**d**ma [그랜마]

M Sarah, did you see this? The Griffith Marathon ________ ________ ________ ________.
W Is that the event to raise money for ________ ________ ________?
M Yes. There are 5-kilometer and 10-kilometer marathons. Let's sign up for the 5-kilometer one.
W Okay. ________ ________ ________ ________?
M It's 50 dollars. The event starts at 8:00 a.m., but we have to line up at 7:45 a.m.
W Got it. Do we need to bring drinks?
M Water ________ ________ ________.

12 목적 고르기

대화를 듣고, 여자가 전화를 건 목적으로 가장 적절한 것을 고르시오.

① 분실물을 찾기 위해서
② 배달을 요청하기 위해서
③ 메뉴를 선주문하기 위해서
④ 예약을 변경하기 위해서
⑤ 식당 정보를 얻기 위해서

적중! Tip May I have your name please?
상대방의 이름을 정중하게 묻는 표현으로, 주로 음식점이나 호텔 등에서 예약을 확인할 때 많이 쓰인다.

[Telephone rings.]
M Good morning. Bistro Italiano. How can I help you?
W Hello. I __________ __________ __________, and I need to make a change.
M May I have your name please?
W It's Rebecca Johnson.
M Alright. You __________ __________ __________ for four on May 15th at 6:30.
W Yes. But I'd like to change the time.
M __________ __________ __________ __________ at our restaurant?
W At 7:30. Also, there will be five people, not four.

13 시간 정보 고르기

대화를 듣고, 두 사람이 만날 시각을 고르시오.

① 2:30 p.m. ② 3:00 p.m. ③ 3:30 p.m.
④ 4:00 p.m. ⑤ 4:30 p.m.

M Bomi, do you want to visit __________ __________ __________ __________ this Saturday?
W Yes. I want to see the parade and fireworks.
M What type of ticket do you want to get?
W How about the half-day ticket? We can get in the park after 4 p.m.
M Okay. __________ __________ __________ in front of the park?
W Sure. I'm so excited!
M Can you meet me at 3:30?
W How about 3? Let's __________ __________ __________ before we go in.
M Okay. See you then!

14 관계 고르기

대화를 듣고, 두 사람의 관계로 가장 적절한 것을 고르시오.

① 소설가 — 독자 ② 디자이너 — 모델
③ 꽃집 직원 — 손님 ④ 기자 — 화가
⑤ 과학 교사 — 학생

W Hello. What can I do for you?
M I'm __________ __________ __________ __________ for my mom.
W What about lilies? They're __________ __________ __________.
M Those look beautiful. I'd also like to get some colorful flowers.
W Hmm... What other flowers __________ __________ __________?
M Well, I'm not sure. *[Pause]* Oh, what are those purple ones?
W Those are lilacs. They __________ __________ __________ lilies.

15 | 부탁·요청한 일 고르기

대화를 듣고, 여자가 남자에게 부탁한 일로 가장 적절한 것을 고르시오.

① 빨래하기 ② 설거지하기
③ 식탁 차리기 ④ 떡볶이 만들기
⑤ 청소기 돌리기

M Honey, your tteokbokki tasted great. _________ _________ _________ tonight.
W You're welcome.
M I'll _________ _________ _________. Why don't you take a break?
W Thanks, but there are still many _________ _________ _________ _________.
M What else should I do?
W Will you _________ _________ _________ for me? I will do the laundry.
M Sure. I'll do that after washing the dishes.

16 | 이유 고르기

대화를 듣고, 여자가 비행기를 놓친 이유로 가장 적절한 것을 고르시오.

① 차가 고장 나서
② 늦게 일어나서
③ 친구가 늦게 와서
④ 여권을 두고 와서
⑤ 공항에서 길을 잃어서

적중! Tip did you
[디드 유]보다는 [디쥬]로 들린다. [d]로 끝나는 단어 뒤에 y-로 시작하는 단어가 이어지면 두 소리가 연결되어 [쥬]로 발음되기 때문이다.
· could you [쿠쥬] · would you [우쥬]

M Hey, Janet. How was your trip to Europe?
W It _________ _________, but I had fun.
M What happened?
W I _________ _________ _________ to London.
M Really? Why?
W I was _________ _________ _________ _________ _________, but my friend, Erica, came late.
M Oh, no! What did you do?
W We had to wait eight hours for _________ _________ _________.

17 | 그림 상황에 적절한 대화 고르기

다음 그림의 상황에 가장 적절한 대화를 고르시오.

① ② ③ ④ ⑤

① **M** What are you planning to do this Saturday?
W I'm going to go to my grandma's house.
② **M** Do you want _________ _________ _________ _________?
W No, thanks. I already drank some.
③ **M** Oh, it _________ _________ _________ here.
W I think there's a garbage can nearby.
④ **M** Please _________ _________ _________ in this recycling can.
W Okay, I will.
⑤ **M** How old is your brother?
W He's 14.

18 | 언급하지 않은 내용 고르기

다음을 듣고, 여자가 Fremont Art Festival에 대해 언급하지 않은 것을 고르시오.

① 행사 목적 ② 행사 날짜 ③ 참가비
④ 전시 품목 ⑤ 공연 장소

적중! Tip Why don't you ~?
상대방에게 제안할 때 사용되는 표현으로 '~하는 게 어떤가요?, 어때?'라는 의미이다.
· Why don't you call her?
그녀에게 전화해보는 게 어때?

W Have you heard about the Fremont Art Festival? This event is held to ________ ________ ________ to the world. It takes place this year on August 6th and 7th. Everything from paintings and drawings to jewelry and clothing will ________ ________ ________. Musical performances will also take place on a stage ________ ________ ________ ________. Why don't you come join us?

19 | 적절한 응답 고르기

대화를 듣고, 남자의 마지막 말에 이어질 여자의 말로 가장 적절한 것을 고르시오.

Woman: ____________________

① She's working out hard.
② No. I don't know the way there.
③ The water is so blue!
④ It's about 500 meters away.
⑤ Two cokes, please.

W It was ________ ________ ________ to ride a bike here!
M Yeah. I love feeling the sea breeze ________ ________ ________.
W Aren't you tired yet? We have ridden for a long time.
M A little bit. I'm also ________ ________ ________.
W Do you know any restaurants near here?
M No. I don't know this area well.
W Then, I'll ________ ________ ________ ________ for a place. *[Pause]* Oh, here's a cafe.
M Where is it?

20 | 적절한 응답 고르기

대화를 듣고, 남자의 마지막 말에 이어질 여자의 말로 가장 적절한 것을 고르시오.

Woman: ____________________

① He won a prize.
② It's a poetry contest.
③ The competition will begin soon.
④ You can begin writing.
⑤ I need a vacation.

M Yejin, you ________ ________ ________.
W Yes. I just talked with my teacher.
M What did you talk about?
W She wants me to participate in ________ ________ ________ ________.
M That's great. Congratulations!
W Thank you. But ________ ________ ________.
M You don't have to be. You're ________ ________ ________. What kind of competition is it?

06회 중학영어듣기 실전 모의고사

실전 모의고사 음성 바로 듣기 ▶

1 다음을 듣고, 대전의 날씨로 가장 적절한 것을 고르시오.

①  ②  ③  ④  ⑤

2 대화를 듣고, 남자가 만든 목도리로 가장 적절한 것을 고르시오.

①  ②  ③ 

④  ⑤ 

3 대화를 듣고, 두 사람이 뮤지컬에 대해 언급하지 <u>않은</u> 것을 고르시오.

① 제목 ② 내용 ③ 배우
④ 예매 시간 ⑤ 예매 방법

고난도

4 대화를 듣고, 여자가 식목일에 한 일로 가장 적절한 것을 고르시오.

① 다큐멘터리 보기 ② 나무 심기
③ 씨앗 나눠주기 ④ 뒷마당 정리하기
⑤ 식물도감 읽기

5 대화를 듣고, 두 사람이 대화하는 장소로 가장 적절한 곳을 고르시오.

① 학교 ② 문구점 ③ 수리점
④ 골프장 ⑤ 휴대폰 가게

6 대화를 듣고, 남자의 마지막 말의 의도로 가장 적절한 것을 고르시오.

① 감사 ② 칭찬 ③ 허락 ④ 후회 ⑤ 조언

7 대화를 듣고, 남자가 대여한 책의 장르를 고르시오.

① 역사 ② 공상 과학 ③ 수필
④ 미스터리 ⑤ 공포

8 대화를 듣고, 남자가 대화 직후에 할 일로 가장 적절한 것을 고르시오.

① 여행 일정 계획하기 ② 기상청에 항의하기
③ 독도 그림 그리기 ④ 수영장 가기
⑤ 일기예보 확인하기

9 대화를 듣고, 남자가 Korea Traditions Expo에 대해 언급하지 <u>않은</u> 것을 고르시오.

① 행사 기간 ② 체험 내용
③ 개최 장소 ④ 티켓 구매 방법
⑤ 티켓 가격

10 다음을 듣고, 여자가 하는 말의 내용으로 가장 적절한 것을 고르시오.

① 침구 정리 방법 ② 공원 이용 수칙
③ 봉사 활동 안내 ④ 방학 숙제 안내
⑤ 학생 선거 절차

11 다음을 듣고, 남자가 좋아하는 화가에 대한 내용으로 일치하지 않는 것을 고르시오.

① 이름은 빈센트 반 고흐이다.
② 네덜란드에서 태어났다.
③ 27살에 그림을 그리기 시작했다.
④ 빨간색 물감을 많이 사용했다.
⑤ 죽고 난 후에 유명해졌다.

12 대화를 듣고, 여자가 전화를 건 목적으로 가장 적절한 것을 고르시오.

① 요가 매트를 구매하기 위해서
② 수업 시간을 확인하기 위해서
③ 수건을 주문하기 위해서
④ 가격을 문의하기 위해서
⑤ 준비물을 확인하기 위해서

고난도

13 대화를 듣고, 여자가 지불해야 할 금액으로 가장 적절한 것을 고르시오.

① $ 55 ② $ 60 ③ $ 65
④ $ 70 ⑤ $ 75

14 대화를 듣고, 두 사람의 관계로 가장 적절한 것을 고르시오.

① 작가 — 편집자 ② 역사 교사 — 학생
③ 요리사 — 손님 ④ 카페 직원 — 손님
⑤ 진행자 — 관객

15 대화를 듣고, 남자가 여자에게 부탁한 일로 가장 적절한 것을 고르시오.

① 소포 보내기 ② 옷 쇼핑하기
③ 딸에게 전화하기 ④ 음식 시식하기
⑤ 회의 참석하기

16 대화를 듣고, 여자가 우산을 산 이유로 가장 적절한 것을 고르시오.

① 친구에게 주기 위해서
② 비를 피하기 위해서
③ 미술 재료로 쓰기 위해서
④ 장마에 대비하기 위해서
⑤ 생일 선물을 하기 위해서

17 다음 그림의 상황에 가장 적절한 대화를 고르시오.

① ② ③ ④ ⑤

18 다음을 듣고, 남자가 강아지에 대해 언급하지 않은 것을 고르시오.

① 이름 ② 나이 ③ 털 색
④ 몸무게 ⑤ 특기

[19-20] 대화를 듣고, 여자의 마지막 말에 이어질 남자의 말로 가장 적절한 것을 고르시오.

19 **Man:** ______________________

① How much is this eraser?
② Of course.
③ I had a great time.
④ Write this down.
⑤ Those stickers are pretty.

20 **Man:** ______________________

① Okay. Let me get my coat.
② I love this color.
③ It's dark here.
④ Don't start without me.
⑤ Keep going straight.

06회 Dictation

Dictation
음성 바로 듣기 ▶

06회 중학영어듣기 실전 모의고사 Dictation 음성을 들으며 빈칸에 알맞은 단어를 채우시오.

1 날씨 고르기

다음을 듣고, 대전의 날씨로 가장 적절한 것을 고르시오.

① ② ③ ④ ⑤

M Good morning, everyone. It's time for the national weather update. Today, strong winds and ________ ________ ________ in Incheon. There will be heavy snowfall in Seoul, but it will be ________ ________ ________ ________. Daejeon will be snowy all day, so be careful when you drive as the roads ________ ________ ________. In Changwon, you'll see cloudy skies, but it won't ________ ________ ________ ________.

2 알맞은 그림 고르기

대화를 듣고, 남자가 만든 목도리로 가장 적절한 것을 고르시오.

① ② ③ ④ ⑤

W Kyle, ________ ________ ________ ________! Did you make it?
M Yes. It's a ________ ________ ________ ________.
W Are those cat faces?
M Yeah. I sewed on those patches because ________ ________ ________ ________.
W What does it say in ________ ________ ________ underneath the cats?
M It says, "LOVE". I hope she likes it.

3 언급하지 않은 내용 고르기

대화를 듣고, 두 사람이 뮤지컬에 대해 언급하지 않은 것을 고르시오.

① 제목 ② 내용 ③ 배우
④ 예매 시간 ⑤ 예매 방법

W Do you want to go to see a musical next week?
M Sure, Mom. ________ ________ ________ ________?
W It's *The Tiger World*.
M Oh, I've heard of it. Isn't it about a little tiger ________ ________ ________ ________ in the forest?
W Right. And a famous actor plays ________ ________ ________.
M When do you want to watch it?
W Is 5:30 on Wednesday okay with you?
M Sure. Let's see it then.
W Okay. I'll ________ ________ ________ then.

고난도

4 | 한 일 고르기

대화를 듣고, 여자가 식목일에 한 일로 가장 적절한 것을 고르시오.

① 다큐멘터리 보기 ② 나무 심기
③ 씨앗 나눠주기 ④ 뒷마당 정리하기
⑤ 식물도감 읽기

적중! Tip important
[임폴턴트]보다는 [임폴은]으로 들린다. 자음 사이에 오는 [t] 발음은 약화되어 거의 들리지 않고, -nt로 끝나는 단어에서 마지막 [t] 발음은 약화되어 거의 들리지 않기 때문이다.

M What are you doing, Christine?
W I'm ________ ________ ________ about National Tree Day, Dad.
M Did you do anything special?
W Yes. I ________ ________ ________ about trees in the Amazon.
M That's nice. How was it?
W ________ ________ ________ ________. I realized how important preserving trees is.
M You're right. ________ ________ ________ a tree in our backyard next week?
W Oh, that's a great idea.

5 | 장소 고르기

대화를 듣고, 두 사람이 대화하는 장소로 가장 적절한 곳을 고르시오.

① 학교 ② 문구점 ③ 수리점
④ 골프장 ⑤ 휴대폰 가게

W Hello. Are you looking for ________ ________ ________?
M Yes, I am. But I don't know what type I want.
W Well, this one here is a good size. It's not ________ ________ ________ ________.
M It looks nice. Do you have it ________ ________ ________?
W This phone comes in blue, pink, and black.
M Can I see ________ ________ ________, please?
W Sure. Just a second.

6 | 의도 고르기

대화를 듣고, 남자의 마지막 말의 의도로 가장 적절한 것을 고르시오.

① 감사 ② 칭찬 ③ 허락 ④ 후회 ⑤ 조언

W Did you buy a new hat?
M Yeah. I ________ ________ ________ ________ at a shopping mall.
W How much was it?
M I paid 50 dollars for this.
W I think I saw ________ ________ ________, and it was only 25 dollars.
M Where did you see it?
W I saw it on an online shop. All the products were 50% off.
M What? That's a huge difference. I ________ ________ ________ ________.

7 | 특정 정보 고르기

대화를 듣고, 남자가 대여한 책의 장르를 고르시오.

① 역사 ② 공상 과학 ③ 수필
④ 미스터리 ⑤ 공포

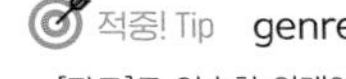
적중! Tip genre
[장르]로 익숙한 외래어이지만 실제로는 [쟌러]로 발음된다.

M Alice, which book did you borrow?
W I got a book about mysteries ________ ________ ________ ________.
M Oh, isn't it scary?
W No way. I'm ________ ________ ________ ________ it. What about you?
M I checked out a science fiction book.
W Science fiction? ________ ________ ________ ________ that genre?
M It's my favorite. I enjoy reading stories about ________ ________ ________ ________.

8 | 할 일 고르기

대화를 듣고, 남자가 대화 직후에 할 일로 가장 적절한 것을 고르시오.

① 여행 일정 계획하기 ② 기상청에 항의하기
③ 독도 그림 그리기 ④ 수영장 가기
⑤ 일기예보 확인하기

M Hey, April. Are you going to _________ _________ _________ _________?

W I'm not planning to _________ _________ _________.

M Then, would you like to take a trip with me?

W Where are you going?

M I want to visit Dokdo.

W Sounds cool, but I heard the weather has to be really nice to go there.

M Oh, no. I heard it will rain this weekend. I'm worried we won't _________ _________ _________ _________!

W But you'd better check _________ _________ _________ first.

M I'll do it right now.

9 | 언급하지 않은 내용 고르기

대화를 듣고, 남자가 Korea Traditions Expo에 대해 언급하지 않은 것을 고르시오.

① 행사 기간 ② 체험 내용
③ 개최 장소 ④ 티켓 구매 방법
⑤ 티켓 가격

적중! Tip activi**t**ies
[액티비티즈]보다는 [액티비리즈]로 들린다. [t]가 모음 사이에서 발음될 때는 약화되어 [r]에 가깝게 발음되기 때문이다.

[Telephone rings.]

M Hello. Korea Traditions Expo information desk. How may I help you?

W I'd like to know _________ _________ _________ _________ _________.

M It will be held from January 1st to 20th.

W What kind of activities _________ _________ _________?

M You can play Korean traditional games like yunnori.

W Do I need to _________ _________ _________ in advance?

M No. You can buy it at the venue.

W Okay. How much is a ticket?

M It's five dollars.

10 | 주제 고르기

다음을 듣고, 여자가 하는 말의 내용으로 가장 적절한 것을 고르시오.

① 침구 정리 방법 ② 공원 이용 수칙
③ 봉사 활동 안내 ④ 방학 숙제 안내
⑤ 학생 선거 절차

W Good morning, everyone. I will _________ _________ _________ _________ during the volunteer activity today. We will pick up trash from the beach. I will give you _________ _________ _________. One is for garbage, and the other is for recyclable materials. When the bags are full, _________ _________ _________ _________. Any questions?

11 | 일치하지 않는 내용 고르기

다음을 듣고, 남자가 좋아하는 화가에 대한 내용으로 일치하지 않는 것을 고르시오.

① 이름은 빈센트 반 고흐이다.
② 네덜란드에서 태어났다.
③ 27살에 그림을 그리기 시작했다.
④ 빨간색 물감을 많이 사용했다.
⑤ 죽고 난 후에 유명해졌다.

M Hello, students. I'd like to tell you about _________ _________ _________, Vincent van Gogh. He was born in Netherlands and moved to France later. _________ _________ _________ when he was 27. Van Gogh often _________ _________ _________ in his paintings. He was an amazing artist, but sadly, he got famous _________ _________ _________.

12 | 목적 고르기

대화를 듣고, 여자가 전화를 건 목적으로 가장 적절한 것을 고르시오.

① 요가 매트를 구매하기 위해서
② 수업 시간을 확인하기 위해서
③ 수건을 주문하기 위해서
④ 가격을 문의하기 위해서
⑤ 준비물을 확인하기 위해서

[Telephone rings.]
M Hello, this is Strong Gym. How can I help you?
W Hello. Is there anything I need to bring ________ ________ ________ ________?
M Is this your first time?
W Yes. I ________ ________ ________ the class yesterday. But I don't know ________ ________ ________.
M Okay. Please bring your own yoga matt.
W Do I also need to ________ ________ ________ ________ for the shower?
M No. Our gym provides towels.
W Great. Thank you.

고난도

13 | 금액 정보 고르기

대화를 듣고, 여자가 지불해야 할 금액으로 가장 적절한 것을 고르시오.

① $ 55　② $ 60　③ $ 65
④ $ 70　⑤ $ 75

적중! Tip　I recommend ~.
상대방에게 무언가를 권유하거나 추천할 때 사용하는 표현으로 '~을 추천해요'라는 의미이다.
· I recommend you wear comfortable clothes.
편한 옷을 입는 것을 추천해요.

M Welcome, what can I do for you?
W I'm looking for a bottle of perfume for my aunt.
M Okay. Would she like ________ ________ ________ ________?
W She'll love it. How much is it?
M It's 55 dollars.
W It ________ ________ ________. She often wears perfume.
M Then, I recommend this bigger one. It's 75 dollars.
W That seems reasonable. I'll take ________ ________ ________.

14 | 관계 고르기

대화를 듣고, 두 사람의 관계로 가장 적절한 것을 고르시오.

① 작가 — 편집자　② 역사 교사 — 학생
③ 요리사 — 손님　④ 카페 직원 — 손님
⑤ 진행자 — 관객

M ________ ________ ________ ________ this evening?
W It was wonderful. I loved the beef stew especially.
M That's ________ ________ ________. It was cooked with my new recipe.
W I thought it tasted different compared to what I had during my last visit.
M I ordered ________ ________ ________ ________ for the stew. What did you think of the cheesecake?
W The fresh raspberries on it were perfect.
M I'm glad you liked it. ________ ________ ________.
W We'll be back soon!

15 | 부탁·요청한 일 고르기

대화를 듣고, 남자가 여자에게 부탁한 일로 가장 적절한 것을 고르시오.

① 소포 보내기 ② 옷 쇼핑하기
③ 딸에게 전화하기 ④ 음식 시식하기
⑤ 회의 참석하기

M Honey, our daughter called today.
W ________ ________ ________ ________ staying at summer camp?
M She is, but she ________ ________ ________ her phone charger.
W Oh, no. What should we do?
M One of us could go to the post office and send it ________ ________ ________.
W Okay. Do you have time to go there?
M Not really. I have to go to a meeting. Could you ________ ________ ________ to her?
W Sure. I'll do it.

16 | 이유 고르기

대화를 듣고, 여자가 우산을 산 이유로 가장 적절한 것을 고르시오.

① 친구에게 주기 위해서
② 비를 피하기 위해서
③ 미술 재료로 쓰기 위해서
④ 장마에 대비하기 위해서
⑤ 생일 선물을 하기 위해서

 적중! Tip Now I see.
상대방의 말을 듣고 이해했음을 나타낼 때 사용되는 표현으로 '이제 이해했어, 이제 알았어'라는 의미이다.

M Claire, why don't we have a picnic in the park today?
W Okay, Charles. ________ ________ ________ ________.
M Is it going to rain later?
W No. It's going to ________ ________ ________ ________.
M Then, why did you ________ ________ ________?
W Actually, I bought it for Harry.
M Why did you buy him an umbrella?
W He lent me his on Friday, but it broke ________ ________ ________ ________.
M Ah! Now I see.

17 | 그림 상황에 적절한 대화 고르기

다음 그림의 상황에 가장 적절한 대화를 고르시오.

① ② ③ ④ ⑤

① **W** This line is so long.
M I agree. Let's go to another restaurant.
② **W** Do you feel okay?
M No. I ________ ________ ________ ________.
③ **W** Do you want to go shopping?
M Yes. I need ________ ________ ________ ________ ________.
④ **W** Excuse me, where is the pasta sauce?
M It's in the Section C, ________ ________ ________ ________.
⑤ **W** Can you pick me up from the subway station?
M Yes. I'll be there in 20 minutes.

18 | 언급하지 않은 내용 고르기

다음을 듣고, 남자가 강아지에 대해 언급하지 않은 것을 고르시오.

① 이름 ② 나이 ③ 털 색
④ 몸무게 ⑤ 특기

적중! Tip in a dark
[인 어 달크]보다는 [이너달크]로 들린다. 앞에 나온 단어의 끝 자음과 뒤에 나온 단어의 첫 모음이 연음되기 때문이다.

M Hello, I'd like to tell you about my puppy. His name is Mori, and he's five months old. He is a small poodle, and he _________ _________ _________ with other dogs. He has dark brown hair, so it's sometimes _________ _________ _________ _________ when he is in a dark room. He can do tricks like _________ _________ _________ _________.

19 | 적절한 응답 고르기

대화를 듣고, 여자의 마지막 말에 이어질 남자의 말로 가장 적절한 것을 고르시오.

Man: ______________________

① How much is this eraser?
② Of course.
③ I had a great time.
④ Write this down.
⑤ Those stickers are pretty.

M Mom, can I go shopping with my friends?
W Sure. Do you _________ _________ _________?
M Yes, please. We are going to the stationery store.
W Okay. What are you going to buy?
M I want _________ _________ _________. My old one is full.
W Alright. Here is 15 dollars. Can you also _________ _________ _________ _________ for me?

20 | 적절한 응답 고르기

대화를 듣고, 여자의 마지막 말에 이어질 남자의 말로 가장 적절한 것을 고르시오.

Man: ______________________

① Okay. Let me get my coat.
② I love this color.
③ It's dark here.
④ Don't start without me.
⑤ Keep going straight.

W What color do you want to paint this room, Honey?
M Hmm... _________ _________ _________ would be nice.
W I like blue better. It will look pretty with our couch.
M That's true. But then we should _________ _________ _________ _________.
W Why? We already have one.
M Yes. But it won't match the new wall color.
W You're right. How about _________ _________ _________ _________ now?

07회 중학영어듣기 실전 모의고사

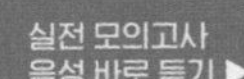

1 다음을 듣고, 금요일의 날씨로 가장 적절한 것을 고르시오.

①  ②  ③  ④  ⑤ 

2 대화를 듣고, 여자가 만든 새집으로 가장 적절한 것을 고르시오.

①  ②  ③ 
④  ⑤ 

3 대화를 듣고, 남자가 다녀온 여행에 대해 언급하지 않은 것을 고르시오.

① 방문 국가 수 ② 방문 국가
③ 날씨 ④ 여행 시작일
⑤ 여행 기간

4 대화를 듣고, 여자가 만든 것으로 가장 적절한 것을 고르시오.

① 인형 ② 비누 ③ 초
④ 기름 ⑤ 책갈피

5 대화를 듣고, 두 사람이 대화하는 장소로 가장 적절한 곳을 고르시오.

① 쇼핑몰 ② 영화관 ③ 식당
④ 은행 ⑤ 약국

6 대화를 듣고, 남자의 마지막 말의 의도로 가장 적절한 것을 고르시오.

① 제안 ② 조언 ③ 부탁 ④ 불평 ⑤ 허락

7 대화를 듣고, 여자가 구매하려는 물건으로 가장 적절한 것을 고르시오.

① 냉장고 ② 세탁기 ③ 청소기
④ 가습기 ⑤ 에어컨

8 대화를 듣고, 남자가 대화 직후에 할 일로 가장 적절한 것을 고르시오.

① 일정 확인하기 ② 알람 시계 사기
③ 샤워하기 ④ 토스트 굽기
⑤ 아침 식사하기

9 대화를 듣고, 두 사람이 캠핑장 이용에 대해 언급하지 않은 것을 고르시오.

① 캠핑장 이용 인원 ② 캠핑장 이용 가격
③ 샤워 시설 유무 ④ 캠프파이어 허용 여부
⑤ 반려견 동반 여부

10 다음을 듣고, 여자가 하는 말의 내용으로 가장 적절한 것을 고르시오.

① 항공편 지연 안내
② 기내 안전 수칙 공지
③ 탑승 위치 변경 공지
④ 비행기 탑승 안내
⑤ 분실물 신고 방법

11 대화를 듣고, 두 사람이 참가할 전시회에 대한 내용으로 일치하지 않는 것을 고르시오.

① 입장료는 30달러이다.
② 다양한 나라의 작가가 출품한다.
③ 전시된 그림을 구매할 수 있다.
④ 남자는 작품을 구매하고 싶어 한다.
⑤ 전시회장에 주차장이 없다.

고난도
12 대화를 듣고, 남자가 경주에 가는 목적으로 가장 적절한 것을 고르시오.

① 사촌을 만나기 위해서
② 전시회를 관람하기 위해서
③ 박물관에 가기 위해서
④ 유적지를 방문하기 위해서
⑤ 사진을 찍기 위해서

13 대화를 듣고, 여자가 미용실에 갈 시각을 고르시오.

① 2:00 p.m. ② 2:30 p.m. ③ 3:00 p.m.
④ 3:30 p.m. ⑤ 4:00 p.m.

14 대화를 듣고, 두 사람의 관계로 가장 적절한 것을 고르시오.

① 학부모 — 교사
② 버스 기사 — 승객
③ 우체국 직원 — 고객
④ 관광 안내소 직원 — 관광객
⑤ 자동차 판매원 — 손님

15 대화를 듣고, 여자가 남자에게 부탁한 일로 가장 적절한 것을 고르시오.

① 숙제 도와주기 ② 낮잠 깨워주기
③ 같이 밤새우기 ④ 과학책 빌려주기
⑤ 샌드위치 사다 주기

16 대화를 듣고, 남자가 스키장에 갈 수 없는 이유로 가장 적절한 것을 고르시오.

① 날씨가 좋지 않아서
② 숙제를 해야 해서
③ 할아버지 생신이어서
④ 교통편이 없어서
⑤ 친구가 감기에 걸려서

17 다음 그림의 상황에 가장 적절한 대화를 고르시오.

① ② ③ ④ ⑤

18 다음을 듣고, 남자가 다람쥐에 대해 언급하지 않은 것을 고르시오.

① 서식지 ② 크기 ③ 수명
④ 주식 ⑤ 먹이 습성

[19-20] 대화를 듣고, 남자의 마지막 말에 이어질 여자의 말로 가장 적절한 것을 고르시오.

고난도
19 **Woman:** ______________________

① I'm interested in playing the guitar.
② The piano contest was held last month.
③ She missed today's lesson.
④ I want to be a professional musician.
⑤ The band will perform tonight.

20 **Woman:** ______________________

① It will finish tomorrow.
② How much is the fine?
③ I think we are lost.
④ You were driving too fast.
⑤ There's a car accident.

07회 Dictation

Dictation
음성 바로 듣기 ▶

07회 중학영어듣기 실전 모의고사 Dictation 음성을 들으며 빈칸에 알맞은 단어를 채우시오.

1 | 날씨 고르기

다음을 듣고, 금요일의 날씨로 가장 적절한 것을 고르시오.

① ② ③ ④ ⑤

M This is Jim with the weekly weather report. Monday and Tuesday will be sunny _____ _____ _____ _____. On Wednesday, it'll _____ _____ _____ _____ in the afternoon. On Thursday, the sky is likely to be clear. On Friday, _____ _____ _____ _____ again and continue through the weekend.

2 | 알맞은 그림 고르기

대화를 듣고, 여자가 만든 새집으로 가장 적절한 것을 고르시오.

① ② ③ ④ ⑤

M What is that little house on the tree in your garden?
W It's a bird house. I _____ _____ _____. Do you like it?
M Yes. It's so pretty! I like _____ _____ _____ on the top.
W Originally, I put it under the hole, but _____ _____ _____ for the birds.
M The windows on the side are also cute. I really like them.
W Thank you.

3 | 언급하지 않은 내용 고르기

대화를 듣고, 남자가 다녀온 여행에 대해 언급하지 않은 것을 고르시오.

① 방문 국가 수 ② 방문 국가
③ 날씨 ④ 여행 시작일
⑤ 여행 기간

W James, _____ _____ _____ _____ to Africa?
M It was exciting! And the weather was better than I expected.
W How many countries did you visit?
M I _____ _____ _____ _____.
W Which was your favorite?
M It was Kenya. I saw many animals while we were on safari. I even saw lions.
W _____ _____ was your trip?
M I traveled for 14 days, but I _____ _____ _____ on the plane.
W That's a long flight.

4 | 특정 정보 고르기

대화를 듣고, 여자가 만든 것으로 가장 적절한 것을 고르시오.

① 인형 ② 비누 ③ 초
④ 기름 ⑤ 책갈피

M Somi, what's _____ _____ _____?
W It's used cooking oil. I used it for my science class.
M Why did you need it?
W We learned _____ _____ _____ soap with used oil.
M Oh, really?
W Yes. We also _____ _____ _____ to the soap so that it will smell nice.
M Will you bring a bar for me?
W Sure. I'll bring you one tomorrow.

5 장소 고르기

대화를 듣고, 두 사람이 대화하는 장소로 가장 적절한 곳을 고르시오.

① 쇼핑몰 ② 영화관 ③ 식당
④ 은행 ⑤ 약국

M Jenny, did you find the shoes _________ _________ _________ _________?
W Yes, I did. And they were _________ _________ too.
M Great. Do you want to go to the food court _________ _________ _________?
W Sure. But don't you want to do more shopping?
M No. I bought a pair of jeans, so I'm fine.
W All right. Let's _________ _________ _________ then.

6 의도 고르기

대화를 듣고, 남자의 마지막 말의 의도로 가장 적절한 것을 고르시오.

① 제안 ② 조언 ③ 부탁 ④ 불평 ⑤ 허락

적중! Tip put it
[풋 잇]보다는 [푸릿]으로 들린다. [t]가 모음 사이에서 발음될 때는 약화되어 [r]에 가깝게 발음되기 때문이다.

M Chloe, are you busy?
W Not really. Why?
M Can you _________ _________ _________ my glasses?
W Dad, they are _________ _________ _________.
M Oh, my! Thank you.
W Do you need anything else?
M Yes. _________ _________ _________ _________ my tablet PC?
W I put it _________ _________ _________ last night.
M Did you? Then, can you bring it to me?

7 특정 정보 고르기

대화를 듣고, 여자가 구매하려는 물건으로 가장 적절한 것을 고르시오.

① 냉장고 ② 세탁기 ③ 청소기
④ 가습기 ⑤ 에어컨

M Welcome to Electroland. May I help you?
W Hi. _________ _________ _________ _________ a refrigerator. Which is the one on your website?
M You mean the one on sale?
W Yes. The one _________ _________ _________.
M You can _________ _________ _________ for that model if you buy it online.
W Hmm... Is there a refrigerator _________ _________ _________ _________ that I can buy in the store?
M This black one is our best seller.
W Oh, that looks nice.

8 | 할 일 고르기

대화를 듣고, 남자가 대화 직후에 할 일로 가장 적절한 것을 고르시오.

① 일정 확인하기 ② 알람 시계 사기
③ 샤워하기 ④ 토스트 굽기
⑤ 아침 식사하기

적중! Tip **wake up**
[웨이크 업]보다는 [웨이컵]으로 들린다. 앞에 나온 단어의 끝 자음과 뒤에 나온 단어의 첫 모음이 연음되고, 이때 강세가 없는 [k]는 된소리로 발음되기 때문이다.

W Nathan, wake up!
M What time is it, Mom?
W It's already 7:30.
M My alarm ________ ________ ________.
W It did, but you didn't wake up.
M I think I need ________ ________ ________ ________.
W Why don't you ________ ________ ________ now? You're going to be late.
M Okay. Will you make me some toast?
W Sure. Hurry up.

9 | 언급하지 않은 내용 고르기

대화를 듣고, 두 사람이 캠핑장 이용에 대해 언급하지 않은 것을 고르시오.

① 캠핑장 이용 인원 ② 캠핑장 이용 가격
③ 샤워 시설 유무 ④ 캠프파이어 허용 여부
⑤ 반려견 동반 여부

[Telephone rings.]
W Good afternoon. Elderberry National Park. How may I help you?
M I want to ________ ________ ________ for July 15th.
W How many people will use the campsite?
M Just two. How much will it be?
W It'll be 10 dollars for each person, so 20 dollars total.
M Okay. Are campfires allowed?
W ________ ________ ________ only at the campgrounds.
M Can we bring our dog?
W Yes. But you need to ________ ________ ________ ________ it at all times.

10 | 주제 고르기

다음을 듣고, 여자가 하는 말의 내용으로 가장 적절한 것을 고르시오.

① 항공편 지연 안내
② 기내 안전 수칙 공지
③ 탑승 위치 변경 공지
④ 비행기 탑승 안내
⑤ 분실물 신고 방법

W Ladies and gentlemen, can I ________ ________ ________, please? We are so sorry for the delay, and we thank you ________ ________ ________. Hankook Airline Flight 727 for Los Angeles is now boarding at Gate H15. Please have your boarding pass ready. Make sure you don't ________ ________ ________. Thank you.

11 | 일치하지 않는 내용 고르기

대화를 듣고, 두 사람이 참가할 전시회에 대한 내용으로 일치하지 않는 것을 고르시오.

① 입장료는 30달러이다.
② 다양한 나라의 작가가 출품한다.
③ 전시된 그림을 구매할 수 있다.
④ 남자는 작품을 구매하고 싶어 한다.
⑤ 전시회장에 주차장이 없다.

W Nick, did you buy the ticket for ________ ________ ________?
M Yeah. It was 30 dollars per person.
W Did you check the artists? *[Clicking sound]* It says the artwork of more than 30 artists ________ ________ ________ ________ will be exhibited.
M Can you also buy paintings there?
W No, you can't. But you can buy souvenirs.
M That's disappointing. I wanted ________ ________ ________ ________. By the way, are we taking the taxi?
W Yes. I heard there isn't a parking lot.

고난도

12 | 목적 고르기

대화를 듣고, 남자가 경주에 가는 목적으로 가장 적절한 것을 고르시오.

① 사촌을 만나기 위해서
② 전시회를 관람하기 위해서
③ 박물관에 가기 위해서
④ 유적지를 보기 위해서
⑤ 사진을 찍기 위해서

적중! Tip have fun
[해브 펀]보다는 [해펀]으로 들린다. [v]와 [f]처럼 발음할 때 혀의 위치가 비슷한 자음이 나란히 나오면 앞 단어의 끝 자음이 탈락되기 때문이다.
· have forever [해포레버] · move forward [무포월드]

W Wilson, are you going to Gyeongju this weekend?
M Yeah. I'm going there tomorrow morning ________ ________ ________ ________ ________.
W What is there to see in Gyeongju?
M There is Bulguksa Temple from the Silla period.
W Wow. Are you a fan of history?
M Yes. I ________ ________ ________ the past.
W I hope you have fun.
M Thanks. I'll ________ ________ ________ ________.

13 | 시간 정보 고르기

대화를 듣고, 여자가 미용실에 갈 시각을 고르시오.

① 2:00 p.m. ② 2:30 p.m. ③ 3:00 p.m.
④ 3:30 p.m. ⑤ 4:00 p.m.

적중! Tip Hair Salon
[헤어 살롱]으로 익숙한 외래어지만 실제로는 [헤얼설로온]으로 발음된다.

[Telephone rings.]
M Hello. Gregory's Hair Salon. What can I do for you?
W Hi. I ________ ________ ________ at 2 o'clock today, but I think I'll ________ ________ ________ the time.
M Sure. May I have your name, please?
W It's Anna Lee.
M Okay. When will you come?
W My meeting will end at 2:30, so I can ________ ________ ________ 3:30.
M Great. I'll see you then.

14 | 관계 고르기

대화를 듣고, 두 사람의 관계로 가장 적절한 것을 고르시오.

① 학부모 — 교사
② 버스 기사 — 승객
③ 우체국 직원 — 고객
④ 관광 안내소 직원 — 관광객
⑤ 자동차 판매원 — 손님

W Hello. Are you looking for a new car?
M Yes. ________ ________ ________ ________.
W Do you want a big car or a small car?
M I ________ ________ ________ ________. I have a wife and three kids.
W What about this one? It has lots of room.
M Hmm... It doesn't look good for ________ ________ ________ ________. We like camping.
W I see. Then, this SUV is perfect for you.

15 | 부탁·요청한 일 고르기

대화를 듣고, 여자가 남자에게 부탁한 일로 가장 적절한 것을 고르시오.

① 숙제 도와주기 ② 낮잠 깨워주기
③ 같이 밤새우기 ④ 과학책 빌려주기
⑤ 샌드위치 사다 주기

적중! Tip No problem.
상대방의 부탁이나 제안에 대해 흔쾌히 승낙할 때 사용하는 표현으로 '문제없어'라는 의미이다. 사과에 대한 응답으로도 사용할 수 있다.

M You look so tired, Amy.
W I couldn't sleep last night.
M What happened?
W I had to ________ ________ ________ ________ to finish my essay.
M But I thought you finished your English essay.
W That was my science report. Could you ________ ________ ________ ________?
M Sure. What is it?
W Could you ________ ________ ________ in an hour? I want to take a nap.
M Of course! No problem.

16 | 이유 고르기

대화를 듣고, 남자가 스키장에 갈 수 없는 이유로 가장 적절한 것을 고르시오.

① 날씨가 좋지 않아서
② 숙제를 해야 해서
③ 할아버지 생신이어서
④ 교통편이 없어서
⑤ 친구가 감기에 걸려서

M Mom, can I go skiing with Paul next Saturday?
W When?
M It's January 14th.
W That's your grandfather's birthday. We are ________ ________ ________ at his house.
M Oh, no! What should I do? ________ ________ ________ Paul.
W I think you should ________ ________ ________ ________ the trip. You can go next time.
M But he'll be so angry.
W Paul will understand if you ________ ________ ________.
M Okay. I'll call him now.

17 | 그림 상황에 적절한 대화 고르기

다음 그림의 상황에 가장 적절한 대화를 고르시오.

① ② ③ ④ ⑤

① **W** Where should we sit?
M How about sitting on that bench ________ ________ ________?
② **W** Should I buy this dress?
M Yes. It looks really nice.
③ **W** Do you want to go to the park today?
M I can't. I'm taking ________ ________ ________.
④ **W** When is soccer practice?
M ________ ________ ________.
⑤ **W** How much are these flowers?
M They're 10 dollars.

18 | 언급하지 않은 내용 고르기

다음을 듣고, 남자가 다람쥐에 대해 언급하지 않은 것을 고르시오.

① 서식지 ② 크기 ③ 수명
④ 주식 ⑤ 먹이 습성

M Hello, everyone. I'd like to tell you about our furry neighbors in the park, squirrels. Squirrels usually live in ________ ________ ________. They live for about 15 years. Squirrels usually ________ ________ ________ ________, but they can also eat insects. Squirrels sometimes ________ ________ ________ in the ground, but they often forget ________ ________ ________ ________. In fact, millions of trees are planted by squirrels.

고난도

19 | 적절한 응답 고르기

대화를 듣고, 남자의 마지막 말에 이어질 여자의 말로 가장 적절한 것을 고르시오.

Woman: ______________________

① I'm interested in playing the guitar.
② The piano contest was held last month.
③ She missed today's lesson.
④ I want to be a professional musician.
⑤ The band will perform tonight.

 적중! Tip I thought ~.

내가 생각했던 것과 사실이 다를 때 쓰는 표현으로 '~인 줄 알았어'라는 의미이다.

· I thought you didn't go to the festival.
난 네가 축제에 안 간 줄 알았어.

M You seem so excited, Grace. What's up?
W I have my first piano lesson today. I ________ ________ ________ start playing.
M Oh, I thought you played the guitar.
W I do, but I want to learn to ________ ________ ________. I will take drum lessons too.
M That's amazing. Why are you ________ ________ ________ so many instruments?

20 | 적절한 응답 고르기

대화를 듣고, 남자의 마지막 말에 이어질 여자의 말로 가장 적절한 것을 고르시오.

Woman: ______________________

① It will finish tomorrow.
② How much is the fine?
③ I think we are lost.
④ You were driving too fast.
⑤ There's a car accident.

M Hello, Officer. What's going on?
W The bus stop is ________ ________, so you can't use it now.
M Then, where should I go?
W Please go straight for two blocks more, and use ________ ________ ________ ________.
M How long will it take to get there?
W It will take 20 minutes on foot.
M That's bad news. ________ ________ ________ for work.
W I'm sorry, sir.
M When does the construction end?

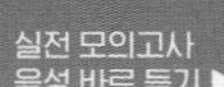

1 다음을 듣고, 광주의 날씨로 가장 적절한 것을 고르시오.

① ② ③ ④ ⑤

2 대화를 듣고, 남자가 두고 온 공책으로 가장 적절한 것을 고르시오.

① 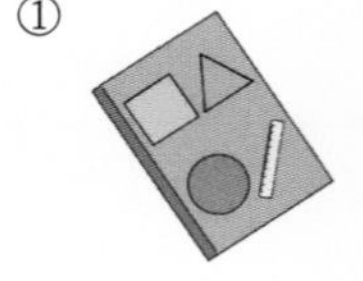 ②  ③ 

④  ⑤ 

3 대화를 듣고, 여자의 심정으로 가장 적절한 것을 고르시오.

① bored ② scared ③ shy
④ satisfied ⑤ excited

4 대화를 듣고, 여자가 오늘 한 일로 가장 적절한 것을 고르시오.

① 책 대여하기 ② 친구들 만나기
③ 도서관 찾기 ④ 카페 가기
⑤ 작가 조사하기

5 대화를 듣고, 두 사람이 대화하는 장소로 가장 적절한 곳을 고르시오.

① 안경원 ② 서점 ③ 교실
④ 사진관 ⑤ 인쇄소

6 대화를 듣고, 여자의 마지막 말의 의도로 가장 적절한 것을 고르시오.

① 감사 ② 거절 ③ 요청 ④ 사과 ⑤ 조언

7 대화를 듣고, 두 사람이 참여하고자 하는 축제를 고르시오.

① 곶감 축제 ② 국화 축제 ③ 김치 축제
④ 얼음 축제 ⑤ 빛 축제

고난도

8 대화를 듣고, 여자가 대화 직후에 할 일로 가장 적절한 것을 고르시오.

① 티셔츠 세탁하기 ② 단체복 맞추기
③ 노래방 가기 ④ 세탁물 분리하기
⑤ 친구에게 전화하기

고난도

9 대화를 듣고, 두 사람이 부엉이에 대해 언급하지 않은 것을 고르시오.

① 다리 길이 ② 깃털 ③ 서식지
④ 활동 시간 ⑤ 산란기

10 다음을 듣고, 남자가 하는 말의 내용으로 가장 적절한 것을 고르시오.

① 거실을 꾸미는 방법 ② 좋은 화분의 중요성
③ 식물을 키우는 방법 ④ 반려동물 관리 사항
⑤ 식물원 이용 예절

11 대화를 듣고, 육상 동아리에 대한 내용으로 일치하지 않는 것을 고르시오.

① 일주일에 세 번 모인다.
② 마라톤 참가를 목표로 한다.
③ 현재 회원은 12명이다.
④ 자유 복장으로 참여할 수 있다.
⑤ 팀 배지가 무료로 제공된다.

12 대화를 듣고, 여자가 영상을 촬영하는 목적으로 가장 적절한 것을 고르시오.

① 사회 숙제로 제출하기 위해서
② 환경 보호 캠페인에 참여하기 위해서
③ 플라스틱 쓰레기를 줄이도록 독려하기 위해서
④ 해변에서 쓰레기 줍기를 홍보하기 위해서
⑤ 친구의 영상 편지에 답하기 위해서

13 대화를 듣고, 남자가 받은 거스름돈으로 가장 적절한 것을 고르시오.

① $ 5 ② $ 10 ③ $ 15
④ $ 20 ⑤ $ 25

14 대화를 듣고, 두 사람의 관계로 가장 적절한 것을 고르시오.

① 의사 — 환자 ② 가구점 직원 — 손님
③ 호텔 직원 — 투숙객 ④ 열차 승무원 — 탑승객
⑤ 식당 점원 — 손님

고난도
15 대화를 듣고, 남자가 여자에게 부탁한 일로 가장 적절한 것을 고르시오.

① 약 사다 주기 ② 아침 준비하기
③ 책 반납하기 ④ 병원 데려가기
⑤ 학교에 전화하기

16 대화를 듣고, 남자가 야구 경기 관람을 하지 못한 이유로 가장 적절한 것을 고르시오.

① 낚시를 하러 가서
② 좌석이 매진 되어서
③ 숙제를 해야 해서
④ 동생이 다리를 다쳐서
⑤ 교통 체증이 심해서

17 다음 그림의 상황에 가장 적절한 대화를 고르시오.

① ② ③ ④ ⑤

18 대화를 듣고, 여자가 피아노 연주회에 관해 언급하지 않은 것을 고르시오.

① 공연 날짜 ② 티켓 가격 ③ 공연 시간
④ 공연 장소 ⑤ 연주자

[19-20] 대화를 듣고, 여자의 마지막 말에 이어질 남자의 말로 가장 적절한 것을 고르시오.

19 **Man:** ______________________

① This is my wife.
② I love your earrings.
③ I'll take a large, please.
④ That's perfect. I'll take it.
⑤ Can you watch over my stuff?

20 **Man:** ______________________

① Thank you for the hard work.
② Let's take a break.
③ Around five hours.
④ Why don't we grow tomatoes?
⑤ We will leave soon.

08회 Dictation

Dictation 음성 바로 듣기 ▶

08회 중학영어듣기 실전 모의고사 Dictation 음성을 들으며 빈칸에 알맞은 단어를 채우시오.

1 | 날씨 고르기

다음을 듣고, 광주의 날씨로 가장 적절한 것을 고르시오.

① ② ③ ④ ⑤

M Good morning, everyone. Let's look at the weather ________ ________ ________. Today, Seoul will be foggy in the morning, and you'll ________ ________ ________ in the afternoon. There will be heavy snow in Daejeon. In Gwangju, ________ ________ ________ ________. Meanwhile, Busan will be sunny again, just like yesterday. ________ ________ ________ ________. Have a good day.

2 | 알맞은 그림 고르기

대화를 듣고, 남자가 두고 온 공책으로 가장 적절한 것을 고르시오.

① ② ③ ④ ⑤

[Cellphone rings.]

M Mom, are you at home?

W Yes. What's up, Junyoung?

M I left ________ ________ ________ in my room. Could you bring it to me?

W Sure. Where did you put it?

M On the desk.

W Do you mean the notebook ________ ________ ________ and a ruler on it?

M No. It has ________ ________ ________ ________ ________.

W Okay. I'll bring it to you.

3 | 심정 고르기

대화를 듣고, 여자의 심정으로 가장 적절한 것을 고르시오.

① bored ② scared ③ shy
④ satisfied ⑤ excited

> 적중! Tip **lately**
> [레이틀리]보다는 [레잇을리]로 들린다. [t]와 [l]처럼 발음할 때 혀의 위치가 비슷한 자음이 나란히 나오면 앞 발음이 탈락되기 때문이다.

M Abby, what are you doing?

W I just ________ ________ ________. What about you?

M I'm going to go to the amusement park with my cousin.

W Sounds great. I wish I had ________ ________ ________ ________.

M Why don't you invite your friends ________ ________ ________?

W I want to, but they are busy with their homework.

M Then, how about ________ ________ ________?

W I don't want to. I've watched too many movies lately. I'm tired of it now.

4 | 한 일 고르기

대화를 듣고, 여자가 오늘 한 일로 가장 적절한 것을 고르시오.

① 책 대여하기 ② 친구들 만나기
③ 도서관 찾기 ④ 카페 가기
⑤ 작가 조사하기

M Sora, how was your day?

W Good. I ________ ________ ________ ________ near my school.

M Did you meet your friends there?

W No. I ________ ________ ________.

M Oh, I see.

W I wanted to read a book ________ ________ ________ ________.

M What did you read?

W I read a book by Charles Dickens.

M He's ________ ________ ________.

5 | 장소 고르기

대화를 듣고, 두 사람이 대화하는 장소로 가장 적절한 곳을 고르시오.

① 안경원 ② 서점 ③ 교실
④ 사진관 ⑤ 인쇄소

W Excuse me, Mr. Stevens. ________ ________ ________ ________ about the homework.
M Sure, Kate. What's your question?
W For the science report, ________ ________ ________ ________?
M Yes, you can. But your essay needs to be five pages long.
W Oh, if I have a picture, does it have to be longer?
M Yes. And ________ ________ ________ at the beginning of class on Monday.

6 | 의도 고르기

대화를 듣고, 여자의 마지막 말의 의도로 가장 적절한 것을 고르시오.

① 감사 ② 거절 ③ 요청 ④ 사과 ⑤ 조언

적중! Tip get it
[겟 잇]보다는 [게릿]으로 들린다. [t]가 모음 사이에서 발음될 때는 약화되어 [r]에 가깝게 발음되기 때문이다.

M My laptop isn't working.
W Again? What's the problem this time?
M ________ ________ ________ ________.
W Oh, no. That's really annoying.
M Yeah. I should take it ________ ________ ________ ________.
W Your computer is ________ ________. When did you get it?
M It was seven years ago.
W I think you should just ________ ________ ________ ________.

7 | 특정 정보 고르기

대화를 듣고, 두 사람이 참여하고자 하는 축제를 고르시오.

① 곶감 축제 ② 국화 축제 ③ 김치 축제
④ 얼음 축제 ⑤ 빛 축제

M Hey, Vanessa. What are you doing?
W I'm ________ ________ ________.
M Is there anything interesting?
W It says that the Seoul Art Fair is next month.
M I went there last year.
W Oh, and there's Yeosu Kimchi Festival next week.
M ________ ________ ________ ________ can you do there?
W You can make your own kimchi! Do you ________ ________ ________ ________?
M Sure. Let's go there!

고난도

8 | 할 일 고르기

대화를 듣고, 여자가 대화 직후에 할 일로 가장 적절한 것을 고르시오.

① 티셔츠 세탁하기 ② 단체복 맞추기
③ 노래방 가기 ④ 세탁물 분리하기
⑤ 친구에게 전화하기

M Taylor, what are you looking for?
W Dad, do you know where my white T-shirt is?
M I think I saw it _________ _________ _________ _________.
W Right. I have to wash it now.
M Why do you need it?
W I need a white T-shirt for choir tomorrow. We _________ _________ _________ matching clothes for the singing contest.
M You'd better _________ _________ _________ first. Don't wash it with dark clothes.
W Okay. I'll do that first.

고난도

9 | 언급하지 않은 내용 고르기

대화를 듣고, 두 사람이 부엉이에 대해 언급하지 <u>않은</u> 것을 고르시오.

① 다리 길이 ② 깃털 ③ 서식지
④ 활동 시간 ⑤ 산란기

적중! Tip **owl**
[아울]이 한 음절씩 들리기보다는 [아우어]로 들릴 수 있다. [w]가 [우]와 [어]의 중간 음으로 발음되기 때문이다.

M Megan, that owl toy is adorable.
W Thanks. I watch a lot of videos about owls.
M Is it true that _________ _________ _________ _________?
W Yes. They also don't make any sound when they fly because _________ _________ _________ _________ _________.
M What else did you learn?
W They usually _________ _________ _________ and are awake at night.
M What do they eat?
W Hmm... I'm not sure.
M _________ _________ on the Internet.

10 | 주제 고르기

다음을 듣고, 남자가 하는 말의 내용으로 가장 적절한 것을 고르시오.

① 거실을 꾸미는 방법 ② 좋은 화분의 중요성
③ 식물을 키우는 방법 ④ 반려동물 관리 사항
⑤ 식물원 이용 예절

M Hello, welcome to my gardening channel. Today, I will talk about _________ _________ _________ _________ _________. First, you need to buy a pot that is _________ _________ for your plant and nice soil. You should also find a place in your house with _________ _________ _________. Finally, you must water your plant regularly.

11 | 일치하지 않는 내용 고르기

대화를 듣고, 육상 동아리에 대한 내용으로 일치하지 <u>않는</u> 것을 고르시오.

① 일주일에 세 번 모인다.
② 마라톤 참가를 목표로 한다.
③ 현재 회원은 12명이다.
④ 자유 복장으로 참여할 수 있다.
⑤ 팀 배지가 무료로 제공된다.

M Nora, what did you do yesterday?
W I _________ _________ _________ _________ with the running club.
M How often does your club meet?
W _________ _________ _________ _________. Our goal is to participate in a marathon this fall.
M Oh, I want to join your club! How many members are there?
W There are 10 members now.
M Do I have to wear athletic clothes?
W No. You can wear whatever you want. And a team badge _________ _________ _________ _________.
M Great!

12 | 목적 고르기

대화를 듣고, 여자가 영상을 촬영하는 목적으로 가장 적절한 것을 고르시오.

① 사회 숙제로 제출하기 위해서
② 환경 보호 캠페인에 참여하기 위해서
③ 플라스틱 쓰레기를 줄이도록 독려하기 위해서
④ 해변에서 쓰레기 줍기를 홍보하기 위해서
⑤ 친구의 영상 편지에 답하기 위해서

적중! Tip **filming**
[필르밍]이 아닌 [필밍]으로 발음된다. [film]은 1음절로 발음되는 단어이기 때문이다.

M What are you up to, Sarah?
W I'm filming a video.
M Oh, ________ ________ ________ ________?
W It's about how much plastic people waste each day.
M Why are you filming it?
W I want to encourage people ________ ________ ________ ________.
M That's really great! It's important to ________ ________ ________.
W Yes. I hope a lot of people watch my video.
M If you ________ ________ ________ ________, I'll share it to my friends.

13 | 금액 정보 고르기

대화를 듣고, 남자가 받은 거스름돈으로 가장 적절한 것을 고르시오.

① $ 5 ② $ 10 ③ $ 15
④ $ 20 ⑤ $ 25

W Welcome. How can I help you?
M ________ ________ ________ ________ a cake for my brother.
W Okay. Would you like to ________ ________ to the cake?
M Yes. Please add "Happy Birthday." How much is it?
W It's 30 dollars ________ ________.
M Alright. Here's 50 dollars.
W ________ ________ ________. Please wait 10 minutes.
M Sure. Thank you!

14 | 관계 고르기

대화를 듣고, 두 사람의 관계로 가장 적절한 것을 고르시오.

① 의사 — 환자 ② 가구점 직원 — 손님
③ 호텔 직원 — 투숙객 ④ 열차 승무원 — 탑승객
⑤ 식당 점원 — 손님

M Hello. I would like ________ ________ ________ ________, please.
W Do you have a reservation?
M No, I don't. ________ ________ ________ right now?
W Yes. We don't have any space in the restaurant ________ ________ ________. But you can ________ ________ ________ on the waiting list.
M Okay. How long is the waiting time?
W A table ________ ________ ________ in about 30 minutes.

고난도

15 | 부탁·요청한 일 고르기

대화를 듣고, 남자가 여자에게 부탁한 일로 가장 적절한 것을 고르시오.

① 약 사다 주기 ② 아침 준비하기
③ 책 반납하기 ④ 병원 데려가기
⑤ 학교에 전화하기

W Jason, are you feeling okay today?
M No, Mom. ________ ________ ________ ________ than yesterday.
W Did you take some medicine?
M Not yet. Mom, I don't think I can go to school today.
W Okay. I'll ________ ________ ________ and tell her that you're still sick.
M Thanks. I also ________ ________ ________ some books to the library.
W Are they due today?
M Yes. Could you return the books for me?
W Sure. ________ ________ ________.

16 | 이유 고르기

대화를 듣고, 남자가 야구 경기 관람을 하지 못한 이유로 가장 적절한 것을 고르시오.

① 낚시를 하러 가서
② 좌석이 매진 되어서
③ 숙제를 해야 해서
④ 동생이 다리를 다쳐서
⑤ 교통 체증이 심해서

M Hey, Heather. What did you ________ ________ ________?
W I went fishing. Did you go to ________ ________ ________?
M No, I didn't.
W What happened? You were ________ ________ ________ the game.
M I was, but my little sister broke her leg on Saturday.
W Oh, poor Sarah. How is she doing now?
M She's ________ ________ ________ now.
W I hope she gets better soon.
M Thank you.

17 | 그림 상황에 적절한 대화 고르기

다음 그림의 상황에 가장 적절한 대화를 고르시오.

① ② ③ ④ ⑤

적중! Tip **beach**
[비이취]로 모음이 길게 발음된다. 자음 사이에 [ea]가 오면 [이] 발음이 길게 되기 때문이다.
· reach [뤼이취] · read [뤼이드]

① **W** Which sport do you like best?
M ________ ________ ________ ________.
② **W** Should I bring an umbrella?
M Yeah. It looks like it's going to rain.
③ **W** Where is the restroom?
M It's ________ ________ ________ ________.
④ **W** Don't run ________ ________ ________. It's dangerous.
M Oh, I'm sorry.
⑤ **W** What are you planning to do at the beach?
M I'm going to ________ ________ ________ ________.

18 | 언급하지 않은 내용 고르기

대화를 듣고, 여자가 피아노 연주회에 관해 언급하지 않은 것을 고르시오.

① 공연 날짜 ② 티켓 가격 ③ 공연 시간
④ 공연 장소 ⑤ 연주자

적중! Tip Do you have plans on ~?
상대방에게 특정 날짜에 계획이 있는지 물어보는 표현으로 '~에 계획이 있니?'라는 의미이다. on 뒤에는 날짜, 요일이 올 수 있다.
· Do you have plans on Friday?
금요일에 계획이 있니?

W Mark, do you have plans on December 31st?
M You mean on New Year's Eve? Not really.
W _______ _______ _______ _______ for a piano concert that evening. Do you want to go?
M That would be great. _______ _______ _______ _______?
W It starts at 6 p.m. Can you meet me at Olympic Concert Hall?
M Where is it?
W It's near Olympic Park Station.
M Okay. Who is playing?
W _______ _______ _______ Seongmin Kim will perform. You'll love it too.

19 | 적절한 응답 고르기

대화를 듣고, 여자의 마지막 말에 이어질 남자의 말로 가장 적절한 것을 고르시오.

Man: _______________

① This is my wife.
② I love your earrings.
③ I'll take a large, please.
④ That's perfect. I'll take it.
⑤ Can you watch over my stuff?

W Hello. Can I help you find something?
M Yes. I'd like _______ _______ _______ _______ for my wife.
W Okay. What style does she like?
M She usually _______ _______ _______.
W Here is a beautiful silver watch _______ _______ _______ _______.
M Do you have anything smaller? That one is too big.
W Sure. What about this one?

20 | 적절한 응답 고르기

대화를 듣고, 여자의 마지막 말에 이어질 남자의 말로 가장 적절한 것을 고르시오.

Man: _______________

① Thank you for the hard work.
② Let's take a break.
③ Around five hours.
④ Why don't we grow tomatoes?
⑤ We will leave soon.

W What are we doing for summer vacation, Dad?
M We will _______ _______ _______.
W That's great. I want to help them with their farm work.
M Excellent. _______ _______ _______ _______.
W Oh, I'm so excited to go.
M Be sure to _______ _______ _______ _______ for the trip. The traffic will be really bad.
W _______ _______ _______ it take to drive to their house?

09회 중학영어듣기 실전 모의고사

실전 모의고사 음성 바로 듣기 ▶

1 다음을 듣고, 인천의 오늘 날씨로 가장 적절한 것을 고르시오.

① 
②  
③  
④  
⑤  

2 대화를 듣고, 남자가 구입할 접시로 가장 적절한 것을 고르시오.

① 
② 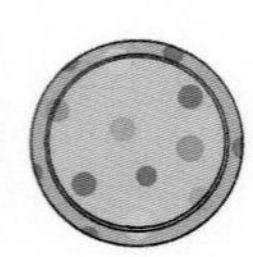
③ 
④ 
⑤ 

고난도

3 대화를 듣고, 여자의 심정으로 가장 적절한 것을 고르시오.

① bored ② upset ③ excited
④ satisfied ⑤ confused

4 대화를 듣고, 여자가 어린이날에 한 일로 가장 적절한 것을 고르시오.

① 동물원 견학하기 ② 집에서 영화 보기
③ 놀이공원 가기 ④ 배드민턴 치기
⑤ 장난감 조립하기

5 대화를 듣고, 두 사람이 대화하는 장소로 가장 적절한 곳을 고르시오.

① 영화관 ② 콘서트장 ③ 농구장
④ 은행 ⑤ 소방서

6 대화를 듣고, 남자의 마지막 말의 의도로 가장 적절한 것을 고르시오.

① 격려 ② 사과 ③ 동의 ④ 감사 ⑤ 충고

7 대화를 듣고, 여자가 카페에서 맛보지 <u>않은</u> 음식을 고르시오.

① 케이크 ② 커피 ③ 샌드위치
④ 녹차 ⑤ 쿠키

8 대화를 듣고, 남자가 대화 직후에 할 일로 가장 적절한 것을 고르시오.

① 교과서 찾아보기 ② 시험지 채점하기
③ 계산 다시 하기 ④ 연습 문제 풀기
⑤ 연습장 사러 가기

9 대화를 듣고, 여자가 지진 발생 시 행동 요령으로 언급하지 <u>않은</u> 것을 고르시오.

① 탁자 다리 붙잡기
② 흔들림이 멈추고 밖으로 나가기
③ 가스 밸브 잠그기
④ 대피 장소로 달려가기
⑤ 라디오 방송의 지시를 따르기

10 다음을 듣고, 여자가 하는 말의 내용으로 가장 적절한 것을 고르시오.

① 채식 식단의 효과 ② 생태계 파괴의 심각성
③ 베푸는 삶의 자세 ④ 규칙적인 생활의 장점
⑤ 긍정적 사고의 중요성

11 다음을 듣고, 사진전에 대한 내용과 일치하지 않는 것을 고르시오.

① 일주일 동안 개최될 예정이다.
② 서울 광장에서 열린다.
③ 파괴된 산림 사진이 전시된다.
④ 환경 오염의 심각성을 보여준다.
⑤ 입장료는 무료이다.

고난도
12 대화를 듣고, 여자가 전화를 건 목적으로 가장 적절한 것을 고르시오.

① 배송일을 확인하기 위해서
② 교환 신청을 하기 위해서
③ 추가 주문을 요청하기 위해서
④ 제품 사용법을 묻기 위해서
⑤ 환불을 받기 위해서

13 대화를 듣고, 두 사람이 만날 시각을 고르시오.

① 6:30 a.m. ② 7:00 a.m. ③ 7:30 a.m.
④ 8:00 a.m. ⑤ 8:30 a.m.

14 대화를 듣고, 두 사람의 관계로 가장 적절한 것을 고르시오.

① 가수 — 팬 ② 연극 감독 — 배우
③ 경찰관 — 시민 ④ 경비원 — 방문객
⑤ 변호사 — 고객

15 대화를 듣고, 남자가 여자에게 부탁한 일로 가장 적절한 것을 고르시오.

① 함께 운동하기 ② 스트레칭 알려주기
③ 허리 치료하기 ④ 병원 예약하기
⑤ 자세 시범 보이기

고난도
16 대화를 듣고, 여자가 남자와의 약속을 취소한 이유로 가장 적절한 것을 고르시오.

① 배탈이 나서 ② 선약이 있어서
③ 폭설이 내려서 ④ 가족 모임이 생겨서
⑤ 동생이 아파서

17 다음 그림의 상황에 가장 적절한 대화를 고르시오.

① ② ③ ④ ⑤

18 다음을 듣고, 여자가 테니스 대회에 대해 언급하지 않은 것을 고르시오.

① 개최 기간 ② 경기 방식 ③ 참가 자격
④ 신청 방법 ⑤ 참가 비용

[19-20] 대화를 듣고, 남자의 마지막 말에 이어질 여자의 말로 가장 적절한 것을 고르시오.

19 **Woman:** ______________________

① That's an amazing idea!
② Let's bring it to the animal shelter.
③ That's a pretty poster.
④ I can't find your house.
⑤ My cat is orange.

20 **Woman:** ______________________

① It was sunny yesterday.
② I packed some chips.
③ Right. I'll put them in my bag.
④ You should protect your eyes.
⑤ Can you buy some apples?

09회 Dictation

Dictation
음성 바로 듣기 ▶

09회 중학영어듣기 실전 모의고사 Dictation 음성을 들으며 빈칸에 알맞은 단어를 채우시오.

1 | 날씨 고르기

다음을 듣고, 인천의 오늘 날씨로 가장 적절한 것을 고르시오.

① ② ③ ④ ⑤

M Good morning. Here is today's local weather forecast. In Dongducheon, it'll be ________ ________ ________ ________ all day. It's cloudy now in Suwon, and ________ ________ ________ will come this afternoon. In Incheon, ________ ________ ________ ________ today, so please be careful. Thank you. And have a nice day.

2 | 알맞은 그림 고르기

대화를 듣고, 남자가 구입할 접시로 가장 적절한 것을 고르시오.

① ② ③ ④ ⑤

W Hello. What can I do for you?

M I'd like to buy a new plate.

W Okay. We have round ones and square ones. ________ ________ ________ ________?

M I like round ones better.

W Then, how about this one ________ ________ ________ on it?

M Can you show me ones with other patterns?

W Of course. This one has ________ ________ ________.

M That's nice. I'll take it.

고난도

3 | 심정 고르기

대화를 듣고, 여자의 심정으로 가장 적절한 것을 고르시오.

① bored ② upset ③ excited
④ satisfied ⑤ confused

> 적중! Tip How come?
> 어떤 상황에 대해 의아한 느낌을 담아 이유를 물을 때 사용되는 표현으로 '어째서?, 왜?'라는 의미이다.

M Amy, did you get your audition results?

W Unfortunately, I didn't ________ ________ ________ for the musical.

M Oh, I'm so sorry ________ ________ ________. You must be upset. You practiced a lot.

W Well... I'm actually okay.

M How come?

W My singing skills really improved ________ ________ ________ for the audition.

M That's good to hear.

W Yeah. I ________ ________ ________ now.

4 | 한 일 고르기

대화를 듣고, 여자가 어린이날에 한 일로 가장 적절한 것을 고르시오.

① 동물원 견학하기 ② 집에서 영화 보기
③ 놀이공원 가기 ④ 배드민턴 치기
⑤ 장난감 조립하기

W What did you do on Children's Day?

M ________ ________ ________ ________ with my family. It was so crowded.

W I can imagine. I wanted to go to an amusement park, but I couldn't.

M Then, did you ________ ________ ________?

W No. I played badminton with my family at a nearby park.

M Did you enjoy it?

W Yeah. I was ________ ________ ________ ________ ________.

5 | 장소 고르기

대화를 듣고, 두 사람이 대화하는 장소로 가장 적절한 곳을 고르시오.

① 영화관 ② 콘서트장 ③ 농구장
④ 은행 ⑤ 소방서

M Hello. I'd like a ticket to see *A New Hero*.
W Alright. What time would you like to watch it?
M I would like to _____ _____ _____ at 2:30 p.m.
W I'm sorry, but _____ _____ _____ _____ for that time.
M No problem. What about _____ _____ _____ _____?
W Seats are available at 4.
M That will do. _____ _____ _____ _____, please.

6 | 의도 고르기

대화를 듣고, 남자의 마지막 말의 의도로 가장 적절한 것을 고르시오.

① 격려 ② 사과 ③ 동의 ④ 감사 ⑤ 충고

W Have you seen my pencil case, Dad?
M No. Did you _____ _____ _____ _____?
W Yes. I searched everywhere, but I couldn't find it.
M Okay. I'll help. What does it look like?
W It's yellow and _____ _____ _____ _____.
M *[Pause]* I found it. It's in the kitchen.
W Oh, right. I left it there this morning after I _____ _____ _____.
M You should put things back after using them.

7 | 특정 정보 고르기

대화를 듣고, 여자가 카페에서 맛보지 않은 음식을 고르시오.

① 케이크 ② 커피 ③ 샌드위치
④ 녹차 ⑤ 쿠키

적중! Tip **tried them**
[트라이드 뎀]보다는 [츄라이뎀]으로 들린다. tr-로 시작하는 단어에서 [t]는 [츄]에 가깝게 발음되고, 비슷하게 발음되는 자음이 나란히 나오면 앞 단어의 끝자음이 탈락되기 때문이다.

W Yongjin, try this cake.
M Thanks. Where did you get it?
W It's from my cousin's new café. It's my favorite dessert .
M _____ _____ _____ _____.
W It tastes really good! The cookies and sandwiches are also popular.
M Have you tried them?
W Yes. They were nice. I _____ _____ _____ _____ too.
M Doesn't the café sell coffee?
W Yes, it does. But _____ _____ _____ _____ because I don't like coffee.

8 할 일 고르기

대화를 듣고, 남자가 대화 직후에 할 일로 가장 적절한 것을 고르시오.

① 교과서 찾아보기 ② 시험지 채점하기
③ 계산 다시 하기 ④ 연습 문제 풀기
⑤ 연습장 사러 가기

M Mom, I can't _________ _________ _________ _________.
W What's the matter?
M I think the answer is 4, but 4 is not one of _________ _________ _________.
W Let me see. *[Pause]* Hmm... You _________ _________ _________ in calculation.
M Oh, I always make mistakes.
W You'd better _________ _________ _________ _________. How about doing this exercise?
M Sure, I'll do that now.

9 언급하지 않은 내용 고르기

대화를 듣고, 여자가 지진 발생 시 행동 요령으로 언급하지 않은 것을 고르시오.

① 탁자 다리 붙잡기
② 흔들림이 멈추고 밖으로 나가기
③ 가스 밸브 잠그기
④ 대피 장소로 달려가기
⑤ 라디오 방송의 지시를 따르기

적중! Tip gas
[가스]로 익숙한 외래어이지만 실제로는 [개스]로 발음된다.

W Hello, students. Today, I'll teach you what to do _________ _________ _________.
M What should I do if I'm inside?
W Good question. You have to _________ _________ _________ _________ and hold its leg.
M When can I go outside?
W _________ _________ _________ _________. But don't forget to turn off the gas before going out.
M I see. Anything else?
W Most importantly, you should follow instructions from the radio.

10 주제 고르기

다음을 듣고, 여자가 하는 말의 내용으로 가장 적절한 것을 고르시오.

① 채식 식단의 효과 ② 생태계 파괴의 심각성
③ 베푸는 삶의 자세 ④ 규칙적인 생활의 장점
⑤ 긍정적 사고의 중요성

W Let me tell you an old story. One day, a fox and a bear decided _________ _________ _________ _________ for the winter. They worked for several weeks. When the house was half finished, the fox gave up. He felt there was still much to do. However, _________ _________ _________ _________. He was happy that lots of work was already done. Finally, the bear had a warm house. This story shows _________ _________ _________ _________ _________.

11 일치하지 않는 내용 고르기

다음을 듣고, 사진전에 대한 내용과 일치하지 않는 것을 고르시오.

① 일주일 동안 개최될 예정이다.
② 서울 광장에서 열린다.
③ 파괴된 산림 사진이 전시된다.
④ 환경 오염의 심각성을 보여준다.
⑤ 입장료는 무료이다.

W Good morning, everyone. A special photo exhibition _________ _________ _________ for one week. It'll be in Seoul Square. We'll display photos of polluted oceans _________ _________ _________. Viewers will be able to see _________ _________ _________ _________ _________. If you are interested, please visit the square at any time. This is _________ _________ _________.

고난도

12 목적 고르기

대화를 듣고, 여자가 전화를 건 목적으로 가장 적절한 것을 고르시오.

① 배송일을 확인하기 위해서
② 교환 신청을 하기 위해서
③ 추가 주문을 요청하기 위해서
④ 제품 사용법을 묻기 위해서
⑤ 환불을 받기 위해서

[Telephone rings.]

M Hello. Best Electronics.
W Hi. I ordered a wireless mouse, but it doesn't work.
M Could you tell me more ________ ________ ________?
W Sure. I put in new batteries, but ________ ________ ________ ________.
M Alright. Do you ________ ________ ________?
W No. I just want to exchange it.
M Okay. Then, please tell me ________ ________ ________.
W It's KG502.

13 시간 정보 고르기

대화를 듣고, 두 사람이 만날 시각을 고르시오.

① 6:30 a.m. ② 7:00 a.m. ③ 7:30 a.m.
④ 8:00 a.m. ⑤ 8:30 a.m.

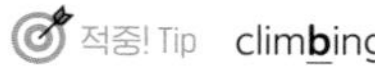
적중! Tip climbing
[클라이밍]으로 발음된다. m- 뒤에 오면서 단어의 맨 마지막에 쓰인 [b]는 묵음이다.
· bomb [밤] · lamb [램]

M Yeji, what are you going to do this Saturday?
W I'm thinking of climbing Dobongsan.
M Sounds good! ________ ________ ________ ________?
W Of course. It's ________ ________ ________ with someone than alone.
M Then, let's meet ________ ________ ________ ________. What time shall we meet?
W How about 7 o'clock in the morning?
M ________ ________ ________ for me. Can we meet an hour later, at 8?
W Okay. See you then.

14 관계 고르기

대화를 듣고, 두 사람의 관계로 가장 적절한 것을 고르시오.

① 가수 — 팬 ② 연극 감독 — 배우
③ 경찰관 — 시민 ④ 경비원 — 방문객
⑤ 변호사 — 고객

M Hi, Ms. Ross. That was an amazing concert. ________ ________ ________ ________.
W I'm glad you enjoyed it.
M Would you ________ ________ ________ for me?
W I would be happy to.
M Can you sign this?
W Sure. Oh, this is ________ ________ ________!
M That's right.
W And what's your name?
M It's Adam Walker.
W Okay. I'll write, "To Adam, thank you ________ ________ ________!"

15 부탁·요청한 일 고르기

대화를 듣고, 남자가 여자에게 부탁한 일로 가장 적절한 것을 고르시오.

① 함께 운동하기　② 스트레칭 알려주기
③ 허리 치료하기　④ 병원 예약하기
⑤ 자세 시범 보이기

M Ouch! My back hurts.
W What's wrong, Luke?
M I think _________ _________ _________ for too long.
W You should do stretches. Do you want me to _________ _________ _________?
M I already did, but it didn't help much.
W You may _________ _________ _________ _________ when you're seated. It's a bad sitting position.
M Oh, I didn't realize that. Can you show me _________ _________ _________?
W No problem. Watch how I sit.

고난도

16 이유 고르기

대화를 듣고, 여자가 남자와의 약속을 취소한 이유로 가장 적절한 것을 고르시오.

① 배탈이 나서　② 선약이 있어서
③ 폭설이 내려서　④ 가족 모임이 생겨서
⑤ 동생이 아파서

적중! Tip supposed to
[서포즈드 투]보다는 [서포즈투]로 들린다. [d]와 [t]처럼 발음할 때 혀의 위치가 비슷한 자음이 나란히 나오면 앞 단어의 끝 자음이 탈락되기 때문이다.

[Cellphone rings.]
M Hi, Sarah. What's up?
W We were supposed to _________ _________ _________ today. Can we make it another time?
M Sure, but why?
W I completely _________ _________ _________ _________ with my professor. It was _________ _________ _________ _________, and it's really important.
M Oh, okay. I understand.
W I'm so sorry. Can I _________ _________ _________ _________?
M Yes. Let's have lunch next Thursday instead.

17 그림 상황에 적절한 대화 고르기

다음 그림의 상황에 가장 적절한 대화를 고르시오.

①　②　③　④　⑤

① **M** Do you know Julie's phone number?
　W Yeah. Let me _________ _________ _________ _________.
② **M** May I take your order?
　W Yes, please. I'd like a chicken burger and a coke.
③ **M** Did you _________ _________ _________ _________?
　W Yes. It was a good game.
④ **M** You look happy. What is going on?
　W I _________ _________ _________ in the singing contest.
⑤ **M** What are you doing on the computer?
　W I'm playing a game.

18 언급하지 않은 내용 고르기

다음을 듣고, 여자가 테니스 대회에 대해 언급하지 않은 것을 고르시오.

① 개최 기간 ② 경기 방식 ③ 참가 자격
④ 신청 방법 ⑤ 참가 비용

W Hello, everyone. Let me tell you about ________ ________ ________ ________. It'll be held from July 10th to 13th. All the amateur tennis players ________ ________ ________ ________ can join. You can simply ________ ________ ________ ________. It will cost 15 dollars. But ________ ________ ________ for participants under 18 and over 60. Thanks for listening.

19 적절한 응답 고르기

대화를 듣고, 남자의 마지막 말에 이어질 여자의 말로 가장 적절한 것을 고르시오.

Woman: ______________________

① That's an amazing idea!
② Let's bring it to the animal shelter.
③ That's a pretty poster.
④ I can't find your house.
⑤ My cat is orange.

 적중! Tip Never mind.

상대방에게 앞서 말한 것에 대해 더 이상 개의치 말라고 말할 때 쓰는 표현으로 '신경 쓰지 마'라는 의미이다. 사과에 대한 응답으로도 쓸 수 있다.

W Hey, Marco. What does your cat look like?
M It's ________ ________ ________ ________.
W Oh, okay. Never mind then.
M Why do you ask?
W I ________ ________ ________ ________ outside of my house. And I'm trying to find its owner.
M ________ ________ ________ ________. How about making posters to ________ ________ ________ ________?

20 적절한 응답 고르기

대화를 듣고, 남자의 마지막 말에 이어질 여자의 말로 가장 적절한 것을 고르시오.

Woman: ______________________

① It was sunny yesterday.
② I packed some chips.
③ Right. I'll put them in my bag.
④ You should protect your eyes.
⑤ Can you buy some apples?

M Minkyung, why don't we go for a picnic ________ ________ ________ this Sunday?
W Sounds great! It will be a beautiful day.
M What shall we take to eat?
W Well, ________ ________ ________ ________.
M What about a picnic mat? Should we buy one?
W Don't worry. I have one. I'll bring it.
M ________ ________ ________ ________ your sunglasses too.

실전 모의고사

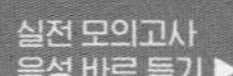

1 다음을 듣고, 토요일의 날씨로 가장 적절한 것을 고르시오.

① ② ③ ④ ⑤

고난도
2 대화를 듣고, 냉장고 안의 음식 배치로 가장 적절한 것을 고르시오.

① 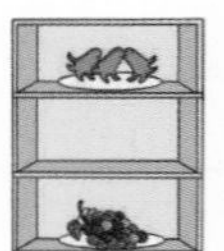 ②  ③ 

④ 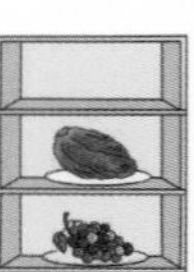 ⑤ 

3 대화를 듣고, 여자의 심정으로 가장 적절한 것을 고르시오.

① excited ② bored ③ disappointed
④ angry ⑤ relaxed

4 대화를 듣고, 여자가 Winter Snow Festival에서 한 일로 가장 적절한 것을 고르시오.

① 기념사진 찍기 ② 스키 타기
③ 눈사람 만들기 ④ 퍼레이드 구경하기
⑤ 눈 조각 감상하기

5 대화를 듣고, 두 사람이 대화하는 장소로 가장 적절한 곳을 고르시오.

① 박물관 ② 미술관 ③ 요리 학원
④ 카페 ⑤ 버스 정류장

6 대화를 듣고, 남자의 마지막 말의 의도로 가장 적절한 것을 고르시오.

① 부탁 ② 칭찬 ③ 충고 ④ 격려 ⑤ 사과

7 대화를 듣고, 남자가 오페라에 대해 언급하지 <u>않은</u> 것을 고르시오.

① 공연 기간 ② 작곡가 ③ 상연 시간
④ 지휘자 ⑤ 출연자

8 대화를 듣고, 두 사람이 대화 직후에 할 일로 가장 적절한 것을 고르시오.

① 책 빌리기 ② 서점 들르기
③ 독후감 쓰기 ④ 자료 복사하기
⑤ 회원증 발급받기

고난도
9 다음을 듣고, 남자가 Pottery Sale Day에 대해 언급하지 <u>않은</u> 것을 고르시오.

① 개최 장소 ② 주최 기관 ③ 판매 물품
④ 결제 방식 ⑤ 주차 안내

10 다음을 듣고, 남자가 하는 말의 내용으로 가장 적절한 것을 고르시오.

① 평화적 갈등 해결법
② 효과적인 의사소통 방법
③ 문화 다양성의 이해
④ 세계 시민 의식 함양
⑤ 환경 보호의 중요성

11 대화를 듣고, 여자가 언급한 내용과 일치하지 않는 것을 고르시오.

① 얼음낚시를 갈 것이다.
② 소나무를 심을 것이다.
③ 서핑을 하러 갈 것이다.
④ 시를 쓸 것이다.
⑤ 수영 연습을 할 것이다.

12 대화를 듣고, 여자가 전화를 건 목적으로 가장 적절한 것을 고르시오.

① 요리법을 묻기 위해서
② 숙제를 함께 하기 위해서
③ 약속 시간을 변경하기 위해서
④ 카메라를 빌리기 위해서
⑤ 저녁 식사에 초대하기 위해서

13 대화를 듣고, 자전거 대회가 개최될 날짜를 고르시오.

① 7월 9일 ② 7월 13일 ③ 7월 17일
④ 7월 20일 ⑤ 7월 24일

14 대화를 듣고, 두 사람의 관계로 가장 적절한 것을 고르시오.

① 환경미화원 — 시민
② 요리사 — 배달원
③ 세탁소 직원 — 손님
④ 경비원 — 아파트 주민
⑤ 바리스타 — 손님

15 대화를 듣고, 남자가 여자에게 부탁한 일로 가장 적절한 것을 고르시오.

① 비행기 표 예약하기 ② 반려견 돌보기
③ 수학 문제 풀기 ④ 여행 계획 세우기
⑤ 약국 다녀오기

16 대화를 듣고, 남자의 친구가 학교에 결석한 이유로 가장 적절한 것을 고르시오.

① 체험 학습을 가서 ② 눈병에 걸려서
③ 가족 여행을 떠나서 ④ 병원에 입원해서
⑤ 폭우로 교통편이 끊겨서

17 다음 그림의 상황에 가장 적절한 대화를 고르시오.

① ② ③ ④ ⑤

고난도

18 다음을 듣고, 여자가 지하철 운행 변경에 대해 언급하지 않은 것을 고르시오.

① 변경 이유 ② 변경 시간대 ③ 배차 간격
④ 막차 시간 ⑤ 무정차 역사

[19-20] 대화를 듣고, 여자의 마지막 말에 이어질 남자의 응답으로 가장 적절한 것을 고르시오.

19 **Man:** ______________________

① It starts next month.
② That's a pity.
③ I don't know how to paint.
④ Sure. If you don't mind.
⑤ He's a close friend.

20 **Man:** ______________________

① I also have an older sister.
② I'm 15 years old.
③ Yes, it was fun.
④ My mother is a lawyer.
⑤ I'll go next time.

10회 Dictation

Dictation 음성 바로 듣기 ▶

10회 중학영어듣기 실전 모의고사 Dictation 음성을 들으며 빈칸에 알맞은 단어를 채우시오.

1 날씨 고르기

다음을 듣고, 토요일의 날씨로 가장 적절한 것을 고르시오.

① ② ③ ④ ⑤

W Now, let's check ________ ________ ________ ________. From Monday to Thursday, there will be lots of ________ ________ ________ ________. On Friday, we will have ________ ________ ________ ________, so try to avoid going out. Fortunately, the rain will stop on Saturday, and it will be ________ ________ ________.

고난도

2 알맞은 그림 고르기

대화를 듣고, 냉장고 안의 음식 배치로 가장 적절한 것을 고르시오.

① ② ③ ④ ⑤

W Dad, can I ________ ________ ________ the table?

M That would be great. Put these side dishes ________ ________ ________, please.

W Okay. Where should I put the kimchi?

M Put it on the middle shelf.

W What about the sausages? ________ ________ ________ ________ on the top shelf?

M No. We'd better ________ ________ ________.

W Alright. There are grapes ________ ________ ________ ________. Why don't we eat some for dessert?

M Sure.

3 심정 고르기

대화를 듣고, 여자의 심정으로 가장 적절한 것을 고르시오.

① excited ② bored ③ disappointed ④ angry ⑤ relaxed

M Honey, wake up.

W ________ ________ ________ ________ now?

M It's already 9. You slept for over two hours after dinner.

W I didn't realize ________ ________ ________ ________.

M It seems that you needed more sleep today.

W Well, I had a lot of work today.

M Then, I'll ________ ________ ________ ________.

W Really? That would be good. I have a stiff neck.

M Tell me if it's too painful.

W Alright. Oh, it ________ ________ ________.

4 한 일 고르기

대화를 듣고, 여자가 Winter Snow Festival에서 한 일로 가장 적절한 것을 고르시오.

① 기념사진 찍기 ② 스키 타기 ③ 눈사람 만들기 ④ 퍼레이드 구경하기 ⑤ 눈 조각 감상하기

M Jane, how was the Winter Snow Festival last weekend?

W It was fantastic. ________ ________ ________ ________, and that made the festival more fun.

M ________ ________ ________ ________ there?

W There was a snowman-making contest.

M That sounds fun. ________ ________ ________ in it?

W No. The event was too crowded with people. So I gave up.

M Then, what did you do instead?

W I ________ ________.

5 | 장소 고르기

대화를 듣고, 두 사람이 대화하는 장소로 가장 적절한 곳을 고르시오.

① 박물관 ② 미술관 ③ 요리 학원
④ 카페 ⑤ 버스 정류장

적중! Tip want to
[원트 투]보다는 [원투]로 들린다. 발음이 같은 자음이 나란히 나오면 앞 단어의 끝 자음이 탈락되기 때문이다.

W What do you want to drink, Kijoon?
M What's ________ ________ ________ ________ here?
W I heard that their milkshakes are delicious.
M I'll take one of those then.
W Great. Do you also ________ ________ ________? They have chocolate cake.
M Yes, please. I'll find a table ________ ________ ________.
W Okay.

6 | 의도 고르기

대화를 듣고, 남자의 마지막 말의 의도로 가장 적절한 것을 고르시오.

① 부탁 ② 칭찬 ③ 충고 ④ 격려 ⑤ 사과

M Jennifer, are you studying for the history exam?
W Yeah. It's ________ ________ ________.
M History is my worst subject too. How about ________ ________ ________ ________?
W Sorry, but I can't.
M Why not?
W I'm going to ________ ________ ________ ________.
M Don't you feel too busy?
W No. I ________ ________ ________ ________.
M You always work so hard! I admire you.

7 | 언급하지 않은 내용 고르기

대화를 듣고, 남자가 오페라에 대해 언급하지 않은 것을 고르시오.

① 공연 기간 ② 작곡가 ③ 상연 시간
④ 지휘자 ⑤ 출연자

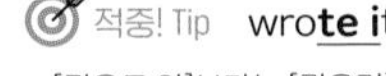

적중! Tip wrote it
[뤄우트 잇]보다는 [뤄우릿]으로 들린다. [t]가 모음 사이에서 발음될 때는 약화되어 [r]에 가깝게 발음되기 때문이다.

M Have you seen the opera *Magic Flute*?
W No, I haven't.
M Then, how about seeing it with me? It ________ ________ ________ from next Friday until April 20th.
W I heard that ________ ________ ________ ________ wrote it.
M Yes. It was Mozart.
W Oh, right. ________ ________ ________ ________ ________?
M Around three hours.
W That's quite long.
M Yeah. But Sumi Jo, the great soprano, will ________ ________ ________. We must see it.

8 할 일 고르기

대화를 듣고, 두 사람이 대화 직후에 할 일로 가장 적절한 것을 고르시오.

① 책 빌리기 ② 서점 들르기
③ 독후감 쓰기 ④ 자료 복사하기
⑤ 회원증 발급받기

M Beth, where are you going?
W Hey, Sanghoon. I'm ________ ________ ________ ________.
M You're looking for the book *Animal Farm*, right?
W Yes. We have to ________ ________ ________ ________ about it by this Friday.
M ________ ________ ________. The book is checked out now.
W Then, what should I do?
M I'm going to the bookstore to ________ ________ ________. Do you want to go together?
W Sure.

고난도

9 언급하지 않은 내용 고르기

다음을 듣고, 남자가 Pottery Sale Day에 대해 언급하지 않은 것을 고르시오.

① 개최 장소 ② 주최 기관 ③ 판매 물품
④ 결제 방식 ⑤ 주차 안내

적중! Tip credit
[크레딧]보다는 [크레릿]으로 들린다. [d]가 모음 사이에서 발음될 때는 약화되어 [r]에 가깝게 발음되기 때문이다.

M Good morning, everyone. Our city will have a Pottery Sale Day at the Hartford Community Center this Sunday. ________ ________ ________ ________ ________ the City Gallery, and local artists will participate as sellers. Many handmade items ________ ________ ________ ________ will be sold there. You can pay by cash or credit card. Since lots of people are ________ ________ ________, please take the bus or the subway. Thank you.

10 주제 고르기

다음을 듣고, 남자가 하는 말의 내용으로 가장 적절한 것을 고르시오.

① 평화적 갈등 해결법
② 효과적인 의사소통 방법
③ 문화 다양성의 이해
④ 세계 시민 의식 함양
⑤ 환경 보호의 중요성

M Hello, class. Let's review ________ ________ ________ in the previous lesson. First, you should listen carefully and show that you're listening. ________ ________ ________ is a good way to do so. Next, you should ________ ________ ________. Also, don't forget to use suitable body language during a conversation. You can ________ ________ ________ ________ using these methods.

11 일치하지 않는 내용 고르기

대화를 듣고, 여자가 언급한 내용과 일치하지 않는 것을 고르시오.

① 얼음낚시를 갈 것이다.
② 소나무를 심을 것이다.
③ 서핑을 하러 갈 것이다.
④ 시를 쓸 것이다.
⑤ 수영 연습을 할 것이다.

W Steve, have you ________ ________ ________ for the next year?
M Not yet. How about you?
W I'm planning to do one thing ________ ________ ________. In spring, I'll plant a pine tree in my yard.
M Wow, what's for winter?
W I'll ________ ________ ________.
M Good. Then, you'll practice swimming in summer, right?
W No. I'll go surfing. And I'll write poems in the fall.
M Awesome. ________ ________ ________ ________ all of those goals.

12 | 목적 고르기

대화를 듣고, 여자가 전화를 건 목적으로 가장 적절한 것을 고르시오.

① 요리법을 묻기 위해서
② 숙제를 함께 하기 위해서
③ 약속 시간을 변경하기 위해서
④ 카메라를 빌리기 위해서
⑤ 저녁 식사에 초대하기 위해서

[Cellphone rings.]

M Hi, Mina. What's up?

W Hello, Kevin. I'm __________ __________ __________ as you taught me.

M Great! It's perfect for dinner.

W Yeah. But can I ask __________ __________ __________ __________ __________?

M What is the problem?

W Well... It doesn't taste __________ __________ __________ __________.

M Did you __________ __________?

W Yes. But maybe I should add a little more.

13 | 시간 정보 고르기

대화를 듣고, 자전거 대회가 개최될 날짜를 고르시오.

① 7월 9일 ② 7월 13일 ③ 7월 17일
④ 7월 20일 ⑤ 7월 24일

적중! Tip Is this ~ speaking?
통화 상황에서 상대방이 누군지 물어보는 표현으로 this 뒤에는 이름을 넣어 쓴다. '~씨이신가요?'라는 의미이다.
· Is this Ms. Davis speaking?
Davis씨이신가요?

[Telephone rings.]

W Hello, this is Julia from the Daehan Cycling Club. Is this Mr. Jones speaking?

M Yes. Can I help you?

W You're going to join our bike race on July 13th, right?

M That's correct. __________ __________ __________ __________?

W I'm sorry, but it'll be delayed because __________ __________ __________ __________.

M Then, when will __________ __________ __________ __________?

W It'll be a week later, on the 20th.

M Alright. Thanks for the call.

14 | 관계 고르기

대화를 듣고, 두 사람의 관계로 가장 적절한 것을 고르시오.

① 환경미화원 — 시민
② 요리사 — 배달원
③ 세탁소 직원 — 손님
④ 경비원 — 아파트 주민
⑤ 바리스타 — 손님

W Welcome. How can I help you?

M I __________ __________ __________ __________. And can you remove this stain from these pants?

W Yes. We can __________ __________ __________.

M Great, thanks. When can I __________ __________ __________ __________?

W They will be ready on Tuesday.

M __________ __________ __________ now?

W Yes. It'll be 10 dollars.

M Here you go. See you on Tuesday.

15 | 부탁·요청한 일 고르기

대화를 듣고, 남자가 여자에게 부탁한 일로 가장 적절한 것을 고르시오.

① 비행기 표 예약하기 ② 반려견 돌보기
③ 수학 문제 풀기 ④ 여행 계획 세우기
⑤ 약국 다녀오기

M Hey, Charlotte.
W Hey, Mike. What's going on?
M I'm traveling to Canada ________ ________ ________ ________.
W When do you leave?
M Next week. But I have a problem. I need a place for my dog to stay ________ ________ ________.
W What about your parents?
M They'll ________ ________ ________ ________ next week. Can you take care of my dog if it's possible?
W Of course. No problem.

16 | 이유 고르기

대화를 듣고, 남자의 친구가 학교에 결석한 이유로 가장 적절한 것을 고르시오.

① 체험 학습을 가서 ② 눈병에 걸려서
③ 가족 여행을 떠나서 ④ 병원에 입원해서
⑤ 폭우로 교통편이 끊겨서

적중! Tip That's a pity.
실망스러운 일이나 안 좋은 일에 대해 유감이나 동정을 나타낼 때 사용되는 표현이다.

W Henry, are you close to Andrew?
M Yeah. ________ ________ ________.
W Then, do you know why Andrew has been ________ ________ ________ since last Friday?
M Yes. He's in the hospital now.
W Oh, what happened to him?
M He broke his leg ________ ________ ________ ________.
W That's a pity.
M I'm going to ________ ________ ________ ________. Would you like to come?
W I'd like that.

17 | 그림 상황에 적절한 대화 고르기

다음 그림의 상황에 가장 적절한 대화를 고르시오.

① ② ③ ④ ⑤

① W Do you want to ________ ________ ________ ________ tomorrow?
M Actually, I'm meeting Lisa for lunch.
② W Can we take some pictures ________ ________ ________ ________ ________?
M Sure! Let's go.
③ W This is a lovely photograph.
M Thanks. That's my family ________ ________ ________.
④ W We should go to the pool.
M Okay. Let me change into my swimsuit.
⑤ W Do you want a room with an ocean view or ________ ________ ________?
M An ocean view, please.

고난도

18 | 언급하지 않은 내용 고르기

다음을 듣고, 여자가 지하철 운행 변경에 대해 언급하지 않은 것을 고르시오.

① 변경 이유 ② 변경 시간대 ③ 배차 간격
④ 막차 시간 ⑤ 무정차 역사

W Hello. I'd like to tell you ________ ________ ________ ________ to our subway service on December 31st. As lots of people will take the subway, we will ________ ________ ________ from 7 to 11 p.m. So, the trains will ________ ________ ________ ________ during those hours. Also, ________ ________ ________ ________ at City Hall Station between 10 p.m. and midnight. Thank you.

19 | 적절한 응답 고르기

대화를 듣고, 여자의 마지막 말에 이어질 남자의 응답으로 가장 적절한 것을 고르시오.

Man: ______________________

① It starts next month.
② That's a pity.
③ I don't know how to paint.
④ Sure. If you don't mind.
⑤ He's a close friend.

 적중! Tip **ex**hibit

[이그지빗]으로 발음된다. [ex]는 [이그즈], [엑스], [익스] 중 하나로 발음된다.

· **ex**hibition [엑서비션] · **ex**treme [익스트림]

M Jia, where are you going?
W Hello, Jaewon. I'm ________ ________ ________ ________ meet a friend at the Wilson Art Gallery.
M Oh, I heard a new exhibit opened there.
W Yeah. There are paintings ________ ________ ________ ________.
M You must be excited.
W Definitely. What about you? ________ ________ ________?
M No. I'm free.
W I see. ________ ________ ________ ________ us at the gallery?

20 | 적절한 응답 고르기

대화를 듣고, 여자의 마지막 말에 이어질 남자의 응답으로 가장 적절한 것을 고르시오.

Man: ______________________

① I also have an older sister.
② I'm 15 years old.
③ Yes, it was fun.
④ My mother is a lawyer.
⑤ I'll go next time.

W How was the festival last night, Taewoo?
M I didn't go.
W Why not? I thought you ________ ________ ________ ________.
M I was, but I had to ________ ________ ________ my little brother.
W Oh, you have a brother?
M Yes. He's four years old now.
W Do you have ________ ________ ________ ________ ________?

중학영어듣기
실전 모의고사

실전 모의고사
음성 바로 듣기 ▶

1 다음을 듣고, 울산의 내일 날씨로 가장 적절한 것을 고르시오.

①  ②  ③  ④  ⑤ 

2 대화를 듣고, 여자가 구입할 커튼으로 가장 적절한 것을 고르시오.

①  ②  ③ 
④  ⑤ 

3 대화를 듣고, 남자의 심정으로 가장 적절한 것을 고르시오.

① worried ② shy ③ bored
④ happy ⑤ nervous

4 대화를 듣고, 여자가 지난 토요일에 한 일로 가장 적절한 것을 고르시오.

① 수산 시장 가기 ② 박물관 방문하기
③ 휴대폰 수리하기 ④ 낚시하기
⑤ 사진 인화하기

5 대화를 듣고, 두 사람이 대화하는 장소로 가장 적절한 곳을 고르시오.

① 옷가게 ② 가구점 ③ 미술관
④ 캠핑용품점 ⑤ 식료품점

6 대화를 듣고, 남자의 마지막 말의 의도로 가장 적절한 것을 고르시오.

① 반대 ② 비난 ③ 반성 ④ 감사 ⑤ 의심

7 대화를 듣고, 남자가 콘서트에 가기 위해 한 일을 고르시오.

① 교통편 알아보기 ② 아르바이트하기
③ 오래된 옷 팔기 ④ 노래 가사 외우기
⑤ 라디오에 사연 보내기

8 대화를 듣고, 남자가 대화 직후에 할 일로 가장 적절한 것을 고르시오.

① 빙상장 가기 ② 스케이트화 구입하기
③ 교통 카드 충전하기 ④ 스케이트보드 타기
⑤ 앱에서 길 찾기

9 대화를 듣고, 두 사람이 달력에 대해 언급하지 <u>않은</u> 것을 고르시오.

① 사진 ② 글씨 크기 ③ 색상
④ 가격 ⑤ 할인율

고난도
10 다음을 듣고, 남자가 하는 말의 내용으로 가장 적절한 것을 고르시오.

① 헌책 기부 방법 ② 좋은 책을 고르는 법
③ 동아리 가입 방법 ④ 도서관 이용 예절
⑤ 속독 추천 이유

11 대화를 듣고, 영화관에 대한 내용과 일치하지 않는 것을 고르시오.

① 지난주에 개관했다.
② 이번 달에는 할인을 한다.
③ 4D 영화를 볼 수 있다.
④ 좌석이 불편하다.
⑤ 다양한 맛의 팝콘을 판다.

12 대화를 듣고, 남자가 전화를 건 목적으로 가장 적절한 것을 고르시오.

① 점심을 함께 먹기 위해서
② 자전거를 빌리기 위해서
③ 주말 계획을 세우기 위해서
④ 수리를 맡기기 위해서
⑤ 학교 준비물을 확인하기 위해서

13 대화를 듣고, 여자가 지불해야 할 금액으로 가장 적절한 것을 고르시오.

① $ 25 ② $ 27 ③ $ 30
④ $ 32 ⑤ $ 35

14 대화를 듣고, 두 사람의 관계로 가장 적절한 것을 고르시오.

① 약사 — 손님 ② 수영 강사 — 수강생
③ 상담사 — 고객 ④ 디자이너 — 모델
⑤ 안경원 직원 — 손님

15 대화를 듣고, 여자가 남자에게 제안한 일로 가장 적절한 것을 고르시오.

① 케이크 주문하기 ② 꽃집 방문하기
③ 손 편지 쓰기 ④ 향수 구매하기
⑤ 경찰서에 전화하기

고난도
16 대화를 듣고, 남자가 일찍 귀가한 이유로 가장 적절한 것을 고르시오.

① 옷을 갈아입으려고 ② 축구 경기를 보려고
③ TV를 수리하려고 ④ 가족과 식사하려고
⑤ 야구를 하러 가려고

17 다음 그림의 상황에 가장 적절한 대화를 고르시오.

① ② ③ ④ ⑤

18 다음을 듣고, 여자가 취미로 하는 일로 언급되지 않은 것을 고르시오.

① 코딩하는 방법을 공부한다.
② 소프트웨어 프로그램을 개발한다.
③ 새로운 부품으로 컴퓨터를 조립한다.
④ 고장 난 컴퓨터를 고친다.
⑤ 컴퓨터 자격증을 취득하려 공부한다.

[19-20] 대화를 듣고, 여자의 마지막 말에 이어질 남자의 말로 가장 적절한 것을 고르시오.

19 **Man:** ________________

① She went to bed early.
② I'll try that tonight.
③ He's feeling better.
④ Do you need to take a nap?
⑤ I'm playing a phone game.

20 **Man:** ________________

① We took the bus.
② No. He is very busy now.
③ Can I buy some stamps?
④ It's pretty expensive.
⑤ Yes. He will love that.

11 회 Dictation

Dictation
음성 바로 듣기 ▶

11회 중학영어듣기 실전 모의고사 Dictation 음성을 들으며 빈칸에 알맞은 단어를 채우시오.

1 | 날씨 고르기

다음을 듣고, 울산의 내일 날씨로 가장 적절한 것을 고르시오.

① ② ③ ④ ⑤

M Good afternoon! Here's the national weather report _________ _________. Seoul will be foggy and cloudy all day long, and _________ _________ _________ _________ dramatically in the evening. It'll be cold in Suwon _________ _________ _________ _________. Heavy snow is expected in Wonju, so try and stay indoors. Lastly in Ulsan, there's _________ _________ _________ _________ rain, so take an umbrella if you go out.

2 | 알맞은 그림 고르기

대화를 듣고, 여자가 구입할 커튼으로 가장 적절한 것을 고르시오.

① ② ③ ④ ⑤

M Hello. May I help you?
W Yes. I'm _________ _________ _________ _________.
M You found the right place! How about this one?
W I really like _________ _________ _________.
M Okay. Which one do you want? The short one or longer one?
W Well, I need it _________ _________ _________ _________. So I'll take the longer one.
M Excellent choice!

3 | 심정 고르기

대화를 듣고, 남자의 심정으로 가장 적절한 것을 고르시오.

① worried ② shy ③ bored
④ happy ⑤ nervous

적중! Tip did it
[디드 잇]보다는 [디릿]으로 들린다. [d]가 모음 사이에서 발음될 때는 약화되어 [r]에 가깝게 발음되기 때문이다.

[Cellphone rings.]
M Hey, Tiffany. What's up?
W Hi, Alex. Did you finish your exam?
M Yes. It's finally over. I'm _________ _________.
W That's good. How did it go?
M It was easy _________ _________ _________ _________. I studied hard for the last three months.
W Oh! I'm really glad to hear that. I knew you _________ _________ _________ on the test.
M Thank you so much.

4 | 한 일 고르기

대화를 듣고, 여자가 지난 토요일에 한 일로 가장 적절한 것을 고르시오.

① 수산 시장 가기 ② 박물관 방문하기
③ 휴대폰 수리하기 ④ 낚시하기
⑤ 사진 인화하기

W Victor, what did you _________ _________ _________?
M I visited the National History Museum. How about you, Emma?
W I _________ _________ with my family.
M That's cool. How was it?
W It was my first time, but I loved it! I caught three fish, and my mom _________ _________ _________.
M Do you have a picture of them?
W Sure. They are on my phone.

5 장소 고르기

대화를 듣고, 두 사람이 대화하는 장소로 가장 적절한 곳을 고르시오.

① 옷가게 ② 가구점 ③ 미술관
④ 캠핑용품점 ⑤ 식료품점

M Hello. Can I help you?
W Yes, please. I'm searching for some new chairs.
M Alright. ________ ________ ________ ________ do you want?
W I want wooden chairs for my kitchen table.
M These chairs are very popular. They would look great in a kitchen.
W They are nice, but ________ ________ ________ ________.
M Okay. ________ ________ these chairs then?
W Oh, those are perfect.

6 의도 고르기

대화를 듣고, 남자의 마지막 말의 의도로 가장 적절한 것을 고르시오.

① 반대 ② 비난 ③ 반성 ④ 감사 ⑤ 의심

적중! Tip next time
[넥스트 타임]보다는 [넥스타임]으로 들린다. 발음이 같은 자음이 나란히 나오면 앞 단어의 끝 자음이 탈락되기 때문이다.

W Jack, today is ________ ________ ________ of your summer vacation, right?
M Yes, Mom. But I didn't finish my vacation homework.
W What is your homework?
M I ________ ________ ________ three reports after reading three books.
W Didn't you read the books?
M Yes. I read them last week. But I didn't have enough time to write reports.
W Jack, you need to ________ ________ ________ ________ next time.
M Okay, Mom. I'll try to ________ ________ ________.

7 한 일 고르기

대화를 듣고, 남자가 콘서트에 가기 위해 한 일을 고르시오.

① 교통편 알아보기 ② 아르바이트하기
③ 오래된 옷 팔기 ④ 노래 가사 외우기
⑤ 라디오에 사연 보내기

W Paul, are you going to Blue Boys' concert?
M Yes. They are ________ ________ ________. What about you?
W I can't go. The tickets are ________ ________.
M Right. I sold some of my old clothes so that I would ________ ________ ________ for a ticket.
W How did you do that?
M Well, I posted them on a website.
W Great idea!
M Yes. You ________ ________ ________ too.

8 | 할 일 고르기

대화를 듣고, 남자가 대화 직후에 할 일로 가장 적절한 것을 고르시오.

① 빙상장 가기 ② 스케이트화 구입하기
③ 교통 카드 충전하기 ④ 스케이트보드 타기
⑤ 앱에서 길 찾기

적중! Tip I am not sure ~.
뭔가를 확실하게 잘 모르겠다고 할 때 사용하는 표현으로 '~인지 잘 모르겠어'라는 의미이다.
· I am not sure if the rumor is true.
나는 그 소문이 사실인지 잘 모르겠어.

M Brenda, are you free on Saturday?
W Yes, I am. _________ _________ _________ _________?
M Would you like to go ice skating with me?
W Sure! Which rink do you want _________ _________ _________?
M My older brother told me that the Westwood Arena has a great rink. But I am not sure how to get there.
W No problem. _________ _________ _________ _________ on the app.
M Oh, I'll check it right now.

9 | 언급하지 않은 내용 고르기

대화를 듣고, 두 사람이 달력에 대해 언급하지 않은 것을 고르시오.

① 사진 ② 글씨 크기 ③ 색상
④ 가격 ⑤ 할인율

M Sara, _________ _________ _________ _________ _________ these calendars?
W I like the one with the pictures of wild animals.
M It's beautiful, but the text is a little small. It could be _________ _________ _________.
W I see. This one with castles is nice too. _________ _________ _________ _________?
M It's 25 dollars. Is that too expensive?
W Look, _________ _________ _________. This calendar is 20% off.
M Let's get it!

고난도

10 | 주제 고르기

다음을 듣고, 남자가 하는 말의 내용으로 가장 적절한 것을 고르시오.

① 헌책 기부 방법 ② 좋은 책을 고르는 법
③ 동아리 가입 방법 ④ 도서관 이용 예절
⑤ 속독 추천 이유

M Good morning. Let's discuss how to _________ _________ _________ _________. There are three ways to do this. First, you can ask your teacher for suggestions. Another way is to read book reviews in _________ _________ _________. Finally, you can join a book club. The club members will _________ _________ _________ for you to read.

11 | 일치하지 않는 내용 고르기

대화를 듣고, 영화관에 대한 내용과 일치하지 않는 것을 고르시오.

① 지난주에 개관했다.
② 이번 달에는 할인을 한다.
③ 4D 영화를 볼 수 있다.
④ 좌석이 불편하다.
⑤ 다양한 맛의 팝콘을 판다.

W Jonathan, did you hear about the new movie theater?
M Yes. It _________ _________ _________.
W It's having a grand opening event. All tickets are 50% off this month.
M Right. I watched a 4D movie there last Friday.
W How was it?
M It felt like _________ _________ _________. And the seat was _________ _________.
W I'd like to visit that theater.
M Do you want to go watch a movie tomorrow? It sells _________ _________ _________ _________ _________ of popcorn too.
W Great! I can't wait.

12 목적 고르기

대화를 듣고, 남자가 전화를 건 목적으로 가장 적절한 것을 고르시오.

① 점심을 함께 먹기 위해서
② 자전거를 빌리기 위해서
③ 주말 계획을 세우기 위해서
④ 수리를 맡기기 위해서
⑤ 학교 준비물을 확인하기 위해서

적중! Tip pick it up
[픽 잇 업]보다는 [피끼럽]으로 들린다. 앞에 나온 단어의 끝 자음과 뒤에 나온 단어의 첫 모음이 연음되고, 이때 강세가 없는 [k]는 된소리로 발음되기 때문이다. 또한 [t]가 모음 사이에서 발음될 때는 약화되어 [r]에 가깝게 발음된다.

[Cellphone rings.]
M Hey, Mindy. I have ________ ________ ________ ________.
W Sure, Jacob. What do you need?
M Could I ________ ________ ________ this weekend?
W Is something wrong with yours?
M Yeah. I broke the seat. But I ________ ________ ________ ________ with some friends on Saturday.
W I can ________ ________ ________ that day.
M Thanks. I'll pick it up at 1.
W See you then!

13 금액 정보 고르기

대화를 듣고, 여자가 지불해야 할 금액으로 가장 적절한 것을 고르시오.

① $ 25 ② $ 27 ③ $ 30
④ $ 32 ⑤ $ 35

M Welcome to our store. ________ ________ ________ ________ you?
W How much are these tumblers?
M The small one is 25 dollars, and ________ ________ ________ is 30 dollars.
W I'll take the medium size. How about ________ ________ ________?
M It's two dollars. Do you want it too?
W Yes, please.
M Then, the total is 32 dollars.

14 관계 고르기

대화를 듣고, 두 사람의 관계로 가장 적절한 것을 고르시오.

① 약사 — 손님 ② 수영 강사 — 수강생
③ 상담사 — 고객 ④ 디자이너 — 모델
⑤ 안경원 직원 — 손님

M Hello. What can I do for you?
W Do you have ________ ________ ________ ________?
M Yes. These pills will help.
W ________ ________ should I take them?
M Take two pills three times per day. Do you need anything else?
W Yes. Can I also have ________ ________ ________ ________?
M Sure. Do you want waterproof ones?
W No. Just the regular bandages, please.

15 제안한 일 고르기

대화를 듣고, 여자가 남자에게 제안한 일로 가장 적절한 것을 고르시오.

① 케이크 주문하기 ② 꽃집 방문하기
③ 손 편지 쓰기 ④ 향수 구매하기
⑤ 경찰서에 전화하기

적중! Tip sweet of you
[스윗 오브 유]보다는 [스위러뷰]로 들린다. [t]가 모음 사이에서 발음될 때는 약화되어 [r]에 가깝게 발음되고, 앞에 나온 단어의 끝 자음과 뒤에 나온 단어의 첫 모음이 연음되기 때문이다.

W Hi, Nick. What are you doing?
M Hi. I'm ________ ________ ________ for my mom.
W That is so sweet of you. Is it her birthday today?
M Actually, it's tomorrow. But I don't know ________ ________ ________ ________.
W Let me help you. What does your mom like the most?
M Well, she likes flowers.
W What about buying a perfume ________ ________ ________ ________? I think she would love it.
M That's a good idea. Thank you.

고난도

16 이유 고르기

대화를 듣고, 남자가 일찍 귀가한 이유로 가장 적절한 것을 고르시오.

① 옷을 갈아입으려고 ② 축구 경기를 보려고
③ TV를 수리하려고 ④ 가족과 식사하려고
⑤ 야구를 하러 가려고

적중! Tip I don't know what you mean.
상대방의 말을 이해하지 못했음을 나타낼 때 사용되는 표현으로 '무슨 말인지 모르겠어'라는 의미이다.

M Karen, I'm home.
W Oh, you came home 30 minutes ________ ________ ________.
M Yes. I had to come home early.
W Why? Are you playing baseball with your friends today?
M Honey, don't you remember ________ ________ ________ ________?
W I'm sorry, but I don't know what you mean.
M There's ________ ________ ________ ________ today!
W Right! Let's order fried chicken and watch it on TV.

17 그림 상황에 적절한 대화 고르기

다음 그림의 상황에 가장 적절한 대화를 고르시오.

① ② ③ ④ ⑤

① **W** ________ ________ ________ tomatoes and onions on your sandwich?
M Just tomatoes, please.
② **W** Do we need to buy any bread?
M Yes. We just ________ ________.
③ **W** What will we eat on our hike?
M I'll pack some strawberries and crackers.
④ **W** What are you ________ ________ ________ ________?
M I've planted some lettuce and cucumbers.
⑤ **W** ________ ________ ________?
M It's March 20th.

18 | 언급하지 않은 내용 고르기

다음을 듣고, 여자가 취미로 하는 일로 언급되지 않은 것을 고르시오.

① 코딩하는 방법을 공부한다.
② 소프트웨어 프로그램을 개발한다.
③ 새로운 부품으로 컴퓨터를 조립한다.
④ 고장 난 컴퓨터를 고친다.
⑤ 컴퓨터 자격증을 취득하려 공부한다.

적중! Tip I'm trying to ~.
어떤 일을 집중해서 하고 있거나 노력해서 하고 있음을 나타낼 때 사용되는 표현으로, to 다음에는 동사원형이 온다.
· I'm trying to read more books.
난 더 많은 책을 읽으려고 노력 중이야.

W Let me tell you about my hobby. I'm very interested in computers. I'm learning _________ _________ _________ code in my free time. I'm trying to develop some software programs with what I've learned. Sometimes, I assemble computers _________ _________ _________. Also, I'm always _________ _________ _________ fix my friends' broken computers. I dream of _________ _________ _________ _________ someday.

19 | 적절한 응답 고르기

대화를 듣고, 여자의 마지막 말에 이어질 남자의 말로 가장 적절한 것을 고르시오.

Man: ____________________________

① She went to bed early.
② I'll try that tonight.
③ He's feeling better.
④ Do you need to take a nap?
⑤ I'm playing a phone game.

W Hi, Matt. You look tired.
M Yes. I can't sleep well nowadays.
W Oh, no. Why not?
M I just _________ _________ _________.
W What have you tried to fall asleep?
M I _________ _________ _________ _________, but it didn't work.
W I see. Do you look at your phone a lot _________ _________ _________?
M I guess I do.
W _________ _________ _________ _________ _________. Next time, read a book instead.

20 | 적절한 응답 고르기

대화를 듣고, 여자의 마지막 말에 이어질 남자의 말로 가장 적절한 것을 고르시오.

Man: ____________________________

① We took the bus.
② No. He is very busy now.
③ Can I buy some stamps?
④ It's pretty expensive.
⑤ Yes. He will love that.

W Hyunmin, that postcard with a picture of Deoksugung is pretty. Who did you _________ _________ _________?
M It's for my friend Edward. He _________ _________ _________.
W How did you meet him?
M I met him at Daejeon Science Camp last summer. He wants to _________ _________ _________ this year.
W I think he will like the postcard then. What about _________ _________ _________ _________ on his visit?

12회 중학영어듣기 실전 모의고사

실전 모의고사 음성 바로 듣기 ▶

1 다음을 듣고, 금요일의 날씨로 가장 적절한 것을 고르시오.

① ② ③ ④ ⑤

2 대화를 듣고, 남자가 만든 가면으로 가장 적절한 것을 고르시오.

①  ②  ③ 

④  ⑤ 

3 대화를 듣고, 남자의 심정으로 가장 적절한 것을 고르시오.

① bored ② excited ③ angry
④ sad ⑤ embarrassed

4 대화를 듣고, 남자가 주말에 한 일로 가장 적절한 것을 고르시오.

① 가족 여행가기 ② 나무 심기
③ 벼룩시장 가기 ④ 요리하기
⑤ 친구 만나기

5 대화를 듣고, 두 사람이 대화하는 장소로 가장 적절한 곳을 고르시오.

① 미술관 ② 수리 센터 ③ 지하철역
④ 백화점 ⑤ 경찰서

6 대화를 듣고, 여자의 마지막 말의 의도로 가장 적절한 것을 고르시오.

① 격려 ② 제안 ③ 충고 ④ 허락 ⑤ 부탁

고난도

7 대화를 듣고, 여자가 현재 아픈 부위로 가장 적절한 것을 고르시오.

① 무릎 ② 발목 ③ 어깨 ④ 허리 ⑤ 머리

8 대화를 듣고, 남자가 대화 직후에 할 일로 가장 적절한 것을 고르시오.

① 스노보드 배우기 ② 동영상 보기
③ 스키 타기 ④ 짐 싸기
⑤ 버스표 구매하기

고난도

9 대화를 듣고, 두 사람이 발레 공연에 대해 언급하지 <u>않은</u> 것을 고르시오.

① 공연명 ② 공연 길이 ③ 등장인물
④ 줄거리 ⑤ 공연 시기

10 다음을 듣고, 여자가 하는 말의 내용으로 가장 적절한 것을 고르시오.

① 할인 쿠폰 사용 ② 매장 공사 안내
③ 할인 행사 안내 ④ 주말농장 판매
⑤ 주차 요금 공지

11 대화를 듣고, Teen Short Film Festival에 대한 내용과 일치하지 않는 것을 고르시오.

① 이번 금요일에 열린다.
② 청소년들끼리 경쟁할 수 있다.
③ 단편 영화를 볼 수 있다.
④ 투표에 참여할 수 있다.
⑤ 학생 입장료는 무료이다.

12 대화를 듣고, 남자가 전화를 건 목적으로 가장 적절한 것을 고르시오.

① 배송 조회를 하기 위해서
② 추가 주문을 하기 위해서
③ 상품을 교환하기 위해서
④ 사용 방법을 물어보기 위해서
⑤ 주문을 취소하기 위해서

13 대화를 듣고, 남자가 구매한 신발의 사이즈를 고르시오.

① 260mm ② 265mm ③ 270mm
④ 275mm ⑤ 280mm

14 대화를 듣고, 두 사람의 관계로 가장 적절한 것을 고르시오.

① 간호사 — 환자 ② 교사 — 학생
③ 영화감독 — 배우 ④ 약사 — 손님
⑤ 택시 기사 — 승객

고난도
15 대화를 듣고, 여자가 남자에게 부탁한 일로 가장 적절한 것을 고르시오.

① 페인트칠하기 ② 새 종이 꺼내주기
③ 붓 빌려주기 ④ 숙제 도와주기
⑤ 빨래하기

16 대화를 듣고, 남자가 우체국에 가는 이유로 가장 적절한 것을 고르시오.

① 택배를 보내기 위해서
② 택배가 분실되어서
③ 돈을 송금하기 위해서
④ 우표를 구매하기 위해서
⑤ 구매한 엽서가 찢어져서

17 다음 그림의 상황에 가장 적절한 대화를 고르시오.

① ② ③ ④ ⑤

18 다음을 듣고, 여자가 Glendale Community Center에 대해 언급하지 않은 것을 고르시오.

① 건물 구성 ② 시설 사용료
③ 수업 종류 ④ 주차장 유무
⑤ 교통편

[19-20] 대화를 듣고, 남자의 마지막 말에 이어질 여자의 말로 가장 적절한 것을 고르시오.

19 Woman: ____________________

① Let's go for a swim.
② I like Yeosu better.
③ How about catching crabs?
④ Have a nice trip.
⑤ We'll need our passports.

20 Woman: ____________________

① I tried that already.
② The screen is broken.
③ Almost 10 years.
④ Thanks for fixing it.
⑤ The service center is on your left.

12회 Dictation

Dictation
음성 바로 듣기 ▶

12회 중학영어듣기 실전 모의고사 Dictation 음성을 들으며 빈칸에 알맞은 단어를 채우시오.

1 날씨 고르기

다음을 듣고, 금요일의 날씨로 가장 적절한 것을 고르시오.

① ② ③ ④ ⑤

W Welcome to the weekly weather report. This week will start with ________ ________ ________ and warm sunshine. From Thursday, however, it'll be partly cloudy and windy. Rain ________ ________ ________ ________ from Friday through the weekend. So, I ________ ________ ________ ________. Thank you.

2 알맞은 그림 고르기

대화를 듣고, 남자가 만든 가면으로 가장 적절한 것을 고르시오.

① ② ③ ④ ⑤

M Mom, look!
W Oh, my! What are you wearing, Sunho?
M It's ________ ________ ________ ________. I made it in class today.
W Why are there three holes?
M It's an alien mask, so I ________ ________ ________ for eyes.
W Did you cut those sharp teeth?
M Ms. Nicholas ________ ________ ________ ________.
W Where is the nose?
M Aliens ________ ________ ________.
W You did a great job. It is scary.

3 심정 고르기

대화를 듣고, 남자의 심정으로 가장 적절한 것을 고르시오.

① bored ② excited ③ angry
④ sad ⑤ embarrassed

적중! Tip Do you want me to ~?
상대방에게 무언가를 제안하며 의향을 물을 때 사용되는 표현으로 '내가 ~해줄까?, 제가 ~할까요?'라는 의미이다.
· Do you want me to make some tea?
내가 차를 타 줄까?

W Brad, did you check the results of ________ ________ ________?
M Not yet. I am so nervous.
W Come on! I know you are a good writer.
M Well, I'm not sure.
W Do you want me to ________ ________ ________ for you?
M Yes, please. I can't check it myself.
W Okay. *[Clicking sound]* Brad, you did it!
M Really? I ________ ________ ________!

4 한 일 고르기

대화를 듣고, 남자가 주말에 한 일로 가장 적절한 것을 고르시오.

① 가족 여행가기 ② 나무 심기
③ 벼룩시장 가기 ④ 요리하기
⑤ 친구 만나기

W What's that small tree on your desk?
M It's a tree-shaped lamp. I got it ________ ________ ________ ________ in Central Park on Saturday.
W Oh, I wanted to go there too. But my family went on a trip to Jeonju.
M ________ ________ ________. What did you do there?
W We went to Jeonju Hanok Village. I had bibimbab for dinner, and it was very delicious.
M It sounds like you ________ ________ ________ ________!

5 | 장소 고르기

대화를 듣고, 두 사람이 대화하는 장소로 가장 적절한 곳을 고르시오.

① 미술관 ② 수리 센터 ③ 지하철역
④ 백화점 ⑤ 경찰서

M Hi, Officer. ________ ________ ________ ________.
W Okay, sir. We'll look into it. What happened?
M Someone ________ ________ ________ ________ and took my bag last night.
W I see. What was inside the bag?
M I keep my laptop in it.
W Alright. I've ________ ________ ________. We will call you if ________ ________ ________ ________.

6 | 의도 고르기

대화를 듣고, 여자의 마지막 말의 의도로 가장 적절한 것을 고르시오.

① 격려 ② 제안 ③ 충고 ④ 허락 ⑤ 부탁

M Kelly, what a surprise! What are you doing here?
W Hi, Minsu. I am getting some chicken and vegetables.
M What are you ________ ________ ________ tonight?
W Today is Thanksgiving in my home country. We usually cook a turkey, but they are ________ ________ ________ in Korea.
M Wow. I've never been to a Thanksgiving dinner before.
W ________ ________ ________ ________ and have dinner with my family?

고난도

7 | 특정 정보 고르기

대화를 듣고, 여자가 현재 아픈 부위로 가장 적절한 것을 고르시오.

① 무릎 ② 발목 ③ 어깨 ④ 허리 ⑤ 머리

적중! Tip **knee**
[니]로 발음된다. -n 앞에 오면서 단어의 맨 처음에 쓰인 [k]는 묵음이다.
· knight [나잇] · knit [닛]

W Good afternoon, Dr. Feldman.
M Ms. Smith, ________ ________ ________ ________ today. What's the matter?
W I fell on the ice yesterday. At first, ________ ________ ________ ________.
M And then?
W This morning, I could hardly walk.
M Does your back still hurt?
W Not anymore. ________ ________ ________ now.
M Okay. I'll take an X-ray. We'll see what's wrong with your knee.

8 | 할 일 고르기

대화를 듣고, 남자가 대화 직후에 할 일로 가장 적절한 것을 고르시오.

① 스노보드 배우기 ② 동영상 보기
③ 스키 타기 ④ 짐 싸기
⑤ 버스표 구매하기

M What is that, Yuna?
W It's a bus ticket to Pyeongchang. ________ ________ ________ in the afternoon.
M I didn't know you like snowboarding.
W Yeah. I learned to snowboard last year, and it's ________ ________ ________ than skiing.
M I want to learn ________ ________ ________ too.
W You can come with me today. I'll teach you how.
M Really?
W Yeah. Go ________ ________ ________. I'll get a ticket for you.
M Okay. Thanks!

고난도

9 | 언급하지 않은 내용 고르기

대화를 듣고, 두 사람이 발레 공연에 대해 언급하지 않은 것을 고르시오.

① 공연명 ② 공연 길이 ③ 등장인물
④ 줄거리 ⑤ 공연 시기

적중! Tip Ballet
[발렛]이 아닌 [발레이]로 발음된다. 프랑스에서 유래한 단어의 맨 끝에 쓰인 t는 묵음인 경우가 있다.
· debut [데뷰] · gourmet [골메이]

M Today, our guest is Sofia Petrov from the National Ballet company. Welcome!
W Good afternoon.
M Could you tell us about ________ ________ ________?
W I danced as Clara in *The Nutcracker*.
M What is the main story of this ballet?
W On Christmas eve, Clara ________ ________ ________ a nutcracker. And ________ ________ ________ the evil Mouse King.
M That sounds interesting. Is the show performed all year?
W No. We usually stage this performance around Christmas time only.

10 | 주제 고르기

다음을 듣고, 여자가 하는 말의 내용으로 가장 적절한 것을 고르시오.

① 할인 쿠폰 사용 ② 매장 공사 안내
③ 할인 행사 안내 ④ 주말농장 판매
⑤ 주차 요금 공지

W Attention, customers. Welcome to Sideshow Supermarket. We are having ________ ________ ________ today. All fruits and vegetables are 10% off. Cucumbers and carrots ________ ________ ________ a 5% discount. Also, download our app, and you can get a pass ________ ________ ________.

11 | 일치하지 않는 내용 고르기

대화를 듣고, Teen Short Film Festival에 대한 내용과 일치하지 않는 것을 고르시오.

① 이번 금요일에 열린다.
② 청소년들끼리 경쟁할 수 있다.
③ 단편 영화를 볼 수 있다.
④ 투표에 참여할 수 있다.
⑤ 학생 입장료는 무료이다.

W Jared, the Teen Short Film Festival ________ ________ ________ this Friday.
M Yeah. Teenagers between 15 and 18 can compete with their short films.
W Cool! Did you ________ ________ ________?
M Yes, I did. You can watch mine and the other participants' short films at the festival. You can also ________ ________ ________ ________ ________.
W I can't wait! Is the festival free?
M No. But it's ________ ________ ________ for students.

12 | 목적 고르기

대화를 듣고, 남자가 전화를 건 목적으로 가장 적절한 것을 고르시오.

① 배송 조회를 하기 위해서
② 추가 주문을 하기 위해서
③ 상품을 교환하기 위해서
④ 사용 방법을 물어보기 위해서
⑤ 주문을 취소하기 위해서

[Telephone rings.]
W Hello, Liberty Electronics customer service. How can I help you?
M Hi, I'd like to ________ ________ ________.
W Okay. Was there anything wrong with your order?
M No. I ________ ________ ________ ________ as a birthday gift.
W Could you tell me the order number?
M Sure. It's MG113.
W Alright. *[Typing sound]* When you receive the headphones, ________ ________ ________ to us. Then, we will provide you with a refund.
M Thank you.

13 | 숫자 정보 고르기

대화를 듣고, 남자가 구매한 신발의 사이즈를 고르시오.

① 260mm ② 265mm ③ 270mm
④ 275mm ⑤ 280mm

M Excuse me. Can you help me?
W Sure. What can I do for you?
M I've tried these sneakers on, but ________ ________ ________ ________.
W Let me see. These are a size 265.
M ________ ________ ________ ________ a size 275?
W Just a second. *[Pause]* Here you go.
M Thank you. *[Pause]* These are ________ ________ ________. I'm sorry, but can I try a smaller size?
W Okay. Here is a size 270.
M These ________ ________. I'll take these.

14 | 관계 고르기

대화를 듣고, 두 사람의 관계로 가장 적절한 것을 고르시오.

① 간호사 — 환자 ② 교사 — 학생
③ 영화감독 — 배우 ④ 약사 — 손님
⑤ 택시 기사 — 승객

적중! Tip lost track
[로스트 트랙]보다는 [로스트랙]으로 들린다. 발음이 같은 자음이 나란히 나오면 앞 단어의 끝 자음이 탈락되기 때문이다.

M Mary, can I speak with you?
W Sure, Mr. Evans. Is something wrong?
M You fell asleep in my class a few times today. Are you alright?
W I'm so sorry. ________ ________ ________ really late last night.
M What were you doing?
W I was playing ________ ________ ________ ________. I lost track of time.
M I see. You should try to ________ ________ ________ ________.

고난도

15 | 부탁·요청한 일 고르기

대화를 듣고, 여자가 남자에게 부탁한 일로 가장 적절한 것을 고르시오.

① 페인트칠하기　② 새 종이 꺼내주기
③ 붓 빌려주기　④ 숙제 도와주기
⑤ 빨래하기

적중! Tip　paint my
[페인트 마이]보다는 [페인마이]로 들린다. 자음 3개가 연속해서 나오면 중간 자음은 발음되지 않기 때문이다.

M Elena, can you help me?
W What's going on, Tom?
M I was painting the wall, and now I have paint ________ ________ ________ ________.
W Oh. What can I do for you?
M Will you ________ ________ ________ ________ ________?
W Sure. Can I ________ ________ ________ later?
M Why do you need them?
W I want to paint my room too.

16 | 이유 고르기

대화를 듣고, 남자가 우체국에 가는 이유로 가장 적절한 것을 고르시오.

① 택배를 보내기 위해서
② 택배가 분실되어서
③ 돈을 송금하기 위해서
④ 우표를 구매하기 위해서
⑤ 구매한 엽서가 찢어져서

M Hello, Kate.
W Hi, Aaron. Where are you ________ ________ ________?
M I'm going to the post office.
W Oh, are you sending something to your sister in France?
M No. I'm going there to ________ ________ ________.
W Oh? What for?
M Actually, ________ ________ is my hobby.
W I see. I hope you find some cool stamps.
M Yes. I heard that they are selling New Year limited-edition stamps today.

17 | 그림 상황에 적절한 대화 고르기

다음 그림의 상황에 가장 적절한 대화를 고르시오.

①　②　③　④　⑤

① **M** How did you get tickets for the concert?
W My friend is in the band.
② **M** What movie do you want to see?
W Let's ________ ________ ________ ________. I don't like scary movies.
③ **M** Why don't we ride the roller coaster?
W You can ride it, but ________ ________ ________ ________.
④ **M** What are you ________ ________?
W I'm watching a funny video of a cat.
⑤ **M** I like your new sweater.
W Thanks. I just bought it.

18 | 언급하지 않은 내용 고르기

다음을 듣고, 여자가 Glendale Community Center에 대해 언급하지 않은 것을 고르시오.

① 건물 구성 ② 시설 사용료
③ 수업 종류 ④ 주차장 유무
⑤ 교통편

적중! Tip sports
[스폴츠]보다는 [스뽈츠]로 들린다. [s] 뒤에 [p] 발음이 오면 된소리로 발음되기 때문이다.
· spell [스뻴] · speak [스삐크]

W Good morning, visitors. Welcome to the newly opened Glendale Community Center. It has two main buildings ________ ________ ________ ________ and a gym. Anyone who lives in Glendale can ________ ________ ________ for free. Our center provides various sports and art classes for children. Our center also ________ ________ ________, so please check the information on our ________ ________ ________ ________.

19 | 적절한 응답 고르기

대화를 듣고, 남자의 마지막 말에 이어질 여자의 말로 가장 적절한 것을 고르시오.

Woman: ____________________

① Let's go for a swim.
② I like Yeosu better.
③ How about catching crabs?
④ Have a nice trip.
⑤ We'll need our passports.

M Honey, where do you want to ________ ________ ________ this year?
W Hmm... What about Namwon? We can climb Jirisan there.
M That sounds nice. But I really want to go ________ ________ ________ ________ instead.
W Okay. Then, how about Taean or Yeosu? They ________ ________ ________ ________.
M Sounds wonderful! Which one ________ ________ ________?

20 | 적절한 응답 고르기

대화를 듣고, 남자의 마지막 말에 이어질 여자의 말로 가장 적절한 것을 고르시오.

Woman: ____________________

① I tried that already.
② The screen is broken.
③ Almost 10 years.
④ Thanks for fixing it.
⑤ The service center is on your left.

M Is there something wrong with your laptop, Susan?
W Yeah. It's ________ ________ ________ right now.
M That's strange. Is it fully charged?
W Yes. I charged it last night.
M It is likely that there's ________ ________ ________ the battery then.
W That could be the problem. It's ________ ________ ________ ________.
M How long have you had it?

13회 중학영어듣기 실전 모의고사

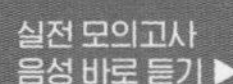

1 다음을 듣고, 뉴욕의 날씨로 가장 적절한 것을 고르시오.

①  ②  ③  ④  ⑤ 

2 대화를 듣고, 여자가 구입할 티로 가장 적절한 것을 고르시오.

①  ②   ③ 

④  ⑤ 

3 대화를 듣고, 여자의 마지막 말의 의도로 가장 적절한 것을 고르시오.

① 거절 ② 충고 ③ 동의 ④ 용서 ⑤ 칭찬

4 대화를 듣고, 남자가 크리스마스에 한 일로 가장 적절한 것을 고르시오.

① 트리 꾸미기 ② 음식 준비하기
③ 이글루 짓기 ④ 선물 포장하기
⑤ 눈사람 만들기

5 대화를 듣고, 두 사람이 대화하는 장소로 가장 적절한 곳을 고르시오.

① 병원 ② 호텔 ③ 기차역
④ 학교 ⑤ 쇼핑몰

6 대화를 듣고, 영화에 대한 내용으로 일치하지 <u>않는</u> 것을 고르시오.

① 애니메이션 영화이다.
② 동물원에서 일어나는 이야기다.
③ 여우가 주인공이다.
④ Kylie Williams가 감독이다.
⑤ 5월 10일에 개봉한다.

7 대화를 듣고, 여자가 할인을 받기 위해 할 일을 고르시오.

① 전단지 보여주기 ② 홈페이지 가입하기
③ 앱 다운 받기 ④ 티셔츠 구매하기
⑤ 문자 메시지 보내기

8 대화를 듣고, 여자가 대화 직후에 할 일로 가장 적절한 것을 고르시오.

① 사진 찍어주기 ② 엽서 고르기
③ 여행 계획하기 ④ 자석 구매하기
⑤ 지도에서 길 찾기

9 대화를 듣고, 여자가 딸기 농장 방문에 대해 언급하지 <u>않은</u> 것을 고르시오.

① 농장 위치 ② 출발 시간 ③ 교통편
④ 활동 ⑤ 입장료

고난도

10 다음을 듣고, 여자가 하는 말의 내용으로 가장 적절한 것을 고르시오.

① 준비 운동의 중요성 ② 부모님 초청 수업
③ 운동 기구 이용 방법 ④ 스키장 안전 수칙
⑤ 스키 강습 신청 방법

정답 및 해설 p.74

맞은 개수 : / 20개

11 대화를 듣고, 종이비행기 대회에 대한 내용과 일치하지 않는 것을 고르시오.

① 운동장에서 열린다.
② 대회는 다음 주에 개최된다.
③ 학생이라면 참가할 수 있다.
④ 우승자에게는 상을 준다.
⑤ 종이의 크기는 정해져 있지 않다.

12 대화를 듣고, 여자가 바자회에 가는 목적으로 가장 적절한 것을 고르시오.

① 가구를 구경하기 위해서
② 장난감을 수집하기 위해서
③ 음반을 찾기 위해서
④ 그림을 구매하기 위해서
⑤ 중고 물건을 판매하기 위해서

13 대화를 듣고, 여자가 지불해야 할 금액으로 가장 적절한 것을 고르시오.

① $ 5 ② $ 10 ③ $ 15
④ $ 20 ⑤ $ 25

14 대화를 듣고, 두 사람의 관계로 가장 적절한 것을 고르시오.

① 과학 교사 — 학생
② 녹음 기사 — 성우
③ 작가 — 독자
④ 조련사 — 수의사
⑤ 박물관 경비원 — 관람객

고난도

15 대화를 듣고, 남자가 여자에게 부탁한 일로 가장 적절한 것을 고르시오.

① 초콜릿 구매하기 ② 옷 수선 맡기기
③ 화분에 물 주기 ④ 커피 머신 구매하기
⑤ 부엌 청소하기

16 대화를 듣고, 여자가 노래방에 가지 못하는 이유로 가장 적절한 것을 고르시오.

① 지갑을 잃어버려서 ② 숙제를 해야 해서
③ 치과에 가야 해서 ④ 감기에 걸려서
⑤ 목이 쉬어서

17 다음 그림의 상황에 가장 적절한 대화를 고르시오.

① ② ③ ④ ⑤

18 다음을 듣고, 여자가 학예회에 대해 언급하지 않은 것을 고르시오.

① 날짜 ② 장소 ③ 시작 시간
④ 사회자 ⑤ 공연 순서

[19-20] 대화를 듣고, 여자의 마지막 말에 이어질 남자의 말로 가장 적절한 것을 고르시오.

19 **Man:** ________________

① The tickets are sold out.
② They open from 5 p.m.
③ Are you finished with your meal?
④ The staff are very friendly.
⑤ I want to invite Jason and Rebecca.

20 **Man:** ________________

① Let me give you my number.
② Be nice to your brother.
③ I think that's for the best.
④ I found my phone.
⑤ Dinner isn't ready.

13회 Dictation

Dictation
음성 바로 듣기 ▶

13회 중학영어듣기 실전 모의고사 Dictation 음성을 들으며 빈칸에 알맞은 단어를 채우시오.

1 | 날씨 고르기

다음을 듣고, 뉴욕의 날씨로 가장 적절한 것을 고르시오.

① ② ③ ④ ⑤

M Good morning! This is the world weather report. In London, it will be rainy _______ _______ _______. Don't forget _______ _______ _______ _______. Paris will be partly cloudy and cold. New York will have a lot of snow today, so be careful of _______ _______ _______. Thank you.

2 | 알맞은 그림 고르기

대화를 듣고, 여자가 구입할 티로 가장 적절한 것을 고르시오.

① ② ③ ④ ⑤

M Welcome. May I help you?
W I'd like to buy a sweatshirt _______ _______ _______ _______.
M Do you have any particular design in mind?
W I don't _______ _______ _______, but I want one with a hood.
M How about this one? It comes _______ _______ _______ _______.
W Hmm... Is there one with no zippers?
M This one doesn't have a zipper.
W I'll _______ _______ _______.

3 | 의도 고르기

대화를 듣고, 여자의 마지막 말의 의도로 가장 적절한 것을 고르시오.

① 거절 ② 충고 ③ 동의 ④ 용서 ⑤ 칭찬

> 적중! Tip **dropped**
> [드랍트]로 발음된다. [p]로 끝나는 동사에 -ed가 붙어 과거형이 되면 [t]로 발음되기 때문이다.
> · po**pped** [팝트] · sto**pped** [스땁트]

M Hey, Mina. What are you doing?
W I'm _______ _______ _______ _______ on my tablet.
M Wow. Is that a new tablet?
W Yes. It's _______ _______ _______ from Four-Star Electronics.
M It looks cool. Can I try it out?
W Sure! Here you go.
M Oh, no! There is _______ _______ _______ on the screen because I dropped your tablet.
W Don't worry about it. I know _______ _______ _______ _______.

4 | 한 일 고르기

대화를 듣고, 남자가 크리스마스에 한 일로 가장 적절한 것을 고르시오.

① 트리 꾸미기 ② 음식 준비하기
③ 이글루 짓기 ④ 선물 포장하기
⑤ 눈사람 만들기

M Jihee, I saw the picture you posted on Christmas.
W _______ _______ _______ _______ the snowman picture? I made it with my sister.
M _______ _______ _______ you had fun.
W Yeah. What did you do on Christmas?
M I _______ _______ _______. I also put mini light bulbs on it.
W Did you put a star on the top of the tree?
M Of course. I can show you the picture if you want.

5 장소 고르기

대화를 듣고, 두 사람이 대화하는 장소로 가장 적절한 곳을 고르시오.

① 병원 ② 호텔 ③ 기차역
④ 학교 ⑤ 쇼핑몰

W Hi. How can I help you?
M Hello. _________ _________ _________ _________ a patient.
W Okay. Who are you looking for?
M Her name is Yasmine Grant. She just _________ _________ _________ _________ this afternoon.
W She'll be on the fifth floor then. You can find the elevator _________ _________ _________.
M Thank you for the help.

6 일치하지 않는 내용 고르기

대화를 듣고, 영화에 대한 내용으로 일치하지 않는 것을 고르시오.

① 애니메이션 영화이다.
② 동물원에서 일어나는 이야기다.
③ 여우가 주인공이다.
④ Kylie Williams가 감독이다.
⑤ 5월 10일에 개봉한다.

적중! Tip What are you up to ~?

무엇을 하는 중인지 물을 때 사용되는 표현이다. 무엇을 할 예정인지 물을 때에도 사용할 수 있다.

· What are you up to tomorrow?
 내일 뭐 할 거야?

M Jane, what are you up to?
W I'm looking at _________ _________ _________ _________.
M It looks interesting. What is the movie about?
W It's a story _________ _________ _________.
M Oh, I love stories about animals.
W Me too. _________ _________ _________ is a fox. It was also made by my favorite director, Kylie Williams.
M _________ _________ _________ _________ _________ so well! When can you watch it?
W It will be released on May 5th.
M You must be excited!

7 할 일 고르기

대화를 듣고, 여자가 할인을 받기 위해 할 일을 고르시오.

① 전단지 보여주기 ② 홈페이지 가입하기
③ 앱 다운 받기 ④ 티셔츠 구매하기
⑤ 문자 메시지 보내기

M Hello, how can I help you?
W I'd like to _________ _________ _________ _________.
M It's 45 dollars in total. You can get a 10% discount if you spend five dollars more.
W Hmm... But I don't know what else to buy now.
M How about buying this T-shirt right here? It's five dollars!
W Then, I'll take it _________ _________ _________ _________.
M You can _________ _________ _________ now.

8 | 할 일 고르기

대화를 듣고, 여자가 대화 직후에 할 일로 가장 적절한 것을 고르시오.

① 사진 찍어주기 ② 엽서 고르기
③ 여행 계획하기 ④ 자석 구매하기
⑤ 지도에서 길 찾기

M Sandy, did you _________ _________ _________ to San Francisco?
W Yes, Dad. Before we go back home, can we go to a gift shop?
M Sure. What do you want to buy?
W I want to _________ _________ _________ to remember this beautiful city.
M If you want to _________ _________ _________ here, why don't you buy postcards?
W That's a great idea! I'll buy some with pictures of the city.
M Oh, there's a shop over there.
W Let's go inside and _________ _________.

9 | 언급하지 않은 내용 고르기

대화를 듣고, 여자가 딸기 농장 방문에 대해 언급하지 않은 것을 고르시오.

① 농장 위치 ② 출발 시간 ③ 교통편
④ 활동 ⑤ 입장료

W Alright, everyone. Tomorrow we will go to _________ _________ _________ in Nonsan.
M Ms. Harris, what time will we leave?
W We will leave at 9 in the morning.
M What activities will we do there?
W We will _________ _________ and make jam.
M Sounds good. Do we _________ _________ _________ _________?
W Yes. Admission is 10 dollars, and you can also buy souvenirs.
M Okay. I can't wait!

고난도

10 | 주제 고르기

다음을 듣고, 여자가 하는 말의 내용으로 가장 적절한 것을 고르시오.

① 준비 운동의 중요성 ② 부모님 초청 수업
③ 운동 기구 이용 방법 ④ 스키장 안전 수칙
⑤ 스키 강습 신청 방법

W Attention, please. _________ _________ _________, please follow these rules. One, please do warm-up exercises _________ _________ _________ _________. Two, please wear protective equipment. You have to wear _________ _________ _________ _________ to stay safe. Three, if you're under 12, do not ski alone. Children under 12 must _________ _________ _________ _________ at all times. Enjoy your time at our ski resort. Thank you.

11 | 일치하지 않는 내용 고르기

대화를 듣고, 종이비행기 대회에 대한 내용과 일치하지 않는 것을 고르시오.

① 운동장에서 열린다.
② 대회는 다음 주에 개최된다.
③ 학생이라면 참가할 수 있다.
④ 우승자에게는 상을 준다.
⑤ 종이의 크기는 정해져 있지 않다.

적중! Tip plane
'평범한'이라는 의미의 형용사 plain의 발음도 [플레인]으로 비슷하다. 이러한 동음이의어는 문맥 속에서 뜻을 파악하는 것이 중요하다.

W Jaehoon, did you hear about _________ _________ _________ _________?
M No, I didn't. When will it be held?
W It will be next week at _________ _________ _________.
M Can I sign up for the competition too?
W Sure. _________ _________ _________ _________. There's also a prize for the winner.
M Great! I will make the biggest paper plane.
W Well, you can't. Everyone's paper will be _________ _________ _________.
M I'll study how to fold it well then.

12 목적 고르기

대화를 듣고, 여자가 바자회에 가는 목적으로 가장 적절한 것을 고르시오.

① 가구를 구경하기 위해서
② 장난감을 수집하기 위해서
③ 음반을 찾기 위해서
④ 그림을 구매하기 위해서
⑤ 중고 물건을 판매하기 위해서

적중! Tip **record**
record는 명사로 쓰일 때는 [레컬드]로, 동사로 쓰일 때는 [리콜드]로 발음된다.

M Bailey, are you going out?
W Yes, Dad. I'm going to a bazaar.
M What are you going to buy?
W ________ ________ ________, so I'll go and find some old records.
M That's a good idea. Please ________ ________ ________ if you find a good one.
W I will. I can look for some of ________ ________ ________ too.
M That would be wonderful!

13 금액 정보 고르기

대화를 듣고, 여자가 지불해야 할 금액으로 가장 적절한 것을 고르시오.

① $ 5 ② $ 10 ③ $ 15
④ $ 20 ⑤ $ 25

W Hello, I'd like to ________ ________ ________.
M Sure. ________ ________ do you need it for?
W Just for one hour, please.
M That's 15 dollars then.
W Can I also rent a helmet?
M Yes. But you have to ________ ________ ________ ________.
W Okay. One helmet please. How much is it in total?
M ________ ________ is 20 dollars.
W Here you go.

14 관계 고르기

대화를 듣고, 두 사람의 관계로 가장 적절한 것을 고르시오.

① 과학 교사 — 학생
② 녹음 기사 — 성우
③ 작가 — 독자
④ 조련사 — 수의사
⑤ 박물관 경비원 — 관람객

적중! Tip **book about**
[북 어바웃]보다는 [부커바웃]으로 들린다. 앞에 나온 단어의 끝 자음과 뒤에 나온 단어의 첫 모음이 연음되기 때문이다.

W Excuse me. Are you Ronald Smith?
M Yes, that's me.
W Wow! I ________ ________ ________ about Lion Man. He's my favorite super hero.
M Thank you. Actually, a new book ________ ________ ________ ________.
W Really? Is it another book about super heroes?
M No. This one is ________ ________ ________.
W That's amazing. I want to be an astronaut in the future.
M Then, you will love it.

고난도

15 | 부탁·요청한 일 고르기

대화를 듣고, 남자가 여자에게 부탁한 일로 가장 적절한 것을 고르시오.

① 초콜릿 구매하기 ② 옷 수선 맡기기
③ 화분에 물 주기 ④ 커피 머신 구매하기
⑤ 부엌 청소하기

M Honey, where are you going?
W I'm _____ _____ _____. I need a new coffee machine.
M Okay. Should I come with you?
W _____ _____. But could you clean the kitchen?
M Sure. I don't mind doing that.
W Thanks. Do you need anything?
M I would love some chocolate. Can you _____ _____ _____?
W Sure. I'll _____ _____ _____.
M Great. Thank you.

16 | 이유 고르기

대화를 듣고, 여자가 노래방에 가지 못하는 이유로 가장 적절한 것을 고르시오.

① 지갑을 잃어버려서 ② 숙제를 해야 해서
③ 치과에 가야 해서 ④ 감기에 걸려서
⑤ 목이 쉬어서

 적중! Tip weekend

[위크엔드]보다는 [위켄드]로 들린다. 강세가 없는 [k]는 된소리로 발음되기 때문이다.

[Telephone rings.]
W Hello?
M Hi, Jihye. Are you _____ _____ _____ to a singing room today?
W Oh, wait. Is that today?
M Yes. We made plans last week.
W I'm sorry, but I have _____ _____ _____. I have a bad toothache.
M Okay. We should go to a singing room next weekend. Let's also have tteokbokki then.
W _____ _____ _____ _____.

17 | 그림 상황에 적절한 대화 고르기

다음 그림의 상황에 가장 적절한 대화를 고르시오.

① ② ③ ④ ⑤

① **W** Why did they _____ _____ _____?
M There is an event today.
② **W** What are you going to wear tonight?
M I will wear a nice shirt and pants.
③ **W** How was _____ _____ _____?
M It was great. I liked the science museum a lot.
④ **W** What should we eat for lunch?
M _____ _____ _____ curry and rice?
⑤ **W** Excuse me. I think you _____ _____ _____.
M Oh, my! Thank you so much.

18 언급하지 않은 내용 고르기

다음을 듣고, 여자가 학예회에 대해 언급하지 않은 것을 고르시오.

① 날짜 ② 장소 ③ 시작 시간
④ 사회자 ⑤ 공연 순서

W Good morning, students. I'd like to tell you about our school's talent show this year. It ________ ________ ________ December 8th, and it ________ ________ ________ in the gym. The talent show will begin at 2 p.m. and will last for two hours. Our school's student president, Paul Mason, will ________ ________ ________. I hope every student comes and enjoys it!

19 적절한 응답 고르기

대화를 듣고, 여자의 마지막 말에 이어질 남자의 말로 가장 적절한 것을 고르시오.

Man: ______________________________

① The tickets are sold out.
② They open from 5 p.m.
③ Are you finished with your meal?
④ The staff are very friendly.
⑤ I want to invite Jason and Rebecca.

적중! Tip **I'd**
[아이드]보다는 [아읻]으로 들린다. 조동사 would의 축약형은 앞에 나오는 주어와 연결해서 약하게 발음되기 때문이다.

M Have you been to that new restaurant, Nara?
W Which restaurant?
M The one next to the park. ________ ________ ________ ________.
W No, I haven't been there. Have you?
M No. But I heard it's great. Do you want to go tomorrow evening?
W I'd love to.
M ________ ________ ________ ________ ________ too.
W Okay. Who do you ________ ________ ________?

20 적절한 응답 고르기

대화를 듣고, 여자의 마지막 말에 이어질 남자의 말로 가장 적절한 것을 고르시오.

Man: ______________________________

① Let me give you my number.
② Be nice to your brother.
③ I think that's for the best.
④ I found my phone.
⑤ Dinner isn't ready.

M Honey, I think we should talk.
W Oh, what's wrong?
M Well, the kids ________ ________ ________ ________ on their phones. I'm worried.
W I totally ________ ________ ________. It is a bad habit.
M How do we stop them from using their phones so much?
W Why don't we ________ ________ ________ ________ for family dinners?

14회 중학영어듣기 실전 모의고사

실전 모의고사 음성 바로 듣기 ▶

1 다음을 듣고, 월요일의 날씨로 가장 적절한 것을 고르시오.

①  ②  ③  ④  ⑤

2 대화를 듣고, 여자가 만든 휴대폰 케이스로 가장 적절한 것을 고르시오.

①

②

③

④

⑤

고난도

3 대화를 듣고, 여자의 마지막 말의 의도로 가장 적절한 것을 고르시오.

① 사과 ② 거절 ③ 불평 ④ 제안 ⑤ 부탁

4 대화를 듣고, 남자가 휴일에 한 일로 가장 적절한 것을 고르시오.

① 수족관 가기 ② 캠핑 가기
③ 등산하기 ④ 스테이크 굽기
⑤ 집 청소하기

5 대화를 듣고, 두 사람이 대화하는 장소로 가장 적절한 곳을 고르시오.

① 병원 ② 미용실 ③ 도서관
④ 카페 ⑤ 사진관

6 대화를 듣고, 책에 관한 정보로 일치하지 않는 것을 고르시오.

① 공상 과학 소설이다.
② 다른 행성으로의 여행에 대한 내용이다.
③ 책 분량은 670쪽이다.
④ 작가는 고등학교 선생님이다.
⑤ 작가는 취미로 소설을 쓰기 시작했다.

7 대화를 듣고, 여자가 빌릴 물건으로 가장 적절한 것을 고르시오.

① 자전거 ② 젓가락 ③ 도시락
④ 헬멧 ⑤ 배낭

8 대화를 듣고, 남자가 대화 직후에 할 일로 가장 적절한 것을 고르시오.

① 체온 재기 ② 병원 가기 ③ 샤워하기
④ 약 먹기 ⑤ 물 끓이기

9 대화를 듣고, 남자가 Ocean Water Park에 대해 언급하지 않은 것을 고르시오.

① 위치 ② 개장일 ③ 놀이 시설
④ 입장료 ⑤ 개장 시간

10 다음을 듣고, 남자가 하는 말의 내용으로 가장 적절한 것을 고르시오.

① 비누 제작 방법 ② 세탁기 사용법
③ 운동화 세탁 방법 ④ 환경 보호 방법
⑤ 분리수거 방법

고난도
11 대화를 듣고, 동영상에 관한 정보로 일치하지 않는 것을 고르시오.

① 10분짜리 영상이다.
② 북극곰에 대한 내용이다.
③ 한국 다큐멘터리 팀이 제작했다.
④ 15년 동안 촬영되었다.
⑤ 북극곰을 보호하기 위해 만들어졌다.

12 대화를 듣고, 여자가 전화를 건 목적으로 가장 적절한 것을 고르시오.

① 위치를 묻기 위해서
② 강습 정보를 얻기 위해서
③ 티켓을 구입하기 위해서
④ 숙소 예약을 변경하기 위해서
⑤ 온라인 수업을 추천 받기 위해서

고난도
13 대화를 듣고, 두 사람이 만날 시각을 고르시오.

① 4:00 p.m. ② 4:30 p.m. ③ 5:00 p.m.
④ 5:30 p.m. ⑤ 6:00 p.m.

14 대화를 듣고, 두 사람의 관계로 가장 적절한 것을 고르시오.

① 역사학자 — 기자 ② 여행 가이드 — 여행객
③ 가수 — 팬 ④ 사진작가 — 모델
⑤ 요리사 — 종업원

15 대화를 듣고, 여자가 남자에게 부탁한 일로 가장 적절한 것을 고르시오.

① 카드 작성하기 ② 편지 보내기
③ 봉투 구매하기 ④ 우표 붙이기
⑤ 책상 정리하기

16 대화를 듣고, 남자가 실망한 이유로 가장 적절한 것을 고르시오.

① 경기가 취소되어서
② 메달을 따지 못해서
③ 서핑보드가 부러져서
④ 동료가 부상을 당해서
⑤ 최선을 다하지 못해서

17 다음 그림의 상황에 가장 적절한 대화를 고르시오.

① ② ③ ④ ⑤

18 다음을 듣고, 여자가 과학 박람회에 대해 언급하지 않은 것을 고르시오.

① 시행 주체 ② 행사 장소 ③ 참가 비용
④ 시작 시간 ⑤ 행사 기간

[19-20] 대화를 듣고, 남자의 마지막 말에 이어질 여자의 말로 가장 적절한 것을 고르시오.

19 **Woman:** ______________________

① It's brown.
② It's in my purse.
③ She ran to the store.
④ Look under the couch.
⑤ I have five dollars.

20 **Woman:** ______________________

① He didn't come to school.
② Sure. I'll try my best.
③ Smile for the camera!
④ It was a funny joke.
⑤ You'll do better next time.

14회 Dictation

Dictation
음성 바로 듣기 ▶

14회 중학영어듣기 실전 모의고사 Dictation 음성을 들으며 빈칸에 알맞은 단어를 채우시오.

1 날씨 고르기

다음을 듣고, 월요일의 날씨로 가장 적절한 것을 고르시오.

① ② ③ ④ ⑤

W Good evening, everyone. This is your end-of-the-weekend weather report from KSBN. Monday will be sunny with ________ ________ ________ ________. From Tuesday, rain will fall, and this signals ________ ________ ________ ________. It'll stop by Thursday, and we'll be able to enjoy ________ ________ ________ again on Friday. The weather will be perfect for outdoor activities on the weekend.

2 알맞은 그림 고르기

대화를 듣고, 여자가 만든 휴대폰 케이스로 가장 적절한 것을 고르시오.

① JESS ② JESS ③ JESS
④ ⑤

M Jess, what did you do today?

W I ________ ________ ________ ________ with a sticker after school, Dad.

M Oh, you decorated this? I like the cat ________ ________ ________.

W Thank you. I really like it too. I wanted to put a dog next to the cat, but I couldn't find a sticker.

M You also put your name ________ ________ ________.

W Yes, I did. That way, my phone case is really personalized. I love it.

고난도

3 의도 고르기

대화를 듣고, 여자의 마지막 말의 의도로 가장 적절한 것을 고르시오.

① 사과 ② 거절 ③ 불평 ④ 제안 ⑤ 부탁

> 적중! Tip Tell me about it.
> 상대방의 의견에 동의할 때 사용되는 표현으로, '제 말이요, 제 말이 그 말이에요'라는 의미이다.

[Knocking sound]

M Who is it?

W Hi, I'm your ________ ________ ________ ________.

M Hi. Is there any problem?

W Could you ________ ________ ________ ________ a bit? I can't sleep because it's too loud.

M Oh, sorry about that. I'll use my headphones.

W Thanks.

M I think the walls in the building are ________ ________.

W Tell me about it. I can even hear another neighbor coughing.

4 한 일 고르기

대화를 듣고, 남자가 휴일에 한 일로 가장 적절한 것을 고르시오.

① 수족관 가기 ② 캠핑 가기
③ 등산하기 ④ 스테이크 굽기
⑤ 집 청소하기

W Hey, Jinsu. How was your holiday? I went to the aquarium.

M Hi, Miso. The aquarium sounds fun. I stayed home ________ ________ ________.

W Why? Didn't you say you were going ________ ________ ________ ________?

M Yeah. But it ________ ________ ________, so my family stayed home.

W Oh, no! Did you do anything else then?

M We ________ ________ ________ instead, and ate delicious steaks.

5 | 장소 고르기

대화를 듣고, 두 사람이 대화하는 장소로 가장 적절한 곳을 고르시오.

① 병원 ② 미용실 ③ 도서관
④ 카페 ⑤ 사진관

M Hi. How do you want your hair cut today?
W Well, I don't want any big changes. I'd like to ________ ________ ________ ________.
M I can just cut a little bit off. It will still ________ ________ ________.
W That's perfect.
M Don't you want to ________ ________ ________ ________?
W No. I want to keep the brown color.
M Okay. I'll get started then.

6 | 일치하지 않는 내용 고르기

대화를 듣고, 책에 관한 정보로 일치하지 <u>않는</u> 것을 고르시오.

① 공상 과학 소설이다.
② 다른 행성으로의 여행에 대한 내용이다.
③ 책 분량은 670쪽이다.
④ 작가는 고등학교 선생님이다.
⑤ 작가는 취미로 소설을 쓰기 시작했다.

M What are you reading, Jamie?
W I'm reading a science fiction novel about a ________ ________ ________ ________.
M The book looks really thick. ________ ________ ________ does it have?
W It's 670 pages long, but it's really exciting.
M Who's the author?
W Surprisingly, the author is ________ ________ ________ ________ in Norway, Jenna Adams.
M Wow. How did she write it?
W She said she ________ ________ ________ ________ as a hobby.

7 | 특정 정보 고르기

대화를 듣고, 여자가 빌릴 물건으로 가장 적절한 것을 고르시오.

① 자전거 ② 젓가락 ③ 도시락
④ 헬멧 ⑤ 배낭

sholu**d I**

[슈드 아이]보다는 [슈라이]로 들린다. [d]가 모음 사이에서 발음될 때는 약화되어 [r]에 가깝게 발음되기 때문이다.

M Sora, are you ready to leave? Did you ________ ________ ________ for bike riding?
W Yeah, I did. Where is the lunch box? I need to ________ ________ ________ in it.
M In the car. Why don't you put it in your backpack?
W Okay. *[Pause]* Oh, no!
M What's wrong?
W There is a hole in ________ ________ ________ ________ ________. What should I do!
M Don't worry. We can ________ ________ ________ at the park.

8 | 할 일 고르기

대화를 듣고, 남자가 대화 직후에 할 일로 가장 적절한 것을 고르시오.

① 체온 재기 ② 병원 가기 ③ 샤워하기
④ 약 먹기 ⑤ 물 끓이기

적중! Tip temperature
[템퍼러쳐]보다는 [템펄쳐]로 들린다. 강세가 없는 [ra]의 발음은 약화되기 때문이다.

W Kevin, what's going on?
M Mom, I think I'm ________ ________ ________.
W Let's check your temperature now.
M How high is it?
W It's 37.3 degrees. You should go see a doctor.
M I'll have to ________ ________ ________ since it's Sunday today.
W Then, take this pill to lower your temperature.
M Okay. I'm going to ________ ________ ________ and get some rest.
W I'll make some tea for you.

9 | 언급하지 않은 내용 고르기

대화를 듣고, 남자가 Ocean Water Park에 대해 언급하지 않은 것을 고르시오.

① 위치 ② 개장일 ③ 놀이 시설
④ 입장료 ⑤ 개장 시간

M Kelly, would you like to go to the Ocean Water Park on Sunday?
W Sure. Is it the new water park on Oak Street?
M Yes. ________ ________ ________ on June 25th.
W What does it have?
M It has more than 12 slides and ________ ________ ________ ________.
W Awesome! Isn't it expensive?
M You can ________ ________ ________ ________ for only 30 dollars.
W Alright. I'll come with you on Sunday.
M See you then!

10 | 주제 고르기

다음을 듣고, 남자가 하는 말의 내용으로 가장 적절한 것을 고르시오.

① 비누 제작 방법 ② 세탁기 사용법
③ 운동화 세탁 방법 ④ 환경 보호 방법
⑤ 분리수거 방법

M Today, I'm going to talk about ________ ________ ________ your sneakers. First, mix baking soda and vinegar with hot water to ________ ________ ________. Second, use a toothbrush and ________ ________ ________ with the paste. Then, let the paste dry for a few hours. Lastly, ________ ________ ________ with warm water. Your shoes will look good as new!

고난도

11 | 일치하지 않는 내용 고르기

대화를 듣고, 동영상에 관한 정보로 일치하지 않는 것을 고르시오.

① 10분짜리 영상이다.
② 북극곰에 대한 내용이다.
③ 한국 다큐멘터리 팀이 제작했다.
④ 15년 동안 촬영되었다.
⑤ 북극곰을 보호하기 위해 만들어졌다.

M What are you watching, Donna?
W It's a video ________ ________ ________. It's only 10 minutes long.
M I want to watch it too. Who filmed it?
W It was made by a Korean documentary team. It took ________ ________ ________ ________.
M Oh, I heard about this. Didn't they make this documentary ________ ________ ________ ________?
W Yeah. They wanted to show ________ ________ ________ ________ these animals.

12 | 목적 고르기

대화를 듣고, 여자가 전화를 건 목적으로 가장 적절한 것을 고르시오.

① 위치를 묻기 위해서
② 강습 정보를 얻기 위해서
③ 티켓을 구입하기 위해서
④ 숙소 예약을 변경하기 위해서
⑤ 온라인 수업을 추천 받기 위해서

[Telephone rings.]

M Hello. Maple Ice Arena. How can I help you today?

W Hi. I'm interested in ________ ________ ________ a skating class.

M Sure. Are you a beginner?

W Yes. I've ________ ________ ________.

M We have beginner classes on Tuesdays and Thursdays at 9 in the morning.

W Okay. ________ ________ is each class?

M Lessons last for an hour, and then there will be 30 minutes for practice.

고난도

13 | 시간 정보 고르기

대화를 듣고, 두 사람이 만날 시각을 고르시오.

① 4:00 p.m. ② 4:30 p.m. ③ 5:00 p.m.
④ 5:30 p.m. ⑤ 6:00 p.m.

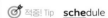

적중! Tip **sche**dule
미국식으로는 [스케쥴]로 발음되고, 영국식으로는 [쉐쥴]로 발음된다.

M Samantha, when do you want to go to the restaurant on Friday? I need to ________ ________ ________.

W Let me check my schedule. *[Pause]* The meeting ends at 4, so how about 6?

M Okay. I'll ________ ________ ________ now.

W Oh, wait a second. I was looking at next week's schedule. I can ________ ________ ________ on Friday.

M That's nice. What about 5 then?

W Let's make it 5:30. Can we meet at 5 and go there together?

M Sure.

14 | 관계 고르기

대화를 듣고, 두 사람의 관계로 가장 적절한 것을 고르시오.

① 역사학자 — 기자 ② 여행 가이드 — 여행객
③ 가수 — 팬 ④ 사진작가 — 모델
⑤ 요리사 — 종업원

M Welcome, everyone. ________ ________ ________ on today's tour is the Louvre Museum.

W Where will we go after the museum?

M ________ ________ ________ ________, so we will visit the Eiffel Tower next.

W Oh, great! I've always wanted to visit the Eiffel Tower.

M After that, we'll eat lunch. ________ ________ ________ ________ to the Seine River, actually.

W Excellent. I ________ ________ ________ ________ French food.

M It's going to be a great day exploring Paris.

15 | 부탁·요청한 일 고르기

대화를 듣고, 여자가 남자에게 부탁한 일로 가장 적절한 것을 고르시오.

① 카드 작성하기　② 편지 보내기
③ 봉투 구매하기　④ 우표 붙이기
⑤ 책상 정리하기

M Honey, what are these? _____ _____ _____.
W Thanks. I made these Christmas cards because I _____ _____ _____ _____ to my friends.
M Is there anything I can do to help you?
W I need to _____ _____ _____ in the cards. Oh, I know what you can do. Is there _____ _____ _____ _____?
M No. But I have some on my desk.
W Good. Will you put the stamps on the envelopes?
M No problem.

16 | 이유 고르기

대화를 듣고, 남자가 실망한 이유로 가장 적절한 것을 고르시오.

① 경기가 취소되어서
② 메달을 따지 못해서
③ 서핑보드가 부러져서
④ 동료가 부상을 당해서
⑤ 최선을 다하지 못해서

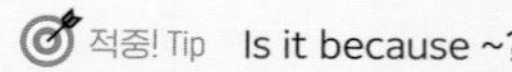
적중! Tip　Is it because ~?

어떤 일에 대한 이유를 물어볼 때 사용되는 표현으로 '~라서인가요, ~이기 때문이니?'의 의미이다. 이때 because 뒤에는 이유라고 생각하는 내용이 온다.

· Is it because you were tired yesterday?
어제 네가 피곤했기 때문이니?

W Today, we have Alex Brown, the surfer, in the studio. Welcome!
M Hello.
W We watched your competition last night. You _____ _____ _____ _____.
M Yes. I'm _____ _____ _____.
W Is it because you didn't win any medals?
M Not because I didn't win, but because I couldn't _____ _____ _____.
W What happened?
M I _____ _____ _____ right before the competition, so I couldn't perform well.

17 | 그림 상황에 적절한 대화 고르기

다음 그림의 상황에 가장 적절한 대화를 고르시오.

①　②　③　④　⑤

① **M** Did you go see a doctor?
　W Yes. I went to the hospital yesterday.
② **M** I'm going to _____ _____ _____.
　W That's a good idea. You look so tired.
③ **M** Did you _____ _____ _____?
　W It was boring. I fell asleep.
④ **M** What time does the shop open?
　W It opens at 8 a.m.
⑤ **M** _____ _____ _____!
　W Sorry. My alarm didn't go off this morning.

18 | 언급하지 않은 내용 고르기

다음을 듣고, 여자가 과학 박람회에 대해 언급하지 않은 것을 고르시오.

① 시행 주체 ② 행사 장소 ③ 참가 비용
④ 시작 시간 ⑤ 행사 기간

W Good morning, everyone. A science fair will be held by our own science club tomorrow. It __________ __________ __________ in the Nara auditorium. Activities like __________ __________ __________ will be held at each booth. It begins at 8:30 a.m. and ends at 5 p.m. The event will __________ __________ __________ __________, so, please come and enjoy the fun activities.

19 | 적절한 응답 고르기

대화를 듣고, 남자의 마지막 말에 이어질 여자의 말로 가장 적절한 것을 고르시오.

Woman: ______________________________

① It's brown.
② It's in my purse.
③ She ran to the store.
④ Look under the couch.
⑤ I have five dollars.

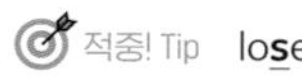 lose

[루즈]로 발음된다. '느슨한'이라는 의미의 형용사 loose가 [루스]로 발음되니 혼동하지 않도록 주의한다.

W Excuse me. __________ __________ __________ a wallet in the store?
M No, I'm sorry. Did you lose one?
W Yes. I think I left it here this morning. I probably __________ __________ __________ __________ __________ from the counter.
M I don't think it's here, but __________ __________ __________.
W Thank you. That would be great.
M What color is it?

20 | 적절한 응답 고르기

대화를 듣고, 남자의 마지막 말에 이어질 여자의 말로 가장 적절한 것을 고르시오.

Woman: ______________________________

① He didn't come to school.
② Sure. I'll try my best.
③ Smile for the camera!
④ It was a funny joke.
⑤ You'll do better next time.

W Hey, Chris. Are you ready for your school photo tomorrow?
M No. I don't like __________ __________.
W Oh, why?
M I get nervous in front of the camera. __________ __________ __________ __________.
W Maybe you need someone to make you laugh __________ __________ __________ __________ __________.
M That's a good idea. Then, I can smile easily.
W Exactly.
M Why don't you do that for me?

중학영어듣기 실전 모의고사

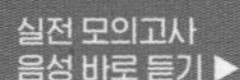

1 다음을 듣고, 대전의 날씨로 가장 적절한 것을 고르시오.

①  ②  ③  ④  ⑤ 

2 대화를 듣고, 여자가 만든 목걸이로 가장 적절한 것을 고르시오.

①  ②  ③ 
④  ⑤ 

3 대화를 듣고, 두 사람이 학생 토론회에 대해 언급하지 <u>않은</u> 것을 고르시오.

① 요일 ② 장소 ③ 시작 시간
④ 참가자 ⑤ 토론 주제

4 대화를 듣고, 여자가 학교 축제에서 한 일로 가장 적절한 것을 고르시오.

① 사진 촬영하기
② 인형 탈 쓰기
③ 포토월 운영하기
④ 가창 대회 참가하기
⑤ 간식 부스에서 일하기

5 대화를 듣고, 두 사람이 대화하는 장소로 가장 적절한 곳을 고르시오.

① 축구장 ② 병원
③ 꽃집 ④ 직업 박람회장
⑤ 운동용품점

6 대화를 듣고, 여자의 마지막 말의 의도로 가장 적절한 것을 고르시오.

① 부탁 ② 충고 ③ 사과 ④ 칭찬 ⑤ 비난

7 대화를 듣고, 남자가 가입하고자 하는 동아리를 고르시오.

① 수영 ② 뜨개질 ③ 테니스
④ 관현악단 ⑤ 미술

8 대화를 듣고, 남자가 대화 직후에 할 일로 가장 적절한 것을 고르시오.

① 잔돈 주기 ② 옷 정리하기
③ 눈 치우기 ④ 우산 가져오기
⑤ 우비 구매하기

9 대화를 듣고, 여자가 Little Italy Restaurant에 대해 언급하지 <u>않은</u> 것을 고르시오.

① 메뉴 ② 음식 가격
③ 영업시간 ④ 위치
⑤ 예약 가능 여부

10 다음을 듣고, 남자가 하는 말의 내용으로 가장 적절한 것을 고르시오.

① 책장 조립 과정 ② 체험학습 공지
③ 강당 이용 수칙 ④ 특별 강연 안내
⑤ 홈페이지 이용 방법

11 다음을 듣고, 남자의 가방에 대한 내용으로 일치하지 않는 것을 고르시오.

① 여동생에게 선물로 받았다.
② 재활용 소재로 만들어졌다.
③ 색상은 한 가지이다.
④ 노트북이 들어가는 크기이다.
⑤ 온라인에서 구매할 수 있다.

12 대화를 듣고, 남자가 서점을 방문한 목적으로 가장 적절한 것을 고르시오.

① 새로운 책을 사기 위해서
② 책을 환불 받기 위해서
③ 책을 대여하기 위해서
④ 중고 책을 팔기 위해서
⑤ 다른 책으로 교환하기 위해서

13 대화를 듣고, 여자가 지불해야 할 금액으로 가장 적절한 것을 고르시오.

① $ 10 ② $ 15 ③ $ 20
④ $ 25 ⑤ $ 30

14 대화를 듣고, 두 사람의 관계로 가장 적절한 것을 고르시오.

① 의사 — 환자
② 기자 — 배우
③ 수리 기사 — 고객
④ 경찰관 — 시민
⑤ 안경원 직원 — 손님

15 대화를 듣고, 남자가 여자에게 부탁한 일로 가장 적절한 것을 고르시오.

① 이삿짐 싸기
② 트럭 빌리기
③ 물건 기부하기
④ 이사할 집 청소하기
⑤ 이삿짐센터에 전화하기

16 대화를 듣고, 여자가 옷을 산 이유로 가장 적절한 것을 고르시오.

① 친구에게 선물하기 위해서
② 날씨가 더워져서
③ 할인율이 높아서
④ 휴가 때 입기 위해서
⑤ 졸업식을 준비하기 위해서

17 다음 그림의 상황에 가장 적절한 대화를 고르시오.

① ② ③ ④ ⑤

고난도
18 다음을 듣고, 남자가 인형에 대해 언급하지 않은 것을 고르시오.

① 이름 ② 유래 ③ 재료 ④ 용도 ⑤ 크기

[19-20] 대화를 듣고, 여자의 마지막 말에 이어질 남자의 말로 가장 적절한 것을 고르시오.

19 **Man:** ______________________

① Yes, they loved my blog.
② I'll send you the link.
③ The results have been posted.
④ I just finished that comic book.
⑤ No, he didn't leave a comment.

20 **Man:** ______________________

① No, I didn't know.
② I've got good news.
③ He missed practice.
④ I definitely will.
⑤ I saw it online.

15회 Dictation

Dictation
음성 바로 듣기 ▶

15회 중학영어듣기 실전 모의고사 Dictation 음성을 들으며 빈칸에 알맞은 단어를 채우시오.

1 | 날씨 고르기

다음을 듣고, 대전의 날씨로 가장 적절한 것을 고르시오.

① ② ③ ④ ⑤

M Good morning, everyone! Here's today's weather report. In Seoul, the air will be _________ _________ _________, so please _________ _________ _________. Suwon will be sunny, but there will be _________ _________ _________ in the afternoon. Sunny and warm weather will continue in Daejeon all day long. Daegu will be _________ _________, but the sky will be clear in the afternoon.

2 | 알맞은 그림 고르기

대화를 듣고, 여자가 만든 목걸이로 가장 적절한 것을 고르시오.

① ② ③ ④ ⑤

M Amy, _________ _________ _________ _________?

W It's mine, Dad. I made it at home today.

M You are so talented. It looks really special with _________ _________.

W Thank you. I thought two-chain necklaces are _________ _________.

M Right. Why did you add the letter *Q* pendant?

W It's _________ _________ _________ of my favorite rock band, Queen.

3 | 언급하지 않은 내용 고르기

대화를 듣고, 두 사람이 학생 토론회에 대해 언급하지 않은 것을 고르시오.

① 요일 ② 장소 ③ 시작 시간
④ 참가자 ⑤ 토론 주제

적중! Tip It says ~.
포스터나 팸플릿에 쓰여 있는 내용을 상대방에게 말해줄 때 쓰는 표현으로 '~라고 쓰여 있어'라는 의미이다.
· It says the museum opens at noon.
그 박물관이 정오에 연다고 쓰여 있어.

M What are you looking at, Dasom?

W I'm reading this poster about _________ _________ _________.

M That is next Friday, isn't it?

W Yes. We should go to the auditorium to watch it.

M Do you know how long it is?

W It says that it _________ _________ _________ _________.

M Who will be debating?

W Four teams will compete. The topics are about _________ _________.

M That sounds interesting.

4 | 한 일 고르기

대화를 듣고, 여자가 학교 축제에서 한 일로 가장 적절한 것을 고르시오.

① 사진 촬영하기
② 인형 탈 쓰기
③ 포토월 운영하기
④ 가창 대회 참가하기
⑤ 간식 부스에서 일하기

W Ollie, did you take these pictures?

M Yes. My teacher asked me _________ _________ _________ at our school festival.

W Are you going to upload them to our school website?

M Yeah. I'm going to choose some good photos first.

W Are there _________ _________ _________ _________?

M I'm not sure. What did you do at the festival?

W I worked at _________ _________ _________.

5 장소 고르기

대화를 듣고, 두 사람이 대화하는 장소로 가장 적절한 곳을 고르시오.

① 축구장 ② 병원
③ 꽃집 ④ 직업 박람회장
⑤ 운동용품점

W You wanted to talk to me, coach?
M Yes, Mary. I need you to play goalkeeper _________ _________ today.
W What about Rose?
M She's not here. She said she _________ _________ _________.
W Oh, that's too bad.
M Here are the goalkeeping gloves. You'll need those.
W Thanks.
M Okay, _________ _________ today!
W I'll _________ _________ _________.

6 의도 고르기

대화를 듣고, 여자의 마지막 말의 의도로 가장 적절한 것을 고르시오.

① 부탁 ② 충고 ③ 사과 ④ 칭찬 ⑤ 비난

W Hey, Jonathan. Why were you late for class today?
M I'm sorry, Ms. Stevens. I had to _________ _________ _________ _________.
W What happened?
M She was looking for the bank, but she _________ _________.
W Did you _________ _________ _________?
M Yes. But she was confused, so I walked to the bank with her.
W Wow. I think you are _________ _________ _________ I know.

7 특정 정보 고르기

대화를 듣고, 남자가 가입하고자 하는 동아리를 고르시오.

① 수영 ② 뜨개질 ③ 테니스
④ 관현악단 ⑤ 미술

적중! Tip orchestra
[오케스트라]로 익숙한 외래어이지만 실제로는 [올키스트라]로 발음된다.

M Olivia, which club are you going to join?
W I _________ _________ _________ _________, so I'll join the school orchestra.
M That's impressive. I want to join a sports club.
W _________ _________ _________ _________ do you like?
M I love swimming. I learned _________ _________ _________ last summer.
W Are you going to join the swimming club then?
M Yes. I want to learn more various swimming styles.

8 | 할 일 고르기

대화를 듣고, 남자가 대화 직후에 할 일로 가장 적절한 것을 고르시오.

① 잔돈 주기 ② 옷 정리하기
③ 눈 치우기 ④ 우산 가져오기
⑤ 우비 구매하기

적중! Tip had to

[해드 투]보다는 [해투]로 들린다. [d]와 [t]처럼 발음할 때 혀의 위치가 비슷한 자음이 나란히 나오면 앞 단어의 끝 자음이 탈락되기 때문이다.

M Honey, I thought you already left the house.
W Yes. But I had to come back.
M Why?
W It's very cold outside, so I needed to ________ ________ ________.
M Oh, right. I heard that it's going to snow in the afternoon.
W Really? I didn't know that.
M ________ ________ ________ an umbrella.
W I lost my umbrella last week. Can I borrow yours?
M Sure. I have ________ ________ in our room. I'll go and get one.

9 | 언급하지 않은 내용 고르기

대화를 듣고, 여자가 Little Italy Restaurant에 대해 언급하지 <u>않은</u> 것을 고르시오.

① 메뉴 ② 음식 가격
③ 영업시간 ④ 위치
⑤ 예약 가능 여부

[Telephone rings.]
W Little Italy Restaurant. How may I help you?
M Hi. I have a question about the menu. Do you ________ ________ ________ ________ dishes?
W Yes. We have several meat-free pastas.
M Great! When do you open?
W We open from 11 a.m. to 10 p.m.
M Could you ________ ________ ________ ________ ________?
W We're on Main Street next to the fountain.
M Okay, I got it. Can I ________ ________ ________ for two on Sunday at 5 p.m.?
W Yes, you can. We'll see you then.

10 | 주제 고르기

다음을 듣고, 남자가 하는 말의 내용으로 가장 적절한 것을 고르시오.

① 책장 조립 과정 ② 체험학습 공지
③ 강당 이용 수칙 ④ 특별 강연 안내
⑤ 홈페이지 이용 방법

M Good morning, students. There will be a special event at our school next week. ________ ________ Emily Miller will visit us and give a lecture. She will ________ ________ ________ about how she wrote her best-selling novel. After that, there will be a question-and-answer session. Please come and ________ ________ ________ ________.

11 | 일치하지 않는 내용 고르기

다음을 듣고, 남자의 가방에 대한 내용으로 일치하지 <u>않는</u> 것을 고르시오.

① 여동생에게 선물로 받았다.
② 재활용 소재로 만들어졌다.
③ 색상은 한 가지이다.
④ 노트북이 들어가는 크기이다.
⑤ 온라인에서 구매할 수 있다.

M Hello, everyone. Let me introduce my special bag. My younger sister bought this for me ________ ________ ________. It's ________ ________ ________ ________. It comes in three different colors, red, black, and blue. I like it because the bag is ________ ________ ________ ________ my laptop. You can buy it online.

12 | 목적 고르기

대화를 듣고, 남자가 서점을 방문한 목적으로 가장 적절한 것을 고르시오.

① 새로운 책을 사기 위해서
② 책을 환불 받기 위해서
③ 책을 대여하기 위해서
④ 중고 책을 팔기 위해서
⑤ 다른 책으로 교환하기 위해서

W Hi. How may I help you?
M Do you ________ ________ ________ here?
W Yes, we do. But it ________ ________ ________ ________ of the books.
M Well, I brought five books. Here they are.
W Let me check them. *[Pause]* This one has a ripped page. ________ ________ ________ ________.
M Okay. I'll sell those four.
W You will receive 15 dollars. Do you want it in ________ ________ ________ ________?
M I would like it in cash.

13 | 금액 정보 고르기

대화를 듣고, 여자가 지불해야 할 금액으로 가장 적절한 것을 고르시오.

① $ 10 ② $ 15 ③ $ 20
④ $ 25 ⑤ $ 30

적중! Tip The total will be ~.
물건을 구입하는 상황에서 총금액을 알려주는 표현으로 '총 ~입니다'라는 의미이다. be 뒤에는 금액이 나온다.
· The total will be 45 dollars.
총 45달러입니다.

M Hello. Are you ready to order?
W Yes. I'd like to ________ ________ ________ ________.
M That will be 11 dollars.
W Oh, can I have ________ ________ ________ too?
M Sure. One order of fried rice and one spicy chicken, right?
W Yes. That's right.
M ________ ________ ________ ________ 30 dollars.
W Hmm... Can I use this 10-dollar ________ ________?
M Of course. Then, the total will be 20 dollars.
W Okay. Here you go.

14 | 관계 고르기

대화를 듣고, 두 사람의 관계로 가장 적절한 것을 고르시오.

① 의사 — 환자
② 기자 — 배우
③ 수리 기사 — 고객
④ 경찰관 — 시민
⑤ 안경원 직원 — 손님

M Welcome to the phone service center. ________ ________ ________ your phone?
W It fell out of my pocket yesterday, and the screen broke.
M I see. It seems like the screen ________ ________ ________ ________.
W How much will a new screen cost?
M It will cost 125 dollars.
W Alright. ________ ________ ________ will it take?
M It will take about an hour.
W Okay. I'll come back in an hour.

15 | 부탁·요청한 일 고르기

대화를 듣고, 남자가 여자에게 부탁한 일로 가장 적절한 것을 고르시오.

① 이삿짐 싸기
② 트럭 빌리기
③ 물건 기부하기
④ 이사할 집 청소하기
⑤ 이삿짐센터에 전화하기

W Honey, let's check our to-do list for the move.
M Okay. We ________ ________ ________ and cleaned the apartment.
W But can we ________ ________ ________ ________ by ourselves?
M I don't think so. We have too much furniture.
W Yeah. ________ ________ ________ a moving service.
M Then, can you call ________ ________ ________?
W Sure. I'll do that.

16 | 이유 고르기

대화를 듣고, 여자가 옷을 산 이유로 가장 적절한 것을 고르시오.

① 친구에게 선물하기 위해서
② 날씨가 더워져서
③ 할인율이 높아서
④ 휴가 때 입기 위해서
⑤ 졸업식을 준비하기 위해서

적중! Tip have it in a
[해브 잇 인 어]보다는 [해빗 이너]로 들린다. 앞에 나온 단어의 끝 자음과 뒤에 나온 단어의 첫 모음이 연음되기 때문이다.

M Good afternoon. Do you need any help?
W I'm looking for ________ ________ ________ ________ on my vacation.
M Okay. Where are you going?
W I'm going to Vietnam. It'll be really hot.
M I ________ ________ ________ ________ here.
W Oh, yes. That is lovely. Do you have it in a medium size?
M Yes, we do. Would you like to ________ ________ ________?
W That would be great. Thanks.
M ________ ________ ________.

17 | 그림 상황에 적절한 대화 고르기

다음 그림의 상황에 가장 적절한 대화를 고르시오.

① ② ③ ④ ⑤

적중! Tip get up
[겟 업]보다는 [게럽]으로 들린다. [t]가 모음 사이에서 발음될 때는 약화되어 [r]에 가깝게 발음되기 때문이다.
· later [레이럴] · pretty [프리리]

① **M** Which scarf should I buy?
W The striped one ________ ________ ________ ________.
② **M** The sunlight is too strong.
W Why don't you ________ ________ ________ ________?
③ **M** Did you get up early to watch the sunrise?
W No. I was too tired.
④ **M** ________ ________ ________ if I turn the air conditioner off?
W Of course not. Go ahead.
⑤ **M** Do you need anything from the supermarket?
W Can you pick up some milk?

고난도

18 언급하지 않은 내용 고르기

다음을 듣고, 남자가 인형에 대해 언급하지 않은 것을 고르시오.

① 이름 ② 유래 ③ 재료 ④ 용도 ⑤ 크기

M Hello, students. Today, I'd like to tell you about worry dolls. These ________ ________ a Guatemalan legend. If you tell your troubles to one and hide it under your pillow, your ________ ________ ________ ________. They are made of ________ ________ ________ ________. They are usually given to children when they're ________ ________ ________. Worry dolls are still very popular today.

19 적절한 응답 고르기

대화를 듣고, 여자의 마지막 말에 이어질 남자의 말로 가장 적절한 것을 고르시오.

Man: ______________________

① Yes, they loved my blog.
② I'll send you the link.
③ The results have been posted.
④ I just finished that comic book.
⑤ No, he didn't leave a comment.

W What are you ________ ________, Minjun?
M I'm writing a new post for my blog.
W Cool! What is your blog about?
M It's about comic books. I like to ________ ________ of them.
W That sounds interesting. Do many people read your posts?
M Yes. ________ ________, 500 people visit every day.
W Great. I'd like to visit your blog too.

20 적절한 응답 고르기

대화를 듣고, 여자의 마지막 말에 이어질 남자의 말로 가장 적절한 것을 고르시오.

Man: ______________________

① No, I didn't know.
② I've got good news.
③ He missed practice.
④ I definitely will.
⑤ I saw it online.

W Is that a newspaper, James?
M Yeah. I'm reading it because there's ________ ________ ________.
W Oh, what is it?
M My favorite rugby team just got a new player.
W That's great. ________ ________ ________ about the player.
M His name is Nick Nelson. He's ________ ________ ________.
W You should try to get tickets to the team's next game.

중학영어듣기

실전 모의고사

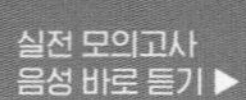

1 다음을 듣고, 토요일의 날씨로 가장 적절한 것을 고르시오.

①  ②  ③  ④  ⑤ 

2 대화를 듣고, 여자가 만든 꽃병으로 가장 적절한 것을 고르시오.

①  ②  ③ 
④  ⑤ 

3 대화를 듣고, 남자가 다녀온 전시회에 대해 언급하지 않은 것을 고르시오.

① 전시 장소 ② 작가 이름 ③ 전시 작품명
④ 전시 기간 ⑤ 입장료

4 대화를 듣고, 남자가 사려는 물건으로 가장 적절한 것을 고르시오.

① 키보드 ② 모니터 ③ 노트북
④ 그래픽 카드 ⑤ 스피커

5 대화를 듣고, 두 사람이 대화하는 장소로 가장 적절한 곳을 고르시오.

① 우체국 ② 은행
③ 버스 터미널 ④ 여행사
⑤ 식료품점

6 대화를 듣고, 여자의 마지막 말의 의도로 가장 적절한 것을 고르시오.

① 사과 ② 충고 ③ 실망 ④ 축하 ⑤ 동의

7 대화를 듣고, 여자가 방문한 적 없는 나라를 고르시오.

① 독일 ② 프랑스 ③ 스위스
④ 이탈리아 ⑤ 스페인

8 대화를 듣고, 남자가 대화 직후에 할 일로 가장 적절한 것을 고르시오.

① 수학 공부하기 ② 일정 확인하기
③ 약속 잡기 ④ 보고서 작성하기
⑤ 친구에게 전화하기

9 대화를 듣고, 남자가 Dino Museum에 대해 언급하지 않은 것을 고르시오.

① 입장료 ② 운영 기관
③ 운영 시간 ④ 운영 요일
⑤ 셔틀버스 운행

10 다음을 듣고, 여자가 하는 말의 내용으로 가장 적절한 것을 고르시오.

① 수업 신청 과정 ② 견학 일정 공지
③ 도서관 이용 방법 ④ 영화관 이용 안내
⑤ 도서관 휴관 공지

11 대화를 듣고, 남자가 판매할 제품에 대한 내용으로 일치하지 않는 것을 고르시오.

① 500달러이다.
② 하늘색이다.
③ 흠집이 약간 있다.
④ 카메라가 잘 작동한다.
⑤ 화면을 교체했다.

고난도
12 대화를 듣고, 남자가 인터넷을 검색하는 목적으로 가장 적절한 것을 고르시오.

① 호주행 비행기표를 예매하기 위해서
② 여름옷을 주문하기 위해서
③ 온라인 게임을 하기 위해서
④ 겨울맞이 옷을 구입하기 위해서
⑤ 백화점으로 가는 길을 찾기 위해서

13 대화를 듣고, 두 사람이 만날 시각을 고르시오.

① 5:00 p.m. ② 6:00 p.m. ③ 7:00 p.m.
④ 8:00 p.m. ⑤ 9:00 p.m.

14 대화를 듣고, 두 사람의 관계로 가장 적절한 것을 고르시오.

① 택배기사 — 고객 ② 학부모 — 교사
③ 제빵사 — 손님 ④ 지휘자 — 피아니스트
⑤ 옷가게 주인 — 손님

15 대화를 듣고, 남자가 여자에게 부탁한 일로 가장 적절한 것을 고르시오.

① 신문지 가져오기 ② 숙제 미리 하기
③ 분리수거 하기 ④ 설거지하기
⑤ 마실 것 가져오기

16 대화를 듣고, 남자가 체육관에 지금 갈 수 없는 이유로 가장 적절한 것을 고르시오.

① 운동화를 잃어버려서
② 빨래를 해야 해서
③ 운동복이 마르지 않아서
④ 정기 휴무일이어서
⑤ 세탁기가 고장 나서

고난도
17 다음 그림의 상황에 가장 적절한 대화를 고르시오.

① ② ③ ④ ⑤

고난도
18 다음을 듣고, 여자가 성에 대해 언급하지 않은 것을 고르시오.

① 이름 ② 위치 ③ 건축 연도
④ 건축가 ⑤ 용도

[19-20] 대화를 듣고, 남자의 마지막 말에 이어질 여자의 말로 가장 적절한 것을 고르시오.

19 **Woman:** ______________________

① Can I read your story?
② Wow, you're so talented!
③ Look at the painting.
④ I'm excited to see it.
⑤ Yes. I want that poster.

20 **Woman:** ______________________

① I just read about that.
② She regularly goes hiking.
③ Almost every week.
④ I'm going to the library.
⑤ I haven't heard of him.

16회 Dictation

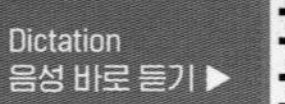

16회 중학영어듣기 실전 모의고사 Dictation 음성을 들으며 빈칸에 알맞은 단어를 채우시오.

1 | 날씨 고르기

다음을 듣고, 토요일의 날씨로 가장 적절한 것을 고르시오.

① ② ③ ④ ⑤

W Good evening. Here is Friday night's weekend weather report. _________ _________ _________ right now. But during the night, it's likely to stop. The temperature will drop in the morning, so _________ _________ _________ _________ when you go outside. Saturday will be cloudy, but there _________ _________ _________ _________. On Sunday, we'll _________ _________ _________ _________ of the year.

2 | 알맞은 그림 고르기

대화를 듣고, 여자가 만든 꽃병으로 가장 적절한 것을 고르시오.

① ② ③ ④ ⑤

W Daniel, look. I made this vase for our grandmother.
M It's beautiful. _________ _________ _________ _________?
W Yeah. I was going to leave it _________ _________ _________, but it looked too boring.
M It looks like snow is falling because of _________ _________ _________ _________.
W I was painting on _________ _________ _________.
M Well, I think grandma will love it.

3 | 언급하지 않은 내용 고르기

대화를 듣고, 남자가 다녀온 전시회에 대해 언급하지 않은 것을 고르시오.

① 전시 장소 ② 작가 이름 ③ 전시 작품명
④ 전시 기간 ⑤ 입장료

W George, did you hear about that _________ _________ _________?
M Do you mean the Salvador Dali exhibition? I've been to it already.
W Where is it held? I really want to see his work.
M _________ _________ _________ the Swan Convention Center.
W I don't want to miss it.
M You can see it until March. His paintings will be on display for four months.
W How much is _________ _________ _________?
M It's only 10 dollars.

4 | 특정 정보 고르기

대화를 듣고, 남자가 사려는 물건으로 가장 적절한 것을 고르시오.

① 키보드 ② 모니터 ③ 노트북
④ 그래픽 카드 ⑤ 스피커

> 적중! Tip **Not at all.**
> 상대방의 말에 대한 응답으로 '전혀 아니다'라고 할 때 쓰는 표현이다. 사과를 받아줄 때에도 쓰며, 빠르게 말할 때는 [나래롤]로 들린다.

M Are you busy now, Jenny?
W Not at all. Why?
M Can you _________ _________ _________? I need to get a new one.
W Do you need a big screen?
M Yeah. I have to _________ _________ _________ with it.
W Okay. Do you _________ _________ _________ _________?
M I rarely play games, so I don't need an expensive graphic card.
W How much can you _________ _________ _________?
M I don't want to spend more than 800 dollars.

5 | 장소 고르기

대화를 듣고, 두 사람이 대화하는 장소로 가장 적절한 곳을 고르시오.

① 우체국 ② 은행
③ 버스 터미널 ④ 여행사
⑤ 식료품점

W Hello. I'd like to ________ ________ ________.
M Okay. Where is it going?
W I'm sending it to Canada.
M How do you want to send it?
W ________ ________ ________, please. It needs to arrive by Friday.
M All right. What is in the package?
W It's just ________ ________ ________ and books.

6 | 의도 고르기

대화를 듣고, 여자의 마지막 말의 의도로 가장 적절한 것을 고르시오.

① 사과 ② 충고 ③ 실망 ④ 축하 ⑤ 동의

적중! Tip look up
[룩 업]보다는 [루껍]으로 들린다. 앞에 나온 단어의 끝 자음과 뒤에 나온 단어의 첫 모음이 연음되고, 이때 강세가 없는 [k]는 된소리로 발음되기 때문이다.

M Wow. Are these people ________ ________ ________ to eat at the restaurant?
W I think so. Do you still want to eat here?
M I really want to ________ ________ ________ ________. But with the line, I'm ________ ________ ________.
W Well, what do you want to do?
M Let's go to another restaurant. We can always ________ ________ ________.
W You are right. I'll look up another place.

7 | 특정 정보 고르기

대화를 듣고, 여자가 방문한 적 없는 나라를 고르시오.

① 독일 ② 프랑스 ③ 스위스
④ 이탈리아 ⑤ 스페인

M Miyoung, how was ________ ________ ________?
W Fantastic! I traveled Europe for a month.
M ________ ________ ________ ________ ________?
W I went to Germany first.
M That sounds awesome! Where else did you go?
W France and Switzerland. It was my first trip to Switzerland.
M ________ ________ ________ ________ France before?
W Yes. I toured France and Italy last year.
M What about Spain? Have you ever traveled there?
W No. But ________ ________ ________ ________ someday.

8 | 할 일 고르기

대화를 듣고, 남자가 대화 직후에 할 일로 가장 적절한 것을 고르시오.

① 수학 공부하기 ② 일정 확인하기
③ 약속 잡기 ④ 보고서 작성하기
⑤ 친구에게 전화하기

W Brian, what are you going to do this afternoon?
M I have to _________ _________ _________ _________ _________ tomorrow.
W It was yesterday, wasn't it?
M Right. I meant I have to _________ _________ _________ _________.
W You worked on it with me last weekend.
M Oh, no. I'm so confused!
W Why don't you _________ _________ _________ _________?
M Okay.

9 | 언급하지 않은 내용 고르기

대화를 듣고, 남자가 Dino Museum에 대해 언급하지 않은 것을 고르시오.

① 입장료 ② 운영 기관
③ 운영 시간 ④ 운영 요일
⑤ 셔틀버스 운행

W Excuse me. Could you help me?
M Yes. What can I do for you?
W I can't _________ _________ _________ _________.
M Our Dino Museum is _________ _________ _________. It's run by the city.
W That's great. _________ _________ _________ _________ today?
M It's open from 9 to 6 on the weekdays. It is closed on the weekends.
W Thanks! Is there any special tours you provide? I'd like to _________ _________ _________ _________.
M We have those only on Wednesdays.

10 | 주제 고르기

다음을 듣고, 여자가 하는 말의 내용으로 가장 적절한 것을 고르시오.

① 수업 신청 과정 ② 견학 일정 공지
③ 도서관 이용 방법 ④ 영화관 이용 안내
⑤ 도서관 휴관 공지

W Hello, everyone. Today, I'll talk about how to use a public library. First, make a library card. _________ _________ _________ _________ will let you use the services that the library provides. The library will lend you _________, _________, _________ _________. Also, you should _________ _________ _________ for special programs. There are many _________ _________ _________ _________.

11 | 일치하지 않는 내용 고르기

대화를 듣고, 남자가 판매할 제품에 대한 내용으로 일치하지 않는 것을 고르시오.

① 500달러이다.
② 하늘색이다.
③ 흠집이 약간 있다.
④ 카메라가 잘 작동한다.
⑤ 화면을 교체했다.

[Telephone rings.]
W Hi, I _________ _________ _________ on the website. Are you still selling your smartphone for 500 dollars?
M Oh, hello. You mean the Universe A12, right?
W Yes. _________ _________ _________ _________?
M It's sky blue. I used it with a case, so there are _________ _________.
W Does the camera work well?
M Yeah. My brother _________ _________ _________ last year, but I fixed it at the repair center.
W Can I pick it up tonight?
M Sure.

고난도

12 | 목적 고르기

대화를 듣고, 남자가 인터넷을 검색하는 목적으로 가장 적절한 것을 고르시오.

① 호주행 비행기표를 예매하기 위해서
② 여름옷을 주문하기 위해서
③ 온라인 게임을 하기 위해서
④ 겨울맞이 옷을 구입하기 위해서
⑤ 백화점으로 가는 길을 찾기 위해서

적중! Tip find them
[파인드 뎀]보다는 [파인뎀]으로 들린다. 비슷하게 발음되는 자음이 나란히 오면 앞 단어의 끝 자음이 탈락되기 때문이다.

W Jay, what are you doing on the Internet?
M I'm looking for __________ __________ __________ __________.
W Why do you need them? It's winter now!
M I'm __________ __________ __________ next week. It's summer there.
W Oh, that's why. Are you going to __________ __________ __________?
M Yes. I couldn't find them __________ __________ __________ __________.
W Right. They must only have winter clothes these days.

13 | 시간 정보 고르기

대화를 듣고, 두 사람이 만날 시각을 고르시오.

① 5:00 p.m. ② 6:00 p.m. ③ 7:00 p.m.
④ 8:00 p.m. ⑤ 9:00 p.m.

M Sarah, what time are we going to meet tomorrow?
W How about 6 p.m.? __________ __________ __________ at 7, so we should get ready __________ __________ __________.
M Ted said that we should __________ __________ __________ one more time before the concert.
W Then, how about 5? I think the rehearsal will take __________ __________ __________ __________.
M Okay. I'll tell the other band members.

14 | 관계 고르기

대화를 듣고, 두 사람의 관계로 가장 적절한 것을 고르시오.

① 택배기사 — 고객 ② 학부모 — 교사
③ 제빵사 — 손님 ④ 지휘자 — 피아니스트
⑤ 옷가게 주인 — 손님

적중! Tip Got it.
상대방의 말을 듣고 이해했음을 나타낼 때 사용되는 표현이다.

[Cellphone rings.]
W Hi. This is Wendy from ABC Bakery. I'm making __________ __________ __________ __________ yesterday.
M Oh, is there something wrong?
W No. I just wanted to check two things. Do you __________ __________ __________?
M Sure.
W Do you want the writing on the cake to be dark blue or light blue?
M Light blue, please.
W I see. And __________ __________ __________ __________?
M Those should be bright pink.
W Got it. Thanks.

15 부탁·요청한 일 고르기

대화를 듣고, 남자가 여자에게 부탁한 일로 가장 적절한 것을 고르시오.

① 신문지 가져오기 ② 숙제 미리 하기
③ 분리수거 하기 ④ 설거지하기
⑤ 마실 것 가져오기

적중! Tip Could you
[쿠드 유]보다는 [쿠쥬]로 들린다. [d]로 끝나는 단어 뒤에 y-로 시작하는 단어가 이어지면 두 소리가 연결되어 [쥬]로 발음되기 때문이다.

W Dad, did you finish reading the newspaper?
M Yes, Mandy. Do you need it?
W Yeah, Dad. I need to ________ ________ ________ and write an essay about it.
M I put it ________ ________ ________ ________ in the kitchen.
W Okay. I'll get it.
M Mandy, will you also ________ ________ ________ ________?
W What is it?
M Could you bring me ________ ________ ________ ________ from the kitchen?
W No problem.

16 이유 고르기

대화를 듣고, 남자가 체육관에 지금 갈 수 없는 이유로 가장 적절한 것을 고르시오.

① 운동화를 잃어버려서
② 빨래를 해야 해서
③ 운동복이 마르지 않아서
④ 정기 휴무일이어서
⑤ 세탁기가 고장 나서

W Danny, are you ready to go to the gym?
M Honey, ________ ________ ________ are missing.
W Didn't you leave them in the bathroom?
M No. They are not there.
W Oh, I think I washed them last night.
M I'll check ________ ________ ________. *[Pause]* I found them!
W Are they dry?
M No. ________ ________ ________ ________. I think I'll stay home today.
W Are you sure?
M Yeah. I'll clean the house ________ ________ ________.

고난도

17 그림 상황에 적절한 대화 고르기

다음 그림의 상황에 가장 적절한 대화를 고르시오.

① ② ③ ④ ⑤

① **M** I'm sorry, but can I have some ketchup?
W Of course. I'll get it for you.
② **M** How should I ________ ________ ________ ________ on the shirt?
W Try to wash it with vinegar.
③ **M** Do you have this coat ________ ________ ________ ________?
W Let me check.
④ **M** ________ ________ ________ on the sofa.
W Oh, I'm sorry.
⑤ **M** Can you open the window?
W Okay. We need ________ ________ ________.

고난도

18 | 언급하지 않은 내용 고르기

다음을 듣고, 여자가 성에 대해 언급하지 않은 것을 고르시오.

① 이름 ② 위치 ③ 건축 연도
④ 건축가 ⑤ 용도

적중! Tip Castle
[캐쓸]로 발음된다. 단어 중간에 st가 연달아 오면 [t]는 묵음이다.
· listen [리쓴] · fasten [패쓴]

W Hello, students. Today, we'll discuss Bran Castle, one of ________ ________ ________ ________ in the world. The castle is located ________ ________ ________ ________ Romania. It was originally built in 1212 as a fortress. However, it became ________ ________ ________ ________ after it was described as Count Dracula's Castle in the novel *Dracula*.

19 | 적절한 응답 고르기

대화를 듣고, 남자의 마지막 말에 이어질 여자의 말로 가장 적절한 것을 고르시오.

Woman: ________________________

① Can I read your story?
② Wow, you're so talented!
③ Look at the painting.
④ I'm excited to see it.
⑤ Yes. I want that poster.

M Cara, do you have an extra pen? Mine has ________ ________ ________ ________.
W Sure. Here you go. What are you writing about in your notebook?
M I'm actually drawing. I do it ________ ________ ________.
W Oh, I didn't know that. What do you like to draw?
M I mostly draw people.
W Can I ________ ________ ________?
M Sorry, it's not finished yet. But you can see it ________ ________ ________.

20 | 적절한 응답 고르기

대화를 듣고, 남자의 마지막 말에 이어질 여자의 말로 가장 적절한 것을 고르시오.

Woman: ________________________

① I just read about that.
② She regularly goes hiking.
③ Almost every week.
④ I'm going to the library.
⑤ I haven't heard of him.

M What are you reading, Sylvia?
W It's called *The Way Up*. It's a book about a famous mountain climber.
M That sounds interesting. Do you like it?
W Yeah. I ________ ________ ________ because I also like to climb.
M Really? Where do you like to climb?
W I usually go to the ________ ________ ________ ________, like Cheonggyesan.
M Wow, that's impressive. ________ ________ do you go?

17회 중학영어듣기 실전 모의고사

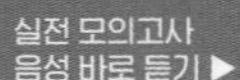

1 다음을 듣고, 예상되는 시드니의 날씨로 가장 적절한 것을 고르시오.

①  ②  ③  ④  ⑤ 

2 대화를 듣고, 여자가 구입할 지갑으로 가장 적절한 것을 고르시오.

①  ②  ③ 

④  ⑤ 

3 대화를 듣고, 남자의 심정으로 가장 적절한 것을 고르시오.

① satisfied ② sorry ③ nervous
④ bored ⑤ disappointed

고난도
4 대화를 듣고, 여자가 지난 주말에 한 일로 가장 적절한 것을 고르시오.

① 동생 데리러 가기
② 운전 연습하기
③ 박물관 방문하기
④ 운전 면허증 발급받기
⑤ 자동차 수리하기

5 대화를 듣고, 두 사람이 대화하는 장소로 가장 적절한 곳을 고르시오.

① 치과 ② 체육관 ③ 공원
④ 신발 가게 ⑤ 세탁소

6 대화를 듣고, 여자의 마지막 말의 의도로 가장 적절한 것을 고르시오.

① 충고 ② 감사 ③ 허락 ④ 제안 ⑤ 거절

고난도
7 대화를 듣고, 여자가 여행하고자 하는 도시를 고르시오.

① 강릉 ② 거제 ③ 부산 ④ 서울 ⑤ 경주

8 대화를 듣고, 남자가 대화 직후에 할 일로 가장 적절한 것을 고르시오.

① 영상 촬영하기 ② 요리책 구매하기
③ 식료품점 가기 ④ 재료 손질하기
⑤ 파스타 요리하기

9 대화를 듣고, 남자가 독도에 대해 언급하지 않은 것을 고르시오.

① 서식 동물 ② 거주 인구 ③ 날씨
④ 크기 ⑤ 교통수단

10 다음을 듣고, 여자가 하는 말의 내용으로 가장 적절한 것을 고르시오.

① 체험 활동 공지 ② 고양이와의 교감법
③ 시험 신청 안내 ④ 동물원 관람 규칙
⑤ 번역 앱 사용법

맞은 개수 : / 20개

11 대화를 듣고, 책에 대한 내용으로 일치하지 않는 것을 고르시오.

① 작가는 Tom Simpson이다.
② 제목이 <The Way Home>이다.
③ 장르는 로맨스다.
④ 도서관에서 빌릴 수 있다.
⑤ 지난주에 출간됐다.

12 대화를 듣고, 남자가 전화를 건 목적으로 가장 적절한 것을 고르시오.

① 요리법을 물어보기 위해서
② 집에 초대하기 위해서
③ 저녁 약속을 잡기 위해서
④ 슈퍼에 함께 가기 위해서
⑤ 숙제를 물어보기 위해서

고난도

13 대화를 듣고, 남자가 지불한 금액으로 가장 적절한 것을 고르시오.

① $ 25 ② $ 30 ③ $ 35
④ $ 45 ⑤ $ 50

14 대화를 듣고, 두 사람의 관계로 가장 적절한 것을 고르시오.

① 경찰관 — 시민 ② 음식 비평가 — 종업원
③ 기자 — 가수 ④ 택시 기사 — 승객
⑤ 배달원 — 손님

15 대화를 듣고, 남자가 여자에게 요청한 일로 가장 적절한 것을 고르시오.

① 원예 잡지 읽기 ② 화분 옮기기
③ 감자 수확하기 ④ 돌멩이 골라내기
⑤ 오렌지 나무 심기

16 대화를 듣고, 남자가 머리를 자르지 못한 이유로 가장 적절한 것을 고르시오.

① 미용실이 문을 닫아서
② 예약 시간에 늦어서
③ 손님이 많아서
④ 예약을 하지 않아서
⑤ 찾는 미용사가 없어서

17 다음 그림의 상황에 가장 적절한 대화를 고르시오.

① ② ③ ④ ⑤

18 대화를 듣고, 남자가 국제 교류 동아리에 관해 언급하지 않은 것을 고르시오.

① 활동 내용 ② 교류 국가 ③ 인원수
④ 가입 방법 ⑤ 지도 선생님

[19-20] 대화를 듣고, 여자의 마지막 말에 이어질 남자의 말로 가장 적절한 것을 고르시오.

19 **Man:** ______________________

① It will keep snowing tomorrow.
② Please turn on the heater.
③ I'll go to the hill.
④ I prefer to ski.
⑤ They're waiting outside.

20 **Man:** ______________________

① That's a good idea.
② I can't find a trash can.
③ Bring a swimsuit.
④ The event begins at 5 p.m.
⑤ Water pollution is a serious problem.

17회 Dictation

Dictation
음성 바로 듣기 ▶

17회 중학영어듣기 실전 모의고사 Dictation 음성을 들으며 빈칸에 알맞은 단어를 채우시오.

1 | 날씨 고르기

다음을 듣고, 예상되는 시드니의 날씨로 가장 적절한 것을 고르시오.

① ② ③ ④ ⑤

M Good morning. This is Jack Duncan with _________ _________ _________ _________. In Hong Kong, it'll be humid and cloudy. London will also be cloudy but chilly, so _________ _________ _________ for outdoor activities. _________ _________ _________ _________ in Sydney today. The forecast for Mexico City is sunny and hot, but it'll cool down _________ _________ _________ in the evening. Thank you.

2 | 알맞은 그림 고르기

대화를 듣고, 여자가 구입할 지갑으로 가장 적절한 것을 고르시오.

① ② ③ ④ ⑤

M Welcome. Can I help you with anything?
W Yes. I need _________ _________ _________.
M Okay. The best-selling purses are these star- and square-shaped ones.
W I like the one that _________ _________ _________ _________. It is cute.
M Great. It will be 9 dollars.
W Hmm... I don't like _________ _________ _________ _________.
M We also have one _________ _________ _________.
W I love it! I'll take it.

3 | 심정 고르기

대화를 듣고, 남자의 심정으로 가장 적절한 것을 고르시오.

① satisfied ② sorry ③ nervous
④ bored ⑤ disappointed

적중! Tip old diaries
[올드 다이어뤼즈]보다는 [올다이어뤼즈]로 들린다. 발음이 같은 자음이 나란히 나오면 앞 단어의 끝 자음이 탈락되기 때문이다.
· had dinner [해디너] · this store [디스토어]

M What do you have there, Jane?
W I _________ _________ _________ in a box.
M Oh, those are my old diaries.
W There are so many of them. Do you _________ _________ _________ _________ every day?
M Yes. I've kept a diary for 10 years.
W Do you have the diaries _________ _________?
M Yeah. It is fun to read them now.
W That's really cool.
M Thanks. I'm glad I _________ _________ _________.

고난도

4 | 한 일 고르기

대화를 듣고, 여자가 지난 주말에 한 일로 가장 적절한 것을 고르시오.

① 동생 데리러 가기
② 운전 연습하기
③ 박물관 방문하기
④ 운전 면허증 발급받기
⑤ 자동차 수리하기

M Penny, how was your weekend?
W It was really wonderful.
M What did you do?
W My mom and I went to the Belleville Car Museum.
M _________ _________ _________ to go there.
W It was great. We saw the first car ever made.
M Awesome. How long _________ _________ _________?
W We were there for about three hours.
M Lucky you. I hope my parents _________ _________ _________.

5 장소 고르기

대화를 듣고, 두 사람이 대화하는 장소로 가장 적절한 곳을 고르시오.

① 치과 ② 체육관 ③ 공원
④ 신발 가게 ⑤ 세탁소

M Hello. Can I help you find something?
W I'm looking for ________ ________ ________.
M Okay. What will you use them for?
W I need them for running. My coach said the ones I have now are ________ ________.
M The running shoes are ________ ________ ________.
W Oh, I really like these here.
M Those are also my favorite. Do you want to ________ ________ ________?
W Yes, please.

6 의도 고르기

대화를 듣고, 여자의 마지막 말의 의도로 가장 적절한 것을 고르시오.

① 충고 ② 감사 ③ 허락 ④ 제안 ⑤ 거절

M Excuse me. Could you tell me ________ ________ ________ ________ on the bookshelf?
W Oh, I did. Why do you ask?
M Wow. ________ ________ ________! I really like your work. Could I buy it?
W Sorry, but it's ________ ________ ________.
M Well... Then, may I ________ ________ ________ of it?
W No problem. I'm happy that someone else loves my work.

고난도

7 특정 정보 고르기

대화를 듣고, 여자가 여행하고자 하는 도시를 고르시오.

① 강릉 ② 거제 ③ 부산 ④ 서울 ⑤ 경주

 적중! Tip I'd love to ~.

어떤 일을 하고 싶음을 강조하여 나타낼 때 사용되는 표현으로, to 다음에는 동사원형이 온다.

· I'd love to go for a walk.
난 산책하러 가고 싶어.

W Jamie, do you have any plan for summer vacation?
M My parents and I will visit my sister.
W Where does she live?
M She lives in Seoul ________ ________ ________ ________. What's your plan?
W I want to go on a trip, but I haven't decided ________ ________ ________.
M How about Gangneung? You can see the ocean there.
W Well, I'd love to enjoy the sea, but ________ ________ ________.
M Oh, I see. Why don't you go to Geoje then?
W I think that would be nice. I'll find out how to get there.

8 | 할 일 고르기

대화를 듣고, 남자가 대화 직후에 할 일로 가장 적절한 것을 고르시오.

① 영상 촬영하기 ② 요리책 구매하기
③ 식료품점 가기 ④ 재료 손질하기
⑤ 파스타 요리하기

적중! Tip recipe
[레시피]로 익숙한 외래어이지만 실제로는 [뤠써피]로 발음된다.

W Chase, is this your recipe book?
M Yeah. I'm really _________ _________ _________ these days.
W _________ _________ _________ _________ so far?
M I've made an omelet, cream pasta, and cheese pizza.
W How did your omelet taste?
M It was salty. I _________ _________ _________ _________.
W Can you make one for me today?
M Sure. I should go to the grocery store to _________ _________ _________ now.

9 | 언급하지 않은 내용 고르기

대화를 듣고, 남자가 독도에 대해 언급하지 않은 것을 고르시오.

① 서식 동물 ② 거주 인구 ③ 날씨
④ 크기 ⑤ 교통수단

M Mom, we learned about Dokdo at school today.
W What did you _________ _________ _________ _________?
M There are a lot of _________ _________ _________ near the island.
W Do people live there?
M Yes. I heard 14 people are living there.
W How's the weather?
M It's usually warm in _________ _________ _________ _________.
W I hope we can visit it someday.
M Me too. We can get there by a ship from Ulleungdo.

10 | 주제 고르기

다음을 듣고, 여자가 하는 말의 내용으로 가장 적절한 것을 고르시오.

① 체험 활동 공지 ② 고양이와의 교감법
③ 시험 신청 안내 ④ 동물원 관람 규칙
⑤ 번역 앱 사용법

W Good afternoon, everyone. Today, I'm going to tell you how to _________ _________ _________ your cat. First, you should pay attention to its body language _________ _________ _________ _________ well. Next, you must respect what your cat likes and dislikes. You should also talk to your cat calmly. Lastly, _________ _________ _________ _________ so that you can bond with it.

11 | 일치하지 않는 내용 고르기

대화를 듣고, 책에 대한 내용으로 일치하지 않는 것을 고르시오.

① 작가는 Tom Simpson이다.
② 제목이 <The Way Home>이다.
③ 장르는 로맨스다.
④ 도서관에서 빌릴 수 있다.
⑤ 지난주에 출간됐다.

M Hello. I'd like to _________ _________ _________ _________ by Tom Simpson.
W Okay. What is the title?
M It's *The Way Home.*
W *[Typing sound]* Well, I see it's a romance novel.
M Yes. Can I borrow it from the library?
W I'm afraid _________ _________ _________ _________ now.
M Oh, no! Wasn't it released last week?
W You're right. But it's _________ _________ _________.

12 목적 고르기

대화를 듣고, 남자가 전화를 건 목적으로 가장 적절한 것을 고르시오.

① 요리법을 물어보기 위해서
② 집에 초대하기 위해서
③ 저녁 약속을 잡기 위해서
④ 슈퍼에 함께 가기 위해서
⑤ 숙제를 물어보기 위해서

[Cellphone rings.]
M Hi, Minji. This is Fred.
W Hello, Fred. ________ ________ ________?
M I want to cook kimchijeon, but I don't know ________ ________ ________ it.
W Do you have ________ ________?
M I have kimchi and flour. How much kimchi do I need?
W I'll come to your house now, and I ________ ________ ________ how to cook it.
M Will you do that?
W Of course.

고난도

13 금액 정보 고르기

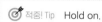

대화를 듣고, 남자가 지불한 금액으로 가장 적절한 것을 고르시오.

① $ 25 ② $ 30 ③ $ 35
④ $ 45 ⑤ $ 50

적중! Tip Hold on.
상대방에게 '잠시만요, 잠깐만요'라고 할 때 사용되는 표현이다. 전화 통화 상황에서도 쓸 수 있다.

W Hello, how can I help you?
M Hi, I'd like to buy ________ ________ ________ ________.
W There are 10 pears in a box, and it costs 30 dollars.
M Can I also get five apples?
W Sure. They are two dollars each. You want a box of pears and five apples, right?
M Yes. ________ ________.
W ________ ________ ________ ________ 40 dollars.
M Oh, hold on. Can I use this five-dollar discount coupon?
W Yes. Then, it's 35 dollars in total.
M Here's 50 dollars.

14 관계 고르기

대화를 듣고, 두 사람의 관계로 가장 적절한 것을 고르시오.

① 경찰관 — 시민 ② 음식 비평가 — 종업원
③ 기자 — 가수 ④ 택시 기사 — 승객
⑤ 배달원 — 손님

[Telephone rings.]
W Hello?
M Hi. I'm ________ ________ ________, but I can't find your house.
W Oh, yes! Where are you?
M I'm ________ ________ ________ of Main Street and Baker Avenue right now. Is your building blue?
W No. It's red. It's right across from the blue building.
M Oh, okay. I see it now. I'll ________ ________ ________.
W Thank you!

15 | 부탁·요청한 일 고르기

대화를 듣고, 남자가 여자에게 요청한 일로 가장 적절한 것을 고르시오.

① 원예 잡지 읽기 ② 화분 옮기기
③ 감자 수확하기 ④ 돌멩이 골라내기
⑤ 오렌지 나무 심기

적중! Tip That's a good idea.
상대방의 제안에 대해 동의할 때 사용되는 표현이다.

W Dan, you are talented _________ _________. Our garden looks amazing.
M Thanks, Mom. Do you remember _________ _________ _________ in the pot?
W Yes. It grew so big.
M It was just a small tree five years ago.
W Yeah. We need to move it _________ _________ _________ _________.
M That's a good idea.
W Do you have a bigger pot?
M Yes. But can you _________ _________ _________ _________?
W No problem.

16 | 이유 고르기

대화를 듣고, 남자가 머리를 자르지 못한 이유로 가장 적절한 것을 고르시오.

① 미용실이 문을 닫아서
② 예약 시간에 늦어서
③ 손님이 많아서
④ 예약을 하지 않아서
⑤ 찾는 미용사가 없어서

M Hey, Marie. How did your weekend go?
W It was good, thanks. Did you _________ _________ _________?
M No, I couldn't.
W Did you have _________ _________ _________ _________ on the weekend?
M No. I went to the hair salon on Sunday, but they said I can't _________ _________ _________ _________.
W What happened?
M I didn't _________ _________ _________ before I went.
W Why don't you call the hair salon today?
M I will. I really need to get my hair cut.

17 | 그림 상황에 적절한 대화 고르기

다음 그림의 상황에 가장 적절한 대화를 고르시오.

① ② ③ ④ ⑤

① **M** Can you _________ _________ _________ of the shelf?
W No. It is too high.
② **M** Please don't run on the stairs.
W Okay. I'll be careful.
③ **M** Is this your sweater?
W No. _________ _________ _________ _________.
④ **M** Do you need any help?
W Yes. Please _________ _________ _________ _________.
⑤ **M** There is a lot of famous artwork in this museum.
W Yes. It's _________ _________.

18 | 언급하지 않은 내용 고르기

대화를 듣고, 남자가 국제 교류 동아리에 관해 언급하지 않은 것을 고르시오.

① 활동 내용 ② 교류 국가 ③ 인원수
④ 가입 방법 ⑤ 지도 선생님

W Jinsoo, what do you do in your ________ ________ ________?
M When ________ ________ ________ our school, I introduce Korean culture to them.
W Where are they from?
M They are usually from the United States.
W Sounds interesting! ________ ________ ________ do you have?
M There are 20 people including me.
W How can I join your club?
M Just ________ ________ ________ to the club president.
W Okay. What's the email address?
M I'll send it by text message.

19 | 적절한 응답 고르기

대화를 듣고, 여자의 마지막 말에 이어질 남자의 말로 가장 적절한 것을 고르시오.

Man: ________________________

① It will keep snowing tomorrow.
② Please turn on the heater.
③ I'll go to the hill.
④ I prefer to ski.
⑤ They're waiting outside.

M Julia, did you see the snow outside?
W No, I didn't. How much did it snow?
M ________ ________ ________. I'm going to ________ ________ ________ later.
W That will be fun. But the weather is very cold.
M It's okay. I'll wear a warm coat and a scarf.
W Good idea. Where will you ________ ________ ________?

20 | 적절한 응답 고르기

대화를 듣고, 여자의 마지막 말에 이어질 남자의 말로 가장 적절한 것을 고르시오.

Man: ________________________

① That's a good idea.
② I can't find a trash can.
③ Bring a swimsuit.
④ The event begins at 5 p.m.
⑤ Water pollution is a serious problem.

적중! Tip last night
[래스트 나잇]보다는 [래스나잇]으로 들린다. 자음 3개가 연속해서 나오면 중간 자음은 발음되지 않기 때문이다.

M Hey, Sophie. What did you do last night?
W I ________ ________ ________ about the trash in the ocean.
M Oh, what did you learn?
W It harms the fish and animals so much, and the problem ________ ________ ________.
M That's terrible. What can we do to clean up the ocean?
W We could pick up trash at the beach. ________ ________ ________ ________?

18회 중학영어듣기 실전 모의고사

실전 모의고사 음성 바로 듣기 ▶

고난도

1 다음을 듣고, 화요일의 날씨로 가장 적절한 것을 고르시오.

①  ②   ③   ④   ⑤  

2 대화를 듣고, 남자가 구입할 탁상 시계로 가장 적절한 것을 고르시오.

①  ②  ③   

④  ⑤ 

3 대화를 듣고, 남자의 심정으로 가장 적절한 것을 고르시오.

① pleased ② bored ③ worried
④ excited ⑤ disappointed

4 대화를 듣고, 여자가 한글날에 한 일로 가장 적절한 것을 고르시오.

① 태극기 게양하기 ② 붓글씨 쓰기
③ 짧은 시 짓기 ④ 한글 창제 배경 알기
⑤ 맞춤법 대회 나가기

5 대화를 듣고, 두 사람이 대화하는 장소로 가장 적절한 곳을 고르시오.

① 옷가게 ② 과학실 ③ 테니스장
④ 카페 ⑤ 볼링장

6 대화를 듣고, 여자의 마지막 말의 의도로 가장 적절한 것을 고르시오.

① 격려 ② 거절 ③ 동의 ④ 부탁 ⑤ 제안

7 대화를 듣고, 남자가 점심에 먹은 음식으로 가장 적절한 것을 고르시오.

① 라면 ② 짬뽕 ③ 비빔밥
④ 볶음밥 ⑤ 카레

8 대화를 듣고, 남자가 대화 직후에 할 일로 가장 적절한 것을 고르시오.

① 소화제 사러 가기 ② 배 찜질하기
③ 동네 산책하기 ④ 매실차 마시기
⑤ 손바닥 마사지하기

9 대화를 듣고, 여자가 투표 시 주의사항으로 언급하지 않은 것을 고르시오.

① 학년별 투표 시간을 따르기
② 학생증 지참하기
③ 투표 전 줄 서서 기다리기
④ 투표 중 사진 찍지 않기
⑤ 투표용지 접기

10 다음을 듣고, 남자가 하는 말의 내용으로 가장 적절한 것을 고르시오.

① 주말의 공연 소식 ② 잘못된 습관의 예
③ 아침 식사의 장점 ④ 돈을 절약하는 방법
⑤ 규칙적인 운동의 중요성

고난도

11 다음을 듣고, 운동회에 대한 내용과 일치하지 않는 것을 고르시오.

① 오후 3시에 행사가 종료된다.
② 단체 줄넘기는 오전에 진행된다.
③ 이어달리기는 오후에 치러진다.
④ 편한 운동화를 신고 와야 한다.
⑤ 점심 식사로 학교 급식이 제공된다.

12 대화를 듣고, 여자가 전화를 건 목적으로 가장 적절한 것을 고르시오.

① 환불을 요청하기 위해서
② 숙소를 예약하기 위해서
③ 배송일을 변경하기 위해서
④ 식사를 주문하기 위해서
⑤ 약속 시간을 확인하기 위해서

13 대화를 듣고, 두 사람이 만날 시각을 고르시오.

① 8:00 a.m. ② 8:30 a.m. ③ 9:00 a.m.
④ 9:30 a.m. ⑤ 10:00 a.m.

14 대화를 듣고, 두 사람의 관계로 가장 적절한 것을 고르시오.

① 안전 요원 — 이용객 ② 영화감독 — 배우
③ 사진작가 — 고객 ④ 리조트 직원 — 손님
⑤ 예술가 — 박물관 직원

15 대화를 듣고, 남자가 여자에게 부탁한 일로 가장 적절한 것을 고르시오.

① 방 청소하기 ② 친구에게 전화하기
③ 영화표 예매하기 ④ 개 산책시키기
⑤ 함께 영화 보기

16 대화를 듣고, 여자가 배구부 주장으로 뽑힌 이유로 가장 적절한 것을 고르시오.

① 카리스마가 있어서 ② 팀을 위해 헌신해서
③ 책임감이 강해서 ④ 배구 실력이 뛰어나서
⑤ 모든 부원과 친해서

17 다음 그림의 상황에 가장 적절한 대화를 고르시오.

① ② ③ ④ ⑤

18 대화를 듣고, 두 사람이 벼룩시장에 대해 언급하지 않은 것을 고르시오.

① 명칭 ② 날짜 ③ 장소
④ 판매 물품 ⑤ 주차 공간

[19-20] 대화를 듣고, 남자의 마지막 말에 이어질 여자의 말로 가장 적절한 것을 고르시오.

19 **Woman:** ______________________

① I'll pay with cash.
② It ended early.
③ Four of them will come tonight.
④ I'm making pasta.
⑤ They're coming at 6 p.m.

20 **Woman:** ______________________

① It takes two hours.
② Let's go to the bakery.
③ I'm using the oven.
④ I would love to.
⑤ The cake is finished.

18회 Dictation

Dictation
음성 바로 듣기 ▶

18회 중학영어듣기 실전 모의고사 Dictation 음성을 들으며 빈칸에 알맞은 단어를 채우시오.

고난도

1 날씨 고르기

다음을 듣고, 화요일의 날씨로 가장 적절한 것을 고르시오.

① ② ③ ④ ⑤

W Good evening. Let's ________ ________ ________ for next week. On Monday, it'll be cloudy all day long. ________ ________ ________ from Tuesday. After it stops on Thursday, we will have clear, sunny skies. But it'll ________ ________ ________ ________. On the weekend, there will be strong winds, so ________ ________ ________.

2 알맞은 그림 고르기

대화를 듣고, 남자가 구입할 탁상 시계로 가장 적절한 것을 고르시오.

① ② ③ ④ ⑤

W Welcome to Luxury Clocks. May I help you?
M I'm looking for ________ ________ ________ ________.
W Okay. How about this one? This square type is very popular.
M But ________ ________ ________. I want something more special.
W Then, ________ ________ ________ from these with legs?
M Oh, I like ________ ________ ________. I'll take it.
W Great.

3 심정 고르기

대화를 듣고, 남자의 심정으로 가장 적절한 것을 고르시오.

① pleased ② bored ③ worried
④ excited ⑤ disappointed

> 적중! Tip Medium
> [미디엄]보다는 [미리엄]으로 들린다. [d]가 모음 사이에서 발음될 때는 약화되어 [r]에 가깝게 발음되기 때문이다.

M Excuse me.
W Yes, sir. May I ________ ________ ________?
M Yes. I'd like to have ________ ________ ________ ________.
W How would you like your steak?
M Medium. Also, can I have lemon cake for dessert?
W I'm sorry, sir. We ________ ________ ________ lemon cake today.
M Oh, no! I was ________ ________ ________ having it.

4 한 일 고르기

대화를 듣고, 여자가 한글날에 한 일로 가장 적절한 것을 고르시오.

① 태극기 게양하기 ② 붓글씨 쓰기
③ 짧은 시 짓기 ④ 한글 창제 배경 알기
⑤ 맞춤법 대회 나가기

W Hi, Minho. ________ ________ ________ ________ Hangul Day?
M I went to the Sejong Festival.
W I've never heard of it. What did you do there?
M I learned how Hangul was created. It was fun. ________ ________ ________, Cathy?
W I wrote ________ ________ ________ in Korean. Do you want to read it?
M I'd love to. *[Pause]* It's really good. Your Korean ________ ________ ________ ________.
W Thank you for the compliment.

5 | 장소 고르기

대화를 듣고, 두 사람이 대화하는 장소로 가장 적절한 곳을 고르시오.

① 옷가게 ② 과학실 ③ 테니스장
④ 카페 ⑤ 볼링장

적중! Tip pick up
[픽 업]보다는 [피컵]으로 들린다. 앞에 나온 단어의 끝 자음과 뒤에 나온 단어의 첫 모음이 연음되고, 이때 강세가 없는 [k]는 된소리로 발음되기 때문이다.

W Wow, you played so well today.
M Thanks. It was ________ ________ ________.
W Can you help me pick up these tennis balls?
M Sure. Let me ________ ________ ________ ________ first.
W Of course. Oh, do you want to get smoothies? I'll pay since ________ ________ ________ ________.
M Thanks! That would be great.
W We should play again next week.
M Good idea. I'll ________ ________ ________ again.

6 | 의도 고르기

대화를 듣고, 여자의 마지막 말의 의도로 가장 적절한 것을 고르시오.

① 격려 ② 거절 ③ 동의 ④ 부탁 ⑤ 제안

M Good morning, Mom.
W Good morning. ________ ________ ________ ________, Jack.
M Yeah. I wanted to drink some milk.
W Oh, can you get me some too?
M Sure. *[Cracking sound]* Oh, I ________ ________ ________. Sorry.
W It's okay. I'll clean up ________ ________ ________.
M Let me help you!
W I don't think it's a good idea. ________ ________ ________.

7 | 특정 정보 고르기

대화를 듣고, 남자가 점심에 먹은 음식으로 가장 적절한 것을 고르시오.

① 라면 ② 짬뽕 ③ 비빔밥
④ 볶음밥 ⑤ 카레

W Sunho, are you okay? You look sleepy.
M I think ________ ________ ________ ________ fried rice at lunch.
W Was it good?
M Yes, it was. I cooked it ________ ________.
W You should tell me ________ ________ ________!
M Chop vegetables and ham. Then, stir fry them with a cup of oil.
W Isn't that too much oil?
M No. It is ________ ________ ________.

8 | 할 일 고르기

대화를 듣고, 남자가 대화 직후에 할 일로 가장 적절한 것을 고르시오.

① 소화제 사러 가기 ② 배 찜질하기
③ 동네 산책하기 ④ 매실차 마시기
⑤ 손바닥 마사지하기

적중! Tip **drawer**

[드로월]보다는 [쥬로월]로 들린다. dr-로 시작하는 단어에서 [d]는 [쥬]에 가깝게 발음되기 때문이다.

· dry [쥬라이] · dress [쥬레스]

W Honey, _________ _________ _________ _________ _________ in that drawer?
M I'm looking for medicine.
W _________ _________ _________ _________?
M I have an upset stomach. I think I ate dinner too quickly.
W Oh, we don't have _________ _________ _________ _________.
M Then, what should I do?
W Why don't you _________ _________ _________ for a while? It will help.
M You're right. I'll walk around the neighborhood.

9 | 언급하지 않은 내용 고르기

대화를 듣고, 여자가 투표 시 주의사항으로 언급하지 않은 것을 고르시오.

① 학년별 투표 시간을 따르기
② 학생증 지참하기
③ 투표 전 줄 서서 기다리기
④ 투표 중 사진 찍지 않기
⑤ 투표용지 접기

M Ms. Evans, when can we go vote for our school president?
W The voting time is _________ _________ _________ _________. Freshmen vote before noon, and the other students _________ _________ _________.
M Alright. Then, I should vote after lunch.
W Oh, remember to _________ _________ _________ _________.
M What else do I have to do?
W Please _________ _________ _________ before voting.
M Okay, I will.
W Also, don't forget to _________ _________ _________ _________.

10 | 주제 고르기

다음을 듣고, 남자가 하는 말의 내용으로 가장 적절한 것을 고르시오.

① 주말의 공연 소식 ② 잘못된 습관의 예
③ 아침 식사의 장점 ④ 돈을 절약하는 방법
⑤ 규칙적인 운동의 중요성

M We're back from the commercial break. Today, we heard useful tips from our guest, Mr. Smith. Let's sum up _________ _________ _________. First, save the _________ _________ _________ _________ regularly. Then, keep a record of your spending. Don't forget to _________ _________ _________ _________ each day. If you follow these tips, _________ _________ _________ _________.

고난도

11 | 일치하지 않는 내용 고르기

다음을 듣고, 운동회에 대한 내용과 일치하지 않는 것을 고르시오.

① 오후 3시에 행사가 종료된다.
② 단체 줄넘기는 오전에 진행된다.
③ 이어달리기는 오후에 치러진다.
④ 편한 운동화를 신고 와야 한다.
⑤ 점심 식사로 학교 급식이 제공된다.

W Okay, class. Tomorrow is our sports day. It'll be from 9 a.m. to 3 p.m. We'll have several fun games. _________ _________ _________ _________ _________ will be played in the morning. After lunch, we'll have soccer games and relay race. Please wear _________ _________ _________ _________ _________. Also, make sure to _________ _________ _________.

12 | 목적 고르기

대화를 듣고, 여자가 전화를 건 목적으로 가장 적절한 것을 고르시오.

① 환불을 요청하기 위해서
② 숙소를 예약하기 위해서
③ 배송일을 변경하기 위해서
④ 식사를 주문하기 위해서
⑤ 약속 시간을 확인하기 위해서

[Telephone rings.]

M Hello. This is Grand Ocean Hotel. What can I do for you?
W Hi. I'd like to ________ ________ ________ for March 27th.
M Sure. How long will you stay?
W Two nights.
M Alright. ________ ________ ________ ________ do you want?
W I want a double room with an ocean view. I'll ________ ________ ________ ________.
M Good. It'll be 300 dollars ________ ________.
W Thank you.

13 | 시간 정보 고르기

대화를 듣고, 두 사람이 만날 시각을 고르시오.

① 8:00 a.m. ② 8:30 a.m. ③ 9:00 a.m.
④ 9:30 a.m. ⑤ 10:00 a.m.

W Alex, did you hear that Tom's Toy Store will sell limited-edition Santa Claus dolls tomorrow?
M No. Maybe I should ________ ________ ________ ________ for Christmas.
W I ________ ________ ________ ________ too. Let's go to the store tomorrow.
M Okay. When does the store open?
W It opens at 9:30.
M Then, let's meet there ________ ________ ________ ________.
W There will be lots of people since ________ ________ ________ ________. Can we meet earlier?
M Sure. How about 8:30?
W Great. See you then.

14 | 관계 고르기

대화를 듣고, 두 사람의 관계로 가장 적절한 것을 고르시오.

① 안전 요원 — 이용객 ② 영화감독 — 배우
③ 사진작가 — 고객 ④ 리조트 직원 — 손님
⑤ 예술가 — 박물관 직원

better

[베털]보다는 [베럴]로 들린다. [t]가 모음 사이에서 발음될 때는 약화되어 [r]에 가깝게 발음되기 때문이다.

W Welcome to Peace Photo Studio.
M Hello. I'm ________ ________ ________ a family portrait.
W I can help you with that.
M Would it be possible to take the pictures ________ ________ ________?
W I charge 100 dollars for photos in the studio or 200 dollars ________ ________ ________.
M It would be better to have the photo shoot in your studio.
W Do you want to schedule ________ ________ ________ ________?
M Yes. How about 10 a.m.?
W Perfect.

15 | 부탁·요청한 일 고르기

대화를 듣고, 남자가 여자에게 부탁한 일로 가장 적절한 것을 고르시오.

① 방 청소하기 ② 친구에게 전화하기
③ 영화표 예매하기 ④ 개 산책시키기
⑤ 함께 영화 보기

W Jaemin, I ________ ________ ________ from your friend Woohyun.
M Oh, what did he say, Mom?
W He wants to ________ ________ ________ ________ with you tonight.
M I'd love to. Is it okay?
W Sure. Then, will you ________ ________ ________ after you come back home?
M Well... I ________ ________ ________. Can you walk the dog for me?
W Alright.

16 | 이유 고르기

대화를 듣고, 여자가 배구부 주장으로 뽑힌 이유로 가장 적절한 것을 고르시오.

① 카리스마가 있어서 ② 팀을 위해 헌신해서
③ 책임감이 강해서 ④ 배구 실력이 뛰어나서
⑤ 모든 부원과 친해서

적중! Tip I can't believe it.
어떤 상황이 너무 놀라워서 믿기지 않을 때 사용되는 표현이다.

M Tina, I have ________ ________ ________ ________.
W What's that, Mr. Parker?
M You ________ ________ ________ ________ of our volleyball club this year.
W Really? I can't believe it.
M You were chosen as the captain by every club member.
W Do you know ________ ________ ________ ________?
M They said you have a strong sense of responsibility.
W ________ ________ ________ ________ to lead our team well.

17 | 그림 상황에 적절한 대화 고르기

다음 그림의 상황에 가장 적절한 대화를 고르시오.

① ② ③ ④ ⑤

① **W** Thanks for ________ ________ ________.
M No problem.
② **W** This dress is too dirty.
M Why don't you wash it?
③ **W** What tools do we need to buy?
M We need ________ ________ ________ ________.
④ **W** Where should we ________ ________ ________?
M Let's put it in the bedroom.
⑤ **W** Do you want some chocolate?
M No, thank you. I'm good.

18 | 언급하지 않은 내용 고르기

대화를 듣고, 두 사람이 벼룩시장에 대해 언급하지 않은 것을 고르시오.

① 명칭 ② 날짜 ③ 장소
④ 판매 물품 ⑤ 주차 공간

적중! Tip Have you heard about ~?
어떤 소식이나 정보에 대해 들어봤는지 물을 때 사용되는 표현으로 '~에 대해 들어본 적 있어?'라는 의미이다.
· Have you heard about his new film?
그의 새 영화에 대해 들어본 적 있어?

W Jeremy, have you heard about the Austin Flea Market?
M Yes, I have. It opens tomorrow, right?
W Yes, it does.
M Where is it ________ ________ ________ ________?
W It will be held on Pine Street.
M That's ________ ________ ________ ________! I can walk there.
W Oh, I didn't know that.
M Do you know what they sell at the flea market?
W There's going to be a lot of used clothes, shoes, and toys.
M I'd love to ________ ________.

19 | 적절한 응답 고르기

대화를 듣고, 남자의 마지막 말에 이어질 여자의 말로 가장 적절한 것을 고르시오.

Woman: ______________________

① I'll pay with cash.
② It ended early.
③ Four of them will come tonight.
④ I'm making pasta.
⑤ They're coming at 6 p.m.

W Do you like these flowers, Honey?
M Yes. Those are pretty.
W They'll look nice ________ ________ ________ ________ the dinner table.
M I agree. Let's buy them. Our guests will love them.
W Okay. What else do we need ________ ________ ________ ________ tonight?
M We need to ________ ________ ________ ________.
W Alright, we can go to the store now.
M What time are ________ ________ ________ ________?

20 | 적절한 응답 고르기

대화를 듣고, 남자의 마지막 말에 이어질 여자의 말로 가장 적절한 것을 고르시오.

Woman: ______________________

① It takes two hours.
② Let's go to the bakery.
③ I'm using the oven.
④ I would love to.
⑤ The cake is finished.

W What are you doing, Sam?
M ________ ________ ________.
W They look tasty. What kind of cookies are you making?
M I'm baking coconut cookies. They're ________ ________ ________.
W I like them the most too. When will they be finished?
M I need to bake them for 20 minutes. Do you ________ ________ ________ ________ when they are done?

19회 중학영어듣기 실전 모의고사

실전 모의고사 음성 바로 듣기 ▶

고난도

1 다음을 듣고, 김해의 날씨로 가장 적절한 것을 고르시오.

①  ②  ③  ④  ⑤ 

고난도

2 대화를 듣고, 스티커 배치로 가장 적절한 것을 고르시오.

①  ②  ③ 

④  ⑤ 

3 대화를 듣고, 여자의 심정으로 가장 적절한 것을 고르시오.

① nervous ② proud ③ annoyed
④ disappointed ⑤ thankful

4 대화를 듣고, 여자가 핼러윈에 한 일로 가장 적절한 것을 고르시오.

① 유령 분장하기 ② 퍼레이드 참여하기
③ 호박파이 굽기 ④ 사탕 받으러 가기
⑤ 장식물 만들기

5 대화를 듣고, 두 사람이 대화하는 장소로 가장 적절한 곳을 고르시오.

① 꽃집 ② 시장 ③ 식당
④ 학교 강당 ⑤ 컨벤션 센터

고난도

6 대화를 듣고, 남자의 마지막 말의 의도로 가장 적절한 것을 고르시오.

① 축하 ② 경고 ③ 약속 ④ 거절 ⑤ 위로

7 대화를 듣고, 여자가 주민센터에서 등록할 프로그램을 고르시오.

① yoga ② jazz dance ③ table tennis
④ ballet ⑤ boxing

8 대화를 듣고, 남자가 대화 직후에 할 일로 가장 적절한 것을 고르시오.

① 일몰 구경하기 ② 호숫가 산책하기
③ 낚시하러 가기 ④ 텐트 설치하기
⑤ 생선 꺼내오기

9 다음을 듣고, 여자가 분실물 센터에 대해 언급하지 <u>않은</u> 것을 고르시오.

① 위치 ② 운영 시간 ③ 전화번호
④ 보관물 현황 ⑤ 운영 방침

10 다음을 듣고, 남자가 하는 말의 내용으로 가장 적절한 것을 고르시오.

① 화재 예방 수칙 ② 인터넷 이용 수칙
③ 올바른 수면 습관 ④ 에너지 절약의 중요성
⑤ 좋은 책을 고르는 방법

맞은 개수 : / 20개

11 다음을 듣고, Paradise Aquarium에 대한 내용으로 일치하지 않는 것을 고르시오.

① 개관 이래로 200만 명이 이곳을 찾았다.
② 약 650여 종의 수중 생물들이 살고 있다.
③ 20개의 구역으로 구분되어 있다.
④ 보통 관람하는 데 2시간 정도 걸린다.
⑤ 바다표범은 현재 보호 중이라 볼 수 없다.

12 대화를 듣고, 여자가 조깅을 시작한 목적으로 가장 적절한 것을 고르시오.

① 건강 증진을 위해서
② 살을 빼기 위해서
③ 인내심을 키우기 위해서
④ 운동 습관을 만들기 위해서
⑤ 마라톤 대회에 나가기 위해서

13 대화를 듣고, 여자가 지불해야 할 금액으로 가장 적절한 것을 고르시오.

① $ 11　② $ 12　③ $ 13
④ $ 14　⑤ $ 15

14 대화를 듣고, 두 사람의 관계로 가장 적절한 것을 고르시오.

① 신발 가게 점원 — 손님
② 감독 — 운동 선수
③ 공원 경비원 — 방문객
④ 안과 의사 — 환자
⑤ 운동 강사 — 수강생

고난도

15 대화를 듣고, 남자가 여자에게 요청한 일로 가장 적절한 것을 고르시오.

① 옷 정리하기　② 신발 세탁하기
③ 설거지하기　④ 샤워하기
⑤ 운동화 구매하기

16 대화를 듣고, 여자가 모자를 던진 이유로 가장 적절한 것을 고르시오.

① 졸업 사진을 찍으려고
② 기부 행사에 참여하려고
③ 모자를 건네주려고
④ 안무 동작을 따라 하려고
⑤ 선수를 축하해주려고

17 다음 그림의 상황에 가장 적절한 대화를 고르시오.

①　②　③　④　⑤

18 대화를 듣고, 두 사람이 현장 학습에 관해 언급하지 않은 것을 고르시오.

① 일시　② 장소　③ 체험 활동
④ 준비물　⑤ 귀가 시간

[19-20] 대화를 듣고, 남자의 마지막 말에 이어질 여자의 응답으로 가장 적절한 것을 고르시오.

19 **Woman:** ______________________

① We practice on Fridays.
② Would you like more water?
③ I'd like apple juice, please.
④ I'll be there in 10 minutes.
⑤ Dinner will be ready soon.

20 **Woman:** ______________________

① I've had so much fun.
② We're sold out.
③ Go straight for two blocks.
④ I'll get them online.
⑤ It runs through the city.

19회 Dictation

Dictation
음성 바로 듣기 ▶

19회 중학영어듣기 실전 모의고사 Dictation 음성을 들으며 빈칸에 알맞은 단어를 채우시오.

고난도

1 | 날씨 고르기

다음을 듣고, 김해의 날씨로 가장 적절한 것을 고르시오.

① ② ③ ④ ⑤

M Good evening. This is the weather report for tomorrow. There is _________ _________ _________ _________ _________ in Seoul. There will be a few showers in Andong, but they will stop in the afternoon. In Gimhae, strong wind is expected. Severe thunderstorms _________ _________ _________ are forecasted in Damyang, so please stay inside for _________ _________ _________. Thank you very much.

고난도

2 | 알맞은 그림 고르기

대화를 듣고, 스티커 배치로 가장 적절한 것을 고르시오.

① ② ③ ④ ⑤

M Honey, I want to _________ _________ _________ with wall stickers.
W I like that idea. Let's _________ _________ _________ _________ _________ first.
M Okay. The deer sticker is the biggest.
W How about putting it _________ _________ _________?
M Good. What should we do about this tree sticker?
W I don't think it looks good there. What else do we have?
M We also have a moon sticker.
W Then, put it _________ _________ _________ on the right side.

3 | 심정 고르기

대화를 듣고, 여자의 심정으로 가장 적절한 것을 고르시오.

① nervous ② proud ③ annoyed
④ disappointed ⑤ thankful

적중! Tip I have butterflies in my stomach.
너무 긴장해서 속이 울렁거리고 가슴이 뛴다고 할 때 사용되는 표현이다.

M It is your turn to bungee jump next. Are you ready?
W Oh, no. Please _________ _________ _________ _________.
M Are you okay?
W Well, I have butterflies in my stomach.
M Do you want to _________ _________ _________ _________?
W No. I expected this.
M Then, calm down and _________ _________ _________ _________.
W Okay, I will.
M Good. Just relax. It will be fun.
W I know. But I can still feel my heart beating.

4 | 한 일 고르기

대화를 듣고, 여자가 핼러윈에 한 일로 가장 적절한 것을 고르시오.

① 유령 분장하기 ② 퍼레이드 참여하기
③ 호박파이 굽기 ④ 사탕 받으러 가기
⑤ 장식물 만들기

W Tom, did you have fun at Halloween?
M Yes. I _________ _________ _________ in a ghost costume.
W I also wanted to join, but I couldn't.
M Then, what did you do on Halloween?
W I made jack-o'-lanterns.
M Do you mean _________ _________ _________ with a scary face?
W Yeah. It's one of _________ _________ _________ _________ of Halloween.
M Nice! I'll make jack-o'-lanterns next year too.

5 | 장소 고르기

대화를 듣고, 두 사람이 대화하는 장소로 가장 적절한 곳을 고르시오.

① 꽃집 ② 시장 ③ 식당
④ 학교 강당 ⑤ 컨벤션 센터

적중! Tip white
[와일]으로 발음된다. 단어의 맨 처음에 쓰인 wh-에서 [w]나 [h] 중 하나는 묵음이다.
· whole [호울] · why [와이]

W Hi. How can I help you?
M I need some flowers for ________ ________ ________ ________.
W I see. How about some white roses?
M Those are beautiful. But I'd like ________ ________ ________ ________.
W Then, maybe you'd like an arrangement with roses, tulips, and carnations.
M ________ ________ ________ ________.
W Do you want to ________ ________ ________?
M Yes. Write a note that says, "Congratulations, Tina!"

고난도

6 | 의도 고르기

대화를 듣고, 남자의 마지막 말의 의도로 가장 적절한 것을 고르시오.

① 축하 ② 경고 ③ 약속 ④ 거절 ⑤ 위로

M Why are you so late, Jackie? ________ ________ ________ ________ already.
W I'm sorry, Dad. Soccer practice lasted until 6.
M Really? Why?
W Our coach ________ ________ ________ extra kicking and running drills.
M Is he worried about the big game on Saturday?
W Yeah. He wants us ________ ________ ________. But I'm so tired!
M I understand. But your effort will be worth it.

7 | 특정 정보 고르기

대화를 듣고, 여자가 주민센터에서 등록할 프로그램을 고르시오.

① yoga ② jazz dance ③ table tennis
④ ballet ⑤ boxing

M Hello, what can I do for you?
W I heard the community center has many interesting programs.
M Do you ________ ________ ________ for a class?
W Yes. I need to exercise ________ ________ ________.
M We have many kinds of sports classes. ________ ________ ________ ________ yoga, table tennis, and boxing.
W I'd love to learn how to play table tennis. Can I sign up now?
M Sure. Please ________ ________ ________ ________.
W Alright.

8 | 할 일 고르기

대화를 듣고, 남자가 대화 직후에 할 일로 가장 적절한 것을 고르시오.

① 일몰 구경하기 ② 호숫가 산책하기
③ 낚시하러 가기 ④ 텐트 설치하기
⑤ 생선 꺼내오기

M Honey, _________ _________ _________ _________ on the lake.
W Wow, it's so wonderful. I'm glad we came here.
M By the way, what are we going to do now?
W _________ _________ _________ _________?
M A little bit. How about making dinner with the fish _________ _________ _________?
W Sounds great. And let's go for a walk _________ _________ _________ after dinner.
M Alright. Then, I'll take the fish out of the cooler.

9 | 언급하지 않은 내용 고르기

다음을 듣고, 여자가 분실물 센터에 대해 언급하지 않은 것을 고르시오.

① 위치 ② 운영 시간 ③ 전화번호
④ 보관물 현황 ⑤ 운영 방침

적중! Tip items
[아이템즈]보다는 [아이럼즈]로 들린다. [t]가 모음 사이에서 발음될 때는 약화되어 [r]에 가깝게 발음되기 때문이다.

W Hello, visitors. Our park has a Lost and Found Center. It is located _________ _________ _________ _________. So please come to check if you _________ _________ _________. The center is open from 10 a.m. to 5 p.m. You can also _________ _________ _________ at 555-6012. We usually keep items for a week and then send them to the police. Thank you.

10 | 주제 고르기

다음을 듣고, 남자가 하는 말의 내용으로 가장 적절한 것을 고르시오.

① 화재 예방 수칙 ② 인터넷 이용 수칙
③ 올바른 수면 습관 ④ 에너지 절약의 중요성
⑤ 좋은 책을 고르는 방법

M Good morning. Did you all sleep well? If you didn't, _________ _________ _________. I'll tell you a few things you should avoid _________ _________ _________ _________. First, don't go online right before bed. Using the Internet _________ _________ _________ _________. Second, avoid drinking water or coffee at night. Lastly, _________ _________ _________ _________ for more than 30 minutes.

11 | 일치하지 않는 내용 고르기

다음을 듣고, Paradise Aquarium에 대한 내용으로 일치하지 않는 것을 고르시오.

① 개관 이래로 200만 명이 이곳을 찾았다.
② 약 650여 종의 수중 생물들이 살고 있다.
③ 20개의 구역으로 구분되어 있다.
④ 보통 관람하는 데 2시간 정도 걸린다.
⑤ 바다표범은 현재 보호 중이라 볼 수 없다.

M Welcome to the Paradise Aquarium. _________ _________ _________ in 2011, more than two million people have visited us. Around 650 kinds of sea creatures are living here in 20 different zones. Generally, it takes two hours _________ _________ _________ _________ at them. Our most popular animals are the seals. They are _________ _________ _________ you will want to watch them for a long time. Thank you. _________ _________ _________ _________ our aquarium.

12 | 목적 고르기

대화를 듣고, 여자가 조깅을 시작한 목적으로 가장 적절한 것을 고르시오.

① 건강 증진을 위해서
② 살을 빼기 위해서
③ 인내심을 키우기 위해서
④ 운동 습관을 만들기 위해서
⑤ 마라톤 대회에 나가기 위해서

적중! Tip It's my first time to ~.
어떤 일이 처음 하는 경험임을 나타낼 때 사용되는 표현으로 '~하는 것은 처음이다'라는 의미이다. 이때 to 다음에는 동사원형이 온다.
· It's my first time to see a panda.
판다를 보는 것은 처음이야.

M Hey, Patricia. What a pleasant surprise! ________ ________ ________ ________?
W Yes. Last week. And it's my first time to jog around here.
M Why did you begin running?
W Lately, I didn't have a lot of energy. So I decided to jog ________ ________ ________ ________.
M Really? You must find it hard.
W Yeah. But ________ ________ ________. I feel more energized.
M That's good.

13 | 금액 정보 고르기

대화를 듣고, 여자가 지불해야 할 금액으로 가장 적절한 것을 고르시오.

① $ 11 ② $ 12 ③ $ 13
④ $ 14 ⑤ $ 15

W Hello, I'm looking for spoons.
M ________ ________ ________ ________ ________?
W I need two large ones.
M I see. You can choose from plastic or wooden spoons.
W What's ________ ________ ________?
M Six dollars each for the plastic ones, and seven dollars each for the wooden ones.
W Then, I'll ________ ________ ________ ________.
M Alright. I'll help you with the payment for a plastic and a wooden spoon.

14 | 관계 고르기

대화를 듣고, 두 사람의 관계로 가장 적절한 것을 고르시오.

① 신발 가게 점원 — 손님
② 감독 — 운동 선수
③ 공원 경비원 — 방문객
④ 안과 의사 — 환자
⑤ 운동 강사 — 수강생

W How can I help you today?
M I'm looking for ________ ________ ________ ________ ________.
W I see. What will you use them for?
M I will use them for ________ ________ ________ ________. I exercise a lot.
W Okay. These shoes are very popular because ________ ________ ________.
M Perfect. Do you have a size 250?
W Yes, we do.

고난도

15 부탁·요청한 일 고르기

대화를 듣고, 남자가 여자에게 요청한 일로 가장 적절한 것을 고르시오.

① 옷 정리하기 ② 신발 세탁하기
③ 설거지하기 ④ 샤워하기
⑤ 운동화 구매하기

W Oh, David. You're all wet.

M Yes, Mom. My shoes are really dirty too.

W _________ _________?

M It suddenly rained _________ _________ _________ _________ _________ at the playground.

W I can see that. _________ _________ _________ in the washing machine, and take a shower.

M Okay. And could you wash my shoes?

W No problem. But you should wear other shoes tomorrow.

16 이유 고르기

대화를 듣고, 여자가 모자를 던진 이유로 가장 적절한 것을 고르시오.

① 졸업 사진을 찍으려고
② 기부 행사에 참여하려고
③ 모자를 건네주려고
④ 안무 동작을 따라 하려고
⑤ 선수를 축하해주려고

적중! Tip just now

[저스트 나우]보다는 [저스나우]로 들린다. 자음 3개가 연속해서 나오면 중간 자음은 발음되지 않기 때문이다.

M Hey, Christine. What did you do just now?

W I _________ _________ _________ onto the ice.

M But why did you throw it?

W Oh, it's just to congratulate the player.

M Sorry, but _________ _________ _________ _________.

W In ice hockey, when a player _________ _________ _________ in a game, we throw our hats.

M Oh, now I see.

17 그림 상황에 적절한 대화 고르기

다음 그림의 상황에 가장 적절한 대화를 고르시오.

① ② ③ ④ ⑤

① M How much did your bike cost?
W It was a Christmas gift from my parents.

② M _________ _________. You can't drive over 30 kilometers per hour here.
W Sorry. I forgot.

③ M Ma'am, you _________ _________ _________.
W Oh, I didn't see the sign. I'll move my car.

④ M Where should I put this box?
W You can leave it on the bench.

⑤ M Excuse me, Officer. I'd like to report a stolen item.
W I'm sorry. _________ _________ _________, please.

18 | 언급하지 않은 내용 고르기

대화를 듣고, 두 사람이 현장 학습에 관해 언급하지 않은 것을 고르시오.

① 일시 ② 장소 ③ 체험 활동
④ 준비물 ⑤ 귀가 시간

적중! Tip field trip
[필드 트립]보다는 [필트립]로 들린다. [d]와 [t]처럼 발음할 때 혀의 위치가 비슷한 자음이 나란히 나오면 앞 단어의 끝 자음이 탈락되기 때문이다.

W Dad, I ________ ________ ________ the field trip.
M When is it, Soyoung?
W This Friday.
M Oh, I remember. You'll visit the Space Center, right?
W Yeah. ________ ________ will be exciting.
M Then, you will arrive home late.
W No. I'll get back home around 5 p.m.
M How is that possible?
W Surprisingly, the center has ________ ________ ________ the sun and stars during the day.
M That's interesting.

19 | 적절한 응답 고르기

대화를 듣고, 남자의 마지막 말에 이어질 여자의 응답으로 가장 적절한 것을 고르시오.

Woman: ____________________

① We practice on Fridays.
② Would you like more water?
③ I'd like apple juice, please.
④ I'll be there in 10 minutes.
⑤ Dinner will be ready soon.

[Cellphone rings.]
M Hi, Honey.
W Hey, Josh. Can you pick me up from the subway station? I'm ________ ________ ________ ________ home from here.
M Sure, but I'll be ________ ________ ________. I'm at the shop right now.
W That's okay. What are you going to buy?
M I'm going to buy ________ ________ ________ ________.
W Oh, can you ________ ________ ________ ________?
M Sure. What do you want?

20 | 적절한 응답 고르기

대화를 듣고, 남자의 마지막 말에 이어질 여자의 응답으로 가장 적절한 것을 고르시오.

Woman: ____________________

① I've had so much fun.
② We're sold out.
③ Go straight for two blocks.
④ I'll get them online.
⑤ It runs through the city.

M What should we do today, Sally?
W How about ________ ________ ________ ________ ________?
M That sounds fun. Where does the boat go?
W It goes down the Sandy River. We can see ________ ________ ________ ________ ________.
M I've never been on a boat before. I want to try it.
W You'll love it.
M Okay. How can we ________ ________ ________?

중학영어듣기 실전 모의고사

실전 모의고사 음성 바로 듣기 ▶

1 다음을 듣고, 제주의 오늘 날씨로 가장 적절한 것을 고르시오.

①  ②  ③  ④  ⑤ 

2 대화를 듣고, 남자가 꺼내준 상자로 가장 적절한 것을 고르시오.

①  ②  ③ 

④  ⑤ 

3 대화를 듣고, 여자의 심정으로 가장 적절한 것을 고르시오.

① sad ② shy ③ pleased
④ angry ⑤ satisfied

4 대화를 듣고, 여자가 지난 겨울 방학에 한 일로 가장 적절한 것을 고르시오.

① 어학연수 ② 국토 대장정
③ 세계 여행 ④ 문학 공부
⑤ 봉사 활동

5 대화를 듣고, 두 사람이 대화하는 장소로 가장 적절한 곳을 고르시오.

① 우체국 ② 박물관
③ 식당 ④ 아이스크림 가게
⑤ 식료품점

6 대화를 듣고, 남자의 마지막 말의 의도로 가장 적절한 것을 고르시오.

① 감사 ② 제안 ③ 조언 ④ 위로 ⑤ 거절

7 대화를 듣고, 남자가 스키 캠프에 대해 언급하지 않은 것을 고르시오.

① 장소 ② 일시 ③ 참여 대상
④ 비용 ⑤ 장비 대여

8 대화를 듣고, 두 사람이 대화 직후에 할 일로 가장 적절한 것을 고르시오.

① 편지 쓰기 ② 차 마시기
③ 시장 가기 ④ 이사 준비하기
⑤ 과일 구입하기

고난도

9 다음을 듣고, 남자가 Community Garage Sale에 대해 언급하지 않은 것을 고르시오.

① 행사 목적 ② 행사 종료 시각
③ 참여 방법 ④ 판매 물건 종류
⑤ 행사 홍보 방식

10 다음을 듣고, 여자가 하는 말의 내용으로 가장 적절한 것을 고르시오.

① 독서의 중요성 ② 포기하지 않는 태도
③ 소화를 돕는 운동 ④ 올바른 학습 방법
⑤ 다양한 의사소통 수단

고난도

11 다음을 듣고, City Eco Center에 대한 내용으로 일치하지 않는 것을 고르시오.

① 친환경적 시설들을 갖추고 있다.
② 목재와 플라스틱 폐기물을 재활용한 미끄럼틀이 있다.
③ 전력을 생산하는 자전거를 타 볼 수 있다.
④ 재활용에 대해 배우는 교육 프로그램이 있다.
⑤ 시립 공원 옆에 위치해 있다.

12 대화를 듣고, 여자가 전화를 건 목적으로 가장 적절한 것을 고르시오.

① 예약 정보를 확인하기 위해서
② 이용 변경 사항을 알려주기 위해서
③ 택배를 전달하기 위해서
④ 분실물을 찾아주기 위해서
⑤ 휴무일을 알려주기 위해서

13 대화를 듣고, 결혼식이 열리는 날짜를 고르시오.

① 6월 15일 ② 6월 16일 ③ 6월 17일
④ 6월 18일 ⑤ 6월 19일

14 대화를 듣고, 두 사람의 관계로 가장 적절한 것을 고르시오.

① TV쇼 진행자 — 연예인
② 영화관 직원 — 손님
③ 서점 직원 — 손님
④ 작가 — 독자
⑤ 과학 교사 — 학생

15 대화를 듣고, 남자가 여자에게 부탁한 일로 가장 적절한 것을 고르시오.

① 사인 대신 받아오기 ② 콘서트 표 예매하기
③ 야구 배트 빌려주기 ④ 함께 사인회장 가기
⑤ 경기 날짜 알려주기

16 대화를 듣고, 남자가 학교에 지각한 이유로 가장 적절한 것을 고르시오.

① 자전거를 도둑맞아서 ② 도로가 공사 중이어서
③ 배탈이 나서 ④ 버스가 오지 않아서
⑤ 시계가 고장 나서

17 다음 그림의 상황에 가장 적절한 대화를 고르시오.

① ② ③ ④ ⑤

18 다음을 듣고, 여자가 미래에 하고 싶은 일로 언급되지 않은 것을 고르시오.

① 운동선수들이 입은 부상을 확인한다.
② 운동선수들이 회복하도록 돕는다.
③ 운동선수들의 훈련 과정을 점검한다.
④ 운동선수들의 건강 관리를 지도한다.
⑤ 운동선수들과 심리 상담을 진행한다.

[19-20] 대화를 듣고, 여자의 마지막 말에 이어질 남자의 응답으로 가장 적절한 것을 고르시오.

19 **Man:** ______________________

① My father is very kind.
② He's from California.
③ The story is so unique.
④ I want to become famous.
⑤ Enjoy the movie in a theater.

20 **Man:** ______________________

① We should see the gardens.
② Yes. We have to buy tickets.
③ We'll have sandwiches.
④ Here is the entrance.
⑤ This is my first time in Paris.

20회 Dictation

Dictation
음성 바로 듣기 ▶

20회 중학영어듣기 실전 모의고사 Dictation 음성을 들으며 빈칸에 알맞은 단어를 채우시오.

1 날씨 고르기

다음을 듣고, 제주의 오늘 날씨로 가장 적절한 것을 고르시오.

① ② ③ ④ ⑤

M Good morning. Here is the weather report for Korea. _________ _________ _________ is expected today in most cities. Seoul will have the most rain. But in Daegu, the _________ _________ _________ with clear sunny skies will continue. In Jeju, there is _________ _________ _________ for strong winds, so please take care. Thank you.

2 알맞은 그림 고르기

대화를 듣고, 남자가 꺼내준 상자로 가장 적절한 것을 고르시오.

① ② ③

④ ⑤

W Dad, can I _________ _________ _________ _________?
M Sure. Go ahead.
W Please grab that box _________ _________ _________ _________. I can't reach it.
M No problem. Which one do you mean?
W The heart-shaped one with _________ _________ _________ _________.
M Okay, I see. _________ _________ _________ _________ with a heart on it. Here it is.
W Thanks a lot.
M Don't mention it.

> 적중! Tip Don't mention it.
> 감사하다는 말에 답할 때 사용되는 표현으로 '천만에' 또는 '별말씀을요'라는 의미이다.

3 심정 고르기

대화를 듣고, 여자의 심정으로 가장 적절한 것을 고르시오.

① sad ② shy ③ pleased
④ angry ⑤ satisfied

M Emily, are you okay? _________ _________ _________ _________.
W My dog, Max, died yesterday.
M I'm so _________ _________ _________ _________.
W I was prepared _________ _________ _________ because he was very old. But it's not easy to let him go.
M I understand.
W I miss him already.
M I _________ _________ _________ _________ it must be for you.
W My heart is broken.

4 한 일 고르기

대화를 듣고, 여자가 지난 겨울 방학에 한 일로 가장 적절한 것을 고르시오.

① 어학연수 ② 국토 대장정
③ 세계 여행 ④ 문학 공부
⑤ 봉사 활동

M Hana, how did you _________ _________ _________ _________?
W I went to Russia as an exchange student.
M Wow, what did you learn there?
W I _________ _________ _________ by Russian writers like Tolstoy.
M Oh, do you want to be a writer?
W Yes. I want _________ _________ _________ _________.
M I'm sure your dream will come true.

5 | 장소 고르기

대화를 듣고, 두 사람이 대화하는 장소로 가장 적절한 곳을 고르시오.

① 우체국 ② 박물관
③ 식당 ④ 아이스크림 가게
⑤ 식료품점

적중! Tip tomato soup
[토마토 수프]로 익숙한 외래어지만 실제로는 [터메이러 수웁]에 가깝게 발음된다.

M Welcome. Are you _________ _________ _________?
W Yes. I'll take the chicken salad and tomato soup, please.
M I'm sorry, but we just _________ _________ _________ tomato soup. What about potato soup instead?
W No, thank you. I'll just _________ _________ _________.
M Okay. Is there anything else you need?
W Can I _________ _________ _________, please?
M Of course. I'll bring that for you right away.

6 | 의도 고르기

대화를 듣고, 남자의 마지막 말의 의도로 가장 적절한 것을 고르시오.

① 감사 ② 제안 ③ 조언 ④ 위로 ⑤ 거절

W Hello, Mr. Randall. I'm here to _________ _________ _________ _________, Ben.
M Okay. Have a seat, please.
W I'm concerned he is too shy in school.
M What _________ _________ _________ _________?
W Actually, he is quiet at home too.
M Don't worry. It's _________ _________ _________ _________.
W How should I treat him then?
M Don't push him. _________ _________ _________ _________ to get ready to talk.

7 | 언급하지 않은 내용 고르기

대화를 듣고, 남자가 스키 캠프에 대해 언급하지 않은 것을 고르시오.

① 장소 ② 일시 ③ 참여 대상
④ 비용 ⑤ 장비 대여

M Amy, why don't we _________ _________ _________ _________ in Pyeongchang?
W I'd love to. When will it be held?
M It's from February 4th to the 6th.
W Good. But I can't ski at all. Is that going to _________ _________ _________?
M Don't worry. The camp is for beginners.
W Alright. _________ _________ _________ _________ _________?
M It's 200 dollars per person.
W It's _________ _________ _________.
M Yeah. But I have a 10% discount coupon.

8 | 할 일 고르기

대화를 듣고, 두 사람이 대화 직후에 할 일로 가장 적절한 것을 고르시오.

① 편지 쓰기 ② 차 마시기
③ 시장 가기 ④ 이사 준비하기
⑤ 과일 구입하기

[Doorbell rings.]
W Hello. Nice to meet you.
M Hi. Are you new here?
W Yes. I just __________ __________ __________ yesterday. Can I ask you something?
M Of course. What is your question?
W Is there __________ __________ __________ __________ __________?
M Yes. It's very close to here.
W That's good. I have lots of things to buy.
M I can show you the way if you want.
W Oh, that would __________ __________ __________.

고난도

9 | 언급하지 않은 내용 고르기

다음을 듣고, 남자가 Community Garage Sale에 대해 언급하지 않은 것을 고르시오.

① 행사 목적 ② 행사 종료 시각
③ 참여 방법 ④ 판매 물건 종류
⑤ 행사 홍보 방식

적중! Tip Community
[커뮤니티]보다는 [커뮤니리]로 들린다. [t]가 모음 사이에서 발음될 때는 약화되어 [r]에 가깝게 발음되기 때문이다.

M Good afternoon, residents. __________ __________ __________ for local charities, we will hold the Community Garage Sale. It'll be on March 19th from 11 a.m. to 3 p.m. If you want to participate, just __________ __________ __________ __________ for sale that day. We will promote this event on many online sites and set up signposts around our town. After the event, feel free to __________ __________ __________ to us. We will __________ __________ __________ to various charities.

10 | 주제 고르기

다음을 듣고, 여자가 하는 말의 내용으로 가장 적절한 것을 고르시오.

① 독서의 중요성 ② 포기하지 않는 태도
③ 소화를 돕는 운동 ④ 올바른 학습 방법
⑤ 다양한 의사소통 수단

W I'd like to tell you a story about an old woman in Korea. She was __________ __________ __________ __________ __________ and couldn't attend school. But she didn't __________ __________ __________. Finally, at age 50, she entered university. Now, she is a great poet. I __________ __________ __________ __________. But after reading her story, I'm __________ __________ __________ __________. I won't give up my dream and will keep trying my best.

고난도

11 | 일치하지 않는 내용 고르기

다음을 듣고, City Eco Center에 대한 내용으로 일치하지 않는 것을 고르시오.

① 친환경적 시설들을 갖추고 있다.
② 목재와 플라스틱 폐기물을 재활용한 미끄럼틀이 있다.
③ 전력을 생산하는 자전거를 타 볼 수 있다.
④ 재활용에 대해 배우는 교육 프로그램이 있다.
⑤ 시립 공원 옆에 위치해 있다.

M Hello. This is City Eco Center. We have many eco-friendly facilities. In our playground, you can __________ __________ __________ slides and swings. They are all made of __________ __________ __________ __________. You can also ride special bicycles. They will __________ __________ while you ride them. We offer educational programs too. You can learn __________ __________ __________. Are you interested? Then, please come visit us. The center is located next to the City Park.

12 | 목적 고르기

대화를 듣고, 여자가 전화를 건 목적으로 가장 적절한 것을 고르시오.

① 예약 정보를 확인하기 위해서
② 이용 변경 사항을 알려주기 위해서
③ 택배를 전달하기 위해서
④ 분실물을 찾아주기 위해서
⑤ 휴무일을 알려주기 위해서

[Cellphone rings.]
W Hi. Is this Mr. Evans speaking?
M Yes. __________ __________?
W This is Muscle Fitness. __________ __________ __________ __________ in the dressing room.
M Really? I didn't know that. I'll come back to __________ __________ __________ now.
W Alright. I'll __________ __________ __________ __________ until you come.
M I really appreciate it.
W You're welcome.

13 | 시간 정보 고르기

대화를 듣고, 결혼식이 열리는 날짜를 고르시오.

① 6월 15일 ② 6월 16일 ③ 6월 17일
④ 6월 18일 ⑤ 6월 19일

적중! Tip I can't wait to ~.
어떤 일을 몹시 기대하고 있음을 나타낼 때 사용되는 표현으로, to 다음에는 동사원형이 온다.
· I can't wait to go to the concert.
콘서트 보러 가는 게 너무 기대돼.

W Jason, did you __________ __________ __________ to Katy's wedding?
M Yes. I can't wait to celebrate her marriage. Are you going too?
W I haven't decided yet. Do you remember __________ __________ __________ __________?
M Hmm... Maybe June 16th? I think it's on the third Saturday of June.
W Let me __________ __________ __________.
M When is it?
W Oh, it's the 19th.

14 | 관계 고르기

대화를 듣고, 두 사람의 관계로 가장 적절한 것을 고르시오.

① TV쇼 진행자 — 연예인
② 영화관 직원 — 손님
③ 서점 직원 — 손님
④ 작가 — 독자
⑤ 과학 교사 — 학생

M Hello. Can I help you find a book?
W Yes. I'm looking for the new book about Einstein.
M Actually, we just __________ __________. I'm so sorry.
W Oh. I will just come back later.
M Well, do you enjoy books about science?
W Yes. I love them.
M Then, I can also __________ __________ __________. It's about famous biologists.
W Wow, thank you. I will __________ __________ __________.

15 | 부탁·요청한 일 고르기

대화를 듣고, 남자가 여자에게 부탁한 일로 가장 적절한 것을 고르시오.

① 사인 대신 받아오기 ② 콘서트 표 예매하기
③ 야구 배트 빌려주기 ④ 함께 사인회장 가기
⑤ 경기 날짜 알려주기

W Daniel, I won the ticket for a fan event. I can see Mark Bonds in person!
M Oh, ________ ________ ________. I'm also a big fan of him.
W I'll get his signature on my baseball, glove and uniform.
M I want to go with you. ________ ________ ________?
W Sorry, but it's not allowed.
M Then, could you ________ ________ ________ on my bat?
W Sure. Give me your bat.
M Thank you so much.

16 | 이유 고르기

대화를 듣고, 남자가 학교에 지각한 이유로 가장 적절한 것을 고르시오.

① 자전거를 도둑맞아서 ② 도로가 공사 중이어서
③ 배탈이 나서 ④ 버스가 오지 않아서
⑤ 시계가 고장 나서

W Sangwon, you look upset.
M I was punished ________ ________ ________ ________ for school today.
W Why were you late? Did you oversleep?
M No. I ________ ________ ________ as always.
W Then, what happened?
M The bus didn't come this morning.
W How did you get to school?
M On foot. It ________ ________ ________ ________.
W I'm sorry you had to do that.

17 | 그림 상황에 적절한 대화 고르기

다음 그림의 상황에 가장 적절한 대화를 고르시오.

① ② ③ ④ ⑤

① **M** It's so hot today.
W Yes. I want to ________ ________ ________ ________.
② **M** Where is the doctor's office?
W It's ________ ________ ________ ________.
③ **M** Do you have these pants in blue?
W I'm sorry. We only have those ________ ________.
④ **M** The concert starts in an hour.
W We should take a taxi then.
⑤ **M** The elevator is on the 10th floor.
W ________ ________ ________ ________.

18 | 언급하지 않은 내용 고르기

다음을 듣고, 여자가 미래에 하고 싶은 일로 언급되지 않은 것을 고르시오.

① 운동선수들이 입은 부상을 확인한다.
② 운동선수들이 회복하도록 돕는다.
③ 운동선수들의 훈련 과정을 점검한다.
④ 운동선수들의 건강 관리를 지도한다.
⑤ 운동선수들과 심리 상담을 진행한다.

적중! Tip **Hopefully**

[호프풀리]보다는 [호풀리]로 들린다. [p]와 [f]처럼 발음할 때 혀의 위치가 비슷한 자음이 나란히 나오면 그중 하나만 발음되기 때문이다.

W Let me tell you ________ ________ ________ ________. I want to become a sports doctor. I'll have to check players' injuries. Also, I'll ________ ________ ________ from their injuries. Sometimes, I'll teach players ________ ________ ________ their health. I will also provide psychological counseling for them. Hopefully, I'll help the players ________ ________ ________.

19 | 적절한 응답 고르기

대화를 듣고, 여자의 마지막 말에 이어질 남자의 응답으로 가장 적절한 것을 고르시오.

Man: ________________________

① My father is very kind.
② He's from California.
③ The story is so unique.
④ I want to become famous.
⑤ Enjoy the movie in a theater.

적중! Tip **role model**

[롤 모델]보다는 [로을 마를]로 들린다. [d]가 모음 사이에서 발음될 때는 약화되어 [r]에 가깝게 발음되기 때문이다.

· video [비리오] · wedding [웨링]

W When did you ________ ________ ________ ________, Rick?
M My father was an actor. So, I loved watching movies ________ ________ ________ ________ ________.
W I see. Then, your father must be your biggest role model, right?
M Of course. He's always helped me ________ ________ ________.
W You've acted in lots of movies. What is ________ ________ ________ among them?
M It is *The Forest*.
W Why is that your favorite?

20 | 적절한 응답 고르기

대화를 듣고, 여자의 마지막 말에 이어질 남자의 응답으로 가장 적절한 것을 고르시오.

Man: ________________________

① We should see the gardens.
② Yes. We have to buy tickets.
③ We'll have sandwiches.
④ Here is the entrance.
⑤ This is my first time in Paris.

M Alright. Our first stop today will be the Palace of Versailles.
W Great! I've always wanted to see it, Dad.
M Me too. We can ________ ________ ________ ________ for a few hours and then get lunch.
W What are we going to do at the palace?
M We can either ________ ________ ________ or join a tour of the palace.
W ________ ________ ________ ________?

해커스북 중·고등

www.HackersBook.com

고난도 모의고사

21~24회 고난도 모의고사

1 다음을 듣고, 부산의 내일 날씨로 가장 적절한 것을 고르시오.

2 대화를 듣고, 여자가 구입할 의자로 가장 적절한 것을 고르시오.

3 대화를 듣고, 여자의 심정으로 가장 적절한 것을 고르시오.

① sorrowful ② bored ③ relaxed
④ shy ⑤ nervous

4 대화를 듣고, 여자가 일요일 오전에 한 일로 가장 적절한 것을 고르시오.

① 피자 만들기 ② 영화 감상하기
③ 유기견 봉사하기 ④ 책 읽기
⑤ 낮잠 자기

5 대화를 듣고, 두 사람이 대화하는 장소로 가장 적절한 곳을 고르시오.

① 등산로 ② 미술관 ③ 낚시용품점
④ 공항 ⑤ 호텔

6 대화를 듣고, 여자의 마지막 말의 의도로 가장 적절한 것을 고르시오.

① 후회 ② 거절 ③ 확신 ④ 칭찬 ⑤ 용서

7 대화를 듣고, 남자가 크리스마스 당일에 한 일로 가장 적절한 것을 고르시오.

① 퍼즐 맞추기 ② 비행기 타기
③ 바다 수영하기 ④ 여행 계획하기
⑤ 영화 보기

8 대화를 듣고, 두 사람이 대화 직후에 할 일로 가장 적절한 것을 고르시오.

① 부엌 청소하기 ② 소파 재배치하기
③ 가구 주문하기 ④ 책 읽기
⑤ 요가 하기

9 대화를 듣고, 두 사람이 라디오 프로그램에 대해 언급하지 <u>않은</u> 것을 고르시오.

① 제목 ② 방송 시간 ③ 방송국
④ 내용 ⑤ 방송 요일

10 다음을 듣고, 남자가 하는 말의 내용으로 가장 적절한 것을 고르시오.

① 수영 수업 등록 안내
② 표 예매 방법
③ 선박 이용 시 주의사항
④ 영화관 이용 예절
⑤ 모형 배 조립 과정

11 대화를 듣고, 휴가에 대한 내용과 일치하지 않는 것을 고르시오.

① 제주도로 휴가를 간다.
② 목요일에 떠난다.
③ 공항에 버스를 타고 간다.
④ 아침은 비행기에서 먹는다.
⑤ 수영할 예정이다.

12 대화를 듣고, 남자가 가방을 구매한 목적으로 가장 적절한 것을 고르시오.

① 바이올린을 넣기 위해서
② 선물을 하기 위해서
③ 비닐 사용을 줄이기 위해서
④ 캠페인에 참여하기 위해서
⑤ 여행을 가기 위해서

13 대화를 듣고, 남자가 지불해야 할 금액으로 가장 적절한 것을 고르시오.

① $ 10 ② $ 15 ③ $ 20 ④ $ 25 ⑤ $ 30

14 대화를 듣고, 두 사람의 관계로 가장 적절한 것을 고르시오.

① 버스 기사 — 승객
② 부동산 중개사 — 집 주인
③ 양초 가게 직원 — 손님
④ 소방관 — 시민
⑤ 요리사 — 기자

15 대화를 듣고, 여자가 남자에게 제안한 일로 가장 적절한 것을 고르시오.

① 함께 사진 찍기 ② 영상 삭제하기
③ 배터리 충전하기 ④ 앱 설치하기
⑤ 우주 영화 보기

16 대화를 듣고, 남자가 점원을 부른 이유로 가장 적절한 것을 고르시오.

① 음식을 포장하려고 ② 추가 주문을 하려고
③ 계산을 하려고 ④ 포크를 교체하려고
⑤ 화장실 위치를 물어보려고

17 다음 그림의 상황에 가장 적절한 대화를 고르시오.

① ② ③ ④ ⑤

18 대화를 듣고, 두 사람이 대회에 대해 언급하지 않은 것을 고르시오.

① 이름 ② 종목 ③ 장소
④ 날짜 ⑤ 참가비

[19-20] 대화를 듣고, 여자의 마지막 말에 이어질 남자의 말로 가장 적절한 것을 고르시오.

19 Man: ______________________

① We spent a month in South Africa.
② That's a tomato plant.
③ Okay. I'll try not to forget it.
④ I'll plant them in the morning.
⑤ I'll move them inside the house.

20 Man: ______________________

① Sorry, but we're closed now.
② He went to the hospital.
③ You should play with your cat more often.
④ How about around 3 in the afternoon?
⑤ Yes. The office is around the corner.

21회 Dictation

Dictation 음성 바로 듣기 ▶

21회 중학영어듣기 고난도 모의고사 Dictation 음성을 들으며 빈칸에 알맞은 단어를 채우시오.

1 | 날씨 고르기

다음을 듣고, 부산의 내일 날씨로 가장 적절한 것을 고르시오.

① ② ③ ④ ⑤

M Good morning, everyone. Tomorrow, Seoul and Incheon ________ ________ ________ ________. In Gangneung, not only heavy rain ________ ________ ________ ________ are expected. ________ ________ ________ ________ of Typhoon Sarah next week, there will be thunderstorms in Jeju. And in Busan, there will be strong winds all day long, so ________ ________ ________ ________ thick clothes when you go out.

2 | 알맞은 그림 고르기

대화를 듣고, 여자가 구입할 의자로 가장 적절한 것을 고르시오.

① ② ③ ④ ⑤

M Welcome to Venice Furniture. What type of furniture are you looking for?

W I'm looking for a chair ________ ________ ________.

M How about this one with a fluffy seat?

W I like the design, but ________ ________ ________ ________.

M Okay. Then, what about these? ________ ________ ________, and the other has four legs.

W I like the one with wheels. I'll buy one.

M ________ ________!

3 | 심정 고르기

대화를 듣고, 여자의 심정으로 가장 적절한 것을 고르시오.

① sorrowful ② bored ③ relaxed
④ shy ⑤ nervous

[Cellphone rings.]

M Rachel, what are you planning to do today? Do you ________ ________ ________ ________?

W Oh, I can't. I'm at the beach with my friends right now.

M Okay. Are you having fun?

W Yes. I really ________ ________ ________ after my math test yesterday.

M Yeah. You studied really hard for that test. You ________ ________ ________ ________.

W That's right. It's great to finally ________ ________ ________ my stress.

4 | 한 일 고르기

대화를 듣고, 여자가 일요일 오전에 한 일로 가장 적절한 것을 고르시오.

① 피자 만들기 ② 영화 감상하기
③ 유기견 봉사하기 ④ 책 읽기
⑤ 낮잠 자기

M Hi, Emma. How did your weekend go?

W Great. I volunteered at ________ ________ ________ ________ on Saturday.

M Really? What did you do there?

W I ________ ________ ________ and took them for walks.

M It sounds like you were busy. ________ ________ ________ on Sunday?

W Yeah. I just read a book in the morning and ________ ________ ________ in the afternoon.

M Well, that sounds like a relaxing day to me.

5 | 장소 고르기

대화를 듣고, 두 사람이 대화하는 장소로 가장 적절한 곳을 고르시오.

① 등산로 ② 미술관 ③ 낚시용품점
④ 공항 ⑤ 호텔

M Hello. Are you _________ _________ _________ _________?
W Yes. My name is Susan Jones.
M Okay, Ms. Jones. You'll be staying here _________ _________ _________, right?
W That's correct.
M Would you like an ocean view or a mountain view from your room?
W I would _________ _________ _________ _________.
M Excellent. _________ _________ _________ _________. You'll be in Room 501.
W Thank you.

6 | 의도 고르기

대화를 듣고, 여자의 마지막 말의 의도로 가장 적절한 것을 고르시오.

① 후회 ② 거절 ③ 확신 ④ 칭찬 ⑤ 용서

I bet ~.
어떤 상황에 대한 확신을 나타낼 때 사용되는 표현으로 '틀림없이 ~이다, 꼭 ~이다'라는 의미이다.
· I bet he'll be late.
틀림없이 그는 늦을 거야.

M Hey, Alice. Did you _________ _________ _________ in the contest?
W Yes! I just sent it. I really hope I win.
M That's great. What did you draw?
W _________ _________ _________ _________ of a coral reef surrounded by fish. I looked up lots of images on the Internet for it.
M I bet _________ _________ _________ _________.
W Yes, I did. I'm sure I'll _________ _________ _________ for it.

7 | 한 일 고르기

대화를 듣고, 남자가 크리스마스 당일에 한 일로 가장 적절한 것을 고르시오.

① 퍼즐 맞추기 ② 비행기 타기
③ 바다 수영하기 ④ 여행 계획하기
⑤ 영화 보기

trip
[트립]보다는 [츄립]으로 들린다. tr-로 시작하는 단어에서 [t]는 [츄]에 가깝게 발음되기 때문이다.

W Hey, Sam! How was your holiday?
M It wasn't bad. How _________ _________ _________ your Christmas?
W Well, I spent the day on a puzzle. I had this one-thousand-piece puzzle.
M Wow. You finished it all?
W Yeah. How was your Christmas in Hawaii? I can't imagine _________ _________ _________ _________ Christmas day.
M Actually, I was _________ _________ _________ that day.
W Oh? What happened?
M I missed my flight, and there weren't _________ _________ _________ on the 24th.
W I'm so sorry to hear that.
M But the rest of the trip was great.

8 | 할 일 고르기

대화를 듣고, 두 사람이 대화 직후에 할 일로 가장 적절한 것을 고르시오.

① 부엌 청소하기 ② 소파 재배치하기
③ 가구 주문하기 ④ 책 읽기
⑤ 요가 하기

W Honey, do you want to do yoga this afternoon?
M Sure! I need to ________ ________ ________.
W Hmm... There's one problem. I don't think there's enough space for ________ ________ ________ to do yoga in our living room.
M ________ ________ ________ ________ the sofa to the kitchen?
W Oh, that will give us much more space.
M Yeah. But I think we should ________ ________ ________ first.
W Okay. Let's do it.

9 | 언급하지 않은 내용 고르기

대화를 듣고, 두 사람이 라디오 프로그램에 대해 언급하지 않은 것을 고르시오.

① 제목 ② 방송 시간 ③ 방송국
④ 내용 ⑤ 방송 요일

W Mike, ________ ________ ________ your new job as a radio show host!
M Thank you. I'm very excited.
W ________ ________ ________ ________ *Morning Catch Up*. Could you tell us more about it?
M It's on from 9 to 11, and I will talk ________ ________ ________.
W That sounds interesting. Will you interview many guests?
M Of course. There will be various experts on the show.
W And when ________ ________ ________ ________?
M The show will air every Monday.

10 | 주제 고르기

다음을 듣고, 남자가 하는 말의 내용으로 가장 적절한 것을 고르시오.

① 수영 수업 등록 안내
② 표 예매 방법
③ 선박 이용 시 주의사항
④ 영화관 이용 예절
⑤ 모형 배 조립 과정

M Welcome aboard, everyone. I'm Jason Smith, the captain of this cruise ship. I will go over ________ ________ ________ with you quickly. Please do not run on the deck. It's dangerous. Also, parents should ________ ________ ________ ________ in the pool. Lastly, please ________ ________ ________ ________ in your room after 11 p.m.

11 | 일치하지 않는 내용 고르기

대화를 듣고, 휴가에 대한 내용과 일치하지 않는 것을 고르시오.

① 제주도로 휴가를 간다.
② 목요일에 떠난다.
③ 공항에 버스를 타고 간다.
④ 아침은 비행기에서 먹는다.
⑤ 수영할 예정이다.

M Honey, are we leaving for Jejudo next Wednesday?
W No. We ________ ________ ________ to May 15th, remember? It's Thursday.
M Right. I'm so excited! We haven't been on a trip for a year.
W I know. Do you want to ride the bus to the airport?
M Why don't we ________ ________ ________? We have to go to the airport early in the morning.
W Sure. ________ ________ ________ ________ before we leave?
M Don't they give you breakfast on the plane?
W Oh, yes. Also, don't forget to ________ ________ ________. We'll go to the beach.

12 | 목적 고르기

대화를 듣고, 남자가 가방을 구매한 목적으로 가장 적절한 것을 고르시오.

① 바이올린을 넣기 위해서
② 선물을 하기 위해서
③ 비닐 사용을 줄이기 위해서
④ 캠페인에 참여하기 위해서
⑤ 여행을 가기 위해서

적중! Tip cotton
[코튼]보다는 [컷은]으로 들린다. [n] 앞에 오는 [t] 발음은 약화되어 거의 들리지 않기 때문이다.
· button [벋은] · badminton [배드민은]

W Ben, ________ ________ ________ ________ for you.
M It must be the bag that I ordered online, Mom.
W Really? You already have a backpack.
M Yes. But I bought a cotton bag for shopping. I don't want to ________ ________ ________.
W That is so thoughtful of you, Ben.
M Thanks, Mom. I just wanted to ________ ________ ________.
W I should also take a cotton bag when I go grocery shopping.

13 | 금액 정보 고르기

대화를 듣고, 남자가 지불해야 할 금액으로 가장 적절한 것을 고르시오.

① $ 10 ② $ 15 ③ $ 20 ④ $ 25 ⑤ $ 30

적중! Tip adult ticket
[어덜트 티켓]보다는 [어덜티킷]으로 들린다. 발음이 같은 자음이 나란히 나오면 앞 단어의 끝 자음이 탈락되기 때문이다.

M Hi. Can I get tickets for ________ ________ ________ ________?
W Sure. ________ ________ ________ do you need?
M One adult ticket and two kid tickets, please.
W How old are the kids?
M They are ________ ________ ________ ________.
W It's 13 dollars for an adult and six dollars for kids under 10.
M Okay. How much do I have to ________ ________ ________?
W It's 25 dollars.
M Here you are.

14 | 관계 고르기

대화를 듣고, 두 사람의 관계로 가장 적절한 것을 고르시오.

① 버스 기사 — 승객
② 부동산 중개사 — 집 주인
③ 양초 가게 직원 — 손님
④ 소방관 — 시민
⑤ 요리사 — 기자

M Hello. Do you live in this apartment?
W Yes, sir. What happened?
M There was a small fire. Luckily, we ________ ________ ________ before it got worse.
W Oh, no! What started the fire?
M It was ________ ________ ________ in the kitchen.
W That's scary!
M It's important to check the wiring regularly ________ ________ ________.
W Okay. I definitely will.

15 | 제안한 일 고르기

대화를 듣고, 여자가 남자에게 제안한 일로 가장 적절한 것을 고르시오.

① 함께 사진 찍기 ② 영상 삭제하기
③ 배터리 충전하기 ④ 앱 설치하기
⑤ 우주 영화 보기

적중! Tip Here you go.
상대방에게 무언가를 건네줄 때 사용되는 표현으로 '여기 있어요'라는 의미이다.

W Alex, can I ________ ________ ________ for a minute?
M Sure. Here you go.
W Thank you. *[Pause]* Why is your phone so slow?
M ________ ________ ________ ________. It got slow recently.
W Maybe your phone's storage space is full.
M What should I do then?
W Why don't you ________ ________ ________ ________ ________? Those take up a lot of space.
M I'll check the photo album and decide which ones to delete.

16 | 이유 고르기

대화를 듣고, 남자가 점원을 부른 이유로 가장 적절한 것을 고르시오.

① 음식을 포장하려고 ② 추가 주문을 하려고
③ 계산을 하려고 ④ 포크를 교체하려고
⑤ 화장실 위치를 물어보려고

M Excuse me.
W Yes? Would you like some more water?
M No. I want to ________ ________ ________, but I need to see a menu.
W Here's a menu for you. *[Pause]* ________ ________ ________ ________?
M Hmm... Can you recommend ________ ________ ________ ________ at this restaurant?
W I recommend the beef steak.
M It ________ ________. I'll have one of those.
W Alright.

17 | 그림 상황에 적절한 대화 고르기

다음 그림의 상황에 가장 적절한 대화를 고르시오.

① ② ③ ④ ⑤

① **W** We should ________ ________ ________ ________ before the movie starts.
M That's a good idea.
② **W** Do you have any water left?
M Yeah. The water bottle is ________ ________ ________.
③ **W** Did you bring your swimming cap?
M Oops. ________ ________.
④ **W** This view from the top of the mountain is incredible.
M Yes. The town ________ ________ ________ ________.
⑤ **W** Oh, it's raining! I don't have an umbrella.
M It's okay. Let's go ________ ________ ________ ________.

18 | 언급하지 않은 내용 고르기

대화를 듣고, 두 사람이 대회에 대해 언급하지 않은 것을 고르시오.

① 이름 ② 종목 ③ 장소
④ 날짜 ⑤ 참가비

적중! Tip Seattle
[시애틀]보다는 [씨애를]로 들린다. [t]가 모음과 단어 끝의 -le 사이에 있으면 약화되어 [r]에 가깝게 발음되기 때문이다.

W Jack, what are you doing?
M I'm buying tickets for the Robot Olympics. It's __________ __________ __________.
W What do the robots do?
M The events involve activities like __________ __________ __________ or folding laundry.
W Where is it held?
M This year, it __________ __________ __________ in our city at the Seattle Stadium.
W I might go then. Is it happening soon?
M It __________ __________ __________ on June 16th.
W Great. I'll buy a ticket as well.

19 | 적절한 응답 고르기

대화를 듣고, 여자의 마지막 말에 이어질 남자의 말로 가장 적절한 것을 고르시오.

Man: ______________________________

① We spent a month in South Africa.
② That's a tomato plant.
③ Okay. I'll try not to forget it.
④ I'll plant them in the morning.
⑤ I'll move them inside the house.

W The garden is so beautiful, Phil.
M Thank you. I __________ __________ in my free time.
W I think it is a good hobby.
M But I __________ __________ __________ now.
W What is it?
M Some plants in my garden are __________ __________.
W Perhaps they need water. __________ __________ __________ every morning.

20 | 적절한 응답 고르기

대화를 듣고, 여자의 마지막 말에 이어질 남자의 말로 가장 적절한 것을 고르시오.

Man: ______________________________

① Sorry, but we're closed now.
② He went to the hospital.
③ You should play with your cat more often.
④ How about around 3 in the afternoon?
⑤ Yes. The office is around the corner.

[Telephone rings.]
M Hello, may I help you?
W Yes. My cat is sick.
M Okay. __________ __________ with your cat?
W She's sleeping a lot and doesn't eat much.
M When did she start acting this way?
W She __________ __________ __________ for two days.
M I think it's best that you __________ __________ __________ __________ __________.
W Okay. When can I come by?

1 다음을 듣고, 내일 오후의 날씨로 가장 적절한 것을 고르시오.

①  ②  ③  ④  ⑤ 

2 대화를 듣고, 여자가 찾는 반지로 가장 적절한 것을 고르시오.

①   ②  ③  

④   ⑤  

3 대화를 듣고, 남자의 심정으로 가장 적절한 것을 고르시오.

① shy ② embarrassed
③ disappointed ④ nervous
⑤ pleased

4 대화를 듣고, 여자가 볼링 대회에 참가하기 위해 한 일을 고르시오.

① 볼링 연습하기 ② 단체복 구매하기
③ 신청서 작성하기 ④ 기차 예매하기
⑤ 작년 경기 영상 보기

5 대화를 듣고, 두 사람이 대화하는 장소로 가장 적절한 곳을 고르시오.

① 역사박물관 ② 보건실
③ 옷가게 ④ 운동장
⑤ 바닷가

6 대화를 듣고, 여자의 마지막 말의 의도로 가장 적절한 것을 고르시오.

① 축하 ② 제안 ③ 실망 ④ 격려 ⑤ 후회

7 대화를 듣고, 남자가 구매한 과일로 가장 적절한 것을 고르시오.

① 바나나 ② 사과 ③ 배
④ 블루베리 ⑤ 키위

8 대화를 듣고, 남자가 대화 직후에 할 일로 가장 적절한 것을 고르시오.

① 점심 준비하기 ② 슈퍼마켓 가기
③ 포크 꺼내오기 ④ 손 씻기
⑤ 설거지하기

9 대화를 듣고, 두 사람이 전학생에 대해 언급하지 <u>않은</u> 것을 고르시오.

① 이름 ② 출신 국가 ③ 언어
④ 가족 수 ⑤ 취미

10 다음을 듣고, 남자가 하는 말의 내용으로 가장 적절한 것을 고르시오.

① 단체 기부 방법 ② 행사 정보 안내
③ 공원 이용 수칙 ④ 게임 출시 정보
⑤ 반려견 입양 현황

11 대화를 듣고, 온라인 투어에 대한 내용과 일치하지 않는 것을 고르시오.

① 매주 토요일에 진행된다.
② 1시간 동안 진행된다.
③ 가이드와 통화할 수 있다.
④ 참가비는 무료이다.
⑤ 단체 참가가 가능하다.

12 대화를 듣고, 남자가 매장을 방문한 목적으로 가장 적절한 것을 고르시오.

① 태블릿 PC를 수리받기 위해서
② 태블릿 PC를 선구매하기 위해서
③ 주문한 물건을 가지러 오기 위해서
④ 제품의 가격을 비교하기 위해서
⑤ 새 휴대폰을 주문하기 위해서

13 대화를 듣고, 여자가 도넛을 몇 박스 구매할지 고르시오.

① 3박스 ② 4박스 ③ 5박스
④ 6박스 ⑤ 7박스

14 대화를 듣고, 두 사람의 관계로 가장 적절한 것을 고르시오.

① 인테리어 디자이너 — 고객
② 식당 직원 — 배달원
③ 피아노 강사 — 수강생
④ 은행원 — 고객
⑤ 소품 가게 주인 — 손님

15 대화를 듣고, 여자가 남자에게 부탁한 일로 가장 적절한 것을 고르시오.

① 집에 데려다주기 ② 탁구 시합하기
③ 간식 사 오기 ④ 봉사활동 하기
⑤ 친구 초대하기

16 대화를 듣고, 남자가 지금 영화를 보고 있는 이유로 가장 적절한 것을 고르시오.

① 영화 감상문을 쓰기 위해서
② 훌륭한 영화감독이 되고 싶어서
③ 좋아하는 장르의 작품이어서
④ 배우의 연기가 훌륭해서
⑤ 대사를 외우기 위해서

17 다음 그림의 상황에 가장 적절한 대화를 고르시오.

① ② ③ ④ ⑤

18 다음을 듣고, 여자가 Bancroft Resort에 대해 언급하지 않은 것을 고르시오.

① 개업일 ② 객실 수 ③ 위치
④ 시설 ⑤ 예약 방법

[19-20] 대화를 듣고, 남자의 마지막 말에 이어질 여자의 응답으로 가장 적절한 것을 고르시오.

19 Woman: ______________________

① It'll be here around 2 p.m.
② There are no more seats.
③ You're here early.
④ Yes. It will be landing in an hour.
⑤ I'm so sorry to hear that terrible news.

20 Woman: ______________________

① Yes. I'm planning to register at the gym.
② Carrots are good for you.
③ I recommend walking.
④ Swimming sounds like a good choice.
⑤ Don't worry. He'll get better soon.

22회 Dictation

Dictation
음성 바로 듣기 ▶

22회 중학영어듣기 고난도 모의고사 Dictation 음성을 들으며 빈칸에 알맞은 단어를 채우시오.

1 | 날씨 고르기

다음을 듣고, 내일 오후의 날씨로 가장 적절한 것을 고르시오.

① ② ③ ④ ⑤

W Good morning, everyone! _________ _________ _________ _________ with bright sunshine and clear skies. But light rain will start falling in the afternoon, and it will _________ _________ _________ _________. It'll be partly cloudy on Sunday afternoon, but _________ _________ _________ _________ by next week. So, _________ _________ _________ on Monday.

2 | 알맞은 그림 고르기

대화를 듣고, 여자가 찾는 반지로 가장 적절한 것을 고르시오.

① ② ③ ④ ⑤

M Mom, are you looking for something?
W Yeah. I can't find my wedding ring.
M Let me help you find it. What does it look like?
W It has _________ _________ _________ in the middle.
M Does it have _________ _________ _________?
W No. That's my grandmother's ring.
M How about this one?
W _________ _________ _________ _________, but the one I'm looking for is thicker.
M Oh, I think I found it.

적중! Tip middle
[미들]보다는 [미를]로 들린다. [d]가 모음과 단어 끝의 -le 사이에 있으면 약화되어 [r]에 가깝게 발음되기 때문이다.

3 | 심정 고르기

대화를 듣고, 남자의 심정으로 가장 적절한 것을 고르시오.

① shy ② embarrassed
③ disappointed ④ nervous
⑤ pleased

M Can I talk to you for a second, Hanna? Did you _________ _________ _________ _________ today?
W I couldn't, sir. My dog, Trevor, _________ _________ _________.
M This is the third time this week you have missed an assignment.
W I know. But there was nothing I could do.
M You _________ _________ _________ your homework this time.
W I'm sorry.
M I expected you to keep your promise, but you _________ _________ _________ again.

4 | 한 일 고르기

대화를 듣고, 여자가 볼링 대회에 참가하기 위해 한 일을 고르시오.

① 볼링 연습하기　② 단체복 구매하기
③ 신청서 작성하기　④ 기차 예매하기
⑤ 작년 경기 영상 보기

W Jake, did you sign up for the bowling tournament?
M Yes, I did. Did you ________ ________ ________ too?
W Not yet. I'll do it tomorrow.
M ________ ________ ________ ________ the tournament since it's my first time competing.
W I'm sure we'll have lots of fun whether ________ ________ ________ ________.
M But I hope we win. I've practiced a lot lately.
W I watched the video of last year's competition. You should watch it.
M Good idea. That will ________ ________ ________.

5 | 장소 고르기

대화를 듣고, 두 사람이 대화하는 장소로 가장 적절한 곳을 고르시오.

① 역사박물관　② 보건실
③ 옷가게　④ 운동장
⑤ 바닷가

W It's such a beautiful day today.
M It really is. Let's ________ ________ ________ ________!
W Okay. But we can't go too far.
M Why not?
W The lifeguards said that we cannot ________ ________ ________ that rock.
M That's fine. Hey, do you have any sunscreen?
W Yes. It's here. I ________ ________ ________ ________ too. I feel like I'm starting to burn.

6 | 의도 고르기

대화를 듣고, 여자의 마지막 말의 의도로 가장 적절한 것을 고르시오.

① 축하　② 제안　③ 실망　④ 격려　⑤ 후회

W Why do you ________ ________ ________ ________, Kevin?
M I didn't win the gold medal. ________ ________ ________.
W You can't win every race.
M I prepared so much for it. I wanted to ________ ________ ________.
W Did something happen? I'm sure you still did well.
M I got really nervous.
W That's alright. ________ ________ ________ next time.

7 | 특정 정보 고르기

대화를 듣고, 남자가 구매한 과일로 가장 적절한 것을 고르시오.

① 바나나　② 사과　③ 배
④ 블루베리　⑤ 키위

적중! Tip　flour
'꽃'이라는 의미의 명사 flower의 발음도 [플라워]로 비슷하다. 이러한 동음이의어는 문맥 속에서 뜻을 파악하는 것이 중요하다.

M Honey, I'm home! I ________ ________ ________ ________, and bought flour and some fruits.
W Thanks! Did you buy any apples? I can ________ ________ ________ ________ for dessert.
M They only had green apples, so I didn't get any.
W How about ________ ________ ________ then?
M Sorry, but they were ________ ________ ________. But I got kiwis. They were on sale.
W Shawn, you know I have allergies to kiwis!
M Oops. I forgot.

8 | 할 일 고르기

대화를 듣고, 남자가 대화 직후에 할 일로 가장 적절한 것을 고르시오.

① 점심 준비하기 ② 슈퍼마켓 가기
③ 포크 꺼내오기 ④ 손 씻기
⑤ 설거지하기

적중! Tip definitely
[데피니틀리]보다는 [데퍼닛을리]로 들린다. [t]와 [l]처럼 발음할 때 혀의 위치가 비슷한 자음이 나란히 나오면 앞 발음이 탈락되기 때문이다.

W David, do you want to try this Spam musubi?
M What is Spam musubi?
W It's ________ ________ ________ made with Spam, rice, and dried seaweed.
M Sounds delicious. I like eating Spam with rice.
W You should definitely try this then.
M Do you have ________ ________ ________?
W Actually, you can eat it with your hands. Why don't you ________ ________ ________ ________?
M Okay. I'll do that now.

9 | 언급하지 않은 내용 고르기

대화를 듣고, 두 사람이 전학생에 대해 언급하지 않은 것을 고르시오.

① 이름 ② 출신 국가 ③ 언어
④ 가족 수 ⑤ 취미

M Hey, Sojin. Have you said hi to the new student?
W Her name is Jamie, right?
M I think so. Do you know ________ ________ ________ ________?
W I heard that she came from Canada.
M Then, ________ ________ ________ ________ too?
W Yeah. I don't remember her hobbies, though.
M I'll ask her ________ ________ ________ ________. I hope she likes taekwondo.
W I agree. It would be ________ ________ ________ ________ to our taekwondo club.

10 | 주제 고르기

다음을 듣고, 남자가 하는 말의 내용으로 가장 적절한 것을 고르시오.

① 단체 기부 방법 ② 행사 정보 안내
③ 공원 이용 수칙 ④ 게임 출시 정보
⑤ 반려견 입양 현황

M Now, ________ ________ ________ about our Dog Day event. It is open to anyone who has a dog. The event ________ ________ ________ at the Blair Dog Park at the corner of Durant Street. There will be fun activities like ________ ________ ________ ________. We'll also provide treats for our furry friends. It's a free event, but we will ask for ________ ________ ________. And this will be used to rescue dogs in danger.

11 | 일치하지 않는 내용 고르기

대화를 듣고, 온라인 투어에 대한 내용과 일치하지 않는 것을 고르시오.

① 매주 토요일에 진행된다.
② 1시간 동안 진행된다.
③ 가이드와 통화할 수 있다.
④ 참가비는 무료이다.
⑤ 단체 참가가 가능하다.

M Hello. This is LiveTour.com. How may I help you?
W Hi, I'd like information about ______ ______ ______ of London.
M Sure. That tour is held every Saturday from 7 to 8 p.m.
W What's the cost?
M There's ______ ______. Any other questions?
W Are we ______ ______ ______ to the guide during the tour?
M Of course. There's an online chat room.
W Okay. Can the tour ______ ______ ______?
M Yes. But you must call our office first.

12 | 목적 고르기

대화를 듣고, 남자가 매장을 방문한 목적으로 가장 적절한 것을 고르시오.

① 태블릿 PC를 수리받기 위해서
② 태블릿 PC를 선구매하기 위해서
③ 주문한 물건을 가지러 오기 위해서
④ 제품의 가격을 비교하기 위해서
⑤ 새 휴대폰을 주문하기 위해서

W Welcome. What can I help you with?
M Do you have the new 4-Star Tablet PC?
W ______ ______ ______.
M I see. When will ______ ______ ______ ______ again?
W Let me check. *[Typing sound]* On Thursday.
M In that case, can I buy one in advance? I will come pick it up.
W You can. Which color do you want?
M I'd like ______ ______ ______.
W That will be 500 dollars.

13 | 숫자 정보 고르기

대화를 듣고, 여자가 도넛을 몇 박스 구매할지 고르시오.

① 3박스 ② 4박스 ③ 5박스
④ 6박스 ⑤ 7박스

M Diana, what are you planning to order for the year-end class party?
W I still ______ ______ ______. Maybe some pizza?
M Hmm... It might get cold. How about donuts?
W Great idea. They would be ______ ______ ______ in class.
M How many donuts will we need?
W There are 24 students in our class. ______ ______ ______ six donuts, so we need four boxes.
M We also have to get one for our homeroom teacher, Mr. Scout.
W Oh, we'll have to buy ______ ______ ______ then.

14 | 관계 고르기

대화를 듣고, 두 사람의 관계로 가장 적절한 것을 고르시오.

① 인테리어 디자이너 — 고객
② 식당 직원 — 배달원
③ 피아노 강사 — 수강생
④ 은행원 — 고객
⑤ 소품 가게 주인 — 손님

적중! Tip I'd appreciate it.
상대방이 내게 뭔가를 해주었을 때 이에 대한 응답으로 사용되는 표현으로 '그래 주시면 감사하겠습니다'라는 의미이다.

W Hello, Mr. Nicoles. I'll show you our living room first.
M Okay. Which color do you want to ______ ______ ______?
W I'd like a light yellow paint.
M And do you want the walls to ______ ______ ______?
W No. The ceiling should be white.
M Okay. I'll start painting the wall next Tuesday.
W Should we ______ ______ ______ out of the living room?
M Yes. I'd appreciate it.

15 | 부탁·요청한 일 고르기

대화를 듣고, 여자가 남자에게 부탁한 일로 가장 적절한 것을 고르시오.

① 집에 데려다주기 ② 탁구 시합하기
③ 간식 사 오기 ④ 봉사활동 하기
⑤ 친구 초대하기

적중! Tip I was wondering if you could ~.
상대방에게 뭔가를 부탁하거나 허락을 구할 때 쓸 수 있는 표현이다.
· I was wondering if you could help me.
네가 나를 도와줄 수 있을지 궁금해.

W Matt, what are you doing this Saturday?
M I'm going to rest at home. I've been _________ _________ _________. Why?
W I'm working at the senior center, and we're having _________ _________ _________ _________ this week.
M That sounds interesting.
W I was wondering if you could volunteer and _________ _________ _________ _________ the event.
M Why not? I can ask my friends _________ _________ _________ if you need more volunteers.
W That would be great!

16 | 이유 고르기

대화를 듣고, 남자가 지금 영화를 보고 있는 이유로 가장 적절한 것을 고르시오.

① 영화 감상문을 쓰기 위해서
② 훌륭한 영화감독이 되고 싶어서
③ 좋아하는 장르의 작품이어서
④ 배우의 연기가 훌륭해서
⑤ 대사를 외우기 위해서

W Andy, _________ _________ _________ this movie before?
M Yeah, I did. This is about the seventh time.
W What? Why have you watched that movie so much? There are lots of _________ _________ _________.
M At first, I watched it for my English homework.
W And did it become your favorite?
M I _________ _________ _________ _________ the actress. Her acting is incredible.
W Wow. I should watch it sometime.
M I think I have memorized her lines now.

17 | 그림 상황에 적절한 대화 고르기

다음 그림의 상황에 가장 적절한 대화를 고르시오.

① ② ③ ④ ⑤

① **W** Did you enjoy your dinner?
M Yes, thank you. Can you _________ _________ _________ _________?
② **W** Would you like your coffee _________ _________?
M I'd like it to go please.
③ **W** I'd like to _________ _________ _________ I bought last week.
M I see. Do you have a receipt?
④ **W** What time does the bank open?
M At 9 o'clock, but _________ _________ _________ _________.
⑤ **W** How do you want to have your hair cut?
M Short, please. I also want to _________ _________ _________ brown.

18 | 언급하지 않은 내용 고르기

다음을 듣고, 여자가 Bancroft Resort에 대해 언급하지 않은 것을 고르시오.

① 개업일 ② 객실 수 ③ 위치
④ 시설 ⑤ 예약 방법

적중! Tip kinds of foods
[카인드즈 오브 푸드즈]보다는 [카인저푸즈]로 들린다. 자음 3개가 연속해서 나오면 중간 자음은 발음되지 않고, [v]와 [f]처럼 발음할 때 혀의 위치가 비슷한 자음이 나란히 나오면 앞 단어의 끝 자음이 탈락되기 때문이다.

W Would you like to ________ ________ ________ ________ ________? Visit us at the Bancroft Resort! We just opened on March 27th. We have more than 100 rooms that come in five different types. We offer various kinds of foods and beverages at our restaurant on the 20th floor. You can also ________ ________ ________ around our hotel from the rooftop swimming pool. ________ ________ ________ ________, call 555-2356 or visit our website at www.BancroftResort.com.

19 | 적절한 응답 고르기

대화를 듣고, 남자의 마지막 말에 이어질 여자의 응답으로 가장 적절한 것을 고르시오.

Woman: ________________

① It'll be here around 2 p.m.
② There are no more seats.
③ You're here early.
④ Yes. It will be landing in an hour.
⑤ I'm so sorry to hear that terrible news.

M Excuse me. Can you tell me the time?
W Sure. It's almost noon.
M Thanks. My friend took a bus from Busan at 8 o'clock. The bus will arrive at 12, right?
W Actually, ________ ________ ________ ________.
M Oh, no. Really?
W Yes. There was ________ ________ ________ ________ on the highway.
M That's terrible! Was it serious?
W Luckily, no one was hurt. But the bus ________ ________ ________ ________.
M Then, what time is the bus arriving?

20 | 적절한 응답 고르기

대화를 듣고, 남자의 마지막 말에 이어질 여자의 응답으로 가장 적절한 것을 고르시오.

Woman: ________________

① Yes. I'm planning to register at the gym.
② Carrots are good for you.
③ I recommend walking.
④ Swimming sounds like a good choice.
⑤ Don't worry. He'll get better soon.

W Hey, Sam. You look worried. What's up?
M I got ________ ________ ________ ________.
W Is there a problem?
M Yeah. I'm a bit overweight.
W Do you have to ________ ________ ________ ________?
M No. But I should eat more vegetables. Also, I need to ________ ________ ________.
W What's your plan?
M I don't know. I don't like ________ ________ ________ ________. What else can I do for exercise?

1 다음을 듣고, 베를린의 날씨로 가장 적절한 것을 고르시오.

2 대화를 듣고, 여자가 선물할 초콜릿 세트로 가장 적절한 것을 고르시오.

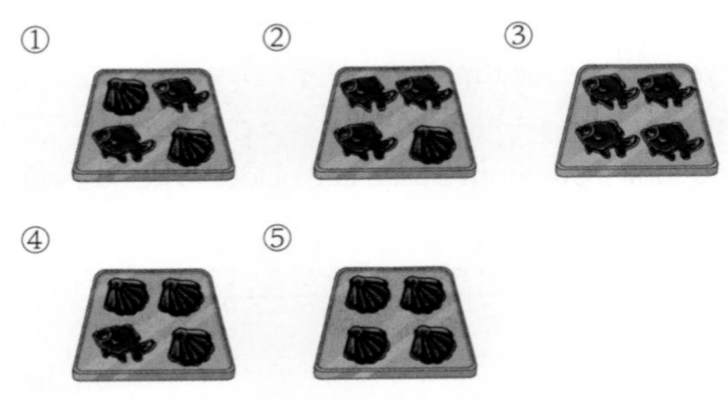

3 대화를 듣고, 남자의 마지막 말의 의도로 가장 적절한 것을 고르시오.

① 비판 ② 설득 ③ 용서 ④ 허락 ⑤ 칭찬

4 대화를 듣고, 여자가 지난 주말에 한 일로 가장 적절한 것을 고르시오.

① 절 방문하기
② 자전거 구매하기
③ 향초 만들기
④ 이불 빨래하기
⑤ 오일 주문하기

5 대화를 듣고, 두 사람이 대화하는 장소로 가장 적절한 곳을 고르시오.

① 공항
② 스터디 룸
③ 병원
④ 식당
⑤ 분실물 보관소

6 대화를 듣고, 제과점에 대한 내용으로 일치하지 않는 것을 고르시오.

① 파크 가에 위치해있다.
② 지난달에 문을 열었다.
③ 많은 사람이 줄을 선다.
④ 오전 8시부터 운영한다.
⑤ 빵 가격이 적당하다.

7 대화를 듣고, 여자가 운동을 하기 위해 할 일을 고르시오.

① 일찍 일어나기
② 기구 구매하기
③ 알람 맞추기
④ 스트레칭 하기
⑤ 체육관 등록하기

8 대화를 듣고, 여자가 대화 직후에 할 일로 가장 적절한 것을 고르시오.

① 고객센터 가기
② 식탁 반품하기
③ 가구 조립하기
④ 의자 구매하기
⑤ 페인트 주문하기

9 대화를 듣고, 자동차에 대해 언급하지 않은 것을 고르시오.

① 제조사
② 출시일
③ 가격
④ 연료
⑤ 색상

10 다음을 듣고, 남자가 하는 말의 내용으로 가장 적절한 것을 고르시오.

① 과학실 이용 수칙
② 방과 후 활동 공지
③ 손 씻는 방법
④ 공장 시설 안내
⑤ 새로운 비누 소개

11 대화를 듣고, Mud Festival에 대한 내용과 일치하지 않는 것을 고르시오.

① 축제는 8월 22일에 열린다.
② 온라인으로 표를 살 수 있다.
③ 표는 10달러이다.
④ 진흙 성 쌓기 체험을 할 수 있다.
⑤ 전통 음악 공연이 있다.

12 대화를 듣고, 남자가 전화를 건 목적으로 가장 적절한 것을 고르시오.

① 예약을 하기 위해서
② 가격을 확인하기 위해서
③ 할인을 요청하기 위해서
④ 위치를 물어보기 위해서
⑤ 물건을 주문하기 위해서

13 대화를 듣고, 여자가 받은 거스름돈으로 가장 적절한 것을 고르시오.

① $ 1 ② $ 2 ③ $ 3 ④ $ 4 ⑤ $ 5

14 대화를 듣고, 두 사람의 관계로 가장 적절한 것을 고르시오.

① 장난감 가게 직원 — 손님
② 양떼목장 주인 — 관광객
③ 반려견 훈련사 — 보호자
④ 동물용품점 직원 — 손님
⑤ 수의사 — 보호자

15 대화를 듣고, 여자가 남자에게 부탁한 일로 가장 적절한 것을 고르시오.

① 숙소 예약하기
② 사진 보내주기
③ 쿠폰 번호 알려주기
④ 카메라 수리하기
⑤ 필름 구매하기

16 대화를 듣고, 여자가 콘서트에 가지 못하는 이유로 가장 적절한 것을 고르시오.

① 표가 매진되어서
② 숙제를 해야 해서
③ 교통편이 좋지 않아서
④ 수업이 있어서
⑤ 동아리 모임이 있어서

17 다음 그림의 상황에 가장 적절한 대화를 고르시오.

① ② ③ ④ ⑤

18 다음을 듣고, 여자가 San Marino City Tour에 대해 언급하지 않은 것을 고르시오.

① 가이드 이름
② 시작 시간
③ 교통편
④ 투어 비용
⑤ 방문 예정지

[19-20] 대화를 듣고, 여자의 마지막 말에 이어질 남자의 말로 가장 적절한 것을 고르시오.

19 **Man:** ______________________________

① Chanwoo is going with me.
② Yes. I start tomorrow.
③ I visited with my teacher.
④ The patients need some help.
⑤ It's a children's hospital.

20 **Man:** ______________________________

① I'm not feeling so good.
② Look over your work.
③ I can't pay attention.
④ The deadline has passed.
⑤ Is Wednesday okay?

23회 Dictation

Dictation
음성 바로 듣기 ▶

23회 중학영어듣기 고난도 모의고사 Dictation 음성을 들으며 빈칸에 알맞은 단어를 채우시오.

1 | 날씨 고르기

다음을 듣고, 베를린의 날씨로 가장 적절한 것을 고르시오.

① ② ③ ④ ⑤

W Hello, everyone. Here's the global weather forecast. In Moscow, _________ _________ _________ are expected. New York is going to be foggy, so _________ _________ _________ _________. The temperature in Berlin will _________ _________ _________, and a snowstorm is expected. Please wear warm clothes and stay inside. Thank you.

2 | 알맞은 그림 고르기

대화를 듣고, 여자가 선물할 초콜릿 세트로 가장 적절한 것을 고르시오.

① ② ③ ④ ⑤

M Mindy, what are you cooking?
W I'm _________ _________ _________ for my friends, Dad.
M The fish-shaped ones are very impressive.
W Thank you, Dad. I also made seashell-shaped chocolates.
M They look delicious. _________ _________ _________ _________ _________ them in boxes?
W Yes. I'll put three fish-shaped chocolates and one seashell-shaped chocolate _________ _________ _________.

3 | 의도 고르기

대화를 듣고, 남자의 마지막 말의 의도로 가장 적절한 것을 고르시오.

① 비판 ② 설득 ③ 용서 ④ 허락 ⑤ 칭찬

적중! Tip this summer
[디스 써머]보다는 [디써머]로 들린다. 발음이 같은 자음이 나란히 나오면 앞 단어의 끝 자음이 탈락되기 때문이다.

W John, you look cheerful.
M Mom, I heard about an _________ _________ _________ in Thailand this summer. I'd really like to go.
W Who do you want to go with?
M I was planning to go by myself.
W You're _________ _________ _________ _________ abroad alone.
M Don't worry. I'll call you every day.
W Well, I don't think I can _________ _________ _________ to do that.
M Please, Mom. The festival sounds incredible.

4 | 한 일 고르기

대화를 듣고, 여자가 지난 주말에 한 일로 가장 적절한 것을 고르시오.

① 절 방문하기 ② 자전거 구매하기
③ 향초 만들기 ④ 이불 빨래하기
⑤ 오일 주문하기

W Neil, what did you do last weekend?
M I visited a temple with my parents. What about you, Bella?
W I _________ _________ _________ _________.
M What a fun thing to do! Was it hard?
W No. It was easy even though it was _________ _________ _________.
M Great! Do your candles smell nice?
W Yeah. I put _________ _________ _________ aroma oil in them.

5 | 장소 고르기

대화를 듣고, 두 사람이 대화하는 장소로 가장 적절한 곳을 고르시오.

① 공항 ② 스터디 룸 ③ 병원
④ 식당 ⑤ 분실물 보관소

W Hello. Can I ________ ________ ________, please?
M Sure. Here you go.
W *[Typing sound]* Here's your ticket to New York. ________ ________ ________ ________ at 3 p.m.
M Thank you. And I'd like to ________ ________.
W Okay. How many suitcases do you have?
M I have two.
W Please place them ________ ________ ________ one at a time.

6 | 일치하지 않는 내용 고르기

대화를 듣고, 제과점에 대한 내용으로 일치하지 않는 것을 고르시오.

① 파크 가에 위치해있다.
② 지난달에 문을 열었다.
③ 많은 사람이 줄을 선다.
④ 오전 8시부터 운영한다.
⑤ 빵 가격이 적당하다.

적중! Tip Can you make it at ~?
상대방에게 '이 시간에 맞출 수 있니?, 이 시간에 되니?'라고 묻는 표현으로, at 다음에는 시간이 온다.
· Can you make it at 3 p.m.?
오후 세 시에 맞출 수 있니?

M Jenna, I bought this cake from the bakery on Park Street.
W I didn't know that there's ________ ________ ________.
M Well, it opened last month.
W Are they expensive?
M No. The bakery has ________ ________ ________.
W I will visit it tomorrow afternoon.
M You should get there at least ________ ________ ________ ________ ________. Can you make it at 8 a.m.?
W I can. But why? Do many people ________ ________ at the store?
M Yes, they do!

7 | 할 일 고르기

대화를 듣고, 여자가 운동을 하기 위해 할 일을 고르시오.

① 일찍 일어나기
② 기구 구매하기
③ 알람 맞추기
④ 스트레칭 하기
⑤ 체육관 등록하기

M Carla, do you run much these days?
W No. I don't like to run in the summer.
M You can go running early in the morning. It will be cooler then.
W I ________ ________ ________ when I wake up early.
M Oh, you could join a gym.
W There isn't one near my house.
M What about ________ ________ ________ ________?
W That would ________ ________ ________. I should order one now.

8 | 할 일 고르기

대화를 듣고, 여자가 대화 직후에 할 일로 가장 적절한 것을 고르시오.

① 고객센터 가기 ② 식탁 반품하기
③ 가구 조립하기 ④ 의자 구매하기
⑤ 페인트 주문하기

M What's wrong, Silvia? ________ ________ ________.
W I ordered a table, and it just arrived. But ________ ________ ________ ________ from what I expected.
M Did the company make a mistake?
W No. But the color ________ ________ ________ online.
M I see. Why don't you paint the table another color?
W That's actually not a bad idea.
M You can ________ ________ ________ on the Internet.
W I'll do that now. I hope there's a nice blue paint.

9 | 언급하지 않은 내용 고르기

대화를 듣고, 자동차에 대해 언급하지 <u>않은</u> 것을 고르시오.

① 제조사 ② 출시일 ③ 가격
④ 연료 ⑤ 색상

적중! Tip Same here.
상대방의 말에 동의할 때 사용되는 표현으로 '나도 마찬가지야'라는 의미이다.

M Wendy, have you heard about the new car from Fast Motors?
W Yes. Wasn't it released yesterday?
M Yeah. I really want to ________ ________ ________ ________.
W Same here. It must be very efficient since it's ________ ________ ________.
M You have a point. If you could buy it, which color would you want?
W Hmm... The dark green one ________ ________ ________ ________.
M I agree. Why don't we go to a motor show to see the car soon?
W Sounds awesome!

10 | 주제 고르기

다음을 듣고, 남자가 하는 말의 내용으로 가장 적절한 것을 고르시오.

① 과학실 이용 수칙 ② 방과 후 활동 공지
③ 손 씻는 방법 ④ 공장 시설 안내
⑤ 새로운 비누 소개

M Good evening, students. I'm your science teacher, Hojin Park. You should follow these rules in the lab ________ ________ ________. First, always follow my directions. Second, do not smell, taste, or ________ ________ ________ we use. Lastly, ________ ________ ________ ________ and tools after you are done. Wash your hands and arms with soap ________ ________ ________ ________.

11 | 일치하지 않는 내용 고르기

대화를 듣고, Mud Festival에 대한 내용과 일치하지 <u>않는</u> 것을 고르시오.

① 축제는 8월 22일에 열린다.
② 온라인으로 표를 살 수 있다.
③ 표는 10달러이다.
④ 진흙 성 쌓기 체험을 할 수 있다.
⑤ 전통 음악 공연이 있다.

W Dad, can I go to the Mud Festival with my friends? It's held on August 22nd.
M Okay. Don't you need a ticket for it?
W Yes. But I can buy one online.
M ________ ________ ________ ________ ________? Is it expensive?
W No. It's only 10 dollars.
M Alright. What will you do there?
W I heard we'll be able to ________ ________ ________ ________.
M That sounds fun. Is there ________ ________ ________ ________?
W There will be a traditional music performance too.

12 | 목적 고르기

대화를 듣고, 남자가 전화를 건 목적으로 가장 적절한 것을 고르시오.

① 예약을 하기 위해서
② 가격을 확인하기 위해서
③ 할인을 요청하기 위해서
④ 위치를 물어보기 위해서
⑤ 물건을 주문하기 위해서

적중! Tip You've reached ~.
전화 통화에서 수신자가 전화를 받으면서 전화를 받은 곳이 어딘지 말해줄 때 사용되는 표현으로, reached 다음에는 전화를 받는 측의 이름이 온다.
· You've reached Nari Hotel.
Nari Hotel입니다.

[Telephone rings.]
W You've reached Star Hair Salon.
M Hi. I ________ ________ ________. How much would that cost?
W The price would be 35 dollars in total.
M That's a little more expensive ________ ________ ________.
W We offer a 5% discount for first-time customers. Would you like to ________ ________ ________?
M Hmm... I need to ________ ________ ________.
W Sure. We are open until 9 p.m., so you can call us before then.
M Thanks.

13 | 금액 정보 고르기

대화를 듣고, 여자가 받은 거스름돈으로 가장 적절한 것을 고르시오.

① $ 1 ② $ 2 ③ $ 3 ④ $ 4 ⑤ $ 5

M Hello, welcome to Moon Sandwich. May I ________ ________ ________?
W Yes, please. I'd like ________ ________ ________ and one sparkling water.
M Which meat do you want in your sandwich, ________ ________ ________?
W I'll have beef. How much is it?
M The sandwich is 15 dollars and the drink is 6 dollars, so they are 21 dollars in total.
W Here's 25 dollars.
M ________ ________ ________. Your sandwich and drink will be ________ ________ ________ ________.
W Alright. Thank you.

14 | 관계 고르기

대화를 듣고, 두 사람의 관계로 가장 적절한 것을 고르시오.

① 장난감 가게 직원 — 손님
② 양떼목장 주인 — 관광객
③ 반려견 훈련사 — 보호자
④ 동물용품점 직원 — 손님
⑤ 수의사 — 보호자

M Hi. I need ________ ________ ________ for my dog.
W This section has all our dog food. How big is your dog?
M She's very small. ________ ________ ________ five kilograms.
W Alright. I recommend this one ________ ________ ________.
M Great. I'll take it. I'm also looking for some toys.
W You can find toys ________ ________ ________ ________.
M Thank you for your help.

15 | 부탁·요청한 일 고르기

대화를 듣고, 여자가 남자에게 부탁한 일로 가장 적절한 것을 고르시오.

① 숙소 예약하기 ② 사진 보내주기
③ 쿠폰 번호 알려주기 ④ 카메라 수리하기
⑤ 필름 구매하기

W Woosik, _________ _________ _________ _________ to San Francisco?
M I had a great time.
W _________ _________ _________ _________ there?
M I visited the Golden Gate Bridge, and I _________ _________ _________.
W Can I see them?
M Sure. Here's the album.
W Oh, wow. Could you _________ _________ _________ _________?
M Of course. What are you going to do with it?
W I want to set this as my phone's wall paper.

16 | 이유 고르기

대화를 듣고, 여자가 콘서트에 가지 못하는 이유로 가장 적절한 것을 고르시오.

① 표가 매진되어서
② 숙제를 해야 해서
③ 교통편이 좋지 않아서
④ 수업이 있어서
⑤ 동아리 모임이 있어서

적중! Tip Can**'t y**ou
[캔트 유]보다는 [캔츄]로 들린다. [t]로 끝나는 단어 뒤에 y-로 시작하는 단어가 이어지면 두 소리가 연결되어 [츄]로 발음되기 때문이다.

M Ashley, didn't you say that you're going to a concert today?
W Yeah. But _________ _________ _________, and now I can't go.
M What happened?
W I have to _________ _________ _________ _________ this afternoon.
M Can't you miss it?
W No, I can't. I'm the president of the club, and we have to _________ _________ _________ today.
M Then, can I go to the concert instead? The tickets are sold out now.
W Sure. I'll give you the ticket.

17 | 그림 상황에 적절한 대화 고르기

다음 그림의 상황에 가장 적절한 대화를 고르시오.

BUS

① ② ③ ④ ⑤

① **M** Did you get my text message?
W No. My phone _________ _________ _________ _________.
② **M** Are we on the right street?
W Yes. We just need to turn right here.
③ **M** Why are you so sad, Anna?
W I _________ _________ _________ _________ on my math test.
④ **M** Oh, no. We just _________ _________ _________.
W It's okay. I'll call a taxi for us.
⑤ **M** Do you need anything from the convenience store?
W I would love _________ _________ _________ _________, please.

18 | 언급하지 않은 내용 고르기

다음을 듣고, 여자가 San Marino City Tour에 대해 언급하지 않은 것을 고르시오.

① 가이드 이름 ② 시작 시간
③ 교통편 ④ 투어 비용
⑤ 방문 예정지

적중! Tip spots
[스팟츠]보다는 [스빳츠]로 들린다. [s] 뒤에 [p] 발음이 오면 된소리로 발음되기 때문이다.

W Good morning, I'm Molly Ashwood. I'll be your guide to a full-day bus trip on the San Marino City Tour. We'll be leaving in five minutes, at 8:30. Our tour ________ ________ ________ ________ to the San Marino City Museum. Lunch will be provided at 12:30 at ________ ________ ________ ________ the Marino Beach Park. Then, we'll travel to popular spots in the city. Please ________ ________ ________ ________ during the trip.

19 | 적절한 응답 고르기

대화를 듣고, 여자의 마지막 말에 이어질 남자의 말로 가장 적절한 것을 고르시오.

Man: ________________

① Chanwoo is going with me.
② Yes. I start tomorrow.
③ I visited with my teacher.
④ The patients need some help.
⑤ It's a children's hospital.

M Can I ________ ________ ________ ________, Mom?
W Sure, Dongwon. When will you volunteer there?
M I'll ________ ________ ________. I start this weekend.
W That sounds good. Do you ________ ________ ________ ________ ________ to the hospital?
M No, thank you. I can take the bus with my friend.
W Oh, okay. Who will volunteer with you?

20 | 적절한 응답 고르기

대화를 듣고, 여자의 마지막 말에 이어질 남자의 말로 가장 적절한 것을 고르시오.

Man: ________________

① I'm not feeling so good.
② Look over your work.
③ I can't pay attention.
④ The deadline has passed.
⑤ Is Wednesday okay?

적중! Tip Do you have a minute?
상대방에게 간단한 대화를 요청할 때 사용되는 표현으로 '잠시 시간 있으세요?'라는 의미이다.

M Hi, Ms. Kimmel. Do you have a minute? I ________ ________ ________ about the English homework.
W ________ ________ ________ the homework due next Monday?
M Yes. ________ ________ ________ for a couple days, so I need more time to work on it.
W That's fine. When can you ________ ________ ________?

1 다음을 듣고, 토요일 저녁의 날씨로 가장 적절한 것을 고르시오.

①　②　③　④　⑤

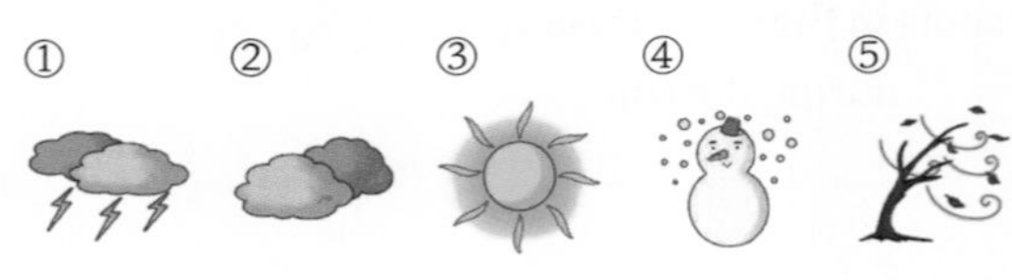

2 대화를 듣고, 여자가 구입할 자전거로 가장 적절한 것을 고르시오.

①　②　③　④　⑤

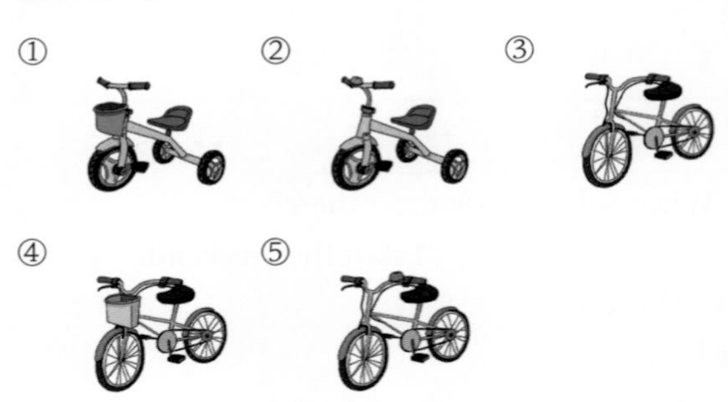

3 대화를 듣고, 남자의 마지막 말의 의도로 가장 적절한 것을 고르시오.

① 충고　② 비난　③ 사과　④ 칭찬　⑤ 용서

4 대화를 듣고, 남자가 어제 한 일로 가장 적절한 것을 고르시오.

① 서핑하기　② 시험 보기　③ 공부하기
④ 게임 하기　⑤ 청소하기

5 대화를 듣고, 두 사람이 대화하는 장소로 가장 적절한 곳을 고르시오.

① 공연장　② 녹음실　③ 슈퍼마켓
④ 제과점　⑤ 수영장

6 대화를 듣고, 그림에 관한 정보로 일치하지 않는 것을 고르시오.

① 1930년대에 그려졌다.
② 파블로 피카소가 그렸다.
③ 제목은 <게르니카>이다.
④ 평화를 상징하고 있다.
⑤ 어두운색만 사용했다.

7 대화를 듣고, 남자가 살 물건으로 가장 적절한 것을 고르시오.

① 스웨터　② 청바지　③ 벨트
④ 셔츠　⑤ 양말

8 대화를 듣고, 남자가 대화 직후에 할 일로 가장 적절한 것을 고르시오.

① 카드로 결제하기　② 서류 작성하기
③ 광고 찾아보기　④ 재고 확인하기
⑤ 온라인 주문하기

9 대화를 듣고, 두 사람이 예약에 대해 언급하지 않은 것을 고르시오.

① 예약 목적　② 이용 날짜
③ 예약 인원 수　④ 예약 시간
⑤ 특별 요청사항

10 다음을 듣고, 남자가 하는 말의 내용으로 가장 적절한 것을 고르시오.

① 식기세척기 사용법　② 충치 예방 교육
③ 배관 수리 공지　④ 청소용품 안내
⑤ 물 절약 방법

11 대화를 듣고, 놀이공원에 대한 내용과 일치하지 않는 것을 고르시오.

① 서울에 있다.
② 큰 롤러코스터가 3개 있다.
③ 범퍼카가 있다.
④ 오전 9시에 문을 연다.
⑤ 입장료가 14달러이다.

12 대화를 듣고, 여자가 학원에 간 목적으로 가장 적절한 것을 고르시오.

① 바이올린 수업을 신청하기 위해서
② 여동생을 만나기 위해서
③ 강습료를 확인하기 위해서
④ 바이올린 강사로 일하기 위해서
⑤ 연주회를 보기 위해서

13 대화를 듣고, 두 사람이 만날 시각을 고르시오.

① 2:30 p.m. ② 3:00 p.m. ③ 3:30 p.m.
④ 4:00 p.m. ⑤ 4:30 p.m.

14 대화를 듣고, 두 사람의 관계로 가장 적절한 것을 고르시오.

① 정원사 — 고객 ② 스튜어디스 — 여행객
③ 치과 의사 — 환자 ④ 경찰관 — 시민
⑤ 항공사 직원 — 승객

15 대화를 듣고, 여자가 남자에게 부탁한 일로 가장 적절한 것을 고르시오.

① 영상 올리기 ② 카메라 찾기
③ 자막 번역하기 ④ 컴퓨터 수리하기
⑤ 영상 촬영하기

16 대화를 듣고, 남자가 축구 동아리를 그만두는 이유로 가장 적절한 것을 고르시오.

① 친구와 싸워서
② 허리를 다쳐서
③ 공부에 집중하려고
④ 다른 동아리에 가입하려고
⑤ 전학을 갈 예정이라서

17 다음 그림의 상황에 가장 적절한 대화를 고르시오.

① ② ③ ④ ⑤

18 다음을 듣고, 여자가 연극에 대해 언급하지 않은 것을 고르시오.

① 장소 ② 제목 ③ 시작 날짜
④ 공연 시간 ⑤ 예매 방법

[19-20] 대화를 듣고, 남자의 마지막 말에 이어질 여자의 말로 가장 적절한 것을 고르시오.

19 **Woman:** ______________________

① Basses and boy sopranos.
② This song is beautiful.
③ You should apply for the audition.
④ A new director was chosen.
⑤ You practiced a lot.

20 **Woman:** ______________________

① That's what friends are for.
② Please forgive me.
③ That's not true.
④ They spoke about it earlier.
⑤ She misunderstood me.

24회 Dictation

Dictation 음성 바로 듣기 ▶

24회 중학영어듣기 고난도 모의고사 Dictation 음성을 들으며 빈칸에 알맞은 단어를 채우시오.

1 | 날씨 고르기

다음을 듣고, 토요일 저녁의 날씨로 가장 적절한 것을 고르시오.

① ② ③ ④ ⑤

W Good evening. This is the Friday night weather report. We're getting ________ ________ ________ right now. The rain will continue all night, and it'll start pouring in the morning. ________ ________ ________ tomorrow evening, so stay indoors and pay attention to the news alerts. You won't be seeing clear skies during the weekend, and it will likely be ________ ________ ________.

2 | 알맞은 그림 고르기

대화를 듣고, 여자가 구입할 자전거로 가장 적절한 것을 고르시오.

① ② ③ ④ ⑤

M Honey, what are we getting our son for Christmas?

W I was thinking about ________ ________ ________ ________.

M What's wrong with the one he has?

W It ________ ________ ________. He is too old for that.

M Right. The old bike has a basket ________ ________ ________. Will he need one for the new one too?

W I don't think he will need it. But we should ________ ________ ________ on the handle.

M That's a good idea. Let's order it online.

3 | 의도 고르기

대화를 듣고, 남자의 마지막 말의 의도로 가장 적절한 것을 고르시오.

① 충고 ② 비난 ③ 사과 ④ 칭찬 ⑤ 용서

> 적중! Tip Excuse me?
>
> 상대방의 말이 터무니없어서 되물을 때 사용되는 표현이다. 상대방의 말을 잘 못 들어서 다시 말해달라고 할 때도 사용된다.

[Cellphone rings.]

M Hey, Kate. Where are you?

W I'm almost there!

M How long will it take? We'll be ________ ________ ________ ________.

W About 30 minutes?

M Excuse me?

W I'm so sorry, Jack. I had a lot to ________ ________ ________.

M You promised ________ ________ ________ ________. And if you are ________ ________ ________, why is it so quiet?

W Uh... I haven't left my apartment yet.

M Oh, Kate... You are late every time!

4 | 한 일 고르기

대화를 듣고, 남자가 어제 한 일로 가장 적절한 것을 고르시오.

① 서핑하기 ② 시험 보기 ③ 공부하기
④ 게임 하기 ⑤ 청소하기

적중! Tip test today
[테스트 투데이]보다는 [테스투데이]로 들린다. 발음이 같은 자음이 나란히 나오면 앞 단어의 끝 자음이 탈락되기 때문이다.

M Hi, Jiyoon. ________ ________ ________ ________ at the beach yesterday?
W Yeah. The weather was warm and sunny. And the ________ ________ ________ for surfing.
M ________ ________ ________. I wanted to go with you.
W How did you do on your test today?
M Well, I ________ ________ ________.
W Are you expecting a good result?
M I missed going surfing to ________ ________ ________ ________, so I hope I get a perfect score.

5 | 장소 고르기

대화를 듣고, 두 사람이 대화하는 장소로 가장 적절한 곳을 고르시오.

① 공연장 ② 녹음실 ③ 슈퍼마켓
④ 제과점 ⑤ 수영장

W Can we ________ ________ ________? I need some water.
M Of course. We'll record again in 10 minutes.
W How did ________ ________ ________? Was the song okay?
M You sounded good, but you should ________ ________ ________.
W So you think it was too fast?
M It was a little fast. But overall, the song sounds great.

6 | 일치하지 않는 내용 고르기

대화를 듣고, 그림에 관한 정보로 일치하지 않는 것을 고르시오.

① 1930년대에 그려졌다.
② 파블로 피카소가 그렸다.
③ 제목은 <게르니카>이다.
④ 평화를 상징하고 있다.
⑤ 어두운색만 사용했다.

M That's a wonderful painting, Vicky.
W I know, right?
M The people in the painting ________ ________ ________.
W Yeah. This is my favorite painting from the 1930s.
M ________ ________ ________ ________?
W Pablo Picasso painted it.
M I see. Do you know the name of the painting?
W It's *Guernica*. Picasso painted it to show the world ________ ________ ________ ________.
M Oh, that's why he only used dark colors.
W That's right.

7 | 특정 정보 고르기

대화를 듣고, 남자가 살 물건으로 가장 적절한 것을 고르시오.

① 스웨터 ② 청바지 ③ 벨트
④ 셔츠 ⑤ 양말

W Did you find any clothes that you liked?
M I think so. I tried on a few things.
W Do you want to ________ ________ ________ ________? I loved the color.
M It was nice, but it was too fancy.
W You're so picky!
M Maybe. But I ________ ________ ________ I want to get. A gray one and a blue one.
W Are you going to get them?
M Yes. Did you buy something?
W I just ________ ________ ________ ________.

8 | 할 일 고르기

대화를 듣고, 남자가 대화 직후에 할 일로 가장 적절한 것을 고르시오.

① 카드로 결제하기 ② 서류 작성하기
③ 광고 찾아보기 ④ 재고 확인하기
⑤ 온라인 주문하기

적중! Tip **w**rist
[뤼스트]로 발음된다. -r 앞에 오면서 단어의 맨 처음에 쓰인 [w]는 묵음이다.
· **w**rong [뤙] · **w**rap [랩]

W May I help you, sir?
M Yes. I want to buy the new T Watch 3. It looked so cool ________ ________ ________ ________.
W We have them over here.
M There are ________ ________ ________.
W You can also change the watch straps easily.
M Do you have ________ ________ ________? This one seems a bit small for my wrist.
W You can only order them now. We ________ ________ ________ ________ in stock.
M Alright. How do I order it?
W Please ________ ________ ________ with your information.

9 | 언급하지 않은 내용 고르기

대화를 듣고, 두 사람이 예약에 대해 언급하지 않은 것을 고르시오.

① 예약 목적 ② 이용 날짜
③ 예약 인원 수 ④ 예약 시간
⑤ 특별 요청사항

[Telephone rings.]
W Hello. Beverly Grill.
M Hi, I'd like to ________ ________ ________ at your restaurant. It's for my son's birthday party.
W On what date?
M His birthday is November 3rd. Do you have ________ ________ ________ ________?
W We do. How many guests will be coming?
M There will be 20 people.
W Okay. Anything else?
M And can I make a special request? Can you serve ________ ________ ________ ________ for dessert?
W Sure. We can do that. I'll just need your name and phone number.

10 | 주제 고르기

다음을 듣고, 남자가 하는 말의 내용으로 가장 적절한 것을 고르시오.

① 식기세척기 사용법 ② 충치 예방 교육
③ 배관 수리 공지 ④ 청소용품 안내
⑤ 물 절약 방법

적중! Tip liter
[리터]로 익숙한 외래어지만 실제로는 [리럴]로 발음된다.

M Hello, everyone. Today, let's talk about __________ __________ __________ __________ at home. First, turn the water off when you brush your teeth. You don't need to run the water while you are brushing your teeth. Second, __________ __________ __________. You can save 12 liters of water by spending __________ __________ __________ in the shower. Lastly, when you wash the dishes, fill up the sink with water first and do the dishes in it.

11 | 일치하지 않는 내용 고르기

대화를 듣고, 놀이공원에 대한 내용과 일치하지 않는 것을 고르시오.

① 서울에 있다.
② 큰 롤러코스터가 3개 있다.
③ 범퍼카가 있다.
④ 오전 9시에 문을 연다.
⑤ 입장료가 14달러이다.

W Hey, Sam. What are you doing this weekend?
M I'm going __________ __________ __________ __________ in Seoul on Saturday.
W That sounds great! What will you do there?
M There are three big roller coasters and bumper cars. I'll __________ __________ __________ __________.
W It must be a big park. Will it be crowded?
M __________ __________ __________, but I am going early. It opens at 9.
W That's a good idea. How much is __________ __________ __________?
M It's 40 dollars.

12 | 목적 고르기

대화를 듣고, 여자가 학원에 간 목적으로 가장 적절한 것을 고르시오.

① 바이올린 수업을 신청하기 위해서
② 여동생을 만나기 위해서
③ 강습료를 확인하기 위해서
④ 바이올린 강사로 일하기 위해서
⑤ 연주회를 보기 위해서

W Brian, what are you doing here?
M Oh, hi Tina. I __________ __________ __________ my violin lesson. Are you signing up for a lesson at this academy?
W Actually, I'm __________ __________ __________ my sister. We are going shopping together after her lesson.
M Your sister goes here? She might be in the same class.
W She's in __________ __________ __________. She just started last month. Oh, there she is.
M Well, it was nice to see you!

13 | 시간 정보 고르기

대화를 듣고, 두 사람이 만날 시각을 고르시오.

① 2:30 p.m. ② 3:00 p.m. ③ 3:30 p.m.
④ 4:00 p.m. ⑤ 4:30 p.m.

W Jerry, are you going to the library today? It's 2 o'clock now.
M Yes, Mom. __________ __________ __________ __________ Jason at 2:30.
W You should hurry then. He doesn't like to wait.
M I know. Can you __________ __________ __________ __________?
W Well, how long will you be there?
M We just need to review for a quiz. I'll __________ __________ __________ in an hour.
W Okay. I'll come get you.

14 | 관계 고르기

대화를 듣고, 두 사람의 관계로 가장 적절한 것을 고르시오.

① 정원사 — 고객 ② 스튜어디스 — 여행객
③ 치과 의사 — 환자 ④ 경찰관 — 시민
⑤ 항공사 직원 — 승객

적중! Tip Can I help you

[캔 아이 헬프 유]보다는 [캐나이 헬퓨]로 들린다. 앞에 나온 단어의 끝 자음과 뒤에 나온 단어의 첫 모음이 연음되기 때문이다.

· have a [해버] · one of [워너브]

M Can I help you?
W I'd like to buy one ticket ________ ________ ________ ________ ________.
M When are you flying out?
W On September 1st, and I'll return on September 13th.
M Would you like economy or business class?
W Economy. Oh, can I ________ ________ ________?
M Yes. An extra fee ________ ________ ________ for more than two bags.
W Alright.
M Let me check ________ ________ ________.

15 | 부탁·요청한 일 고르기

대화를 듣고, 여자가 남자에게 부탁한 일로 가장 적절한 것을 고르시오.

① 영상 올리기 ② 카메라 찾기
③ 자막 번역하기 ④ 컴퓨터 수리하기
⑤ 영상 촬영하기

적중! Tip uploaded video

[업로디드 비디오]보다는 [업로리드 비리오]로 들린다. [d]가 모음 사이에서 발음될 때는 약화되어 [r]에 가깝게 발음되기 때문이다.

M Irene, is this the video that you shot yesterday?
W Yeah. I still ________ ________ ________ ________.
M Can I help you with anything?
W You know ________ ________ ________ ________ ________, right?
M Sure. I can do that.
W Will you ________ ________ ________ ________ on the blog?
M Okay. *[Pause]* I got it. I uploaded video 33.
W Oh, no! I'm ________ ________ ________ that one yet!

16 | 이유 고르기

대화를 듣고, 남자가 축구 동아리를 그만두는 이유로 가장 적절한 것을 고르시오.

① 친구와 싸워서
② 허리를 다쳐서
③ 공부에 집중하려고
④ 다른 동아리에 가입하려고
⑤ 전학을 갈 예정이라서

W I heard you are ________ ________ ________ ________, Jared.
M Yeah. Tomorrow is my last day on the team.
W Is it because you ________ ________ ________ ________, Mason?
M No. That's not a problem anymore. We're good friends again.
W Then, why are you quitting the team?
M I decided to join ________ ________ ________ this year.
W Really? Why can't you do both of them?
M Well, I want to ________ ________ ________ ________.

17 | 그림 상황에 적절한 대화 고르기

다음 그림의 상황에 가장 적절한 대화를 고르시오.

① ② ③ ④ ⑤

① M Can you ______ ______ ______?
W There's a great one on Main Street.
② M Excuse me. Are these your glasses?
W Oh, thank you. ______ ______ ______ ______ ______ at our table.
③ M Should we clean the house today?
W Yes. Let's take the dog ______ ______ ______ first.
④ M The neighbors invited us over for dinner tomorrow.
W That's nice. We should ______ ______ ______.
⑤ M Can you tell me where the swimming pool is?
W It's on the roof of the hotel.

18 | 언급하지 않은 내용 고르기

다음을 듣고, 여자가 연극에 대해 언급하지 않은 것을 고르시오.

① 장소 ② 제목 ③ 시작 날짜
④ 공연 시간 ⑤ 예매 방법

W Welcome to Pasadena Art Theater. I'd like to tell you about ______ ______ ______, *The Family Tree*. Some great actors will ______ ______ ______ ______, and it will be held in the Grand Hall. Shows will begin on Friday, March 29th. Tickets will ______ ______ ______ next week. You can get the ticket ______ ______ ______. We would love to see you there!

19 | 적절한 응답 고르기

대화를 듣고, 남자의 마지막 말에 이어질 여자의 말로 가장 적절한 것을 고르시오.

Woman: ______________________

① Basses and boy sopranos.
② This song is beautiful.
③ You should apply for the audition.
④ A new director was chosen.
⑤ You practiced a lot.

W Brian, you look very sad. What's the problem?
M I didn't ______ ______ ______ in the school musical.
W Cheer up! ______ ______ ______ ______ the next one.
M Yes. But I have to wait a while for the next musical.
W Well, you can audition for the school choir instead.
M ______ ______ ______ ______ does the choir need?

20 | 적절한 응답 고르기

대화를 듣고, 남자의 마지막 말에 이어질 여자의 말로 가장 적절한 것을 고르시오.

Woman: ______________________

① That's what friends are for.
② Please forgive me.
③ That's not true.
④ They spoke about it earlier.
⑤ She misunderstood me.

W Michael, you look upset. Are you okay?
M Not really. I ______ ______ ______ ______ with Chris.
W What happened ______ ______ ______?
M I made a joke, and it hurt his feelings. But I didn't mean ______ ______ ______.
W Well, in my opinion, ______ ______ ______ to him.
M You're right. Thanks for the advice.

MEMO

영어듣기 만점을 위한 **완벽한 실전 대비서**

해커스 중학영어듣기 모의고사 24회

초판 2쇄 발행 2023년 1월 2일

초판 1쇄 발행 2022년 9월 1일

지은이	해커스 어학연구소
펴낸곳	㈜해커스 어학연구소
펴낸이	해커스 어학연구소 출판팀
주소	서울특별시 서초구 강남대로61길 23 ㈜해커스 어학연구소
고객센터	02-537-5000
교재 관련 문의	publishing@hackers.com 해커스북 사이트(HackersBook.com) 고객센터 Q&A 게시판
동영상강의	star.Hackers.com
ISBN	978-89-6542-490-1 (53740)
Serial Number	01-02-01

영어듣기 만점을 위한 **완벽한 실전 대비서**

해커스 중학영어듣기 모의고사 24회

LEVEL 2

정답 및 해설

영어듣기 만점을 위한 **완벽한 실전 대비서**

해커스 중학영어듣기 모의고사 24회

정답 및 해설

해커스 어학연구소

01회 실전 모의고사

| 문제 pp.26-27

1	①	2	③	3	④	4	④	5	③	6	④	7	⑤	8	④	9	③	10	②
11	③	12	②	13	②	14	②	15	④	16	①	17	①	18	②	19	①	20	②

1 날씨 고르기

정답 ①

W I went on a backpacking trip to Hawaii last February. I thought it was always sunny and warm there, so I brought only light clothing. However, I was surprised because it was rainy throughout my trip. I got caught in rain showers several times, and I felt very cold.

여 저는 지난 2월에 하와이로 배낭여행을 갔습니다. 그곳은 항상 화창하고 따뜻할 것으로 생각해서, 저는 가벼운 옷만 가져갔습니다. 하지만 여행 내내 비가 와서 놀랐습니다. 저는 소나기를 여러 번 만났고, 매우 추웠습니다.

해설 | 여자가 하와이 여행 내내 비가 왔다고 했으므로 정답은 ①이다.

어휘 | backpacking trip 배낭여행 clothing [klóuðiŋ] 명 옷 throughout [θru:áut] 전 ~ 내내; 도처에 rain shower 소나기

2 알맞은 그림 고르기

정답 ③

W Welcome to Happy Flowers. May I help you?
M Yes, please. I'd like to buy flowers for my sister.
W What about these tulips?
M Well, my sister prefers roses and sunflowers.
W Okay. Would you like to put them in a basket?
M Hmm... No. My sister would want to put them in a vase later.
W Then, what about wrapping them in paper?
M That'll be great.

여 Happy Flowers에 오신 걸 환영합니다. 무엇을 도와드릴까요?
남 네, 부탁드려요. 제 여동생에게 꽃을 사주고 싶어요.
여 이 튤립들은 어떠신가요?
남 글쎄요, 제 여동생은 장미와 해바라기를 선호해요.
여 알겠습니다. 바구니에 담아드릴까요?
남 흠... 아니요. 제 여동생은 나중에 그걸 꽃병에 담고 싶어 할 거예요.
여 그러면, 종이에 싸드리는 건 어떠세요?
남 그게 좋겠어요.

해설 | 남자는 여동생이 장미와 해바라기를 선호한다고 했고, 여자가 종이에 꽃을 싸주는 것이 어떨지 묻자 그게 좋겠다고 했으므로 정답은 ③이다.

어휘 | sunflower [sʌ́nflauər] 명 해바라기 vase [veis] 명 꽃병 wrap [ræp] 동 싸다, 포장하다

3 심정 고르기

정답 ④

W Hello. Take a seat, please. What is bothering you?
M I have a toothache.
W Alright. Can you open your mouth?
M One moment, please. My heart is beating too fast. I'm so afraid now.
W What's the problem?
M Sorry, I always get nervous at the dentist.
W It's okay. Take a minute to relax. I'm just going to do a simple checkup.

여 안녕하세요. 자리에 앉아주세요. 어디가 불편하신가요?
남 치통이 있어요.
여 그러시군요. 입을 벌려 보시겠어요?
남 잠시만요. 제 심장이 너무 빨리 뛰어요. 지금 너무 무서워요.
여 무슨 문제가 있으신가요?
남 죄송해요, 저는 치과에서 항상 긴장돼요.
여 괜찮아요. 잠시 긴장을 풀어보세요. 전 그냥 간단한 검사만 할 거예요.

해설 | 남자가 지금 너무 무섭다고 하며 자신은 치과에서 항상 긴장된다고 했으므로 정답은 ④ 'scared'이다.

선택지 해석

① 수줍은 ② 지루한 ③ 신난 ④ 무서운 ⑤ 자랑스러운

어휘 | toothache [tú:θeik] 명 치통 beat [bi:t] 동 뛰다, 고동치다; 이기다 nervous [nə́:rvəs] 형 긴장되는, 불안한 relax [rilǽks] 동 (긴장을) 풀다 checkup [tʃékʌp] 명 검사, 건강 진단

4 한 일 고르기

정답 ④

M Hi, Sunjoo. Did you enjoy your weekend?
W Yes. I visited the Philippines.
M Really? How long did you spend there?
W Three days. I went scuba diving on Friday. It was fantastic.
M That's cool! What else did you do?
W I visited a night market the next day and then flew back to Korea on Sunday.

남 안녕, 선주야. 주말 잘 보냈니?
여 응. 나는 필리핀에 다녀왔어.
남 정말? 거기서 얼마나 있었어?
여 3일. 금요일에는 스쿠버 다이빙을 하러갔어. 환상적이었어.
남 그거 멋지다! 그밖에는 뭘 했니?
여 그다음 날은 야시장을 방문했고, 일요일에는 비행기를 타고 한국으로 돌아왔어.

해설 | 여자가 금요일에는 스쿠버 다이빙을 갔다고 했으므로 정답은 ④ '스쿠버 다이빙'이다.

어휘 | weekend [wíːkend] 명 주말 fantastic [fæntǽstik] 형 환상적인

5 장소 고르기

정답 ③

W Hello. How much are these strawberries?
M They're only five dollars for a box.
W Wow. That's so cheap.
M Our store is having a sale this week.
W Is any other fruit on sale?
M The bananas and blueberries are 50% off.
W Nice! I'll get some of each.
M And most of the meat is on sale right now too.

여 안녕하세요. 이 딸기들은 얼마인가요?
남 그것들은 한 상자에 5달러밖에 안 해요.
여 우와. 엄청나게 싸네요.
남 저희 가게는 이번 주에 할인을 하고 있어요.
여 다른 과일도 할인 중인가요?
남 바나나와 블루베리는 50% 할인 중이에요.
여 좋네요! 각각 조금씩 주세요.
남 그리고 고기 대부분도 지금 할인 중이에요.

해설 | 딸기를 비롯한 과일이 할인 중이라고 언급했고, 고기 대부분도 할인 중이라고 말하는 것으로 보아 정답은 ③ '식료품점'이다.

어휘 | cheap [tʃiːp] 형 싼, 저렴한 on sale 할인 중인

6 의도 고르기

정답 ④

W Tim, do you have any plans this Friday?
M Nothing special. Why?
W I was invited to a pizza-tasting event. There will be various types of pizza to try. Do you want to come?
M Well, I'm on a diet. I'd better not go.
W Come on. You won't gain weight if you don't eat too much.
M You're right. I'll go with you.

여 Tim, 이번 금요일에 무슨 계획 있니?
남 특별한 건 없어. 왜?
여 내가 피자 시식 행사에 초대받았거든. 다양한 종류의 피자들을 먹어볼 수 있을 거야. 같이 갈래?
남 음, 나는 다이어트 중이야. 가지 않는 게 좋겠어.
여 말도 안 돼. 너무 많이 먹지만 않으면 체중이 늘지 않을 거야.
남 네 말이 맞아. 같이 갈게.

해설 | 여자가 너무 많이 먹지만 않으면 체중이 늘지 않을 것이라고 설득하자 남자가 여자의 말이 맞는다며 동의했으므로 정답은 ④ '동의'이다.

어휘 | various [vɛ́riəs] 형 다양한 be on a diet 다이어트 중이다 gain weight 체중이 늘다

7 특정 정보 고르기

정답 ⑤

M Hi, Angela. You look so happy.
W Yeah. I have some good news.
M What is it?
W My parents are finally allowing me to have a pet.
M That's good. Which animal will you adopt, a cat or a dog?
W Neither of them. I'm going to get a parrot.
M Oh, I didn't know you liked parrots.
W They are so smart and cute. I really like them.

남 안녕, Angela. 너 매우 행복해 보인다.
여 응. 나 좋은 소식이 있어.
남 뭔데?
여 우리 부모님이 드디어 내가 반려동물을 키우는 걸 허락해 주셨어.
남 잘됐다. 고양이와 개 중 어떤 동물을 입양할 거니?
여 둘 다 아냐. 나는 앵무새를 데려올 거야.
남 오, 나는 네가 앵무새를 좋아하는지 몰랐어.
여 그들은 매우 똑똑하고 귀여워. 난 앵무새를 정말 좋아해.

해설 | 여자가 앵무새를 데려올 것이라고 했으므로 정답은 ⑤ 'parrot'이다.

선택지 해석

① 고양이 ② 개 ③ 거북 ④ 햄스터 ⑤ 앵무새

어휘 | finally [fáinəli] 부 드디어, 마침내 allow [əláu] 동 허락하다 adopt [ədɑ́pt] 동 입양하다

8 할 일 고르기

정답 ④

M Mom, I smell something burning in the kitchen.
W Oh, no! I forgot to turn off the gas stove.
M Let me check. *[Pause]* The pot was burned.
W I guess I'll need to cook something else.
M Can I help you?
W Sure. But we need to get rid of the smell of the burned food first.
M Alright. I'll open the windows to let some fresh air in.

남 엄마, 주방에서 무언가 타는 냄새가 나요.
여 오, 안돼! 가스레인지 끄는 것을 잊어버렸어.
남 확인해 볼게요. *[잠시 멈춤]* 냄비가 탔어요.
여 다른 걸 요리해야 할 것 같구나.
남 도와드릴까요?
여 물론이지. 그렇지만 먼저 탄 음식 냄새를 없애야 해.
남 네. 신선한 공기가 들어오게 제가 창문을 열게요.

해설 | 여자가 먼저 탄 음식 냄새부터 없애야 한다고 하자, 남자가 신선한 공기가 들어오게 창문을 열겠다고 했으므로 정답은 ④ '환기하기'이다.

어휘 | smell [smel] 동 냄새가 나다 명 냄새 burn [bəːrn] 동 타다, 태우다 turn off 끄다 pot [pɑt] 명 냄비 get rid of ~을 없애다

9 언급하지 않은 내용 고르기

정답 ③

W Welcome to the Winter Sports Arena. We have several ice rinks for skating, ice hockey, and curling. The general public can use them for up to three hours a day. Only professional athletes can rent our ice rinks for a full day or longer. If you are interested in renting one of our rinks, please send the application form by e-mail. Thank you. Have a nice day.

여 동계 스포츠 경기장에 오신 것을 환영합니다. 저희는 스케이트, 아이스하키, 그리고 컬링을 위한 여러 개의 빙상 경기장을 가지고 있습니다. 일반 대중은 하루에 세 시간까지 이용하실 수 있습니다. 프로 선수만이 저희 경기장을 하루 종일 또는 더 길게 대관할 수 있습니다. 저희 경기장 중 하나를 빌리고 싶으시다면, 이메일로 신청서를 보내주십시오. 감사합니다. 좋은 하루 되십시오.

해설 | ① 시설 종류(스케이트, 아이스하키, 컬링용 빙상 경기장), ② 사용 시간(하루에 3시간까지), ④ 대관 자격(프로 선수), ⑤ 대관 신청 방법(이메일로 신청서 보내기)에 대해 언급했으므로 정답은 ③ '사용료'이다.

어휘 | general public 일반 대중 up to ~까지 professional athlete 프로 선수 rent [rent] 동 대관하다, 빌리다 application form 신청서, 지원서

10 주제 고르기

정답 ②

M Hello, visitors. Please follow these rules so that everyone can enjoy the ballet. First, please get to your seat 10 minutes before the ballet begins. Second, you should not talk loudly or move around during the show. Lastly, make sure to turn off or silence your phone before the performance begins. Thank you.

남 안녕하십니까, 관람객 여러분. 모든 분이 발레를 즐길 수 있도록 이 규칙들을 지켜 주십시오. 먼저, 발레가 시작되기 10분 전에는 자리에 앉아 주십시오. 두 번째로, 공연 중에는 크게 말하거나 돌아다니시면 안 됩니다. 마지막으로, 공연 시작 전에 휴대폰은 끄거나 무음으로 해주십시오. 감사합니다.

해설 | 남자가 관람객 모두가 발레를 즐기기 위해 지켜야 하는 규칙들을 말하고 있으므로 정답은 ② '공연장 관람 예절'이다.

어휘 | visitor [vízitər] 명 관람객, 방문객 rule [ruːl] 명 규칙 lastly [lǽstli] 부 마지막으로 silence [sáiləns] 동 무음으로 하다, 조용히 시키다

11 일치하지 않는 내용 고르기

정답 ③

W Jinsu, do you have any plans for next weekend?
M No, I don't. Why?
W My school choir will have a charity concert on Saturday. Can you come and give us a hand?
M Where will it be held?
W At Green Hospital. We're going to sing the *Arirang* medley.
M That sounds great! I'd love to help. What can I do for you?
W I want you to hand out the pamphlets before the concert begins.
M My pleasure.

여 진수야, 너 다음 주말에 무슨 계획 있니?
남 아니, 없어. 왜?
여 우리 학교 합창단이 토요일에 자선 공연을 할 거야. 와서 우리를 도와줄 수 있어?
남 어디서 열릴 예정인데?
여 그린 병원에서. 우리는 <아리랑> 메들리를 부를 거야.
남 그거 멋지다! 돕고 싶어. 내가 뭘 하면 될까?
여 공연이 시작되기 전에 네가 팸플릿을 나눠줬으면 좋겠어.
남 도울 수 있어 기뻐.

해설 | 여자가 그린 병원에서 학교 합창단이 자선 공연을 할 것이라고 했으므로 정답은 ③ '공연은 양로원에서 열린다.'이다.

어휘 | choir [kwaiər] 명 합창단 charity [tʃǽrəti] 명 자선 give a hand 도와주다 hand out 나눠주다

12 목적 고르기

정답 ②

M Hey, Miranda. Long time no see.
W Hi, Jeff. It's nice to see you again.
M You too. I teach physics at this university. What brings you here?
W I'm here to attend the graduation ceremony.
M Oh, who is graduating this year?
W My little brother. He majored in art history.
M Good for him. Please give him my congratulations.

남 안녕, Miranda. 오랜만이야.
여 안녕, Jeff. 다시 만나서 반가워.
남 동감이야. 난 이 대학교에서 물리학을 가르쳐. 너는 무슨 일로 왔니?
여 나는 졸업식에 참석하려고 왔어.
남 오, 누가 올해 졸업을 하는데?
여 내 남동생. 그는 미술사를 전공했어.
남 잘됐다. 그에게 축하한다고 전해줘.

해설 I 여자가 남동생의 졸업식에 참석하기 위해 왔다고 했으므로 정답은 ② '졸업식에 참석하기 위해서'이다.

어휘 I physics [fíziks] 명 물리학 attend [əténd] 동 참석하다 graduation [grædʒuéiʃən] 명 졸업 (graduate [grǽdʒuət] 동 졸업하다) major [méidʒər] 동 전공하다 art history 미술사

13 금액 정보 고르기

정답 ②

W Excuse me. I'd like to rent a rubber boat for four people.
M How long will you rent it?
W Two hours. How much will it cost?
M It costs 15 dollars per hour.
W Okay. We'll take it.
M If you are local residents, you can get a five-dollar discount.
W Great. We're all locals.
M Then, your total will be 25 dollars.

여 실례합니다. 4인용 고무보트를 빌리고 싶어요.
남 얼마 동안 빌릴 예정이신가요?
여 두 시간이요. 비용은 얼마나 들까요?
남 시간당 15달러입니다.
여 알겠습니다. 빌릴게요.
남 만약 지역 주민이시라면, 5달러 할인을 받으실 수 있습니다.
여 좋네요. 저희 모두 지역민이에요.
남 그러면, 총 25달러 되겠습니다.

해설 I 고무보트를 빌리는 데 시간당 15달러이고, 5달러를 할인받았으므로 정답은 ② '$ 25'이다.

어휘 I rubber [rʌ́bər] 형 고무 cost [kɔːst] 동 비용이 들다 local [lóukəl] 형 지역의 명 지역민 resident [rézədnt] 명 주민, 거주자

14 관계 고르기

정답 ②

W Hi. How can I help you today, sir?
M Hello. I'd like to exchange some money.
W What type of money do you need?
M I want some British pounds, please. I have 500,000 won here.
W Alright. Can I do anything else for you?
M Actually, I also need a new credit card. Mine doesn't work sometimes.
W No problem. I'll get one for you right away.

여 안녕하세요. 오늘은 어떻게 도와드릴까요, 고객님?
남 안녕하세요. 돈을 약간 환전하고 싶어서요.
여 어떤 종류의 화폐가 필요하신가요?
남 영국 파운드화로 부탁드려요. 여기 50만원이 있습니다.
여 알겠습니다. 다른 것도 도와드릴 것이 있을까요?
남 사실, 새 신용카드도 필요해요. 제 것은 가끔 잘 안 돼요.
여 알겠습니다. 바로 한 장 드릴게요.

해설 I 남자가 원화를 파운드화로 환전해주길 요청하고 있는 것으로 보아 정답은 ② '은행원 — 고객'이다.

어휘 I exchange [ikstʃéindʒ] 동 환전하다; 교환하다

15 제안한 일 고르기

정답 ④

W Ian, what are you doing?
M I'm making a webtoon on my tablet PC.
W Wow. That's amazing. Did you do it all on your own?
M No. My friend Joe wrote the main story.
W And you did all the drawing and coloring, right?
M Yes, I did. I want to hear other people's opinions about it though.
W I can take a look and give you mine.
M I'd love that.

여 Ian, 뭐 하고 있니?
남 내 태블릿 PC로 웹툰을 제작하고 있어.
여 우와. 그거 대단하다. 너 혼자서 그걸 다 한 거니?
남 아냐. 내 친구 Joe가 줄거리를 썼어.
여 그리고 네가 스케치와 채색을 다 했고, 그렇지?
남 응, 그랬지. 이것에 대한 다른 사람의 의견을 들어보고 싶어 근데.
여 내가 보고 의견을 줄 수 있어.
남 그럼 좋지.

해설 I 여자가 남자에게 웹툰을 보고 의견을 주겠다고 제안하고 있으므로 정답은 ④ '감상평 말해주기'이다.

어휘 I on one's own ~ 혼자서, 스스로 opinion [əpínjən] 명 의견

16 이유 고르기

정답 ①

M Lisa, it'll take another hour to set up for our school's art festival.
W But I have a piano lesson soon.
M Why don't you call your instructor and tell him you'll be late?
W Okay. *[Pause]* My phone isn't working.
M What happened?
W It ran out of battery. Can I borrow yours?
M Of course. Do you know your instructor's cellphone number?
W It's on the academy's website.

남 Lisa, 우리 학교 미술 축제를 준비하는 데 한 시간 더 걸릴 것 같아.
여 하지만 나 곧 피아노 레슨이 있어.
남 선생님께 전화해서 네가 늦을 거라고 말씀드리는 게 어때?
여 그래. *[잠시 멈춤]* 내 전화기가 작동하지 않아.
남 무슨 일이야?
여 배터리가 나갔어. 네 것을 빌릴 수 있을까?
남 당연하지. 선생님 휴대폰 번호는 아니?
여 학원 홈페이지에 있어.

해설 | 여자가 남자에게 전화기의 배터리가 나갔다고 말했으므로 정답은 ① '휴대폰 배터리가 없어서'이다.

어휘 | another [ənʌ́ðər] 형 더, 또 하나의; 다른 set up 준비하다 instructor [instrʌ́ktər] 명 선생님, 교사 run out of ~가 떨어지다, ~을 다 써버리다

17 그림 상황에 적절한 대화 고르기

정답 ①

① W What would you like to order, sir?
M I'd like a coffee and a piece of cake, please.
② W What are you doing today?
M I'm baking cookies for my class.
③ W I have a sore throat and a headache.
M I will get you a cup of warm water.
④ W Do you see my phone? I can't find it.
M It's here! It was next to the sink.
⑤ W What is that smell? It's so nice.
M It's my new candle.

① 여 무엇을 주문하시겠습니까, 고객님?
남 커피 한 잔과 케이크 한 조각 주세요.
② 여 넌 오늘 뭐 할 거니?
남 우리 반을 위해서 쿠키를 구울 거야.
③ 여 나는 인후통과 두통이 있어.
남 따뜻한 물 한 잔 가져다줄게.
④ 여 내 전화기 보이니? 못 찾겠어.
남 여기 있어! 싱크대 옆에 있었어.
⑤ 여 이 냄새는 뭐야? 너무 좋다.
남 그건 내 새 양초야.

해설 | 여자가 주문을 받고 있고 남자가 커피와 케이크를 주문하는 상황이므로 정답은 ①이다.

어휘 | sore throat 인후통 headache [hédeik] 명 두통 candle [kǽndl] 명 양초

18 언급하지 않은 내용 고르기

정답 ②

W Minsu, did you know the Golden Comic Convention is coming up?
M No. When will it be held?
W It's from March 15th to 20th. Do you want to go together?
M Sure. How much do tickets cost?
W They are 10 dollars each.
M Do you know how to buy them?
W Yes. We can order them from the convention's website.
M Okay. When do you want to go?
W How about March 17th?
M Alright. It should be fun.

여 민수야, 너 Golden Comic Convention이 다가오는 걸 알았니?
남 아니. 언제 열리는데?
여 그건 3월 15일부터 20일까지야. 같이 갈래?
남 물론이지. 표는 얼마야?
여 각각 10달러씩이야.
남 어떻게 사는지 아니?
여 응. 박람회 웹사이트에서 주문하면 돼.
남 그래. 언제 갈래?
여 3월 17일이 어때?
남 좋아. 재미있겠다.

해설 | ① 명칭(Golden Comic Convention), ③ 개최 기간(3월 15일부터 20일), ④ 티켓 가격(10달러), ⑤ 티켓 구매 방법(박람회 웹사이트에서 주문)에 대해 언급했으므로 정답은 ② '개최 장소'이다.

어휘 | convention [kənvénʃən] 명 박람회

19 적절한 응답 고르기

정답 ①

M Excuse me. What is this line for?
W This is the line for the newly released sneakers.
M Oh, really? The line is so long.
W Yes. They are very popular.
M Will the store still have any of the sneakers tomorrow?
W I don't think so. They will probably sell out today.
M I see. How long will I need to wait in line then?
W At least 45 minutes.

남 실례합니다. 이 줄은 무엇을 위한 거죠?
여 이건 새로 출시된 운동화를 위한 줄이에요.
남 오, 정말요? 줄이 정말 기네요.
여 네. 그것들은 매우 인기 있거든요.
남 매장에 내일도 운동화가 남아있을까요?
여 그렇지 않을 것 같아요. 오늘 아마 다 팔릴 거예요.
남 그렇군요. 줄 서서 얼마나 기다려야 할까요 그럼?
여 적어도 45분이요.

해설 | 남자가 줄 서서 얼마나 기다려야 할지 묻고 있으므로 정답은 기다리는 시간을 언급하는 ① 'At least 45 minutes.'이다.

선택지 해석

① 적어도 45분이요. ② 제가 다음 차례예요. ③ 저희는 그 신발을 살 거예요. ④ 거긴 오전 9시에 열어요. ⑤ 전 현금이 약간 필요해요.

어휘 | release [rilíːs] 동 출시하다, 발표하다 sell out 다 팔리다, 매진되다

20 적절한 응답 고르기

정답 ②

M What are you doing, Eunji?
W I'm reviewing my notes for the history test, but I'll take a break soon.
M You're already preparing for the exam. I admire you!
W Are you having trouble studying?
M Yes. I can't focus on the textbook when I read it.
W Well, you listen to music while studying. You should turn it off.
M I've tried that, but it didn't change anything. What else can I do?
W How about studying in a library?

남 뭐 하고 있니, 은지야?
여 역사 시험에 대비해서 필기를 복습하고 있는데, 곧 잠깐 쉴 거야.
남 벌써 시험을 준비하고 있구나. 칭찬해!
여 공부하는 데 어려움을 겪고 있니?
남 응. 난 교과서를 읽을 때 집중을 할 수가 없어.
여 음, 너는 공부하는 동안 음악을 듣잖아. 그걸 꺼야 해.
남 그것도 시도해 봤는데, 바뀐 게 없었어. 다른 걸 뭘 할 수 있을까?
여 도서관에서 공부하는 건 어때?

해설 | 음악을 끄는 것 외에 공부할 때 집중할 수 있는 방법이 뭐가 있을지 묻고 있으므로 정답은 공부 방식에 대해 조언하는 ② 'How about studying in a library?'이다.

선택지 해석

① 우리는 제2차 세계 대전을 공부하고 있어. ② 도서관에서 공부하는 건 어때? ③ 음량을 줄여줘. ④ 그녀는 방금 온라인에 뭔가를 올렸어. ⑤ 나는 숙제를 하지 않았어.

어휘 | review [rivjúː] 동 복습하다 prepare [pripέər] 동 준비하다 admire [ædmáiər] 동 ~을 칭찬하다; 존경하다 focus on ~에 집중하다

02회 실전 모의고사

| 문제 pp.34-35

1	③	2	②	3	④	4	①	5	④	6	③	7	③	8	④	9	④	10	④
11	⑤	12	④	13	②	14	④	15	②	16	③	17	①	18	③	19	②	20	⑤

1 날씨 고르기

정답 ③

M Good morning. Here's the weather report. Tomorrow, Seoul and Daejeon will be cloudy. In Chuncheon, there will be a lot of rain, so try to avoid going outside. And in Changwon, strong wind is expected, so please dress warmly. Thank you for listening.

남 안녕하세요. 일기 예보입니다. 내일 서울과 대전은 흐리겠습니다. 춘천에는 많은 비가 내릴 예정이므로, 야외에 나가는 것을 피하십시오. 그리고 창원에는 강한 바람이 예상되므로, 따뜻하게 입으십시오. 청취해 주셔서 감사합니다.

해설 | 창원에는 강한 바람이 예상된다고 했으므로 정답은 ③이다.

어휘 | avoid [əvɔ́id] 동 피하다 warmly [wɔ́ːrmli] 부 따뜻하게

2 알맞은 그림 고르기

정답 ②

M Hello. How can I help you?
W I'm looking for a mirror.
M Okay. How about these round ones?
W They look nice. I'll take one of them.
M Good. Do you prefer the mirror with the smiley face or the heart?
W The one with the heart, please.
M Great choice!

남 안녕하세요. 어떻게 도와드릴까요?
여 저는 거울을 찾고 있어요.
남 그러시군요. 이 둥근 것들은 어떠신가요?
여 좋아 보여요. 그것 중 하나로 할게요.
남 좋습니다. 스마일이 있는 것과 하트가 있는 거울 중 어떤 것을 더 선호하시나요?
여 하트가 있는 것으로 부탁드려요.
남 좋은 선택이세요!

해설 | 여자가 하트가 있는 둥근 거울로 하겠다고 했으므로 정답은 ②이다.

어휘 | mirror [mírər] 명 거울 prefer [prifə́ːr] 동 선호하다 choice [tʃɔis] 명 선택

3 심정 고르기

정답 ④

[Cellphone rings.]
W Ben, why are you so late?
M I'm sorry. I left my wallet at home, and I had to go back to get it.
W But the movie starts in 15 minutes. Where are you now?
M I just reached the subway station.
W I'm afraid you'll miss the start of the movie.
M I will run to the theater as fast as I can!

[휴대폰이 울린다.]
여 Ben, 너 왜 이렇게 늦어?
남 미안해. 지갑을 집에 놓고 와서, 가지러 돌아가야 했어.
여 그렇지만 영화가 15분 후에 시작해. 지금 어디 있어?
남 지금 막 지하철역에 도착했어.
여 난 네가 영화 도입부를 놓칠 것 같아.
남 내가 할 수 있는 만큼 빠르게 영화관으로 뛰어갈게!

해설 | 여자는 영화가 15분 후에 시작한다며 남자가 영화 도입부를 놓칠 것 같다고 했으므로 정답은 ④ 'worried'이다.

선택지 해석

① 수줍은 ② 무서운 ③ 기쁜 ④ 걱정되는 ⑤ 지루한

어휘 | wallet [wálit] 명 지갑 reach [riːtʃ] 동 도착하다 miss [mis] 동 놓치다

4 한 일 고르기

정답 ①

M Claire, what did you do last weekend?
W I went to a swimming pool. What about you, Connor?
M I knitted a muffler.
W How did you learn to knit?
M My sister taught me to knit. It's her hobby.
W Wow. I want to learn, but I'm not good with my hands.
M Practice makes perfect! I can help you if you want.

남 Claire, 너 지난 주말에 뭐 했니?
여 나는 수영장에 갔어. 넌 뭐 했니, Connor?
남 나는 목도리를 떴어.
여 뜨개질을 어떻게 배웠어?
남 우리 누나가 내게 뜨개질을 가르쳐줬어. 그게 그녀의 취미야.
여 우와. 나도 배우고 싶은데, 나는 손재주가 없어.
남 연습이 완벽을 만든다고! 원한다면 내가 도와줄 수 있어.

해설 | 남자는 목도리를 떴다고 했으므로 정답은 ① '목도리 뜨기'이다.

어휘 | knit [nit] 동 (실로 옷 등을) 뜨다, 뜨개질을 하다 muffler [mʌ́flər] 명 목도리

5 장소 고르기

정답 ④

M Hello. Do you need any help?
W That would be great. I want to buy a book.
M Alright. What kind of book do you want?
W I'm going to be on an airplane for a long time. So, I want an exciting story.
M What about *The Game*? It's a novel about a detective who solves crimes.
W That sounds interesting. I'll buy it.

남 안녕하세요. 도움이 필요하신가요?
여 그러면 좋을 것 같아요. 저는 책을 사고 싶어요.
남 그러시군요. 어떤 종류의 책을 원하시나요?
여 저는 장시간 비행기를 탈 예정이에요. 그래서 저는 신나는 이야기를 원해요.
남 <The Game>은 어떠신가요? 이것은 범죄를 해결하는 탐정에 대한 소설이에요.
여 흥미롭게 들리는데요. 그걸 살게요.

해설 | 여자가 책을 사고 싶다고 했고, 남자가 책을 추천해 주는 것으로 보아 정답은 ④ '서점'이다.

어휘 | detective [ditéktiv] 명 탐정 solve [salv] 동 해결하다 crime [kraim] 명 범죄

6 의도 고르기

정답 ③

W Do you have a minute, Mr. Jones?
M Of course. What can I do for you, Mary?
W I'm a little worried about the essay you asked me to write.
M What's wrong?
W I can't choose a topic.
M I suggested a few in yesterday's class.
W Yes. But none of them are interesting to me.
M You should make a list of possible topics. Then, pick the one that is most appealing.

여 잠시 시간이 있으신가요, Jones 선생님?
남 물론이지. 내가 무엇을 도와줄까, Mary?
여 저는 저에게 쓰라고 하신 에세이에 대해 약간 걱정이 돼요.
남 뭐가 문제니?
여 주제를 못 고르겠어요.
남 어제 수업에서 몇 가지를 제안해줬잖니.
여 네. 그런데 제게는 흥미로운 것이 아무것도 없어요.
남 가능한 주제들의 목록을 만드는 것이 좋겠구나. 그다음에, 가장 끌리는 것 하나를 고르렴.

해설 | 여자가 에세이 주제를 못 고르겠다는 말에 남자가 가능한 주제의 목록을 만들고 가장 끌리는 것 하나를 고르라고 했으므로 정답은 ③ '조언'이다.

어휘 | essay [ései] 명 에세이, 작문 topic [tápik] 명 주제 suggest [səgdʒést] 동 제안하다 possible [pásəbl] 형 가능한 appealing [əpí:liŋ] 형 마음을 끄는, 매력적인

7 한 일 고르기

정답 ③

W Carter, do you know about the Eco Festival?
M No, I don't. What is it?
W It's a festival to encourage people to protect the environment.
M Have you been there?
W Yes. I did a lot of fun things there last year.
M What did you do?
W I learned how to use less plastic. I even made a bamboo toothbrush.
M Wow! That's great.

여 Carter, 너 Eco Festival에 대해 아니?
남 아니, 몰라. 그게 뭔데?
여 그것은 사람들이 환경을 보호하도록 장려하는 축제야.
남 너는 거기 가봤니?
여 응. 나는 작년에 거기서 재미있는 것들을 많이 했어.
남 뭘 했는데?
여 어떻게 하면 플라스틱을 적게 쓰는지 배웠어. 나는 심지어 대나무 칫솔도 만들었어.
남 우와! 굉장하다.

해설 | 여자가 대나무 칫솔을 만들었다고 했으므로 정답은 ③ '대나무 칫솔 만들기'이다.

어휘 | encourage [inkə́:rdʒ] 동 장려하다, 권장하다 protect [prətékt] 동 보호하다 environment [inváiərənmənt] 명 환경 bamboo [bæmbú:] 명 대나무

8 할 일 고르기

정답 ④

M Your brother came in first in the speech contest.
W I know, Dad. He has talked about it all day.
M I'm very proud of him. It is an impressive achievement.
W Why don't we throw a party for him?
M That's what I was thinking. How about going to a bakery to buy a cake now?
W Okay. Can we also get some lemonade? It'll go well with the cake.
M Sure. I'll search for a café online now.

남 네 남동생이 말하기 대회에서 1등을 했단다.
여 알아요, 아빠. 그는 온종일 그것에 대해 이야기했어요.
남 그가 매우 자랑스럽구나. 그건 놀라운 성적이야.
여 그를 위해 파티를 열어주는 것이 어때요?
남 그게 바로 내가 생각하던 거야. 지금 케이크를 사러 제과점에 가는 게 어떠니?
여 그래요. 레모네이드도 좀 사도 돼요? 케이크와 잘 어울릴 거예요.
남 물론이지. 내가 지금 온라인으로 카페를 찾아볼게.

해설 | 여자가 레모네이드도 좀 사도 되는지 묻자 남자가 지금 온라인으로 카페를 찾겠다고 했으므로 정답은 ④ '카페 검색하기'이다.

어휘 | impressive [imprésiv] 형 놀라운; 인상적인 achievement [ətʃí:vmənt] 명 성적, 달성 throw a party 파티를 열다 go well with ~와 잘 어울리다 search [sə:rtʃ] 동 찾다

9 언급하지 않은 내용 고르기

정답 ④

M Hello. We have musical director Jess Hwang on our show today.
W I'm honored to be here.
M Our pleasure. So, tell us about your new musical, *LA to New York*.
W It's about a rock band traveling around the country.
M Who plays the main character?
W Paul Klein. His acting and singing are unbelievable.
M I also heard the news that *LA to New York* was nominated for a musical award. Congratulations!
W Thank you so much.

남 안녕하세요. 오늘은 저희 쇼에 뮤지컬 감독 Jess Hwang을 모셨습니다.
여 여기 나오게 되어 영광입니다.
남 저희가 감사하지요. 그럼, 새로운 뮤지컬 <LA to New York>에 대해 말씀해 주세요.
여 전국을 여행하는 록 밴드에 대한 내용이에요.
남 누가 주인공을 연기하나요?
여 Paul Klein이요. 그의 연기와 노래는 믿을 수 없을 정도로 대단해요.
남 <LA to New York>이 한 뮤지컬 상의 후보로 선정되었다는 소식도 들었어요. 축하드립니다!
여 정말 감사합니다.

해설 | ① 제목(<LA to New York>), ② 내용(전국을 여행하는 록 밴드), ③ 주연 배우(Paul Klein), ⑤ 수상 후보 여부(뮤지컬 상 후보 선정)에 대해 언급했으므로 정답은 ④ '관객 수'이다.

어휘 | honored [ánərd] 형 영광으로 생각하는 main character 주인공 nominate [námənèit] 동 후보에 오르다

10 주제 고르기

정답 ④

W Hello, fellow students. My name is Jimin. As your new student leader, I will make our school cleaner and safer. To do so, I will put trash cans in the hallway and install more security cameras. I will also make new clubs. Thank you for voting for me in the last student election. I promise to do my best.

여 안녕하세요, 학생 여러분. 제 이름은 지민입니다. 여러분의 새 학생회장으로서, 저는 저희 학교를 더 깨끗하고 안전하게 만들겠습니다. 그렇게 하기 위해, 저는 복도에 쓰레기통을 놓고 더 많은 보안 카메라를 설치할 것입니다. 저는 또한 새로운 동아리들을 만들 것입니다. 지난 학생 선거에서 저에게 투표해주셔서 감사합니다. 저는 최선을 다하겠다고 약속드립니다.

해설 | 여자가 자신이 학생회장이 되어서 실행할 내용과 소감을 말하고 있으므로 정답은 ④ '당선 포부'이다.

어휘 | hallway [hɔ́:lwei] 명 복도 install [instɔ́:l] 동 설치하다 vote [vout] 동 투표하다 election [ilékʃən] 명 선거 promise [prámis] 동 약속하다

11 일치하지 않는 내용 고르기

정답 ⑤

W Sam, have you ever been to the Miracle Science Museum?
M Where is it?
W It's the big green building across the street from our school.
M Oh, I know the one you mean. It opened last year, right?
W That's the one. So, have you ever visited it?
M No. I'd like to someday.
W Why don't we go on Saturday? It offers special discounts for students.
M Okay. It opens at 10, so let's meet there at 11 a.m.
W Perfect.

여 Sam, 너 미라클 과학 박물관에 가봤니?
남 어디에 있는데?
여 그건 우리 학교 길 건너편에 있는 큰 초록색 건물이야.
남 오, 네가 뭘 말하는지 알아. 그곳은 작년에 열었어, 그렇지?
여 바로 그거야. 그래서, 방문해본 적 있니?
남 아니. 언젠가 가보고 싶어.
여 우리 토요일에 가는 게 어때? 학생들에게는 특별 할인을 제공해줘.
남 그래. 그곳은 10시에 여니까, 거기서 오전 11시에 만나자.
여 완벽해.

해설 | 남자가 박물관이 10시에 여니 오전 11시에 만나자고 했으므로 정답은 ⑤ '오전 11시에 문을 연다.'이다.

어휘 | across [əkrɔ́:s] 전 건너서 someday [sʌ́mdei] 부 언젠가 discount [dískaunt] 명 할인

12 목적 고르기

정답 ④

[Cellphone rings.]
M Hey, Gracie.
W Hi, Brad. What's up?
M Didn't you say that you have visited Jeonju?
W Right. I've been there twice.
M I'm traveling there next week. Can you let me know some good places to visit?
W Sure. You should visit the Hanok Village and Nambu Market.
M Thanks! I'll definitely go there and take pictures.
W I hope you have a great time. Show me your pictures later.

[휴대폰이 울린다.]
남 안녕, Gracie.
여 안녕, Brad. 무슨 일이야?
남 너 전주에 가봤다고 하지 않았니?
여 맞아. 난 거기에 두 번 가봤어.
남 나는 다음 주에 거기로 여행을 갈 거야. 방문할만한 좋은 장소들을 알려줄 수 있어?
여 물론이지. 너는 한옥 마을과 남부 시장을 방문해야 해.
남 고마워! 반드시 거기에 가서 사진을 찍을게.
여 좋은 시간 보내길 바라. 나중에 사진 보여줘.

해설 | 남자가 다음 주에 전주에 여행을 가니 방문하기 좋은 장소를 알려달라고 했으므로 정답은 ④ '관광 명소를 물어보기 위해서'이다.
어휘 | twice [twais] 부 두 번 definitely [défənitli] 부 반드시

13 금액 정보 고르기

정답 ②

M Good afternoon. What would you like to order?
W Yes. I'd like to have one hamburger set and one sandwich set.
M Which size would you like, regular or large?
W Both regular, please. How much are they?
M They're 18 dollars in total.
W Here's 20 dollars.
M Here's your change. I'll get the hamburger and sandwich sets right away.
W Thanks a lot.

남 안녕하세요. 무엇을 주문하시겠어요?
여 저는 햄버거 세트 하나와 샌드위치 세트 하나 주세요.
남 레귤러와 라지 중 어떤 사이즈를 원하시나요?
여 둘 다 레귤러로 주세요. 얼마인가요?
남 총 18달러입니다.
여 여기 20달러요.
남 여기 거스름돈이 있습니다. 햄버거와 샌드위치 세트를 바로 가져다드리겠습니다.
여 정말 감사합니다.

해설 | 햄버거 세트 하나와 샌드위치 세트 하나의 총액이 18달러이고 여자는 20달러를 냈으므로 정답은 ② '$ 2'이다.
어휘 | change [tʃeindʒ] 명 거스름돈

14 관계 고르기

정답 ④

W Hello. Can I help you with anything?
M Yes. I would like to sign up for a programming class.
W Okay. Have you learned anything related to programming before?
M No. This is my first time.
W I recommend our beginner's class then. It starts at 1 p.m. Does that work for you?
M Sure. What do you teach on the first day of the class?
W You will learn basics of coding.

여 안녕하세요. 무엇을 도와드릴까요?
남 네. 저는 프로그래밍 수업을 등록하고 싶어요.
여 그러시군요. 전에 프로그래밍과 관련 있는 것을 배워본 적이 있으신가요?
남 아니요. 이번이 처음이에요.
여 그렇다면 초보자반을 추천해 드려요. 그건 오후 1시에 시작합니다. 가능하신가요?
남 물론이죠. 수업 첫 날에는 무엇을 가르치시나요?
여 코딩의 기초를 배우시게 될 거예요.

해설 | 남자가 여자에게 프로그래밍 수업을 등록하고 싶다고 했고 여자가 반을 추천해주고 있는 것으로 보아 정답은 ④ '컴퓨터 학원 직원 — 학생'이다.
어휘 | sign up for ~을 등록하다, 신청하다 recommend [rèkəménd] 동 추천하다 beginner [bigínər] 명 초보자 basic [béisik] 명 기초

15 제안한 일 고르기

정답 ②

M Good afternoon. How may I help you?
W Could you check if you have these shoes in a size 250?
M There should be some on the shelves in the women's shoe section.
W I looked there, but I couldn't find them.
M Hmm... Let me check. *[Typing sound]* Sorry, they are all sold out.
W I need them by Saturday for a wedding. Do you have any suggestions?
M If you order the shoes on our website today, you can get them delivered to your house by then.
W Great. Thanks.

남 안녕하세요. 어떻게 도와드릴까요?
여 이 신발이 250 사이즈가 있는지 확인해 주시겠어요?
남 여성용 신발 구역의 선반에 몇 켤레 있을 거예요.
여 거기를 봤는데, 못 찾았어요.
남 흠... 확인해 보겠습니다. *[타자치는 소리]* 죄송하지만, 그것들은 모두 품절입니다.
여 저는 결혼식을 위해 토요일까지 그것들이 필요해요. 제안해 주실 것이 있나요?
남 만약 오늘 저희 웹사이트에서 신발을 주문하시면, 그때까지 집으로 배송 받으실 수 있어요.
여 좋네요. 감사합니다.

해설 | 남자가 오늘 웹사이트에서 신발을 주문하면 토요일까지 집으로 신발을 배송 받을 수 있다고 말했으므로 정답은 ② '온라인 주문하기'이다.

어휘 | shelf [ʃelf] 명 선반 suggestion [səgdʒéstʃən] 명 제안 deliver [dilívər] 동 배송하다, 배달하다

16 이유 고르기

정답 ③

M Mom, I'm home.
W Hi, Jonghyun. Why are you so sweaty?
M I walked all the way home after school.
W Why? Were you trying to get some exercise?
M No. The pedal on my bike fell off.
W Oh, no. You must be exhausted from pushing your bike home.
M I am. Now I have to try to fix it.
W I can help you with that.

남 엄마, 저 집에 왔어요.
여 종현아, 왜 그렇게 땀투성이니?
남 방과 후에 집까지 걸어왔어요.
여 왜? 운동을 하려고 한 거니?
남 아니요. 자전거의 페달이 떨어졌어요.
여 오, 저런. 집까지 자전거를 밀면서 오느라 지쳤겠구나.
남 그랬어요. 이제 그것을 고쳐 봐야 해요.
여 내가 도와줄 수 있단다.

해설 | 남자는 자전거의 페달이 떨어져서 걸어왔다고 말했으므로 정답은 ③ '자전거가 고장 나서'이다.

어휘 | sweaty [swéti] 형 땀투성이의 fall off (붙어 있던 것이) 떨어지다 exhausted [igzɔ́:stid] 형 지친 fix [fiks] 동 고치다

17 그림 상황에 적절한 대화 고르기

정답 ①

① M Was the soccer game canceled?
W Yes. It's raining outside.
② M Is that your favorite player?
W Yes. He's the best on the team.
③ M What do you usually do on Saturdays?
W I go to my favorite café.
④ M Our flight is delayed.
W Yeah. It's snowing a lot.
⑤ M Where are the kids?
W They're playing on the playground with a ball.

① 남 축구 경기가 취소됐니?
여 응. 밖에 비가 오고 있어.
② 남 저 사람이 네가 가장 좋아하는 선수니?
여 응. 그는 팀에서 제일 뛰어나.
③ 남 너는 토요일에 보통 뭘 하니?
여 나는 내가 가장 좋아하는 카페에 가.
④ 남 우리 비행기가 지연됐어.
여 맞아. 눈이 많이 오고 있어.
⑤ 남 아이들은 어디 있어?
여 공을 가지고 놀이터에서 놀고 있어.

해설 | 남자가 축구 경기가 취소됐냐고 묻자 여자가 그렇다고 하며 밖에 비가 온다고 하는 상황이므로 정답은 ①이다.

어휘 | canceled [kǽnsəld] 형 취소된 player [pléiər] 명 선수 flight [flait] 명 비행기

18 언급하지 않은 내용 고르기

정답 ③

W Hi, Michael. What's the matter?
M Hey, Janet. My phone is getting so slow.
W Have you tried Safe Cleaner?
M What is it?
W It's an app to remove all unnecessary files from a mobile phone.
M I'll install it now. *[Pause]* Wow, more than one million people have already downloaded it.
W Yeah. And it has a high rating from users. It almost has five stars.
M Thanks for letting me know about this.
W You're welcome.

여 안녕, Michael. 무슨 일이야?
남 안녕, Janet. 내 핸드폰이 너무 느려지고 있어.
여 Safe Cleaner를 시도해 봤니?
남 그게 뭔데?
여 그건 휴대폰에서 필요 없는 파일을 모두 제거해 주는 앱이야.
남 지금 설치할게. *[잠시 멈춤]* 우와, 백만 명이 넘는 사람들이 이미 다운로드 했네.
여 맞아. 그리고 그건 사용자들에게 높은 평가를 받았어. 그건 거의 별 다섯 개를 받았어.
남 이거 알려줘서 고마워.
여 천만에.

해설 | ① 이름(Safe Cleaner), ② 기능(휴대폰에서 필요 없는 파일을 모두 제거), ④ 평점(별 다섯 개), ⑤ 다운로드 횟수(백만 이상)에 대해 언급했으므로 정답은 ③ '가격'이다.

어휘 | matter [mætər] 명 일; 문제 remove [rimúːv] 동 제거하다 unnecessary [ʌnnésəseri] 형 필요 없는 rating [réitiŋ] 명 평가 almost [ɔ́ːlmoust] 부 거의

19 적절한 응답 고르기

정답 ②

M Hello. Welcome to Central Gym. How may I help you?
W I want to sign up for a class.
M Okay. What kind of class do you want to register for?
W What are the options?
M Well, there are kickboxing and swimming classes in the mornings.
W Oh, I like exercising at night.
M No problem. There's a popular golf class in the evening. Are you interested?
W Yes. That sounds good.

남 안녕하세요. 센트럴 체육관에 오신 것을 환영합니다. 어떻게 도와드릴까요?
여 수업에 등록하고 싶어요.
남 그러시군요. 어떤 종류의 수업에 등록하고 싶으신가요?
여 어떤 선택지가 있나요?
남 음, 아침에는 킥복싱과 수영 수업이 있습니다.
여 오, 저는 밤에 운동하는 것을 좋아해요.
남 괜찮습니다. 저녁에는 인기 있는 골프 수업이 있어요. 관심 있으신가요?
여 네. 그거 좋은 것 같아요.

해설 | 남자가 저녁에는 인기 있는 골프 수업이 있다고 하며 관심이 있는지 묻고 있으므로 정답은 그에 동의하는 ② 'Yes. That sounds good.'이다.

선택지 해석

① 일정을 바꿀 수 있나요? ② 네. 그거 좋은 것 같아요. ③ 늦지 않도록 해주세요. ④ 제가 가장 좋아하는 운동은 수영이에요. ⑤ 오실 수 있어서 기뻐요.

어휘 | kind [kaind] 명 종류 register [rédʒistər] 동 등록하다 option [ápʃən] 명 선택지 interested [íntərəstid] 형 관심이 있는, 흥미 있는

20 적절한 응답 고르기

정답 ⑤

[Cellphone rings.]
M Hey, Martha. What are you doing?
W I just bought a new shirt.
M Then, are you in the department store now?
W Yes. I'm on the third floor.
M Who are you shopping with?
W I'm shopping alone. Why do you ask that?
M I need to buy a new backpack. Can I join you?
W Of course you can.
M Good. I'm really close to the store. Let's meet on the first floor.
W Okay. I'll go there.

[휴대폰이 울린다.]
남 안녕, Martha. 뭐 하고 있니?
여 나 방금 새로운 셔츠를 샀어.
남 그럼, 너 지금 백화점에 있니?
여 응. 나 3층에 있어.
남 누구랑 쇼핑 중이야?
여 혼자 쇼핑 중이야. 그건 왜 물어봐?
남 나 새 배낭을 사야 해. 함께 해도 될까?
여 당연히 그래도 되지.
남 좋아. 나 백화점과 정말 가까이에 있어. 1층에서 만나자.
여 알겠어. 거기로 갈게.

해설 | 남자가 1층에서 만나자고 제안했으므로 정답은 제안을 수락하는 ⑤ 'Okay. I'll go there.'이다.

선택지 해석

① 이 쇼핑몰은 거대해. ② 미안하지만, 나는 더 이상 걸을 수 없어. ③ 가격이 너무 싸. ④ 화장실은 아래층에 있어. ⑤ 알겠어. 거기로 갈게.

어휘 | department store 백화점 alone [əlóun] 부 혼자 backpack [bǽkpæk] 명 배낭 close to 가까이에

03회 실전 모의고사

| 문제 pp.42-43

1	①	2	④	3	⑤	4	①	5	③	6	③	7	②	8	②	9	③	10	③
11	④	12	③	13	⑤	14	③	15	④	16	③	17	③	18	⑤	19	④	20	②

1 날씨 고르기

정답 ①

W Good evening, everyone. Here's the weekly weather report. On Monday and Tuesday, it'll be rainy, so bring your umbrella. On Wednesday, however, it'll be sunny all day. The weather will be perfect for a picnic. Starting Thursday, it'll be cloudy, and it will rain throughout the weekend.

여 안녕하세요, 여러분. 주간 일기예보입니다. 월요일과 화요일에는 비가 올 것이니, 우산을 가져가십시오. 하지만 수요일은 하루 종일 화창하겠습니다. 소풍에 완벽한 날씨가 될 것입니다. 목요일부터는 날이 흐려지기 시작하겠고, 주말 내내 비가 오겠습니다.

해설 | 수요일은 하루 종일 화창하겠다고 했으므로 정답은 ①이다.

어휘 | throughout [θru:áut] 전 내내

2 알맞은 그림 고르기

정답 ④

M May I help you?
W I'm looking for a mug for my friend.
M Okay. This cup with the tail-shaped handle is our best seller.
W It looks uncomfortable to hold.
M How about these ones with letters on them? They just came in yesterday.
W Actually, my friend's name is Karen, so I think the one with the letter *K* is perfect.
M Do you want the one without a handle?
W No. I'll take the one with a handle.

남 도와드릴까요?
여 친구를 위해 머그잔을 찾고 있어요.
남 그러시군요. 이 꼬리 모양 손잡이가 있는 컵이 저희 베스트셀러입니다.
여 그건 손에 쥐기 불편해 보여요.
남 글씨가 쓰여 있는 건 어떠신가요? 어제 막 들어왔어요.
여 사실, 제 친구의 이름이 Karen이니, 철자 K가 있는 것이 딱 좋은 것 같아요.
남 손잡이가 없는 걸 원하세요?
여 아니요. 손잡이가 있는 걸로 할게요.

해설 | 여자는 K라는 글자가 있고, 손잡이가 있는 머그잔을 살 것이라고 했으므로 정답은 ④이다.

어휘 | mug [mʌg] 명 머그잔 come in 상품이 들어오다 handle [hǽndl] 명 손잡이

3 심정 고르기

정답 ⑤

[Cellphone rings.]
W Hi, Jake.
M Hello, Cathy. I'm calling to ask you about our camping trip this weekend.
W We have a problem.
M What's wrong?
W The weather forecast said that it's going to rain all weekend.
M Oh, no! I was so excited to go!
W I know. Sorry, but I think we need to go camping later.
M I can't believe this!

[휴대폰이 울린다.]
여 안녕, Jake.
남 안녕, Cathy. 이번 주말 우리의 캠핑 여행에 대해 물어보려고 전화했어.
여 우리 문제가 생겼어.
남 뭐가 문제야?
여 일기예보에서 주말 내내 비가 올 거라고 했어.
남 오, 이런! 가게 되어서 정말 신났었는데!
여 나도 알지. 유감이지만, 캠핑은 나중에 가야 할 것 같아.
남 믿을 수가 없네!

해설 | 여자가 캠핑은 나중에 가야 할 것 같다고 하자 남자가 믿을 수가 없다고 했으므로 정답은 ⑤ 'disappointed'이다.

선택지 해석
① 행복한 ② 자랑스러운 ③ 수줍은 ④ 지루한 ⑤ 실망한

어휘 | weekend [wí:kend] 명 주말 problem [prábləm] 명 문제 believe [bilí:v] 동 믿다

4 한 일 고르기

정답 ①

M Janet, this is my present for you.
W Thanks, Tim. What's in the box?
M They are cookies that I baked with my younger sister yesterday.
W They smell delicious. What did you put in the cookies?
M Chocolate chips and nuts.
W I want to learn how to bake cookies too.
M You should come to my house next weekend. I'll show you how to bake them.

남 Janet, 널 위한 내 선물이야.
여 고마워, Tim. 상자 안에 뭐가 들었니?
남 어제 여동생과 함께 구운 쿠키야.
여 맛있는 냄새가 나. 쿠키에 뭘 넣었니?
남 초콜릿 칩이랑 견과류야.
여 나도 쿠키 굽는 법을 배우고 싶어.
남 다음 주말에 우리 집에 와. 어떻게 굽는지 알려줄게.

해설 | 남자는 어제 여동생과 함께 쿠키를 구웠다고 했으므로 정답은 ① '쿠키 굽기'이다.
어휘 | bake [beik] 통 굽다 nut [nʌt] 명 견과류

5 장소 고르기

정답 ③

W Which animal do you want to see first, Will?
M I don't know. Let's look at the map.
W It says that the elephants are near here. We could go there.
M The lions are also nearby.
W Oh, I really want to see the lions. Can we go there first?
M Sure. After that, we can see the elephants and have lunch.
W That sounds like a good plan.

여 어떤 동물을 먼저 보고 싶니, Will?
남 잘 모르겠어. 지도를 보자.
여 코끼리가 이 근처에 있다고 하네. 거기 가도 되겠어.
남 사자들도 근처에 있어.
여 오, 나는 사자를 정말 보고 싶어. 거기 먼저 가도 될까?
남 물론이지. 그 후에 코끼리를 보고 점심을 먹자.
여 좋은 계획인 것 같아.

해설 | 어떤 동물을 보고 싶은지 물었고, 지도를 보면서 동물들의 위치를 파악하고 있으므로 정답은 ③ '동물원'이다.
어휘 | nearby [nìərbái] 전 근처의 plan [plæn] 명 계획

6 의도 고르기

정답 ③

W Ron, can I talk to you for a minute?
M Yes, Ms. Robinson.
W What happened with your math quiz score?
M I think I didn't really understand the equations. They were so confusing.
W That's too bad.
M Can I ask some questions about that part now?
W Of course! I'm always happy to help.

여 Ron, 잠깐 얘기 좀 할 수 있을까?
남 네, Robinson 선생님.
여 네 수학 쪽지 시험 점수는 어떻게 된 거니?
남 제가 공식들을 잘 이해하지 못한 것 같아요. 그것들은 너무 헷갈렸어요.
여 안타깝구나.
남 지금 그 부분에 대해 몇 가지 질문을 해도 될까요?
여 물론이지! 언제든 도와주마.

해설 | 남자가 이해하지 못한 부분에 대해 몇 가지 질문을 해도 될지 묻자 여자가 물론이라고 한 후 언제든 도와주겠다는 말을 했으므로 정답은 ③ '승낙'이다.
어휘 | quiz [kwiz] 명 쪽지 시험, 퀴즈 equation [ikwéiʒən] 명 공식; 방정식 confusing [kənfjúːziŋ] 형 헷갈리는; 혼란스러운

7 특정 정보 고르기

정답 ②

M Are you ready to place your order?
W Yes. I'll get a steak, please.
M Okay. Would you like soup or salad with that?
W Soup. I would also like some French fries.
M Of course. I'll add that to your order. Do you want something to drink?
W An orange juice would be nice. Oh, one more thing. Do you sell cheesecake?
M We do. It's the chef's specialty.
W Wonderful. I'll have that for dessert.

남 주문할 준비가 되셨나요?
여 네. 저는 스테이크를 주세요.
남 알겠습니다. 수프나 샐러드도 함께 드시겠어요?
여 수프요. 감자튀김도 주세요.
남 물론이죠. 주문에 추가해 드릴게요. 마실 것 좀 드릴까요?
여 오렌지 주스가 좋겠어요. 오, 한 가지 더요. 치즈 케이크를 파나요?
남 팝니다. 주방장의 특기예요.
여 아주 좋네요. 후식으로 그걸 먹을게요.

해설 | 여자는 ① 수프, ③ 감자튀김, ④ 주스, ⑤ 케이크를 주문했으므로 정답은 ② '샐러드'이다.
어휘 | place an order 주문을 하다 add [æd] 통 추가하다, 더하다 specialty [spéʃəlti] 명 특기

8 할 일 고르기

정답 ②

W Matt, do you have a ladder?
M No. Why?
W I need to change the light bulb in the living room, but my ladder broke.
M Why don't you buy a new one?
W I ordered one, but it won't arrive until next week.
M Hmm... You should ask James if he has one.
W That's a good idea. But I don't know his phone number.
M I'll text you his number.

여 Matt, 너 사다리 있니?
남 아니. 왜?
여 거실에 전구를 갈아야 하는데, 내 사다리가 부러졌어.
남 새것을 사는 게 어때?
여 하나 주문했는데, 다음 주까지 도착하지 않을 거야.
남 흠... James에게 하나 가지고 있는지 물어봐.
여 좋은 생각이야. 그런데 나는 그의 전화번호를 몰라.
남 그의 번호를 문자로 보내줄게.

해설 | 여자가 James의 전화번호를 모른다고 하자 남자가 그의 번호를 문자로 보내 준다고 했으므로 정답은 ② '문자 보내기'이다.

어휘 | ladder [lǽdər] 명 사다리 light bulb 전구 order [ɔ́:rdər] 동 주문하다 arrive [əráiv] 동 도착하다 text [tekst] 동 문자를 보내다

9 언급하지 않은 내용 고르기

정답 ③

W Michael, have you tried the pizza place in Itaewon?
M You mean Louise's Pizzeria, right?
W Yeah. I haven't been there yet.
M Really? The chef came to Korea to open the restaurant a few years ago.
W I heard that they sell the best pizza in the city.
M They open at 5 p.m., so we can get their pizza for dinner now.
W Or, we can get it delivered. It only costs 2 dollars for the delivery service.
M That's cheap.

여 Michael, 너 이태원에 있는 피자집 가봤니?
남 Louise's Pizzeria 말이지, 그렇지?
여 응. 난 아직 거기에 가본 적이 없어.
남 정말? 그 주방장이 몇 년 전에 식당을 열기 위해 한국에 왔잖아.
여 시내에서 가장 맛있는 피자를 판다고 들었어.
남 오후 5시에 문을 여니까, 지금 저녁으로 피자를 사 올 수 있겠다.
여 아니면, 배달받을 수도 있어. 배달 요금이 2달러밖에 안 들어.
남 싸네.

해설 | ① 위치(이태원), ② 이름(Louise's Pizzeria), ④ 개점 시간(오후 5시), ⑤ 배달 요금(2달러)에 대해 언급했으므로 정답은 ③ '개업 연도'이다.

어휘 | chef [ʃef] 명 주방장, 요리사 deliver [dilívər] 동 배달하다 cost [kɔ́:st] 동 (값·비용이) 들다

10 주제 고르기

정답 ③

W Hello, everyone. Today, I'll talk about the safety rules at the Madison Swimming Center. First, do not run in the pool area. The floor is wet, so you might slip and hurt yourself. Second, do not dive. The water is not deep, so diving may cause a head injury. Finally, food and drinks are not allowed in the pool area.

여 안녕하세요, 여러분. 오늘 저는 메디슨 수영 센터의 안전 수칙에 대해 말씀드리겠습니다. 첫째, 수영장 구역에서 뛰지 마세요. 바닥이 젖었으므로 미끄러져서 다칠 수 있습니다. 둘째, 다이빙하지 마세요. 물이 깊지 않기 때문에 다이빙하는 것은 머리 부상을 야기할 수 있습니다. 마지막으로, 수영장 구역에서는 음식과 마실 것이 허용되지 않습니다.

해설 | 여자가 메디슨 수영 센터의 안전 수칙에 대해 말하고 있으므로 정답은 ③ '수영장 안전 수칙'이다.

어휘 | safety [séifti] 명 안전 area [ɛ́əriə] 명 구역 slip [slip] 동 미끄러지다 cause [kɔ:z] 동 야기하다, 발생시키다 injury [índʒəri] 명 부상 allow [əláu] 동 허용하다; 허락하다

11 일치하지 않는 내용 고르기

정답 ④

W Mr. Benson, when is our next basketball game?
M It's this Saturday.
W I have a dentist's appointment on Saturday at 11 a.m.
M That's fine. The game starts at 3 p.m.
W What about the practice?
M You'll have to miss it, but that won't be a problem.
W Okay. By the way, my parents want to buy tickets for the game. Are they sold out?
M No, they aren't. And the tickets are free for family members.

여 Benson 선생님, 저희 다음 농구 경기가 언제죠?
남 이번 토요일이란다.
여 저는 토요일 오전 11시에 치과 예약이 있어요.
남 괜찮아. 경기는 오후 3시에 시작한단다.
여 연습은요?
남 그건 빠져야 할 것 같지만, 문제없을 거야.
여 알겠습니다. 그나저나, 저희 부모님이 경기를 위해 티켓을 사고 싶어 하셔요. 매진되었나요?
남 아니, 그렇지 않아. 그리고 가족들은 티켓이 무료란다.

해설 | 여자가 경기 티켓이 매진되었냐고 묻자 남자가 아니라고 했으므로 정답은 ④ '티켓이 이미 매진이다.'이다.
어휘 | appointment [əpɔ́intmənt] 명 예약 practice [prǽktis] 명 연습 miss [mis] 동 빠지다; 놓치다

12 목적 고르기

정답 ③

W May I help you?
M I'm looking for a patient. She's in Room 405.
W Take the stairs on the right. That room's on the fourth floor.
M Okay.
W Are you visiting a friend?
M No. My sister was in a car accident yesterday.
W Oh, no. I hope she gets well soon.
M I hope so too.

여 무엇을 도와드릴까요?
남 저는 환자를 찾고 있어요. 그녀는 405호에 있어요.
여 오른쪽에 있는 계단을 이용하세요. 그 병실은 4층에 있습니다.
남 알겠습니다.
여 친구분을 방문하시는 건가요?
남 아니요. 제 여동생이 어제 교통사고를 당했어요.
여 오, 이런. 그녀가 빨리 회복되기를 바랄게요.
남 저도 그러길 바라요.

해설 | 남자가 환자를 찾고 있다며 405호에 있다고 했고, 여동생이 어제 교통사고를 당했다고 했으므로 정답은 ③ '병문안을 가기 위해서'이다.
어휘 | patient [péiʃənt] 명 환자 accident [ǽksidənt] 명 사고 get well 회복하다

13 숫자 정보 고르기

정답 ⑤

W Hi, Jason. I didn't recognize you! When did you get so tall?
M Hey, Amanda. I grew 10 centimeters this year.
W How tall are you?
M I was 175 centimeters tall when you saw me last year.
W Then, you are now 185 centimeters tall?
M Yeah. Now, I am taller than my dad.
W Wow. You should really try out for the volleyball team.
M Maybe I will.

여 안녕, Jason. 못 알아봤어! 언제 이렇게 키가 컸니?
남 안녕, Amanda. 난 올해 10센티미터가 컸어.
여 키가 몇이야?
남 작년에 네가 나를 봤을 때 175센티미터였어.
여 그럼, 너 지금 185센티미터인 거야?
남 응. 이제 우리 아빠보다 내가 더 커.
여 우와. 너 정말 배구팀에 지원해 봐야겠다.
남 그럴지도 몰라.

해설 | 여자가 185센티미터인 거냐고 묻자 남자가 그렇다고 했으므로 정답은 ⑤ '185cm'이다.
어휘 | grow [grou] 동 크다, 자라다 try out for (팀원·배역 선발 등을 위한 경쟁에) 지원하다

14 관계 고르기

정답 ③

M Hi, Ms. Simmons.
W Hey, Richard. Did you choose a topic for your history project?
M I want to do my presentation on the Joseon Dynasty.
W That's a good choice. Why did you pick the Joseon Dynasty?
M I want to learn more about King Sejo.
W Okay. I can recommend a book to read for your project.
M I'd like that.
W Remember, you also have to hand in the report on Friday.

남 안녕하세요, Simmons 선생님.
여 안녕, Richard. 역사 과제 주제를 정했니?
남 저는 조선 왕조에 대해서 발표하고 싶어요.
여 좋은 선택이구나. 왜 조선 왕조를 골랐니?
남 세조 왕에 대해서 더 배우고 싶어서요.
여 그래. 네 과제를 위해 읽을 책을 추천해줄 수 있단다.
남 좋아요.
여 기억하렴, 금요일에는 보고서도 제출해야 한단다.

해설 | 남자가 여자를 Simmons 선생님이라고 불렀고 여자가 역사 과제 주제를 정했는지 물어보는 것으로 보아 정답은 ③ '역사 교사 — 학생'이다.
어휘 | project [prádʒekt] 명 과제 dynasty [dáinəsti] 명 왕조; 시대 choice [tʃɔis] 명 선택 pick [pik] 동 고르다 hand in 제출하다

15 부탁·요청한 일 고르기

정답 ④

M Honey, what is this delicious smell?
W I'm making gimbab and egg soup for dinner.
M Great. I'll set the table. Uh, what are these ingredients for?
W Oh, I forgot. I was going to use them to make japchae, but we didn't have enough carrots.
M Do you want me to get those now?
W Yes, please. Can you go buy two carrots?
M Sure.

남 여보, 이 맛있는 냄새는 뭐야?
여 저녁으로 김밥과 계란국을 만들고 있어.
남 좋아. 내가 상을 차릴게. 어, 이 재료들은 뭘 위한 거야?
여 오, 깜빡했어. 잡채 만들 때 쓰려고 했는데, 당근이 충분히 없었어.
남 내가 지금 그것들을 사 올까?
여 응, 부탁할게. 가서 당근 두 개 사 올 수 있어?
남 물론이지.

해설 | 여자가 남자에게 당근 두 개 사 오는 것을 부탁했으므로 정답은 ④ '당근 사 오기'다.

어휘 | set [set] 동 (상에 수저 등을) 차리다 ingredient [ingríːdiənt] 명 재료

16 이유 고르기

정답 ③

M Hi, Tara!
W Hey, Paul! Where are you going?
M I'm going to the library.
W Oh, are you going to borrow some books for the science report?
M No. I already bought the books I need from the bookstore.
W Then, why are you going to the library?
M My favorite author is coming to the library. He is going to read a chapter of his new book for his fans.
W That's cool. Can I come with you?
M Why not?

남 안녕, Tara!
여 안녕, Paul! 너 어디 가는 중이야?
남 나 도서관에 가고 있어.
여 오, 과학 보고서를 위해 책을 좀 빌릴 거니?
남 아니. 나는 서점에서 필요한 책들을 이미 샀어.
여 그럼, 도서관에는 왜 가는 거야?
남 내가 좋아하는 작가가 도서관에 올 거야. 그는 팬들을 위해서 그의 신간 한 챕터를 읽어 줄 거야.
여 멋지다. 나도 같이 가도 돼?
남 왜 안 되겠어?

해설 | 여자가 도서관에는 왜 가는지 묻자 남자는 자신이 좋아하는 작가가 도서관에 와서 신간 한 챕터를 읽어 줄 거라고 말했으므로 정답은 ③ '행사에 참석하기 위해서'이다.

어휘 | already [ɔːlrédi] 부 이미, 벌써 author [ɔ́ːθər] 명 작가

17 그림 상황에 적절한 대화 고르기

정답 ③

① M I got your postcard. Your trip looked amazing.
W Yes. I didn't want to come back.
② M What should we eat tonight?
W I'll order a chicken.
③ M How can I help you?
W I need to mail a package.
④ M Let me help you carry those boxes. They look heavy.
W Thank you for your help.
⑤ M What do you want for your birthday present?
W I'd like a new coat.

① 남 네 엽서를 받았어. 여행 멋져 보이더라.
여 맞아. 돌아오고 싶지 않았어.
② 남 우리 오늘 밤에 뭐 먹을까?
여 내가 치킨을 시킬게.
③ 남 어떻게 도와 드릴까요?
여 저는 택배를 보내야 해요.
④ 남 그 상자들 나르는 걸 도와드릴게요. 무거워 보이네요.
여 도와주셔서 감사해요.
⑤ 남 네 생일 선물로 무엇을 원하니?
여 새 코트를 갖고 싶어.

해설 | 남자가 어떻게 도와줄지 묻자 여자가 택배를 보내야 한다고 말하는 상황이므로 정답은 ③이다.

어휘 | postcard [póustkard] 명 엽서 mail [meil] 동 보내다 명 우편 package [pǽkidʒ] 명 택배 carry [kǽri] 동 나르다

18 언급하지 않은 내용 고르기

정답 ⑤

W Did you know that a hot dog eating contest is held on Coney Island? This event has been held every year since 1972. The winner of this event is awarded a yellow belt. In 2021, a man set a new record by eating 76 hotdogs in 10 minutes.

여 코니아일랜드에서 핫도그 먹기 대회가 열린다는 것을 알고 계셨나요? 이 행사는 1972년부터 매해 열려 왔습니다. 행사의 승자는 노란색 허리띠를 수여 받습니다. 2021년에는 한 남성이 10분 안에 핫도그 76개를 먹음으로써 신기록을 세웠습니다.

해설 | ① 개최 장소(코니아일랜드), ② 시작 연도(1972년), ③ 상품(노란색 허리띠), ④ 최고 기록(핫도그 76개)에 대해 언급했으므로 정답은 ⑤ '우승자 이름'이다.
어휘 | award [əwɔ́ːrd] 동 수여하다 set a record 기록을 세우다

19 적절한 응답 고르기

정답 ④

M Hello. Do you need help to find a poster?
W Yes. I'm looking for a poster of my favorite band.
M Okay. What is your favorite band?
W I am a big fan of Red Punk.
M Oh, they're very popular. Here are two of their posters.
W I love the one with them in the car.
M Okay. Do you want the smaller or bigger poster?
W The smaller one is perfect.

남 안녕하세요. 포스터 찾는 데 도움이 필요하신가요?
여 네. 제가 가장 좋아하는 밴드의 포스터를 찾고 있어요.
남 그러시군요. 당신이 가장 좋아하는 밴드가 무엇인가요?
여 저는 Red Punk의 열혈 팬이에요.
남 오, 그들은 매우 인기가 있죠. 여기 그들의 포스터 중 두 장이 있어요.
여 그들이 차 안에 있는 이것이 정말 맘에 드네요.
남 그러시군요. 작은 포스터를 원하세요, 큰 포스터를 원하세요?
여 작은 것이 좋겠네요.

해설 | 남자가 작은 포스터를 원하는지 큰 포스터를 원하는지 묻고 있으므로 정답은 작은 포스터라고 답하는 ④ 'The smaller one is perfect.'이다.

선택지 해석

① 그들의 새 앨범이 막 발매됐어요. ② 환불을 받고 싶어요. ③ 그녀는 빨간 차를 좋아해요. ④ 작은 것이 좋겠네요. ⑤ 저는 파티에 초대되지 않았어요.

어휘 | popular [pápjulər] 형 인기 있는 release [rilíːs] 동 발매하다; 발표하다

20 적절한 응답 고르기

정답 ②

M It smells so good in here. What is that scent?
W It's a new candle that I bought. It has a coffee smell.
M That's one of my favorite scents. I love vanilla candles too.
W I don't really like vanilla, but I like the smell of lavender a lot. It helps me relax.
M I need to relax more often. What else do you do to relax?
W I like to do yoga.

남 여기 냄새가 정말 좋네. 무슨 향이야?
여 내가 산 새 양초야. 그건 커피 향이 나.
남 그건 내가 가장 좋아하는 향 중 하나야. 나는 바닐라 양초도 좋아해.
여 나는 바닐라는 별로 좋아하지 않지만, 라벤더 향은 정말 좋아해. 긴장을 푸는 데 도움이 되거든.
남 나는 더 자주 긴장을 풀어야 할 필요가 있어. 너는 긴장을 풀기 위해 그밖에는 뭘 하니?
여 나는 요가 하는 것을 좋아해.

해설 | 남자가 긴장을 풀기 위해 그밖에는 무엇을 하냐고 묻고 있으므로 정답은 요가 하는 것을 좋아한다고 답하는 ② 'I like to do yoga.'이다.

선택지 해석

① 이 양초는 좋은 향이 나. ② 나는 요가 하는 것을 좋아해. ③ 아니. 나는 바닐라 아이스크림을 원해. ④ 나는 딸기를 선호해. ⑤ 나는 스트레스를 풀어야 해.

어휘 | scent [sent] 명 향, 냄새 relax [rilǽks] 동 긴장을 풀다; 휴식을 취하다 relieve stress 스트레스를 풀다

04회 실전 모의고사

| 문제 pp.50-51

1	②	2	③	3	①	4	②	5	④	6	⑤	7	③	8	③	9	⑤	10	④
11	⑤	12	②	13	④	14	②	15	④	16	④	17	②	18	②	19	⑤	20	③

1 날씨 고르기

정답 ②

M Good morning! Here is today's global weather. In Seoul, there will be a bit of snow and strong wind. London will have heavy rain, and there is a chance of flooding. In San Francisco, however, it's going to be sunny and the sky will be clear. Thank you.

남 안녕하십니까! 오늘의 세계 날씨입니다. 서울에는 약간의 눈이 오고 강한 바람이 불겠습니다. 런던에는 폭우가 내릴 예정이며, 홍수가 날 가능성이 있습니다. 하지만 샌프란시스코는 화창하고 하늘이 맑겠습니다. 감사합니다.

해설 | 런던에는 폭우가 내릴 예정이라고 했으므로 정답은 ②이다.
어휘 | global [glóubəl] 형 세계적인 strong [strɔːŋ] 형 강한 chance [tʃæns] 명 가능성, 기회 flooding [flʌ́diŋ] 명 홍수

2 알맞은 그림 고르기

정답 ③

M Melinda, how was your day?
W It was great. I made a hair pin for Mom.
M Is this it? I like the diamond-shaped jewel between the square jewels. Where did you get that jewel?
W I bought it at a Seoul Market yesterday. I also bought a shell-shaped jewel.
M Oh, why didn't you put it in the middle?
W I didn't think Mom would like it.

남 Melinda, 오늘 하루는 어땠니?
여 아주 좋았어. 나는 엄마를 위한 머리핀을 만들었어.
남 이게 그거니? 사각형 보석들 사이에 있는 다이아몬드 모양 보석이 마음에 드네. 그 보석은 어디서 샀니?
여 어제 서울 시장에서 그걸 샀어. 그리고 조개 모양 보석도 샀어.
남 오, 왜 그것을 가운데에 붙이지 않았니?
여 엄마가 좋아하지 않으실 것 같았어.

해설 | 남자가 사각형 보석들 사이에 있는 다이아몬드 모양 보석이 마음에 든다고 했으므로 정답은 ③이다.

어휘 | jewel [dʒú:əl] 명 보석 square [skwεər] 형 사각형의

3 의도 고르기

정답 ①

W Good morning, Dad. You woke up so early today.
M Yes. I'm going on a business trip to Pyeongchang today.
W I heard that it's going to snow a lot there this week. Please be careful when you drive on the highway.
M Alright, I'll be careful. Take a seat, and have some cereal.
W Okay, Dad. Can you give me a ride to school today?
M I'm sorry, but could you take the bus?

여 좋은 아침이에요, 아빠. 오늘 매우 일찍 일어나셨네요.
남 그래. 나는 오늘 평창으로 출장을 간단다.
여 이번 주에 거기 눈이 많이 올 거라고 들었어요. 고속도로에서 운전하실 때 조심하세요.
남 알겠어, 조심할게. 앉아서 시리얼을 좀 먹으렴.
여 네, 아빠. 오늘 학교까지 태워 주실 수 있으세요?
남 미안하지만, 버스를 탈 수 있겠니?

해설 | 여자가 학교까지 태워 줄 수 있는지 묻는 말에 미안하지만 버스를 탈 수 있냐고 했으므로 정답은 ① '거절'이다.

어휘 | business trip 출장 highway [háiwèi] 명 고속도로 give a ride 태워 주다

4 한 일 고르기

정답 ②

W Andy, what are you watching on your cellphone?
M I'm watching a video that I took on Teachers' Day, Grandma.
W Oh, who is the girl singing in front of the class?
M That's Christine, and she also played the guitar.
W Her voice sounds beautiful. Did you give your teacher something for Teachers' Day?
M Yes. My classmates and I wrote a letter on a big piece of paper.
M That is so sweet of you.

여 Andy, 휴대폰으로 무엇을 보고 있니?
남 스승의 날에 제가 찍은 영상을 보고 있어요, 할머니.
여 오, 동급생들 앞에서 노래를 부르고 있는 소녀는 누구니?
남 그건 Christine이고, 그녀는 기타도 쳤어요.
여 그녀의 목소리는 아름답구나. 스승의 날에 선생님께 무언가를 드렸니?
남 네. 반 친구들과 저는 커다란 종이 한 장에 편지를 썼어요.
여 너희 정말 다정하구나.

해설 | 남자는 스승의 날에 반 친구들과 커다란 종이 한 장에 편지를 썼다고 했으므로 정답은 ② '편지 쓰기'이다.

어휘 | guitar [gitɑ́r] 명 기타 voice [vɔis] 명 목소리 classmate [klǽsmeit] 명 반 친구 sweet [swi:t] 형 다정한; 달콤한

5 장소 고르기

정답 ④

M I can't wait to watch this basketball game.
W Me too. It's going to be so exciting!
M Do you want to buy some snacks?
W Yes. And I want to buy a T-shirt at the gift shop.
M Okay. Let's go there first.
W We have so much to do. Hurry!
M Relax. We still have an hour before the game starts.

남 나는 이 농구 경기를 빨리 보고 싶어.
여 나도. 매우 흥미진진할 거야!
남 간식을 좀 살래?
여 그래. 그리고 선물 가게에서 티셔츠를 사고 싶어.
남 알겠어. 거기 먼저 가자.
여 우리 할 것이 너무 많아. 서둘러!
남 진정해. 우리 아직 경기가 시작하기 전에 한 시간이 있어.

해설 | 남자가 이 농구 경기를 빨리 보고 싶다고 언급했고, 경기 시작 전에 한 시간이 있다고 하는 것으로 보아 정답은 ④ '농구 경기장'이다.

어휘 | hurry [hə́:ri] 동 서두르다 hour [auər] 명 시간

6 일치하지 않는 내용 고르기

정답 ⑤

W Kevin, what are you reading?
M I'm reading an article about the new library in the downtown area.
W I heard it opens next week, doesn't it?
M Right. And it was built by an excellent architect, Nicole Williams.
W Oh, really?
M Yeah! And there will be a huge children's section.
W Wow, I had no idea.
M They'll also hold events at the library every week.
W I really want to visit soon.

여 Kevin, 뭘 읽고 있니?
남 시내 지역의 새 도서관에 대한 기사를 읽고 있어.
여 그곳은 다음 주에 개관한다고 들었어, 그렇지 않니?
남 맞아. 그리고 그건 뛰어난 건축가인 Nicole Williams에 의해 지어졌어.
여 오, 정말이니?
남 응! 그리고 거기에는 매우 큰 아동용 구역이 있을 거야.
여 우와, 난 전혀 몰랐어.
남 그들은 또 매주 도서관에서 행사를 열 거야.
여 정말 빨리 방문하고 싶다.

해설 | 남자가 매주 도서관에서 행사를 열 것이라고 했으므로 정답은 ⑤ '한 달에 한 번 행사를 한다.'이다.

어휘 | article [ɑ́:rtikl] 명 기사 downtown [dáuntaun] 명 시내 architect [ɑ́rkətèkt] 명 건축가 section [sékʃən] 명 구역

7 할 일 고르기

정답 ③

W Hey, Paul. How are you doing?
M To be honest, I'm really bored these days.
W Then, why don't you try something new?
M That's not a bad idea. Learning Italian could be fun.
W How are you going to study it?
M I'll watch an Italian movie for kids and learn some basic words first.
W That sounds like a good way to learn a new language.

여 안녕, Paul. 잘 지내니?
남 솔직히 말하면, 요즘 너무 지루해.
여 그럼, 뭔가 새로운 걸 해보는 게 어때?
남 나쁘지 않은 생각이야. 이탈리아어를 배우는 것도 재미있겠다.
여 어떻게 공부할 거니?
남 어린이들을 위한 이탈리아 영화를 보고 기본적인 어휘를 먼저 배울 거야.
여 그거 새로운 언어를 배우기에 좋은 방법 같다.

해설 | 남자가 어린이들을 위한 이탈리아 영화를 보고 기본 어휘를 먼저 배울 것이라고 했으므로 정답은 ③ '이탈리아 영화 보기'이다.

어휘 | honest [ɑ́nist] 형 솔직한 Italian [itǽljən] 명 이탈리아어 형 이탈리아의 basic [béisik] 형 기본적인

8 할 일 고르기

정답 ③

M Brenda, what are you up to?
W I'm going to the running track now.
M That's why you're wearing running shoes.
W Yes. I love these shoes. They are so light that I can run fast.
M That's exactly what I need. Where did you buy those?
W The shoe shop on 3rd Street. These shoes are on sale now.
M Then, I'll go there right now.

남 Brenda, 뭐 하고 있어?
여 난 지금 육상 트랙에 갈 거야.
남 그래서 운동화를 신었구나.
여 맞아. 난 이 신발을 정말 좋아해. 이건 매우 가벼워서 빠르게 달릴 수 있어.
남 그게 바로 내가 필요한 거야. 어디서 샀니?
여 3번가에 있는 신발 가게에서 샀어. 이 신발 지금 세일 중이야.
남 그럼, 지금 바로 거기 가야겠다.

해설 | 여자가 3번가에 있는 신발 가게에서 신발을 샀다고 하며 신발이 지금 세일 중이라고 하자 남자가 지금 바로 거기 가야겠다고 했으므로 정답은 ③ '신발 가게 가기'이다.

어휘 | light [lait] 형 가벼운 on sale 세일 중인

9 언급하지 않은 내용 고르기

정답 ⑤

W Tomorrow, our class will go on a field trip to a farm.
M Ms. Green, how will we get there?
W We'll take a bus to the farm.
M Is there anything we should bring?
W Good question! You need to bring your own gloves.
M Why do we need gloves?
W We will plant potatoes at the farm, so you'll need them to protect your hands.
M Okay.

여 내일, 우리 반은 농장으로 체험 학습을 갈 거예요.
남 Green 선생님, 거기에 어떻게 가나요?
여 우리는 농장에 버스를 타고 갈 거야.
남 저희가 가져가야 할 것이 있나요?
여 좋은 질문이야! 각자의 장갑을 가져와야 한단다.
남 왜 장갑이 필요한가요?
여 우리는 농장에서 감자를 심을 예정이니, 손을 보호하기 위해 그것들이 필요해.
남 알겠습니다.

해설 | ① 체험 장소(농장), ② 교통편(버스), ③ 준비물(장갑), ④ 체험 내용(감자 심기)에 대해 언급했으므로 정답은 ⑤ '종료 시간'이다.

어휘 | field trip 체험 학습 glove [glʌv] 명 장갑 plant [plænt] 동 심다 protect [prətékt] 동 보호하다

10 주제 고르기

정답 ④

M Welcome to the National Science Museum. Please follow our safety rules in the Typhoon Experience Exhibit. First of all, a strong wind will blow, so hold on to the rail in front of you. Also, do not take out your cellphone. Lastly, keep your raincoat on. If you take it off, your clothes will get wet.

남 국립 과학 박물관에 오신 것을 환영합니다. 태풍 체험전에서는 저희의 안전 수칙을 지켜 주십시오. 가장 먼저, 강한 바람이 불 것이므로, 앞에 있는 난간을 꼭 붙잡으십시오. 또, 휴대폰을 꺼내지 마십시오. 마지막으로, 우비를 착용한 채로 있으십시오. 만약 그것을 벗으시면, 옷이 젖을 것입니다.

해설 | 남자가 태풍 체험전에서 지켜야 할 안전 수칙에 대해 말하고 있으므로 정답은 ④ '태풍 체험전 안전 수칙'이다.

어휘 | exhibit [igzíbit] 명 전시회 blow [blou] 동 불다 hold on 꼭 붙잡다 rail [reil] 명 난간 take out 꺼내다 raincoat [réinkòut] 명 우비

11 일치하지 않는 내용 고르기

정답 ⑤

W Harry, do you want to go to a classical music concert held at the Opera House?
M Sure. When is it?
W It's going to be held this Sunday.
M I've never been there before. Are tickets expensive?
W No. They are free. I also heard that a famous singer will perform that day.
M It will be crowded. I think we should get there early.
W It begins at 6, so let's meet at 5.
M Perfect!

여 Harry, 오페라 하우스에서 열리는 클래식 음악 연주회에 가고 싶니?
남 물론이지. 언제야?
여 그건 이번 일요일에 열릴 거야.
남 나는 전에 거기 가본 적이 없어. 티켓이 비싸니?
여 아니. 무료야. 그날 그리고 유명한 가수가 공연할 예정이라고 들었어.
남 붐비겠네. 우리 거기에 일찍 도착해야 할 것 같아.
여 6시에 시작하니까, 5시에 만나자.
남 좋아!

해설 | 여자가 음악 연주회가 6시에 시작한다고 했고, 5시에 만나자고 했으므로 정답은 ⑤ '오후 5시 30분에 시작한다.'이다.

어휘 | hold [hould] 동 열다 expensive [ikspénsiv] 형 비싼 free [friː] 형 무료의 perform [pərfɔ́ːrm] 동 공연하다 crowded [kráudid] 형 붐비는

12 목적 고르기

정답 ②

M Hi, Kate. Where are you going?
W I'm heading to a department store.
M The one next to the police station?
W Yes. I need to buy a birthday gift for my friend.
M Have you decided what to buy?
W Yes. I searched for shirts on the Internet, but I want to see them in person.
M Yeah. Sometimes products look different online.
W Do you want to come with me?
M Okay. I'm free now.

남 안녕, Kate. 어디 가는 중이니?
여 백화점으로 향하는 중이야.
남 경찰서 옆에 있는 거 말이야?
여 응. 친구 생일 선물을 사야 해.
남 뭐 살지 정했어?
여 응. 인터넷으로 셔츠들을 검색했는데, 직접 보고 싶었어.
남 그래. 온라인으로는 가끔 상품들이 다르게 보여.
여 나랑 같이 갈래?
남 그래. 나 지금 한가해.

해설 | 여자가 백화점에서 친구의 생일 선물을 사야 한다고 했으므로 정답은 ② '친구 선물을 사기 위해서'이다.
어휘 | department store 백화점 in person 직접, 실제로 하는

13 금액 정보 고르기

정답 ④

M Good morning. Would you like to order?
W I'd like to order a bulgogi hamburger set.
M Okay. It's 10 dollars.
W Could I have a large drink instead of a medium one?
M Sure, but it will cost two dollars more. Would you like to change your French fries to a large size too?
W Yes. How much is it in total?
M It's 13 dollars.
W Here you are.
M Thank you. Have a good day.

남 좋은 아침입니다. 주문하시겠어요?
여 불고기 햄버거 세트를 주문하고 싶어요.
남 네. 10달러입니다.
여 중간 것 대신 큰 음료로 바꿀 수 있을까요?
남 물론이죠, 하지만 2달러 더 내셔야 해요. 감자튀김도 큰 사이즈로 변경하고 싶으신가요?
여 네. 총 얼마인가요?
남 13달러입니다.
여 여기 있어요.
남 감사합니다. 좋은 하루 되세요.

해설 | 여자가 총 얼마인지 묻자 남자가 13달러라고 했으므로 정답은 ④ '$ 13'이다.
어휘 | instead of ~ 대신 in total 총, 전체로

14 관계 고르기

정답 ②

W Hi. I'm sorry, but there is a mistake.
M What's wrong?
W I ordered an iced coffee, but I got a hot one.
M Oh, I see. Can I see your receipt, please?
W Sure. Here you go.
M You are right. Let me get you an iced coffee right away.
W Thank you so much!
M Please take this cookie too. We apologize for the mistake.

여 안녕하세요. 실례지만, 실수가 있어요.
남 무엇이 잘못되었나요?
여 저는 아이스 커피를 주문했는데, 뜨거운 것을 받았어요.
남 오, 그렇군요. 영수증을 볼 수 있을까요?
여 물론이죠. 여기 있어요.
남 맞네요. 아이스 커피를 바로 가져다드릴게요.
여 정말 감사합니다!
남 이 쿠키도 가져가세요. 실수에 대해 사과 드립니다.

해설 | 남자가 여자에게 잘못 주문된 커피를 교환해 주고 있는 것으로 보아 정답은 ② '바리스타 — 손님'이다.
어휘 | mistake [mistéik] 명 실수 receipt [risí:t] 명 영수증 apologize [əpálədʒàiz] 동 사과하다

15 부탁·요청한 일 고르기

정답 ④

M Olivia, can I borrow your earphones?
W Sure. They're in my bag. *[Pause]* Oh, no!
M What's wrong?
W I think I left them on a bench in the park.
M What did you do there?
W I sat down on a bench after taking a walk. Can you go to the park with me to find my earphones?
M Of course.
W Thank you so much. I hope they are still there.

남 Olivia, 네 이어폰을 빌릴 수 있을까?
여 물론이지. 그것들은 내 가방 안에 있어. *[잠시 멈춤]* 오, 이런!
남 무슨 일이야?
여 그것들을 공원에 있는 벤치 위에 두고 온 것 같아.
남 거기서 뭘 했는데?
여 산책한 후에 벤치에 앉아 있었어. 내 이어폰을 찾으러 공원에 같이 가줄 수 있니?
남 당연하지.
여 정말 고마워. 거기에 여전히 있으면 좋겠다.

해설 | 여자가 남자에게 공원에 같이 가 줄 수 있을지 요청했으므로 정답은 ④ '공원에 함께 가기'이다.
어휘 | take a walk 산책하다 still [stil] 부 여전히

16 이유 고르기

정답 ④

M Hey, Yura. What is this box?
W It's a present for you. Open it up.
M Really? Thanks a lot. *[Pause]* Wow, there are macarons in the box!
W You're welcome.
M Why are you giving these to me? It's not my birthday today.
W I know. I just want to cheer you up. You seem exhausted recently.
M You're so kind.
W I'm glad you like them.

남 안녕, 유라야. 이 상자는 뭐니?
여 그건 널 위한 선물이야. 열어 봐.
남 정말? 진짜 고마워. *[잠시 멈춤]* 우와, 상자 안에 마카롱이 들어 있네!
여 천만에.
남 왜 내게 마카롱을 주는 거야? 오늘은 내 생일이 아닌데.
여 알아. 그냥 기운을 북돋아 주고 싶었어. 너 요즘 지쳐 보여.
남 너 정말 친절하구나.
여 네가 좋아해서 기쁘다.

해설 | 여자가 남자의 기운을 북돋아 주고 싶어서 마카롱을 줬다고 말했으므로 정답은 ④ '응원하는 마음을 전하기 위해서'이다.

어휘 | present [préznt] 명 선물 exhausted [igɔ́:stid] 형 지친, 기진맥진한

17 그림 상황에 적절한 대화 고르기

정답 ②

① M Would you like something to drink?
W Yes. I'd like a glass of apple juice, please.
② M Is there something wrong with my dog?
W Actually, he is a bit overweight for his age.
③ M Your rabbit is so cute!
W Thanks. Her name is Bella.
④ M What's your favorite animal?
W I really love dolphins.
⑤ M Can I borrow your pen?
W Yes. Here you go.

① 남 마실 것 좀 드릴까요?
여 네. 사과주스 한 잔 주세요.
② 남 제 개에게 뭔가 문제가 있나요?
여 사실, 그는 자기 나이에 비해 약간 과체중이에요.
③ 남 네 토끼 정말 귀엽다!
여 고마워. 그녀의 이름은 Bella야.
④ 남 네가 가장 좋아하는 동물은 뭐니?
여 나는 돌고래를 정말 좋아해.
⑤ 남 네 펜 좀 빌려도 될까?
여 그래. 여기 있어.

해설 | 남자가 자신의 개의 상태에 대해 묻자 이에 대해 여자가 알려주는 상황이므로 정답은 ②이다.

어휘 | overweight [òuvərwéit] 형 과체중의 dolphin [dálfin] 명 돌고래

18 언급하지 않은 내용 고르기

정답 ②

W Hello, everyone. I'd like to introduce our new TV program *History Mystery Show*. This amazing new show will be aired on Channel 4 tonight. Jisoo, a popular celebrity in Korea, will be the host. Don't miss the first episode on the mystery of the pyramids. Tune in tonight at 7 p.m.

여 안녕하세요, 여러분. 저는 오늘 저희의 새 TV 프로그램 <History Mystery Show>를 소개해 드리려고 합니다. 이 멋진 새 프로는 오늘 밤 4 채널에서 방영될 것입니다. 한국의 인기 있는 연예인인 지수가 진행자가 될 예정입니다. 피라미드의 신비에 대한 첫 번째 에피소드를 놓치지 마세요. 오늘 밤 오후 7시에 채널 고정하세요.

해설 | ① 방영 채널(4 채널), ③ 진행자(지수), ④ 방송 주제(피라미드의 신비), ⑤ 방송 시간(오후 7시)에 대해 언급했으므로 정답은 ② '방영 요일'이다.

어휘 | introduce [ìntrədjú:s] 동 소개하다 celebrity [səlébrəti] 명 연예인 mystery [místəri] 명 신비, 수수께끼 tune in 채널을 고정하다

19 적절한 응답 고르기

정답 ⑤

M What are you playing on your phone, Olivia?
W It's Quiz Mania. It's a new game I bought.
M What are the quizzes about?
W You can choose from several topics including science, culture, and history.
M Is it difficult?
W Yes. But it's also fun. Are you interested in taking quizzes too?
M Yes. I think I'll download it now.
W Then, I can invite you to this game. What about playing against me now?
M Sure. I'll install it right away.

남 휴대폰으로 뭘 하고 있니, Olivia?
여 이건 Quiz Mania야. 내가 산 새 게임이야.
남 퀴즈들은 뭐에 관한 거야?
여 과학, 문화, 그리고 역사를 포함한 여러 주제 중에서 고를 수 있어.
남 그거 어렵니?
여 응. 하지만 재미도 있어. 너도 퀴즈 푸는 것에 흥미가 있니?
남 응. 나도 지금 그걸 다운받아야겠다.
여 그럼, 내가 너를 이 게임에 초대할 수 있어. 지금 나를 상대로 해보는 게 어때?
남 그래. 지금 바로 설치할게.

해설 | 여자가 지금 자신을 상대로 게임을 해보는 것이 어떤지 제안하고 있으므로 정답은 제안을 수락하는 ⑤ 'Sure. I'll install it right away.'이다.

선택지 해석

① 나는 답을 몰라. ② 나는 과학 퀴즈를 낙제했어. ③ 그녀가 경기에 이겼어. ④ 그것들이 규칙이야. ⑤ 그래. 지금 바로 설치할게.

어휘 | choose [tʃu:z] 동 고르다, 선택하다 include [inklú:d] 동 포함하다 against [əgénst] 전 ~을 상대하여

20 적절한 응답 고르기

정답 ③

W What should we do at your house tonight, Blake?
M Why don't we watch a movie?
W Okay. What kind of movies do you prefer?
M I love scary movies.
W Me too! What about the new zombie movie?
M That's perfect. Should we also have some snacks?
W Absolutely! I can bring nachos or popcorn. Which one do you want?
M Popcorn, please.

여 오늘 밤에 너희 집에서 우리 뭘 할까, Blake?
남 영화를 보는 건 어때?
여 그래. 어떤 종류의 영화를 좋아하니?
남 나는 무서운 영화를 좋아해.
여 나도 그래! 새로 나온 좀비 영화는 어때?
남 완벽해. 간식도 좀 먹을까?
여 물론이지! 내가 나초나 팝콘을 가져올 수 있어. 어떤 걸 원해?
남 팝콘으로 부탁해.

해설 | 여자가 나초나 팝콘을 가져올 수 있다고 하며 어떤 걸 원하는지 묻고 있으므로 정답은 하나를 선택하는 ③ 'Popcorn, please.'이다.

선택지 해석

① 그래, 그럼 그때 봐. ② 그건 정말 무서워. ③ 팝콘으로 부탁해. ④ 그건 그녀가 가장 좋아하는 영화야. ⑤ 티켓이 매진되었어.

어휘 | absolutely [ǽbsəlu:tli] 부 물론; 절대적으로

05회 실전 모의고사

| 문제 pp.58-59

1	③	2	④	3	①	4	④	5	⑤	6	②	7	⑤	8	③	9	①	10	②
11	⑤	12	④	13	②	14	③	15	⑤	16	③	17	④	18	③	19	④	20	②

1 날씨 고르기

정답 ③

W It's time for the weekend weather forecast. On Saturday morning, you'll have bright sunshine and clear skies. In the afternoon, however, it'll be cloudy and gray. On Sunday, it's going to snow heavily until noon. The snow will stop in the evening, and then the sky will clear. It'll be perfect for an evening walk in the snow.

여 주말 일기 예보 시간입니다. 토요일 아침에는 밝은 햇살과 맑은 하늘이 이어지겠습니다. 하지만 오후에는 구름이 끼고 우중충할 예정입니다. 일요일에는 정오까지 눈이 많이 올 것입니다. 눈은 저녁에 그칠 것이고, 하늘이 갤 예정입니다. 눈 속에서의 저녁 산책에 완벽한 날씨일 것입니다.

해설 | 일요일에는 정오까지 눈이 많이 올 것이라고 했으므로 정답은 ③이다.

어휘 | bright [brait] 형 밝은, 눈부신 gray [grei] 형 우중충한, 흐린 noon [nu:n] 명 정오

2 알맞은 그림 고르기

정답 ④

W	Hi. I'm looking for a hat for my nephew.	여	안녕하세요. 제 조카를 위한 모자를 찾고 있어요.
M	Welcome to our store. We have a variety of children's hats.	남	저희 가게에 오신 것을 환영합니다. 저희는 다양한 어린이 모자를 가지고 있습니다.
W	Wow, they all look cute.	여	우와, 모두 귀여워 보이네요.
M	What about this cap with a little duck on it?	남	작은 오리가 있는 이 야구 모자는 어떠신가요?
W	I prefer the ones in animal shapes.	여	저는 동물 모양인 것들이 더 좋아요.
M	Okay. We have one with rabbit ears. And this one has frog eyes instead of ears. Which one do you like better?	남	그러시군요. 저희는 토끼 귀가 있는 것이 하나 있어요. 그리고 이건 귀 대신 개구리 눈이 있어요. 어떤 게 더 좋으신가요?
W	I'll take the one with frog eyes.	여	개구리 눈이 있는 것을 살게요.

해설 | 여자는 동물 모양 모자가 더 좋다고 한 후 개구리 눈이 있는 것을 산다고 했으므로 정답은 ④이다.

어휘 | nephew [néfjuː] 명 (남자) 조카 a variety of 다양한

3 의도 고르기

정답 ①

M	Hey, Minji. Have you made up with Nara?	남	안녕, 민지야. 나라와 화해했니?
W	No, not yet.	여	아니, 아직 안 했어.
M	What's wrong? Why didn't you tell her you're sorry?	남	뭐가 문제야? 왜 그녀에게 미안하다고 말하지 않았니?
W	Well, she also hurt my feelings.	여	음, 그녀도 내 기분을 상하게 했잖아.
M	Listen. The fight was your fault. You told her a lie.	남	들어봐. 싸움은 네 잘못이었어. 네가 그녀에게 거짓말을 했잖아.
W	But I didn't mean to hurt her.	여	그렇지만 그녀에게 상처를 주려는 의도는 아니었어.
M	I know you didn't. But that's not an excuse. You should apologize.	남	네가 그런 의도가 아니었다는 건 나도 알지. 하지만 그건 변명이 안 돼. 넌 사과해야 해.

해설 | 남자가 상처를 주려는 의도가 아니었어도 사과를 해야 한다고 했으므로 정답은 ① '조언'이다.

어휘 | make up with ~와 화해하다 fault [fɔːlt] 명 잘못 lie [lai] 명 거짓말

4 한 일 고르기

정답 ④

W	Suho, long time no see.	여	수호야, 오랜만이야.
M	Hi, Jihyun. It's nice to see you. How was your summer vacation?	남	안녕, 지현아. 보니까 반갑다. 여름방학은 어땠어?
W	I had a great time. I visited my cousin in Hong Kong.	여	정말 즐거웠어. 홍콩에 있는 사촌을 방문했거든.
M	That sounds exciting! What did you like the most?	남	재미있었겠다! 뭐가 제일 좋았니?
W	My favorite was going to a theme park. I also had a lot of delicious food. What about you?	여	내가 제일 좋았던 것은 놀이공원에 가는 거였어. 맛있는 음식도 많이 먹었어. 너는 어땠니?
M	I finally learned how to swim.	남	나는 드디어 수영하는 법을 배웠어.
W	I'm glad to hear that!	여	그 말을 들으니 기쁘다!

해설 | 남자는 드디어 수영하는 법을 배웠다고 했으므로 정답은 ④ '수영 배우기'이다.

어휘 | theme park 놀이공원; 테마파크

5 장소 고르기

정답 ⑤

W	What should we look at first, Jinsu?	여	우리 뭐부터 봐야 할까, 진수야?
M	I would like to see the exhibit on dinosaurs. I find them interesting.	남	나는 공룡에 관한 전시를 보고 싶어. 난 그것들이 흥미롭다고 생각하거든.
W	Me too. This museum has the biggest collection of dinosaur bones in our country.	여	나도. 이 박물관은 우리나라에서 가장 많은 공룡 뼈를 소장하고 있어.
M	I didn't know that. That's amazing.	남	그건 몰랐어. 대단하다.
W	Let's go there now.	여	지금 거기로 가자.
M	The brochure says that the collection is on the third floor.	남	책자에 그 전시는 3층에 있다고 나와 있어.
W	Okay. I can't wait!	여	알았어. 너무 기대돼!

해설 | 이 박물관은 우리나라에서 가장 많은 공룡 뼈를 소장하고 있다는 말을 하는 것으로 보아 정답은 ⑤ '박물관'이다.

어휘 | find [faind] 동 생각하다; 찾다 brochure [brouʃúər] 명 (안내·광고용) 책자

6 일치하지 않는 내용 고르기

정답 ②

M Stacy, look at this poster. There's a Vegetarians for Beginners Workshop next Friday.
W Are you interested?
M Yes. Let's sign up for it. We can learn how to cook delicious meals without using meat.
W Is it a free class?
M No. But it costs only five dollars. The event starts at 9 a.m.
W It ends before 12 p.m., right?
M Yes. It lasts for two hours.
W I'll see you then.
M Don't forget to bring an apron.

남 Stacy, 이 포스터 좀 봐. 다음 금요일에 Vegetarians for Beginners Workshop이 있어.
여 너 관심이 있니?
남 응. 그거 신청하자. 고기를 사용하지 않고 어떻게 맛있는 음식을 요리하는지를 배울 수 있어.
여 무료 수업이니?
남 아니. 하지만 5달러밖에 안 해. 행사는 오전 9시에 시작해.
여 오후 12시 전에 끝나지, 그렇지?
남 응. 그건 두 시간 동안 진행돼.
여 그럼 그때 봐.
남 앞치마 가져오는 거 잊지 마.

해설 | 남자가 다음 금요일에 Vegetarians for Beginners Workshop이 있다고 했으므로 정답은 ② '다음 일요일에 열린다.'이다.

어휘 | sign up for ~을 신청하다 apron [éiprən] 명 앞치마

7 특정 정보 고르기

정답 ⑤

W Who is that in the picture, Aaron?
M This is Harry Kane, an English soccer player.
W I think I read about him in a magazine.
M He's famous, so you can find many interviews. Who's your favorite athlete?
W I like Lee Sanghwa. She was a Korean speed skater.
M I know her. She won a gold medal at the Olympics, right?
W Yeah. Speed skating became my favorite sport after watching her races.

여 사진 속의 저 사람은 누구니, Aaron?
남 이 사람은 영국 축구 선수인 해리 케인이야.
여 잡지에서 그에 대해 읽어 본 것 같아.
남 그는 유명해서, 인터뷰들을 많이 찾을 수 있어. 네가 가장 좋아하는 운동선수는 누구니?
여 나는 이상화를 좋아해. 그녀는 한국의 스피드 스케이팅 선수였어.
남 그녀를 알아. 올림픽에서 금메달을 땄잖아, 그렇지?
여 응. 그녀의 경주를 본 후 스피드 스케이팅은 내가 가장 좋아하는 스포츠가 되었어.

해설 | 여자는 이상화의 경주를 본 후 스피드 스케이팅이 가장 좋아하는 스포츠가 되었다고 했으므로 정답은 ⑤ '스피드 스케이팅'이다.

어휘 | athlete [ǽθliːt] 명 운동선수 race [reis] 명 경주

8 할 일 고르기

정답 ③

M Good afternoon. What can I do for you?
W Hi, I want to purchase these.
M Okay. One jacket, two shirts, and a pair of socks. Will that be all?
W Yes. I don't need anything else.
M Did you check the sizes of all the items?
W Uh, wait. This isn't medium. Do you have this jacket in medium?
M Just a minute. Let me check in storage.

남 안녕하세요. 무엇을 도와 드릴까요?
여 안녕하세요, 저는 이것들을 구매하고 싶어요.
남 알겠습니다. 재킷 하나, 셔츠 두 개, 그리고 양말 한 켤레요. 이게 전부이신가요?
여 네. 다른 건 필요 없어요.
남 모든 품목의 사이즈는 확인하셨나요?
여 어, 잠시만요. 이건 미디엄이 아니네요. 이 재킷 미디엄으로 있나요?
남 잠시만요. 창고를 확인해볼게요.

해설 | 남자가 창고를 확인해본다고 했으므로 정답은 ③ '창고 확인하기'이다.

어휘 | purchase [pə́ːrtʃəs] 동 구매하다 item [áitəm] 명 품목; 항목 storage [stɔ́ːridʒ] 명 창고

9 언급하지 않은 내용 고르기

정답 ①

W Welcome to the Hamilton Park Information Center. How can I help you today?
M Hi. I was wondering if I could buy a map of the park.
W It's two dollars. Here you go. Anything else?
M How big is the park?
W It's the size of 70 soccer fields.
M Wow, that's really big. What's in the park?
W It has a rose garden, four tennis courts, and a restaurant.
M Do I need a reservation to use the tennis court?
W Yes. You can reserve a court on our website.

여 해밀턴 공원 안내소에 오신 것을 환영합니다. 오늘 어떻게 도와드릴까요?
남 안녕하세요. 혹시 공원 지도를 살 수 있을까 해서요.
여 2달러예요. 여기 있습니다. 또 다른 건 없으세요?
남 공원이 얼마나 큰가요?
여 축구장 70개 크기예요.
남 우와, 정말 크네요. 공원에는 뭐가 있나요?
여 장미 정원, 테니스 코트 네 개, 그리고 식당이 있어요.
남 테니스 코트를 이용하려면 예약이 필요한가요?
여 네. 저희 웹사이트에서 코트를 예약하실 수 있어요.

해설 | ② 지도 가격(2달러), ③ 공원 크기(축구장 70개 크기), ④ 공원 시설(장미 정원, 테니스 코트 네 개, 식당), ⑤ 시설 예약 방법(웹사이트)에 대해 언급했으므로 정답은 ① '공원 입장료'이다.

어휘 | wonder [wʌ́ndər] 동 ~일까 생각하다; 궁금하다 soccer field 축구장 reserve [rizə́:rv] 동 예약하다

10 주제 고르기

정답 ②

M Hello, everyone. Today, I'm going to tell you how to improve your grades. First, you should pay attention in class. Listening to your teacher during class is the best way to learn the materials. Second, get enough sleep. If you are tired, it's hard to concentrate in class. Lastly, don't start studying right before the test. You should study a little every day.

남 안녕하세요, 여러분. 오늘은 성적을 향상하는 방법을 말씀드리겠습니다. 첫 번째로, 수업 시간에 집중해야 합니다. 수업 중에 선생님의 말씀을 듣는 것이 학습 자료를 익히는 가장 좋은 방법입니다. 두 번째로, 충분한 잠을 주무십시오. 만약 여러분이 피곤하다면, 수업 시간에 집중하기가 어렵습니다. 마지막으로, 시험 직전에 공부를 시작하지 마세요. 매일 조금씩 공부해야 합니다.

해설 | 남자가 성적을 향상하는 방법을 알려주겠다고 했으므로 정답은 ② '성적을 향상하는 법'이다.

어휘 | improve [imprú:v] 동 향상하다 material [mətíəriəl] 명 학습 자료 concentrate [kánsəntrèit] 동 집중하다

11 일치하지 않는 내용 고르기

정답 ⑤

M Sarah, did you see this? The Griffith Marathon is scheduled next Saturday.
W Is that the event to raise money for wild animal protection?
M Yes. There are 5-kilometer and 10-kilometer marathons. Let's sign up for the 5-kilometer one.
W Okay. How much is it?
M It's 50 dollars. The event starts at 8:00 a.m., but we have to line up at 7:45 a.m.
W Got it. Do we need to bring drinks?
M Water will be provided.

남 Sarah, 이거 봤어? Griffith Marathon이 다음 주 토요일에 예정되어 있어.
여 그거 야생동물 보호를 위해 기금을 모으기 위한 행사니?
남 응. 5킬로미터 마라톤과 10킬로미터 마라톤이 있어. 5킬로미터짜리를 신청하자.
여 그래. 얼마야?
남 50달러야. 행사는 오전 8시에 시작하지만 우리는 오전 7시 45분에 줄을 서야 해.
여 알겠어. 마실 것을 들고 가야 하니?
남 물은 제공될 거야.

해설 | 남자가 물은 제공될 거라고 했으므로 정답은 ⑤ '참가자가 물을 준비해야 한다.'이다.

어휘 | schedule [skédʒu:l] 동 예정하다, 일정을 잡다 raise [reiz] 동 (자금·사람 등을) 모으다 protection [prətékʃən] 명 보호 line up 줄을 서다 provide [prəváid] 동 제공하다

12 목적 고르기

정답 ④

[Telephone rings.]
M Good morning. Bistro Italiano. How can I help you?
W Hello. I booked a table, and I need to make a change.
M May I have your name please?
W It's Rebecca Johnson.
M Alright. You reserved a table for four on May 15th at 6:30.
W Yes. But I'd like to change the time.
M When will you arrive at our restaurant?
W At 7:30. Also, there will be five people, not four.

[전화기가 울린다.]
남 좋은 아침입니다. Bistro Italiano입니다. 어떻게 도와드릴까요?
여 안녕하세요. 테이블을 예약했는데, 변경을 해야 해서요.
남 성함이 어떻게 되시나요?
여 Rebecca Johnson이에요.
남 알겠습니다. 5월 15일 6시 30분에 4인 테이블을 예약하셨네요.
여 네. 그런데 시간을 변경하고 싶어요.
남 저희 식당에 언제 도착할 예정이신가요?
여 7시 30분이요. 그리고 네 명이 아니라, 다섯 명일 거예요.

해설 | 여자가 테이블을 예약했는데 변경을 해야 할 것 같다고 했으므로 정답은 ④ '예약을 변경하기 위해서'이다.
어휘 | book [buk] 동 예약하다 명 책 arrive [əráiv] 동 도착하다

13 시간 정보 고르기

정답 ②

M Bomi, do you want to visit the new amusement park this Saturday?
W Yes. I want to see the parade and fireworks.
M What type of ticket do you want to get?
W How about the half-day ticket? We can get in the park after 4 p.m.
M Okay. Should we meet in front of the park?
W Sure. I'm so excited!
M Can you meet me at 3:30?
W How about 3? Let's have some coffee before we go in.
M Okay. See you then!

남 보미야, 이번 토요일에 새로운 놀이공원에 갈래?
여 응. 나는 퍼레이드와 불꽃놀이를 보고 싶어.
남 어떤 종류의 티켓을 사고 싶니?
여 반나절 짜리 티켓은 어때? 오후 4시 이후에 공원에 들어갈 수 있어.
남 좋아. 우리 공원 앞에서 만날까?
여 그래. 너무 기대돼!
남 3시 30분에 만날 수 있니?
여 3시는 어때? 들어가기 전에 커피를 좀 마시자.
남 알겠어. 그때 보자!

해설 | 여자가 3시는 어떠냐고 묻자 남자가 알겠다고 했으므로 정답은 ② '3:00 p.m.'이다.
어휘 | parade [pəréid] 명 퍼레이드; 행진 firework [fáiərwə:rk] 명 불꽃놀이

14 관계 고르기

정답 ③

W Hello. What can I do for you?
M I'm looking for some flowers for my mom.
W What about lilies? They're really fresh today.
M Those look beautiful. I'd also like to get some colorful flowers.
W Hmm... What other flowers do you prefer?
M Well, I'm not sure. *[Pause]* Oh, what are those purple ones?
W Those are lilacs. They go well with lilies.

여 안녕하세요. 무엇을 도와 드릴까요?
남 저는 엄마를 위해 꽃을 찾고 있어요.
여 백합은 어떠신가요? 오늘 그것들이 아주 신선해요.
남 이것들은 아름답네요. 저는 알록달록한 꽃도 약간 사고 싶어요.
여 흠... 다른 꽃은 어떤 것을 좋아하세요?
남 글쎄요, 잘 모르겠어요. *[잠시 멈춤]* 오, 저 보라색 꽃들은 뭐예요?
여 저것들은 라일락이에요. 백합과 잘 어울려요.

해설 | 남자가 엄마를 위해 꽃을 찾고 있다고 했고, 여자가 꽃을 추천해 주고 있는 것으로 보아 정답은 ③ '꽃집 직원 — 손님'이다.
어휘 | lily [líli] 명 백합 go well with 잘 어울리다

15 부탁·요청한 일 고르기

정답 ⑤

M Honey, your tteokbokki tasted great. Thanks for cooking tonight.
W You're welcome.
M I'll do the dishes. Why don't you take a break?
W Thanks, but there are still many other things to do.
M What else should I do?
W Will you vacuum the floor for me? I will do the laundry.
M Sure. I'll do that after washing the dishes.

남 여보, 당신 떡볶이는 정말 맛있었어. 오늘 밤 요리해 줘서 고마워.
여 천만에.
남 내가 설거지할게. 당신은 쉬는 게 어때?
여 고맙지만, 아직 할 일이 많아.
남 내가 또 뭘 하면 될까?
여 나 대신 진공청소기로 바닥을 청소해줄래? 난 빨래를 할게.
남 물론이지. 설거지한 후에 할게.

해설 | 여자가 진공청소기로 바닥을 청소해달라고 부탁했으므로 정답은 ⑤ '청소기 돌리기'이다.
어휘 | vacuum [vǽkjuəm] 동 진공청소기로 청소하다 floor [flɔ:r] 명 바닥 do the laundry 빨래하다, 세탁하다

16 이유 고르기

정답 ③

M Hey, Janet. How was your trip to Europe?
W It began badly, but I had fun.
M What happened?
W I missed my flight to London.
M Really? Why?
W I was at the airport on time, but my friend, Erica, came late.
M Oh, no! What did you do?
W We had to wait eight hours for the next flight.

남 안녕, Janet. 유럽 여행은 어땠어?
여 시작은 좋지 않았지만, 그래도 즐거웠어.
남 무슨 일 있었어?
여 런던행 비행기를 놓쳤어.
남 정말? 왜?
여 나는 공항에 제때 도착했는데, 내 친구 Erica가 늦게 왔어.
남 오, 이런! 어떻게 했어?
여 다음 비행기를 타기 위해 8시간을 기다려야 했어.

해설 | 여자는 친구 Erica가 늦게 왔기 때문이라고 말했으므로 정답은 ③ '친구가 늦게 와서'이다.
어휘 | miss [mis] 동 놓치다 on time 제때

17 그림 상황에 적절한 대화 고르기

정답 ④

① M What are you planning to do this Saturday?
W I'm going to go to my grandma's house.
② M Do you want a glass of water?
W No, thanks. I already drank some.
③ M Oh, it smells so bad here.
W I think there's a garbage can nearby.
④ M Please put glass bottles in this recycling can.
W Okay, I will.
⑤ M How old is your brother?
W He's 14.

① 남 이번 토요일에 뭐 할 계획이니?
여 할머니 댁에 갈 거야.
② 남 물 한 잔 마실래?
여 아니 괜찮아. 이미 좀 마셨어.
③ 남 오, 여기 냄새가 너무 고약하다.
여 근처에 쓰레기통이 있는 것 같아.
④ 남 유리병은 이 재활용 쓰레기통에 넣어줘.
여 그래, 그럴게.
⑤ 남 네 남동생은 몇 살이니?
여 14살이야.

해설 | 남자가 유리병을 재활용 쓰레기통에 넣어달라고 요청하고 있고 여자가 그러겠다고 하는 상황이므로 정답은 ④이다.
어휘 | garbage can 쓰레기통 nearby [nìərbái] 부 근처에

18 언급하지 않은 내용 고르기

정답 ③

W Have you heard about the Fremont Art Festival? This event is held to introduce new artists to the world. It takes place this year on August 6th and 7th. Everything from paintings and drawings to jewelry and clothing will be on display. Musical performances will also take place on a stage near the main entrance. Why don't you come join us?

여 Fremont Art Festival에 대해 들어본 적 있으신가요? 이 행사는 세상에 새로운 예술가들을 소개하기 위해 개최됩니다. 이것은 올해 8월 6일과 7일에 열립니다. 그림과 소묘부터 보석과 옷에 이르기까지 모든 것이 전시될 것입니다. 음악 공연도 정문 근처의 무대에서 펼쳐질 예정입니다. 오셔서 저희와 함께하는 게 어떠신가요?

해설 | ① 행사 목적(세상에 새로운 예술가들을 소개함), ② 행사 날짜(올해 8월 6일과 7일), ④ 전시 품목(그림, 소묘, 보석, 옷 등), ⑤ 공연 장소(정문 근처 무대)에 대해 언급했으므로 정답은 ③ '참가비'이다.
어휘 | take place 개최되다 drawing [drɔ́:iŋ] 명 소묘 jewelry [dʒú:əlri] 명 보석 clothing [klóuðiŋ] 명 옷 on display 전시된

19 적절한 응답 고르기

정답 ④

W It was a great decision to ride a bike here!
M Yeah. I love feeling the sea breeze while I'm riding.
W Aren't you tired yet? We have ridden for a long time.
M A little bit. I'm also thirsty and hungry.
W Do you know any restaurants near here?
M No. I don't know this area well.
W Then, I'll look on my phone for a place. *[Pause]* Oh, here's a cafe.
M Where is it?
W It's about 500 meters away.

여 여기서 자전거를 타기로 한 것은 좋은 결정이었어!
남 맞아. 타는 동안 바닷바람을 느끼는 것이 정말 좋다.
여 아직 안 피곤하니? 우리 오랜 시간 동안 탔잖아.
남 조금. 난 목도 마르고 배도 고파.
여 이 주변에 식당 아는 곳이 있니?
남 아니. 이 지역은 잘 몰라.
여 그럼 내 휴대폰에서 한 군데 찾아볼게. *[잠시 멈춤]* 오, 여기 카페가 있어.
남 어디에 있어?
여 500미터 정도 떨어져 있어.

해설 | 남자가 카페가 어디 있냐고 묻고 있으므로 정답은 위치를 언급하는 ④ 'It's about 500 meters away.'이다.

선택지 해석

① 그녀는 열심히 운동하고 있어. ② 아니. 나는 거기에 가는 길을 몰라. ③ 물이 정말 파랗다! ④ 500미터 정도 떨어져 있어. ⑤ 콜라 두 잔 주세요.

어휘 | decision [disíʒən] 명 결정 sea breeze 바닷바람, 해풍 area [ɛ́əriə] 명 지역 work out 운동하다

20 적절한 응답 고르기

정답 ②

M Yejin, you seem very stressed.
W Yes. I just talked with my teacher.
M What did you talk about?
W She wants me to participate in a national writing competition.
M That's great. Congratulations!
W Thank you. But I'm so nervous.
M You don't have to be. You're great at writing. What kind of competition is it?
W It's a poetry contest.

남 예진아, 너 스트레스를 많이 받은 것처럼 보여.
여 응. 방금 우리 선생님과 이야기했어.
남 뭐에 대해 이야기했니?
여 선생님은 내가 전국 글짓기 대회에 참가하기를 바라셔.
남 잘됐네. 축하해!
여 고마워. 하지만 난 너무 걱정돼.
남 그럴 필요 없어. 너는 글을 잘 쓰잖아. 어떤 종류의 대회야?
여 그건 시 대회야.

해설 | 남자가 어떤 종류의 대회인지 물었으므로 정답은 대회 종류를 알려주는 ② 'It's a poetry contest.'이다.

선택지 해석

① 그는 상을 탔어. ② 그건 시 대회야. ③ 대회가 곧 시작할 거야. ④ 글을 쓰기 시작해도 돼. ⑤ 나는 휴가가 필요해.

어휘 | national [nǽʃənəl] 형 전국의; 국가의 competition [kàmpətíʃən] 명 대회 poetry [póuitri] 명 시 contest [kántest] 명 대회

06회 실전 모의고사

| 문제 pp.66-67

1	⑤	2	③	3	⑤	4	①	5	⑤	6	④	7	②	8	⑤	9	③	10	③
11	④	12	⑤	13	⑤	14	③	15	①	16	①	17	④	18	④	19	②	20	①

1 날씨 고르기

정답 ⑤

M Good morning, everyone. It's time for the national weather update. Today, strong winds and rainfall are expected in Incheon. There will be heavy snowfall in Seoul, but it will be sunny in the afternoon. Daejeon will be snowy all day, so be careful when you drive as the roads will be slippery. In Changwon, you'll see cloudy skies, but it won't snow until next week.

남 안녕하십니까, 여러분. 국내 날씨 정보 시간입니다. 오늘 인천에는 강한 바람과 강우가 예상됩니다. 서울에는 폭설이 예상되나, 오후에는 화창할 것입니다. 대전은 온종일 눈이 내릴 예정이므로, 도로가 미끄러울 것이니 운전하실 때 조심하십시오. 창원에서는 흐린 하늘을 보시겠지만 다음 주까지는 눈이 내리지 않을 예정입니다.

해설 | 대전은 눈이 내릴 예정이라고 했으므로 정답은 ⑤이다.

어휘 | rainfall [reinfɔl] 명 강우 heavy snowfall 폭설 slippery [slípəri] 형 미끄러운

2 알맞은 그림 고르기

정답 ③

W Kyle, what a cute scarf! Did you make it?
M Yes. It's a present for my grandmother.
W Are those cat faces?
M Yeah. I sewed on those patches because my grandmother loves cats.
W What does it say in the small letters underneath the cats?
M It says, "LOVE". I hope she likes it.

여 Kyle, 정말 귀여운 목도리다! 네가 만들었니?
남 응. 이건 우리 할머니를 위한 선물이야.
여 그것들은 고양이 얼굴이니?
남 응. 할머니가 고양이를 좋아하셔서 내가 그 헝겊 조각들을 꿰맸어.
여 고양이들 아래에 작은 글자로는 뭐라고 쓰여있니?
남 'LOVE'라고 쓰여 있어. 할머니가 좋아하시면 좋겠다.

해설 | 남자는 고양이 얼굴 모양의 헝겊 조각들을 꿰맸고 아래에 작은 글자로 'LOVE'라고 쓰여 있는 목도리를 만들었다고 했으므로 정답은 ③이다.

어휘 | sew [sou] 동 꿰매다 patch [pætʃ] 명 헝겊 조각 letter [létər] 명 글자, 철자 underneath [ʌ̀ndərní:θ] 전 아래의

3 언급하지 않은 내용 고르기

정답 ⑤

W Do you want to go to see a musical next week?
M Sure, Mom. What is it called?
W It's *The Tiger World*.
M Oh, I've heard of it. Isn't it about a little tiger looking for his dad in the forest?
W Right. And a famous actor plays the main character.
M When do you want to watch it?
W Is 5:30 on Wednesday okay with you?
M Sure. Let's see it then.
W Okay. I'll book two tickets then.

여 다음 주에 뮤지컬 보러 갈래?
남 좋아요, 엄마. 제목이 뭐예요?
여 <The Tiger World>란다.
남 오, 그것에 대해 들어봤어요. 어린 호랑이가 숲에서 그의 아빠를 찾는 것에 대한 것 아닌가요?
여 맞아. 그리고 유명한 배우가 주인공을 연기해.
남 언제 보고 싶으세요?
여 수요일 5시 30분 괜찮니?
남 물론이죠. 그때 봐요 그럼.
여 그래. 그럼 티켓을 두 장 예매할게.

해설 | ① 제목(<The Tiger World>), ② 내용(어린 호랑이가 숲에서 그의 아빠를 찾는 것), ③ 배우(유명한 배우), ④ 예매 시간(수요일 5시 30분)을 언급했으므로 정답은 ⑤ '예매 방법'이다.

어휘 | forest [fɔ́:rist] 명 숲 famous [féiməs] 형 유명한 main character 주인공, 주요 인물

4 한 일 고르기

정답 ①

M What are you doing, Christine?
W I'm writing a diary about National Tree Day, Dad.
M Did you do anything special?
W Yes. I watched a documentary about trees in the Amazon.
M That's nice. How was it?
W It was really interesting. I realized how important preserving trees is.
M You're right. How about planting a tree in our backyard next week?
W Oh, that's a great idea.

남 뭐 하고 있니, Christine?
여 식목일에 대해 일기를 쓰고 있어요, 아빠.
남 뭔가 특별한 것을 했니?
여 네. 아마존의 나무들에 대한 다큐멘터리를 봤어요.
남 그거 좋구나. 어땠니?
여 정말 흥미로웠어요. 저는 나무를 보존하는 것이 얼마나 중요한지 깨달았어요.
남 그렇단다. 다음 주에 우리 뒷마당에 나무를 심는 것이 어떠니?
여 오, 그거 좋은 생각이에요.

해설 | 여자는 식목일에 아마존의 나무들에 대한 다큐멘터리를 봤다고 했으므로 정답은 ① '다큐멘터리 보기'이다.

어휘 | interesting [íntərəstiŋ] 형 흥미로운 realize [rí:əlàiz] 동 깨닫다 preserve [prizə́:rv] 동 보존하다 plant [plænt] 동 심다 backyard [bǽkjàrd] 명 뒷마당

5 장소 고르기

정답 ⑤

W Hello. Are you looking for a new cellphone?
M Yes, I am. But I don't know what type I want.
W Well, this one here is a good size. It's not too big or small.
M It looks nice. Do you have it in other colors?
W This phone comes in blue, pink, and black.
M Can I see the blue one, please?
W Sure. Just a second.

여 안녕하세요. 새 휴대폰을 찾으시나요?
남 네, 맞아요. 그런데 제가 어떤 종류를 원하는지 잘 모르겠어요.
여 음, 여기 이건 사이즈가 괜찮아요. 너무 크거나 작지 않아요.
남 좋아 보이네요. 다른 색상으로도 있나요?
여 이 휴대폰은 파란색, 분홍색, 그리고 검은색으로 나와요.
남 파란색을 볼 수 있을까요?
여 물론이죠. 잠시만요.

해설 | 새 휴대폰을 찾고 있다고 언급했고, 여자가 사이즈를 추천해주고 남자가 휴대폰의 색상을 고르는 것으로 보아 정답은 ⑤ '휴대폰 가게'이다.

어휘 | type [taip] 명 종류 come [kʌm] 동 (물품, 상품 등이) 나오다; 오다

6 의도 고르기

정답 ④

W Did you buy a new hat?
M Yeah. I bought it last week at a shopping mall.
W How much was it?
M I paid 50 dollars for this.
W I think I saw the same hat, and it was only 25 dollars.
M Where did you see it?
W I saw it on an online shop. All the products were 50% off.
M What? That's a huge difference. I spent too much money.

여 새 모자 샀니?
남 응. 쇼핑몰에서 지난주에 샀어.
여 얼마였어?
남 50달러를 냈어.
여 같은 모자를 봤던 것 같은데, 그건 겨우 25달러였어.
남 어디서 봤는데?
여 온라인 쇼핑몰에서 봤어. 모든 제품이 50% 할인이었어.
남 뭐? 그거 큰 차이인데. 난 돈을 너무 많이 썼네.

해설 | 남자가 새로 산 모자를 보고 여자가 온라인에 50% 할인하는 쇼핑몰이 있었다고 하자, 남자가 자신이 돈을 너무 많이 썼다고 했으므로 정답은 ④ '후회'이다.

어휘 | product [prάdʌkt] 명 제품 huge [hjuːdʒ] 형 큰, 거대한 difference [dífərəns] 명 차이

7 특정 정보 고르기

정답 ②

M Alice, which book did you borrow?
W I got a book about mysteries all over the world.
M Oh, isn't it scary?
W No way. I'm looking forward to reading it. What about you?
M I checked out a science fiction book.
W Science fiction? Why did you choose that genre?
M It's my favorite. I enjoy reading stories about robots and space travel.

남 Alice, 너는 어떤 책을 빌렸니?
여 나는 온 세상의 미스터리 관한 책을 빌렸어.
남 오, 그거 무섭지 않니?
여 전혀. 그걸 읽는 것이 기대돼. 너는 어때?
남 나는 공상 과학책을 빌렸어.
여 공상 과학? 왜 그 장르를 골랐어?
남 내가 제일 좋아하는 장르야. 나는 로봇과 우주여행에 대한 이야기를 읽는 것을 좋아하거든.

해설 | 남자가 공상 과학책을 빌렸다고 했으므로 정답은 ② '공상 과학'이다.

어휘 | mystery [místəri] 명 미스터리, 수수께끼 look forward to ~을 기대하다, 고대하다 check out 빌리다, 대출하다 science fiction 공상 과학

8 할 일 고르기

정답 ⑤

M Hey, April. Are you going to your hometown this weekend?
W I'm not planning to do anything special.
M Then, would you like to take a trip with me?
W Where are you going?
M I want to visit Dokdo.
W Sounds cool, but I heard the weather has to be really nice to go there.
M Oh, no. I heard it will rain this weekend. I'm worried we won't be able to go!
W But you'd better check the weather forecast first.
M I'll do it right now.

남 안녕, April. 이번 주말에 고향에 갈 거니?
여 나는 아직 특별한 것을 계획하고 있지 않아.
남 그럼, 나와 함께 여행하지 않을래?
여 어디 가는데?
남 나는 독도를 방문하고 싶어.
여 멋질 것 같은데, 거기 가려면 날씨가 정말 좋아야 한다고 들었어.
남 오, 안돼. 이번 주말에 비가 올 거라고 들었어. 갈 수 없을까 봐 걱정돼!
여 하지만 먼저 일기예보를 확인해보는 게 좋겠어.
남 지금 바로 해볼게.

해설 | 여자가 먼저 일기예보를 확인해 보는 게 좋겠다고 하자 남자가 지금 바로 해보겠다고 했으므로 정답은 ⑤ '일기예보 확인하기'이다.

어휘 | hometown [hoúmtaùn] 명 고향 plan [plæn] 동 계획하다

9 언급하지 않은 내용 고르기

정답 ③

[Telephone rings.]
M Hello. Korea Traditions Expo information desk. How may I help you?
W I'd like to know when the expo will be.
M It will be held from January 1st to 20th.
W What kind of activities will be offered?
M You can play Korean traditional games like yunnori.
W Do I need to get a ticket in advance?
M No. You can buy it at the venue.
W Okay. How much is a ticket?
M It's five dollars.

[전화기가 울린다.]
남 안녕하세요. 한국 전통 엑스포 안내소입니다. 어떻게 도와 드릴까요?
여 엑스포가 언제일지 알고 싶어서요.
남 1월 1일부터 20일까지 열릴 예정입니다.
여 어떤 활동들이 제공되나요?
남 윷놀이 같은 한국 전통 놀이를 하실 수 있어요.
여 미리 티켓을 구매해야 하나요?
남 아니요. 현장에서 구매하실 수 있어요.
여 그렇군요. 티켓은 얼마인가요?
남 5달러입니다.

해설 | ① 행사 기간(1월 1일부터 20일까지), ② 체험 내용(한국 전통 놀이), ④ 티켓 구매 방법(현장 구매), ⑤ 티켓 가격(5달러)에 대해 언급했으므로 정답은 ③ '개최 장소'이다.

어휘 | offer [ɔ́:fər] 동 제공하다 traditional [trədíʃənəl] 형 전통적인 in advance 미리 venue [vénju:] 명 현장

10 주제 고르기

정답 ③

W Good morning, everyone. I will explain what to do during the volunteer activity today. We will pick up trash from the beach. I will give you two plastic bags. One is for garbage, and the other is for recyclable materials. When the bags are full, bring them back here. Any questions?

여 좋은 아침입니다, 여러분. 저는 오늘 봉사활동 시간에 무엇을 할지 설명할 것입니다. 우리는 해변에서 쓰레기를 주울 것입니다. 제가 여러분께 비닐봉지 두 장을 드릴 것입니다. 하나는 쓰레기를 위한 것이고, 다른 하나는 재활용이 가능한 물건을 위한 것입니다. 봉지가 가득 차면, 여기로 그것들을 가져오세요. 질문 있으신가요?

해설 | 여자가 오늘 봉사활동 시간에 할 일들을 말하고 있으므로 정답은 ③ '봉사활동 안내'이다.

어휘 | explain [ikspléin] 동 설명하다 plastic bag 비닐봉지 garbage [gá:rbidʒ] 명 쓰레기 recyclable [ri:sáikləbl] 형 재활용이 가능한 material [mətíəriəl] 명 물건, 재료

11 일치하지 않는 내용 고르기

정답 ④

M Hello, students. I'd like to tell you about my favorite artist, Vincent van Gogh. He was born in Netherlands and moved to France later. He started painting when he was 27. Van Gogh often used yellow paint in his paintings. He was an amazing artist, but sadly, he got famous after he died.

남 안녕하세요, 학생 여러분. 제가 가장 좋아하는 예술가인 빈센트 반 고흐에 대해 말씀드리려고 합니다. 그는 네덜란드에서 태어났고, 후에 프랑스로 이사했습니다. 그는 27살에 그림을 그리기 시작했습니다. 반 고흐는 그의 그림에 노란 물감을 자주 사용했습니다. 그는 대단한 미술가였지만, 슬프게도 그는 사후에 유명해졌습니다.

해설 | 남자가 반 고흐는 그의 그림에 노란 물감을 자주 사용했다고 했으므로 정답은 ④ '빨간색 물감을 많이 사용했다.'이다.

어휘 | be born 태어나다 move [mu:v] 동 이사하다 use [ju:z] 동 사용하다 sadly [sǽdli] 부 슬프게도

12 목적 고르기

정답 ⑤

[Telephone rings.]
M Hello, this is Strong Gym. How can I help you?
W Hello. Is there anything I need to bring for my yoga class?
M Is this your first time?
W Yes. I signed up for the class yesterday. But I don't know what I need.
M Okay. Please bring your own yoga matt.
W Do I also need to bring my own towel for the shower?
M No. Our gym provides towels.
W Great. Thank you.

[전화기가 울린다.]
남 안녕하세요, Strong Gym입니다. 어떻게 도와드릴까요?
여 안녕하세요. 요가 수업에 가져가야 할 것이 있나요?
남 처음이신가요?
여 네. 어제 수업을 등록했어요. 근데 무엇이 필요한지 몰라서요.
남 그러시군요. 개인 요가 매트를 가져와 주세요.
여 샤워를 하기 위해서는 제 수건을 가져가야 하나요?
남 아니요. 저희 체육관은 수건을 제공합니다.
여 좋네요. 감사합니다.

해설 | 여자가 남자에게 요가 수업에 가져가야 할 것이 있는지 물었으므로 정답은 ⑤ '준비물을 확인하기 위해서'이다.

어휘 | towel [táuəl] 명 수건 provide [prəváid] 동 제공하다

13 금액 정보 고르기

정답 ⑤

M Welcome, what can I do for you?
W I'm looking for a bottle of perfume for my aunt.
M Okay. Would she like a fresh lemon scent?
W She'll love it. How much is it?
M It's 55 dollars.
W It seems quite small. She often wears perfume.
M Then, I recommend this bigger one. It's 75 dollars.
W That seems reasonable. I'll take the bigger one.

남 어서 오세요, 무엇을 도와드릴까요?
여 저는 이모를 위한 향수 한 병을 찾고 있어요.
남 그러시군요. 상쾌한 레몬 향을 좋아하실까요?
여 정말 좋아하실 거예요. 얼마인가요?
남 55달러예요.
여 이건 조금 작아 보이네요. 그녀는 향수를 자주 뿌리시거든요.
남 그럼, 더 큰 이것을 추천해요. 이건 75달러예요.
여 이게 합리적으로 보이네요. 더 큰 것을 살게요.

해설 | 남자가 75달러인 더 큰 것을 추천하자 여자가 그것을 산다고 했으므로 정답은 ⑤ '$ 75'이다.

어휘 | perfume [pə́ːrfjuːm] 명 향수 scent [sent] 명 향, 냄새 recommend [rèkəménd] 동 추천하다 reasonable [ríːzənəbl] 형 합리적인

14 관계 고르기

정답 ③

M How was your meal this evening?
W It was wonderful. I loved the beef stew especially.
M That's good to hear. It was cooked with my new recipe.
W I thought it tasted different compared to what I had during my last visit.
M I ordered special beef from Australia for the stew. What did you think of the cheesecake?
W The fresh raspberries on it were perfect.
M I'm glad you liked it. Thanks for coming.
W We'll be back soon!

남 오늘 저녁 식사 어떠셨나요?
여 굉장했어요. 특히 소고기 스튜가 좋았어요.
남 그것참 다행이네요. 그건 제 새 요리법으로 조리되었어요.
여 지난번 방문했을 때 먹었던 것과 비교해서 맛이 다르다고 생각했어요.
남 스튜에 넣기 위해 호주에서 특별한 소고기를 주문했어요. 치즈케이크는 어떠셨나요?
여 위에 올라간 신선한 산딸기가 완벽했어요.
남 좋아하셨다니 기쁘네요. 방문해주셔서 감사합니다.
여 곧 또 올게요!

해설 | 남자가 저녁 식사에 대해 물으며 방문해줘서 감사하다고 하고 있는 것으로 보아 정답은 ③ '요리사 — 손님'이다.

어휘 | meal [miːl] 명 식사 wonderful [wʌ́ndərfəl] 형 굉장한 recipe [résəpi] 명 요리법 different [dífərənt] 형 다른 glad [glæd] 형 기쁜

15 부탁·요청한 일 고르기

정답 ①

M Honey, our daughter called today.
W Is she having fun staying at summer camp?
M She is, but she forgot to take her phone charger.
W Oh, no. What should we do?
M One of us could go to the post office and send it by express mail.
W Okay. Do you have time to go there?
M Not really. I have to go to a meeting. Could you send the package to her?
W Sure. I'll do it.

남 여보, 우리 딸이 오늘 전화했어.
여 여름 캠프에서 재미있게 지내고 있대?
남 그렇긴 한데, 휴대폰 충전기 가져가는 것을 잊어버렸대.
여 오, 이런. 어떻게 하지?
남 우리 중 한 명이 우체국에 가서 그걸 특급 우편으로 보낼 수 있어.
여 그래. 당신 거기 갈 시간 있어?
남 사실 없어. 회의에 가야 하거든. 그녀에게 소포를 보내줄 수 있어?
여 물론이지. 내가 할게.

해설 | 남자가 여자에게 소포를 보내줄 수 있는지 물었으므로 정답은 ① '소포 보내기'다.

어휘 | phone charger 휴대폰 충전기 express mail 특급 우편 package [pǽkidʒ] 명 소포

16 이유 고르기

정답 ①

M Claire, why don't we have a picnic in the park today?
W Okay, Charles. The weather is perfect.
M Is it going to rain later?
W No. It's going to be sunny all day.
M Then, why did you bring an umbrella?
W Actually, I bought it for Harry.
M Why did you buy him an umbrella?
W He lent me his on Friday, but it broke in the strong wind.
M Ah! Now I see.

남 Claire, 우리 오늘 공원으로 소풍을 가는 게 어때?
여 그래, Charles. 날씨가 완벽해.
남 나중에 비가 올까?
여 아니. 온종일 화창할 거야.
남 그럼 우산은 왜 가지고 온 거야?
여 사실, 이건 Harry를 위해 샀어.
남 그에게 우산을 왜 사주는 거야?
여 금요일에 나에게 그의 우산을 빌려줬는데, 그게 강한 바람에 부러졌거든.
남 아! 이제 이해했어.

해설 | 여자는 남자에게 Harry를 위해 우산을 샀다고 말했으므로 정답은 ① '친구에게 주기 위해서'이다.

어휘 | lend [lend] 통 빌려주다 break [breik] 통 부러지다

17 그림 상황에 적절한 대화 고르기

정답 ④

① W This line is so long.
M I agree. Let's go to another restaurant.
② W Do you feel okay?
M No. I ate too much pizza.
③ W Do you want to go shopping?
M Yes. I need a new pair of jeans.
④ W Excuse me, where is the pasta sauce?
M It's in the Section C, next to the bakery.
⑤ W Can you pick me up from the subway station?
M Yes. I'll be there in 20 minutes.

① 여 이 줄은 너무 길어.
남 나도 동의해. 다른 식당에 가자.
② 여 너 괜찮니?
남 아니. 나 피자를 너무 많이 먹었어.
③ 여 쇼핑 갈래?
남 응. 나 새로운 청바지 한 벌이 필요해.
④ 여 실례합니다, 파스타 소스는 어디에 있나요?
남 그건 제과점 옆의 C 구역에 있어요.
⑤ 여 지하철역으로 나를 데리러 올 수 있니?
남 응. 내가 20분 후에 거기로 갈게.

해설 | 여자가 파스타 소스가 어디 있는지 묻고 있고, 남자가 C 구역에 있다고 답하는 상황이므로 정답은 ④이다.

어휘 | agree [əgríː] 통 동의하다 section [sékʃən] 명 구역

18 언급하지 않은 내용 고르기

정답 ④

M Hello, I'd like to tell you about my puppy. His name is Mori, and he's five months old. He is a small poodle, and he loves to play with other dogs. He has dark brown hair, so it's sometimes hard to find him when he is in a dark room. He can do tricks like shaking hands and bowing.

남 안녕하세요, 저는 제 강아지에 대해 말씀드리려고 합니다. 그의 이름은 Mori이고, 생후 5개월입니다. 그는 작은 푸들이고, 다른 개들과 노는 것을 매우 좋아합니다. 그는 어두운 갈색 털을 가지고 있어서, 그가 어두운 방에 있을 때는 가끔 그를 찾는 것이 어렵습니다. 그는 악수하기나 엎드리기 같은 묘기를 부릴 수 있습니다.

해설 | ① 이름(Mori), ② 나이(생후 5개월), ③ 털 색(어두운 갈색 털), ⑤ 특기(묘기 부리기)에 대해 언급했으므로 정답은 ④ '몸무게'이다.

어휘 | dark [daːrk] 형 어두운 trick [trik] 명 묘기 shake hands 악수하다 bow [bau] 통 엎드리다, 절하다

19 적절한 응답 고르기

정답 ②

M Mom, can I go shopping with my friends?
W Sure. Do you need some money?
M Yes, please. We are going to the stationery store.
W Okay. What are you going to buy?
M I want a new journal. My old one is full.
W Alright. Here is 15 dollars. Can you also buy two black pens for me?
M Of course.

남 엄마, 제 친구들이랑 쇼핑가도 돼요?
여 물론이지. 돈이 좀 필요하니?
남 네, 부탁드려요. 저희는 문구점에 갈 거예요.
여 그래. 뭘 살 거니?
남 저는 새 일기장이 갖고 싶어요. 예전 것은 가득 찼거든요.
여 그렇구나. 여기 15달러다. 나에게 검은색 펜 2개도 사다 줄 수 있니?
남 물론이죠.

해설 | 여자가 남자에게 검은색 펜을 사다 줄 수 있는지 묻고 있으므로 정답은 부탁을 수락하는 ② 'Of course.'이다.

선택지 해석

① 이 지우개는 얼마인가요? ② 물론이죠. ③ 정말 즐거웠어요. ④ 이걸 받아쓰세요. ⑤ 스티커가 예쁘네요.

어휘 | stationery store 문구점, 문방구 journal [dʒə́ːrnəl] 명 일기장, 일지 write down 받아쓰다, 적다

20 적절한 응답 고르기

정답 ①

W What color do you want to paint this room, Honey?
M Hmm... Blue or yellow would be nice.
W I like blue better. It will look pretty with our couch.
M That's true. But then we should buy a new lamp.
W Why? We already have one.
M Yes. But it won't match the new wall color.
W You're right. How about going to the store now?
M Okay. Let me get my coat.

여 이 방을 무슨 색으로 칠하고 싶어, 여보?
남 흠... 파란색이나 노란색이 좋을 것 같아.
여 나는 파란색이 더 좋아. 우리 소파에 잘 어울릴 거야.
남 그건 맞아. 하지만 그럼 우리는 새 전등을 사야 해.
여 왜? 우리 이미 하나 있잖아.
남 맞아. 하지만 그건 새 벽 색깔과 어울리지 않을 거야.
여 당신 말이 맞아. 지금 상점에 가는 것이 어때?
남 좋아. 내 코트 가지고 올게.

해설 | 여자가 지금 상점에 가는 것이 어떤지 제안하고 있으므로 정답은 제안을 승낙하는 ① 'Okay. Let me get my coat.'이다.

선택지 해석

① 좋아. 내 코트 가지고 올게. ② 난 이 색이 정말 좋아. ③ 여기 어둡다. ④ 나 없이 시작하지 마. ⑤ 계속 직진해.

어휘 | couch [kautʃ] 명 소파 true [truː] 형 맞는, 사실인 already [ɔːlrédi] 부 이미 match [mætʃ] 동 어울리다, 맞다

07회 실전 모의고사

| 문제 pp.74-75

1	②	2	③	3	④	4	②	5	①	6	③	7	①	8	③	9	③	10	④
11	③	12	④	13	④	14	⑤	15	②	16	③	17	①	18	②	19	④	20	①

1 날씨 고르기

정답 ②

M This is Jim with the weekly weather report. Monday and Tuesday will be sunny with a warm breeze. On Wednesday, it'll get cloudy and rainy in the afternoon. On Thursday, the sky is likely to be clear. On Friday, rain will start falling again and continue through the weekend.

남 주간 일기예보를 맡고 있는 Jim입니다. 월요일과 화요일에는 따뜻한 바람이 불며 화창하겠습니다. 수요일에는 오후부터 구름이 끼고 비가 오겠습니다. 목요일에는 하늘이 갤 것으로 예상됩니다. 금요일에는 다시 비가 떨어지기 시작해 주말까지 이어지겠습니다.

해설 | 금요일에는 다시 비가 떨어지기 시작한다고 했으므로 정답은 ②이다.

어휘 | likely [láikli] 형 ~할 것으로 예상되는

2 알맞은 그림 고르기

정답 ③

M What is that little house on the tree in your garden?
W It's a bird house. I made it myself. Do you like it?
M Yes. It's so pretty! I like the little star on the top.
W Originally, I put it under the hole, but it looked uncomfortable for the birds.
M The windows on the side are also cute. I really like them.
W Thank you.

남 네 정원의 나무 위에 있는 작은 집은 뭐니?
여 그건 새집이야. 내가 직접 만들었어. 마음에 드니?
남 응. 정말 예뻐! 맨 위에 있는 작은 별이 마음에 들어.
여 원래 그걸 구멍 아래에 달았는데, 새들에게 불편해 보였어.
남 옆에 있는 창문도 귀여워. 정말 마음에 들어.
여 고마워.

해설 | 남자가 위에 있는 작은 별이 마음에 든다고 했고, 옆에 있는 창문도 귀엽다고 했으므로, 정답은 ③이다.

어휘 | top [tɑp] 명 맨 위, 정상 originally [ərídʒənəli] 부 원래 hole [houl] 명 구멍 uncomfortable [ənkʌ́mfərtəbəl] 형 불편한 side [said] 명 옆

3 언급하지 않은 내용 고르기

정답 ④

W James, how was your trip to Africa?
M It was exciting! And the weather was better than I expected.
W How many countries did you visit?
M I went to four countries.
W Which was your favorite?
M It was Kenya. I saw many animals while we were on safari. I even saw lions.
W How long was your trip?
M I traveled for 14 days, but I spent two days on the plane.
W That's a long flight.

여 James, 아프리카 여행은 어땠어?
남 흥미진진했어! 그리고 날씨는 내가 기대했던 것보다 좋았어.
여 몇 개 국가를 방문했니?
남 4개국에 다녀왔어.
여 어디가 가장 좋았어?
남 케냐야. 우리가 사파리에 있는 동안 많은 동물을 봤어. 심지어 사자도 봤어.
여 여행은 얼마나 오래 했어?
남 나는 14일 동안 여행했지만, 비행기에서 이틀을 보냈어.
여 정말 긴 비행이었구나.

해설 | ① 방문 국가 수(4개국), ② 방문 국가(케냐), ③ 날씨(기대했던 것보다 좋았음), ⑤ 여행 기간(14일)에 대해 언급했으므로 정답은 ④ '여행 시작일'이다.
어휘 | expect [ikspékt] 동 기대하다 country [kʌ́ntri] 명 국가, 나라 flight [flait] 명 비행

4 특정 정보 고르기

정답 ②

M Somi, what's in that bottle?
W It's used cooking oil. I used it for my science class.
M Why did you need it?
W We learned how to make soap with used oil.
M Oh, really?
W Yes. We also added dried flowers to the soap so that it will smell nice.
M Will you bring a bar for me?
W Sure. I'll bring you one tomorrow.

남 소미야, 저 병 안에 뭐가 있니?
여 그건 사용한 식용유야. 과학 수업을 위해 사용했어.
남 그게 왜 필요했어?
여 우리는 사용한 기름으로 비누 만드는 법을 배웠거든.
남 오, 정말?
여 응. 좋은 냄새가 나도록 비누에 말린 꽃도 넣었어.
남 나 하나 가져다줄래?
여 물론이지. 내일 하나 갖다줄게.

해설 | 여자는 사용한 기름으로 비누를 만드는 법을 배웠다고 했으므로 정답은 ② '비누'이다.
어휘 | used [ju:st] 형 사용한, 중고의 cooking oil 식용유

5 장소 고르기

정답 ①

M Jenny, did you find the shoes you were looking for?
W Yes, I did. And they were on sale too.
M Great. Do you want to go to the food court before we leave?
W Sure. But don't you want to do more shopping?
M No. I bought a pair of jeans, so I'm fine.
W All right. Let's grab some food then.

남 Jenny, 네가 찾고 있던 신발은 찾았니?
여 응, 찾았어. 그리고 그것들은 할인 중이기도 했어.
남 잘됐다. 우리 떠나기 전에 푸드코트에 갈래?
여 그래. 근데 쇼핑을 더 하고 싶지는 않니?
남 아니. 나는 청바지를 사서 괜찮아.
여 좋아. 그럼 밥을 좀 먹자.

해설 | 남자가 떠나기 전에 푸드코트에 가자고 하자 여자가 쇼핑을 더 하고 싶지 않냐고 묻는 것으로 보아 정답은 ① '쇼핑몰'이다.
어휘 | on sale 할인 중인

6 의도 고르기

정답 ③

M Chloe, are you busy?
W Not really. Why?
M Can you help me find my glasses?
W Dad, they are on your head.
M Oh, my! Thank you.
W Do you need anything else?
M Yes. Have you also seen my tablet PC?
W I put it on your desk last night.
M Did you? Then, can you bring it to me?

남 Chloe, 바쁘니?
여 별로요. 왜요?
남 내 안경 찾는 것 좀 도와줄래?
여 아빠, 그건 아빠 머리 위에 있어요.
남 오, 이런! 고맙구나.
여 더 필요한 건 없으세요?
남 응. 내 태블릿 PC도 본 적 있니?
여 어젯밤에 아빠 책상 위에 놓았어요.
남 그랬니? 그럼 내게 그걸 가져다줄 수 있겠니?

해설 | 여자가 남자의 태블릿 PC를 어젯밤에 아빠의 책상 위에 놓았다고 하자, 자신에게 그걸 가져다줄 수 있겠냐고 말했으므로 정답은 ③ '부탁'이다.

어휘 | bring [briŋ] 동 가지고 오다

7 특정 정보 고르기

정답 ①

M Welcome to Electroland. May I help you?
W Hi. I'd like to buy a refrigerator. Which is the one on your website?
M You mean the one on sale?
W Yes. The one with pink doors.
M You can get a discount for that model if you buy it online.
W Hmm... Is there a refrigerator with a similar price that I can buy in the store?
M This black one is our best seller.
W Oh, that looks nice.

남 Electroland에 오신 걸 환영합니다. 도와드릴까요?
여 안녕하세요. 냉장고를 사고 싶어서요. 웹사이트에 있는 것이 어느 것인가요?
남 할인 중인 것 말씀이신가요?
여 네. 분홍색 문이 있는 거요.
남 그 모델은 온라인에서 구매하셔야 할인받으실 수 있어요.
여 흠... 매장에서 살 수 있는 비슷한 가격의 냉장고가 있나요?
남 이 검은색이 제일 잘 팔리는 거예요.
여 오, 좋아 보이네요.

해설 | 여자는 냉장고를 사고 싶다고 했으므로 정답은 ① '냉장고'이다.

어휘 | refrigerator [rifrídʒərèitər] 명 냉장고 discount [dískaunt] 명 할인 similar [símələr] 형 비슷한

8 할 일 고르기

정답 ③

W Nathan, wake up!
M What time is it, Mom?
W It's already 7:30.
M My alarm didn't go off.
W It did, but you didn't wake up.
M I think I need a louder alarm clock.
W Why don't you take a shower now? You're going to be late.
M Okay. Will you make me some toast?
W Sure. Hurry up.

여 Nathan, 일어나렴!
남 지금 몇 시예요, 엄마?
여 벌써 7시 30분이야.
남 제 알람이 안 울렸어요.
여 울렸는데, 네가 일어나지 않더구나.
남 저는 소리가 더 큰 알람 시계가 필요한 것 같아요.
여 이제 샤워를 하는 게 어떠니? 늦겠구나.
남 알겠어요. 토스트 좀 만들어 주시겠어요?
여 물론이지. 서두르렴.

해설 | 여자가 이제 샤워를 하는 게 어떠냐고 묻자 남자가 알겠다고 했으므로 정답은 ③ '샤워하기'이다.

어휘 | go off (알람, 경보기 등이) 울리다 loud [laud] 형 (소리가) 큰, 시끄러운 take a shower 샤워를 하다

9 언급하지 않은 내용 고르기

정답 ③

[Telephone rings.]
W Good afternoon. Elderberry National Park. How may I help you?
M I want to book a campsite for July 15th.
W How many people will use the campsite?
M Just two. How much will it be?
W It'll be 10 dollars for each person, so 20 dollars total.
M Okay. Are campfires allowed?
W Fires are allowed only at the campgrounds.
M Can we bring our dog?
W Yes. But you need to keep an eye on it at all times.

[전화기가 울린다.]
여 안녕하세요. 엘더베리 국립공원입니다. 어떻게 도와드릴까요?
남 7월 15일에 캠핑장을 예약하고 싶어요.
여 몇 명이 캠핑장을 사용하실 예정인가요?
남 단 두 명이요. 얼마인가요?
여 한 사람당 10달러이니, 총 20달러입니다.
남 알겠습니다. 캠프파이어가 허용되나요?
여 모닥불은 캠핑장에서만 허용됩니다.
남 개를 데리고 가도 되나요?
여 네. 하지만 항상 주시하고 계셔야 합니다.

해설 | ① 캠핑장 이용 인원(두 명), ② 캠핑장 이용 가격(총 20달러), ④ 캠프파이어 허용 여부(캠핑장에서 가능), ⑤ 반려견 동반 여부(가능함)에 대해 언급했으므로 정답은 ③ '샤워 시설 유무'이다.

어휘 | campsite [kǽmpsait] 명 캠핑장 allow [əláu] 동 허용하다 fire [faiər] 명 모닥불; 불 keep an eye on 주시하다, 눈을 떼지 않다

10 주제 고르기

정답 ④

W Ladies and gentlemen, can I have your attention, please? We are so sorry for the delay, and we thank you for your patience. Hankook Airline Flight 727 for Los Angeles is now boarding at Gate H15. Please have your boarding pass ready. Make sure you don't leave your belongings. Thank you.

여 신사 숙녀 여러분, 주목해 주시겠습니까? 지연되어 대단히 죄송하며, 양해해주셔서 감사합니다. 로스앤젤레스행 한국 항공 727편은 지금 H15번 게이트에서 탑승 중입니다. 탑승권을 준비해 주십시오. 소지품을 두고 가지 않도록 주의하십시오. 감사합니다.

해설 | 여자가 항공편 지연에 대해 사과한 후에 지금 탑승 중이라고 말했기 때문에 정답은 ④ '비행기 탑승 안내'이다.

어휘 | delay [diléi] 명 지연 board [bɔːrd] 동 탑승하다 belonging [bilɔ́ːŋiŋ] 명 소지품

11 일치하지 않는 내용 고르기

정답 ③

W Nick, did you buy the ticket for the art exhibition?
M Yeah. It was 30 dollars per person.
W Did you check the artists? *[Clicking sound]* It says the artwork of more than 30 artists from around the world will be exhibited.
M Can you also buy paintings there?
W No, you can't. But you can buy souvenirs.
M That's disappointing. I wanted to buy a painting. By the way, are we taking the taxi?
W Yes. I heard there isn't a parking lot.

여 Nick, 미술 전시회 티켓 샀니?
남 응. 1인당 30달러였어.
여 화가들은 확인해봤어? *[딸깍하는 소리]* 전 세계의 30명이 넘는 화가들의 미술품이 전시되어 있을 거라고 되어있어.
남 거기서 그림도 살 수 있니?
여 아니, 못 사. 하지만 기념품은 살 수 있어.
남 실망스럽네. 나는 그림을 사고 싶었어. 그건 그렇고, 우리 택시 탈 거야?
여 응. 주차장이 없다고 들었거든.

해설 | 남자가 거기서 그림도 살 수 있는지 묻자 여자가 못 산다고 했으므로 정답은 ③ '전시품은 구매할 수 있다.'이다.

어휘 | per [pəːr] 전 ~당, 마다 artwork [ártwərk] 명 미술품 exhibit [igzíbit] 동 전시하다 souvenir [sùːvəníər] 명 기념품

12 목적 고르기

정답 ④

W Wilson, are you going to Gyeongju this weekend?
M Yeah. I'm going there tomorrow morning to visit famous historic sites.
W What is there to see in Gyeongju?
M There is Bulguksa Temple from the Silla period.
W Wow. Are you a fan of history?
M Yes. I love learning about the past.
W I hope you have fun.
M Thanks. I'll send you some photos.

여 Wilson, 이번 주말에 경주에 가니?
남 응. 내일 아침에 유명한 유적지를 방문하러 거기 갈 거야.
여 경주에서 볼 것이 뭐가 있니?
남 신라 시대의 불국사가 있어.
여 우와. 너 역사 애호가니?
남 응. 나는 과거에 대해 배우는 것을 정말 좋아해.
여 재미있게 보내길 바랄게.
남 고마워. 사진 몇 장 보내줄게.

해설 | 여자가 이번 주말에 경주에 가는지 묻자 남자가 유명한 유적지를 방문하러 간다고 했으므로 정답은 ④ '유적지를 방문하기 위해서'이다.

어휘 | historic site 유적지 period [píːriəd] 명 시대

13 시간 정보 고르기

정답 ④

[Telephone rings.]
M Hello. Gregory's Hair Salon. What can I do for you?
W Hi. I have a reservation at 2 o'clock today, but I think I'll have to change the time.
M Sure. May I have your name, please?
W It's Anna Lee.
M Okay. When will you come?
W My meeting will end at 2:30, so I can be there by 3:30.
M Great. I'll see you then.

[전화기가 울린다.]
남 안녕하세요. Gregory's Hair Salon입니다. 무엇을 도와 드릴까요?
여 안녕하세요. 오늘 2시에 예약했는데, 시간을 변경해야 할 것 같아요.
남 그러세요. 성함이 어떻게 되시죠?
여 Anna Lee예요.
남 알겠습니다. 언제 올 예정이신가요?
여 회의가 2시 30분에 끝날 예정이라, 3시 30분까지 갈 수 있어요.
남 좋습니다. 그때 뵐게요.

해설 | 여자가 3시 30분까지 갈 수 있다고 했으므로 정답은 ④ '3:30 p.m.'이다.

어휘 | reservation [rèzərvéiʃən] 명 예약

14 관계 고르기

정답 ⑤

W Hello. Are you looking for a new car?
M Yes. Mine is too old.
W Do you want a big car or a small car?
M I need a big one. I have a wife and three kids.
W What about this one? It has lots of room.
M Hmm... It doesn't look good for driving in the mountains. We like camping.
W I see. Then, this SUV is perfect for you.

여 안녕하세요. 새 차를 찾고 계신가요?
남 네. 제 차는 너무 오래됐어요.
여 큰 차를 원하세요, 아니면 작은 차를 원하세요?
남 전 큰 것이 필요해요. 아내와 세 명의 아이들이 있거든요.
여 이건 어떤가요? 이건 공간이 많아요.
남 흠... 산에서 운전하기에는 좋아 보이지 않네요. 저희는 캠핑을 좋아해서요.
여 그러시군요. 그렇다면, 이 SUV가 고객님에게 딱 맞겠네요.

해설 | 여자가 남자에게 차를 추천하고 있는 것으로 보아 정답은 ⑤ '자동차 판매원 — 손님'이다.

어휘 | room [ruːm] 명 공간; 방 mountain [máuntən] 명 산

15 부탁·요청한 일 고르기

정답 ②

M You look so tired, Amy.
W I couldn't sleep last night.
M What happened?
W I had to stay up all night to finish my essay.
M But I thought you finished your English essay.
W That was my science report. Could you do me a favor?
M Sure. What is it?
W Could you wake me up in an hour? I want to take a nap.
M Of course! No problem.

남 너 되게 피곤해 보여, Amy.
여 어젯밤에 잠을 못 잤어.
남 무슨 일이 있었니?
여 에세이를 끝내기 위해 밤을 새워야 했어.
남 하지만 영어 에세이는 다 끝낸 줄 알았는데.
여 그건 내 과학 보고서였어. 내 부탁 하나만 들어 줄래?
남 물론이지. 뭔데?
여 한 시간 후에 날 깨워 줄래? 낮잠을 자고 싶어.
남 물론이지! 문제없어.

해설 | 여자가 남자에게 낮잠을 자고 싶다며 한 시간 후에 깨워달라고 부탁했으므로 정답은 ② '낮잠 깨워주기'이다.

어휘 | stay up all night 밤을 새우다 favor [féivər] 명 부탁 take a nap 낮잠을 자다

16 이유 고르기

정답 ③

M Mom, can I go skiing with Paul next Saturday?
W When?
M It's January 14th.
W That's your grandfather's birthday. We are having dinner together at his house.
M Oh, no! What should I do? I already promised Paul.
W I think you should say sorry and cancel the trip. You can go next time.
M But he'll be so angry.
W Paul will understand if you explain the situation.
M Okay. I'll call him now.

남 엄마, 다음 토요일에 Paul이랑 스키 타러 가도 돼요?
여 언제?
남 1월 14일이에요.
여 그날은 네 할아버지 생신이야. 할아버지 댁에서 함께 저녁을 먹을 거란다.
남 오, 이런! 어떻게 해야 하죠? 저 이미 Paul과 약속했어요.
여 미안하다고 말하고 여행을 취소해야 할 것 같구나. 다음에 가면 되잖니.
남 하지만 그는 매우 화낼 거예요.
여 Paul은 네가 상황을 설명하면 이해할 거야.
남 알겠어요. 그에게 지금 전화를 걸게요.

해설 | 남자가 스키를 타러 가도 되냐고 묻자 여자가 그날은 할아버지 생신이라고 한 후 할아버지 댁에서 함께 저녁을 먹을 거라고 했으므로 정답은 ③ '할아버지 생신이어서'이다.

어휘 | promise [prámis] 동 약속하다 cancel [kǽnsəl] 동 취소하다 explain [ikspléin] 동 설명하다 situation [sìtʃuéiʃən] 명 상황

17 그림 상황에 적절한 대화 고르기

정답 ①

① W Where should we sit?
M How about sitting on that bench by the fountain?
② W Should I buy this dress?
M Yes. It looks really nice.
③ W Do you want to go to the park today?
M I can't. I'm taking a French class.
④ W When is soccer practice?
M It's on Mondays.
⑤ W How much are these flowers?
M They're 10 dollars.

① 여 우리 어디 앉을까?
남 분수 옆에 있는 저 벤치에 앉는 게 어때?
② 여 나 이 원피스를 살까?
남 응. 그거 정말 좋아 보여.
③ 여 오늘 공원에 갈래?
남 못 가. 난 프랑스어 수업을 들어.
④ 여 축구 연습이 언제니?
남 월요일마다 있어.
⑤ 여 이 꽃들은 얼마예요?
남 그것들은 10달러예요.

해설 | 여자가 어디에 앉을지 물었고, 남자가 분수 옆에 있는 저 벤치에 앉는 게 어떤지 제안하는 상황이므로 정답은 ①이다.
어휘 | fountain [fáuntən] 명 분수

18 언급하지 않은 내용 고르기

정답 ②

M Hello, everyone. I'd like to tell you about our furry neighbors in the park, squirrels. Squirrels usually live in trees in forests. They live for about 15 years. Squirrels usually eat nuts and grains, but they can also eat insects. Squirrels sometimes save their nuts in the ground, but they often forget where those are hidden. In fact, millions of trees are planted by squirrels.

남 안녕하세요, 여러분. 저는 공원에 있는 우리의 털북숭이 이웃인 다람쥐에 대해 말씀드리고 싶습니다. 다람쥐는 보통 숲속의 나무에 삽니다. 그들은 약 15년 동안 삽니다. 다람쥐는 보통 견과류와 곡물을 먹지만, 곤충도 먹을 수 있습니다. 그들은 보통 땅속에 견과류를 저장하는데, 그것들이 어디에 숨겨져 있는지 종종 잊어버립니다. 사실상, 수백만 그루의 나무들이 다람쥐들에 의해 심어집니다.

해설 | ① 서식지(숲속의 나무), ③ 수명(약 15년), ④ 주식(견과류와 곡물), ⑤ 먹이 습성(땅속에 견과류를 저장함)에 대해 언급했으므로 정답은 ② '크기'이다.
어휘 | furry [fə́:ri] 형 털북숭이의 grain [grein] 명 곡물 insect [ínsekt] 명 곤충 ground [graund] 명 땅

19 적절한 응답 고르기

정답 ④

M You seem so excited, Grace. What's up?
W I have my first piano lesson today. I can't wait to start playing.
M Oh, I thought you played the guitar.
W I do, but I want to learn to play more instruments. I will take drum lessons too.
M That's amazing. Why are you learning to play so many instruments?
W I want to be a professional musician.

남 너 정말 신나 보여, Grace. 무슨 일이야?
여 오늘 첫 피아노 레슨이 있어. 빨리 연주를 시작하고 싶어.
남 오, 난 네가 기타를 치는 줄 알았어.
여 맞아, 하지만 더 많은 악기 연주를 배우고 싶어. 드럼 레슨도 받을 거야.
남 정말 놀랍다. 왜 그렇게 많은 악기 연주를 배우는 거니?
여 나는 전문적인 음악가가 되고 싶어.

해설 | 남자가 왜 그렇게 많은 악기 연주를 배우는지 묻고 있으므로 정답은 이유를 알려주는 ④ 'I want to be a professional musician.'이다.

선택지 해석

① 나는 기타 치는 것에 관심이 있어. ② 피아노 대회는 지난달에 열렸어. ③ 그녀는 오늘 수업을 빠졌어. ④ 나는 전문적인 음악가가 되고 싶어.
⑤ 그 밴드는 오늘 밤 공연할 거야.

어휘 | instrument [ínstrəmənt] 명 악기 professional [prəféʃənəl] 형 전문적인 perform [pərfɔ́:rm] 동 공연하다

20 적절한 응답 고르기

정답 ①

M Hello, Officer. What's going on?
W The bus stop is under construction, so you can't use it now.
M Then, where should I go?
W Please go straight for two blocks more, and use the next bus stop.
M How long will it take to get there?
W It will take 20 minutes on foot.
M That's bad news. I'm running late for work.
W I'm sorry, sir.
M When does the construction end?
W It will finish tomorrow.

남 안녕하세요, 경관님. 무슨 일인가요?
여 버스 정류장이 공사 중이라, 지금은 이용하실 수 없습니다.
남 그럼 어디로 가야 하나요?
여 두 블록 더 직진하셔서, 다음 버스 정류장을 이용하세요.
남 거기까지 가는 데 얼마나 걸릴까요?
여 걸어서 20분 걸릴 거예요.
남 그거 안 좋은 소식이네요. 제가 직장에 늦었거든요.
여 유감입니다, 선생님.
남 공사는 언제 끝나나요?
여 내일 끝날 거예요.

해설 | 남자가 공사가 언제 끝나는지 물었으므로 정답은 끝나는 날을 알려주는 ① 'It will finish tomorrow.'이다.

선택지 해석

① 내일 끝날 거예요. ② 벌금이 얼마예요? ③ 저희는 길을 잃은 것 같아요. ④ 당신은 너무 빠르게 운전하고 있었어요. ⑤ 교통사고가 났어요.

어휘 | under construction 공사 중인 be running late 늦다, 늦어지다 fine [fain] 명 벌금

08회 실전 모의고사

| 문제 pp.82-83

1	④	2	③	3	①	4	④	5	③	6	⑤	7	③	8	④	9	⑤	10	③
11	③	12	③	13	④	14	⑤	15	③	16	④	17	④	18	②	19	④	20	③

1 날씨 고르기

정답 ④

M Good morning, everyone. Let's look at the weather around the country. Today, Seoul will be foggy in the morning, and you'll see clear skies in the afternoon. There will be heavy snow in Daejeon. In Gwangju, strong winds are expected. Meanwhile, Busan will be sunny again, just like yesterday. Thank you for watching. Have a good day.

남 안녕하십니까, 여러분. 전국의 날씨를 보시겠습니다. 오늘 서울은 오전에 안개가 낄 예정이며, 오후에는 맑은 하늘을 보실 수 있을 것입니다. 대전에는 폭설이 내릴 예정입니다. 광주는 강한 바람이 예상됩니다. 한편, 부산은 어제와 같이 다시 화창한 날씨가 이어지겠습니다. 시청해주셔서 감사합니다. 좋은 하루 되십시오.

해설 | 광주는 강한 바람이 예상된다고 했으므로 정답은 ④이다.

어휘 | foggy [fɔ́:gi] 형 안개가 낀 meanwhile [mí:nwàil] 부 한편, 그 동안에

2 알맞은 그림 고르기

정답 ③

[Cellphone rings.]
M Mom, are you at home?
W Yes. What's up, Junyoung?
M I left my math notebook in my room. Could you bring it to me?
W Sure. Where did you put it?
M On the desk.
W Do you mean the notebook with two triangles and a ruler on it?
M No. It has two circles and a compass.
W Okay. I'll bring it to you.

[휴대폰이 울린다.]
남 엄마, 집에 계세요?
여 그래. 무슨 일이니, 준영아?
남 제 방에 수학 공책을 두고 왔어요. 제게 가져다주실 수 있으신가요?
여 물론이지. 어디에 뒀니?
남 책상 위에요.
여 위에 삼각형 두 개와 자가 그려진 공책을 말하는 거니?
남 아니요. 동그라미 두 개랑 컴퍼스 한 개가 그려져 있어요.
여 알겠다. 내가 가져다줄게.

해설 | 남자가 동그라미 두 개와 컴퍼스 한 개가 그려진 공책을 가져다 달라고 했으므로 정답은 ③이다.

어휘 | triangle [tráiæŋgl] 명 삼각형 ruler [rú:lər] 명 자 circle [sə́:rkl] 명 동그라미 compass [kʌ́mpəs] 명 컴퍼스

3 심정 고르기

정답 ①

M Abby, what are you doing?
W I just finished my homework. What about you?
M I'm going to go to the amusement park with my cousin.
W Sounds great. I wish I had something fun to do.
M Why don't you invite your friends to hang out?
W I want to, but they are busy with their homework.
M Then, how about watching a movie?
W I don't want to. I've watched too many movies lately. I'm tired of it now.

남 Abby, 뭐 하고 있니?
여 나는 막 숙제를 끝냈어. 너는?
남 나는 내 사촌과 놀이공원에 갈 거야.
여 좋겠다. 나도 재미있는 무언가를 할 수 있으면 좋을 텐데.
남 친구들을 초대해서 노는 것이 어때?
여 그러고 싶은데, 그들은 숙제 하느라 바빠.
남 그럼, 영화를 보는 건 어때?
여 그러고 싶지 않아. 난 최근에 영화를 너무 많이 봤어. 이제 싫증이 나.

해설 | 여자는 재미있는 무언가를 할 수 있으면 좋겠다고 한 후, 친구들은 숙제하느라 바쁘고 최근에 영화를 너무 많이 봐서 이제 싫증이 난다고 했으므로 정답은 ① 'bored'이다.

선택지 해석

① 지루한 ② 두려운 ③ 수줍은 ④ 만족한 ⑤ 흥분한

어휘 | amusement park 놀이공원 hang out 놀다 lately [léitli] 부 최근에 tired of ~에 싫증이 난

4 한 일 고르기

정답 ④

M Sora, how was your day?
W Good. I went to a café near my school.
M Did you meet your friends there?
W No. I went by myself.
M Oh, I see.
W I wanted to read a book in a quiet place.
M What did you read?
W I read a book by Charles Dickens.
M He's a great author.

남 소라야, 너의 하루는 어땠니?
여 좋았어. 우리 학교 근처의 카페에 갔었어.
남 거기서 친구들을 만났니?
여 아니. 나 혼자 갔어.
남 오, 그렇구나.
여 조용한 장소에서 책을 읽고 싶었거든.
남 뭘 읽었니?
여 찰스 디킨스가 쓴 책을 읽었어.
남 그는 훌륭한 작가지.

해설 | 여자는 어제 학교 근처의 카페에 갔다고 했으므로 정답은 ④ '카페 가기'이다.

어휘 | quiet [kwáiət] 형 조용한 author [ɔ́:θər] 명 작가

5 장소 고르기

정답 ③

W Excuse me, Mr. Stevens. I have a question about the homework.
M Sure, Kate. What's your question?
W For the science report, can I use pictures?
M Yes, you can. But your essay needs to be five pages long.
W Oh, if I have a picture, does it have to be longer?
M Yes. And it is due at the beginning of class on Monday.

여 실례합니다, Stevens 선생님. 숙제에 대해서 질문이 있어요.
남 물론이지, Kate. 질문이 뭐니?
여 과학 보고서에 사진을 써도 되나요?
남 그럼, 써도 된단다. 하지만 글이 다섯 장 길이여야 해.
여 오, 사진이 있으면 더 길어야 하는 건가요?
남 그럼. 그리고 월요일 수업 시작 시 제출해야 한단다.

해설 | 여자가 남자에게 숙제에 대해서 질문을 했고, 남자는 월요일 수업 시작 시 보고서를 제출해야 한다고 말하는 것으로 보아 정답은 ③ '교실'이다.

어휘 | question [kwéstʃən] 명 질문 due [dju:] 형 ~을 하기로 되어 있는, ~할 예정인

6 의도 고르기

정답 ⑤

M My laptop isn't working.
W Again? What's the problem this time?
M The screen keeps blinking.
W Oh, no. That's really annoying.
M Yeah. I should take it to the repair shop.
W Your computer is pretty old. When did you get it?
M It was seven years ago.
W I think you should just get a new laptop.

남 내 노트북이 작동하지 않아.
여 또? 이번에는 뭐가 문제야?
남 화면이 계속 깜빡거려.
여 오, 저런. 그거 정말 짜증 나지.
남 응. 수리점에 가져가야겠어.
여 네 노트북은 꽤 오래됐잖아. 언제 샀어?
남 7년 전이었어.
여 난 네가 그냥 새 노트북을 사는 것이 좋을 것 같아.

해설 | 여자가 남자의 노트북이 꽤 오래됐다고 말한 후 새 노트북을 사는 것이 좋겠다는 말을 했으므로 정답은 ⑤ '조언'이다.
어휘 | work [wəːrk] 동 작동하다; 일하다 again [əgén] 부 또, 다시 blink [bliŋk] 동 깜빡이다 annoying [ənɔ́iiŋ] 형 짜증 나는, 성가신 pretty [príti] 부 꽤

7 특정 정보 고르기

정답 ③

M Hey, Vanessa. What are you doing?
W I'm reading a magazine.
M Is there anything interesting?
W It says that the Seoul Art Fair is next month.
M I went there last year.
W Oh, and there's Yeosu Kimchi Festival next week.
M What kind of activities can you do there?
W You can make your own kimchi! Do you want to join me?
M Sure. Let's go there!

남 안녕, Vanessa. 뭐 하고 있니?
여 잡지를 읽고 있어.
남 흥미로운 것이 있니?
여 Seoul Art Fair가 다음 달이라고 쓰여 있어.
남 나는 작년에 거기에 갔었어.
여 오, 그리고 다음 주에는 Yeosu Kimchi Festival이 있어.
남 거기서 어떤 종류의 활동을 할 수 있니?
여 네가 직접 너의 김치를 만들 수 있어! 나랑 같이 갈래?
남 좋아. 거기 가자!

해설 | 여자는 다음 주에 Yeosu Kimchi Festival이 있다고 했고 남자에게 같이 갈지 묻고 있으므로 정답은 ③ '김치 축제'이다.
어휘 | magazine [mæ̀gəzíːn] 명 잡지 fair [fɛər] 명 박람회 own [oun] 형 자신의

8 할 일 고르기

정답 ④

M Taylor, what are you looking for?
W Dad, do you know where my white T-shirt is?
M I think I saw it in a laundry basket.
W Right. I have to wash it now.
M Why do you need it?
W I need a white T-shirt for choir tomorrow. We decided to wear matching clothes for the singing contest.
M You'd better separate the laundry first. Don't wash it with dark clothes.
W Okay. I'll do that first.

남 Taylor, 너 뭘 찾고 있니?
여 아빠, 제 흰색 티셔츠가 어디 있는지 아세요?
남 내 생각에 세탁물 바구니에서 그걸 본 것 같아.
여 맞네요. 지금 그걸 빨아야겠어요.
남 그게 왜 필요하니?
여 내일 합창단을 위해 흰색 티셔츠가 필요해요. 저희는 노래 대회에서 비슷한 옷을 입기로 결정했거든요.
남 먼저 세탁물을 분리하는 것이 좋겠다. 어두운 옷과 같이 빨지 말렴.
여 알겠어요. 그거 먼저 할게요.

해설 | 남자가 빨래를 하기 전에 먼저 세탁물을 분리하는 것이 좋겠다고 했고 여자가 알겠다고 했으므로 정답은 ④ '세탁물 분리하기'이다.
어휘 | laundry [lɔ́ːndri] 명 세탁물 choir [kwaiər] 명 합창단 decide [disáid] 동 결정하다 matching [mǽtʃiŋ] 형 비슷한, 어울리는
separate [sépərèit] 동 분리하다

9 언급하지 않은 내용 고르기

정답 ⑤

M Megan, that owl toy is adorable.
W Thanks. I watch a lot of videos about owls.
M Is it true that their legs are long?
W Yes. They also don't make any sound when they fly because their feathers are so soft.
M What else did you learn?
W They usually live in forests and are awake at night.
M What do they eat?
W Hmm... I'm not sure.
M Let's check on the Internet.

남 Megan, 그 부엉이 장난감 귀엽다.
여 고마워. 난 부엉이에 대한 영상을 많이 봐.
남 부엉이의 다리가 길다는 게 사실이야?
여 응. 또 그들은 깃털이 매우 부드러워서 날아갈 때 어떤 소리도 내지 않아.
남 또 무엇을 배웠니?
여 그들은 보통 숲속에 살고 밤에 깨어있어.
남 그들은 무엇을 먹니?
여 음... 잘 모르겠어.
남 인터넷에서 확인해보자.

해설 | ① 다리 길이(다리가 김), ② 깃털(부드러움), ③ 서식지(숲속), ④ 활동 시간(밤)에 대해 언급했으므로 정답은 ⑤ '산란기'이다.

어휘 | owl [aul] 명 부엉이 adorable [ədɔ́:rəbl] 형 귀여운, 사랑스러운 feather [féðər] 명 깃털 forest [fɔ́:rist] 명 숲 awake [əwéik] 형 깨어있는

10 주제 고르기

정답 ③

M Hello, welcome to my gardening channel. Today, I will talk about how to raise a plant. First, you need to buy a pot that is big enough for your plant and nice soil. You should also find a place in your house with lots of sunlight. Finally, you must water your plant regularly.

남 안녕하세요, 저의 원예 채널에 오신 걸 환영합니다. 오늘은 식물을 키우는 방법에 대해 말씀드리겠습니다. 먼저, 식물을 위한 충분히 큰 화분과 좋은 흙을 사야 합니다. 집안에서 햇빛이 많이 드는 공간도 찾으셔야 합니다. 마지막으로, 식물에 규칙적으로 물을 줘야 합니다.

해설 | 남자가 식물을 키우는 방법을 말하고 있으므로 정답은 ③ '식물을 키우는 방법'이다.

어휘 | gardening [gɑ́:rdniŋ] 명 원예 pot [pat] 명 화분; 항아리 soil [sɔil] 명 흙 sunlight [sʌ́nlait] 명 햇빛 regularly [régjulərli] 부 규칙적으로

11 일치하지 않는 내용 고르기

정답 ③

M Nora, what did you do yesterday?
W I went for a run with the running club.
M How often does your club meet?
W Three times a week. Our goal is to participate in a marathon this fall.
M Oh, I want to join your club! How many members are there?
W There are 10 members now.
M Do I have to wear athletic clothes?
W No. You can wear whatever you want. And a team badge is provided for free.
M Great!

남 Nora, 너는 어제 뭘 했니?
여 나는 육상 동아리와 함께 달리기를 하러 갔어.
남 너희 동아리는 얼마나 자주 만나니?
여 일주일에 세 번. 우리의 목표는 이번 가을 마라톤에 참가하는 거야.
남 오, 나도 너희 동아리에 가입하고 싶어! 거기 회원이 몇 명이나 있니?
여 지금은 10명의 회원이 있어.
남 운동복을 입어야 하니?
여 아니. 네가 원하는 것을 아무거나 입어도 돼. 그리고 팀 배지가 무료로 제공돼.
남 좋다!

해설 | 여자가 지금은 10명의 회원이 있다고 했으므로 정답은 ③ '현재 회원은 12명이다.'이다.

어휘 | participate [pa:rtísəpèit] 동 참가하다, 참여하다 marathon [mǽrəθɑ̀n] 명 마라톤 member [mémbər] 명 회원 athletic [æθlétik] 형 운동의 provide [prəváid] 동 제공하다

12 목적 고르기

정답 ③

M What are you up to, Sarah?
W I'm filming a video.
M Oh, what is it about?
W It's about how much plastic people waste each day.
M Why are you filming it?
W I want to encourage people to reduce plastic waste.
M That's really great! It's important to protect the environment.
W Yes. I hope a lot of people watch my video.
M If you post the video online, I'll share it to my friends.

남 뭐 하고 있니, Sarah?
여 나는 영상을 촬영하고 있어.
남 오, 그건 뭐에 관한 거니?
여 이건 사람들이 매일 얼마나 많은 플라스틱을 소비하는지에 대한 거야.
남 그걸 왜 찍는 거야?
여 난 사람들이 플라스틱 쓰레기를 줄이도록 권장하고 싶어.
남 그거 정말 좋다! 환경을 보호하는 것은 중요해.
여 맞아. 많은 사람이 내 영상을 보면 좋겠어.
남 만약 그 영상을 온라인에 게시하면, 내가 친구들에게 그것을 공유할게.

해설 | 여자가 사람들이 플라스틱 쓰레기를 줄이도록 권장하고 싶다고 말했으므로 정답은 ③ '플라스틱 쓰레기 줄이도록 독려하기 위해서'이다.

어휘 | waste [weist] 통 소비하다; 낭비하다 명 쓰레기 encourage [inkə́:ridʒ] 통 권장하다, 격려하다 reduce [ridjú:s] 통 줄이다 post [poust] 통 게시하다

13 금액 정보 고르기

정답 ④

W Welcome. How can I help you?
M I'd like to order a cake for my brother.
W Okay. Would you like to add lettering to the cake?
M Yes. Please add "Happy Birthday." How much is it?
W It's 30 dollars in total.
M Alright. Here's 50 dollars.
W Here's your change. Please wait 10 minutes.
M Sure. Thank you!

여 어서 오세요. 어떻게 도와드릴까요?
남 저희 남동생을 위한 케이크를 주문하고 싶어요.
여 알겠습니다. 케이크에 레터링을 추가하시겠어요?
남 네. '생일 축하해'를 추가해주세요. 얼마인가요?
여 총 30달러입니다.
남 알겠습니다. 여기 50달러입니다.
여 여기 잔돈이 있습니다. 10분만 기다려주세요.
남 물론이죠. 감사합니다!

해설 | 여자가 총 30달러라고 하자 남자가 50달러를 냈으므로 정답은 ④ '$ 20'이다.

어휘 | lettering [létəriŋ] 명 레터링, 글자 새기기 change [tʃeindʒ] 명 잔돈; 변화

14 관계 고르기

정답 ⑤

M Hello. I would like a table for two, please.
W Do you have a reservation?
M No, I don't. Are you full right now?
W Yes. We don't have any space in the restaurant at the moment. But you can put your name on the waiting list.
M Okay. How long is the waiting time?
W A table will be available in about 30 minutes.

남 안녕하세요. 2인석 테이블 부탁드려요.
여 예약하셨나요?
남 아니요, 안 했어요. 지금 자리가 꽉 찼나요?
여 네. 현재는 식당에 자리가 없습니다. 하지만 대기자 명단에 이름을 쓰실 수 있어요.
남 알겠습니다. 대기 시간이 얼마나 되나요?
여 30분 정도 후에 테이블을 이용하실 수 있을 거예요.

해설 | 남자가 식당에 자리가 있는지 묻고 있고, 여자가 현재 식당에 자리가 없다고 하는 것으로 보아 정답은 ⑤ '식당 점원 — 손님'이다.

어휘 | reservation [rèzərvéiʃən] 명 예약 space [speis] 명 공간 at the moment 현재는, 지금은 available [əvéiləbl] 형 이용 가능한

15 부탁·요청한 일 고르기

정답 ③

W Jason, are you feeling okay today?
M No, Mom. My headache is worse than yesterday.
W Did you take some medicine?
M Not yet. Mom, I don't think I can go to school today.
W Okay. I'll call your teacher and tell her that you're still sick.
M Thanks. I also need to return some books to the library.
W Are they due today?
M Yes. Could you return the books for me?
W Sure. Get some rest.

여 Jason, 오늘은 좀 괜찮니?
남 아니요, 엄마. 어제보다 두통이 심해요.
여 약 먹었니?
남 아직이요. 엄마, 오늘 학교에 갈 수 없을 것 같아요.
여 그래. 선생님께 전화해서 네가 아직 아프다고 말씀드릴게.
남 감사해요. 도서관에 책도 몇 권 반납해야 해요.
여 오늘까지니?
남 네. 절 위해 책을 반납해 주실 수 있으신가요?
여 물론이지. 쉬도록 하렴.

해설 | 남자가 여자에게 책을 반납해 줄 수 있는지 물었으므로 정답은 ③ '책 반납하기'이다.

어휘 | headache [hédeik] 명 두통 medicine [médisn] 명 약 still [stil] 부 아직, 여전히 return [ritə́:rn] 통 반납하다

16 이유 고르기

정답 ④

M Hey, Heather. What did you do last weekend?
W I went fishing. Did you go to the baseball game?
M No, I didn't.
W What happened? You were looking forward to the game.
M I was, but my little sister broke her leg on Saturday.
W Oh, poor Sarah. How is she doing now?
M She's in the hospital now.
W I hope she gets better soon.
M Thank you.

남 안녕, Heather. 지난 주말에 뭐 했니?
여 나는 낚시를 갔어. 너는 야구 시합에 갔니?
남 아니, 안 갔어.
여 무슨 일 있었어? 너 그 경기를 기대하고 있었잖아.
남 그랬는데, 내 여동생이 토요일에 다리가 부러졌어.
여 오, 안쓰러운 Sarah. 그녀는 지금 어때?
남 그녀는 지금 병원에 있어.
여 곧 나았으면 좋겠다.
남 고마워.

해설 | 남자의 여동생이 토요일에 다리가 부러져서 야구 경기 관람을 하지 못했다고 말했으므로 정답은 ④ '동생이 다리를 다쳐서'이다.

어휘 | go fishing 낚시를 가다 hospital [háspitl] 명 병원

17 그림 상황에 적절한 대화 고르기

정답 ④

① W Which sport do you like best?
M I like swimming best.
② W Should I bring an umbrella?
M Yeah. It looks like it's going to rain.
③ W Where is the restroom?
M It's next to the kitchen.
④ W Don't run near the pool. It's dangerous.
M Oh, I'm sorry.
⑤ W What are you planning to do at the beach?
M I'm going to build a huge sandcastle.

① 여 넌 어떤 운동을 가장 좋아하니?
남 나는 수영을 가장 좋아해.
② 여 내가 우산을 가져가야 할까?
남 응. 비가 올 것처럼 보여.
③ 여 화장실이 어디 있나요?
남 부엌 옆에 있어요.
④ 여 수영장 근처에서 뛰지 마세요. 위험해요.
남 오, 죄송합니다.
⑤ 여 넌 해변에서 뭘 할 계획이니?
남 나는 거대한 모래성을 쌓을 거야.

해설 | 여자가 수영장 근처에서 뛰지 말라고 하고 남자가 사과하고 있는 상황이므로 정답은 ④이다.

어휘 | restroom [réstru:m] 명 화장실 kitchen [kítʃən] 명 부엌, 주방 near [niər] 전 근처에 dangerous [déindʒərəs] 형 위험한 sandcastle [sǽndkæsl] 명 모래성

18 언급하지 않은 내용 고르기

정답 ②

W Mark, do you have plans on December 31st?
M You mean on New Year's Eve? Not really.
W I have two tickets for a piano concert that evening. Do you want to go?
M That would be great. When does it begin?
W It starts at 6 p.m. Can you meet me at Olympic Concert Hall?
M Where is it?
W It's near Olympic Park Station.
M Okay. Who is playing?
W My favorite pianist Seongmin Kim will perform. You'll love it too.

여 Mark, 12월 31일에 계획이 있니?
남 새해 전야 말이야? 별 계획 없어.
여 나 그날 밤에 피아노 연주회 표가 두 장 있어. 갈래?
남 정말 좋을 것 같아. 언제 시작하는데?
여 그건 오후 여섯 시에 시작해. 올림픽 콘서트홀에서 만날 수 있니?
남 그건 어디 있는데?
여 올림픽 공원 역 근처에 있어.
남 그래. 누가 연주하는데?
여 내가 제일 좋아하는 피아니스트인 김성민이 공연할 예정이야. 네가 좋아할 거야.

해설 | ① 공연 날짜(12월 31일), ③ 공연 시간(오후 6시), ④ 공연 장소(올림픽 콘서트홀), ⑤ 연주자(김성민)에 대해 언급했으므로 정답은 ② '티켓 가격'이다.

어휘 | play [plei] 동 연주하다; 놀다 perform [pərfɔ́:rm] 동 공연하다, 연주하다

19 적절한 응답 고르기

정답 ④

W Hello. Can I help you find something?
M Yes. I'd like to buy a watch for my wife.
W Okay. What style does she like?
M She usually wears silver jewelry.
W Here is a beautiful silver watch with a blue face.
M Do you have anything smaller? That one is too big.
W Sure. What about this one?
M That's perfect. I'll take it.

여 안녕하세요. 뭔가 찾으시는 것을 도와드릴까요?
남 네. 제 부인을 위한 시계를 사고 싶은데요.
여 알겠습니다. 그녀는 어떤 스타일을 좋아하시나요?
남 그녀는 보통 은 장신구를 착용해요.
여 여기 앞면이 파란 아름다운 은시계가 있어요.
남 더 작은 것이 있나요? 그건 너무 커요.
여 물론이죠. 이건 어떠신가요?
남 딱 좋아요. 그걸 살게요.

해설 | 남자가 더 작은 것이 있냐고 묻는 말에 여자가 물론이라며 더 작은 것을 제안하고 있으므로 정답은 제안을 수락하는 ④ 'That's perfect. I'll take it.'이다.

선택지 해석

① 이쪽은 제 부인이에요. ② 저는 당신의 귀걸이가 마음에 들어요. ③ 라지로 주세요. ④ 딱 좋아요. 그걸 살게요. ⑤ 제 물건들 좀 지켜봐 주시겠어요?

어휘 | watch [watʃ] 명 시계 동 지켜보다 wear [wεər] 동 착용하다, 입다 silver [sílvər] 명 은 jewelry [dʒúːəlri] 명 장신구, 보석 face [feis] 명 (시계의) 앞면; 얼굴 stuff [stʌf] 명 물건

20 적절한 응답 고르기

정답 ③

W What are we doing for summer vacation, Dad?
M We will visit your grandparents.
W That's great. I want to help them with their farm work.
M Excellent. They would love that.
W Oh, I'm so excited to go.
M Be sure to pack a neck pillow for the trip. The traffic will be really bad.
W How long will it take to drive to their house?
M Around five hours.

여 우리는 여름 방학에 무엇을 할 건가요, 아빠?
남 우리는 네 조부모님을 방문할 거란다.
여 좋아요. 저는 농장 일을 돕고 싶어요.
남 훌륭하구나. 그분들이 정말 좋아하실 거야.
여 오, 가게 되어서 정말 신나요.
남 여행을 위해 목 베개를 꼭 챙기도록 해. 교통 상황이 정말 좋지 않을 거야.
여 조부모님 댁까지 가는 데 얼마나 오래 걸릴까요?
남 다섯 시간 정도.

해설 | 여자가 조부모님 댁까지 가는 데 얼마나 오래 걸릴지 묻고 있으므로 정답은 걸리는 시간을 답하는 ③ 'Around five hours.'이다.

선택지 해석

① 노고에 감사드립니다. ② 잠깐 쉬자. ③ 다섯 시간 정도. ④ 토마토를 키우는 게 어때? ⑤ 우리는 곧 떠날 거야.

어휘 | farm [faːrm] 명 농장 pack [pæk] 동 챙기다 pillow [pílou] 명 베개 take a break (잠깐) 쉬다, 휴식을 취하다 grow [grou] 동 키우다

09회 실전 모의고사

| 문제 pp.90-91

1	③	2	③	3	④	4	④	5	①	6	⑤	7	②	8	④	9	④	10	⑤
11	③	12	②	13	④	14	①	15	⑤	16	②	17	⑤	18	②	19	①	20	③

1 날씨 고르기

정답 ③

M Good morning. Here is today's local weather forecast. In Dongducheon, it'll be very cold and snowy all day. It's cloudy now in Suwon, and lots of rain will come this afternoon. In Incheon, strong winds are expected today, so please be careful. Thank you. And have a nice day.

남 안녕하십니까. 오늘의 지역 일기 예보입니다. 동두천은 온종일 매우 춥고 눈이 내리겠습니다. 현재 수원은 흐리며, 오늘 오후에 많은 비가 오겠습니다. 인천에서는 오늘 강한 바람이 예상되므로 주의하시기 바랍니다. 감사합니다. 그럼 좋은 하루 보내십시오.

해설 | 인천은 강한 바람이 예상된다고 했으므로 정답은 ③이다.

어휘 | local [lóukəl] 명 지역의 expect [ikspékt] 동 예상하다, 기대하다

2 알맞은 그림 고르기

정답 ③

W Hello. What can I do for you?
M I'd like to buy a new plate.
W Okay. We have round ones and square ones. Which do you prefer?
M I like round ones better.
W Then, how about this one with polka dots on it?
M Can you show me ones with other patterns?
W Of course. This one has a leaf pattern.
M That's nice. I'll take it.

여 안녕하세요. 무엇을 도와드릴까요?
남 저는 새 접시를 사고 싶어요.
여 그러시군요. 저희는 둥근 것과 네모난 것이 있습니다. 어떤 것을 더 선호하시나요?
남 저는 둥근 것들이 더 좋아요.
여 그렇다면, 겉에 물방울무늬가 있는 이것은 어떠신가요?
남 다른 무늬가 있는 것들을 보여줄 수 있으신가요?
여 물론이죠. 이것은 잎사귀 무늬가 있어요.
남 그거 좋네요. 그걸 살게요.

해설 | 남자는 잎사귀 무늬가 있는 둥근 접시를 산다고 했으므로 정답은 ③이다.

어휘 | round [raund] 형 둥근 square [skwɛər] 형 네모난 polka dot 물방울무늬 pattern [pǽtərn] 명 무늬

3 심정 고르기

정답 ④

M Amy, did you get your audition results?
W Unfortunately, I didn't get the part for the musical.
M Oh, I'm so sorry to hear that. You must be upset. You practiced a lot.
W Well... I'm actually okay.
M How come?
W My singing skills really improved when I practiced for the audition.
M That's good to hear.
W Yeah. I feel more confident now.

남 Amy, 오디션 결과 받았니?
여 불행히도, 난 뮤지컬에서 배역을 맡지 못했어.
남 오, 그것참 안됐다. 정말 속상하겠네. 많이 연습했잖아.
여 음... 난 사실 괜찮아.
남 어째서?
여 오디션을 위해 연습할 때 내 노래 실력이 정말 많이 향상되었거든.
남 다행이네.
여 응. 나 이제 더 자신 있어.

해설 | 여자는 오디션을 위해 연습할 때 노래 실력이 많이 향상되었다며 이제 더 자신 있다고 했으므로 정답은 ④ 'satisfied'이다.

선택지 해석

① 지루한 ② 화난 ③ 신난 ④ 만족한 ⑤ 혼란스러운

어휘 | result [rizʌ́lt] 명 결과 unfortunately [ənfɔ́rtʃənətli] 부 불행히도, 안타깝게도 part [pa:rt] 명 배역; 부분, 역할 practice [prǽktis] 동 연습하다 confident [kɑ́nfədənt] 형 자신 있는

4 한 일 고르기

정답 ④

W What did you do on Children's Day?
M I visited the zoo with my family. It was so crowded.
W I can imagine. I wanted to go to an amusement park, but I couldn't.
M Then, did you stay at home?
W No. I played badminton with my family at a nearby park.
M Did you enjoy it?
W Yeah. I was happy to spend time outside.

여 너는 어린이날에 뭐 했니?
남 나는 우리 가족과 동물원에 다녀왔어. 정말 붐볐어.
여 상상이 되네. 나는 놀이공원에 가고 싶었는데, 갈 수 없었어.
남 그럼, 집에 있었니?
여 아니. 나는 우리 가족이랑 근처 공원에서 배드민턴을 쳤어.
남 재미있었어?
여 응. 밖에서 시간을 보내서 행복했어.

해설 | 여자는 어린이날에 가족이랑 근처 공원에서 배드민턴을 쳤다고 했으므로 정답은 ④ '배드민턴 치기'이다.

어휘 | amusement park 놀이공원 outside [àutsáid] 부 밖에서

5 장소 고르기

정답 ①

M Hello. I'd like a ticket to see *A New Hero.*
W Alright. What time would you like to watch it?
M I would like to see the movie at 2:30 p.m.
W I'm sorry, but we are sold out for that time.
M No problem. What about later in the afternoon?
W Seats are available at 4.
M That will do. I'll take one ticket, please.

남 안녕하세요. <A New Hero>의 티켓 한 장 주세요.
여 알겠습니다. 몇 시에 보고 싶으신가요?
남 저는 오후 2시 30분에 영화를 보고 싶어요.
여 죄송합니다만, 그 시간은 매진이에요.
남 괜찮아요. 오후 더 늦게는 어떤가요?
여 4시에 이용 가능한 좌석이 있습니다.
남 그거면 되겠어요. 티켓 한 장 주세요.

해설 | 2시 30분의 영화 티켓을 사고 싶다고 하는 것으로 보아 정답은 ① '영화관'이다.

어휘 | sold out 매진된 available [əvéiləbl] 형 이용 가능한

6 의도 고르기

정답 ⑤

W Have you seen my pencil case, Dad?
M No. Did you look on your desk?
W Yes. I searched everywhere, but I couldn't find it.
M Okay. I'll help. What does it look like?
W It's yellow and has cherries on it.
M *[Pause]* I found it. It's in the kitchen.
W Oh, right. I left it there this morning after I took some notes.
M You should put things back after using them.

여 제 필통 보셨어요, 아빠?
남 아니. 네 책상 위는 봤니?
여 네. 모든 곳을 찾아봤는데, 찾을 수 없었어요.
남 그래. 내가 도와주마. 어떻게 생겼니?
여 그건 노란색이고 체리가 그려져 있어요.
남 *[잠시 멈춤]* 찾았다. 주방에 있구나.
여 오, 맞다. 오늘 아침에 메모를 하고 거기 두고 갔어요.
남 사용한 후에는 물건들을 제자리에 가져다 놔야 해.

해설 | 남자가 사용한 후에는 물건들을 제자리에 가져다 놔야 한다고 했으므로 정답은 ⑤ '충고'이다.

어휘 | search [səːrtʃ] 동 찾다 take notes 메모하다, 필기하다

7 특정 정보 고르기

정답 ②

W Yongjin, try this cake.
M Thanks. Where did you get it?
W It's from my cousin's new café. It's my favorite dessert.
M The cake looks delicious.
W It tastes really good! The cookies and sandwiches are also popular.
M Have you tried them?
W Yes. They were nice. I like the green tea too.
M Doesn't the café sell coffee?
W Yes, it does. But I've never tried it because I don't like coffee.

여 용진아, 이 케이크 먹어봐.
남 고마워. 어디서 났어?
여 내 사촌의 새 카페에서 가져온 거야. 내가 가장 좋아하는 디저트야.
남 케이크 맛있어 보인다.
여 정말 맛있어! 쿠키와 샌드위치도 인기 있어.
남 넌 먹어봤니?
여 응. 그것들은 맛있었어. 녹차도 좋았고.
남 카페에서 커피를 팔지 않니?
여 응, 팔아. 하지만 난 커피를 좋아하지 않기 때문에 마셔보지 않았어.

해설 | 여자가 커피를 좋아하지 않기 때문에 마셔보지 않았다고 했으므로 정답은 ② '커피'이다.

어휘 | cousin [kʌ́zn] 명 사촌 popular [pάpjulər] 형 인기 있는

8 할 일 고르기

정답 ④

M Mom, I can't solve this math problem.
W What's the matter?
M I think the answer is 4, but 4 is not one of the answer choices.
W Let me see. *[Pause]* Hmm... You made an error in calculation.
M Oh, I always make mistakes.
W You'd better solve more math problems. How about doing this exercise?
M Sure, I'll do that now.

남 엄마, 이 수학 문제 못 풀겠어요.
여 뭐가 문제니?
남 저는 답이 4인 것 같은데, 4는 정답 선택지 중 하나가 아니에요.
여 어디 보자. *[잠시 멈춤]* 흠... 너 계산에서 실수했구나.
남 오, 저는 항상 실수를 해요.
여 너 수학 문제를 좀 더 풀어야겠다. 이 연습 문제를 푸는 건 어떠니?
남 물론이죠, 지금 할게요.

해설 | 여자가 연습 문제를 푸는 것이 어떤지 묻자 남자가 지금 하겠다고 했으므로 정답은 ④ '연습 문제 풀기'이다.

어휘 | solve [salv] 동 풀다, 해결하다 choice [tʃɔis] 명 선택지, 선택 error [érər] 명 실수; 오류 calculation [kælkjuléiʃən] 명 계산 mistake [mistéik] 명 실수

9 언급하지 않은 내용 고르기

정답 ④

W Hello, students. Today, I'll teach you what to do during an earthquake.
M What should I do if I'm inside?
W Good question. You have to get under a table and hold its leg.
M When can I go outside?
W After the shaking stops. But don't forget to turn off the gas before going out.
M I see. Anything else?
W Most importantly, you should follow instructions from the radio.

여 안녕하세요, 학생 여러분. 오늘 저는 지진 시에 무엇을 해야 하는지 알려드릴 거예요.
남 만약 제가 실내에 있다면 뭘 해야 하나요?
여 좋은 질문이에요. 탁자 아래에 들어가서 탁자 다리를 붙잡아야 해요.
남 밖에는 언제 나갈 수 있나요?
여 흔들리는 게 끝나고 나서요. 하지만 나가기 전에 가스를 끄는 것을 잊지 마세요.
남 그렇군요. 또 다른 것이 있나요?
여 무엇보다도, 라디오에서 나오는 지시를 따라야 해요.

해설 | ① 탁자 다리 붙잡기, ② 흔들림이 멈추고 밖으로 나가기, ③ 가스 밸브 잠그기, ⑤ 라디오 방송의 지시를 따르기를 언급했으므로 정답은 ④ '대피 장소로 달려가기'이다.

어휘 | earthquake [ə:rθkweik] 명 지진 hold [hould] 동 붙잡다 shake [ʃeik] 동 흔들리다 instruction [instrʌ́kʃən] 명 지시

10 주제 고르기

정답 ⑤

W Let me tell you an old story. One day, a fox and a bear decided to build a house for the winter. They worked for several weeks. When the house was half finished, the fox gave up. He felt there was still much to do. However, the bear kept working. He was happy that lots of work was already done. Finally, the bear had a warm house. This story shows the importance of thinking positively.

여 옛이야기를 하나 해드리겠습니다. 하루는 여우와 곰이 겨울을 대비해 집을 짓기로 결심했습니다. 그들은 몇 주 동안 일했습니다. 집의 절반이 완성되었을 때, 여우는 포기했습니다. 그는 여전히 너무 할 것이 많다고 생각했습니다. 그러나 곰은 계속해서 일했습니다. 그는 많은 것들이 이미 완성되어서 기뻤습니다. 마침내, 곰은 따뜻한 집을 갖게 되었습니다. 이 이야기는 긍정적으로 생각하는 것의 중요성을 보여줍니다.

해설 | 곰과 여우의 이야기를 통해 긍정적으로 생각하는 것의 중요성을 말하고 있으므로 정답은 ⑤ '긍정적 사고의 중요성'이다.

어휘 | decide [disáid] 동 결심하다 several [sévərəl] 형 몇, 여러 give up 포기하다 importance [impɔ́:rtəns] 명 중요성 positively [pάzətivli] 부 긍정적으로

11 일치하지 않는 내용 고르기

정답 ③

W Good morning, everyone. A special photo exhibition will be held for one week. It'll be in Seoul Square. We'll display photos of polluted oceans around the world. Viewers will be able to see the seriousness of environmental pollution. If you are interested, please visit the square at any time. This is a free event.

여 좋은 아침입니다, 여러분. 특별한 사진전이 일주일 동안 개최될 예정입니다. 이것은 서울 광장에서 열릴 것입니다. 저희는 전 세계의 오염된 바다 사진을 전시할 것입니다. 관람객들은 환경 오염의 심각성을 볼 수 있을 것입니다. 관심이 있으시다면, 언제든지 광장을 방문해주십시오. 이것은 무료 행사입니다.

해설 | 여자가 사진전에서 전 세계의 오염된 바다 사진을 전시할 것이라고 했으므로 정답은 ③ '파괴된 산림 사진이 전시된다.'이다.

어휘 | photo exhibition 사진전 polluted [pəlú:tid] 형 오염된 (pollution [pəlú:ʃən] 명 오염) ocean [óuʃən] 명 바다 seriousness [síəriəsnis] 명 심각성

12 목적 고르기

정답 ②

[Telephone rings.]
M Hello. Best Electronics.
W Hi. I ordered a wireless mouse, but it doesn't work.
M Could you tell me more about the problem?
W Sure. I put in new batteries, but it didn't turn on.
M Alright. Do you want a refund?
W No. I just want to exchange it.
M Okay. Then, please tell me your order number.
W It's KG502.

[전화기가 울린다.]
남 안녕하세요. Best Electronics입니다.
여 안녕하세요. 제가 무선 마우스를 주문했는데, 작동이 안 돼요.
남 문제에 대해서 더 말씀해 주시겠어요?
여 물론이죠. 새 건전지를 넣었는데, 켜지지 않았어요.
남 그러시군요. 환불을 원하시나요?
여 아니요. 저는 그냥 그것을 교환하고 싶어요.
남 알겠습니다. 그럼, 주문 번호를 알려주세요.
여 KG502입니다.

해설 | 여자가 무선 마우스를 교환해달라고 했으므로 정답은 ② '교환 신청을 하기 위해서'이다.

어휘 | wireless [wáiərlis] 형 무선의 problem [prάbləm] 명 문제 turn on 켜지다 refund [rifʌ́nd] 명 환불 exchange [ikstʃéindʒ] 동 교환하다

13 시간 정보 고르기

정답 ④

M Yeji, what are you going to do this Saturday?
W I'm thinking of climbing Dobongsan.
M Sounds good! Can I join you?
W Of course. It's better to go with someone than alone.
M Then, let's meet at the subway station. What time shall we meet?
W How about 7 o'clock in the morning?
M That's too early for me. Can we meet an hour later, at 8?
W Okay. See you then.

남 예지야, 이번 토요일에는 뭐 할 거니?
여 나는 도봉산을 등산할까 생각 중이야.
남 좋은 것 같아! 나도 같이 가도 돼?
여 물론이지. 혼자 가는 것보다 누군가와 같이 가는 게 낫지.
남 그럼, 지하철역에서 만나자. 몇 시에 만나야 할까?
여 아침 7시가 어때?
남 나에게는 너무 일러. 한 시간 후인 8시에 만나도 될까?
여 그래. 그때 봐.

해설 | 남자가 아침 7시는 너무 이르다며 한 시간 후인 8시에 만나자고 했으므로 정답은 ④ '8:00 a.m.'이다.

어휘 | alone [əlóun] 형 혼자의 early [ə́:rli] 형 이른

14 관계 고르기

정답 ①

M Hi, Ms. Ross. That was an amazing concert. Your voice sounded beautiful.
W I'm glad you enjoyed it.
M Would you sign an autograph for me?
W I would be happy to.
M Can you sign this?
W Sure. Oh, this is my first album!
M That's right.
W And what's your name?
M It's Adam Walker.
W Okay. I'll write, "To Adam, thank you for your support!"

남 안녕하세요, Ross씨. 굉장한 콘서트였어요. 당신의 목소리는 아름다웠어요.
여 즐거우셨다니 저도 기쁘네요.
남 절 위해 사인을 해주시겠어요?
여 기꺼이 해드릴게요.
남 이것에 사인해 주시겠어요?
여 물론이죠. 오, 이건 제 첫 앨범이네요!
남 맞아요.
여 성함이 어떻게 되시죠?
남 Adam Walker입니다.
여 그래요. 'Adam에게, 응원해 주셔서 감사합니다!'라고 쓸게요.

해설 | 남자가 여자에게 콘서트가 굉장했으며 목소리가 아름다웠다고 하며 첫 앨범에 사인해 달라고 요청하고 있는 것으로 보아 정답은 ① '가수 — 팬'이다.

어휘 | amazing [əméiziŋ] 형 굉장한, 놀라운 autograph [ɔ́:təgræf] 명 사인 support [səpɔ́:rt] 명 응원, 지지, 지원

15 부탁·요청한 일 고르기

정답 ⑤

M Ouch! My back hurts.
W What's wrong, Luke?
M I think I sat still for too long.
W You should do stretches. Do you want me to teach some exercises?
M I already did, but it didn't help much.
W You may lean too far forward when you're seated. It's a bad sitting position.
M Oh, I didn't realize that. Can you show me the correct position?
W No problem. Watch how I sit.

남 아야! 등이 아파.
여 뭐가 문제니, Luke?
남 너무 오랫동안 가만히 앉아 있었던 것 같아.
여 너는 스트레칭을 좀 해야 해. 내가 운동 몇 가지를 가르쳐 줄까?
남 이미 했는데, 별로 도움이 되지 않았어.
여 앉아 있을 때 앞으로 너무 많이 숙이는지도 몰라. 그건 좋지 않은 앉은 자세야.
남 오, 그건 몰랐어. 바른 자세를 보여줄 수 있니?
여 그럼. 내가 어떻게 앉는지 봐봐.

해설 | 남자가 여자에게 바르게 앉는 자세를 보여달라고 부탁했으므로 정답은 ⑤ '자세 시범 보이기'이다.

어휘 | back [bæk] 명 등 lean [li:n] 동 숙이다, 기대다 forward [fɔ́:rwərd] 부 앞으로 position [pəzíʃən] 명 자세 realize [rí:əlàiz] 동 알다, 깨닫다

16 이유 고르기

정답 ②

[Cellphone rings.]
M Hi, Sarah. What's up?
W We were supposed to have dinner together today. Can we make it another time?
M Sure, but why?
W I completely forgot about the appointment with my professor. It was scheduled a month ago, and it's really important.
M Oh, okay. I understand.
W I'm so sorry. Can I take a rain check?
M Yes. Let's have lunch next Thursday instead.

[휴대폰이 울린다.]
남 안녕, Sarah. 무슨 일이니?
여 우리 오늘 같이 저녁 먹기로 되어 있었잖아. 다음번에 먹어도 될까?
남 물론이지, 근데 왜?
여 내가 교수님과의 약속을 완전히 잊어버렸어. 한 달 전에 일정을 잡은 거였는데, 정말 중요해.
남 오, 그래. 이해해.
여 정말 미안해. 다음에 만나도 될까?
남 그래. 대신에 다음 목요일에 점심을 먹자.

해설 | 여자가 교수님과의 약속을 완전히 잊어버렸다며 정말 중요한 거라고 말했으므로 정답은 ② '선약이 있어서'이다.

어휘 | be supposed to ~하기로 되어 있다, ~할 예정이다 take a rain check 다음에 만나다, 다음을 기약하다

17 그림 상황에 적절한 대화 고르기

정답 ⑤

① M Do you know Julie's phone number?
W Yeah. Let me look on my phone.
② M May I take your order?
W Yes, please. I'd like a chicken burger and a coke.
③ M Did you win your soccer match?
W Yes. It was a good game.
④ M You look happy. What is going on?
W I won first prize in the singing contest.
⑤ M What are you doing on the computer?
W I'm playing a game.

① 남 너 Julie의 전화번호 아니?
여 응. 내 휴대폰에서 볼게.
② 남 주문 도와드릴까요?
여 네, 주문할게요. 치킨버거 하나와 콜라 한 잔 주세요.
③ 남 너 축구 경기 이겼니?
여 응. 좋은 경기였어.
④ 남 너 행복해 보인다. 무슨 일이야?
여 나 노래 대회에서 1등 상을 탔어.
⑤ 남 컴퓨터로 뭘 하고 있니?
여 게임을 하고 있어.

해설 | 여자가 컴퓨터로 게임을 하고 있는 상황이므로 정답은 ⑤이다.

어휘 | match [mætʃ] 명 경기, 시합 prize [praiz] 명 상

18 언급하지 않은 내용 고르기

정답 ②

W Hello, everyone. Let me tell you about our fourth tennis tournament. It'll be held from July 10th to 13th. All the amateur tennis players living in our city can join. You can simply register on our website. It will cost 15 dollars. But it is free for participants under 18 and over 60. Thanks for listening.

여 안녕하세요, 여러분. 제4회 테니스 대회에 대해 말씀드리겠습니다. 대회는 7월 10일부터 13일까지 열릴 예정입니다. 우리 도시에 거주하는 모든 아마추어 테니스 선수들은 참가하실 수 있습니다. 저희 웹사이트에서 간단히 등록하실 수 있습니다. 비용은 15달러입니다. 하지만 18세 이하와 60세 이상의 참가자들에게는 무료입니다. 들어주셔서 감사합니다.

해설 | ① 개최 기간(7월 10일부터 13일), ③ 참가 자격(우리 도시에 거주하는 아마추어 선수), ④ 신청 방법(웹사이트에서 등록), ⑤ 참가 비용(15달러, 18세 이하와 60세 이상은 무료)에 대해 언급했으므로 정답은 ② '경기 방식'이다.

어휘 | tournament [túərnəmənt] 명 대회 register [rédʒistər] 동 등록하다 cost [kɔːst] 동 비용이 들다 participant [paːrtísəpənt] 명 참가자

19 적절한 응답 고르기

정답 ①

W Hey, Marco. What does your cat look like?
M It's black with white ears.
W Oh, okay. Never mind then.
M Why do you ask?
W I found a lost cat outside of my house. And I'm trying to find its owner.
M I can help you. How about making posters to put around the neighborhood?
W That's an amazing idea!

여 안녕, Marco. 네 고양이는 어떻게 생겼니?
남 까만색이고 귀가 하얘.
여 오, 그렇구나. 신경 쓰지 마 그럼.
남 왜 물어보는 거야?
여 우리 집 밖에서 길 잃은 고양이를 발견했거든. 그리고 주인을 찾아주려고 노력하는 중이야.
남 내가 도와줄 수 있어. 인근에 붙일 포스터를 만드는 게 어때?
여 그거 좋은 생각이다!

해설 | 남자가 인근에 붙일 포스터를 만드는 것을 제안하고 있으므로 정답은 제안을 수락하는 ① 'That's an amazing idea!'이다.

선택지 해석

① 그거 좋은 생각이다! ② 동물 보호소에 데려가자. ③ 그거 예쁜 포스터구나. ④ 너희 집을 못 찾겠어. ⑤ 내 고양이는 오렌지색이야.

어휘 | lost [lɔːst] 형 길 잃은, 잃어버린 owner [óunər] 명 주인 neighborhood [néibərhùd] 명 인근, 근처, 이웃 animal shelter 동물 보호소

20 적절한 응답 고르기

정답 ③

M Minkyung, why don't we go for a picnic by the lake this Sunday?
W Sounds great! It will be a beautiful day.
M What shall we take to eat?
W Well, sandwiches would be good.
M What about a picnic mat? Should we buy one?
W Don't worry. I have one. I'll bring it.
M Don't forget to bring your sunglasses too.
W Right. I'll put them in my bag.

남 민경아, 우리 이번 일요일에 호숫가로 소풍 가는 것이 어때?
여 좋아! 아름다운 날이 될 거야.
남 먹을 것을 뭘 가져가야 할까?
여 음, 샌드위치가 좋을 것 같아.
남 소풍용 돗자리는 어떻게 할까? 하나 사야 할까?
여 걱정하지 마. 나한테 하나 있어. 내가 가져갈게.
남 선글라스도 가져오는 것도 잊지 마.
여 그래. 내 가방에 넣어둘게.

해설 | 남자가 선글라스도 가져오는 것을 잊지 말라고 당부하고 있으므로 정답은 당부에 응답하는 ③ 'Right. I'll put them in my bag.'이다.

선택지 해석

① 어제 화창했어. ② 내가 감자 칩을 챙겼어. ③ 그래. 내 가방에 넣어둘게. ④ 너는 눈을 보호해야 해. ⑤ 네가 사과를 좀 살 수 있을까?

어휘 | lake [leik] 명 호수 mat [mæt] 명 돗자리

10회 실전 모의고사

| 문제 pp.98-99

1	①	2	④	3	⑤	4	②	5	④	6	②	7	④	8	②	9	⑤	10	②
11	⑤	12	①	13	④	14	③	15	②	16	④	17	③	18	④	19	④	20	①

1 날씨 고르기

정답 ①

W Now, let's check next week's weather report. From Monday to Thursday, there will be lots of clouds and strong winds. On Friday, we will have heavy rain and lightning, so try to avoid going out. Fortunately, the rain will stop on Saturday, and it will be sunny and warm.

여 이제, 다음 주의 일기 예보를 확인하겠습니다. 월요일부터 목요일까지 많은 구름이 끼고 강한 바람이 불겠습니다. 금요일에는 폭우가 내리고 번개가 칠 예정이니, 외출을 피하십시오. 다행히, 토요일에는 비가 그칠 예정이며, 날이 화창하고 따뜻하겠습니다.

해설 | 토요일에는 비가 그칠 예정이며, 날이 화창하고 따뜻하겠다고 했으므로 정답은 ①이다.

어휘 | heavy rain 폭우 avoid [əvɔ́id] 동 피하다 fortunately [fɔ́ːrtʃənətli] 부 다행히

2 알맞은 그림 고르기

정답 ④

W Dad, can I help you clear the table?
M That would be great. Put these side dishes in the refrigerator, please.
W Okay. Where should I put the kimchi?
M Put it on the middle shelf.
W What about the sausages? Should I place them on the top shelf?
M No. We'd better throw them away.
W Alright. There are grapes on the bottom shelf. Why don't we eat some for dessert?
M Sure.

여 아빠, 식탁 치우는 것을 도와드릴까요?
남 그러면 좋겠구나. 이 반찬들을 냉장고에 넣어 주렴.
여 네. 김치를 어디에 넣어야 할까요?
남 가운데 선반에 올려두렴.
여 소시지는요? 맨 위의 선반에 놓을까요?
남 아니. 그건 버리는 게 낫겠구나.
여 알겠어요. 맨 아래 선반에 포도가 있어요. 후식으로 좀 먹는 것이 어때요?
남 그러자.

해설 | 남자가 김치를 가운데 선반에 올려두고 소시지는 버리라고 했고, 여자가 맨 밑의 선반에 포도가 있다고 했으므로 정답은 ④이다.

어휘 | clear [kliər] 동 치우다, 깨끗이 하다 side dish 반찬 refrigerator [rifrídʒərèitər] 명 냉장고 throw away 버리다 dessert [dizə́ːrt] 명 후식

3 심정 고르기

정답 ⑤

M Honey, wake up.
W What time is it now?
M It's already 9. You slept for over two hours after dinner.
W I didn't realize I was so sleepy.
M It seems that you needed more sleep today.
W Well, I had a lot of work today.
M Then, I'll give you a massage.
W Really? That would be good. I have a stiff neck.
M Tell me if it's too painful.
W Alright. Oh, it feels so good.

남 여보, 일어나.
여 지금 몇 시야?
남 벌써 9시야. 저녁 식사 후에 2시간 넘게 잤어.
여 내가 그렇게 졸린 줄 몰랐어.
남 당신 오늘 잠이 더 필요했던 것처럼 보여.
여 음, 오늘 일이 많았어.
남 그럼, 내가 마사지해줄게.
여 정말? 그거 좋겠다. 나 목이 뻐뻐해.
남 너무 아프면 말해줘.
여 알았어. 오, 정말 좋다.

해설 | 남자가 마사지를 해주자 여자가 정말 좋다고 했으므로 정답은 ⑤ 'relaxed'이다.

선택지 해석

① 신난 ② 지루한 ③ 실망한 ④ 화난 ⑤ 편안한

어휘 | sleepy [slíːpi] 형 졸린 stiff [stif] 형 뻣뻣한 painful [péinfəl] 형 아픈, 고통스러운

4 한 일 고르기

정답 ②

M Jane, how was the Winter Snow Festival last weekend?
W It was fantastic. It snowed a lot, and that made the festival more fun.
M What events were held there?
W There was a snowman-making contest.
M That sounds fun. Did you participate in it?
W No. The event was too crowded with people. So I gave up.
M Then, what did you do instead?
W I went skiing.

남 Jane, 지난 주말의 Winter Snow Festival은 어땠니?
여 환상적이었어. 눈이 많이 내렸는데, 그게 축제를 더 재미있게 만들었어.
남 거기서 무슨 행사가 열렸니?
여 눈사람 만들기 대회가 있었어.
남 재미있었겠다. 너는 거기 참여했니?
여 아니. 행사가 사람들로 너무 붐볐어. 그래서 나는 포기했어.
남 그럼, 대신 뭘 했니?
여 나는 스키를 타러 갔어.

해설 | 여자가 눈사람 만들기 대회는 너무 붐벼서 포기했고, 대신 스키를 타러 갔다고 했으므로 정답은 ② '스키 타기'이다.

어휘 | fantastic [fæntǽstik] 형 환상적인, 멋진 participate [paːrtísəpèit] 동 참여하다, 참가하다 crowded [kráudid] 형 붐비는 give up 포기하다

5 장소 고르기

정답 ④

W What do you want to drink, Kijoon?
M What's the most popular drink here?
W I heard that their milkshakes are delicious.
M I'll take one of those then.
W Great. Do you also want a dessert? They have chocolate cake.
M Yes, please. I'll find a table while you order.
W Okay.

여 뭘 마실래, 기준아?
남 여기서 가장 유명한 음료가 뭐니?
여 밀크셰이크가 맛있다고 들었어.
남 그럼 그거 한 잔 마실래.
여 좋아. 디저트도 먹을래? 초콜릿케이크가 있어.
남 응, 부탁할게. 네가 주문하는 동안 내가 자리를 찾을게.
여 알겠어.

해설 | 밀크셰이크가 맛있다고 언급되었고, 여자가 주문하는 동안 남자가 자리를 찾겠다고 말하는 것으로 보아 정답은 ④ '카페'이다.

어휘 | popular [pápjulər] 형 유명한, 인기 있는 while [hwail] 접 ~ 동안에

6 의도 고르기

정답 ②

M Jennifer, are you studying for the history exam?
W Yeah. It's my weakest subject.
M History is my worst subject too. How about studying together this weekend?
W Sorry, but I can't.
M Why not?
W I'm going to volunteer at a hospital.
M Don't you feel too busy?
W No. I enjoy helping other people.
M You always work so hard! I admire you.

남 Jennifer, 너 역사 시험공부 하고 있니?
여 응. 그건 내가 가장 약한 과목이거든.
남 나도 역사가 최악의 과목이야. 이번 주말에 같이 공부하는 게 어때?
여 미안한데, 그럴 수 없어.
남 어째서?
여 나는 병원에 봉사 활동을 하러 갈 거야.
남 너 너무 바쁘다고 느끼지 않니?
여 아니야. 난 다른 사람들을 돕는 게 좋아.
남 넌 항상 매우 열심이구나! 네가 존경스러워.

해설 | 남자가 여자에게 항상 열심이라고 감탄한 이후 존경한다고 했으므로 정답은 ② '칭찬'이다.

어휘 | weak [wi:k] 형 약한 subject [sʌ́bdʒikt] 명 과목; 주제 volunteer [vὰləntíər] 동 봉사 활동하다 admire [ædmáiər] 동 존경하다

7 언급하지 않은 내용 고르기

정답 ④

M Have you seen the opera *Magic Flute*?
W No, I haven't.
M Then, how about seeing it with me? It will be performed from next Friday until April 20th.
W I heard that a very famous composer wrote it.
M Yes. It was Mozart.
W Oh, right. How long does it last?
M Around three hours.
W That's quite long.
M Yeah. But Sumi Jo, the great soprano, will play the queen. We must see it.

남 너 오페라 <마술 피리>를 본 적 있니?
여 아니, 없어.
남 그럼 나랑 그걸 보는 게 어때? 다음 금요일부터 4월 20일까지 공연될 거야.
여 매우 유명한 작곡가가 그걸 썼다고 들었는데.
남 응. 모차르트야.
여 오, 맞아. 공연이 얼마나 기니?
남 3시간 정도야.
여 꽤 길다.
남 맞아. 하지만 훌륭한 소프라노인 조수미가 여왕을 연기할 거야. 우리는 그걸 꼭 봐야 해.

해설 | ① 공연 기간(다음 금요일부터 4월 20일까지), ② 작곡가(모차르트), ③ 상연 시간(3시간 정도), ⑤ 출연자(조수미)에 대해 언급했으므로 정답은 ④ '지휘자'이다.

어휘 | perform [pərfɔ́:rm] 동 공연하다 composer [kəmpóuzər] 명 작곡가

8 할 일 고르기

정답 ②

M Beth, where are you going?
W Hey, Sanghoon. I'm heading to the library.
M You're looking for the book *Animal Farm*, right?
W Yes. We have to write a book report about it by this Friday.
M It's no use. The book is checked out now.
W Then, what should I do?
M I'm going to the bookstore to buy the book. Do you want to go together?
W Sure.

남 Beth, 어디 가는 중이니?
여 안녕, 상훈아. 난 도서관에 가는 중이야.
남 <동물 농장> 책을 찾는 거구나, 그렇지?
여 맞아. 우리 그것에 대해 이번 금요일까지 독후감을 써야 하잖아.
남 소용없어. 그 책은 지금 대출 중이야.
여 그럼, 난 뭘 해야 할까?
남 나 그 책을 사러 서점에 가는 중이야. 같이 갈래?
여 그래.

해설 | 남자가 책을 사러 서점에 가는 중이라고 했고, 여자가 같이 가겠다고 했으므로 정답은 ② '서점 들르기'이다.

어휘 | head [hed] 동 가다, 향하다 book report 독후감 check out 대출하다, 빌리다

9 언급하지 않은 내용 고르기

정답 ⑤

M Good morning, everyone. Our city will have a Pottery Sale Day at the Hartford Community Center this Sunday. This event is run by the City Gallery, and local artists will participate as sellers. Many handmade items including cups and dishes will be sold there. You can pay by cash or credit card. Since lots of people are expected to come, please take the bus or the subway. Thank you.

남 좋은 아침입니다, 여러분. 우리 시는 이번 일요일에 하트포드 시민 회관에서 Pottery Sale Day를 가질 예정입니다. 이 행사는 시립 미술관에 의해 열리며, 지역 미술가들이 판매자로 참가할 것입니다. 컵과 접시를 포함한 많은 수제 물품들이 판매될 것입니다. 현금 또는 신용카드로 지불이 가능합니다. 많은 사람이 방문할 것으로 예상되니, 버스나 지하철을 이용해 주시기 바랍니다. 감사합니다.

해설 | ① 개최 장소(하트포드 시민 회관), ② 주최 기관(시립 미술관), ③ 판매 물품(컵과 접시를 포함한 많은 수제 물품), ④ 결제 방식(현금 또는 신용카드)에 대해 언급했으므로 정답은 ⑤ '주차 안내'이다.

어휘 | pottery [pátəri] 명 도자기 seller [sélər] 명 판매자 including [inklúːdiŋ] 전 ~을 포함하여 cash [kæʃ] 명 현금 credit card 신용 카드

10 주제 고르기

정답 ②

M Hello, class. Let's review what you learned in the previous lesson. First, you should listen carefully and show that you're listening. Making eye contact is a good way to do so. Next, you should use positive words. Also, don't forget to use suitable body language during a conversation. You can effectively communicate with others using these methods.

남 안녕하세요, 학생 여러분. 지난 수업에서 배웠던 것을 복습해 봅시다. 먼저, 여러분은 주의 깊게 듣고서 여러분이 경청하고 있다는 것을 보여주어야 합니다. 시선을 마주치는 것은 그렇게 하는 좋은 방법입니다. 그다음, 긍정적인 단어들을 사용해야 합니다. 또, 대화 도중 적절한 보디랭귀지를 사용하는 것을 잊지 마십시오. 이런 방법들을 사용하면 다른 사람들과 효과적으로 의사소통을 할 수 있습니다.

해설 | 남자가 다른 사람들과 효과적으로 의사소통할 수 있는 방법을 말하고 있으므로 정답은 ② '효과적인 의사소통 방법'이다.

어휘 | review [rivjúː] 동 복습하다 previous [príːviəs] 형 지난, 이전의 suitable [súːtəbl] 형 적절한 effectively [iféktivli] 부 효과적으로 method [méθəd] 명 방법

11 일치하지 않는 내용 고르기

정답 ⑤

W Steve, have you set your goals for the next year?
M Not yet. How about you?
W I'm planning to do one thing for each season. In spring, I'll plant a pine tree in my yard.
M Wow, what's for winter?
W I'll go ice fishing.
M Good. Then, you'll practice swimming in summer, right?
W No. I'll go surfing. And I'll write poems in the fall.
M Awesome. I hope you achieve all of those goals.

여 Steve, 너는 내년 목표를 세웠니?
남 아직 안 세웠어. 너는?
여 나는 계절마다 한 가지씩 하는 걸 계획 중이야. 봄에는 마당에 소나무를 심을 거야.
남 우와, 겨울에는 뭔데?
여 얼음낚시를 갈 거야.
남 좋다. 그럼, 여름에는 수영 연습을 하겠다, 그렇지?
여 아니. 난 서핑을 하러 갈 거야. 그리고 가을에는 시를 쓸 거야.
남 멋있다. 네가 이 모든 목표들을 달성할 수 있으면 좋겠어.

해설 | 남자가 여름에 수영 연습을 할지 묻자, 여자가 부정하며 서핑을 하러 갈 것이라고 했으므로 정답은 ⑤ '수영 연습을 할 것이다.'이다.

어휘 | goal [goul] 명 목표 pine tree 소나무 yard [jaːrd] 명 마당 go surfing 서핑하러 가다 poem [póuəm] 명 시 achieve [ətʃíːv] 동 달성하다, 성취하다

12 목적 고르기

정답 ①

[Cellphone rings.]
M Hi, Mina. What's up?
W Hello, Kevin. I'm cooking chicken pasta as you taught me.
M Great! It's perfect for dinner.
W Yeah. But can I ask a question about the recipe?
M What is the problem?
W Well... It doesn't taste as spicy as yours.
M Did you add pepper?
W Yes. But maybe I should add a little more.

[휴대폰이 울린다.]
남 안녕, 미나야. 무슨 일이야?
여 안녕, Kevin. 난 네가 가르쳐준 대로 치킨 파스타를 요리하고 있어.
남 잘됐다! 그건 저녁 식사로 딱 좋아.
여 맞아. 그런데 요리법에 대해 질문 하나 해도 될까?
남 뭐가 문제니?
여 음... 네 것만큼 맵지 않아.
남 후추를 넣었니?
여 응. 하지만 아마 조금 더 넣어야 하나 봐.

해설 | 여자가 남자에게 요리법에 대해 질문을 해도 되는지 물었으므로 정답은 ① '요리법을 묻기 위해서'이다.

어휘 | recipe [résəpi] 명 요리법 problem [prábləm] 명 문제 pepper [pépər] 명 후추; 고추

13 시간 정보 고르기

정답 ④

[Telephone rings.]
W Hello, this is Julia from the Daehan Cycling Club. Is this Mr. Jones speaking?
M Yes. Can I help you?
W You're going to join our bike race on July 13th, right?
M That's correct. Is there something wrong?
W I'm sorry, but it'll be delayed because a typhoon is expected.
M Then, when will the event be held?
W It'll be a week later, on the 20th.
M Alright. Thanks for the call.

[전화기가 울린다.]
여 안녕하세요, 대한 사이클링 클럽의 Julia입니다. Jones씨이신가요?
남 네. 무엇을 도와드릴까요?
여 Jones씨는 7월 13일에 저희 자전거 경주에 참가하실 예정이셨어요, 맞으시죠?
남 맞습니다. 뭔가 잘못되었나요?
여 죄송합니다만, 태풍이 예상되어서 경주가 미뤄질 예정입니다.
남 그렇다면, 언제 행사가 열릴 예정인가요?
여 일주일 후인 20일에요.
남 알겠습니다. 전화주셔서 감사합니다.

해설 | 여자가 7월 13일의 일주일 후인 20일에 대회가 열린다고 했으므로 정답은 ④ '7월 20일'이다.

어휘 | delay [diléi] 동 미루다, 연기하다 typhoon [taifú:n] 명 태풍 later [léitər] 부 후에, 나중에

14 관계 고르기

정답 ③

W Welcome. How can I help you?
M I need this suit cleaned. And can you remove this stain from these pants?
W Yes. We can get that out.
M Great, thanks. When can I pick up my clothes?
W They will be ready on Tuesday.
M Should I pay now?
W Yes. It'll be 10 dollars.
M Here you go. See you on Tuesday.

여 어서 오세요. 어떻게 도와드릴까요?
남 이 양복을 세탁해야 해요. 그리고 이 바지에서 이 얼룩을 제거할 수 있을까요?
여 네. 그건 제거할 수 있어요.
남 좋아요, 감사합니다. 언제 제 옷을 찾으러 오면 되나요?
여 화요일에는 준비가 되어 있을 거예요.
남 지금 지불해야 하나요?
여 네. 10달러입니다.
남 여기 있습니다. 화요일에 뵐게요.

해설 | 남자가 여자에게 양복 세탁과 바지의 얼룩 제거를 요청하고 있는 것으로 보아 정답은 ③ '세탁소 직원 — 손님'이다.

어휘 | remove [rimú:v] 동 제거하다 stain [stein] 명 얼룩 pick up ~을 찾아오다 ready [rédi] 형 준비가 된

15 부탁·요청한 일 고르기

정답 ②

M Hey, Charlotte.
W Hey, Mike. What's going on?
M I'm traveling to Canada to visit some friends.
W When do you leave?
M Next week. But I have a problem. I need a place for my dog to stay during my trip.
W What about your parents?
M They'll be out of town next week. Can you take care of my dog if it's possible?
W Of course. No problem.

남 안녕, Charlotte.
여 안녕, Mike. 무슨 일이야?
남 난 친구 몇 명을 만나러 캐나다로 여행을 갈 거야.
여 언제 떠나는데?
남 다음 주에. 그런데 문제가 있어. 내가 여행을 간 동안 내 개가 지낼 장소를 구해야 해.
여 너희 부모님은?
남 다음 주에 출장을 가실 거야. 만약 가능하다면, 네가 내 개를 돌봐줄 수 있을까?
여 물론이지. 문제없어.

해설 | 남자가 여자에게 자신이 여행 간 동안 개를 돌봐달라고 부탁했으므로 정답은 ② '반려견 돌보기'이다.

어휘 | place [pleis] 명 장소 동 놓다 take care of ~를 돌보다 possible [pάsəbl] 형 가능한

16 이유 고르기

정답 ④

W Henry, are you close to Andrew?
M Yeah. We're best friends.
W Then, do you know why Andrew has been absent from school since last Friday?
M Yes. He's in the hospital now.
W Oh, what happened to him?
M He broke his leg in a car accident.
W That's a pity.
M I'm going to visit him after class. Would you like to come?
W I'd like that.

여 Henry, 너 Andrew랑 친하니?
남 응. 우리는 단짝 친구야.
여 그러면, 지난 금요일부터 Andrew가 왜 학교에 결석했는지 아니?
남 응. 그는 지금 병원에 있어.
여 오, 그에게 무슨 일이 일어난 거야?
남 차 사고로 다리가 부러졌어.
여 유감이다.
남 나는 수업이 끝나고 병문안을 갈 거야. 너도 갈래?
여 그렇게 할게.

해설 | 남자의 친구가 차 사고로 다리가 부러져서 지금 병원에 있다고 했으므로 정답은 ④ '병원에 입원해서'이다.

어휘 | close [klouz] 형 친한; 가까운 absent [ǽbsənt] 형 결석한 happen [hǽpən] 동 일어나다 pity [píti] 명 유감

17 그림 상황에 적절한 대화 고르기

정답 ③

① W Do you want to eat lunch with me tomorrow?
M Actually, I'm meeting Lisa for lunch.
② W Can we take some pictures in front of that statue?
M Sure! Let's go.
③ W This is a lovely photograph.
M Thanks. That's my family at the beach.
④ W We should go to the pool.
M Okay. Let me change into my swimsuit.
⑤ W Do you want a room with an ocean view or a mountain view?
M An ocean view, please.

① 여 내일 나와 함께 점심 먹을래?
남 사실, 난 내일 점심에 Lisa를 만날 거야.
② 여 우리 저 동상 앞에서 사진 찍어도 될까?
남 당연하지! 가자.
③ 여 이건 사랑스러운 사진이네.
남 고마워. 저건 해변에 있는 우리 가족이야.
④ 여 우리 수영장에 가야 해.
남 알겠어. 수영복으로 갈아입을게.
⑤ 여 바다 전망 또는 산 전망 중에서 어떤 방으로 하시겠어요?
남 바다 전망으로 부탁드려요.

해설 | 남자와 여자가 해변에서 찍은 사진을 함께 보면서 대화하고 있는 상황이므로 정답은 ③이다.

어휘 | statue [stǽtʃuː] 명 동상 photograph [fóutəgræf] 명 사진 swimsuit [swímsuːt] 명 수영복 mountain [máuntən] 명 산

18 언급하지 않은 내용 고르기

정답 ④

W Hello. I'd like to tell you about a few changes to our subway service on December 31st. As lots of people will take the subway, we will have extra trains from 7 to 11 p.m. So, the trains will run every three minutes during those hours. Also, the trains won't stop at City Hall Station between 10 p.m. and midnight. Thank you.

여 안녕하세요. 12월 31일의 지하철 운영에 있어 몇 가지 변경 사항을 알려드리려고 합니다. 많은 사람이 지하철을 이용할 예정이므로, 저희는 오후 7시부터 11시까지 추가 열차를 배차할 것입니다. 그러므로, 열차는 그 시간 동안 3분마다 운행할 것입니다. 또한, 오후 10시부터 자정까지는 열차가 시청역에 정차하지 않을 것입니다. 감사합니다.

해설 | ① 변경 이유(많은 사람이 지하철을 이용할 예정임), ② 변경 시간대(오후 7시부터 11시), ③ 배차 간격(3분), ⑤ 무정차 역사(시청역)에 대해 언급했으므로 정답은 ④ '막차 시간'이다.

어휘 | extra [ékstrə] 형 추가의, 여분의 midnight [mídnàit] 명 자정

19 적절한 응답 고르기

정답 ④

M Jia, where are you going?
W Hello, Jaewon. I'm on my way to meet a friend at the Wilson Art Gallery.
M Oh, I heard a new exhibit opened there.
W Yeah. There are paintings by my favorite artist.
M You must be excited.
W Definitely. What about you? Are you busy?
M No. I'm free.
W I see. Why don't you join us at the gallery?
M Sure. If you don't mind.

남 지아야, 어디 가니?
여 안녕, 재원아. 나는 윌슨 미술관에 친구를 만나러 가는 길이야.
남 오, 거기 새 전시가 열렸다고 들었어.
여 맞아. 내가 가장 좋아하는 작가의 그림이 있어.
남 신났겠구나.
여 물론이지. 너는 어때? 바쁘니?
남 아니. 나 한가해.
여 그렇구나. 우리와 같이 미술관에 가는 게 어때?
남 좋아. 너만 괜찮다면.

해설 | 여자가 미술관에 함께 갈 것을 제안하고 있으므로 정답은 제안을 수락하는 ④ 'Sure. If you don't mind.'이다.

선택지 해석

① 그건 다음 달에 시작해. ② 유감이야. ③ 어떻게 칠할지 모르겠어. ④ 좋아. 너만 괜찮다면. ⑤ 그는 친한 친구야.

어휘 | art gallery 미술관 exhibit [igzíbit] 명 전시 definitely [défənitli] 부 물론; 분명히 free [fri:] 형 한가한

20 적절한 응답 고르기

정답 ①

W How was the festival last night, Taewoo?
M I didn't go.
W Why not? I thought you were excited about it.
M I was, but I had to take care of my little brother.
W Oh, you have a brother?
M Yes. He's four years old now.
W Do you have any other brothers or sisters?
M I also have an older sister.

여 어젯밤 축제는 어땠니, 태우야?
남 나 안 갔어.
여 왜 안 갔어? 네가 그걸 기대하는 줄 알았는데.
남 그랬지, 그런데 내 남동생을 돌봐야 했어.
여 오, 너 남동생이 있어?
남 응. 그는 이제 4살이야.
여 다른 형제도 있어?
남 누나도 한 명 있어.

해설 | 남자에게 다른 형제가 있는지 묻고 있으므로 정답은 형제 관계를 언급하는 ① 'I also have an older sister.'이다.

선택지 해석

① 누나도 한 명 있어. ② 난 15살이야. ③ 응, 재미있었어. ④ 우리 엄마는 변호사야. ⑤ 다음에 갈 거야.

어휘 | festival [féstəvəl] 명 축제 lawyer [lɔ́:jər] 명 변호사

11회 실전 모의고사

| 문제 pp.106-107

1	③	2	①	3	④	4	④	5	②	6	③	7	③	8	⑤	9	③	10	②
11	④	12	②	13	④	14	①	15	④	16	②	17	①	18	⑤	19	②	20	⑤

1 날씨 고르기

정답 ③

M Good afternoon! Here's the national weather report for tomorrow. Seoul will be foggy and cloudy all day long, and the temperature will drop dramatically in the evening. It'll be cold in Suwon because of strong winds. Heavy snow is expected in Wonju, so try and stay indoors. Lastly in Ulsan, there's a high chance of rain, so take an umbrella if you go out.

남 안녕하십니까! 내일의 전국 일기 예보입니다. 서울은 하루 종일 안개가 끼고 흐릴 예정이며, 저녁에는 기온이 급격히 떨어질 것입니다. 수원은 강풍으로 인해 춥겠습니다. 원주에는 폭설이 예상되어 있으니, 실내에 머무르시길 바랍니다. 마지막으로 울산에는 비가 올 확률이 높으니 외출 시 우산을 챙기십시오.

해설 | 울산에는 비가 올 확률이 높을 것이라고 했으므로 정답은 ③이다.

어휘 | national [næʃənəl] 형 전국적인; 국가의 foggy [fɔ́:gi] 형 안개가 낀 dramatically [drəmǽtikəli] 부 급격히

2 알맞은 그림 고르기

정답 ①

M Hello. May I help you?
W Yes. I'm looking for a curtain.
M You found the right place! How about this one?
W I really like its flower pattern.
M Okay. Which one do you want? The short one or longer one?
W Well, I need it for my living room. So I'll take the longer one.
M Excellent choice!

남 안녕하세요. 도와드릴까요?
여 네. 저는 커튼을 찾고 있어요.
남 잘 찾아오셨어요! 이건 어떠신가요?
여 꽃무늬가 정말 마음에 드네요.
남 알겠습니다. 어떤 게 필요하시나요? 짧은 커튼인가요, 더 긴 것인가요?
여 글쎄요, 거실에 필요한 거라서요. 그러니 더 긴 걸로 살게요.
남 훌륭한 선택이세요!

해설 | 여자가 커튼의 꽃무늬가 마음에 든다고 했고, 거실용의 긴 커튼으로 사겠다고 했으므로 정답은 ①이다.

어휘 | living room 거실 excellent [éksələnt] 형 훌륭한, 우수한

3 심정 고르기

정답 ④

[Cellphone rings.]
M Hey, Tiffany. What's up?
W Hi, Alex. Did you finish your exam?
M Yes. It's finally over. I'm so relieved.
W That's good. How did it go?
M It was easy to answer the questions. I studied hard for the last three months.
W Oh! I'm really glad to hear that. I knew you would do great on the test.
M Thank you so much.

[휴대폰이 울린다.]
남 안녕, Tiffany. 무슨 일이야?
여 안녕, Alex. 너 시험 끝났니?
남 응. 드디어 끝났어. 너무 다행이야.
여 잘 됐다. 어떻게 됐어?
남 문제 푸는 게 쉬웠어. 지난 세 달 동안 열심히 공부했거든.
여 오! 그렇다니 정말 기쁘다. 네가 이번 시험에서 잘할 줄 알고 있었어.
남 정말 고마워.

해설 | 남자가 시험이 끝나서 다행이며, 문제 푸는 게 쉬웠다고 했으므로 정답은 ④ 'happy'이다.

선택지 해석

① 걱정스러운 ② 수줍은 ③ 지루한 ④ 행복한 ⑤ 초조한

어휘 | finally [fáinəli] 부 드디어, 마침내 relieved [rilí:vd] 형 다행으로 여기는, 안심한

4 한 일 고르기

정답 ④

W Victor, what did you do last Saturday?
M I visited the National History Museum. How about you, Emma?
W I went fishing with my family.
M That's cool. How was it?
W It was my first time, but I loved it! I caught three fish, and my mom caught an octopus.
M Do you have a picture of them?
W Sure. They are on my phone.

여 Victor, 지난 토요일에 뭐 했니?
남 나는 국립 역사박물관에 갔어. 너는 뭐 했니, Emma?
여 난 우리 가족과 함께 낚시하러 갔어.
남 그거 멋진걸. 어땠어?
여 난 낚시가 처음이었지만, 정말 좋았어! 내가 물고기 세 마리를 잡았고, 엄마는 문어를 잡으셨어.
남 그것들 사진 있니?
여 물론이지. 내 휴대폰에 있어.

해설 | 여자가 지난 토요일에 가족과 함께 낚시하러 갔다고 했으므로 정답은 ④ '낚시하기'이다.
어휘 | catch [kætʃ] 동 잡다 octopus [ɑ́ktəpəs] 명 문어

5 장소 고르기

정답 ②

M Hello. Can I help you?
W Yes, please. I'm searching for some new chairs.
M Alright. What kind of chairs do you want?
W I want wooden chairs for my kitchen table.
M These chairs are very popular. They would look great in a kitchen.
W They are nice, but I want darker chairs.
M Okay. How about these chairs then?
W Oh, those are perfect.

남 안녕하세요. 도와드릴까요?
여 네, 부탁드려요. 전 새 의자들을 좀 찾고 있어요.
남 그러시군요. 어떤 종류의 의자를 원하시나요?
여 부엌 식탁에 쓸 나무 의자를 원해요.
남 이 의자들이 매우 인기가 있답니다. 그것들은 부엌에 아주 잘 어울릴 거예요.
여 멋지긴 한데, 좀 더 어두운색의 의자였으면 좋겠어요.
남 알겠습니다. 그럼 이 의자들은 어떠세요?
여 오, 그것들이 딱이네요.

해설 | 여자가 새 의자들을 찾고 있다고 하는 것으로 보아 정답은 ② '가구점'이다.
어휘 | wooden [wúdn] 형 나무로 된, 목재의 kitchen [kítʃən] 명 부엌, 주방

6 의도 고르기

정답 ③

W Jack, today is your last day of your summer vacation, right?
M Yes, Mom. But I didn't finish my vacation homework.
W What is your homework?
M I have to write three reports after reading three books.
W Didn't you read the books?
M Yes. I read them last week. But I didn't have enough time to write reports.
W Jack, you need to start your homework earlier next time.
M Okay, Mom. I'll try to be more responsible.

여 Jack, 오늘이 네 여름 방학의 마지막 날이구나, 그렇지?
남 네, 엄마. 하지만 전 방학 숙제를 끝내지 못했어요.
여 숙제가 뭐니?
남 책 세 권을 읽고 나서 보고서 세 개를 써야 해요.
여 책은 읽지 않았니?
남 네. 지난주에 읽었어요. 그런데 보고서를 쓸 시간이 충분하지 않았어요.
여 Jack, 다음번에는 숙제를 더 일찍 시작해야겠구나.
남 네, 엄마. 더 책임감을 가지도록 노력할게요.

해설 | 여자가 다음 번에는 숙제를 더 일찍 시작하라고 충고하자, 남자가 더 책임감을 가지도록 노력하겠다고 했으므로 정답은 ③ '반성'이다.
어휘 | last [læst] 형 지난; 마지막의, 최후의 enough [inʌ́f] 형 충분한 responsible [rispɑ́nsəbl] 형 책임감 있는, 책임이 있는

7 한 일 고르기

정답 ③

W Paul, are you going to Blue Boys' concert?
M Yes. They are my favorite band. What about you?
W I can't go. The tickets are too expensive.
M Right. I sold some of my old clothes so that I would have enough money for a ticket.
W How did you do that?
M Well, I posted them on a website.
W Great idea!
M Yes. You should try it too.

여 Paul, 너 Blue Boys' 콘서트에 갈 거야?
남 응. 그들은 내가 가장 좋아하는 밴드야. 너는?
여 난 못 가. 티켓이 너무 비싸.
남 맞아. 난 티켓을 위해 충분한 돈을 마련하려고 오래된 옷 중 몇 벌을 팔았어.
여 그걸 어떻게 했어?
남 음, 웹사이트에 그것들을 올렸어.
여 좋은 생각이다!
남 그래. 너도 한번 시도해봐.

해설 | 남자가 콘서트 티켓을 살 돈을 마련하기 위해 오래된 옷들을 팔았다고 했으므로 정답은 ③ '오래된 옷 팔기'이다.
어휘 | expensive [ikspénsiv] 형 비싼 post [poust] 동 올리다, 게시하다, 붙이다 명 기둥

8 할 일 고르기

정답 ⑤

M Brenda, are you free on Saturday?
W Yes, I am. Why do you ask?
M Would you like to go ice skating with me?
W Sure! Which rink do you want to skate at?
M My older brother told me that the Westwood Arena has a great rink. But I am not sure how to get there.
W No problem. We can find directions on the app.
M Oh, I'll check it right now.

남 Brenda, 너 토요일에 한가하니?
여 응, 한가해. 왜 물어보는데?
남 나랑 스케이트를 타러 갈래?
여 물론이지! 어떤 빙상장에서 스케이트를 타고 싶니?
남 우리 형이 웨스트우드 경기장에 좋은 빙상장이 있다고 말했어. 그런데 거기에 어떻게 가는지는 잘 모르겠네.
여 문제없어. 앱으로 길을 찾을 수 있잖아.
남 오, 내가 지금 바로 확인할게.

해설 | 여자가 앱으로 경기장까지의 길을 찾을 수 있다고 하자 남자가 바로 확인하겠다고 했으므로 정답은 ⑤ '앱에서 길 찾기'이다.
어휘 | free [friː] 형 한가한; 자유로운 directions [dirékʃənz] 명 길; 길 안내 (direction [dirékʃən] 명 방향) check [tʃek] 동 확인하다

9 언급하지 않은 내용 고르기

정답 ③

M Sara, what do you think of these calendars?
W I like the one with the pictures of wild animals.
M It's beautiful, but the text is a little small. It could be hard to read.
W I see. This one with castles is nice too. How much is it?
M It's 25 dollars. Is that too expensive?
W Look, it's on sale. This calendar is 20% off.
M Let's get it!

남 Sara, 이 달력들에 대해 어떻게 생각해?
여 나는 야생 동물 사진이 있는 게 마음에 들어.
남 그게 예쁘긴 한데, 글자가 약간 작아. 읽기 어려울 수 있어.
여 그렇구나. 성 사진이 있는 이것도 괜찮은데. 이건 얼마야?
남 25달러야. 너무 비싼가?
여 저기 봐, 이건 할인 중이야. 이 달력은 20% 할인되네.
남 이걸로 사자!

해설 | ① 사진(야생 동물, 성) ② 글씨 크기(약간 작음), ④ 가격(25달러), ⑤ 할인율(20%)에 대해 언급했으므로 정답은 ③ '색상'이다.
어휘 | calendar [kǽləndər] 명 달력 wild [waild] 형 야생의 castle [kǽsl] 명 성

10 주제 고르기

정답 ②

M Good morning. Let's discuss how to choose a good book. There are three ways to do this. First, you can ask your teacher for suggestions. Another way is to read book reviews in newspapers and magazines. Finally, you can join a book club. The club members will recommend different books for you to read.

남 좋은 아침입니다. 좋은 책을 고르는 방법을 이야기해봅시다. 이를 할 수 있는 세 가지 방법이 있습니다. 첫째로, 선생님께 추천을 부탁할 수 있습니다. 다른 방법은 신문과 잡지에 실린 서평을 읽는 것입니다. 마지막으로, 독서 동아리에 가입할 수 있습니다. 동아리 회원들이 여러분이 읽을 다양한 책들을 추천해 줄 겁니다.

해설 | 남자가 좋은 책을 고르는 방법 세 가지를 말하고 있으므로 정답은 ② '좋은 책을 고르는 법'이다.
어휘 | discuss [diskʌ́s] 동 이야기하다; 논의하다 ask A for B A에게 B를 부탁하다, 요구하다 suggestion [səgdʒéstʃən] 명 추천; 제안
recommend [rèkəménd] 동 추천하다

11 일치하지 않는 내용 고르기

정답 ④

W Jonathan, did you hear about the new movie theater?
M Yes. It opened last week.
W It's having a grand opening event. All tickets are 50% off this month.
M Right. I watched a 4D movie there last Friday.
W How was it?
M It felt like I was flying. And the seat was very comfortable.
W I'd like to visit that theater.
M Do you want to go watch a movie tomorrow? It sells a lot of different flavors of popcorn too.
W Great! I can't wait.

여 Jonathan, 새 영화관에 대해 들었니?
남 응. 지난주에 문을 열었잖아.
여 개관 행사를 하고 있어. 이번 달에는 모든 표가 50% 할인이 돼.
남 맞아. 나 지난 금요일에 거기서 4D 영화를 봤어.
여 어땠어?
남 내가 날고 있는 것처럼 느껴졌어. 그리고 좌석이 정말 편안했어.
여 나도 그 영화관에 가보고 싶어.
남 내일 영화 보러 갈래? 거기는 다양한 맛의 팝콘도 팔아.
여 좋아! 너무 기대된다.

해설 | 남자가 좌석이 매우 편안했다고 했으므로 정답은 ④ '좌석이 불편하다.'이다.

어휘 | comfortable [kʌ́mfərtəbl] 형 편안한 flavor [fléivər] 명 맛

12 목적 고르기

정답 ②

[Cellphone rings.]
M Hey, Mindy. I have a favor to ask.
W Sure, Jacob. What do you need?
M Could I borrow your bicycle this weekend?
W Is something wrong with yours?
M Yeah. I broke the seat. But I promised to go riding with some friends on Saturday.
W I can lend you mine that day.
M Thanks. I'll pick it up at 1.
W See you then!

[휴대폰이 울린다.]
남 안녕, Mindy. 나 부탁할 게 있어.
여 물론이지, Jacob. 뭐가 필요하니?
남 이번 주말에 네 자전거를 빌릴 수 있을까?
여 네 것에 무슨 문제가 있니?
남 응. 내가 안장을 망가뜨렸어. 그런데 토요일에 친구들 몇 명과 자전거를 타러 가기로 약속했거든.
여 그날은 내 걸 빌려줄 수 있어.
남 고마워. 내가 1시에 가지러 갈게.
여 그때 보자!

해설 | 남자가 여자의 자전거를 주말에 빌릴 수 있을지 물었으므로 정답은 ② '자전거를 빌리기 위해서'이다.

어휘 | break [breik] 동 망가뜨리다; 깨다 lend [lend] 동 빌려주다

13 금액 정보 고르기

정답 ④

M Welcome to our store. How can I help you?
W How much are these tumblers?
M The small one is 25 dollars, and the medium one is 30 dollars.
W I'll take the medium size. How about this red straw?
M It's two dollars. Do you want it too?
W Yes, please.
M Then, the total is 32 dollars.

남 저희 가게에 오신 걸 환영합니다. 어떻게 도와드릴까요?
여 이 텀블러들은 얼마인가요?
남 작은 건 25달러이고, 중간 것은 30달러입니다.
여 중간 사이즈로 살게요. 이 빨간 빨대는요?
남 그건 2달러입니다. 그것도 원하시나요?
여 네, 주세요.
남 그러면, 총 32달러입니다.

해설 | 중간 사이즈 텀블러가 30달러, 빨대가 2달러로 총 32달러라고 했으므로 정답은 ④ '$ 32'이다.

어휘 | tumbler [tʌ́mblər] 명 텀블러, 큰 컵 medium [míːdiəm] 명 중간 straw [strɔː] 명 빨대; 지푸라기

14 관계 고르기

정답 ①

M Hello. What can I do for you?
W Do you have any medicine for headaches?
M Yes. These pills will help.
W How often should I take them?
M Take two pills three times per day. Do you need anything else?
W Yes. Can I also have a box of bandages?
M Sure. Do you want waterproof ones?
W No. Just the regular bandages, please.

남 안녕하세요. 무엇을 도와드릴까요?
여 두통약이 있나요?
남 네. 이 알약이 도움이 될 거예요.
여 얼마나 자주 복용해야 하나요?
남 하루에 세 번 두 알씩 드세요. 더 필요하신 것 있으세요?
여 네. 반창고도 한 상자 주실래요?
남 그럼요. 방수 반창고로 드릴까요?
여 아니요. 그냥 보통 반창고로 주세요.

해설 | 여자가 두통약을 찾자 남자가 약을 추천해주면서 복용법을 설명해주고 있는 것으로 보아 정답은 ① '약사 — 손님'이다.

어휘 | pill [pil] 명 알약, 약 bandage [bǽndidʒ] 명 반창고, 붕대 waterproof [wɔ́tərpruf] 형 방수의 regular [régjulər] 형 보통의; 규칙적인

15 제안한 일 고르기

정답 ④

W Hi, Nick. What are you doing?
M Hi. I'm writing a letter for my mom.
W That is so sweet of you. Is it her birthday today?
M Actually, it's tomorrow. But I don't know what to buy her.
W Let me help you. What does your mom like the most?
M Well, she likes flowers.
W What about buying a perfume that smells like flowers? I think she would love it.
M That's a good idea. Thank you.

여 안녕, Nick. 뭐 하고 있니?
남 안녕. 난 엄마께 편지를 쓰는 중이야.
여 너 참 다정하구나. 오늘이 어머니 생신이니?
남 사실, 내일이야. 그런데 뭘 사드려야 할지 모르겠어.
여 내가 도와줄게. 너희 어머니는 뭘 가장 좋아하시니?
남 음, 꽃을 좋아하셔.
여 꽃향기가 나는 향수를 사는 건 어때? 정말 좋아하실 것 같아.
남 그거 좋은 생각이다. 고마워.

해설 | 여자가 남자에게 꽃향기가 나는 향수를 살 것을 제안하고 있으므로 정답은 ④ '향수 구매하기'이다.
어휘 | letter [létər] 명 편지 perfume [pə́ːrfjuːm] 명 향수 smell [smel] 동 향기가 나다, 냄새가 나다

16 이유 고르기

정답 ②

M Karen, I'm home.
W Oh, you came home 30 minutes earlier than usual.
M Yes. I had to come home early.
W Why? Are you playing baseball with your friends today?
M Honey, don't you remember what day it is?
W I'm sorry, but I don't know what you mean.
M There's an Olympic soccer match today!
W Right! Let's order fried chicken and watch it on TV.

남 Karen, 나 집에 왔어.
여 오, 평소보다 30분이나 일찍 집에 왔네.
남 응. 집에 일찍 와야 했어.
여 왜? 오늘 친구들이랑 야구하러 가?
남 여보, 오늘이 무슨 날인지 기억 안 나?
여 미안하지만, 무슨 말인지 모르겠어.
남 오늘 올림픽 축구 경기가 있잖아!
여 그랬지! 프라이드 치킨을 주문하고 TV로 경기를 보자.

해설 | 남자가 오늘 올림픽 축구 경기가 있어서 집에 일찍 왔다고 했으므로 정답은 ② '축구 경기를 보려고'이다.
어휘 | early [ə́ːrli] 부 일찍 usual [júːuəl] 형 평소의 baseball [béisbɔ̀ːl] 명 야구 match [mætʃ] 명 경기 order [ɔ́ːrdər] 동 주문하다

17 그림 상황에 적절한 대화 고르기

정답 ①

① W Would you like tomatoes and onions on your sandwich?
M Just tomatoes, please.
② W Do we need to buy any bread?
M Yes. We just ran out.
③ W What will we eat on our hike?
M I'll pack some strawberries and crackers.
④ W What are you growing in your garden?
M I've planted some lettuce and cucumbers.
⑤ W What's today's date?
M It's March 20th.

① 여 샌드위치에 토마토와 양파를 넣으시겠습니까?
남 그냥 토마토만요.
② 여 빵을 좀 사야 할까?
남 응. 막 다 떨어졌어.
③ 여 하이킹 가서 뭘 먹을까?
남 내가 딸기와 크래커를 챙길게.
④ 여 정원에서 뭘 재배하고 있니?
남 상추랑 오이를 조금 심었어.
⑤ 여 오늘이 며칠이지?
남 3월 20일이야.

해설 | 여자가 남자의 샌드위치를 주문받고 있고, 남자가 토마토를 넣어달라고 하는 상황이므로 정답은 ①이다.
어휘 | run out 다 떨어지다, 다하다 grow [grou] 동 재배하다; 자라다 lettuce [létis] 명 상추 cucumber [kjúːkʌmbər] 명 오이

18 언급하지 않은 내용 고르기

정답 ⑤

W Let me tell you about my hobby. I'm very interested in computers. I'm learning how to write code in my free time. I'm trying to develop some software programs with what I've learned. Sometimes, I assemble computers using new parts. Also, I'm always happy to help fix my friends' broken computers. I dream of becoming a computer programmer someday.

여 제 취미에 대해 말씀드리겠습니다. 저는 컴퓨터에 관심이 많습니다. 저는 여가 시간에는 코드 짜는 법을 배우고 있습니다. 제가 배운 것으로 소프트웨어 프로그램을 개발하려고 노력 중입니다. 가끔, 저는 새로운 부품들을 사용해서 컴퓨터를 조립합니다. 또, 저는 항상 제 친구들의 고장 난 컴퓨터를 고치는 것을 도울 수 있어 행복합니다. 저는 언젠가 컴퓨터 프로그래머가 되는 것을 꿈꿉니다.

해설 | 여자가 취미로 하는 일로 컴퓨터 관련 자격증을 취득하기 위해 공부한다는 말은 언급되지 않았으므로 정답은 ⑤이다.

어휘 | free time 여가 시간 develop [divéləp] 동 개발하다 assemble [əsémbl] 동 조립하다 fix [fiks] 동 고치다, 수리하다

19 적절한 응답 고르기

정답 ②

W Hi, Matt. You look tired.
M Yes. I can't sleep well nowadays.
W Oh, no. Why not?
M I just can't fall asleep.
W What have you tried to fall asleep?
M I listened to calming music, but it didn't work.
W I see. Do you look at your phone a lot before you sleep?
M I guess I do.
W That must be the problem. Next time, read a book instead.
M I'll try that tonight.

여 안녕, Matt. 너 피곤해 보인다.
남 응. 나 요즘 잠을 잘 잘 수가 없어.
여 오, 저런. 왜 못 자?
남 그냥 잠들 수가 없어.
여 잠들기 위해 뭘 해 봤니?
남 차분하게 해주는 음악을 들었는데, 효과가 없었어.
여 그렇구나. 너 자기 전에 휴대폰을 많이 보니?
남 아마 그런 것 같아.
여 그게 분명 문제일 거야. 다음에는, 대신 책을 읽어봐.
남 오늘 밤에 그렇게 해볼게.

해설 | 여자가 자기 전에 휴대폰을 보는 대신 책을 읽어보라고 조언하고 있으므로 정답은 조언을 수락하는 ② 'I'll try that tonight.'이다.

선택지 해석

① 그녀는 일찍 자러 갔어. ② 오늘 밤에 그렇게 해볼게. ③ 그는 좀 괜찮아졌어. ④ 낮잠을 자야 하니? ⑤ 나는 휴대폰 게임을 하는 중이야.

어휘 | nowadays [náuədèiz] 부 요즈음 calm [ka:m] 동 차분하게 하다 형 고요한 work [wə:rk] 동 효과가 있다; 일하다 instead [instéd] 부 대신에 nap [næp] 명 낮잠

20 적절한 응답 고르기

정답 ⑤

W Hyunmin, that postcard with a picture of Deoksugung is pretty. Who did you buy it for?
M It's for my friend Edward. He lives in England.
W How did you meet him?
M I met him at Daejeon Science Camp last summer. He wants to visit Korea again this year.
W I think he will like the postcard then. What about showing him the palace on his visit?
M Yes. He will love that.

여 현민아, 저 덕수궁 사진이 있는 엽서 예쁘다. 누구를 위해 산 거야?
남 내 친구 Edward를 위한 거야. 그는 영국에 살아.
여 어떻게 만났어?
남 지난여름 대전 과학 캠프에서 만났어. Edward는 올해도 다시 한국을 방문하고 싶어 해.
여 그럼 그 친구가 이 엽서를 좋아할 거 같네. 친구가 오면 덕수궁을 보여주는 건 어때?
남 그래. 그가 좋아할 거야.

해설 | 남자의 친구에게 덕수궁을 보여줄 것을 제안하고 있으므로 정답은 제안에 동의하는 ⑤ 'Yes. He will love that.'이다.

선택지 해석

① 우리는 버스를 탔어. ② 아니. 그는 지금 바빠. ③ 우표 몇 장 사도 될까? ④ 그건 꽤 비싸. ⑤ 그래. 그가 좋아할 거야.

어휘 | postcard [póustkɑ:rd] 명 엽서 palace [pǽlis] 명 궁전 stamp [stæmp] 명 우표

12회 실전 모의고사

| 문제 pp.114-115

1	①	2	④	3	②	4	③	5	⑤	6	②	7	①	8	④	9	②	10	③
11	⑤	12	⑤	13	③	14	②	15	③	16	④	17	②	18	④	19	②	20	③

1 날씨 고르기

정답 ①

W Welcome to the weekly weather report. This week will start with beautiful spring weather and warm sunshine. From Thursday, however, it'll be partly cloudy and windy. Rain is expected to fall from Friday through the weekend. So, I recommend bringing an umbrella. Thank you.

여 주간 일기예보에 오신 것을 환영합니다. 이번 주는 아름다운 봄 날씨와 따뜻한 햇살로 시작하겠습니다. 하지만, 목요일부터는 부분적으로 흐리고 바람이 불겠습니다. 금요일부터 주말까지는 비가 내릴 것으로 예상됩니다. 그러니, 우산을 가지고 가시는 것을 추천합니다. 감사합니다.

해설 | 금요일부터 주말까지는 비가 내릴 것으로 예상된다고 했으므로 정답은 ①이다.

어휘 | expect [ikspékt] 동 예상하다

2 알맞은 그림 고르기

정답 ④

M Mom, look!
W Oh, my! What are you wearing, Sunho?
M It's a paper bag mask. I made it in class today.
W Why are there three holes?
M It's an alien mask, so I put three holes for eyes.
W Did you cut those sharp teeth?
M Ms. Nicholas helped me cut these.
W Where is the nose?
M Aliens don't have noses.
W You did a great job. It is scary.

남 엄마, 보세요!
여 오, 이런! 선호야, 무엇을 쓰고 있니?
남 종이가방 가면이에요. 오늘 수업 시간에 만들었어요.
여 왜 구멍이 세 개니?
남 이건 외계인 가면이라서, 눈구멍을 세 개 뚫었어요.
여 네가 그 날카로운 이빨을 오렸니?
남 Nicholas 선생님이 이걸 오리는 걸 도와주셨어요.
여 코는 어디 있니?
남 외계인은 코가 없어요.
여 정말 잘했구나. 무서워.

해설 | 남자는 눈구멍을 세 개 뚫고 날카로운 이빨을 오렸으며, 외계인이라 코가 없다고 했으므로 정답은 ④이다.

어휘 | mask [mæsk] 명 가면 hole [houl] 명 구멍 alien [éiljən] 명 외계인 sharp [ʃa:rp] 형 날카로운, 뾰족한

3 심정 고르기

정답 ②

W Brad, did you check the results of the writing contest?
M Not yet. I am so nervous.
W Come on! I know you are a good writer.
M Well, I'm not sure.
W Do you want me to check the website for you?
M Yes, please. I can't check it myself.
W Okay. *[Clicking sound]* Brad, you did it!
M Really? I can't believe it!

여 Brad, 글짓기 대회 결과 확인했니?
남 아직 안 했어. 나 너무 떨려.
여 왜 이래! 나는 네가 좋은 작가라는 것을 알고 있어.
남 음, 난 잘 모르겠어.
여 내가 홈페이지를 확인해 줄까?
남 응, 그렇게 해줘. 내가 직접 확인을 못 하겠어.
여 알았어. *[클릭하는 소리]* Brad, 네가 해냈어!
남 정말? 믿을 수가 없어!

해설 | 여자는 네가 해냈다고 하자 남자가 믿을 수가 없다고 했으므로 정답은 ② 'excited'이다.

선택지 해석

① 지루한 ② 흥분한 ③ 화난 ④ 슬픈 ⑤ 민망한

어휘 | result [rizʌ́lt] 명 결과 contest [kɑ́ntest] 명 대회 embarrassed [imbǽrəst] 형 민망한

4 한 일 고르기

정답 ③

W What's that small tree on your desk?
M It's a tree-shaped lamp. I got it from the flea market in Central Park on Saturday.
W Oh, I wanted to go there too. But my family went on a trip to Jeonju.
M That sounds interesting. What did you do there?
W We went to Jeonju Hanok Village. I had bibimbab for dinner, and it was very delicious.
M It sounds like you had a great day!

여 책상 위에 있는 저 작은 나무는 뭐니?
남 나무 모양의 램프야. 토요일에 센트럴 공원의 벼룩시장에서 샀어.
여 오, 나도 거기 가고 싶었어. 하지만 우리 가족은 전주로 여행을 갔었어.
남 그거 흥미롭게 들리는데. 거기서 뭘 했니?
여 우리는 전주 한옥마을에 갔어. 저녁으로 비빔밥을 먹었는데, 그건 정말 맛있었어.
남 좋은 하루를 보낸 것 같네!

해설 | 남자는 토요일에 센트럴 공원의 벼룩시장에서 나무 모양의 램프를 샀다고 했으므로 정답은 ③ '벼룩시장 가기'이다.
어휘 | flea market 벼룩시장

5 장소 고르기

정답 ⑤

M Hi, Officer. My bag was stolen.
W Okay, sir. We'll look into it. What happened?
M Someone broke into my car and took my bag last night.
W I see. What was inside the bag?
M I keep my laptop in it.
W Alright. I've got your report. We will call you if your bag is found.

남 안녕하세요, 경관님. 제 가방을 도둑맞았어요.
여 알겠습니다, 선생님. 저희가 조사하겠습니다. 무슨 일이 있었습니까?
남 어젯밤 누군가가 제 차에 침입해서 제 가방을 가져갔어요.
여 그렇군요. 가방 안에는 무엇이 들어있었나요?
남 저는 노트북을 그 안에 보관해요.
여 알겠습니다. 신고가 완료됐습니다. 만약 가방이 발견되면 전화 드리겠습니다.

해설 | 남자가 가방을 도둑맞았다고 했고, 여자가 신고가 완료됐다는 말을 하는 것으로 보아 정답은 ⑤ '경찰서'이다.
어휘 | look into 조사하다 break into 침입하다 keep [kiːp] 동 보관하다; 유지하다 call [kɔːl] 동 전화하다

6 의도 고르기

정답 ②

M Kelly, what a surprise! What are you doing here?
W Hi, Minsu. I am getting some chicken and vegetables.
M What are you cooking for dinner tonight?
W Today is Thanksgiving in my home country. We usually cook a turkey, but they are difficult to find in Korea.
M Wow. I've never been to a Thanksgiving dinner before.
W Why don't you come and have dinner with my family?

남 Kelly, 웬일이야! 여기서 뭐해?
여 안녕, 민수야. 나는 닭고기와 채소를 사고 있어.
남 오늘 저녁으로 뭘 요리하는데?
여 우리나라에서는 오늘이 추수감사절이야. 우리는 보통 칠면조를 요리하는데, 한국에서는 칠면조를 찾기가 어렵네.
남 우와. 난 추수감사절 저녁 식사에 한 번도 가본 적이 없어.
여 와서 우리 가족과 함께 저녁을 먹는 게 어때?

해설 | 남자가 추수감사절 저녁 식사에 한 번도 가본 적이 없다고 하자 여자가 자신의 가족과 함께 저녁을 먹는 게 어떠냐고 말했으므로 정답은 ② '제안'이다.
어휘 | vegetable [védʒətəbl] 명 채소 turkey [tə́ːrki] 명 칠면조 difficult [dífikəlt] 형 어려운

7 특정 정보 고르기

정답 ①

W Good afternoon, Dr. Feldman.
M Ms. Smith, you look so pale today. What's the matter?
W I fell on the ice yesterday. At first, my back was sore.
M And then?
W This morning, I could hardly walk.
M Does your back still hurt?
W Not anymore. My knee hurts now.
M Okay. I'll take an X-ray. We'll see what's wrong with your knee.

여 안녕하세요, Feldman 선생님.
남 Smith씨, 오늘 매우 창백해 보이세요. 무슨 일인가요?
여 어제 빙판 위에서 넘어졌어요. 처음에는, 허리가 아팠어요.
남 그리고서는요?
여 오늘 아침에는 거의 걸을 수가 없었어요.
남 허리는 아직도 아픈가요?
여 더 이상 아프지 않아요. 지금은 무릎이 아파요.
남 알겠습니다. 엑스레이를 찍을게요. 무릎에 무슨 문제가 있는지 알아보겠습니다.

해설 | 여자가 지금은 무릎이 아프다고 했으므로 정답은 ① '무릎'이다.
어휘 | pale [peil] 형 창백한 sore [sɔːr] 형 아픈; 몸이 아픈 hardly [háːrdli] 부 거의 ~않다

8 할 일 고르기

정답 ④

M What is that, Yuna?
W It's a bus ticket to Pyeongchang. I'm going snowboarding in the afternoon.
M I didn't know you like snowboarding.
W Yeah. I learned to snowboard last year, and it's even more fun than skiing.
M I want to learn how to snowboard too.
W You can come with me today. I'll teach you how.
M Really?
W Yeah. Go pack your bag. I'll get a ticket for you.
M Okay. Thanks!

남 저건 뭐니, 유나야?
여 평창으로 가는 버스표야. 나는 오후에 스노보드를 타러 가.
남 네가 스노보드를 좋아하는지 몰랐어.
여 응. 나는 작년에 스노보드를 배웠는데, 스키보다 훨씬 더 재미있어.
남 나도 스노보드를 타는 법을 배우고 싶어.
여 나랑 오늘 같이 가도 돼. 내가 어떻게 타는지 가르쳐 줄게.
남 정말?
여 응. 가서 가방을 챙겨. 내가 네 표를 살게.
남 알겠어. 고마워!

해설 | 여자가 남자에게 가서 가방을 챙기라고 하자 남자가 알겠다고 했으므로 정답은 ④ '짐 싸기'이다.

어휘 | pack [pæk] 동 (짐을) 챙기다

9 언급하지 않은 내용 고르기

정답 ②

M Today, our guest is Sofia Petrov from the National Ballet company. Welcome!
W Good afternoon.
M Could you tell us about your last performance?
W I danced as Clara in *The Nutcracker*.
M What is the main story of this ballet?
W On Christmas eve, Clara becomes friends with a nutcracker. And she fights against the evil Mouse King.
M That sounds interesting. Is the show performed all year?
W No. We usually stage this performance around Christmas time only.

남 오늘 저희 게스트는 국립 발레단의 Sofia Petrov씨입니다. 어서 오세요!
여 안녕하세요.
남 지난 공연에 대해 말씀해 주시겠어요?
여 저는 <호두까기 인형>에서 Clara로 춤을 췄습니다.
남 이 발레의 주요 줄거리가 무엇인가요?
여 크리스마스이브에 Clara는 호두까기 인형과 친구가 돼요. 그리고 그녀는 사악한 Mouse King에 대항하여 싸우죠.
남 흥미로울 것 같네요. 이 작품은 일 년 내내 공연되나요?
여 아니요. 저희는 보통 크리스마스 때쯤에만 상연해요.

해설 | ① 공연명(<호두까기 인형>), ③ 등장인물(Clara), ④ 줄거리(호두까기 인형과 친구가 되고 Mouse King과 싸움), ⑤ 공연 시기(크리스마스 때쯤)에 대해 언급했으므로 정답은 ② '공연 길이'이다.

어휘 | last [læst] 형 지난; 마지막의 performance [pərfɔ́:rməns] 명 공연 fight [fait] 동 싸우다 evil [í:vəl] 형 사악한 stage [steidʒ] 동 상연하다

10 주제 고르기

정답 ③

W Attention, customers. Welcome to Sideshow Supermarket. We are having a special sale today. All fruits and vegetables are 10% off. Cucumbers and carrots are available at a 5% discount. Also, download our app, and you can get a pass for free parking.

여 주목해주십시오, 고객 여러분. 사이드쇼 슈퍼마켓에 오신 것을 환영합니다. 저희는 오늘 특별 할인을 하고 있습니다. 모든 과일과 채소는 10% 할인됩니다. 오이와 당근은 5% 할인된 가격에 구매하실 수 있습니다. 그리고, 저희 앱을 다운받으시면 무료 주차권을 받으실 수 있습니다.

해설 | 여자가 오늘은 특별 할인을 한다고 했고, 할인하는 품목을 말하고 있으므로 정답은 ③ '할인 행사 안내'이다.

어휘 | customer [kʌ́stəmər] 명 고객 cucumber [kjú:kʌmbər] 명 오이 available [əvéiləbl] 형 이용 가능한 discount [dískaunt] 명 할인 pass [pæs] 명 무료입장권

11 일치하지 않는 내용 고르기

정답 ⑤

W Jared, the Teen Short Film Festival will be held this Friday.
M Yeah. Teenagers between 15 and 18 can compete with their short films.
W Cool! Did you submit your film?
M Yes, I did. You can watch mine and the other participants' short films at the festival. You can also vote for the best work.
W I can't wait! Is the festival free?
M No. But it's just a dollar for students.

여 Jared, Teen Short Film Festival이 이번 금요일에 열릴 거야.
남 맞아. 15세에서 18세 사이의 십대들은 그들의 단편 영화를 가지고 경쟁할 수 있어.
여 멋지다! 너는 영화를 제출했니?
남 응, 했어. 나와 다른 참가자들의 단편 영화들은 영화제에서 볼 수 있어. 최고의 작품에 투표할 수도 있어.
여 기대된다! 그 축제는 무료니?
남 아니. 하지만 학생들은 1달러밖에 안 해.

해설 | 학생들은 1달러밖에 안 한다고 했으므로 정답은 ⑤ '학생 입장료는 무료이다.'이다.

어휘 | compete [kəmpíːt] 동 경쟁하다 submit [səbmít] 동 제출하다 participant [paːrtísəpənt] 명 참가자 vote [vout] 동 투표하다 work [wəːrk] 명 작품 동 일하다

12 목적 고르기

정답 ⑤

[Telephone rings.]
W Hello, Liberty Electronics customer service. How can I help you?
M Hi, I'd like to cancel my order.
W Okay. Was there anything wrong with your order?
M No. I got the same headphones as a birthday gift.
W Could you tell me the order number?
M Sure. It's MG113.
W Alright. *[Typing sound]* When you receive the headphones, send them back to us. Then, we will provide you with a refund.
M Thank you.

[전화기가 울린다.]
여 여보세요, Liberty Electronics 고객 센터입니다. 무엇을 도와드릴까요?
남 안녕하세요, 제 주문을 취소하고 싶은데요.
여 네. 주문에 무슨 문제가 있었나요?
남 아니요. 생일 선물로 똑같은 헤드폰을 받았어요.
여 주문 번호를 말씀해주시겠습니까?
남 물론이죠. MG113이에요.
여 알겠습니다. *[타자 치는 소리]* 헤드폰을 받으시면, 저희에게 반송해주세요. 그 이후에 환불해드리겠습니다.
남 감사합니다.

해설 | 남자가 주문했던 것과 똑같은 헤드폰을 생일 선물로 받아서 주문을 취소하고 싶다고 했으므로 정답은 ⑤ '주문을 취소하기 위해서'이다.

어휘 | cancel [kǽnsəl] 동 취소하다 receive [risíːv] 동 받다 send back 반송하다, 돌려주다

13 숫자 정보 고르기

정답 ③

M Excuse me. Can you help me?
W Sure. What can I do for you?
M I've tried these sneakers on, but they are too small.
W Let me see. These are a size 265.
M Can I try on a size 275?
W Just a second. *[Pause]* Here you go.
M Thank you. *[Pause]* These are a bit large. I'm sorry, but can I try a smaller size?
W Okay. Here is a size 270.
M These fit perfectly. I'll take these.

남 실례합니다. 도와주실 수 있나요?
여 물론이죠. 무엇을 도와드릴까요?
남 이 운동화를 신어봤는데, 너무 작아요.
여 제가 볼게요. 이건 265 사이즈입니다.
남 275 사이즈를 신어볼 수 있을까요?
여 잠시만요. *[잠시 멈춤]* 여기 있습니다.
남 감사합니다. *[잠시 멈춤]* 이건 약간 크네요. 죄송하지만 더 작은 사이즈로 신어볼 수 있을까요?
여 알겠습니다. 여기 270 사이즈가 있습니다.
남 완벽하게 맞네요. 이걸로 할게요.

해설 | 여자가 270 사이즈를 주었고, 남자가 완벽하게 맞는다고 했으므로 정답은 ③ '270mm'이다.

어휘 | perfectly [pə́ːrfiktli] 부 완벽하게

14 관계 고르기

정답 ②

M	Mary, can I speak with you?
W	Sure, Mr. Evans. Is something wrong?
M	You fell asleep in my class a few times today. Are you alright?
W	I'm so sorry. I stayed up really late last night.
M	What were you doing?
W	I was playing my favorite video game. I lost track of time.
M	I see. You should try to go to sleep earlier.

남 Mary, 이야기 좀 할 수 있을까?
여 물론이죠, Evans 선생님. 뭔가 잘못됐나요?
남 오늘 내 수업 중에 몇 번 잠들더라. 괜찮니?
여 정말 죄송해요. 어젯밤에 정말 늦게까지 깨어 있었어요.
남 뭘 하고 있었니?
여 제가 가장 좋아하는 비디오 게임을 하고 있었어요. 시간 가는 줄 몰랐어요.
남 그렇구나. 더 일찍 자기 위해 노력해보렴.

해설 | 남자가 여자에게 자신의 수업 중에 몇 번 잠들었다고 말하며, 더 일찍 자기 위해 노력하라고 조언하는 것으로 보아 정답은 ② '교사 — 학생'이다.

어휘 | fall asleep 잠들다 lose track of ~을 모르다, 잊어버리다

15 부탁·요청한 일 고르기

정답 ③

M	Elena, can you help me?
W	What's going on, Tom?
M	I was painting the wall, and now I have paint all over my hands.
W	Oh. What can I do for you?
M	Will you bring me a wet towel?
W	Sure. Can I borrow your brushes later?
M	Why do you need them?
W	I want to paint my room too.

남 Elena, 나 좀 도와줄래?
여 무슨 일이야, Tom?
남 벽에 페인트칠을 하고 있었는데, 이젠 손 전체에 페인트가 묻었어.
여 오. 내가 뭘 해줄까?
남 젖은 수건 좀 가져다줄래?
여 물론이지. 나중에 네 붓 좀 빌릴 수 있을까?
남 그게 왜 필요하니?
여 내 방도 페인트칠을 하고 싶어.

해설 | 여자가 남자에게 나중에 붓 좀 빌려 달라고 부탁했으므로 정답은 ③ '붓 빌려주기'이다.

어휘 | wall [wɔːl] 명 벽 wet [wet] 형 젖은 borrow [bɑ́rou] 동 빌리다

16 이유 고르기

정답 ④

M	Hello, Kate.
W	Hi, Aaron. Where are you going so early?
M	I'm going to the post office.
W	Oh, are you sending something to your sister in France?
M	No. I'm going there to buy some stamps.
W	Oh? What for?
M	Actually, collecting stamps is my hobby.
W	I see. I hope you find some cool stamps.
M	Yes. I heard that they are selling New Year limited-edition stamps today.

남 안녕, Kate.
여 안녕, Aaron. 이렇게 일찍 어디 가니?
남 나는 우체국에 가고 있어.
여 오, 프랑스에 있는 누나에게 무언가를 보내는 거니?
남 아니. 난 우표를 몇 장 사러 가는 중이야.
여 오? 뭐 때문에?
남 사실, 우표 수집이 내 취미거든.
여 그렇구나. 멋진 우표를 구하길 바랄게.
남 응. 오늘 신년 한정판 우표를 판매한다고 들었어.

해설 | 남자는 여자에게 우표를 사러 가는 중이라고 말했으므로 정답은 ④ '우표를 구매하기 위해서'이다.

어휘 | stamp [stæmp] 명 우표 collect [kəlékt] 동 수집하다, 모으다 limited-edition 명 한정판

17 그림 상황에 적절한 대화 고르기

정답 ②

① M How did you get tickets for the concert?
W My friend is in the band.
② M What movie do you want to see?
W Let's see the romantic comedy. I don't like scary movies.
③ M Why don't we ride the roller coaster?
W You can ride it, but I'm afraid of heights.
④ M What are you laughing at?
W I'm watching a funny video of a cat.
⑤ M I like your new sweater.
W Thanks. I just bought it.

① 남 그 콘서트 티켓 어떻게 구했니?
여 내 친구가 그 밴드에 있거든.
② 남 무슨 영화를 보고 싶니?
여 로맨틱 코미디를 보자. 나는 무서운 영화를 좋아하지 않아.
③ 남 우리 롤러코스터 타는 게 어때?
여 너는 타도 되는데, 나는 높은 곳을 무서워해.
④ 남 뭘 보고 웃고 있니?
여 웃긴 고양이 비디오를 보고 있어.
⑤ 남 네 새 스웨터 맘에 든다.
여 고마워. 방금 샀어.

해설 | 남자가 무슨 영화를 보고 싶은지 묻고 있고, 여자가 로맨틱 코미디를 보자고 하는 상황이므로 정답은 ②이다.

어휘 | height [hait] 명 높은 곳; 높이

18 언급하지 않은 내용 고르기

정답 ④

W Good morning, visitors. Welcome to the newly opened Glendale Community Center. It has two main buildings with a large auditorium and a gym. Anyone who lives in Glendale can use our facilities for free. Our center provides various sports and art classes for children. Our center also runs shuttle buses, so please check the information on our website for the schedule.

여 안녕하세요, 방문객 여러분. 새롭게 문을 연 글렌데일 주민 센터에 오신 걸 환영합니다. 이곳은 대형 강당과 체육관이 있는 두 개의 본관이 있습니다. 글렌데일에 사는 누구든 시설을 무료로 이용할 수 있습니다. 저희 센터는 어린이들을 위해 다양한 스포츠와 미술 수업을 제공합니다. 저희 센터는 셔틀버스도 운행하고 있으니, 시간표는 저희 웹사이트의 정보를 확인해 주십시오.

해설 | ① 건물 구성(대형 강당과 체육관이 있는 두 개의 본관), ② 시설 사용료(무료), ③ 수업 종류(어린이를 위한 다양한 스포츠와 미술 수업), ⑤ 교통편(셔틀버스)에 대해 언급했으므로 정답은 ④ '주차장 유무'이다.

어휘 | auditorium [ɔ̀:ditɔ́:riəm] 명 강당 facility [fəsíləti] 명 시설 provide [prəváid] 동 제공하다 various [vɛ́əriəs] 형 다양한
run [rʌn] 동 운행하다; 운영하다

19 적절한 응답 고르기

정답 ②

M Honey, where do you want to go on vacation this year?
W Hmm... What about Namwon? We can climb Jirisan there.
M That sounds nice. But I really want to go somewhere with a beach instead.
W Okay. Then, how about Taean or Yeosu? They both have beautiful beaches.
M Sounds wonderful! Which one do you prefer?
W I like Yeosu better.

남 여보, 올해는 어디로 휴가를 가고 싶어?
여 흠... 남원은 어때? 그곳에서 지리산을 등반할 수 있어.
남 좋은 생각이네. 하지만 나는 그보다는 해변이 있는 곳으로 꼭 가고 싶어.
여 알겠어. 그럼, 태안이나 여수는 어때? 둘 다 아름다운 해변을 가지고 있어.
남 아주 멋질 것 같아! 어디가 더 좋아?
여 나는 여수가 더 좋아.

해설 | 남자가 어디가 더 좋은지 물어보고 있으므로 정답은 더 좋은 곳을 말하는 ② 'I like Yeosu better.'이다.

선택지 해석

① 수영하러 가자. ② 나는 여수가 더 좋아. ③ 게를 잡는 것은 어때? ④ 즐거운 여행 되길 바라. ⑤ 우리는 여권이 필요할 거야.

어휘 | instead [instéd] 부 그보다는; 대신에 prefer [prifə́:r] 동 더 좋아하다; 선호하다 passport [pǽspɔ:rt] 명 여권

20 적절한 응답 고르기

정답 ③

M Is there something wrong with your laptop, Susan?
W Yeah. It's not turning on right now.
M That's strange. Is it fully charged?
W Yes. I charged it last night.
M It is likely that there's something wrong with the battery then.
W That could be the problem. It's a really old laptop.
M How long have you had it?
W Almost 10 years.

남 네 노트북에 무슨 문제라도 있니, Susan?
여 응. 지금 안 켜지고 있어.
남 이상하네. 충전은 다 됐어?
여 응. 어젯밤에 충전했어.
남 그렇다면 배터리에 뭔가 문제가 있는 것 같아.
여 그게 문제일 수도 있지. 정말 오래된 노트북이거든.
남 얼마나 오랫동안 가지고 있었니?
여 거의 10년 됐어.

해설 | 남자가 얼마나 오랫동안 가지고 있었는지를 물었으므로 정답은 기한을 말하는 ③ 'Almost 10 years.'이다.

선택지 해석

① 그건 벌써 해봤어. ② 화면이 망가졌어. ③ 거의 10년 됐어. ④ 고쳐줘서 고마워. ⑤ 서비스 센터는 왼편에 있어.

어휘 | turn on 켜지다, 켜다 strange [streindʒ] 형 이상한 charge [tʃaːrdʒ] 동 충전하다 likely [láikli] 형 할 것 같은 almost [ɔ́ːlmoust] 부 거의

13회 실전 모의고사

| 문제 pp.122-123

1	④	2	④	3	④	4	①	5	①	6	⑤	7	④	8	②	9	③	10	④
11	⑤	12	③	13	④	14	③	15	①	16	③	17	①	18	⑤	19	⑤	20	③

1 날씨 고르기

정답 ④

M Good morning! This is the world weather report. In London, it will be rainy all day long. Don't forget your umbrella or raincoat. Paris will be partly cloudy and cold. New York will have a lot of snow today, so be careful of the slippery streets. Thank you.

남 안녕하십니까! 세계 일기 예보입니다. 런던은 온종일 비가 오겠습니다. 우산이나 우비를 잊지 마십시오. 파리는 부분적으로 흐리고 춥겠습니다. 뉴욕에는 오늘 많은 눈이 예상되니, 미끄러운 거리를 조심하십시오. 감사합니다.

해설 | 뉴욕에서는 많은 눈이 예상된다고 했으므로 정답은 ④이다.

어휘 | raincoat [réinkout] 명 우비 partly [pɑ́ːrtli] 부 부분적으로 slippery [slípəri] 형 미끄러운

2 알맞은 그림 고르기

정답 ④

M Welcome. May I help you?
W I'd like to buy a sweatshirt for my gym class.
M Do you have any particular design in mind?
W I don't want any pockets, but I want one with a hood.
M How about this one? It comes in many different colors.
W Hmm... Is there one with no zippers?
M This one doesn't have a zipper.
W I'll take that one.

남 어서 오세요. 도와드릴까요?
여 체육 시간에 입을 운동복 상의를 사고 싶어요.
남 특별히 생각해 둔 디자인이 있나요?
여 주머니는 원하지 않지만, 후드가 달린 것을 원해요.
남 이것은 어떠세요? 이건 많은 다른 색상으로 나와요.
여 흠... 지퍼가 없는 것이 있나요?
남 이것에는 지퍼가 없어요.
여 그걸로 할게요.

해설 | 여자는 주머니는 없지만 후드가 달려있고, 지퍼가 없는 것을 구입할 것이라고 했으므로 정답은 ④이다.

어휘 | sweatshirt [swétʃɜːrt] 명 운동복 상의 particular [pərtíkjulər] 형 특별한; 특정한 pocket [pɑ́kit] 명 주머니 hood [hud] 명 후드; 모자

3 의도 고르기

정답 ④

M Hey, Mina. What are you doing?
W I'm searching for pasta recipes on my tablet.
M Wow. Is that a new tablet?
W Yes. It's the latest model from Four-Star Electronics.
M It looks cool. Can I try it out?
W Sure! Here you go.
M Oh, no! There is a small scratch on the screen because I dropped your tablet.
W Don't worry about it. I know it was an accident.

남 안녕, 미나야. 뭐 하고 있니?
여 태블릿으로 파스타 요리법을 검색 중이야.
남 우와. 그거 새 태블릿이야?
여 응. Four-Star Electronics의 최신 모델이야.
남 멋져 보인다. 내가 한 번 써봐도 될까?
여 물론이지! 여기 있어.
남 오, 이런! 내가 떨어뜨려서 화면 위에 작은 흠집이 났어.
여 걱정하지 마. 사고였다는 걸 알아.

해설 | 태블릿을 떨어뜨린 남자에게 여자가 사고였으니 걱정하지 말라고 했으므로 정답은 ④ '용서'이다.

어휘 | search [sə:rtʃ] 동 검색하다, 찾다 recipe [résəpi] 명 요리법, 조리법 latest [léitist] 형 최신의; 가장 늦은 scratch [skrætʃ] 명 흠집 동 긁다

4 한 일 고르기

정답 ①

M Jihee, I saw the picture you posted on Christmas.
W Are you talking about the snowman picture? I made it with my sister.
M It looks like you had fun.
W Yeah. What did you do on Christmas?
M I decorated a tree. I also put mini light bulbs on it.
W Did you put a star on the top of the tree?
M Of course. I can show you the picture if you want.

남 지희야, 나 네가 크리스마스에 올린 사진 봤어.
여 눈사람 사진을 말하는 거니? 내 여동생이랑 그걸 만들었어.
남 재미있게 보낸 거 같더라.
여 맞아. 넌 크리스마스에 뭐 했니?
남 나는 트리를 장식했어. 거기에 작은 전구들도 달았어.
여 나무 꼭대기에는 별을 달았니?
남 당연하지. 네가 원한다면 사진을 보여줄 수 있어.

해설 | 남자가 크리스마스에 트리를 장식했다고 했으므로 정답은 ① '트리 꾸미기'이다.

어휘 | light bulb 전구

5 장소 고르기

정답 ①

W Hi. How can I help you?
M Hello. I'm here to see a patient.
W Okay. Who are you looking for?
M Her name is Yasmine Grant. She just got out of surgery this afternoon.
W She'll be on the fifth floor then. You can find the elevator down the hall.
M Thank you for the help.

여 안녕하세요. 어떻게 도와드릴까요?
남 안녕하세요. 여기 환자를 보러 왔는데요.
여 알겠습니다. 누구를 찾으시나요?
남 그녀의 이름은 Yasmine Grant예요. 오늘 오후에 막 수술이 끝났어요.
여 그럼 그분은 5층에 계시겠네요. 엘리베이터는 복도 끝에서 찾으실 수 있어요.
남 도와주셔서 감사합니다.

해설 | 남자가 환자를 보러왔다고 하며 오후에 수술이 끝났다고 하는 것으로 보아 정답은 ① '병원'이다.

어휘 | patient [péiʃənt] 명 환자 get out of ~에서 나오다, 나가다 surgery [sə́:rdʒəri] 명 수술 hall [hɔ:l] 명 복도; 홀, 집회장, 강당

6 일치하지 않는 내용 고르기

정답 ⑤

M Jane, what are you up to?
W I'm looking at this animated movie poster.
M It looks interesting. What is the movie about?
W It's a story about a zoo.
M Oh, I love stories about animals.
W Me too. The main character is a fox. It was also made by my favorite director, Kylie Williams.
M That's why you know it so well! When can you watch it?
W It will be released on May 5th.
M You must be excited!

남 Jane, 뭐하고 있어?
여 이 애니메이션 영화 포스터를 보고 있어.
남 그거 흥미로워 보인다. 그 영화는 뭐에 관한 거니?
여 이건 동물원에 관한 이야기야.
남 오, 난 동물에 관한 이야기를 정말 좋아해.
여 나도 그래. 주인공이 여우야. 그리고 이건 내가 가장 좋아하는 감독인 Kylie Williams가 만들었어.
남 그래서 네가 그렇게 잘 아는구나! 언제 볼 수 있는데?
여 그건 5월 5일에 개봉해.
남 너 정말 기대되겠다!

해설 | 여자가 5월 5일에 개봉한다고 했으므로 정답은 ⑤ '5월 10일에 개봉한다.'이다.

어휘 | animated [ǽnəmèitid] 형 애니메이션 영화의, 만화 영화의 director [diréktər] 명 감독; 지도자 release [rilíːs] 동 개봉하다, 발표하다; 해방하다

7 할 일 고르기

정답 ④

M Hello, how can I help you?
W I'd like to pay for these clothes.
M It's 45 dollars in total. You can get a 10% discount if you spend five dollars more.
W Hmm... But I don't know what else to buy now.
M How about buying this T-shirt right here? It's five dollars!
W Then, I'll take it in a large size.
M You can get the discount now.

남 안녕하세요, 어떻게 도와드릴까요?
여 이 옷들을 계산하고 싶어요.
남 총 45달러입니다. 5달러만 더 쓰시면 10% 할인을 받으실 수 있어요.
여 흠... 그렇지만 이제 뭘 더 사야 할지 모르겠어요.
남 바로 여기 있는 이 티셔츠를 구매하시는 건 어떠세요? 5달러예요!
여 그럼, 라지 사이즈로 살게요.
남 이제 할인을 받으실 수 있어요.

해설 | 남자가 5달러를 더 쓰면 할인을 받을 수 있다고 하며 여자에게 티셔츠 구매를 권하자 여자가 그것을 사겠다고 했으므로 정답은 ④ '티셔츠 구매하기'이다.

어휘 | discount [dískaunt] 명 할인 spend [spend] 동 쓰다, 보내다

8 할 일 고르기

정답 ②

M Sandy, did you enjoy our trip to San Francisco?
W Yes, Dad. Before we go back home, can we go to a gift shop?
M Sure. What do you want to buy?
W I want to buy a magnet to remember this beautiful city.
M If you want to remember the scenery here, why don't you buy postcards?
W That's a great idea! I'll buy some with pictures of the city.
M Oh, there's a shop over there.
W Let's go inside and pick some.

남 Sandy, 샌프란시스코 여행은 재미있었니?
여 네, 아빠. 집에 돌아가기 전에, 기념품 가게에 가도 돼요?
남 물론이지. 뭘 사고 싶니?
여 이 아름다운 도시를 기억하기 위해 자석을 사고 싶어요.
남 이곳의 풍경을 기억하고 싶다면, 엽서를 사는 건 어떠니?
여 좋은 생각이에요! 도시 사진이 있는 엽서 몇 장을 사야겠어요.
남 오, 저쪽에 가게가 하나 있구나.
여 우리 안에 들어가서 몇 장 골라봐요.

해설 | 남자가 엽서를 살 것을 제안하자 여자가 기념품 가게에 들어가서 몇 장을 골라보겠다고 했으므로 정답은 ② '엽서 고르기'이다.

어휘 | magnet [mǽgnit] 명 자석 scenery [síːnəri] 명 풍경, 경치 postcard [póustkaːrd] 명 엽서

9 언급하지 않은 내용 고르기

정답 ③

W Alright, everyone. Tomorrow we will go to a strawberry farm in Nonsan.
M Ms. Harris, what time will we leave?
W We will leave at 9 in the morning.
M What activities will we do there?
W We will pick strawberries and make jam.
M Sounds good. Do we need to bring cash?
W Yes. Admission is 10 dollars, and you can also buy souvenirs.
M Okay. I can't wait!

여 자, 여러분. 내일 우리는 논산에 있는 딸기 농장에 갈 거예요.
남 Harris 선생님, 저희는 몇 시에 출발하나요?
여 오전 9시에 출발할 거란다.
남 거기에서는 어떤 활동들을 하게 되나요?
여 우리는 딸기를 따고 잼을 만들 거야.
남 좋네요. 현금을 들고 가야 하나요?
여 그래. 입장료는 10달러이고, 기념품을 사도 돼.
남 알겠습니다. 기대되네요!

해설 | ① 농장 위치(논산), ② 출발 시간(오전 9시), ④ 활동(딸기 따기, 잼 만들기), ⑤ 입장료(10달러)에 대해 언급했으므로 정답은 ③ '교통편'이다.
어휘 | activity [æktívəti] 명 활동 cash [kæʃ] 명 현금 admission [ædmíʃən] 명 입장료 souvenir [sù:vəníər] 명 기념품

10 주제 고르기

정답 ④

W Attention, please. For your safety, please follow these rules. One, please do warm-up exercises before you go skiing. Two, please wear protective equipment. You have to wear a helmet and goggles to stay safe. Three, if you're under 12, do not ski alone. Children under 12 must stay with a parent at all times. Enjoy your time at our ski resort. Thank you.

여 집중해 주십시오. 안전을 위해서, 다음의 규칙들을 따라 주십시오. 하나, 스키를 타러 가기 전에 준비 운동을 해주십시오. 둘, 보호 장비를 착용하십시오. 안전을 위해서 헬멧과 고글을 써야 합니다. 셋, 만약 12세 이하라면, 혼자 스키를 타지 마십시오. 12세 이하의 어린이는 항상 부모님과 같이 있어야 합니다. 저희 스키 리조트에서 즐거운 시간 보내십시오. 감사합니다.

해설 | 여자가 안전을 위해서 스키장에서 따라야 할 규칙들을 말하고 있으므로 정답은 ④ '스키장 안전 수칙'이다.
어휘 | safety [séifti] 명 안전 follow [fálou] 동 따르다 warm-up exercise 준비 운동 protective [prətéktiv] 형 보호하는 equipment [ikwípmənt] 명 장비

11 일치하지 않는 내용 고르기

정답 ⑤

W Jaehoon, did you hear about the paper plane competition?
M No, I didn't. When will it be held?
W It will be next week at the school playground.
M Can I sign up for the competition too?
W Sure. All students can participate. There's also a prize for the winner.
M Great! I will make the biggest paper plane.
W Well, you can't. Everyone's paper will be the same size.
M I'll study how to fold it well then.

여 재훈아, 종이비행기 대회에 대해 들었니?
남 아니, 못 들었어. 언제 열리는데?
여 학교 운동장에서 다음 주에 열릴 거야.
남 나도 대회 참가 신청을 할 수 있을까?
여 물론이지. 모든 학생이 참가할 수 있어. 우승자에게는 상도 있어.
남 좋다! 나는 가장 큰 종이비행기를 만들 거야.
여 응, 그건 안돼. 모든 사람의 종이는 같은 크기일 거야.
남 그럼 잘 접는 방법을 연구해야겠다.

해설 | 모든 사람들의 종이는 같은 크기일 것이라고 했으므로 정답은 ⑤ '종이의 크기는 정해져 있지 않다.'이다.
어휘 | competition [kàmpətíʃən] 명 대회; 경쟁 playground [pléigràund] 명 운동장, 놀이터 sign up for ~을 신청하다 fold [fould] 동 접다

12 목적 고르기

정답 ③

M Bailey, are you going out?
W Yes, Dad. I'm going to a bazaar.
M What are you going to buy?
W I'm collecting records, so I'll go and find some old records.
M That's a good idea. Please let me know if you find a good one.
W I will. I can look for some of your favorite music too.
M That would be wonderful!

남 Bailey, 너 외출할 거니?
여 네, 아빠. 저는 바자회에 갈 거예요.
남 뭘 살 거니?
여 음반을 모으는 중이라서, 가서 오래된 음반들을 좀 찾아볼 거예요.
남 좋은 생각이구나. 좋은 물건을 찾으면 나도 알려주렴.
여 그럴게요. 아빠가 좋아하시는 음악도 좀 찾아봐드릴 수 있어요.
남 그러면 아주 좋겠구나!

해설 | 여자가 바자회에 가서 오래된 음반들을 찾아볼 것이라고 했으므로 정답은 ③ '음반을 찾기 위해서'이다.
어휘 | bazaar [bəzá:r] 명 바자회; 상점가 collect [kəlékt] 동 모으다, 수집하다 record [rékərd] 명 음반, 레코드 [rikɔ́:rd] 동 기록하다

13 금액 정보 고르기

정답 ④

W Hello, I'd like to rent a bike.
M Sure. How long do you need it for?
W Just for one hour, please.
M That's 15 dollars then.
W Can I also rent a helmet?
M Yes. But you have to pay five dollars more.
W Okay. One helmet please. How much is it in total?
M Your total is 20 dollars.
W Here you go.

여 안녕하세요, 자전거를 빌리고 싶은데요.
남 그래요. 얼마나 오래 필요하신가요?
여 딱 한 시간만이요.
남 그럼 15달러입니다.
여 헬멧도 빌릴 수 있을까요?
남 네. 하지만 5달러를 더 내셔야 해요.
여 알겠어요. 헬멧 하나 주세요. 총 얼마죠?
남 총 20달러예요.
여 여기 있습니다.

해설 | 자전거는 한 시간 대여에 15달러, 헬멧은 5달러로 총 20달러라고 했으므로 정답은 ④ '$ 20'이다.

어휘 | rent [rent] 동 빌리다

14 관계 고르기

정답 ③

W Excuse me. Are you Ronald Smith?
M Yes, that's me.
W Wow! I love your books about Lion Man. He's my favorite super hero.
M Thank you. Actually, a new book is coming out soon.
W Really? Is it another book about super heroes?
M No. This one is about space travel.
W That's amazing. I want to be an astronaut in the future.
M Then, you will love it.

여 실례합니다. Ronald Smith씨 되시나요?
남 네, 접니다.
여 우와! 저는 Lion Man에 대한 당신의 책들을 정말 좋아해요. 그는 제가 가장 좋아하는 슈퍼히어로예요.
남 감사합니다. 사실, 새 책이 곧 나올 거예요.
여 정말요? 그것도 슈퍼히어로에 관한 책인가요?
남 아니요. 우주여행에 관한 것이에요.
여 놀랍네요. 저는 미래에 우주 비행사가 되고 싶거든요.
남 그럼, 마음에 드실 거예요.

해설 | 여자가 남자의 책들을 정말 좋아한다고 하는 것으로 보아 정답은 ③ '작가 — 독자'이다.

어휘 | come out 나오다, 출판되다 space [speis] 명 우주; 공간 astronaut [ǽstrənɔ:t] 명 우주 비행사

15 부탁·요청한 일 고르기

정답 ①

M Honey, where are you going?
W I'm going shopping downtown. I need a new coffee machine.
M Okay. Should I come with you?
W That's fine. But could you clean the kitchen?
M Sure. I don't mind doing that.
W Thanks. Do you need anything?
M I would love some chocolate. Can you get me some?
W Sure. I'll stop by the supermarket.
M Great. Thank you.

남 여보, 어디 가?
여 시내에 쇼핑하러 갈 거야. 새 커피 머신이 필요하거든.
남 알겠어. 내가 같이 가야 할까?
여 괜찮아. 그런데 부엌 청소 좀 해줄 수 있어?
남 물론이지. 나는 상관없어.
여 고마워. 필요한 거 있어?
남 초콜릿이 좀 있으면 좋겠어. 사다 줄 수 있어?
여 그럼. 슈퍼마켓에 들를게.
남 좋아. 고마워.

해설 | 남자가 여자에게 초콜릿을 사다 달라고 부탁했으므로 정답은 ① '초콜릿 구매하기'이다.

어휘 | downtown [dáuntaun] 부 시내에, 상업 지구로 stop by (도중에) 들르다

16 이유 고르기

정답 ③

[Telephone rings.]
W Hello?
M Hi, Jihye. Are you ready to go to a singing room today?
W Oh, wait. Is that today?
M Yes. We made plans last week.
W I'm sorry, but I have a dentist appointment. I have a bad toothache.
M Okay. We should go to a singing room next weekend. Let's also have tteokbokki then.
W Thank you for understanding.

[전화기가 울린다.]
여 여보세요?
남 안녕, 지혜야. 오늘 노래방 갈 준비 됐니?
여 오, 잠깐만. 그게 오늘이야?
남 응. 지난주에 계획을 세웠잖아.
여 미안한데, 나 치과 예약이 있어. 치통이 심해.
남 그래. 노래방은 다음 주말에 가야겠네. 그때 떡볶이도 먹자.
여 이해해줘서 고마워.

해설 | 오늘 노래방에 가기로 했었다고 말하는 남자에게 여자가 미안하지만 치과 예약이 있다고 했으므로 정답은 ③ '치과에 가야 해서'이다.
어휘 | singing room 노래방 toothache [túːθeik] 명 치통

17 그림 상황에 적절한 대화 고르기

정답 ①

① W Why did they block the sidewalk?
M There is an event today.
② W What are you going to wear tonight?
M I will wear a nice shirt and pants.
③ W How was your field trip?
M It was great. I liked the science museum a lot.
④ W What should we eat for lunch?
M How about having curry and rice?
⑤ W Excuse me. I think you dropped this key.
M Oh, my! Thank you so much.

① 여 왜 인도를 막은 거예요?
남 오늘 행사가 있어요.
② 여 오늘 밤에 뭐 입을 거니?
남 근사한 셔츠와 바지를 입을 거야.
③ 여 현장 학습은 어땠어?
남 훌륭했어. 과학 박물관이 아주 좋았어.
④ 여 점심 식사로 뭘 먹을까?
남 카레 라이스를 먹는 건 어때?
⑤ 여 실례합니다. 이 열쇠를 떨어뜨리신 것 같아요.
남 오, 이런! 정말 감사합니다.

해설 | 진입이 금지된 인도를 두고 두 사람이 대화를 하는 상황이므로 정답은 ①이다.
어휘 | block [blak] 동 (길을) 막다 field trip 현장 학습, 견학 여행 drop [drap] 동 떨어뜨리다

18 언급하지 않은 내용 고르기

정답 ⑤

W Good morning, students. I'd like to tell you about our school's talent show this year. It is scheduled for December 8th, and it will be held in the gym. The talent show will begin at 2 p.m. and will last for two hours. Our school's student president, Paul Mason, will host the event. I hope every student comes and enjoys it!

여 좋은 아침입니다, 학생 여러분. 올해 우리 학교의 학예회에 대해 말씀드리고 싶습니다. 12월 8일로 예정되어 있으며, 체육관에서 열릴 것입니다. 학예회는 오후 2시에 시작되어서 2시간 동안 이어질 것입니다. 우리 학교의 학생회장인 Paul Mason이 행사의 사회를 맡을 것입니다. 학생 여러분 모두 오셔서 즐기시면 좋겠습니다!

해설 | ① 날짜(12월 8일), ② 장소(체육관), ③ 시작 시간(오후 2시), ④ 사회자(학생회장 Paul Mason)에 대해 언급했으므로 정답은 ⑤ '공연 순서'이다.
어휘 | school's talent show 학예회 president [prézədənt] 명 회장; 대통령 host [houst] 동 사회를 맡다 명 주인, 주최자

19 적절한 응답 고르기

정답 ⑤

M Have you been to that new restaurant, Nara? W Which restaurant? M The one next to the park. It serves Italian food. W No, I haven't been there. Have you? M No. But I heard it's great. Do you want to go tomorrow evening? W I'd love to. M Let's invite our other friends too. W Okay. Who do you want to ask? M I want to invite Jason and Rebecca.	남 너는 새로 생긴 식당에 가봤니, 나라야? 여 어떤 식당? 남 공원 옆에 있는 곳. 그곳은 이탈리아 음식을 제공해. 여 아니, 안 가봤어. 너는 가봤어? 남 아니. 그렇지만 거기가 훌륭하다고 들었어. 내일 저녁에 갈래? 여 좋아. 남 우리 다른 친구들도 몇 명 초대하자. 여 그래. 누굴 초대하고 싶니? 남 나는 Jason과 Rebecca를 초대하고 싶어.

해설 | 여자가 누구를 초대하고 싶은지 묻고 있으므로 정답은 초대할 사람을 언급하는 ⑤ 'I want to invite Jason and Rebecca.'이다.

선택지 해석

① 표가 매진됐어. ② 그곳은 오후 5시부터 열어. ③ 식사 다 했니? ④ 직원들이 매우 친절해. ⑤ 나는 Jason과 Rebecca를 초대하고 싶어.

어휘 | serve [sə:rv] 동 제공하다 staff [stæf] 명 직원 friendly [fréndli] 형 친절한

20 적절한 응답 고르기

정답 ③

M Honey, I think we should talk. W Oh, what's wrong? M Well, the kids spend too much time on their phones. I'm worried. W I totally agree with you. It is a bad habit. M How do we stop them from using their phones so much? W Why don't we take their phones away for family dinners? M I think that's for the best.	남 여보, 우리 얘기 좀 해야겠어. 여 오, 무슨 일인데? 남 그게, 우리 아이들이 휴대폰에 시간을 너무 많이 써. 난 걱정 돼. 여 당신 말에 완전히 동의해. 그건 나쁜 습관이야. 남 아이들이 휴대폰을 그렇게 많이 쓰는 걸 어떻게 막을 수 있을까? 여 가족 저녁 식사 동안에는 아이들의 휴대폰을 치워두는 건 어때? 남 그게 최선인 것 같아.

해설 | 여자가 가족 저녁 식사 동안에는 아이들의 휴대폰을 치워두자고 제안하고 있으므로 정답은 제안에 동의하는 ③ 'I think that's for the best.'이다.

선택지 해석

① 내 전화번호를 줄게. ② 남동생에게 잘해줘. ③ 그게 최선인 것 같아. ④ 내 휴대폰 찾았어. ⑤ 저녁 식사 준비가 아직 안 됐어.

어휘 | totally [tóutəli] 부 완전히, 전부 habit [hǽbit] 명 습관 take away ~을 치우다, 옮겨 버리다

14회 실전 모의고사

| 문제 pp.130-131

1	②	2	③	3	③	4	⑤	5	②	6	④	7	①	8	④	9	⑤	10	③
11	④	12	②	13	③	14	②	15	④	16	⑤	17	②	18	③	19	①	20	②

1 날씨 고르기

정답 ②

W Good evening, everyone. This is your end-of-the-weekend weather report from KSBN. Monday will be sunny with a warm spring breeze. From Tuesday, rain will fall, and this signals the beginning of spring. It'll stop by Thursday, and we'll be able to enjoy the bright sunshine again on Friday. The weather will be perfect for outdoor activities on the weekend.	여 안녕하세요, 여러분. KSBN에서 보내드리는 주말의 마지막 일기예보입니다. 월요일은 따뜻한 봄바람과 함께 화창하겠습니다. 화요일부터는 비가 내릴 것이며, 봄의 시작을 알리겠습니다. 목요일까지는 비가 그치겠고, 금요일에는 다시 밝은 햇살을 즐길 수 있겠습니다. 주말은 야외 활동에 완벽한 날씨일 것입니다.

해설 | 월요일은 따뜻한 봄바람과 함께 화창할 것이라고 했으므로 정답은 ②이다.

어휘 | breeze [bri:z] 명 바람 signal [sígnəl] 동 알리다 명 신호 bright [brait] 형 밝은

2 알맞은 그림 고르기

정답 ③

M Jess, what did you do today?
W I decorated my phone case with a sticker after school, Dad.
M Oh, you decorated this? I like the cat in the middle.
W Thank you. I really like it too. I wanted to put a dog next to the cat, but I couldn't find a sticker.
M You also put your name under the cat.
W Yes, I did. That way, my phone case is really personalized. I love it.

남 Jess, 오늘 뭐 했니?
여 방과 후에 스티커로 휴대폰 케이스를 꾸몄어요, 아빠.
남 오, 네가 이걸 꾸몄어? 가운데의 고양이가 마음에 드는구나.
여 고맙습니다. 저도 그게 정말 좋아요. 고양이 옆에 개도 붙이고 싶었는데, 스티커를 못 찾았어요.
남 고양이 아래에는 네 이름도 붙였네!
여 네, 그랬어요. 그렇게 하니까, 휴대폰 케이스가 제게 맞춘 것이 되었어요. 아주 마음에 들어요.

해설 | 남자가 가운데에 있는 고양이가 좋다고 했고, 고양이 아래에 여자의 이름이 있다고 했으므로 정답은 ③이다.

어휘 | decorate [dékərèit] 동 꾸미다, 장식하다 sticker [stíkər] 명 스티커 personalize [pə́:rsənəlaiz] 동 개인에 맞추다; ~을 개인의 문제로 생각하다

3 의도 고르기

정답 ③

[Knocking sound]
M Who is it?
W Hi, I'm your neighbor from next door.
M Hi. Is there any problem?
W Could you turn down the music a bit? I can't sleep because it's too loud.
M Oh, sorry about that. I'll use my headphones.
W Thanks.
M I think the walls in the building are too thin.
W Tell me about it. I can even hear another neighbor coughing.

[노크하는 소리]
남 누구세요?
여 안녕하세요, 저는 옆집에 사는 사람입니다.
남 안녕하세요. 무슨 문제라도 있나요?
여 음악 소리 좀 낮춰주시겠어요? 너무 시끄러워서 잠을 잘 수가 없어요.
남 오, 죄송합니다. 헤드폰을 사용할게요.
여 감사합니다.
남 건물 벽이 너무 얇은 것 같아요.
여 제 말이요. 심지어 다른 이웃이 기침하는 소리도 들을 수 있어요.

해설 | 남자가 건물 벽이 너무 얇은 것 같다고 하자 여자가 동의하며 심지어 다른 이웃이 기침하는 소리도 들을 수 있다는 말을 했으므로 정답은 ③ '불평'이다.

어휘 | turn down (라디오 등의) 소리를 낮추다 thin [θin] 형 얇은

4 한 일 고르기

정답 ⑤

W Hey, Jinsu. How was your holiday? I went to the aquarium.
M Hi, Miso. The aquarium sounds fun. I stayed home for the holiday.
W Why? Didn't you say you were going camping in the mountains?
M Yeah. But it rained too much, so my family stayed home.
W Oh, no! Did you do anything else then?
M We cleaned the house instead, and ate delicious steaks.

여 안녕, 진수야. 네 휴일은 어땠니? 나는 수족관에 갔어.
남 안녕, 미소야. 수족관 재미있었겠다. 나는 휴일 동안 집에 있었어.
여 왜? 산으로 캠핑 간다고 하지 않았어?
남 그랬지. 하지만 비가 너무 많이 와서, 우리 가족은 집에 있었어.
여 오, 이런! 그 외에 다른 걸 했니 그럼?
남 우리는 그 대신에 집을 청소했고, 맛있는 스테이크를 먹었어.

해설 | 남자는 휴일에 집을 청소했다고 했으므로 정답은 ⑤ '집 청소하기'이다.

어휘 | holiday [hɑ́lədei] 명 휴일 mountain [máuntən] 명 산 instead [instéd] 부 그 대신에

5 장소 고르기

정답 ②

M Hi. How do you want your hair cut today?
W Well, I don't want any big changes. I'd like to keep my hair long.
M I can just cut a little bit off. It will still reach your shoulders.
W That's perfect.
M Don't you want to change your hair color?
W No. I want to keep the brown color.
M Okay. I'll get started then.

남 안녕하세요. 오늘 머리를 어떻게 잘라 드릴까요?
여 음, 큰 변화는 원하지 않아요. 저는 긴 머리를 유지하고 싶어요.
남 아주 조금만 잘라낼 수 있어요. 여전히 어깨에는 닿을 거예요.
여 완벽해요.
남 머리 색을 바꾸고 싶지 않으신가요?
여 아니요. 갈색은 유지하고 싶어요.
남 알겠습니다. 그럼 시작할게요.

해설 | 남자가 오늘 머리를 어떻게 자를지 물었고, 머리 색깔을 바꾸고 싶지 않냐고 말하는 것으로 보아 정답은 ② '미용실'이다.

어휘 | reach [ri:tʃ] 동 닿다; 도달하다

6 일치하지 않는 내용 고르기

정답 ④

M What are you reading, Jamie?
W I'm reading a science fiction novel about a trip to another planet.
M The book looks really thick. How many pages does it have?
W It's 670 pages long, but it's really exciting.
M Who's the author?
W Surprisingly, the author is a high school student in Norway, Jenna Adams.
M Wow. How did she write it?
W She said she started it for fun as a hobby.

남 뭘 읽고 있니, Jamie?
여 다른 행성으로의 여행에 대한 공상 과학 소설을 읽고 있어.
남 그 책 정말 두꺼워 보인다. 몇 쪽이나 되니?
여 670쪽이지만, 이건 정말 흥미진진해.
남 작가가 누구니?
여 놀랍게도, 작가는 노르웨이에 사는 고등학생인 Jenna Adams야.
남 우와. 그녀는 그걸 어떻게 썼을까?
여 그녀는 재미를 위해서 취미로 시작했대.

해설 | 작가가 고등학생이라고 했으므로 정답은 ④ '작가는 고등학교 선생님이다.'이다.

어휘 | science fiction novel 공상 과학 소설 planet [plǽnit] 명 행성 thick [θik] 형 두꺼운 author [ɔ́:θər] 명 작가

7 특정 정보 고르기

정답 ①

M Sora, are you ready to leave? Did you pack your helmet for bike riding?
W Yeah, I did. Where is the lunch box? I need to put these chopsticks in it.
M In the car. Why don't you put it in your backpack?
W Okay. *[Pause]* Oh, no!
M What's wrong?
W There is a hole in one of the bike tires. What should I do!
M Don't worry. We can borrow a bike at the park.

남 소라야, 떠날 준비 됐니? 자전거 탈 때 쓸 헬멧은 챙겼어?
여 응, 챙겼어. 도시락은 어디에 있어? 이 젓가락을 안에 넣어야 해.
남 차 안에. 그건 네 배낭에 넣는 게 어때?
여 그래. *[잠시 멈춤]* 오, 이런!
남 무슨 일이야?
여 자전거 타이어 중 하나에 구멍이 났어. 어떻게 해!
남 걱정 마. 공원에서 자전거를 빌릴 수 있어.

해설 | 여자가 자전거 타이어에 구멍이 났다고 하자 남자가 공원에서 자전거를 빌릴 수 있다고 했으므로 정답은 ① '자전거'이다.

어휘 | chopstick [tʃɑ́:pstik] 명 젓가락 backpack [bǽkpæk] 명 배낭

8 할 일 고르기

정답 ④

W Kevin, what's going on?
M Mom, I think I'm getting the flu.
W Let's check your temperature now.
M How high is it?
W It's 37.3 degrees. You should go see a doctor.
M I'll have to wait until tomorrow since it's Sunday today.
W Then, take this pill to lower your temperature.
M Okay. I'm going to take this medicine and get some rest.
W I'll make some tea for you.

여 Kevin, 무슨 일이야?
남 엄마, 저 독감에 걸린 것 같아요.
여 지금 체온을 재보자.
남 얼마나 높아요?
여 37.3도야. 너 진찰을 받아야겠다.
남 오늘은 일요일이라서 내일까지 기다려야겠네요.
여 그럼, 체온을 낮추기 위해 이 알약을 먹으렴.
남 알겠어요. 이 약을 먹고 휴식을 좀 취할게요.
여 네게 차를 끓여주마.

해설 | 남자는 약을 먹고 휴식을 좀 취해야겠다고 했으므로 정답은 ④ '약 먹기'이다.

어휘 | flu [flu:] 명 독감 temperature [témpərətʃər] 명 체온, 온도 see a doctor 진찰을 받다

9 언급하지 않은 내용 고르기

정답 ⑤

M Kelly, would you like to go to the Ocean Water Park on Sunday?
W Sure. Is it the new water park on Oak Street?
M Yes. It finally opened on June 25th.
W What does it have?
M It has more than 12 slides and a huge wave pool.
W Awesome! Isn't it expensive?
M You can enjoy all these rides for only 30 dollars.
W Alright. I'll come with you on Sunday.
M See you then!

남 Kelly, 일요일에 Ocean Water Park에 가지 않을래?
여 그래. 그게 오크 가에 새로 생긴 워터 파크야?
남 응. 6월 25일에 드디어 문을 열었어.
여 거기에는 뭐가 있니?
남 12개 이상의 미끄럼틀과 거대한 파도 풀장이 있어.
여 굉장하다! 비싸지 않아?
남 30달러만 내면 이 모든 놀이기구를 즐길 수 있어.
여 알았어. 일요일에 같이 갈게.
남 그때 봐!

해설 | ① 위치(오크 가), ② 개장일(6월 25일), ③ 놀이 시설(12개 이상의 미끄럼틀, 거대한 파도 풀장), ④ 입장료(30달러)에 대해 언급했으므로 정답은 ⑤ '개장 시간'이다.

어휘 | slide [slaid] 명 미끄럼틀 huge [hjuːdʒ] 형 거대한 wave [weiv] 명 파도 ride [raid] 명 놀이기구; 탈 것

10 주제 고르기

정답 ③

M Today, I'm going to talk about how to clean your sneakers. First, mix baking soda and vinegar with hot water to make a paste. Second, use a toothbrush and rub your shoes with the paste. Then, let the paste dry for a few hours. Lastly, remove the paste with warm water. Your shoes will look good as new!

남 오늘은 운동화 세탁법에 대해 이야기하려고 합니다. 먼저, 반죽을 만들기 위해 베이킹소다와 식초를 뜨거운 물에 섞으세요. 두 번째로, 칫솔을 사용해서 반죽을 신발에 문지르세요. 다음에, 몇 시간 동안 반죽을 마르게 두세요. 마지막으로, 따뜻한 물로 반죽을 제거하세요. 여러분의 신발은 새것처럼 보일 거예요!

해설 | 남자가 운동화 세탁법에 대해 이야기하겠다고 했으므로 정답은 ③ '운동화 세탁 방법'이다.

어휘 | vinegar [vínəgər] 명 식초 paste [peist] 명 반죽 rub [rʌb] 동 문지르다 remove [rimúːv] 동 제거하다

11 일치하지 않는 내용 고르기

정답 ④

M What are you watching, Donna?
W It's a video about polar bears. It's only 10 minutes long.
M I want to watch it too. Who filmed it?
W It was made by a Korean documentary team. It took five years to film.
M Oh, I heard about this. Didn't they make this documentary to protect the bears?
W Yeah. They wanted to show how climate change affects these animals.

남 뭘 보는 중이니, Donna?
여 북극곰에 관한 동영상이야. 겨우 10분밖에 안 돼.
남 나도 보고 싶어. 누가 찍은 거니?
여 이건 한국 다큐멘터리 팀에 의해 만들어졌어. 촬영하는 데 5년이 걸렸어.
남 오, 나 이것에 대해 들어봤어. 그들은 곰을 보호하기 위해 이 다큐멘터리를 만들지 않았니?
여 맞아. 그들은 기후 변화가 이 동물들에게 어떻게 영향을 미치는지 보여주고 싶어 했어.

해설 | 여자가 촬영하는 데 5년이 걸렸다고 했으므로 정답은 ④ '15년 동안 촬영되었다.'이다.

어휘 | polar bear 북극곰 climate change 기후 변화 affect [əfékt] 동 영향을 미치다

12 목적 고르기

정답 ②

[Telephone rings.]
M Hello. Maple Ice Arena. How can I help you today?
W Hi. I'm interested in signing up for a skating class.
M Sure. Are you a beginner?
W Yes. I've never skated before.
M We have beginner classes on Tuesdays and Thursdays at 9 in the morning.
W Okay. How long is each class?
M Lessons last for an hour, and then there will be 30 minutes for practice.

[전화기가 울린다.]
남 안녕하세요. 메이플 빙상 경기장입니다. 오늘은 어떻게 도와드릴까요?
여 안녕하세요. 스케이트 강습 등록에 관심이 있어요.
남 그러시군요. 초보이신가요?
여 네. 저는 스케이트를 타본 적이 없어요.
남 저희는 화요일과 목요일 아침 9시에 초급반 수업이 있어요.
여 그렇군요. 각 수업은 얼마나 길게 진행되나요?
남 수업은 한 시간 동안 진행되고, 연습 시간이 30분 있어요.

해설 | 여자가 스케이트 강습 등록에 관심이 있다고 한 후 수업은 얼마나 길게 진행되는지 물었으므로 정답은 ② '강습 정보를 얻기 위해서'이다.

어휘 | sign up for ~을 등록하다, 신청하다 beginner [bigínər] 명 초보자

13 시간 정보 고르기

정답 ③

M Samantha, when do you want to go to the restaurant on Friday? I need to reserve a table.
W Let me check my schedule. *[Pause]* The meeting ends at 4, so how about 6?
M Okay. I'll call the restaurant now.
W Oh, wait a second. I was looking at next week's schedule. I can be there earlier on Friday.
M That's nice. What about 5 then?
W Let's make it 5:30. Can we meet at 5 and go there together?
M Sure.

남 Samantha, 금요일 몇 시에 식당에 가고 싶니? 자리를 예약해야 해.
여 내 스케줄을 확인해 볼게. *[잠시 멈춤]* 회의가 4시에 끝나니까, 6시는 어때?
남 알았어. 지금 식당에 전화할게.
여 오, 잠깐만. 나 다음 주 일정을 보고 있었어. 금요일에는 그곳에 더 일찍 갈 수 있어.
남 잘됐네. 그럼 5시는 어때?
여 5시 30분으로 하자. 우리 5시에 만나서 그곳에 같이 갈 수 있을까?
남 물론이지.

해설 | 여자가 5시에 만나서 같이 가자고 하자 남자가 물론이라고 했으므로 정답은 ③ '5:00 p.m.'이다.
어휘 | reserve [rizə́:rv] 통 예약하다

14 관계 고르기

정답 ②

M Welcome, everyone. Our first stop on today's tour is the Louvre Museum.
W Where will we go after the museum?
M It's a beautiful day, so we will visit the Eiffel Tower next.
W Oh, great! I've always wanted to visit the Eiffel Tower.
M After that, we'll eat lunch. The restaurant is close to the Seine River, actually.
W Excellent. I can't wait to try French food.
M It's going to be a great day exploring Paris.

남 환영합니다, 여러분. 오늘 관광의 첫 번째 목적지는 루브르 박물관입니다.
여 박물관 다음에는 어디에 갈 예정인가요?
남 날씨가 좋으니, 그다음엔 에펠탑을 방문할 거예요.
여 오, 좋아요! 저는 늘 에펠탑에 가보고 싶었어요.
남 그 후에, 저희는 점심을 먹을 예정입니다. 그 식당은 사실 센 강과 가까워요.
여 아주 좋네요. 빨리 프랑스 음식을 먹어보고 싶어요.
남 파리를 탐험하시는 멋진 날이 될 겁니다.

해설 | 남자가 오늘 관광의 첫 번째 목적지는 루브르 박물관이라고 하며 관광 일정을 말하고 있는 것으로 보아 정답은 ② '여행 가이드 — 여행객'이다.
어휘 | close [klouz] 형 가까운 try [trai] 통 먹어보다; 시식하다 explore [ikspl5:r] 통 탐험하다

15 부탁·요청한 일 고르기

정답 ④

M Honey, what are these? They are lovely.
W Thanks. I made these Christmas cards because I wanted to send them to my friends.
M Is there anything I can do to help you?
W I need to finish writing messages in the cards. Oh, I know what you can do. Is there glue on the table?
M No. But I have some on my desk.
W Good. Will you put the stamps on the envelopes?
M No problem.

남 여보, 이것들은 뭐야? 아름답다.
여 고마워. 친구들에게 보내고 싶어서 이 크리스마스카드들을 만들었어.
남 내가 도와줄 수 있는 일이 있을까?
여 나는 카드에 메시지 쓰는 것을 끝내야 해. 오, 당신이 할 수 있는 게 뭔지 알겠어. 테이블 위에 풀 있어?
남 아니. 하지만 내 책상 위에 몇 개 있어.
여 좋아. 봉투에 우표를 붙여 줄래?
남 물론이지.

해설 | 여자가 남자에게 봉투에 우표를 붙여달라고 부탁했으므로 정답은 ④ '우표 붙이기'이다.
어휘 | glue [glu:] 명 풀 envelope [énvəloup] 명 봉투

16 이유 고르기

정답 ⑤

W Today, we have Alex Brown, the surfer, in the studio. Welcome!
M Hello.
W We watched your competition last night. You came in fourth place.
M Yes. I'm a little disappointed.
W Is it because you didn't win any medals?
M Not because I didn't win, but because I couldn't do my best.
W What happened?
M I hurt my back right before the competition, so I couldn't perform well.

여 오늘, 저희는 서퍼 Alex Brown을 스튜디오에 모셨습니다. 환영합니다!
남 안녕하세요.
여 어젯밤에 당신의 시합을 봤어요. 4등을 하셨잖아요.
남 네. 저는 약간 실망했습니다.
여 메달을 하나도 못 따서인가요?
남 제가 메달을 못따서가 아니라, 최선을 다할 수 없었기 때문이에요.
여 무슨 일이 있었나요?
남 대회 직전에 허리를 다쳐서, 좋은 성적을 낼 수 없었습니다.

해설 | 남자는 약간 실망했다고 말한 후, 최선을 다할 수 없었기 때문이라고 말했으므로 정답은 ⑤ '최선을 다하지 못해서'이다.

어휘 | competition [kàmpətíʃən] 명 시합 place [pleis] 명 입상 순위 disappointed [dìsəpɔ́intid] 형 실망한 hurt [həːrt] 동 다치다

17 그림 상황에 적절한 대화 고르기

정답 ②

① M Did you go see a doctor?
W Yes. I went to the hospital yesterday.
② M I'm going to take a nap.
W That's a good idea. You look so tired.
③ M Did you enjoy the movie?
W It was boring. I fell asleep.
④ M What time does the shop open?
W It opens at 8 a.m.
⑤ M You're so late!
W Sorry. My alarm didn't go off this morning.

① 남 너 진찰 받으러 갔었니?
여 응. 어제 병원에 갔었어.
② 남 나는 낮잠을 잘 거야.
여 좋은 생각이야. 너 정말 피곤해 보여.
③ 남 영화 재미있게 봤니?
여 지루했어. 나는 잠들었어.
④ 남 그 가게는 몇 시에 여니?
여 거긴 오전 8시에 열어.
⑤ 남 너 엄청나게 늦었어!
여 미안해. 오늘 아침에 알람이 울리지 않았어.

해설 | 남자가 낮잠을 잘 거라고 하자 여자가 좋은 생각이라며 정말 피곤해 보인다고 하는 상황이므로 정답은 ②이다.

어휘 | take a nap 낮잠을 자다 fall asleep 잠들다 go off 울리다

18 언급하지 않은 내용 고르기

정답 ③

W Good morning, everyone. A science fair will be held by our own science club tomorrow. It will take place in the Nara auditorium. Activities like volcano eruption experiments will be held at each booth. It begins at 8:30 a.m. and ends at 5 p.m. The event will continue for two days, so, please come and enjoy the fun activities.

여 좋은 아침입니다, 여러분. 내일 저희 과학 동아리에서 주최하는 과학 박람회가 열릴 예정입니다. 박람회는 나라 강당에서 열릴 것입니다. 각 부스에서는 화산 폭발 실험과 같은 활동들이 진행될 것입니다. 박람회는 오전 8시 30분에 시작해서 오후 5시에 끝납니다. 행사는 이틀 동안 진행될 예정이니, 오셔서 재미있는 활동들을 즐겨주세요.

해설 | ① 시행 주체(과학 동아리), ② 행사 장소(나라 강당), ④ 시작 시간(8시 30분), ⑤ 행사 기간(이틀)에 대해 언급했으므로 정답은 ③ '참가 비용'이다.

어휘 | science fair 과학 박람회 take place 열리다 volcano [valkéinou] 명 화산 eruption [irʌ́pʃən] 명 폭발; 분출 experiment [ikspérəmənt] 명 실험

19 적절한 응답 고르기

정답 ①

W Excuse me. Have you seen a wallet in the store?
M No, I'm sorry. Did you lose one?
W Yes. I think I left it here this morning. I probably forgot to pick it up from the counter.
M I don't think it's here, but I'll look around.
W Thank you. That would be great.
M What color is it?
W It's brown.

여 실례합니다. 가게에서 지갑을 본 적이 있으신가요?
남 아니요, 죄송합니다. 잃어버리셨나요?
여 네. 오늘 아침에 여기에 두고 간 것 같아요. 아마 계산대에서 가져가는 것을 잊어버렸을 거예요.
남 여기 없는 것 같지만, 제가 둘러볼게요.
여 감사합니다. 그래 주시면 좋겠어요.
남 그것은 무슨 색인가요?
여 그건 갈색이에요.

해설 | 남자가 무슨 색이냐고 물었으므로 정답은 색을 말해주는 ① 'It's brown.'이다.

선택지 해석

① 그건 갈색이에요. ② 그것은 제 지갑 안에 있어요. ③ 그녀는 가게로 달려갔어요. ④ 소파 아래를 보세요. ⑤ 저는 5달러가 있어요.

어휘 | probably [prábəbli] 부 아마도 counter [káuntər] 명 계산대 look around 둘러보다 purse [pəːrs] 명 지갑 couch [kautʃ] 명 소파

20 적절한 응답 고르기

정답 ②

W Hey, Chris. Are you ready for your school photo tomorrow?
M No. I don't like taking photos.
W Oh, why?
M I get nervous in front of the camera. I can't smile naturally.
W Maybe you need someone to make you laugh when you take your picture.
M That's a good idea. Then, I can smile easily.
W Exactly.
M Why don't you do that for me?
W Sure. I'll try my best.

여 안녕, Chris. 내일 학교 사진 찍을 준비 됐니?
남 아니. 나는 사진 찍는 것을 좋아하지 않아.
여 오, 왜?
남 나는 카메라 앞에서 긴장해. 자연스럽게 미소를 지을 수가 없어.
여 사진 찍을 때 너를 웃게 해줄 누군가가 필요한 걸지도 몰라.
남 그거 좋은 생각이다. 그럼, 나도 쉽게 미소 지을 수 있어.
여 바로 그거야.
남 네가 그렇게 해주는 게 어때?
여 물론이지. 최선을 다할게.

해설 | 남자가 사진을 찍을 때 웃게 해달라고 부탁했으므로 정답은 부탁을 들어주는 ② 'Sure. I'll try my best.'이다.

선택지 해석

① 그는 학교에 오지 않았어. ② 물론이지. 최선을 다할게. ③ 카메라를 보고 미소 지어! ④ 그건 웃긴 농담이었어. ⑤ 다음에는 더 잘할 거야.

어휘 | nervous [nɔ́ːrvəs] 형 긴장한 laugh [læf] 동 웃다 easily [íːzili] 부 쉽게

15회 실전 모의고사

| 문제 pp.138-139

1	①	2	④	3	③	4	⑤	5	①	6	④	7	①	8	④	9	②	10	④
11	③	12	④	13	③	14	③	15	⑤	16	④	17	①	18	⑤	19	②	20	④

1 날씨 고르기

정답 ①

M Good morning, everyone! Here's today's weather report. In Seoul, the air will be bad and dusty, so please wear a mask. Suwon will be sunny, but there will be a few showers in the afternoon. Sunny and warm weather will continue in Daejeon all day long. Daegu will be partly cloudy, but the sky will be clear in the afternoon.

남 안녕하십니까, 여러분! 오늘의 일기 예보입니다. 서울은 공기가 좋지 않고 먼지가 많을 예정이니, 마스크를 착용하십시오. 수원은 화창하겠지만, 오후에는 몇 차례 소나기가 내리겠습니다. 대전은 온종일 따뜻하고 화창하겠습니다. 대구는 일부 흐리겠지만, 오후에는 하늘이 맑아질 것입니다.

해설 | 대전은 온종일 따뜻하고 화창하겠다고 했으므로 정답은 ①이다.

어휘 | wear [wɛər] 동 착용하다, 입다 partly [páːrtli] 부 일부분은, 부분적으로

2 알맞은 그림 고르기

정답 ④

M Amy, whose necklace is this?	남 Amy, 이거 누구 목걸이니?
W It's mine, Dad. I made it at home today.	여 그건 제 거예요, 아빠. 오늘 집에서 만들었어요.
M You are so talented. It looks really special with two chains.	남 넌 정말 재능이 있구나. 체인 두 줄이 있는 것이 정말 특별해 보이네.
W Thank you. I thought two-chain necklaces are more unique.	여 감사해요. 두 줄짜리 체인 목걸이가 좀 더 독특하다고 생각했어요.
M Right. Why did you add the letter *Q* pendant?	남 맞아. 글자 Q 펜던트는 왜 추가했니?
W It's the first letter of my favorite rock band, Queen.	여 그건 제가 가장 좋아하는 록 밴드인 퀸의 첫 글자예요.

해설 | 남자는 두 줄짜리 체인 목걸이가 특별해 보인다고 했고, 글자 Q 펜던트를 추가한 이유를 물었으므로 정답은 ④이다.

어휘 | necklace [néklis] 명 목걸이 talented [tǽləntid] 형 재능이 있는 unique [juːníːk] 형 독특한; 유일한
pendant [péndənt] 명 펜던트(귀걸이·목걸이 등의 늘어뜨린 장식)

3 언급하지 않은 내용 고르기

정답 ③

M What are you looking at, Dasom?	남 뭘 보고 있니, 다솜아?
W I'm reading this poster about the student debate.	여 학생 토론회에 대한 포스터를 읽고 있어.
M That is next Friday, isn't it?	남 그거 다음 금요일이지, 그렇지 않니?
W Yes. We should go to the auditorium to watch it.	여 맞아. 그걸 보려면 강당으로 가야 해.
M Do you know how long it is?	남 얼마나 오래 하는지 아니?
W It says that it will take two hours.	여 2시간 걸릴 거라고 쓰여 있어.
M Who will be debating?	남 누가 토론할 예정이야?
W Four teams will compete. The topics are about climate change.	여 네 개 팀이 경쟁할 거야. 주제는 기후 변화에 관한 거고.
M That sounds interesting.	남 흥미롭게 들리네.

해설 | ① 요일(다음 금요일), ② 장소(강당), ④ 참가자(네 개 팀), ⑤ 토론 주제(기후 변화)에 대해 언급했으므로 정답은 ③ '시작 시간'이다.

어휘 | debate [dibéit] 명 토론회; 토론, 논쟁 동 토론하다 auditorium [ɔ̀ːditɔ́ːriəm] 명 강당 climate [kláimit] 명 기후

4 한 일 고르기

정답 ⑤

W Ollie, did you take these pictures?	여 Ollie, 이 사진들 네가 찍었니?
M Yes. My teacher asked me to take pictures at our school festival.	남 응. 우리 선생님께서 학교 축제 때 나한테 사진을 찍어달라고 요청하셨어.
W Are you going to upload them to our school website?	여 이것들을 학교 웹사이트에 올릴 거니?
M Yeah. I'm going to choose some good photos first.	남 응. 우선 좋은 사진들 몇 장을 고를 거야.
W Are there any photos of me?	여 거기 내 사진들도 좀 있어?
M I'm not sure. What did you do at the festival?	남 잘 모르겠어. 축제에서 뭐 했었는데?
W I worked at the snack booth.	여 난 간식 부스에서 일했어.

해설 | 여자가 학교 축제에서 간식 부스에서 일했다고 했으므로 정답은 ⑤ '간식 부스에서 일하기'이다.

어휘 | snack [snæk] 명 간식 booth [buːθ] 명 부스, 노점, 매점

5 장소 고르기

정답 ①

W You wanted to talk to me, coach?	여 저와 대화하고 싶으셨다고요, 코치님?
M Yes, Mary. I need you to play goalkeeper during practice today.	남 그래, Mary. 오늘 연습하는 동안 네가 골키퍼를 해주려무나.
W What about Rose?	여 Rose는요?
M She's not here. She said she was feeling sick.	남 그녀는 여기 없단다. 아프다고 하더구나.
W Oh, that's too bad.	여 오, 안됐네요.
M Here are the goalkeeping gloves. You'll need those.	남 여기 골키퍼 장갑이 있어. 이것들이 필요할 거야.
W Thanks.	여 감사합니다.
M Okay, play hard today!	남 그래, 오늘도 열심히 해보자!
W I'll do my best.	여 최선을 다할게요.

해설 | 남자가 여자에게 오늘 연습에서 골키퍼를 맡아달라고 부탁하는 것으로 보아 정답은 ① '축구장'이다.

어휘 | goalkeeper [góulkiːpər] 명 골키퍼 glove [glʌv] 명 장갑 hard [haːrd] 부 열심히 형 단단한

6 의도 고르기

정답 ④

W Hey, Jonathan. Why were you late for class today? M I'm sorry, Ms. Stevens. I had to help an old lady. W What happened? M She was looking for the bank, but she got lost. W Did you give her directions? M Yes. But she was confused, so I walked to the bank with her. W Wow. I think you are the nicest person I know.	여 얘, Jonathan. 왜 오늘 수업에 늦었니? 남 죄송해요, Stevens 선생님. 한 할머니를 도와드려야 했어요. 여 무슨 일이 있었니? 남 그분은 은행을 찾고 계셨는데, 길을 잃으셨더라고요. 여 네가 길을 알려 드렸니? 남 네. 그런데 할머니가 헷갈려 하셔서, 제가 그분과 함께 은행까지 걸어갔어요. 여 우와. 너는 내가 아는 사람 중 가장 친절한 것 같구나.

해설 | 여자가 길을 잃은 할머니를 도와드린 남자를 향해 자신이 아는 사람 중에서 가장 친절한 것 같다고 말했으므로 정답은 ④ '칭찬'이다.

어휘 | get lost 길을 잃다 give directions 길을 알려주다 confused [kənfjúːzd] 형 헷갈리는; 혼란한, 당황한

7 특정 정보 고르기

정답 ①

M Olivia, which club are you going to join? W I used to play violin, so I'll join the school orchestra. M That's impressive. I want to join a sports club. W What kind of sports do you like? M I love swimming. I learned how to swim last summer. W Are you going to join the swimming club then? M Yes. I want to learn more various swimming styles.	남 Olivia, 너는 어떤 동아리에 가입할 거니? 여 나는 바이올린을 연주했었어서, 학교 관현악단에 가입할 거야. 남 인상적이네. 나는 운동 동아리에 가입하고 싶어. 여 어떤 종목의 운동을 좋아하는데? 남 나는 수영을 정말 좋아해. 작년 여름에 수영하는 법을 배웠어. 여 그러면 수영부에 가입할 거야? 남 응. 난 더 다양한 영법을 배우고 싶어.

해설 | 여자가 수영부에 가입할 것인지 묻자 남자가 그렇다고 했으므로 정답은 ① '수영'이다.

어휘 | orchestra [ɔ́ːrkəstrə] 명 관현악단, 오케스트라 impressive [imprésiv] 형 인상적인 various [vɛ́əriəs] 형 다양한

8 할 일 고르기

정답 ④

M Honey, I thought you already left the house. W Yes. But I had to come back. M Why? W It's very cold outside, so I needed to change my clothes. M Oh, right. I heard that it's going to snow in the afternoon. W Really? I didn't know that. M You'd better take an umbrella. W I lost my umbrella last week. Can I borrow yours? M Sure. I have extra umbrellas in our room. I'll go and get one.	남 여보, 난 당신이 이미 집을 나선 줄 알았어. 여 맞아. 그런데 다시 돌아와야 했어. 남 왜? 여 밖이 너무 추워서, 옷을 갈아입어야 했어. 남 오, 맞아. 오후에는 눈이 내릴 거라고 들었어. 여 정말? 그건 몰랐어. 남 우산을 들고 가는 게 좋겠어. 여 내 우산은 지난주에 잃어버렸어. 당신 것을 빌려도 될까? 남 물론이지. 우리 방에 여분의 우산이 있어. 내가 가서 하나 가져올게.

해설 | 남자가 방에 여분의 우산이 있으니 가서 가져오겠다고 했으므로 정답은 ④ '우산 가져오기'이다.

어휘 | change clothes 옷을 갈아입다 extra [ékstrə] 형 여분의

9 언급하지 않은 내용 고르기

정답 ②

[Telephone rings.] W Little Italy Restaurant. How may I help you? M Hi. I have a question about the menu. Do you serve any vegetarian pasta dishes? W Yes. We have several meat-free pastas. M Great! When do you open? W We open from 11 a.m. to 10 p.m. M Could you let me know the location? W We're on Main Street next to the fountain. M Okay, I got it. Can I make a reservation for two on Sunday at 5 p.m.? W Yes, you can. We'll see you then.	*[전화기가 울린다.]* 여 Little Italy Restaurant입니다. 무엇을 도와드릴까요? 남 안녕하세요. 메뉴에 대해 질문이 있어서요. 채식주의자용 파스타 요리를 제공하나요? 여 네. 고기가 들지 않은 파스타가 몇 가지 있어요. 남 좋네요! 언제 여시죠? 여 저희는 오전 11시부터 오후 10시까지 열어요. 남 위치를 알려주실 수 있으신가요? 여 메인 가 분수대 옆에 있습니다. 남 네, 알겠습니다. 일요일 오후 5시에 두 명 예약할 수 있을까요? 여 네, 가능하세요. 그때 뵙겠습니다.

해설 | ① 메뉴(고기가 들지 않은 파스타), ③ 영업시간(오전 11시부터 오후 10시까지), ④ 위치(메인 가 분수대 옆), ⑤ 예약 가능 여부(일요일 오후 5시에 예약 가능)에 대해 언급했으므로 정답은 ② '음식 가격'이다.

어휘 | vegetarian [vèdʒətɛ́əriən] 형 채식주의자를 위한 명 채식주의자 location [loukéiʃən] 명 위치 fountain [fáuntən] 명 분수대 make a reservation 예약하다

10 주제 고르기

정답 ④

M Good morning, students. There will be a special event at our school next week. Famous novelist Emily Miller will visit us and give a lecture. She will share her story about how she wrote her best-selling novel. After that, there will be a question-and-answer session. Please come and enjoy this unique experience.

남 좋은 아침입니다, 학생 여러분. 다음 주에는 우리 학교에서 특별한 행사가 있을 예정입니다. 유명한 소설가인 Emily Miller가 우리를 방문해서 강연을 할 것입니다. 그녀는 어떻게 그녀가 베스트셀러 소설을 썼는지에 대한 이야기를 나눌 예정입니다. 그 후에, 질의응답 시간이 있겠습니다. 부디 와서 이 특별한 경험을 즐기길 바랍니다.

해설 | 남자가 유명한 소설가가 다음 주에 학교를 방문하여 강연할 것이라고 말하고 있으므로 정답은 ④ '특별 강연 안내'이다.

어휘 | novelist [návəlist] 명 소설가 (novel [návəl] 명 소설) lecture [léktʃər] 명 강연, 강의 session [séʃən] 명 시간, 기간

11 일치하지 않는 내용 고르기

정답 ③

M Hello, everyone. Let me introduce my special bag. My younger sister bought this for me as a gift. It's made of recycled material. It comes in three different colors, red, black, and blue. I like it because the bag is big enough to hold my laptop. You can buy it online.

남 안녕하세요, 여러분. 제 특별한 가방을 소개해드리겠습니다. 제 여동생이 선물로 제게 이것을 사주었습니다. 이것은 재활용한 재료로 만들어졌습니다. 이것은 빨간색, 검은색, 파란색의 세 가지 다른 색상으로 나옵니다. 저는 제 노트북이 들어갈 정도로 충분히 크기 때문에 이 가방을 좋아합니다. 이것은 온라인에서 사실 수 있습니다.

해설 | 남자가 빨간색, 검은색, 파란색의 세 가지 색상으로 나와 있다고 했으므로 정답은 ③ '색상은 한 가지이다.'이다.

어휘 | recycle [ri:sáikl] 동 재활용하다 material [mətíəriəl] 명 재료

12 목적 고르기

정답 ④

W Hi. How may I help you?
M Do you buy used books here?
W Yes, we do. But it depends on the condition of the books.
M Well, I brought five books. Here they are.
W Let me check them. *[Pause]* This one has a ripped page. The others look fine.
M Okay. I'll sell those four.
W You will receive 15 dollars. Do you want it in cash or store credit?
M I would like it in cash.

여 안녕하세요. 어떻게 도와드릴까요?
남 여기서 중고 책을 사시나요?
여 네, 맞아요. 하지만 책 상태에 따라 달라요.
남 음, 저는 다섯 권의 책을 가지고 왔어요. 여기 있습니다.
여 확인해 볼게요. *[잠시 멈춤]* 이것은 찢어진 페이지가 있네요. 다른 것들은 괜찮아 보여요.
남 알겠습니다. 그 네 권을 팔게요.
여 15달러 받으실 예정입니다. 현금으로 드릴까요, 매장 포인트로 드릴까요?
남 현금으로 주세요.

해설 | 남자가 여자에게 여기서 중고 책을 사는지 물어본 후 다섯 권의 책을 가지고 왔다고 했으므로 정답은 ④ '중고 책을 팔기 위해서'이다.

어휘 | used [ju:sd] 형 중고의, 사용된 depend on ~에 따라 다르다 condition [kəndíʃən] 명 상태 ripped [ript] 형 찢어진 receive [risí:v] 동 받다

13 금액 정보 고르기

정답 ③

M Hello. Are you ready to order?
W Yes. I'd like to order some fried rice.
M That will be 11 dollars.
W Oh, can I have the spicy chicken too?
M Sure. One order of fried rice and one spicy chicken, right?
W Yes. That's right.
M The total comes to 30 dollars.
W Hmm... Can I use this 10-dollar discount coupon?
M Of course. Then, the total will be 20 dollars.
W Okay. Here you go.

남 안녕하세요. 주문할 준비가 되셨나요?
여 네. 저는 볶음밥을 주문하고 싶어요.
남 11달러입니다.
여 오, 그리고 매운 닭요리도 하나 주시겠어요?
남 물론이죠. 볶음밥 하나와 매운 닭요리 하나, 맞으시죠?
여 네. 맞아요.
남 총 30달러입니다.
여 흠... 이 10달러 할인 쿠폰 사용할 수 있나요?
남 물론이죠. 그럼, 총 20달러입니다.
여 그렇군요. 여기 있어요.

해설 | 남자가 총 20달러라고 했으므로 정답은 ③ '$ 20'이다.

어휘 | order [ɔ́:rdər] 동 주문하다 spicy [spáisi] 형 매운 come to (총계가) ~이 되다 discount [dískaunt] 명 할인

14 관계 고르기

정답 ③

M	Welcome to the phone service center. What's wrong with your phone?	남	휴대폰 서비스 센터에 오신 것을 환영합니다. 휴대폰에 무슨 문제가 있나요?
W	It fell out of my pocket yesterday, and the screen broke.	여	어제 주머니에서 떨어져서, 화면이 깨졌어요.
M	I see. It seems like the screen needs to be replaced.	남	그렇군요. 화면을 교체해야 할 것 같습니다.
W	How much will a new screen cost?	여	새 화면은 얼마나 드나요?
M	It will cost 125 dollars.	남	125달러가 들겠습니다.
W	Alright. How much time will it take?	여	알겠습니다. 시간은 얼마나 오래 걸리나요?
M	It will take about an hour.	남	대략 한 시간 정도 걸릴 거예요.
W	Okay. I'll come back in an hour.	여	네. 한 시간 후에 돌아올게요.

해설 | 남자가 여자에게 휴대폰 서비스 센터에 오신 것을 환영한다면서 휴대폰에 무슨 문제가 있는지 묻는 것으로 보아 정답은 ③ '수리 기사 — 고객'이다.

어휘 | fall out of 떨어지다 pocket [pákit] 명 주머니 replace [ripléis] 동 교체하다, 바꾸다; 대신하다 cost [kɔ:st] 동 (값·비용이) 들다

15 부탁·요청한 일 고르기

정답 ⑤

W	Honey, let's check our to-do list for the move.	여	여보, 이사를 위해 해야 할 일 목록을 확인하자.
M	Okay. We packed the clothes and cleaned the apartment.	남	알겠어. 옷은 다 쌌고 아파트 청소도 했어.
W	But can we move all the furniture by ourselves?	여	그런데 모든 가구를 우리가 직접 옮길 수 있을까?
M	I don't think so. We have too much furniture.	남	안 될 것 같아. 가구가 너무 많아.
W	Yeah. We'd better use a moving service.	여	그래. 이사 서비스를 이용하는 게 낫겠어.
M	Then, can you call a moving company?	남	그럼, 이삿짐센터에 전화해 줄 수 있어?
W	Sure. I'll do that.	여	물론이지. 내가 할게.

해설 | 여자가 이사 서비스를 이용하는 것이 좋겠다고 하자, 남자가 여자에게 이삿짐센터에 전화해 달라고 부탁했으므로 정답은 ⑤ '이삿짐센터에 전화하기'이다.

어휘 | move [mu:v] 명 이사 동 옮기다 pack [pæk] 동 (짐을) 싸다 furniture [fə́:rnitʃər] 명 가구

16 이유 고르기

정답 ④

M	Good afternoon. Do you need any help?	남	안녕하세요. 도움이 필요하신가요?
W	I'm looking for some clothes to wear on my vacation.	여	휴가 때 입을 옷을 좀 찾고 있어요.
M	Okay. Where are you going?	남	알겠습니다. 어디로 가시나요?
W	I'm going to Vietnam. It'll be really hot.	여	저는 베트남에 갈 거예요. 정말 더울 거예요.
M	I recommend this yellow dress here.	남	저는 여기 이 노란색 원피스를 추천드려요.
W	Oh, yes. That is lovely. Do you have it in a medium size?	여	오, 네. 사랑스럽네요. 미디움 사이즈가 있나요?
M	Yes, we do. Would you like to try it on?	남	네, 있어요. 입어 보시겠어요?
W	That would be great. Thanks.	여	그게 좋겠어요. 감사해요.
M	Here you go.	남	여기 있습니다.

해설 | 여자가 휴가 때 입을 옷을 찾고 있다고 했으므로 정답은 ④ '휴가 때 입기 위해서'이다.

어휘 | vacation [veikéiʃən] 명 휴가, 방학 Vietnam [vì:etná:m] 명 베트남 recommend [rèkəménd] 동 추천하다 try on 입어 보다

17 그림 상황에 적절한 대화 고르기

정답 ①

① M Which scarf should I buy?
W The striped one looks nice on you.
② M The sunlight is too strong.
W Why don't you put on your sunglasses?
③ M Did you get up early to watch the sunrise?
W No. I was too tired.
④ M Do you mind if I turn the air conditioner off?
W Of course not. Go ahead.
⑤ M Do you need anything from the supermarket?
W Can you pick up some milk?

① 남 어떤 목도리를 사야 할까?
여 줄무늬 목도리가 네게 잘 어울려.
② 남 햇빛이 너무 강해.
여 선글라스를 쓰는 건 어때?
③ 남 해돋이를 보기 위해 일찍 일어났니?
여 아니. 너무 피곤했어.
④ 남 에어컨을 꺼도 괜찮을까?
여 물론 괜찮지. 그렇게 해.
⑤ 남 슈퍼마켓에서 뭐 필요한 거 있니?
여 우유 좀 사다 줄래?

해설 | 옷 가게에서 남자가 목도리를 살피고 있고 여자는 줄무늬 목도리를 추천하고 있는 상황이므로 정답은 ①이다.

어휘 | scarf [ska:rf] 명 목도리, 스카프 striped [straipt] 형 줄무늬의 sunrise [sʌ́nraiz] 명 해돋이, 일출 pick up 사다, 얻다; 집다

18 언급하지 않은 내용 고르기

정답 ⑤

M Hello, students. Today, I'd like to tell you about worry dolls. These originate from a Guatemalan legend. If you tell your troubles to one and hide it under your pillow, your troubles will go away. They are made of wire and colorful wool. They are usually given to children when they're sad or upset. Worry dolls are still very popular today.

남 안녕하세요, 학생 여러분. 오늘은 여러분에게 걱정 인형에 대해 말씀드리고 싶습니다. 걱정 인형은 과테말라의 전설에서 유래됐습니다. 만약 걱정 인형에게 여러분의 고민을 말하고 그것을 베개 아래에 숨기면, 고민이 사라질 것입니다. 그것들은 철사와 알록달록한 털실로 만들어집니다. 이것은 보통 아이들이 슬프거나 화가 났을 때 주어집니다. 걱정 인형은 오늘날도 여전히 매우 인기가 있습니다.

해설 | ① 이름(걱정 인형), ② 유래(과테말라의 전설), ③ 재료(철사와 털실), ④ 용도(고민이 사라짐)에 대해 언급했으므로 정답은 ⑤ '크기'이다.

어휘 | originate from ~에서 유래하다, 기원하다 legend [lédʒənd] 명 전설 go away 사라지다 wire [waiər] 명 철사 wool [wul] 명 털실; 양털

19 적절한 응답 고르기

정답 ②

W What are you working on, Minjun?
M I'm writing a new post for my blog.
W Cool! What is your blog about?
M It's about comic books. I like to write reviews of them.
W That sounds interesting. Do many people read your posts?
M Yes. On average, 500 people visit every day.
W Great. I'd like to visit your blog too.
M I'll send you the link.

여 뭐 하고 있니, 민준아?
남 블로그에 올릴 새 게시글을 쓰고 있어.
여 멋지다! 네 블로그는 뭐에 관한 거야?
남 만화책에 관한 거야. 나는 만화책 감상평 쓰는 걸 좋아해.
여 흥미로운걸. 많은 사람이 네 게시글을 읽니?
남 응. 평균적으로, 매일 500명의 사람이 방문해.
여 훌륭하다. 나도 네 블로그를 방문하고 싶어.
남 내가 링크를 보내 줄게.

해설 | 여자가 남자의 블로그를 방문하고 싶다 했으므로 정답은 링크를 보내주겠다고 답하는 ② 'I'll send you the link.'이다.

선택지 해석

① 응, 그들은 내 블로그를 정말 좋아했어. ② 내가 링크를 보내 줄게. ③ 결과가 게시됐어. ④ 난 방금 저 만화책을 다 읽었어.
⑤ 아니, 그는 댓글을 남기지 않았어.

어휘 | on average 평균적으로

20 적절한 응답 고르기

정답 ④

W Is that a newspaper, James?
M Yeah. I'm reading it because there's some exciting news.
W Oh, what is it?
M My favorite rugby team just got a new player.
W That's great. Tell me more about the player.
M His name is Nick Nelson. He's a top player.
W You should try to get tickets to the team's next game.
M I definitely will.

여 그거 신문이니, James?
남 응. 흥미진진한 뉴스가 있어서 읽는 중이야.
여 오, 뭔데?
남 내가 좋아하는 럭비팀이 새 선수를 막 영입했어.
여 잘됐네. 그 선수에 대해 좀 더 얘기해줘.
남 그의 이름은 Nick Nelson이야. 그는 최고의 선수야.
여 너 그 팀의 다음 경기 표를 꼭 구해봐야겠는걸.
남 물론 그렇게 할 거야.

해설 | 남자에게 럭비팀의 다음 경기 표를 구해보라고 권유하고 있으므로 정답은 권유를 받아들이는 ④ 'I definitely will.'이다.

선택지 해석

① 아니, 난 몰랐어. ② 내게 좋은 소식이 있어. ③ 그는 연습에 빠졌어. ④ 물론 그렇게 할 거야. ⑤ 나는 그걸 온라인으로 봤어.

어휘 | rugby [rʌ́gbi] 명 럭비 definitely [défənitli] 부 물론, 틀림없이; 분명히

16회 실전 모의고사

| 문제 pp.146-147

1	①	2	⑤	3	③	4	③	5	①	6	⑤	7	⑤	8	②	9	⑤	10	③
11	③	12	②	13	①	14	③	15	⑤	16	③	17	②	18	④	19	④	20	③

1 날씨 고르기

정답 ①

W Good evening. Here is Friday night's weekend weather report. It's raining hard right now. But during the night, it's likely to stop. The temperature will drop in the morning, so wear a warm jacket when you go outside. Saturday will be cloudy, but there won't be any rain. On Sunday, we'll get the first snow of the year.

여 안녕하십니까. 금요일 밤의 주말 일기 예보입니다. 현재 세차게 비가 내리고 있습니다. 하지만 밤 동안 그칠 가능성이 높습니다. 아침에는 기온이 떨어질 예정이니, 외출 시 따뜻한 재킷을 입으시기 바랍니다. 토요일은 흐릴 예정이나 비는 오지 않겠습니다. 일요일에는 올해의 첫눈이 내리겠습니다.

해설 | 토요일은 흐릴 예정이나 비는 내리지 않겠다고 했으므로 정답은 ①이다.

어휘 | hard [ha:rd] 부 세게

2 알맞은 그림 고르기

정답 ⑤

W Daniel, look. I made this vase for our grandmother.
M It's beautiful. Did you paint it?
W Yeah. I was going to leave it without a pattern, but it looked too boring.
M It looks like snow is falling because of the dark background color.
W I was painting on a snowy night.
M Well, I think grandma will love it.

여 Daniel, 봐. 우리 할머니를 위해 이 꽃병을 만들었어.
남 아름답다. 네가 칠한 거야?
여 응. 무늬 없이 남겨두려고 했는데, 너무 따분해 보였어.
남 어두운 배경색 때문에 눈이 내리는 것처럼 보여.
여 눈이 많이 내리는 밤에 칠하고 있었어.
남 음, 할머니가 그걸 좋아하실 것 같아.

해설 | 여자는 어두운 배경색 때문에 눈이 내리는 것 같아 보이는 꽃병을 만들었다고 했으므로 정답은 ⑤이다.

어휘 | vase [veis] 명 꽃병 leave [li:v] 동 남기다 pattern [pǽtərn] 명 무늬, 패턴 fall [fɔ:l] 동 내리다; 떨어지다 snowy [snóui] 형 눈이 많이 내리는

3 언급하지 않은 내용 고르기

정답 ③

W George, did you hear about that new art exhibition?
M Do you mean the Salvador Dali exhibition? I've been to it already.
W Where is it held? I really want to see his work.
M It's held at the Swan Convention Center.
W I don't want to miss it.
M You can see it until March. His paintings will be on display for four months.
W How much is the entrance fee?
M It's only 10 dollars.

여 George, 새 미술 전시회에 대해 들었니?
남 살바도르 달리 전시회 말하는 거야? 나는 이미 다녀왔어.
여 어디에서 열리는 거야? 그의 작품을 정말 보고 싶어.
남 그건 스완 컨벤션 센터에서 개최돼.
여 난 그걸 놓치고 싶지 않아.
남 3월까지 볼 수 있어. 그의 작품은 4개월 동안 전시될 거야.
여 입장료는 얼마야?
남 10달러밖에 안 해.

해설 | ① 전시 장소(스완 컨벤션 센터), ② 작가 이름(살바도르 달리), ④ 전시 기간(4개월), ⑤ 입장료(10달러)에 대해 언급했으므로 정답은 ③ '전시 작품명'이다.

어휘 | exhibition [èksəbíʃən] 명 전시회 miss [mis] 동 놓치다 entrance fee 입장료

4 특정 정보 고르기

정답 ③

M Are you busy now, Jenny?
W Not at all. Why?
M Can you recommend a laptop? I need to get a new one.
W Do you need a big screen?
M Yeah. I have to take online classes with it.
W Okay. Do you need any special features?
M I rarely play games, so I don't need an expensive graphic card.
W How much can you spend on it?
M I don't want to spend more than 800 dollars.

남 지금 바쁘니, Jenny?
여 전혀. 왜?
남 노트북을 추천해 줄 수 있어? 나 새 노트북을 사야 해.
여 큰 화면이 필요하니?
남 응. 난 그걸로 온라인 수업을 들어야 해.
여 그렇구나. 필요한 특별한 기능이 있니?
남 난 게임을 거의 하지 않으니, 비싼 그래픽 카드는 필요 없어.
여 그것에 얼마나 쓸 수 있니?
남 800달러 이상은 쓰고 싶지 않아.

해설 | 남자가 노트북을 추천해 줄 수 있는지 물은 후에 새 노트북을 사야 한다고 했으므로 정답은 ③ '노트북'이다.

어휘 | feature [fíːtʃər] 명 기능; 특색 expensive [ikspénsiv] 형 비싼

5 장소 고르기

정답 ①

W Hello. I'd like to send this package.
M Okay. Where is it going?
W I'm sending it to Canada.
M How do you want to send it?
W By express mail, please. It needs to arrive by Friday.
M All right. What is in the package?
W It's just Korean traditional snacks and books.

여 안녕하세요. 이 소포를 보내고 싶어요.
남 알겠습니다. 어디로 가는 거죠?
여 캐나다로 보낼 거예요.
남 어떻게 보내고 싶으신가요?
여 특급 우편으로 부탁드립니다. 금요일까지 도착해야 해요.
남 알겠습니다. 소포에는 무엇이 들어 있나요?
여 그냥 한국 전통 과자와 책이에요.

해설 | 여자가 소포를 보내고 싶다고 하며 특급 우편으로 보낸다는 말을 하는 것으로 보아 정답은 ① '우체국'이다.

어휘 | package [pǽkidʒ] 명 소포

6 의도 고르기

정답 ⑤

M Wow. Are these people waiting in line to eat at the restaurant?
W I think so. Do you still want to eat here?
M I really want to try their fried salmon. But with the line, I'm not sure anymore.
W Well, what do you want to do?
M Let's go to another restaurant. We can always come back later.
W You are right. I'll look up another place.

남 우와. 이 사람들 식당에서 먹기 위해 줄을 서서 기다리고 있는 거야?
여 그런 것 같아. 여전히 여기서 먹고 싶니?
남 난 연어 튀김을 정말 먹어보고 싶었어. 하지만 줄을 보니까, 이제는 잘 모르겠어.
여 음, 어떻게 하고 싶어?
남 다른 식당으로 가자. 나중에 언제든 다시 오면 돼.
여 네 말이 맞아. 내가 다른 곳을 찾아볼게.

해설 | 남자가 다른 식당으로 가자는 말을 하자 여자가 동의하며 다른 식당을 찾아보겠다는 말을 했으므로 정답은 ⑤ '동의'이다.

어휘 | in line 줄 서서 still [stil] 부 여전히, 아직도 salmon [sǽmən] 명 연어

7 특정 정보 고르기

정답 ⑤

M Miyoung, how was your summer vacation? W Fantastic! I traveled Europe for a month. M Which countries did you visit? W I went to Germany first. M That sounds awesome! Where else did you go? W France and Switzerland. It was my first trip to Switzerland. M Have you been to France before? W Yes. I toured France and Italy last year. M What about Spain? Have you ever traveled there? W No. But I hope to go someday.	남 미영아, 여름 방학은 어땠니? 여 굉장했어! 난 한 달 동안 유럽을 여행했어. 남 어떤 나라들을 방문했니? 여 나는 먼저 독일에 갔어. 남 정말 멋지다! 또 어디에 갔니? 여 프랑스와 스위스. 스위스로는 첫 여행이었어. 남 프랑스는 전에 가본 적 있었어? 여 응. 나는 작년에 프랑스와 이탈리아를 여행했어. 남 스페인은 어때? 거기는 가본 적 있니? 여 아니. 그렇지만 언젠가 가보고 싶어.

해설 | 여자가 스페인은 가본 적이 없지만 언젠가 가보고 싶다고 했으므로 정답은 ⑤ '스페인'이다.

어휘 | country [kʌ́ntri] 명 나라, 국가 trip [trip] 명 여행 someday [sʌ́mdei] 부 언젠가

8 할 일 고르기

정답 ②

W Brian, what are you going to do this afternoon? M I have to study for the math test tomorrow. W It was yesterday, wasn't it? M Right. I meant I have to write a history report. W You worked on it with me last weekend. M Oh, no. I'm so confused! W Why don't you check your schedule again? M Okay.	여 Brian, 오늘 오후에 뭐 할 거야? 남 내일 수학 시험을 위해 공부해야 해. 여 그건 어제였어, 그렇지 않니? 남 맞아. 내 말은 역사 보고서를 써야 한다는 거였어. 여 지난 주말에 나랑 같이했잖아. 남 오, 이런. 너무 헷갈려! 여 일정을 다시 한번 확인해 보는 게 어때? 남 알겠어.

해설 | 여자가 일정을 다시 한번 확인해 보는 게 어떠냐고 하자 남자가 알겠다고 했으므로 정답은 ② '일정 확인하기'이다.

어휘 | confused [kənfjúːzd] 형 헷갈리는, 혼란한

9 언급하지 않은 내용 고르기

정답 ⑤

W Excuse me. Could you help me? M Yes. What can I do for you? W I can't find the ticket booth. M Our Dino Museum is free for everyone. It's run by the city. W That's great. When does it close today? M It's open from 9 to 6 on the weekdays. It is closed on the weekends. W Thanks! Is there any special tours you provide? I'd like to learn more about dinosaurs. M We have those only on Wednesdays.	여 실례합니다. 저 좀 도와주시겠어요? 남 네. 무엇을 도와드릴까요? 여 매표소를 못 찾겠어요. 남 저희 다이노 박물관은 모두에게 무료입니다. 이곳은 시에 의해 운영되고 있어요. 여 잘 됐네요. 오늘 몇 시에 닫나요? 남 평일에는 9시부터 6시까지 운영합니다. 주말에는 닫아요. 여 감사합니다! 박물관에서 제공하는 특별한 투어가 있나요? 저는 공룡에 대해 더 배우고 싶어요. 남 그것은 수요일에만 있어요.

해설 | ① 입장료(무료), ② 운영 기관(시), ③ 운영 시간(9시부터 6시까지), ④ 운영 요일(주말에 닫음)에 대해 말하고 있으므로 정답은 ⑤ '셔틀버스 운행'이다.

어휘 | run [rʌn] 동 운영하다 weekday [wíkdei] 명 평일, 주중 dinosaur [dáinəsɔ̀ːr] 명 공룡

10 주제 고르기

정답 ③

W Hello, everyone. Today, I'll talk about how to use a public library. First, make a library card. Making a library card will let you use the services that the library provides. The library will lend you books, movies, and more. Also, you should check the schedule for special programs. There are many interesting events like lectures.	여 안녕하세요, 여러분. 오늘은 공공 도서관을 이용하는 방법에 대해 이야기하겠습니다. 먼저, 도서관 카드를 만드세요. 도서관 카드를 만드는 것은 도서관이 제공하는 서비스를 이용할 수 있게 해줍니다. 도서관은 당신에게 책, 영화 등을 빌려줄 것입니다. 또, 특별 프로그램의 일정을 확인하십시오. 강의와 같은 많은 재미있는 행사들이 있습니다.

해설 | 여자가 공공 도서관을 이용하는 방법에 대해 말하고 있으므로 정답은 ③ '도서관 이용 방법'이다.
어휘 | public [pʌ́blik] 형 공공의 provide [prəváid] 동 제공하다 lend [lend] 동 빌려주다 special [spéʃəl] 형 특별한 lecture [léktʃər] 명 강의

11 일치하지 않는 내용 고르기

정답 ③

[Telephone rings.]
W Hi, I saw your post on the website. Are you still selling your smartphone for 500 dollars?
M Oh, hello. You mean the Universe A12, right?
W Yes. What color is it?
M It's sky blue. I used it with a case, so there are no scratches.
W Does the camera work well?
M Yeah. My brother broke the screen last year, but I fixed it at the repair center.
W Can I pick it up tonight?
M Sure.

[전화기가 울린다.]
여 안녕하세요, 웹사이트에서 당신의 게시글을 봤어요. 아직도 스마트폰을 500달러에 팔고 있으신가요?
남 오, 안녕하세요. Universe A12 말씀하시는 거죠, 그렇죠?
여 네. 무슨 색인가요?
남 하늘색이에요. 제가 케이스와 함께 사용해서 흠집은 없어요.
여 카메라는 잘 작동하나요?
남 네. 작년에 제 남동생이 화면을 깨트렸는데, 수리 센터에서 고쳤어요.
여 오늘 밤에 가지러 가도 될까요?
남 물론이죠.

해설 | 남자가 흠집은 없다고 했으므로 정답은 ③ '흠집이 약간 있다.'이다.
어휘 | mean [miːn] 동 가리켜 말하다, 의미하다 scratch [skrætʃ] 명 흠집 work [wəːrk] 동 작동하다; 일하다 fix [fiks] 동 고치다, 수리하다

12 목적 고르기

정답 ②

W Jay, what are you doing on the Internet?
M I'm looking for some clothes for summer.
W Why do you need them? It's winter now!
M I'm going to Australia next week. It's summer there.
W Oh, that's why. Are you going to order them online?
M Yes. I couldn't find them at the department store.
W Right. They must only have winter clothes these days.

여 Jay, 인터넷으로 뭘 하고 있니?
남 여름옷을 좀 찾아보고 있어.
여 그것들이 왜 필요해? 지금은 겨울이잖아!
남 나는 다음 주에 호주에 가. 거기는 여름이야.
여 오, 그래서구나. 온라인으로 주문할 거니?
남 응. 백화점에서는 찾을 수 없었어.
여 그렇구나. 요즘은 겨울옷만 있겠구나.

해설 | 여자가 인터넷으로 뭘 하고 있는지 묻자 남자가 여름옷을 좀 찾아보고 있다고 하며 온라인으로 그것들을 주문할 것이라고 했으므로 정답은 ② '여름옷을 주문하기 위해서'이다.
어휘 | look for 찾다 order [ɔ́ːrdər] 동 주문하다 department store 백화점

13 시간 정보 고르기

정답 ①

M Sarah, what time are we going to meet tomorrow?
W How about 6 p.m.? The concert begins at 7, so we should get ready before it starts.
M Ted said that we should practice our songs one more time before the concert.
W Then, how about 5? I think the rehearsal will take at least an hour.
M Okay. I'll tell the other band members.

남 Sarah, 우리 내일 몇 시에 만날까?
여 오후 6시는 어때? 공연이 7시에 시작하니까, 공연 시작 전에 준비해야 해.
남 Ted는 우리가 공연 전에 노래를 한 번 더 연습해야 한다고 했어.
여 그럼, 5시는 어때? 리허설은 적어도 한 시간은 걸릴 것 같아.
남 알겠어. 내가 다른 밴드 멤버들에게 말할게.

해설 | 여자가 5시는 어떠냐고 물어보자 남자가 알겠다고 했으므로 정답은 ① '5:00 p.m'이다.
어휘 | get ready 준비하다 at least 적어도; 최소한

14 관계 고르기

정답 ③

[Cellphone rings.]
W Hi. This is Wendy from ABC Bakery. I'm making the cake you ordered yesterday.
M Oh, is there something wrong?
W No. I just wanted to check two things. Do you have a moment?
M Sure.
W Do you want the writing on the cake to be dark blue or light blue?
M Light blue, please.
W I see. And what about the candles?
M Those should be bright pink.
W Got it. Thanks.

[휴대폰이 울린다.]
여 안녕하세요. ABC 베이커리의 Wendy입니다. 어제 주문하신 케이크를 만들고 있는데요.
남 오, 무슨 문제가 있나요?
여 아니요. 두 가지를 확인하고 싶어서요. 잠깐 시간 있으세요?
남 물론이죠.
여 케이크의 글씨를 진한 파란색으로 해드릴까요, 아니면 연한 파란색으로 해드릴까요?
남 연한 파란색으로 해 주세요.
여 그렇군요. 그리고 양초는요?
남 그것들은 밝은 분홍색이어야 해요.
여 알겠습니다. 감사해요.

해설 | 여자가 ABC 베이커리의 Wendy라고 하며 어제 주문 받은 케이크에 대해 물어보고 있는 것으로 보아 정답은 ③ '제빵사 — 손님'이다.
어휘 | candle [kǽndl] 명 양초 bright [brait] 형 밝은

15 부탁·요청한 일 고르기

정답 ⑤

W Dad, did you finish reading the newspaper?
M Yes, Mandy. Do you need it?
W Yeah, Dad. I need to find an article and write an essay about it.
M I put it in the recycling box in the kitchen.
W Okay. I'll get it.
M Mandy, will you also do me a favor?
W What is it?
M Could you bring me a glass of water from the kitchen?
W No problem.

여 아빠, 신문 다 읽으셨어요?
남 그래, Mandy. 그게 필요하니?
여 네, 아빠. 기사를 하나 찾아서 그것에 대한 글을 써야 해요.
남 부엌에 있는 재활용 상자에 넣었단다.
여 알겠어요. 제가 가져올게요.
남 Mandy, 내 부탁도 들어줄 수 있겠니?
여 뭔데요?
남 부엌에서 물 한 잔만 가져다줄 수 있니?
여 물론이죠.

해설 | 남자가 여자에게 부엌에서 물을 한 잔 가져다줄 수 있냐고 부탁했으므로 정답은 ⑤ '마실 것 가져오기'이다.
어휘 | article [áːrtikl] 명 기사 do a favor 부탁을 들어주다

16 이유 고르기

정답 ③

W Danny, are you ready to go to the gym?
M Honey, my gym clothes are missing.
W Didn't you leave them in the bathroom?
M No. They are not there.
W Oh, I think I washed them last night.
M I'll check the washing machine. *[Pause]* I found them!
W Are they dry?
M No. They are soaking wet. I think I'll stay home today.
W Are you sure?
M Yeah. I'll clean the house while you exercise.

여 Danny, 체육관에 갈 준비 됐어?
남 여보, 내 운동복이 없어졌어.
여 화장실에 두지 않았어?
남 아니. 거기에 없어.
여 오, 어젯밤에 내가 그것들을 빤 것 같아.
남 세탁기를 확인해 볼게. *[잠시 멈춤]* 찾았어!
여 말랐어?
남 아니. 흠뻑 젖었어. 나 오늘은 집에 있을까 봐.
여 확실해?
남 응. 당신이 운동하는 동안 내가 집 청소를 할게.

해설 | 남자는 운동복이 흠뻑 젖었다며 오늘은 집에 있겠다고 말했으므로 정답은 ③ '운동복이 마르지 않아서'이다.
어휘 | washing machine 명 세탁기 soaking [sóukiŋ] 형 흠뻑 젖은 while [hwail] 접 ~하는 동안 exercise [éksərsàiz] 동 운동하다

17 그림 상황에 적절한 대화 고르기

정답 ②

① M I'm sorry, but can I have some ketchup?
W Of course. I'll get it for you.
② M How should I remove this ketchup stain on the shirt?
W Try to wash it with vinegar.
③ M Do you have this coat in a small size?
W Let me check.
④ M Don't eat food on the sofa.
W Oh, I'm sorry.
⑤ M Can you open the window?
W Okay. We need some fresh air.

① 남 죄송하지만, 케첩 좀 주시겠어요?
여 물론이죠. 제가 가져다드릴게요.
② 남 셔츠에 있는 케첩 자국을 어떻게 제거하지?
여 식초로 닦아봐.
③ 남 이 코트 스몰 사이즈 있어요?
여 확인해 볼게요.
④ 남 소파에서 음식을 먹지 마.
여 오, 미안해.
⑤ 남 창문 좀 열어줄래?
여 그래. 우린 신선한 공기가 좀 필요해.

해설 | 남자가 셔츠의 케첩 자국을 어떻게 제거하는지 묻고 있고, 여자가 식초로 닦아보라고 하는 상황이므로 정답은 ②이다.
어휘 | stain [stein] 명 자국, 얼룩 vinegar [vínəgər] 명 식초

18 언급하지 않은 내용 고르기

정답 ④

W Hello, students. Today, we'll discuss Bran Castle, one of the most beautiful castles in the world. The castle is located in the middle of Romania. It was originally built in 1212 as a fortress. However, it became a popular tourist attraction after it was described as Count Dracula's Castle in the novel *Dracula*.

여 안녕하세요, 학생 여러분. 오늘은 세계에서 가장 아름다운 성 중 하나인 브란 성에 대해 이야기해보겠습니다. 이 성은 루마니아의 중앙에 위치해 있습니다. 이곳은 원래 1212년에 요새로 지어졌습니다. 하지만 이곳은 소설 <드라큘라>에서 드라큘라 백작의 성으로 묘사된 이후, 인기 있는 관광 명소가 되었습니다.

해설 | ① 이름(브란 성), ② 위치(루마니아의 중앙), ③ 건축 연도(1212년), ⑤ 용도(요새, 관광 명소)에 대해 언급했으므로 정답은 ④ '건축가'이다.
어휘 | tourist attraction 관광 명소 describe [diskráib] 동 묘사하다 count [kaunt] 명 백작 novel [nάvəl] 명 소설

19 적절한 응답 고르기

정답 ④

M Cara, do you have an extra pen? Mine has run out of ink.
W Sure. Here you go. What are you writing about in your notebook?
M I'm actually drawing. I do it all the time.
W Oh, I didn't know that. What do you like to draw?
M I mostly draw people.
W Can I see your picture?
M Sorry, it's not finished yet. But you can see it when I'm done.
W I'm excited to see it.

남 Cara, 여분의 펜이 있니? 내 것은 잉크가 다 떨어졌어.
여 물론이지. 여기 있어. 공책에 무엇에 대해 쓰고 있니?
남 난 사실 그림을 그리고 있어. 난 늘 그림을 그려.
여 오, 그건 몰랐네. 뭘 그리는 걸 좋아하니?
남 나는 대부분 사람을 그려.
여 네 그림을 볼 수 있을까?
남 미안, 아직 안 끝났어. 하지만 내가 다 끝내면 봐도 돼.
여 그걸 보는 게 기대돼.

해설 | 남자가 그림을 다 끝내면 봐도 된다고 했으므로 정답은 기대감을 나타내는 ④ 'I'm excited to see it.'이다.

선택지 해석

① 네 이야기를 읽어도 될까? ② 우와, 너는 정말 재능이 있구나! ③ 저 그림을 봐. ④ 그걸 보는 게 기대돼. ⑤ 응. 나는 그 포스터를 원해.

어휘 | run out of ~가 다 떨어지다 all the time 늘; 항상 mostly [móustli] 부 대부분

20 적절한 응답 고르기

정답 ③

M What are you reading, Sylvia?
W It's called *The Way Up*. It's a book about a famous mountain climber.
M That sounds interesting. Do you like it?
W Yeah. I find it fascinating because I also like to climb.
M Really? Where do you like to climb?
W I usually go to the mountains around the city, like Cheonggyesan.
M Wow, that's impressive. How often do you go?
W Almost every week.

남 뭘 읽고 있니, Sylvia?
여 이건 <The Way Up>이야. 유명한 등산가에 관한 책이야.
남 흥미롭게 들리네. 마음에 드니?
여 응. 나도 등산을 좋아하기 때문에 매우 흥미롭게 느껴져.
남 정말? 넌 어디를 등산하는 걸 좋아하니?
여 나는 보통 청계산 같은 도시 주변의 산에 가.
남 우와, 인상적이다. 얼마나 자주 가?
여 거의 매주.

해설 | 남자가 얼마나 자주 가는지 물었으므로 정답은 주기를 말하는 ③ 'Almost every week.'이다.

선택지 해석

① 나는 방금 그것에 대해 읽었어. ② 그녀는 정기적으로 등산을 가. ③ 거의 매주. ④ 나는 도서관에 가고 있어. ⑤ 그에 대해 들어보지 못했어.

어휘 | fascinating [fǽsəneitiŋ] 형 매우 흥미로운 impressive [imprésiv] 형 인상적인

17회 실전 모의고사

| 문제 pp.154-155

1	③	2	③	3	①	4	③	5	④	6	③	7	②	8	③	9	④	10	②
11	④	12	①	13	③	14	⑤	15	②	16	④	17	④	18	⑤	19	③	20	①

1 날씨 고르기

정답 ③

M Good morning. This is Jack Duncan with the global weather report. In Hong Kong, it'll be humid and cloudy. London will also be cloudy but chilly, so wear long sleeves for outdoor activities. Light showers are expected in Sydney today. The forecast for Mexico City is sunny and hot, but it'll cool down after it rains in the evening. Thank you.

남 안녕하십니까. 세계 일기 예보의 Jack Duncan입니다. 홍콩은 습하고 구름이 끼겠습니다. 런던 또한 구름이 끼겠으나, 쌀쌀할 예정이므로 야외 활동을 위해서는 긴소매를 입으십시오. 오늘 시드니에는 가벼운 소나기가 예상됩니다. 멕시코시티의 예보는 화창하고 더울 예정이나, 저녁에 비 온 뒤에 시원해지겠습니다. 감사합니다.

해설 | 시드니는 오늘 가벼운 소나기가 예상된다고 했으므로 정답은 ③이다.

어휘 | global [glóubəl] 형 세계적인 humid [hjú:mid] 형 습한 shower [ʃáuər] 명 소나기

2 알맞은 그림 고르기

정답 ③

M Welcome. Can I help you with anything?
W Yes. I need a new purse.
M Okay. The best-selling purses are these star- and square-shaped ones.
W I like the one that looks like a star. It is cute.
M Great. It will be 9 dollars.
W Hmm... I don't like the squirrel on it.
M We also have one without a squirrel.
W I love it! I'll take it.

남 어서 오세요. 무엇을 도와드릴까요?
여 네. 저는 새 지갑이 필요해요.
남 그러시군요. 가장 잘 팔리는 지갑들은 저 별과 사각형 모양들이에요.
여 저는 별처럼 보이는 것이 좋네요. 귀여워요.
남 잘됐네요. 9달러입니다.
여 흠... 겉에 있는 다람쥐가 맘에 들지 않아요.
남 다람쥐가 없는 것도 있어요.
여 맘에 들어요! 그걸로 살게요.

해설 | 여자는 별처럼 보이고 다람쥐가 없는 것을 사겠다고 했으므로 정답은 ③이다.

어휘 | purse [pə:rs] 명 지갑 without [wiðáut] 전 ~없이

3 심정 고르기

정답 ①

M What do you have there, Jane?
W I found these notebooks in a box.
M Oh, those are my old diaries.
W There are so many of them. Do you write in a diary every day?
M Yes. I've kept a diary for 10 years.
W Do you have the diaries from childhood?
M Yeah. It is fun to read them now.
W That's really cool.
M Thanks. I'm glad I kept them all.

남 거기에 뭐가 있어, Jane?
여 상자에서 이 공책들을 찾았어.
남 오, 그것들은 내 예전 일기장들이야.
여 정말 많이 있네. 너는 매일 일기를 쓰니?
남 응. 나는 10년 동안 일기를 써왔어.
여 어린 시절 일기장도 있니?
남 응. 지금 읽으면 재미있어.
여 정말 멋지다.
남 고마워. 전부 간직하고 있어서 다행이야.

해설 | 남자는 예전 일기장들을 전부 간직하고 있어서 다행이라고 했으므로 정답은 ① 'satisfied'이다.

선택지 해석

① 만족스러운 ② 미안한 ③ 초조한 ④ 지루한 ⑤ 실망한

어휘 | keep a diary 일기를 쓰다 childhood [tʃáildhùd] 명 어린 시절

4 한 일 고르기

정답 ③

M Penny, how was your weekend?
W It was really wonderful.
M What did you do?
W My mom and I went to the Belleville Car Museum.
M I've always wanted to go there.
W It was great. We saw the first car ever made.
M Awesome. How long did you stay?
W We were there for about three hours.
M Lucky you. I hope my parents take me soon.

남 Penny, 주말 어땠니?
여 정말 멋졌어.
남 뭘 했는데?
여 우리 엄마와 나는 벨빌 자동차 박물관에 갔어.
남 나도 항상 거기 가보고 싶었는데.
여 정말 좋았어. 우리는 최초로 만들어진 자동차도 봤어.
남 굉장하다. 얼마나 오래 있었어?
여 우리는 거기에 세 시간 정도 있었어.
남 부럽다. 우리 부모님도 조만간 데려가 주시면 좋겠어.

해설 | 여자가 주말에 엄마와 함께 자동차 박물관에 갔다고 했으므로 정답은 ③ '박물관 방문하기'이다.

어휘 | awesome [ɔ́:səm] 형 굉장한, 멋진

5 장소 고르기

정답 ④

M Hello. Can I help you find something?
W I'm looking for comfortable new sneakers.
M Okay. What will you use them for?
W I need them for running. My coach said the ones I have now are too old.
M The running shoes are in this section.
W Oh, I really like these here.
M Those are also my favorite. Do you want to try them on?
W Yes, please.

남 안녕하세요. 뭐 찾으시는 거라도 있으세요?
여 저는 편안한 새 운동화를 찾고 있어요.
남 알겠습니다. 무슨 용도로 쓰실 건가요?
여 달리기용으로 필요해요. 제 코치님이 제가 지금 가지고 있는 것은 너무 낡았다고 하셨거든요.
남 운동화는 이 구역에 있어요.
여 오, 여기 이게 정말 마음에 드네요.
남 그건 제가 가장 좋아하는 것들이기도 해요. 신어보시겠어요?
여 네, 그럴게요.

해설 | 여자가 편안한 새 운동화를 찾고 있다고 말했고, 남자가 운동화는 이 구역에 있다고 하는 것으로 보아 정답은 ④ '신발 가게'이다.

어휘 | comfortable [kʌ́mfərtəbl] 형 편안한 sneakers [sní:kərz] 명 운동화 try on 신어보다, 입어보다

6 의도 고르기

정답 ③

M Excuse me. Could you tell me who made the sculpture on the bookshelf?
W Oh, I did. Why do you ask?
M Wow. You're so talented! I really like your work. Could I buy it?
W Sorry, but it's not for sale.
M Well... Then, may I take a photograph of it?
W No problem. I'm happy that someone else loves my work.

남 실례합니다. 책장 위에 있는 저 조각을 누가 만들었는지 알려주실 수 있으신가요?
여 오, 제가요. 왜 물어보시죠?
남 우와. 정말 실력 있으시네요! 작품이 정말 마음에 들어요. 제가 살 수 있을까요?
여 죄송하지만, 판매하는 게 아니에요.
남 음... 그럼, 사진을 찍어도 될까요?
여 물론이죠. 다른 사람이 제 작품을 좋아하니 기쁘네요.

해설 | 남자가 사진을 찍어도 되냐고 묻자 여자가 물론이라고 했으므로 정답은 ③ '허락'이다.

어휘 | sculpture [skʌ́lptʃər] 명 조각 bookshelf [bùkʃélf] 명 책장 talented [tǽləntid] 형 실력이 있는, 재능 있는 for sale 판매하는, 팔려고 내놓은

7 특정 정보 고르기

정답 ②

W Jamie, do you have any plan for summer vacation?
M My parents and I will visit my sister.
W Where does she live?
M She lives in Seoul because of her university. What's your plan?
W I want to go on a trip, but I haven't decided where to go.
M How about Gangneung? You can see the ocean there.
W Well, I'd love to enjoy the sea, but it's too far.
M Oh, I see. Why don't you go to Geoje then?
W I think that would be nice. I'll find out how to get there.

여 Jamie, 여름 방학 계획이 있니?
남 우리 부모님이랑 나는 누나를 방문할 거야.
여 누나가 어디 사는데?
남 대학 때문에 서울에 살아. 네 계획은 뭐니?
여 여행을 가고 싶은데, 어디로 갈지 못 정했어.
남 강릉은 어때? 거기서는 바다를 볼 수 있잖아.
여 글쎄, 바다를 즐기고 싶긴 한데, 너무 멀어.
남 오, 그렇구나. 그럼 거제에 가는 건 어때?
여 그거 좋을 것 같다. 거기에 어떻게 갈지 찾아봐야겠어.

해설 | 남자가 거제에 가는 것을 제안하자 여자가 좋을 것 같다고 했으므로 정답은 ② '거제'이다.

어휘 | because of ~ 때문에 university [jù:nəvə́:rsəti] 명 대학 ocean [óuʃən] 명 바다

8 할 일 고르기

정답 ③

W Chase, is this your recipe book?
M Yeah. I'm really interested in cooking these days.
W What have you made so far?
M I've made an omelet, cream pasta, and cheese pizza.
W How did your omelet taste?
M It was salty. I need to practice more.
W Can you make one for me today?
M Sure. I should go to the grocery store to buy some ingredients now.

여 Chase, 이거 네 요리책이니?
남 응. 요즘 요리에 정말 관심이 많거든.
여 지금까지 뭘 만들어 봤니?
남 오믈렛, 크림 파스타, 그리고 치즈피자를 만들어봤어.
여 오믈렛 맛은 어땠어?
남 짰어. 나는 더 연습해야 해.
여 오늘 내게 하나 만들어줄래?
남 물론이지. 재료 좀 사려면 지금 식료품점에 가야겠다.

해설 | 남자가 오믈렛 재료를 사기 위해 지금 식료품점에 가야겠다고 했으므로 정답은 ③ '식료품점 가기'이다.

어휘 | these days 요즘 so far 지금까지 salty [sɔ́:lti] 형 짠 ingredient [ingrí:diənt] 명 재료

9 언급하지 않은 내용 고르기

정답 ④

M Mom, we learned about Dokdo at school today.
W What did you find out about it?
M There are a lot of squid and salmon near the island.
W Do people live there?
M Yes. I heard 14 people are living there.
W How's the weather?
M It's usually warm in both summer and winter.
W I hope we can visit it someday.
M Me too. We can get there by a ship from Ulleungdo.

남 엄마, 오늘 학교에서 독도에 대해 배웠어요.
여 독도에 대해 뭘 알았니?
남 독도 주변에는 오징어와 연어가 많아요.
여 거기에 사람들이 사니?
남 네. 14명이 사람들이 그곳에 살고 있다고 들었어요.
여 날씨는 어떠니?
남 보통 여름과 겨울 모두 따뜻해요.
여 언젠가 거길 방문할 수 있으면 좋겠구나.
남 저도요. 울릉도에서 배를 타고 거기 갈 수 있어요.

해설 | ① 서식 동물(오징어와 연어), ② 거주 인구(14명), ③ 날씨(여름과 겨울 모두 따뜻), ⑤ 교통수단(배)에 대해 언급했으므로 정답은 ④ '크기'이다.

어휘 | squid [skwid] 명 오징어 salmon [sǽmən] 명 연어

10 주제 고르기

정답 ②

W Good afternoon, everyone. Today, I'm going to tell you how to get along with your cat. First, you should pay attention to its body language to understand its emotions well. Next, you must respect what your cat likes and dislikes. You should also talk to your cat calmly. Lastly, play with it often so that you can bond with it.

여 안녕하세요, 여러분. 오늘, 저는 여러분의 고양이와 잘 지내는 방법에 대해 말씀드리겠습니다. 먼저, 고양이의 감정을 잘 이해하기 위해서는 고양이의 몸짓에 주의를 기울여야 합니다. 다음으로, 여러분의 고양이가 무엇을 좋아하고 싫어하는지를 존중해야 합니다. 또한 고양이에게는 차분하게 말을 해야 합니다. 마지막으로, 고양이와 유대감을 맺을 수 있도록 자주 놀아줘야 합니다.

해설 | 여자가 고양이와 잘 지내는 방법에 대해 말하고 있으므로 정답은 ② '고양이와의 교감법'이다.

어휘 | get along with ~와 잘 지내다 pay attention to ~에 주의를 기울이다 emotion [imóuʃən] 명 감정 respect [rispékt] 동 존중하다 bond [bɑːnd] 동 유대감을 맺다

11 일치하지 않는 내용 고르기

정답 ④

M Hello. I'd like to borrow a new book by Tom Simpson.
W Okay. What is the title?
M It's *The Way Home*.
W *[Typing sound]* Well, I see it's a romance novel.
M Yes. Can I borrow it from the library?
W I'm afraid we don't have it now.
M Oh, no! Wasn't it released last week?
W You're right. But it's already checked out.

남 안녕하세요. Tom Simpson의 신간을 빌리고 싶은데요.
여 알겠습니다. 제목이 뭔가요?
남 <The Way Home>이에요.
여 *[타자 치는 소리]* 음, 로맨스 소설인가 보네요.
남 네. 도서관에서 빌릴 수 있을까요?
여 현재로서는 그 책이 없는 것 같네요.
남 오, 이런! 지난주에 발매되지 않았나요?
여 맞아요. 하지만 그건 이미 대출 중이에요.

해설 | 여자가 책이 이미 대출 중이어서 현재 도서관에 없다고 했으므로 정답은 ④ '도서관에서 빌릴 수 있다.'이다.

어휘 | novel [nάvəl] 명 소설 release [rilíːs] 동 발매하다, 발표하다 check out 대출하다, 빌리다

12 목적 고르기

정답 ①

[Cellphone rings.]
M Hi, Minji. This is Fred.
W Hello, Fred. What's going on?
M I want to cook kimchijeon, but I don't know how to make it.
W Do you have the ingredients?
M I have kimchi and flour. How much kimchi do I need?
W I'll come to your house now, and I can show you how to cook it.
M Will you do that?
W Of course.

[휴대폰이 울린다.]
남 안녕, 민지야. 나 Fred야.
여 안녕, Fred. 무슨 일이야?
남 김치전을 요리하고 싶은데, 어떻게 만드는지를 몰라.
여 재료는 있니?
남 김치와 밀가루는 있어. 김치가 얼마나 필요하니?
여 내가 지금 너희 집으로 가서 어떻게 요리하는지 보여줄 수 있어.
남 그렇게 해줄래?
여 물론이지.

해설 | 남자가 김치전을 요리하고 싶은데, 어떻게 만드는지 모르겠다고 했으므로 정답은 ① '요리법을 물어보기 위해서'이다.

어휘 | ingredient [ingríːdiənt] 명 재료 flour [fláuər] 명 밀가루

13 금액 정보 고르기

정답 ③

W Hello, how can I help you?
M Hi, I'd like to buy a box of pears.
W There are 10 pears in a box, and it costs 30 dollars.
M Can I also get five apples?
W Sure. They are two dollars each. You want a box of pears and five apples, right?
M Yes. That's correct.
W The total comes to 40 dollars.
M Oh, hold on. Can I use this five-dollar discount coupon?
W Yes. Then, it's 35 dollars in total.
M Here's 50 dollars.

여 안녕하세요, 무엇을 도와드릴까요?
남 안녕하세요, 배 한 상자를 사고 싶어요.
여 한 상자에 배 10개가 들어있고, 가격은 30달러입니다.
남 사과도 5개 살 수 있을까요?
여 물론이죠. 개당 2달러입니다. 배 한 상자와 사과 5개 구매하시는 거죠, 맞죠?
남 네. 맞아요.
여 총 40달러 되겠습니다.
남 오, 잠시만요. 이 5달러 할인 쿠폰을 쓸 수 있을까요?
여 네. 그러면 총 35달러입니다.
남 여기 50달러 드릴게요.

해설 | 총 40달러에서 5달러 할인 쿠폰을 써서 총 35달러라고 했으므로 정답은 ③ '$ 35'이다.

어휘 | correct [kərékt] 형 맞는, 정확한, 올바른 hold on 잠시 기다리다

14 관계 고르기

정답 ⑤

[Telephone rings.]
W Hello?
M Hi. I'm delivering your pizza, but I can't find your house.
W Oh, yes! Where are you?
M I'm on the corner of Main Street and Baker Avenue right now. Is your building blue?
W No. It's red. It's right across from the blue building.
M Oh, okay. I see it now. I'll be there shortly.
W Thank you!

[전화기가 울린다.]
여 여보세요?
남 안녕하세요. 제가 피자를 배달 중인데, 손님 댁을 못 찾겠네요.
여 오, 그러시군요! 어디 계세요?
남 지금 메인 가와 베이커 가의 모퉁이에 있어요. 건물이 파란색인가요?
여 아니요. 붉은색이에요. 파란 건물 바로 맞은편이에요.
남 오, 알겠습니다. 이제 보이네요. 곧 갑니다.
여 감사합니다.

해설 | 남자가 여자의 피자를 배달하는 중이라고 하는 것으로 보아 정답은 ⑤ '배달원 — 손님'이다.

어휘 | deliver [dilívər] 동 배달하다 across [əkrɔ́:s] 전 ~의 맞은편에; ~을 건너서 shortly [ʃɔ́:rtli] 부 곧, 금방

15 부탁·요청한 일 고르기

정답 ②

W Dan, you are talented at gardening. Our garden looks amazing.
M Thanks, Mom. Do you remember planting this tree in the pot?
W Yes. It grew so big.
M It was just a small tree five years ago.
W Yeah. We need to move it to a bigger pot.
M That's a good idea.
W Do you have a bigger pot?
M Yes. But can you help me carry it?
W No problem.

여 Dan, 너는 원예에 재능이 있구나. 우리 정원이 멋져 보여.
남 고마워요, 엄마. 화분에 이 나무 심었던 것 기억하세요?
여 그래. 정말 많이 자랐네.
남 5년 전에는 참 작은 나무였잖아요.
여 그러게. 더 큰 화분에 옮겨야겠다.
남 좋은 생각이에요.
여 더 큰 화분이 있니?
남 네. 그런데 제가 그걸 옮기는 걸 도와줄 수 있으세요?
여 물론이지.

해설 | 남자가 여자에게 화분을 옮기는 것을 도와달라고 요청했으므로 정답은 ② '화분 옮기기'이다.

어휘 | gardening [gɑ́:rdniŋ] 명 원예 pot [pat] 명 화분

16 이유 고르기

정답 ④

M Hey, Marie. How did your weekend go?
W It was good, thanks. Did you get a haircut?
M No, I couldn't.
W Did you have other things to do on the weekend?
M No. I went to the hair salon on Sunday, but they said I can't get my hair cut.
W What happened?
M I didn't make a reservation before I went.
W Why don't you call the hair salon today?
M I will. I really need to get my hair cut.

남 안녕, Marie. 주말 어떻게 보냈니?
여 좋았어, 고마워. 너 이발했니?
남 아니, 못 했어.
여 주말에 다른 할 일이 있었던 거야?
남 아니. 일요일에 미용실에 갔는데, 이발이 안 된다고 했어.
여 무슨 일 있었어?
남 가기 전에 예약을 안 했거든.
여 오늘 미용실에 전화해보는 건 어때?
남 그러려고. 나 이발이 정말 필요해.

해설 | 남자가 미용실에 가기 전에 예약을 하지 않아서 이발할 수 없었다고 했으므로 정답은 ④ '예약을 하지 않아서'이다.

어휘 | get a haircut 이발하다, 머리를 자르다 hair salon 미용실 reservation [rèzərvéiʃən] 명 예약

17 그림 상황에 적절한 대화 고르기

정답 ④

① M Can you reach the top of the shelf?
W No. It is too high.
② M Please don't run on the stairs.
W Okay. I'll be careful.
③ M Is this your sweater?
W No. Mine has green stripes.
④ M Do you need any help?
W Yes. Please pass me the paintbrush.
⑤ M There is a lot of famous artwork in this museum.
W Yes. It's quite impressive.

① 남 너 선반 맨 위에 닿을 수 있니?
여 아니. 너무 높아.
② 남 계단에서는 뛰지 마세요.
여 알겠어요. 조심할게요.
③ 남 이거 네 스웨터니?
여 아니. 내 건 초록색 줄무늬가 있어.
④ 남 도와줄까?
여 응. 페인트 붓 좀 건네줘.
⑤ 남 여기 박물관에는 유명한 예술작품이 많아.
여 응. 꽤 인상적이야.

해설 | 여자가 사다리 위에 서 있고, 남자에게 떨어진 페인트 붓을 건네달라고 요청하고 있는 상황이므로 정답은 ④이다.

어휘 | reach [riːtʃ] 동 ~에 닿다 stair [stɛər] 명 계단 artwork [ártwərk] 명 예술작품 quite [kwait] 부 꽤 impressive [imprésiv] 형 인상적인

18 언급하지 않은 내용 고르기

정답 ⑤

W Jinsoo, what do you do in your international exchange club?
M When foreign students visit our school, I introduce Korean culture to them.
W Where are they from?
M They are usually from the United States.
W Sounds interesting! How many members do you have?
M There are 20 people including me.
W How can I join your club?
M Just send an email to the club president.
W Okay. What's the email address?
M I'll send it by text message.

여 진수야, 국제 교류 동아리에서 너는 무슨 일을 하니?
남 외국 학생들이 우리 학교를 방문하면, 내가 그들에게 한국 문화를 소개해줘.
여 어느 나라에서 오는데?
남 그들은 보통 미국인이야.
여 흥미로운걸! 동아리 회원은 몇 명이나 돼?
남 나를 포함해서 20명이 있어.
여 내가 어떻게 가입할 수 있을까?
남 동아리 회장에게 이메일을 보내봐.
여 알겠어. 이메일 주소가 어떻게 돼?
남 내가 문자로 보내줄게.

해설 | ① 활동 내용(한국 문화 소개), ② 교류 국가(미국), ③ 인원수(20명), ④ 가입 방법(동아리 회장에게 이메일 발송)에 대해 언급했으므로 정답은 ⑤ '지도 선생님'이다.

어휘 | international [ìntərnǽʃənəl] 형 국제의, 국제적인 exchange [ikstʃéindʒ] 명 교류, 교환 foreign [fɔ́ːrən] 형 외국의 including [inklúːdiŋ] 전 ~을 포함하여

19 적절한 응답 고르기

정답 ③

M Julia, did you see the snow outside?
W No, I didn't. How much did it snow?
M Quite a lot. I'm going to ride my sled later.
W That will be fun. But the weather is very cold.
M It's okay. I'll wear a warm coat and a scarf.
W Good idea. Where will you take your sled?
M I'll go to the hill.

남 Julia, 밖에 눈 온 거 봤어?
여 아니, 못 봤어. 눈이 얼마나 왔는데?
남 꽤 많이 왔어. 난 이따가 썰매를 타러 갈 거야.
여 재미있겠다. 그런데 날이 너무 추워.
남 괜찮아. 나는 따뜻한 코트를 입고 목도리를 할 거야.
여 좋은 생각이야. 썰매를 어디로 가지고 갈 거니?
남 언덕으로 갈 거야.

해설 | 여자가 어디에서 썰매를 탈 것인지 물었으므로 정답은 썰매 탈 장소를 언급하는 ③ 'I'll go to the hill.'이다.

선택지 해석

① 내일도 계속 눈이 올 거야. ② 난방을 켜줘. ③ 언덕으로 갈 거야. ④ 나는 스키 타는 것이 더 좋아. ⑤ 그들이 밖에서 기다리고 있어.

어휘 | sled [sled] 명 썰매 heat [hiːt] 명 난방; 열

20 적절한 응답 고르기

정답 ①

M Hey, Sophie. What did you do last night?
W I watched a documentary about the trash in the ocean.
M Oh, what did you learn?
W It harms the fish and animals so much, and the problem is getting worse.
M That's terrible. What can we do to clean up the ocean?
W We could pick up trash at the beach. What do you think?
M That's a good idea.

남 안녕, Sophie. 어젯밤에 뭐 했니?
여 해양 쓰레기에 대한 다큐멘터리를 시청했어.
남 오, 무엇을 배웠니?
여 물고기와 동물들에 매우 많은 해를 끼치고 있고, 문제가 점점 심각해지고 있대.
남 끔찍하다. 바다를 깨끗하게 하기 위해 우리가 뭘 할 수 있을까?
여 바닷가에서 쓰레기를 주울 수 있을 것 같아. 어떻게 생각해?
남 그거 좋은 생각이다.

해설 | 여자가 바닷가로 쓰레기 주우러 가는 것을 제안하며 어떻게 생각하는지 물었으므로 정답은 제안에 동의하는 ① 'That's a good idea.'이다.

선택지 해석

① 그거 좋은 생각이다. ② 쓰레기통을 못 찾겠어. ③ 수영복을 가져와. ④ 행사는 오후 5시에 시작해. ⑤ 수질 오염은 심각한 문제야.

어휘 | harm [haːrm] 동 해를 끼치다 terrible [térəbl] 형 끔찍한 trash can 쓰레기통 serious [síəriəs] 형 심각한

18회 실전 모의고사

| 문제 pp.162-163

1	②	2	③	3	⑤	4	③	5	③	6	②	7	④	8	③	9	④	10	④
11	⑤	12	②	13	②	14	③	15	④	16	③	17	③	18	⑤	19	⑤	20	④

1 날씨 고르기

정답 ②

W Good evening. Let's check the weather for next week. On Monday, it'll be cloudy all day long. Snow is expected from Tuesday. After it stops on Thursday, we will have clear, sunny skies. But it'll get colder from Friday. On the weekend, there will be strong winds, so wear warm clothes.

여 안녕하십니까. 다음 주의 날씨를 확인해 보겠습니다. 월요일에는 온종일 흐리겠습니다. 화요일부터는 눈이 올 것으로 예상됩니다. 목요일에 눈이 그치고 나면, 맑고 화창한 하늘을 보실 수 있을 겁니다. 하지만 금요일부터는 더 추워지겠습니다. 주말에는 강한 바람이 예상되니, 따뜻한 옷을 입으십시오.

해설 | 화요일에는 눈이 올 것으로 예상된다고 했으므로 정답은 ②이다.

어휘 | clothes [klouz] 명 옷 (cloth [klɔːθ] 명 천)

2 알맞은 그림 고르기

정답 ③

W Welcome to Luxury Clocks. May I help you?
M I'm looking for a digital alarm clock.
W Okay. How about this one? This square type is very popular.
M But it looks plain. I want something more special.
W Then, how about choosing from these with legs?
M Oh, I like the round one. I'll take it.
W Great.

여 Luxury Clocks에 오신 것을 환영합니다. 도와드릴까요?
남 저는 전자 알람 시계를 찾고 있어요.
여 그러시군요. 이것은 어떠신가요? 이 네모난 종류가 아주 인기 있어요.
남 하지만 평범해 보여요. 저는 더 특별한 무언가를 원해요.
여 그렇다면 다리가 있는 이것 중에서 고르시는 건 어떤가요?
남 오, 저는 둥근 것이 마음에 들어요. 그걸 살게요.
여 좋아요.

해설 | 남자가 전자시계 중에서 다리가 있고 둥근 것을 사겠다고 했으므로 정답은 ③이다.

어휘 | digital [dídʒətl] 형 전자의, 디지털의 plain [plein] 형 평범한; 분명한

3 심정 고르기

정답 ⑤

M Excuse me.
W Yes, sir. May I take your order?
M Yes. I'd like to have a steak with salad.
W How would you like your steak?
M Medium. Also, can I have lemon cake for dessert?
W I'm sorry, sir. We are out of lemon cake today.
M Oh, no! I was looking forward to having it.

남 실례합니다.
여 네, 고객님. 주문하시겠어요?
남 네. 저는 스테이크와 샐러드를 먹고 싶어요.
여 스테이크는 어떻게 해 드릴까요?
남 미디엄이요. 그리고, 후식으로 레몬 케이크를 먹을 수 있을까요?
여 죄송합니다, 고객님. 오늘은 레몬 케이크가 다 떨어졌어요.
남 오, 이런! 그걸 먹길 기대하고 있었거든요.

해설 | 레몬 케이크가 다 떨어졌다는 여자의 말에 대해 남자가 그걸 먹길 기대하고 있었다고 했으므로 정답은 ⑤ 'disappointed'이다.

선택지 해석

① 기쁜 ② 지루한 ③ 걱정스러운 ④ 신난 ⑤ 실망한

어휘 | look forward to ~을 기대하다

4 한 일 고르기

정답 ③

W Hi, Minho. How did you spend Hangul Day?
M I went to the Sejong Festival.
W I've never heard of it. What did you do there?
M I learned how Hangul was created. It was fun. What about you, Cathy?
W I wrote a short poem in Korean. Do you want to read it?
M I'd love to. *[Pause]* It's really good. Your Korean has gotten much better.
W Thank you for the compliment.

여 안녕, 민호야. 넌 한글날을 어떻게 보냈니?
남 나는 세종 축제에 갔어.
여 난 그것에 대해 들어본 적이 없어. 거기서 뭐 했니?
남 한글이 어떻게 창제되었는지 배웠어. 재미있었어. 너는 어땠니, Cathy?
여 나는 한국어로 짧은 시를 썼어. 읽어볼래?
남 좋지. *[잠시 멈춤]* 이거 정말 좋다. 너 한국어가 많이 늘었구나.
여 칭찬 고마워.

해설 | 여자가 한글날에 한국어로 짧은 시를 썼다고 했으므로 정답은 ③ '짧은 시 짓기'이다.

어휘 | spend [spend] 동 보내다, 쓰다 learn [ləːrn] 동 배우다 create [kriéit] 동 창제하다, 창조하다 poem [póuəm] 명 시
compliment [kámpləmənt] 명 칭찬

5 장소 고르기

정답 ③

W Wow, you played so well today.
M Thanks. It was a great game.
W Can you help me pick up these tennis balls?
M Sure. Let me pack up my racket first.
W Of course. Oh, do you want to get smoothies? I'll pay since you won the game.
M Thanks! That would be great.
W We should play again next week.
M Good idea. I'll reserve the court again.

여 우와, 너 오늘 정말 잘 치더라.
남 고마워. 좋은 경기였어.
여 이 테니스공들 줍는 거 도와줄래?
남 물론이지. 먼저 내 라켓을 좀 챙길게.
여 당연하지. 오, 스무디 마실래? 네가 이겼으니까 내가 살게.
남 고마워! 그러면 정말 좋지.
여 우리 다음 주에도 치자.
남 좋은 생각이야. 내가 코트를 또 예약할게.

해설 | 여자가 테니스공 줍는 것을 도와달라고 했고, 남자가 코트를 또 예약하겠다고 말하는 것으로 보아 정답은 ③ '테니스장'이다.

어휘 | pick up 줍다 pack up 챙기다 reserve [rizə́ːrv] 동 예약하다 court [kɔːrt] 명 (테니스, 배구 등의) 코트

6 의도 고르기

정답 ②

M Good morning, Mom.
W Good morning. You woke up early, Jack.
M Yeah. I wanted to drink some milk.
W Oh, can you get me some too?
M Sure. *[Cracking sound]* Oh, I dropped the glass. Sorry.
W It's okay. I'll clean up the broken pieces.
M Let me help you!
W I don't think it's a good idea. It's too dangerous.

남 좋은 아침이에요, 엄마.
여 좋은 아침이야. 일찍 일어났구나, Jack.
남 네. 우유를 마시고 싶었거든요.
여 오, 나도 좀 줄래?
남 물론이죠. *[깨지는 소리]* 오, 제가 유리잔을 떨어뜨렸어요. 죄송해요.
여 괜찮아. 내가 깨진 조각들을 치우마.
남 제가 도와드릴게요!
여 좋은 생각 같지 않구나. 너무 위험해.

해설 | 남자가 깨진 조각 치우는 것을 돕겠다고 하자, 여자가 좋은 생각 같지 않다고 했으므로 정답은 ② '거절'이다.

어휘 | drop [drap] 동 떨어뜨리다 clean up 치우다, 청소하다 dangerous [déindʒərəs] 형 위험한

7 특정 정보 고르기

정답 ④

W Sunho, are you okay? You look sleepy.
M I think I ate too much fried rice at lunch.
W Was it good?
M Yes, it was. I cooked it by myself.
W You should tell me your secret recipe!
M Chop vegetables and ham. Then, stir fry them with a cup of oil.
W Isn't that too much oil?
M No. It is the right amount.

여 선호야, 괜찮아? 너 졸려 보여.
남 점심에 볶음밥을 너무 많이 먹은 것 같아.
여 맛있었니?
남 응, 맛있었어. 내가 직접 만들었거든.
여 네 요리 비법을 알려줘!
남 채소와 햄을 다져. 그러고 나서, 기름 한 컵과 함께 센 불에 재빨리 볶아.
여 기름이 너무 많은 거 아니야?
남 아니야. 그게 맞는 양이야.

해설 | 남자는 점심에 볶음밥을 너무 많이 먹은 것 같다고 했으므로 정답은 ④ '볶음밥'이다.

어휘 | sleepy [slíːpi] 형 졸린 secret recipe 요리 비법 chop [tʃap] 동 다지다; 썰다 stir fry 센 불에 재빨리 볶다 amount [əmáunt] 명 양

8 할 일 고르기

정답 ③

W Honey, what are you searching for in that drawer?
M I'm looking for medicine.
W Are you feeling sick?
M I have an upset stomach. I think I ate dinner too quickly.
W Oh, we don't have any medicine for that.
M Then, what should I do?
W Why don't you take a walk for a while? It will help.
M You're right. I'll walk around the neighborhood.

여 여보, 서랍에서 뭘 찾는 중이야?
남 약을 찾고 있어.
여 어디 아파?
남 배탈이 났어. 저녁을 너무 빨리 먹었나 봐.
여 오, 우리 그것에 듣는 약은 없는데.
남 그럼, 어떡하지?
여 잠깐 산책을 하는 게 어때? 도움이 될 거야.
남 당신 말이 맞아. 동네 주변을 걸어야겠어.

해설 | 여자가 산책하는 것을 제안하자 남자가 동의하며 동네 주변을 걸어야겠다고 했으므로 정답은 ③ '동네 산책하기'이다.
어휘 | search [səːrtʃ] 동 찾다 medicine [médisn] 명 약 upset stomach 배탈 neighborhood [néibərhùd] 명 동네, 인근, 이웃

9 언급하지 않은 내용 고르기

정답 ④

M Ms. Evans, when can we go vote for our school president?
W The voting time is different for each grade. Freshmen vote before noon, and the other students go after lunch.
M Alright. Then, I should vote after lunch.
W Oh, remember to take your student card.
M What else do I have to do?
W Please wait in line before voting.
M Okay, I will.
W Also, don't forget to fold the voting paper.

남 Evans 선생님, 저희는 언제 학생회장 선거를 하러 갈 수 있나요?
여 투표 시간이 학년별로 다르단다. 1학년은 점심 전에 하고, 다른 학년 학생들은 점심 후란다.
남 그렇군요. 그럼, 저는 점심 후에 투표해야겠네요.
여 오, 학생증 가져가는 것을 기억하렴.
남 그 외에는 또 뭘 해야 하나요?
여 투표하기 전에 줄 서서 기다리렴.
남 네, 그럴게요.
여 그리고, 투표용지 접는 것도 잊지 말렴.

해설 | ① 학년별 투표 시간을 따르기, ② 학생증 지참하기, ③ 투표 전 줄 서서 기다리기, ⑤ 투표용지 접기를 언급했으므로 정답은 ④ '투표 중 사진 찍지 않기'이다.
어휘 | vote [vout] 동 투표하다 different [dífərənt] 형 다른 freshman [fréʃmən] 명 1학년, 신입생 fold [fould] 동 접다

10 주제 고르기

정답 ④

M We're back from the commercial break. Today, we heard useful tips from our guest, Mr. Smith. Let's sum up the main points. First, save the same amount of money regularly. Then, keep a record of your spending. Don't forget to write down your purchases each day. If you follow these tips, you will save money.

남 광고 듣고 왔습니다. 오늘 저희는 초대 손님인 Smith씨께 유용한 조언을 들었습니다. 요점을 요약해 봅시다. 먼저, 같은 액수의 돈을 규칙적으로 저축하세요. 그리고 나서, 여러분의 소비를 기록해 두세요. 매일 구매 내역을 기록하는 것을 잊지 마세요. 만약 이 조언들을 따른다면, 여러분은 돈을 아끼실 것입니다.

해설 | 남자가 돈을 아낄 수 있는 방법에 대해 말하고 있으므로 정답은 ④ '돈을 절약하는 방법'이다.
어휘 | commercial [kəmə́ːrʃəl] 명 광고 형 상업의 sum up 요약하다 keep a record 기록해 두다 purchase [pə́ːrtʃəs] 명 구매 동 구매하다

11 일치하지 않는 내용 고르기

정답 ⑤

W Okay, class. Tomorrow is our sports day. It'll be from 9 a.m. to 3 p.m. We'll have several fun games. Group jump rope and basketball will be played in the morning. After lunch, we'll have soccer games and relay race. Please wear gym clothes and comfortable sneakers. Also, make sure to bring your lunch.

여 좋습니다, 학생 여러분. 내일은 운동회 날입니다. 운동회는 오전 9시부터 오후 3시까지입니다. 여러 재미있는 게임이 진행될 것입니다. 단체 줄넘기와 농구는 아침에 경기가 있을 것입니다. 점심 이후에는, 축구와 이어달리기 경기가 있겠습니다. 체육복을 입고 편안한 운동화를 신어주십시오. 그리고, 꼭 점심 도시락을 가지고 와주십시오.

해설 | 여자가 꼭 점심 도시락을 가지고 와 달라했으므로 정답은 ⑤ '점심 식사로 학교 급식이 제공된다.'이다.
어휘 | jump rope 줄넘기 relay race 이어달리기, 계주 wear [wεər] 동 입다 comfortable [kʌ́mfərtəbl] 형 편안한

12 목적 고르기

정답 ②

[Telephone rings.]
M Hello. This is Grand Ocean Hotel. What can I do for you?
W Hi. I'd like to make a reservation for March 27th.
M Sure. How long will you stay?
W Two nights.
M Alright. What type of room do you want?
W I want a double room with an ocean view. I'll stay with my husband.
M Good. It'll be 300 dollars including breakfast.
W Thank you.

[전화기가 울린다.]
남 안녕하세요. 그랜드 오션 호텔입니다. 무엇을 도와드릴까요?
여 안녕하세요. 3월 27일에 예약하고 싶어서요.
남 알겠습니다. 얼마나 묵으실 예정인가요?
여 이틀 밤이요.
남 알겠습니다. 어떤 종류의 방을 원하시나요?
여 저는 바다가 보이는 더블룸을 원해요. 남편과 함께 묵을 거예요.
남 좋습니다. 조식을 포함해서 300달러 되겠습니다.
여 감사합니다.

해설 | 여자가 호텔 예약을 하고 싶다고 했으므로 정답은 ② '숙소를 예약하기 위해서'이다.
어휘 | reservation [rèzərvéiʃən] 명 예약 including [inklúːdiŋ] 전 ~을 포함하여

13 시간 정보 고르기

정답 ②

W Alex, did you hear that Tom's Toy Store will sell limited-edition Santa Claus dolls tomorrow?
M No. Maybe I should buy my nephew one for Christmas.
W I want to get one too. Let's go to the store tomorrow.
M Okay. When does the store open?
W It opens at 9:30.
M Then, let's meet there at its opening time.
W There will be lots of people since these dolls are popular. Can we meet earlier?
M Sure. How about 8:30?
W Great. See you then.

여 Alex, 내일 Tom's Toy Store에서 한정판 산타클로스 인형을 팔 예정이라는 거 들었니?
남 아니. 크리스마스 선물로 조카에게 하나 사주는 것도 좋겠다.
여 나도 하나 가지고 싶어. 내일 가게에 가자.
남 그래. 가게가 언제 여니?
여 9시 30분에 열어.
남 그럼, 개점 시간에 거기서 만나자.
여 이 인형들은 인기가 있어서 사람들이 많을 거야. 더 일찍 만날 수 있을까?
남 물론이지. 8시 30분은 어때?
여 좋아. 그때 보자.

해설 | 여자가 인형이 인기가 있으니 개점 시간보다 일찍 만날 수 있는지 물었고, 8시 30분에 보자는 남자의 제안에 그때 보자고 했으므로 정답은 ② '8:30 a.m.'이다.

어휘 | limited-edition 명 한정판 nephew [néfjuː] 명 조카

14 관계 고르기

정답 ③

W Welcome to Peace Photo Studio.
M Hello. I'm interested in getting a family portrait.
W I can help you with that.
M Would it be possible to take the pictures by the river?
W I charge 100 dollars for photos in the studio or 200 dollars in another location.
M It would be better to have the photo shoot in your studio.
W Do you want to schedule a session for Saturday?
M Yes. How about 10 a.m.?
W Perfect.

여 피스 사진관에 오신 것을 환영합니다.
남 안녕하세요. 가족사진 촬영에 관심이 있어요.
여 제가 도와드릴 수 있겠군요.
남 강가에서 사진을 찍는 게 가능할까요?
여 사진관에서 촬영하는 사진은 100달러를 받고, 다른 장소에서는 200달러를 받고 있어요.
남 사진관에서 사진 촬영을 하는 게 낫겠네요.
여 토요일에 시간을 잡아드릴까요?
남 네. 오전 10시는 어떤가요?
여 완벽합니다.

해설 | 남자가 여자에게 가족사진을 찍는 것에 대해 문의하고 있는 것으로 보아 정답은 ③ '사진작가 — 고객'이다.

어휘 | portrait [pɔ́ːrtrit] 명 (얼굴) 사진, 초상화 charge [tʃaːrdʒ] 동 값을 받다; 청구하다 schedule [skédʒuːl] 동 시간을 잡다

15 부탁·요청한 일 고르기

정답 ④

W Jaemin, I got a call from your friend Woohyun.
M Oh, what did he say, Mom?
W He wants to go to a movie with you tonight.
M I'd love to. Is it okay?
W Sure. Then, will you walk the dog after you come back home?
M Well... I may be late. Can you walk the dog for me?
W Alright.

여 재민아, 네 친구 우현이에게서 전화가 왔었단다.
남 오, 그가 뭐라고 하던가요, 엄마?
여 오늘 밤에 너랑 영화를 보러 가고 싶어 해.
남 저도 그러고 싶어요. 그래도 돼요?
여 물론이지. 그럼, 집에 온 후에 개를 산책시켜주겠니?
남 음... 늦을지도 몰라요. 저 대신 개를 산책시켜주실 수 있으세요?
여 알겠어.

해설 | 남자가 자기 대신 개를 산책시켜 달라고 부탁했으므로 정답은 ④ '개 산책시키기'이다.

어휘 | walk the dog 개를 산책시키다

16 이유 고르기

정답 ③

M Tina, I have good news for you.
W What's that, Mr. Parker?
M You will be the captain of our volleyball club this year.
W Really? I can't believe it.
M You were chosen as the captain by every club member.
W Do you know why they recommended me?
M They said you have a strong sense of responsibility.
W I'll do my best to lead our team well.

남 Tina, 네게 좋은 소식이 있단다.
여 그게 뭔가요, Parker 선생님?
남 네가 올해 배구 동아리의 주장이 될 거란다.
여 정말요? 믿을 수가 없어요.
남 모든 부원이 널 주장으로 원했어.
여 왜 저를 추천했는지 아시나요?
남 그들은 네가 강한 책임감을 가지고 있다고 했단다.
여 저희 팀을 잘 이끌 수 있도록 최선을 다할게요.

해설 | 배구부원들이 여자가 강한 책임감을 가지고 있어서 주장으로 추천했다고 했으므로 정답은 ③ '책임감이 강해서'이다.

어휘 | recommend [rèkəménd] 통 추천하다 responsibility [rispɑ̀nsəbíləti] 명 책임감 lead [li:d] 통 이끌다

17 그림 상황에 적절한 대화 고르기

정답 ③

① W Thanks for fixing my guitar.
M No problem.
② W This dress is too dirty.
M Why don't you wash it?
③ W What tools do we need to buy?
M We need a hammer and nails.
④ W Where should we hang this painting?
M Let's put it in the bedroom.
⑤ W Do you want some chocolate?
M No, thank you. I'm good.

① 여 내 기타를 고쳐줘서 고마워.
남 천만에.
② 여 이 원피스 너무 더럽네.
남 세탁하는 게 어때?
③ 여 우리 무슨 도구를 사야 해?
남 망치와 못이 필요해.
④ 여 이 그림을 어디에 걸어야 할까?
남 침실에 두자.
⑤ 여 초콜릿 좀 먹을래?
남 아니, 괜찮아. 난 됐어.

해설 | 남자와 여자가 상점에서 망치와 못을 찾고 있는 상황이므로 정답은 ③이다.

어휘 | fix [fiks] 통 고치다 tool [tu:l] 명 도구 hammer [hǽmər] 명 망치 nail [neil] 명 못

18 언급하지 않은 내용 고르기

정답 ⑤

W Jeremy, have you heard about the Austin Flea Market?
M Yes, I have. It opens tomorrow, right?
W Yes, it does.
M Where is it going to be held?
W It will be held on Pine Street.
M That's close to my house! I can walk there.
W Oh, I didn't know that.
M Do you know what they sell at the flea market?
W There's going to be a lot of used clothes, shoes, and toys.
M I'd love to look around.

여 Jeremy, 너 Austin Flea Market에 대해 들어본 적 있어?
남 응, 들어봤어. 내일 열리잖아, 그렇지?
여 응, 맞아.
남 어디에서 열려?
여 파인 가에서 열릴 거야.
남 우리 집에서 가깝잖아! 거기는 걸어서 갈 수 있어.
여 오, 그건 몰랐네.
남 벼룩 시장에서 뭘 파는지 알고 있니?
여 많은 중고 의류, 신발, 그리고 장난감들이 있을 거야.
남 꼭 둘러보고 싶네.

해설 | ① 명칭(Austin Flea Market), ② 날짜(내일), ③ 장소(파인 가), ④ 판매 물품(중고 의류, 신발, 장난감)에 대해 언급했으므로 정답은 ⑤ '주차 공간'이다.

어휘 | flea market 벼룩 시장 hold [hould] 통 열다, 개최하다 used [ju:st] 형 중고의, 사용된; 익숙한 look around (주위를) 둘러보다; 돌아다니다

19 적절한 응답 고르기

정답 ⑤

W Do you like these flowers, Honey?
M Yes. Those are pretty.
W They'll look nice in the middle of the dinner table.
M I agree. Let's buy them. Our guests will love them.
W Okay. What else do we need to do before dinner tonight?
M We need to pick up some groceries.
W Alright, we can go to the store now.
M What time are our friends coming over?
W They're coming at 6 p.m.

여 이 꽃들 마음에 들어, 여보?
남 응. 예쁘네.
여 식탁 가운데 있으면 근사해 보일 거야.
남 나도 그렇게 생각해. 그거 사자. 손님들이 좋아할 거야.
여 좋아. 오늘 밤 저녁 식사 전에 또 뭘 해야 하지?
남 식료품을 좀 사야 해.
여 좋아, 지금 가게에 가면 되겠다.
남 우리 친구들은 몇 시에 오지?
여 그들은 오후 6시에 올 거야.

해설 | 남자가 친구들이 몇 시에 오는지 묻고 있으므로 정답은 도착 시간을 언급하는 ⑤ 'They're coming at 6 p.m.'이다.

선택지 해석

① 현금으로 계산할게. ② 그건 일찍 끝났어. ③ 그들 중 네 명이 오늘 밤에 올 거야. ④ 내가 파스타를 만들 거야. ⑤ 그들은 오후 6시에 올 거야.

어휘 | middle [mídl] 명 가운데, 중간 grocery [gróusəri] 명 식료품

20 적절한 응답 고르기

정답 ④

W What are you doing, Sam?
M I'm baking cookies.
W They look tasty. What kind of cookies are you making?
M I'm baking coconut cookies. They're my favorite dessert.
W I like them the most too. When will they be finished?
M I need to bake them for 20 minutes. Do you want to try one when they are done?
W I would love to.

여 뭐 하고 있니, Sam?
남 쿠키를 굽고 있어.
여 맛있어 보인다. 어떤 종류의 쿠키를 만들고 있는 거야?
남 코코넛 쿠키를 굽고 있어. 내가 가장 좋아하는 디저트야.
여 나도 그것들을 가장 좋아해. 언제 완성될까?
남 20분 동안 구워야 해. 다 되면 하나 시식해볼래?
여 좋아.

해설 | 남자가 쿠키가 다 구워지면 시식해보겠는지 의사를 묻고 있으므로 정답은 긍정적 의사를 나타내는 ④ 'I would love to.'이다.

선택지 해석

① 두 시간 걸려. ② 제과점에 가자. ③ 내가 오븐을 쓰고 있어. ④ 좋아. ⑤ 케이크가 완성됐어.

어휘 | bake [beik] 동 굽다 finish [fíniʃ] 동 완성하다, 끝내다

19회 실전 모의고사

| 문제 pp.170-171

1	③	2	①	3	①	4	⑤	5	①	6	⑤	7	③	8	⑤	9	④	10	③
11	⑤	12	①	13	③	14	①	15	②	16	⑤	17	③	18	④	19	③	20	④

1 날씨 고르기

정답 ③

M Good evening. This is the weather report for tomorrow. There is a high chance of rain in Seoul. There will be a few showers in Andong, but they will stop in the afternoon. In Gimhae, strong wind is expected. Severe thunderstorms with frequent lightning are forecasted in Damyang, so please stay inside for your own safety. Thank you very much.

남 안녕하십니까. 내일의 일기 예보입니다. 서울에는 비가 올 가능성이 높습니다. 안동에는 소나기가 몇 차례 내릴 예정이나, 오후에는 그칠 예정입니다. 김해에는 강풍이 예상됩니다. 담양에는 잦은 번개를 동반한 심한 뇌우가 예측되니, 안전을 위해 실내에 머무르시길 바랍니다. 정말 감사합니다.

해설 | 김해에서는 강풍이 예상된다고 했으므로 정답은 ③이다.

어휘 | shower [ʃáuər] 명 소나기 severe [siviər] 형 심한, 심각한 thunderstorm [θʌndərstɔ̀ːrm] 명 뇌우, 폭풍우 frequent [fríːkwənt] 형 잦은 forecast [fɔ́rkæst] 동 예측하다, 예보하다 safety [séifti] 명 안전

2 알맞은 그림 고르기

정답 ①

M Honey, I want to decorate our bedroom with wall stickers.
W I like that idea. Let's put up the biggest one first.
M Okay. The deer sticker is the biggest.
W How about putting it on the left?
M Good. What should we do about this tree sticker?
W I don't think it looks good there. What else do we have?
M We also have a moon sticker.
W Then, put it above the deer on the right side.

남 여보, 나 우리 침실을 벽면 스티커로 꾸미고 싶어.
여 그 생각 마음에 든다. 가장 큰 것부터 붙이자.
남 그래. 사슴 스티커가 가장 크네.
여 그걸 왼쪽에 붙이는 게 어때?
남 좋아. 이 나무 스티커는 어떻게 하지?
여 그건 거기에 잘 안 어울리는 것 같아. 우리 또 뭐가 있어?
남 달 스티커도 있어.
여 그럼, 그건 사슴 위 오른쪽에 붙이자.

해설 | 여자가 가장 큰 사슴 스티커를 왼쪽에 붙이고, 달 스티커는 사슴 위 오른쪽에 붙이자고 했으므로 정답은 ①이다.

어휘 | decorate [dékərèit] 동 꾸미다, 장식하다 deer [diər] 명 사슴

3 심정 고르기

정답 ①

M It is your turn to bungee jump next. Are you ready?
W Oh, no. Please give me a minute.
M Are you okay?
W Well, I have butterflies in my stomach.
M Do you want to give up your turn?
W No. I expected this.
M Then, calm down and take a deep breath.
W Okay, I will.
M Good. Just relax. It will be fun.
W I know. But I can still feel my heart beating.

남 다음 번지 점프하실 차례에요. 준비되셨나요?
여 오, 아니요. 1분만 주세요.
남 괜찮으세요?
여 음, 속이 울렁거려요.
남 차례를 포기하시겠어요?
여 아니요. 이럴 줄 알았어요.
남 그럼, 침착하시고 숨을 깊게 들이쉬세요.
여 네, 그럴게요.
남 좋아요. 긴장을 푸세요. 재미있을 거예요.
여 알아요. 하지만 여전히 심장이 뛰는 게 느껴져요.

해설 | 여자가 속이 울렁거린다고 하며 심장이 뛰는 게 느껴진다고 했으므로 정답은 ① 'nervous'이다.

선택지 해석

① 긴장한 ② 자랑스러운 ③ 짜증이 난 ④ 실망한 ⑤ 고마운

어휘 | have butterflies in one's stomach 속이 울렁거리다, 두근거리다 deep [diːp] 형 깊은 breath [breθ] 명 숨

4 한 일 고르기

정답 ⑤

W Tom, did you have fun at Halloween?
M Yes. I joined a parade in a ghost costume.
W I also wanted to join, but I couldn't.
M Then, what did you do on Halloween?
W I made jack-o'-lanterns.
M Do you mean the pumpkin decoration with a scary face?
W Yeah. It's one of the most popular symbols of Halloween.
M Nice! I'll make jack-o'-lanterns next year too.

여 Tom, 핼러윈 때 재미있었니?
남 응. 난 유령 분장을 하고 퍼레이드에 참가했어.
여 나도 참가하고 싶었는데, 못했어.
남 그럼, 핼러윈에 뭘 했니?
여 잭오랜턴을 만들었어.
남 무서운 얼굴을 한 호박 장식을 말하는 거야?
여 응. 그건 핼러윈의 가장 유명한 상징 중 하나잖아.
남 좋네! 내년에는 나도 잭오랜턴을 만들어야겠어.

해설 | 여자가 핼러윈에 무서운 얼굴을 한 호박 장식인 잭오랜턴을 만들었다고 했으므로 정답은 ⑤ '장식물 만들기'이다.

어휘 | join [dʒɔin] 동 참가하다 pumpkin [pʌ́mpkin] 명 호박 decoration [dèkəréiʃən] 명 장식 symbol [símbəl] 명 상징

5 장소 고르기

정답 ①

W Hi. How can I help you?
M I need some flowers for my sister's graduation ceremony.
W I see. How about some white roses?
M Those are beautiful. But I'd like a variety of flowers.
W Then, maybe you'd like an arrangement with roses, tulips, and carnations.
M That would be perfect.
W Do you want to add a message?
M Yes. Write a note that says, "Congratulations, Tina!"

여 안녕하세요. 무엇을 도와드릴까요?
남 저는 제 여동생의 졸업식을 위해 꽃이 좀 필요해요.
여 그러시군요. 하얀 장미는 어떠신가요?
남 아름답네요. 그런데 꽃이 다양하면 좋겠어요.
여 그럼 아마 장미, 튤립, 그리고 카네이션의 배합을 좋아하실 것 같아요.
남 완벽할 것 같네요.
여 메시지를 추가하시겠어요?
남 네. '축하해, Tina!'라고 메모를 적어주세요.

해설 | 여동생의 졸업식을 위해 꽃이 필요하다고 했고, 다양한 꽃들을 원한다고 하는 것으로 보아 정답은 ① '꽃집'이다.

어휘 | graduation [grædʒuéiʃən] 명 졸업 variety [vəráiəti] 명 다양, 여러 종류 arrangement [əréindʒmənt] 명 배합

6 의도 고르기

정답 ⑤

M Why are you so late, Jackie? We started eating dinner already.
W I'm sorry, Dad. Soccer practice lasted until 6.
M Really? Why?
W Our coach made us do extra kicking and running drills.
M Is he worried about the big game on Saturday?
W Yeah. He wants us to be ready. But I'm so tired!
M I understand. But your effort will be worth it.

남 왜 이렇게 늦었니, Jackie? 우리는 이미 저녁을 먹기 시작했단다.
여 죄송해요, 아빠. 축구 연습이 6시까지 계속되었어요.
남 정말? 왜?
여 코치님이 추가적인 발차기와 달리기 훈련을 하게 했어요.
남 토요일에 있을 큰 경기에 대해 걱정하시니?
여 네. 그는 저희가 준비되어 있길 원하세요. 하지만 너무 피곤해요!
남 이해한단다. 그래도 너희의 노력은 가치가 있을 거야.

해설 | 여자가 추가적인 훈련 때문에 피곤하다는 말을 하자 남자는 노력은 가치가 있을 것이라는 말을 했으므로 정답은 ⑤ '위로'이다.

어휘 | last [læst] 동 계속하다, 지속하다 extra [ékstrə] 형 추가의 drill [dril] 명 훈련 effort [éfərt] 명 노력 worth [wəːrθ] 형 ~의 가치가 있는

7 특정 정보 고르기

정답 ③

M Hello, what can I do for you?
W I heard the community center has many interesting programs.
M Do you want to register for a class?
W Yes. I need to exercise for my health.
M We have many kinds of sports classes. You can choose from yoga, table tennis, and boxing.
W I'd love to learn how to play table tennis. Can I sign up now?
M Sure. Please fill out this form.
W Alright.

남 안녕하세요, 무엇을 도와드릴까요?
여 주민센터에 흥미로운 프로그램이 많다고 들었어요.
남 수업에 등록하고 싶으신가요?
여 네. 전 건강을 위해 운동을 해야 해요.
남 저희는 많은 종류의 스포츠 수업이 있어요. 요가, 탁구와 복싱 중에 고르실 수 있어요.
여 탁구치는 법을 배워보고 싶어요. 지금 등록할 수 있나요?
남 물론이죠. 이 양식을 채워주세요.
여 알겠습니다.

해설 | 여자가 탁구치는 법을 배워보고 싶다고 했으므로 정답은 ③ 'table tennis'이다.

선택지 해석

① 요가 ② 재즈 댄스 ③ 탁구 ④ 발레 ⑤ 복싱

어휘 | register [rédʒistər] 동 등록하다 table tennis 탁구 sign up 등록하다 fill out 채우다

8 할 일 고르기

정답 ⑤

M Honey, look at the sunset on the lake.
W Wow, it's so wonderful. I'm glad we came here.
M By the way, what are we going to do now?
W Are you feeling hungry?
M A little bit. How about making dinner with the fish that we caught?
W Sounds great. And let's go for a walk along the lake after dinner.
M Alright. Then, I'll take the fish out of the cooler.

남 여보, 호수 위에 일몰 좀 봐.
여 우와, 정말 멋지다. 여기 오길 잘했어.
남 그나저나, 우리 이제 뭐 해?
여 당신 배고파?
남 약간. 우리가 잡은 생선으로 저녁 식사를 차리는 게 어때?
여 좋아. 그리고 저녁 식사 후에는 호수를 따라서 산책하자.
남 그래. 그럼, 아이스박스에서 생선을 꺼낼게.

해설 | 남자가 자신들이 잡은 생선으로 저녁을 만들자고 한 후 아이스박스에서 생선을 꺼내겠다고 했으므로 정답은 ⑤ '생선 꺼내오기'이다.

어휘 | sunset [sʌ́nset] 명 일몰 along [əlɔ́:ŋ] 전 ~을 따라서

9 언급하지 않은 내용 고르기

정답 ④

W Hello, visitors. Our park has a Lost and Found Center. It is located near the park entrance. So please come to check if you lose an item. The center is open from 10 a.m. to 5 p.m. You can also call the center at 555-6012. We usually keep items for a week and then send them to the police. Thank you.

여 안녕하세요, 방문객 여러분. 저희 공원에는 분실물 센터가 있습니다. 그것은 공원 입구 근처에 위치해 있습니다. 그러니 만약 물건을 잃어버리셨다면 확인하러 와 주시기 바랍니다. 센터는 오전 10시부터 오후 5시까지 운영합니다. 555-6012로 센터에 전화주셔도 됩니다. 저희는 보통 물건을 일주일 동안 보관한 후 경찰서로 보냅니다. 감사합니다.

해설 | ① 위치(공원 입구 근처), ② 운영 시간(오전 10시부터 오후 5시까지), ③ 전화번호(555-6012), ⑤ 운영 방침(일주일 동안 보관한 후 경찰서로 보냄)에 대해 언급했으므로 정답은 ④ '보관물 현황'이다.

어휘 | item [áitəm] 명 물건, 물품 send [send] 동 보내다

10 주제 고르기

정답 ③

M Good morning. Did you all sleep well? If you didn't, please pay attention. I'll tell you a few things you should avoid before going to bed. First, don't go online right before bed. Using the Internet keeps you from sleeping. Second, avoid drinking water or coffee at night. Lastly, don't take a nap for more than 30 minutes.

남 좋은 아침입니다. 모두 잘 주무셨나요? 그렇지 않으셨다면, 집중해 주세요. 잠자리에 들기 전에 피해야 할 몇 가지를 말씀드리겠습니다. 먼저, 자러 가기 직전에 인터넷에 접속하지 마세요. 인터넷을 사용하는 것은 여러분을 잠들지 못하게 합니다. 두 번째로, 밤에 물이나 커피 마시는 것을 피하세요. 마지막으로, 30분 이상 낮잠을 자지 마세요.

해설 | 남자가 잠자리에 들기 전에 피해야 할 몇 가지를 말하고 있으므로 정답은 ③ '올바른 수면 습관'이다.

어휘 | avoid [əvɔ́id] 동 피하다 go online 인터넷에 접속하다 nap [næp] 명 낮잠

11 일치하지 않는 내용 고르기

정답 ⑤

M Welcome to the Paradise Aquarium. Since we opened in 2011, more than two million people have visited us. Around 650 kinds of sea creatures are living here in 20 different zones. Generally, it takes two hours to take a look at them. Our most popular animals are the seals. They are so cute that you will want to watch them for a long time. Thank you. I hope you enjoy our aquarium.

남 파라다이스 수족관에 오신 걸 환영합니다. 2011년에 개장한 이래로, 2백만 명 이상이 저희를 방문해 주셨습니다. 약 650종의 해양 생물이 이곳 20여 개의 다른 구역에서 살고 있습니다. 일반적으로, 그것들을 관람하는 데는 두 시간이 걸립니다. 가장 인기 있는 동물은 바다표범입니다. 바다표범들은 정말 귀여워서 오랫동안 보고 싶으실 겁니다. 감사합니다. 저희 수족관을 즐겨주시면 좋겠습니다.

해설 | 남자가 방문객들이 오랫동안 귀여운 바다표범들을 보고 싶을 것이라고 했으므로 정답은 ⑤ '바다표범은 현재 보호 중이라 볼 수 없다.'이다.

어휘 | million [míljən] 명 백만 around [əráund] 부 약, 대략 creature [krí:tʃər] 명 생물 generally [dʒénərəli] 부 일반적으로 seal [si:l] 명 바다표범

12 목적 고르기

정답 ①

M Hey, Patricia. What a pleasant surprise! Did you start jogging?
W Yes. Last week. And it's my first time to jog around here.
M Why did you begin running?
W Lately, I didn't have a lot of energy. So I decided to jog to improve my health.
M Really? You must find it hard.
W Yeah. But it works great. I feel more energized.
M That's good.

남 안녕, Patricia. 정말 반가워! 너 조깅 시작했니?
여 응. 지난주에. 여기 주변을 조깅하는 건 처음이야.
남 왜 달리기를 시작한 거야?
여 최근에 기운이 많이 없었거든. 그래서, 건강을 향상시키기 위해 조깅하기로 결심했어.
남 정말? 힘들겠다.
여 응. 그렇지만 효과가 좋아. 나는 더 활력이 생긴 것 같아.
남 그거 좋네.

해설 | 여자가 건강을 향상시키기 위해 조깅하기로 결심했다고 했으므로 정답은 ① '건강 증진을 위해서'이다.

어휘 | lately [léitli] 부 최근에 improve [imprú:v] 동 향상시키다 energize [énərdʒàiz] 동 활력을 주다, 활발하게 하다

13 금액 정보 고르기

정답 ③

W Hello, I'm looking for spoons.
M How many do you need?
W I need two large ones.
M I see. You can choose from plastic or wooden spoons.
W What's the price difference?
M Six dollars each for the plastic ones, and seven dollars each for the wooden ones.
W Then, I'll take one of each.
M Alright. I'll help you with the payment for a plastic and a wooden spoon.

여 안녕하세요, 숟가락을 찾고 있는데요.
남 몇 개가 필요하신가요?
여 큰 것 2개가 필요해요.
남 그러시군요. 플라스틱과 나무 숟가락 중 고르실 수 있어요.
여 가격 차이가 얼마나 나나요?
남 플라스틱 숟가락은 각 6달러이고, 나무 숟가락은 각 7달러입니다.
여 그렇다면, 각각 한 개씩 살게요.
남 좋습니다. 플라스틱 숟가락 하나와 나무 숟가락 하나의 계산을 도와드릴게요.

해설 | 남자가 플라스틱 숟가락은 6달러이고 나무 숟가락은 7달러라고 했고, 여자가 각각 하나씩 사겠다고 했으므로 정답은 ③ '$ 13'이다.

어휘 | wooden [wúdn] 형 나무의, 목재의 difference [dífərəns] 명 차이, 다름

14 관계 고르기

정답 ①

W How can I help you today?
M I'm looking for a new pair of shoes.
W I see. What will you use them for?
M I will use them for running and playing basketball. I exercise a lot.
W Okay. These shoes are very popular because they are comfortable.
M Perfect. Do you have a size 250?
W Yes, we do.

여 오늘 어떻게 도와드릴까요?
남 새 신발을 찾고 있어요.
여 그러시군요. 어디에 쓰실 건가요?
남 달리기와 농구를 하는 데 쓸 거예요. 저는 운동을 많이 하거든요.
여 알겠습니다. 이 신발들은 편해서 매우 인기가 많아요.
남 완벽하네요. 250사이즈가 있나요?
여 네, 있어요.

해설 | 남자가 여자에게 신발을 추천 받고 있는 것으로 보아 정답은 ① '신발 가게 점원 — 손님'이다.

어휘 | exercise [éksərsàiz] 동 운동하다 명 운동 perfect [pə́ːrfikt] 형 완벽한

15 부탁·요청한 일 고르기

정답 ②

W Oh, David. You're all wet.
M Yes, Mom. My shoes are really dirty too.
W What happened?
M It suddenly rained while I was playing soccer at the playground.
W I can see that. Put your clothes in the washing machine, and take a shower.
M Okay. And could you wash my shoes?
W No problem. But you should wear other shoes tomorrow.

여 오, David. 너 다 젖었구나.
남 네, 엄마. 제 신발도 정말 더러워요.
여 무슨 일이 있었니?
남 운동장에서 축구를 하는 동안 갑자기 비가 내렸어요.
여 그래 보이는구나. 옷을 세탁기에 넣고 샤워를 하렴.
남 알겠어요. 그리고 제 신발을 빨아주실 수 있으세요?
여 물론이지. 하지만 내일은 다른 신발을 신어야 해.

해설 | 남자가 여자에게 신발을 세탁해 달라고 요청했으므로 정답은 ② '신발 세탁하기'이다.

어휘 | suddenly [sʌ́dnli] 부 갑자기 playground [pléigràund] 명 운동장, 놀이터

16 이유 고르기

정답 ⑤

M Hey, Christine. What did you do just now?
W I threw my hat onto the ice.
M But why did you throw it?
W Oh, it's just to congratulate the player.
M Sorry, but I still can't understand.
W In ice hockey, when a player scores three times in a game, we throw our hats.
M Oh, now I see.

남 이봐, Christine. 지금 막 뭘 한 거야?
여 내 모자를 얼음 위로 던졌어.
남 아니 그걸 왜 던졌는데?
여 오, 그건 그냥 선수를 축하하기 위한 거야.
남 미안해, 하지만 아직도 이해할 수가 없어.
여 아이스하키에서는 선수가 경기에서 골을 세 번 넣으면 모자를 던져.
남 오, 이제 알겠다.

해설 | 여자가 아이스하키 선수를 축하하기 위해 모자를 던졌다고 했으므로 정답은 ⑤ '선수를 축하해주려고'이다.

어휘 | throw [θrou] 동 던지다 congratulate [kəngrǽtʃulèit] 동 축하하다 score [skɔːr] 동 골을 넣다

17 그림 상황에 적절한 대화 고르기

정답 ③

① M How much did your bike cost?
W It was a Christmas gift from my parents.
② M Slow down. You can't drive over 30 kilometers per hour here.
W Sorry. I forgot.
③ M Ma'am, you cannot park here.
W Oh, I didn't see the sign. I'll move my car.
④ M Where should I put this box?
W You can leave it on the bench.
⑤ M Excuse me, Officer. I'd like to report a stolen item.
W I'm sorry. Have a seat, please.

① 남 저 자전거 얼마 들었니?
여 그건 부모님의 크리스마스 선물이었어.
② 남 천천히 가. 여기서는 시속 30km 이상으로 달릴 수 없어.
여 미안. 잊어버렸어.
③ 남 선생님, 여기 주차하시면 안 돼요.
여 오, 표지판을 못 봤어요. 차를 옮길게요.
④ 남 이 상자를 어디에 둬야 할까?
여 벤치 위에 둬도 돼.
⑤ 남 실례합니다, 경관님. 도둑맞은 물건을 신고하고 싶어요.
여 유감입니다. 앉으세요.

해설 | 남자가 주차 금지 표지판을 가리키면서 운전석에 앉은 여자에게 말을 하고 있는 상황이므로 정답은 ③이다.

어휘 | cost [kɔːst] 동 비용이 들다 park [pɑːrk] 동 주차하다 stolen [stóulən] 형 도둑맞은

18 언급하지 않은 내용 고르기

정답 ④

W Dad, I can't wait for the field trip.
M When is it, Soyoung?
W This Friday.
M Oh, I remember. You'll visit the Space Center, right?
W Yeah. Observing stars will be exciting.
M Then, you will arrive home late.
W No. I'll get back home around 5 p.m.
M How is that possible?
W Surprisingly, the center has equipment to see the sun and stars during the day.
M That's interesting.

여 아빠, 전 현장 학습이 정말 기대돼요.
남 그게 언제지, 소영아?
여 이번 금요일이에요.
남 오, 기억난다. 우주 센터를 방문할 예정이지, 맞지?
여 네. 별을 관찰하는 건 재미있을 거예요.
남 그럼, 집에 늦게 도착하겠구나.
여 아니요. 집에 오후 5시 정도면 돌아올 거예요.
남 어떻게 그게 가능하니?
여 놀랍게도, 그 센터에는 낮 동안 태양과 별을 볼 수 있는 장비가 있어요.
남 그거 흥미롭구나.

해설 | ① 일시(이번 금요일), ② 장소(우주 센터), ③ 체험 활동(별 관찰), ⑤ 귀가 시간(오후 5시)에 대해 언급했으므로 정답은 ④ '준비물'이다.

어휘 | field trip 현장 학습 observe [əbzə́ːrv] 동 관찰하다 surprisingly [sərpráiziŋli] 부 놀랍게도 equipment [ikwípmənt] 명 장비

19 적절한 응답 고르기

정답 ③

[Cellphone rings.]
M Hi, Honey.
W Hey, Josh. Can you pick me up from the subway station? I'm too tired to walk home from here.
M Sure, but I'll be a little late. I'm at the shop right now.
W That's okay. What are you going to buy?
M I'm going to buy some food for dinner.
W Oh, can you get me a drink?
M Sure. What do you want?
W I'd like apple juice, please.

[휴대폰이 울린다.]
남 안녕, 여보.
여 안녕, Josh. 지하철역에 날 데리러 올 수 있어? 여기서 집까지 걸어가기엔 너무 피곤해.
남 물론이지, 그런데 약간 늦을 거야. 나 지금 상점에 있거든.
여 괜찮아. 뭘 사려고?
남 저녁 식사를 위한 음식을 좀 살 거야.
여 오, 음료수를 사다 줄 수 있어?
남 물론이지. 뭘 원해?
여 사과주스 부탁해.

해설 | 여자가 음료수를 사달라고 하자 남자가 무엇을 원하는지 물었으므로 정답은 음료의 종류를 언급하는 ③ 'I'd like apple juice, please.'이다.

선택지 해석

① 우리는 금요일마다 연습해. ② 물을 더 줄까? ③ 사과주스 부탁해. ④ 10분 후에 거기 도착할 거야. ⑤ 저녁이 곧 준비될 거야.

어휘 | drink [driŋk] 명 음료수 동 마시다 soon [suːn] 부 곧, 이내

20 적절한 응답 고르기

정답 ④

M What should we do today, Sally?
W How about going on a boat ride?
M That sounds fun. Where does the boat go?
W It goes down the Sandy River. We can see beautiful views of the city.
M I've never been on a boat before. I want to try it.
W You'll love it.
M Okay. How can we get the tickets?
W I'll get them online.

남 오늘 우리 뭘 할까, Sally?
여 보트 타러 가는 게 어때?
남 재미있겠다. 보트가 어디로 가는데?
여 그건 샌디강을 따라 내려가. 우리는 도시의 아름다운 경치를 볼 수 있어.
남 난 보트를 타본 적이 없어. 시도해 보고 싶어.
여 네가 좋아할 거야.
남 그래. 표는 어떻게 사면 돼?
여 내가 온라인으로 살게.

해설 | 남자가 표를 어떻게 사는지 묻고 있으므로 정답은 구매 방법을 언급하는 ④ 'I'll get them online.'이다.

선택지 해석

① 정말 너무 재미있었어. ② 다 팔렸어. ③ 두 블록 직진해. ④ 내가 온라인으로 살게. ⑤ 그건 도시를 통과해서 흘러.

어휘 | go down 내려가다 view [vjuː] 명 경치 through [θruː] 전 ~을 통과하여

20회 실전 모의고사

| 문제 pp.178-179

1	③	2	②	3	①	4	④	5	③	6	③	7	⑤	8	③	9	④	10	②
11	④	12	④	13	⑤	14	③	15	①	16	④	17	②	18	③	19	③	20	①

1 날씨 고르기

정답 ③

M Good morning. Here is the weather report for Korea. Lots of rain is expected today in most cities. Seoul will have the most rain. But in Daegu, the hot summer weather with clear sunny skies will continue. In Jeju, there is a weather warning for strong winds, so please take care. Thank you.

남 안녕하십니까. 한국의 일기 예보입니다. 오늘 대부분의 도시에 많은 비가 예상됩니다. 서울에 가장 비가 많이 올 예정입니다. 하지만 대구는 맑고 화창한 하늘과 함께 무더운 여름 날씨가 이어지겠습니다. 제주에는 강풍 경보가 내려져 있으니, 조심하시기 바랍니다. 감사합니다.

해설 | 제주에는 강풍 경보가 내려져 있다고 했으므로 정답은 ③이다.

어휘 | most [moust] 형 대부분의 warning [wɔ́ːrniŋ] 명 경보

2 알맞은 그림 고르기

정답 ②

W Dad, can I ask you a favor?
M Sure. Go ahead.
W Please grab that box on the top shelf. I can't reach it.
M No problem. Which one do you mean?
W The heart-shaped one with a ribbon around it.
M Okay, I see. It's behind the box with a heart on it. Here it is.
W Thanks a lot.
M Don't mention it.

여 아빠, 부탁 하나만 드려도 돼요?
남 물론이지. 말하렴.
여 선반 맨 위에 있는 저 상자 좀 집어주세요. 저는 닿지가 않아요.
남 문제없지. 어떤 걸 말하는 거니?
여 리본이 둘러져 있는 하트 모양 상자요.
남 그래, 알겠다. 위에 하트가 그려진 상자 뒤에 있구나. 여기 있다.
여 정말 감사합니다.
남 천만에.

해설 | 여자가 리본이 둘러져 있는 하트 모양 상자라고 했으므로 정답은 ②이다.

어휘 | grab [græb] 동 집다, 붙잡다 reach [riːtʃ] 동 닿다 behind [biháind] 전 뒤에

3 심정 고르기

정답 ①

M Emily, are you okay? You look so pale.	남 Emily, 괜찮니? 너 몹시 창백해 보여.
W My dog, Max, died yesterday.	여 내 반려견 Max가 어제 죽었어.
M I'm so sorry to hear that.	남 정말 유감이야.
W I was prepared for losing him because he was very old. But it's not easy to let him go.	여 Max의 나이가 매우 많았기 때문에 그를 잃을 것을 준비하긴 했어. 하지만 놓아주는 게 쉽지 않네.
M I understand.	남 이해해.
W I miss him already.	여 벌써 그가 보고 싶어.
M I can't imagine how hard it must be for you.	남 얼마나 힘들지 상상도 안돼.
W My heart is broken.	여 마음이 찢어져.

해설 | 여자가 반려견이 죽었다고 하며 벌써 보고 싶고 마음이 찢어진다고 했으므로 정답은 ① 'sad'이다

선택지 해석

① 슬픈 ② 수줍은 ③ 기쁜 ④ 화난 ⑤ 만족스러운

어휘 | pale [peil] 형 창백한 prepare [pripέər] 동 준비하다 understand [ʌ̀ndərstǽnd] 동 이해하다 imagine [imǽdʒin] 동 상상하다

4 한 일 고르기

정답 ④

M Hana, how did you spend your winter vacation?	남 하나야, 겨울 방학은 어떻게 보냈니?
W I went to Russia as an exchange student.	여 나는 교환학생으로 러시아에 다녀왔어.
M Wow, what did you learn there?	남 우와, 거기서 뭘 배웠어?
W I studied great novels by Russian writers like Tolstoy.	여 톨스토이 같은 러시아 작가들이 쓴 명작 소설들을 공부했어.
M Oh, do you want to be a writer?	남 오, 너 작가가 되고 싶은 거야?
W Yes. I want to become a novelist.	여 응. 난 소설가가 되고 싶어.
M I'm sure your dream will come true.	남 네 꿈은 꼭 이뤄질 거라고 확신해.

해설 | 여자가 겨울 방학 동안 교환학생으로 러시아에 가서 러시아 작가의 소설을 공부했다고 했으므로 정답은 ④ '문학 공부'이다.

어휘 | exchange student 교환학생 novel [nάvəl] 명 소설 (novelist [nάvəlist] 명 소설가)

5 장소 고르기

정답 ③

M Welcome. Are you ready to order?	남 어서 오세요. 주문하실 준비 되셨나요?
W Yes. I'll take the chicken salad and tomato soup, please.	여 네. 저는 치킨 샐러드와 토마토수프를 먹을게요.
M I'm sorry, but we just ran out of tomato soup. What about potato soup instead?	남 죄송하지만, 토마토수프가 막 다 떨어졌어요. 대신에 감자수프는 어떠신가요?
W No, thank you. I'll just have the salad.	여 아니요, 괜찮습니다. 그냥 샐러드만 먹을게요.
M Okay. Is there anything else you need?	남 알겠습니다. 더 필요한 건 없으신가요?
W Can I have some coffee, please?	여 커피 좀 마실 수 있을까요?
M Of course. I'll bring that for you right away.	남 물론이죠. 바로 가져다드리겠습니다.

해설 | 남자가 주문할 준비가 되었는지를 묻자, 여자가 샐러드와 수프 등 음식을 주문하는 것으로 보아 정답은 ③ '식당'이다.

어휘 | run out of ~가 다 떨어지다

6 의도 고르기

정답 ③

W Hello, Mr. Randall. I'm here to talk about my son, Ben.
M Okay. Have a seat, please.
W I'm concerned he is too shy in school.
M What makes you think that?
W Actually, he is quiet at home too.
M Don't worry. It's common for teenage boys.
W How should I treat him then?
M Don't push him. Give him some time to get ready to talk.

여 안녕하세요, Randall 선생님. 제 아들 Ben에 관해 이야기를 하러 왔어요.
남 그러시군요. 앉아주세요.
여 제 아들이 학교에서 너무 수줍음을 많이 타서 걱정이에요.
남 무엇 때문에 그렇게 생각하시나요?
여 실은, 제 아들은 집에서도 조용하거든요.
남 걱정하지 마세요. 그건 십 대 남자 아이들에게 흔한 일이에요.
여 제가 어떻게 대해야 할까요 그럼?
남 강요하지 마세요. 말할 준비를 할 시간을 주세요.

해설 | 여자가 아들을 어떻게 대해야 하냐고 묻는 말에 남자가 강요하지 말고 말할 준비를 할 시간을 주라고 했으므로 정답은 ③ '조언'이다.

어휘 | concerned [kənsə́ːrnd] 형 걱정하는 shy [ʃai] 형 수줍음을 많이 타는 common [kámən] 형 흔한 push [puʃ] 동 강요하다; 밀다

7 언급하지 않은 내용 고르기

정답 ⑤

M Amy, why don't we attend the ski camp in Pyeongchang?
W I'd love to. When will it be held?
M It's from February 4th to the 6th.
W Good. But I can't ski at all. Is that going to be a problem?
M Don't worry. The camp is for beginners.
W Alright. How much does it cost?
M It's 200 dollars per person.
W It's a bit expensive.
M Yeah. But I have a 10% discount coupon.

남 Amy, 우리 평창 스키 캠프에 참가하는 게 어때?
여 좋아. 언제 열리는데?
남 2월 4일부터 6일까지야.
여 좋아. 하지만 난 스키를 전혀 못 타. 그게 문제가 될까?
남 걱정하지 마. 그 캠프는 초보자를 위한 거야.
여 그렇구나. 비용이 얼마나 들어?
남 인당 200달러야.
여 약간 비싸네.
남 응. 그렇지만 나한테 10% 할인 쿠폰이 있어.

해설 | ① 장소(평창), ② 일시(2월 4일부터 6일까지), ③ 참여 대상(초보자), ④ 비용(인당 200달러)에 대해 언급했으므로 정답은 ⑤ '장비 대여'이다.

어휘 | not ~ at all 전혀 ~이 아닌 expensive [ikspénsiv] 형 비싼 discount [dískaunt] 명 할인

8 할 일 고르기

정답 ③

[Doorbell rings.]
W Hello. Nice to meet you.
M Hi. Are you new here?
W Yes. I just moved in downstairs yesterday. Can I ask you something?
M Of course. What is your question?
W Is there a traditional market around here?
M Yes. It's very close to here.
W That's good. I have lots of things to buy.
M I can show you the way if you want.
W Oh, that would be very helpful.

[초인종이 울린다.]
여 안녕하세요. 만나서 반가워요.
남 안녕하세요. 이사 오셨나요?
여 네. 어제 막 아래층으로 이사 왔어요. 뭐 좀 물어봐도 될까요?
남 물론이죠. 질문이 뭔가요?
여 이 주변에 전통 시장이 있나요?
남 네. 여기서 매우 가까워요.
여 좋네요. 제가 살 것들이 많거든요.
남 원하신다면 제가 길을 안내해 드릴 수 있어요.
여 오, 그러면 정말 도움이 될 거예요.

해설 | 남자가 전통 시장으로 길을 안내해주겠다고 제안하자 여자가 동의했으므로 정답은 ③ '시장 가기'이다.

어휘 | move in 이사 오다 downstairs [dáunstɛ̀ərz] 부 아래층으로 traditional [trədíʃənəl] 형 전통의 helpful [hélpfəl] 형 도움이 되는

9 언급하지 않은 내용 고르기

정답 ④

M Good afternoon, residents. To raise funds for local charities, we will hold the Community Garage Sale. It'll be on March 19th from 11 a.m. to 3 p.m. If you want to participate, just have your items out for sale that day. We will promote this event on many online sites and set up signposts around our town. After the event, feel free to donate your profits to us. We will send the money to various charities.

남 좋은 오후입니다, 거주민 여러분. 지역 자선 단체를 위한 기금 모금을 위해, 저희는 Community Garage Sale을 열 예정입니다. 이는 3월 19일 오전 11시부터 오후 3시까지 열릴 것입니다. 참여하고 싶으시다면, 그날 판매를 위해 그냥 물건들을 내놓으시면 됩니다. 저희는 이 행사를 많은 온라인 사이트에 홍보할 것이며 마을 주변에 표지판을 설치할 것입니다. 행사 후에는, 저희에게 수익을 얼마든지 기부하십시오. 저희는 다양한 자선단체에 돈을 보낼 예정입니다.

해설 | ① 행사 목적(지역 자선 단체를 위한 기금 모금), ② 행사 종료 시각(오후 3시), ③ 참여 방법(물건 내놓기), ⑤ 행사 홍보 방식(온라인 사이트에 홍보 및 마을 주변에 표지판 세우기)에 대해 언급했으므로 정답은 ④ '판매 물건 종류'이다.

어휘 | raise funds 기금을 모금하다 charity [tʃǽrəti] 명 자선 단체 set up 설치하다 donate [dóuneit] 동 기부하다 profit [práfit] 명 수익

10 주제 고르기

정답 ②

W I'd like to tell you a story about an old woman in Korea. She was born into a poor family and couldn't attend school. But she didn't give up learning. Finally, at age 50, she entered university. Now, she is a great poet. I used to quit easily. But after reading her story, I'm trying to change that. I won't give up my dream and will keep trying my best.

여 저는 한국의 한 할머니에 대한 이야기를 말씀드리려고 합니다. 그녀는 가난한 가정에서 태어났고, 학교에 다닐 수가 없었습니다. 그렇지만 그녀는 배우는 것을 포기하지 않았습니다. 마침내 50세에, 그녀는 대학에 입학했습니다. 이제, 그녀는 훌륭한 시인입니다. 저는 쉽게 포기하곤 했었습니다. 하지만 그녀의 이야기를 읽은 후, 저는 그것을 바꾸려고 노력 중입니다. 저는 제 꿈을 포기하지 않고 최선을 다하기 위해 노력할 것입니다.

해설 | 여자가 배움을 포기하지 않고 대학에 입학해 시인이 된 할머니의 이야기를 들려주며, 자신도 꿈을 포기하지 않고 최선을 다하려 노력하겠다 하고 있으므로 정답은 ② '포기하지 않는 태도'이다.

어휘 | poor [pur] 형 가난한 enter [éntər] 동 입학하다 quit [kwit] 동 포기하다, 그만두다

11 일치하지 않는 내용 고르기

정답 ④

M Hello. This is City Eco Center. We have many eco-friendly facilities. In our playground, you can have fun with slides and swings. They are all made of recycled wood and plastic. You can also ride special bicycles. They will produce electricity while you ride them. We offer educational programs too. You can learn about climate change. Are you interested? Then, please come visit us. The center is located next to the City Park.

남 안녕하세요. City Eco Center입니다. 저희는 친환경적인 시설을 많이 갖추고 있습니다. 저희 놀이터에서는 미끄럼틀과 그네로 재미있게 노실 수 있습니다. 그것들은 모두 재활용된 나무와 플라스틱으로 만들어져 있습니다. 또한 특별한 자전거도 타실 수 있습니다. 그 자전거는 그것을 타는 동안 전력을 생산합니다. 저희는 교육적인 프로그램도 제공합니다. 기후 변화에 대해 배우실 수 있습니다. 흥미가 있으신가요? 그렇다면, 저희를 방문하러 와 주십시오. 센터는 시립 공원 옆에 위치해 있습니다.

해설 | 남자가 City Eco Center에서 교육적인 프로그램을 제공하며, 기후 변화에 대해 배울 수 있다고 했으므로 정답은 ④ '재활용에 대해 배우는 교육 프로그램이 있다.'이다.

어휘 | eco-friendly 형 친환경적인 facility [fəsíləti] 명 시설 produce [prədjúːs] 동 생산하다 electricity [ilektrísəti] 명 전력, 전기 educational [èdʒukéiʃənəl] 형 교육적인

12 목적 고르기

정답 ④

[Cellphone rings.]

W Hi. Is this Mr. Evans speaking?

M Yes. Who's calling?

W This is Muscle Fitness. You left your wallet in the dressing room.

M Really? I didn't know that. I'll come back to pick it up now.

W Alright. I'll keep the center open until you come.

M I really appreciate it.

W You're welcome.

[휴대폰이 울린다.]

여 안녕하세요. Evans씨이신가요?

남 네. 누구시죠?

여 Muscle Fitness입니다. 탈의실에 지갑을 두고 가셨어요.

남 정말요? 몰랐네요. 지금 가지러 돌아갈게요.

여 알겠습니다. 오실 때까지 센터를 열어두도록 할게요.

남 정말 감사합니다.

여 천만에요.

해설 | 여자가 남자에게 탈의실에 지갑을 두고 갔다고 알렸으므로 정답은 ④ '분실물을 찾아주기 위해서'이다.

어휘 | dressing room 탈의실 appreciate [əpríːʃièit] 동 감사하다

13 시간 정보 고르기

정답 ⑤

W Jason, did you get an invitation to Katy's wedding?
M Yes. I can't wait to celebrate her marriage. Are you going too?
W I haven't decided yet. Do you remember when the wedding is?
M Hmm... Maybe June 16th? I think it's on the third Saturday of June.
W Let me check the calendar.
M When is it?
W Oh, it's the 19th.

여 Jason, 너 Katy의 결혼식 초대장을 받았니?
남 응. 그녀의 결혼을 축하하는 게 너무 기대돼. 너도 가니?
여 아직 결정 못했어. 결혼식이 언제인지 기억해?
남 흠... 아마 6월 16일? 6월의 셋째 주 토요일이었던 것 같아.
여 달력을 확인해볼게.
남 언제니?
여 오, 19일이야.

해설 | 6월의 셋째 주 토요일을 달력으로 확인한 여자가 19일이라고 했으므로 정답은 ⑤ '6월 19일'이다.

어휘 | invitation [ìnvitéiʃən] 명 초대장 celebrate [séləbreit] 동 축하하다 marriage [mǽridʒ] 명 결혼 calendar [kǽləndər] 명 달력

14 관계 고르기

정답 ③

M Hello. Can I help you find a book?
W Yes. I'm looking for the new book about Einstein.
M Actually, we just sold out. I'm so sorry.
W Oh. I will just come back later.
M Well, do you enjoy books about science?
W Yes. I love them.
M Then, I can also recommend this book. It's about famous biologists.
W Wow, thank you. I will take a look.

남 안녕하세요. 책 찾는 것을 도와드릴까요?
여 네. 저는 아인슈타인에 관한 신간을 찾고 있어요.
남 사실, 그건 막 다 팔렸어요. 죄송합니다.
여 오. 그냥 나중에 다시 올게요.
남 음, 과학에 관한 책을 좋아하시나요?
여 네. 정말 좋아해요.
남 그럼, 저는 이 책도 추천해 드려요. 이건 유명한 생물학자들에 관한 것이에요.
여 우와, 감사합니다. 살펴볼게요.

해설 | 남자가 여자가 구매하려는 책이 다 팔렸다고 알려준 후 다른 책을 추천해 주는 것으로 보아 정답은 ③ '서점 직원 — 손님'이다.

어휘 | recommend [rèkəménd] 동 추천하다 biologist [baiáləd3ist] 명 생물학자 take a look 살펴보다

15 부탁·요청한 일 고르기

정답 ①

W Daniel, I won the ticket for a fan event. I can see Mark Bonds in person!
M Oh, I envy you. I'm also a big fan of him.
W I'll get his signature on my baseball, glove and uniform.
M I want to go with you. Is it possible?
W Sorry, but it's not allowed.
M Then, could you get his signature on my bat?
W Sure. Give me your bat.
M Thank you so much.

여 Daniel, 나 팬 행사 표를 얻었어. Mark Bonds를 직접 볼 수 있어!
남 오, 부럽다. 나도 그의 열렬한 팬이야.
여 나는 야구공이랑, 장갑, 그리고 유니폼에 그의 사인을 받을 거야.
남 나도 같이 가고 싶어. 가능할까?
여 미안하지만, 그건 안돼.
남 그럼, 내 야구 배트에 그의 사인을 받아 줄 수 있니?
여 물론이지. 네 야구 배트를 줘.
남 정말 고마워.

해설 | 남자가 여자에게 자신의 야구 배트에 사인을 받아와 달라고 부탁했으므로 정답은 ① '사인 대신 받아오기'이다.

어휘 | win [win] 동 얻다, 따다 in person 직접 envy [énvi] 동 부러워하다 possible [pásəbl] 형 가능한 allow [əláu] 동 허용하다; 허락하다

16 이유 고르기

정답 ④

W Sangwon, you look upset.
M I was punished because I was late for school today.
W Why were you late? Did you oversleep?
M No. I got up early as always.
W Then, what happened?
M The bus didn't come this morning.
W How did you get to school?
M On foot. It took half an hour.
W I'm sorry you had to do that.

여 상원아, 너 속상해 보여.
남 오늘 학교에 늦어서 벌을 받았어.
여 왜 늦었니? 늦잠을 잤니?
남 아니. 언제나처럼 일찍 일어났어.
여 그럼, 무슨 일이 있었던 거야?
남 아침에 버스가 오지 않았어.
여 학교에 어떻게 갔니?
남 걸어서. 30분이 걸렸어.
여 그래야만 했다니 유감이야.

해설 | 남자가 아침에 버스가 오지 않아서 학교에 늦었다고 했으므로 정답은 ④ '버스가 오지 않아서'이다.
어휘 | punish [pʌ́niʃ] 동 벌주다, 처벌하다 oversleep [òuvərslíːp] 동 늦잠 자다 on foot 걸어서, 도보로

17 그림 상황에 적절한 대화 고르기

정답 ②

① M It's so hot today.
W Yes. I want to have some ice cream.
② M Where is the doctor's office?
W It's on the third floor.
③ M Do you have these pants in blue?
W I'm sorry. We only have those in black.
④ M The concert starts in an hour.
W We should take a taxi then.
⑤ M The elevator is on the 10th floor.
W Let's take the stairs.

① 남 오늘 너무 덥다.
여 맞아. 아이스크림을 먹고 싶어.
② 남 병원은 어디 있나요?
여 3층에 있어요.
③ 남 이 바지 파란색으로 있나요?
여 죄송합니다. 그건 검은색만 있어요.
④ 남 공연이 한 시간 후에 시작해.
여 그럼 우리 택시 타야겠다.
⑤ 남 엘리베이터가 10층에 있어.
여 계단으로 가자.

해설 | 남자가 병원을 찾고 있고 여자가 3층을 가리키고 있는 상황이므로 정답은 ②이다.
어휘 | floor [flɔːr] 명 층; 바닥 stair [stɛər] 명 계단

18 언급하지 않은 내용 고르기

정답 ③

W Let me tell you about my dream job. I want to become a sports doctor. I'll have to check players' injuries. Also, I'll help them recover from their injuries. Sometimes, I'll teach players how to improve their health. I will also provide psychological counseling for them. Hopefully, I'll help the players do their best.

여 제 꿈의 직업에 관해 말씀드리겠습니다. 저는 스포츠 의사가 되고 싶습니다. 저는 선수들의 부상을 확인해야 할 것입니다. 그리고, 그들이 부상에서 회복할 수 있도록 도울 것입니다. 가끔은, 선수들에게 그들의 건강을 어떻게 증진시키는지 가르쳐 줄 것입니다. 저는 또한 그들을 위해 심리 상담을 제공할 것입니다. 바라건대, 저는 선수들이 최선을 다할 수 있도록 도울 것입니다.

해설 | 여자가 미래에 하고 싶은 일로 운동선수들의 훈련 과정을 점검한다는 말은 언급되지 않았으므로 정답은 ③이다.
어휘 | injury [índʒəri] 명 부상 recover [rikʌ́vər] 동 회복하다 provide [prəváid] 동 제공하다 psychological [sàikəládʒikəl] 형 심리의, 심리적인 counseling [káunsəliŋ] 명 상담

19 적절한 응답 고르기

정답 ③

W When did you become interested in acting, Rick?
M My father was an actor. So, I loved watching movies when I was a kid.
W I see. Then, your father must be your biggest role model, right?
M Of course. He's always helped me with my career.
W You've acted in lots of movies. What is your favorite movie among them?
M It is *The Forest*.
W Why is that your favorite?
M The story is so unique.

여 언제 연기에 흥미를 가지셨나요, Rick?
남 제 아버지가 배우셨어요. 그래서, 저는 어릴 때 영화 보는 것을 좋아했어요.
여 그러시군요. 그럼, 아버님이 가장 큰 롤모델이시겠군요, 그렇죠?
남 당연하죠. 아버지는 항상 저의 진로를 도와주셨어요.
여 많은 영화에서 연기를 하셨어요. 그중에서 가장 좋아하는 영화는 뭔가요?
남 <The Forest>예요.
여 왜 그걸 가장 좋아하시나요?
남 줄거리가 매우 독특해서요.

해설 | 여자가 왜 그 영화를 가장 좋아하는지 물었으므로 정답은 영화에 관해 설명하는 ③ 'The story is so unique.'이다.

선택지 해석

① 제 아버지는 정말 친절하세요. ② 그는 캘리포니아에서 왔어요. ③ 줄거리가 매우 독특해서요. ④ 저는 유명해지고 싶어요. ⑤ 극장에서 영화를 즐기세요.

어휘 | career [kəríər] 명 진로 unique [juːníːk] 형 독특한

20 적절한 응답 고르기

정답 ①

M Alright. Our first stop today will be the Palace of Versailles.
W Great! I've always wanted to see it, Dad.
M Me too. We can look around the area for a few hours and then get lunch.
W What are we going to do at the palace?
M We can either explore the gardens or join a tour of the palace.
W What should we do?
M We should see the gardens.

남 좋아. 오늘 첫 번째로 들를 곳은 베르사유 궁전이란다.
여 좋아요! 저는 항상 그곳을 보고 싶었어요, 아빠.
남 나도 그렇단다. 몇 시간 동안 그 장소를 둘러보고 점심을 먹도록 하자.
여 궁전에서는 뭘 할 건가요?
남 우리는 정원을 탐험하거나 궁전 탐방에 참여할 수 있단다.
여 뭘 해야 할까요?
남 정원을 보자.

해설 | 여자가 어떤 활동을 할지 물었으므로 정답은 할 활동을 말하는 ① 'We should see the gardens.'이다.

선택지 해석

① 정원을 보자. ② 응. 표를 사야 해. ③ 우리는 샌드위치를 먹을 거야. ④ 여기 입구가 있어. ⑤ 이건 내 첫 파리 방문이야.

어휘 | palace [pǽlis] 명 궁전 explore [ikspl5ːr] 동 탐험하다 entrance [éntrəns] 명 입구

21회 고난도 모의고사

| 문제 pp.188-189

1	②	2	④	3	③	4	④	5	⑤	6	③	7	②	8	①	9	③	10	③
11	③	12	③	13	④	14	④	15	②	16	②	17	④	18	⑤	19	③	20	④

1 날씨 고르기

정답 ②

M Good morning, everyone. Tomorrow, Seoul and Incheon will be partly cloudy. In Gangneung, not only heavy rain but also low temperatures are expected. Due to the arrival of Typhoon Sarah next week, there will be thunderstorms in Jeju. And in Busan, there will be strong winds all day long, so make sure to wear thick clothes when you go out.

남 안녕하십니까, 여러분. 내일 서울과 인천은 일부 흐리겠습니다. 강릉에는 폭우뿐만 아니라 낮은 기온도 예상됩니다. 다음 주 태풍 사라의 북상으로 인해 제주에는 천둥과 번개가 치는 곳이 있겠습니다. 그리고 부산에서는 강한 바람이 온종일 불겠으니, 외출하실 때 반드시 두꺼운 옷을 입으십시오.

해설 | 부산에는 강한 바람이 불겠다고 했으므로 정답은 ②이다.

어휘 | not only A but also B A뿐만 아니라 B도 make sure 반드시 ~하다; 확인하다

2 알맞은 그림 고르기

정답 ④

M Welcome to Venice Furniture. What type of furniture are you looking for?
W I'm looking for a chair for my office.
M How about this one with a fluffy seat?
W I like the design, but I need an armrest.
M Okay. Then, what about these? One has wheels, and the other has four legs.
W I like the one with wheels. I'll buy one.
M Great choice!

남 Venice Furniture에 오신 걸 환영합니다. 어떤 종류의 가구를 찾고 계시나요?
여 제 사무실을 위한 의자를 찾고 있어요.
남 푹신한 좌석이 있는 이건 어떠세요?
여 디자인은 좋은데, 저는 팔걸이가 필요해요.
남 알겠습니다. 그럼, 이것들은 어떠세요? 하나는 바퀴가 달려 있고, 나머지 하나는 다리가 4개예요.
여 바퀴 달린 게 좋네요. 그걸로 하나 살게요.
남 훌륭한 선택이세요!

해설 | 여자가 팔걸이가 필요하다고 했고 바퀴 달린 게 좋다고 했으므로 정답은 ④이다.

어휘 | furniture [fə́ːrnitʃər] 명 가구 armrest [áːrmrest] 명 팔걸이 wheel [hwiːl] 명 바퀴

3 심정 고르기

정답 ③

[Cellphone rings.]
M Rachel, what are you planning to do today? Do you want to hang out?
W Oh, I can't. I'm at the beach with my friends right now.
M Okay. Are you having fun?
W Yes. I really needed a break after my math test yesterday.
M Yeah. You studied really hard for that test. You must be so tired.
W That's right. It's great to finally get rid of my stress.

[휴대폰이 울린다.]
남 Rachel, 오늘 무엇을 할 계획이니? 같이 놀래?
여 오, 그럴 수 없어. 나 지금 친구들과 해변에 와있어.
남 알겠어. 재미있게 보내고 있니?
여 응. 어제 수학 시험이 끝나고 휴식이 정말 필요했거든.
남 그래. 너 그 시험을 위해 정말 열심히 공부했잖아. 분명 많이 지쳤을 거야.
여 맞아. 마침내 스트레스를 없애게 돼서 좋아.

해설 | 여자가 수학 시험이 끝나고 휴식이 정말 필요했다고 하며, 마침내 스트레스를 없애게 돼서 좋다고 했으므로 정답은 ③ 'relaxed'이다.

선택지 해석
① 슬픈 ② 지루한 ③ 편안한 ④ 수줍은 ⑤ 긴장한

어휘 | hang out 놀다; 많은 시간을 보내다 break [breik] 명 휴식 동 깨다 get rid of 없애다, 제거하다

4 한 일 고르기

정답 ④

M Hi, Emma. How did your weekend go?
W Great. I volunteered at a local dog shelter on Saturday.
M Really? What did you do there?
W I fed the dogs and took them for walks.
M It sounds like you were busy. Were you tired on Sunday?
W Yeah. I just read a book in the morning and took a nap in the afternoon.
M Well, that sounds like a relaxing day to me.

남 안녕, Emma. 주말 어떻게 보냈니?
여 좋았어. 나는 토요일에 지역 유기견 보호소에서 자원봉사를 했어.
남 정말? 거기서 뭐 했니?
여 나는 개들에게 먹이를 주고 산책을 시켜줬어.
남 바빴던 것 같네. 일요일에는 피곤했니?
여 응. 오전에는 그냥 책을 읽고 오후에는 낮잠을 잤어.
남 음, 그거 나한테는 느긋한 하루였던 걸로 들리네.

해설 | 남자가 여자에게 일요일에는 피곤했는지 묻자 여자가 일요일 오전에는 그냥 책을 읽었다고 했으므로 정답은 ④ '책 읽기'이다.

어휘 | dog shelter 유기견 보호소 feed [fi:d] 동 음식, 먹이를 주다 take a nap 낮잠을 자다 relaxing [rilǽksiŋ] 형 느긋한, 사람을 느슨해지게 하는

5 장소 고르기

정답 ⑤

M Hello. Are you here to check in?
W Yes. My name is Susan Jones.
M Okay, Ms. Jones. You'll be staying here for two nights, right?
W That's correct.
M Would you like an ocean view or a mountain view from your room?
W I would prefer an ocean view.
M Excellent. Here is your key. You'll be in Room 501.
W Thank you.

남 안녕하세요. 체크인하러 오셨나요?
여 네. 제 이름은 Susan Jones예요.
남 알겠습니다, Jones씨. 여기에서 이틀 밤 묵는 것, 맞으시죠?
여 맞아요.
남 바다 전망 객실을 원하시나요, 아니면 산 전망 객실을 원하시나요?
여 바다 전망이면 좋겠어요.
남 좋습니다. 여기 열쇠가 있습니다. 501호 객실에 묵으실 예정입니다.
여 감사합니다.

해설 | 남자가 여자에게 체크인하러 왔는지 물으며 이틀 밤을 묵을 것이라는 점을 확인하는 것으로 보아 정답은 ⑤ '호텔'이다.

어휘 | correct [kərékt] 형 맞는, 정확한 view [vju:] 명 전망

6 의도 고르기

정답 ③

M Hey, Alice. Did you enter your drawing in the contest?
W Yes! I just sent it. I really hope I win.
M That's great. What did you draw?
W I drew a picture of a coral reef surrounded by fish. I looked up lots of images on the Internet for it.
M I bet you tried your best.
W Yes, I did. I'm sure I'll get a medal for it.

남 안녕, Alice. 너 대회에 그림 출품했니?
여 응! 방금 보냈어. 내가 우승하면 정말 좋겠어.
남 잘됐다. 뭘 그렸니?
여 물고기로 둘러싸인 산호초 그림을 그렸어. 그걸 위해 인터넷으로 많은 이미지들을 찾아봤었어.
남 틀림없이 넌 최선을 다했을 거야.
여 응, 그랬어. 내가 메달을 딸 거라고 확신해.

해설 | 여자가 최선을 다했고 대회에서 메달을 딸 거라고 확신한다고 했으므로 정답은 ③ '확신'이다.

어휘 | coral reef 산호초 surround [səráund] 동 둘러싸다 look up 찾아보다

7 한 일 고르기

정답 ②

W Hey, Sam! How was your holiday?
M It wasn't bad. How did you spend your Christmas?
W Well, I spent the day on a puzzle. I had this one-thousand-piece puzzle.
M Wow. You finished it all?
W Yeah. How was your Christmas in Hawaii? I can't imagine a warm and sunny Christmas day.
M Actually, I was on the airplane that day.
W Oh? What happened?
M I missed my flight, and there weren't any tickets left on the 24th.
W I'm so sorry to hear that.
M But the rest of the trip was great.

여 안녕, Sam! 네 휴일은 어땠니?
남 나쁘지 않았어. 크리스마스는 어떻게 보냈니?
여 음, 난 퍼즐로 하루를 보냈어. 나는 이 천 조각 짜리 퍼즐이 있었거든.
남 우와. 네가 다 끝냈어?
여 응. 하와이에서의 크리스마스는 어땠어? 나는 따뜻하고 화창한 크리스마스 날이 상상이 안 돼.
남 사실, 나는 그날 비행기에 있었어.
여 오? 무슨 일이 있었어?
남 내가 비행기를 놓쳤는데, 24일에는 남은 표가 하나도 없었거든.
여 정말 안됐네.
남 하지만 여행의 나머지 부분은 정말 좋았어.

해설 | 여자가 하와이에서의 크리스마스는 어땠냐고 물었고 남자가 그날 비행기에 있었다고 했으므로 정답은 ② '비행기 타기'이다.

어휘 | imagine [imǽdʒin] 동 상상하다

8 할 일 고르기

정답 ①

W Honey, do you want to do yoga this afternoon?
M Sure! I need to stretch my back.
W Hmm... There's one problem. I don't think there's enough space for both of us to do yoga in our living room.
M Why don't we move the sofa to the kitchen?
W Oh, that will give us much more space.
M Yeah. But I think we should clean the kitchen first.
W Okay. Let's do it.

여 여보, 오늘 오후에 요가 할래?
남 물론이지! 난 등을 스트레칭해야 해.
여 흠... 한 가지 문제가 있어. 우리 거실은 둘 다 요가를 하기엔 공간이 충분하지 않은 것 같아.
남 소파를 부엌으로 옮기는 건 어때?
여 오, 그러면 우리에게 훨씬 더 많은 공간이 생기겠네.
남 맞아. 그런데 우리 먼저 부엌 청소부터 해야 할 것 같아.
여 알겠어. 그러자.

해설 | 남자가 여자에게 먼저 부엌 청소부터 해야 할 것 같다고 제안하자 여자가 그러자고 했으므로 정답은 ① '부엌 청소하기'이다.

어휘 | space [speis] 명 공간 both of 둘 다, 양쪽 모두

9 언급하지 않은 내용 고르기

정답 ③

W Mike, congratulations on starting your new job as a radio show host!
M Thank you. I'm very excited.
W Your show is called *Morning Catch Up*. Could you tell us more about it?
M It's on from 9 to 11, and I will talk about world news.
W That sounds interesting. Will you interview many guests?
M Of course. There will be various experts on the show.
W And when will it be aired?
M The show will air every Monday.

여 Mike, 라디오 쇼 호스트로 새 일을 시작하게 된 걸 축하드려요!
남 감사합니다. 정말 신나네요.
여 당신의 프로는 <Morning Catch Up>이라고 불리는데요. 저희에게 그 프로에 대해 좀 더 말해주실래요?
남 9시부터 11시까지 방송되고, 저는 세계 뉴스에 대해 이야기할 거예요.
여 흥미롭네요. 많은 게스트도 인터뷰할 건가요?
남 물론입니다. 프로에는 다양한 전문가들이 나올 거예요.
여 그리고 언제 방송이 될 예정인가요?
남 그 프로는 매주 월요일마다 방송될 거예요.

해설 | ① 제목(<Morning Catch Up>), ② 방송 시간(9시부터 11시까지), ④ 내용(세계 뉴스), ⑤ 방송 요일(월요일)에 대해 언급했으므로 정답은 ③ '방송국'이다.

어휘 | various [vέəriəs] 형 다양한 expert [ékspəːrt] 명 전문가 air [εər] 동 방송하다 명 공기

10 주제 고르기

정답 ③

M Welcome aboard, everyone. I'm Jason Smith, the captain of this cruise ship. I will go over the ship's regulations with you quickly. Please do not run on the deck. It's dangerous. Also, parents should watch their children closely in the pool. Lastly, please avoid making loud noises in your room after 11 p.m.

남 탑승하신 걸 환영합니다, 여러분. 저는 Jason Smith이고, 이 유람선의 선장입니다. 여러분들과 빠르게 선박의 규정을 훑어보겠습니다. 갑판 위에서는 뛰지 말아 주십시오. 위험합니다. 또한, 부모님들은 수영장에서 자녀분들을 주의 깊게 지켜봐 주십시오. 마지막으로, 오후 11시 이후엔 객실에서 큰 소음을 내지 말아 주십시오.

해설 | 남자가 탑승객들에게 선박의 규정을 말하고 있으므로 정답은 ③ '선박 이용 시 주의사항'이다.

어휘 | aboard [əbɔ́ːrd] 부 탑승하여, (배 등을) 타고 captain [kǽptin] 명 선장 go over 훑어보다 regulation [règjuléiʃən] 명 규정, 규칙
deck [dek] 명 갑판 closely [klóusli] 부 주의 깊게

11 일치하지 않는 내용 고르기

정답 ③

M Honey, are we leaving for Jejudo next Wednesday?
W No. We changed the date to May 15th, remember? It's Thursday.
M Right. I'm so excited! We haven't been on a trip for a year.
W I know. Do you want to ride the bus to the airport?
M Why don't we take the car? We have to go to the airport early in the morning.
W Sure. Should we eat something before we leave?
M Don't they give you breakfast on the plane?
W Oh, yes. Also, don't forget to pack your swimsuit. We'll go to the beach.

남 여보, 우리 다음 수요일에 제주도로 떠나?
여 아니. 5월 15일로 날짜 바꿨잖아, 기억나? 목요일이야.
남 맞네. 나 너무 신나! 우리 1년 동안 여행을 가지 않았잖아.
여 맞아. 공항에는 버스를 타고 갈래?
남 차를 가져가는 게 어때? 공항에 아침 일찍 가야 하잖아.
여 그래. 떠나기 전에 뭐 좀 먹어야 할까?
남 비행기에서 아침 식사를 주지 않니?
여 오, 맞아. 그리고, 수영복 챙기는 것 잊지 마. 우리는 해변에 갈 거야.

해설 | 남자가 차를 가져가는 게 어떠냐고 물었고 여자가 그러자고 했으므로 정답은 ③ '공항에 버스를 타고 간다.'이다.

어휘 | leave for ~로 떠나다 breakfast [brékfəst] 명 아침 식사 swimsuit [swímsùt] 명 수영복

12 목적 고르기

정답 ③

W Ben, a package was delivered for you.
M It must be the bag that I ordered online, Mom.
W Really? You already have a backpack.
M Yes. But I bought a cotton bag for shopping. I don't want to use plastic bags.
W That is so thoughtful of you, Ben.
M Thanks, Mom. I just wanted to protect the environment.
W I should also take a cotton bag when I go grocery shopping.

여 Ben, 너에게 택배가 왔어.
남 그건 분명 제가 온라인으로 주문한 가방이예요, 엄마.
여 정말? 너 이미 배낭이 있잖니.
남 네. 그런데 제가 산 건 장 보기용 면 가방이에요. 비닐봉지를 쓰고 싶지 않아요.
여 참 사려 깊구나, Ben.
남 고마워요, 엄마. 전 그냥 환경을 보호하고 싶었어요.
여 나도 장을 보러 갈 때는 면 가방을 가져가야겠구나.

해설 | 남자는 환경을 보호하고 싶어서 비닐봉지를 쓰길 원하지 않는다고 했으므로 정답은 ③ '비닐 사용을 줄이기 위해서'이다.

어휘 | package [pǽkidʒ] 명 택배, 소포 cotton [kɑ́tn] 명 면, 솜 plastic [plǽstik] 형 비닐의; 플라스틱의 thoughtful [θɔ́:tfəl] 형 사려 깊은

13 금액 정보 고르기

정답 ④

M Hi. Can I get tickets for the night palace tour?
W Sure. How many tickets do you need?
M One adult ticket and two kid tickets, please.
W How old are the kids?
M They are both nine years old.
W It's 13 dollars for an adult and six dollars for kids under 10.
M Okay. How much do I have to pay in total?
W It's 25 dollars.
M Here you are.

남 안녕하세요. 야간 궁 투어 표를 살 수 있을까요?
여 물론이죠. 표는 몇 장 필요하세요?
남 어른 1장이랑 어린이 2장으로 부탁드립니다.
여 아이들은 몇 살인가요?
남 둘 다 9살이에요.
여 어른은 13달러이고 10살 이하 어린이는 6달러입니다.
남 알겠습니다. 총 얼마 내야 하는 거죠?
여 25달러입니다.
남 여기 있어요.

해설 | 어른은 13달러, 10살 이하 어린이는 6달러로 총 25달러라고 했으므로 정답은 ④ '$ 25'이다.

어휘 | adult [ədʌ́lt] 명 어른, 성인

14 관계 고르기

정답 ④

M Hello. Do you live in this apartment?
W Yes, sir. What happened?
M There was a small fire. Luckily, we put it out before it got worse.
W Oh, no! What started the fire?
M It was an electrical problem in the kitchen.
W That's scary!
M It's important to check the wiring regularly to prevent fires.
W Okay. I definitely will.

남 안녕하세요. 이 아파트에 사시나요?
여 네, 선생님. 무슨 일이죠?
남 작은 화재가 있었어요. 다행히, 심각해지기 전에 저희가 불을 껐어요.
여 오, 이런! 무엇이 화재를 일으켰나요?
남 부엌에 전기 문제가 있었어요.
여 무섭네요!
남 화재를 예방하려면 정기적으로 전선을 점검하는 게 중요합니다.
여 알겠습니다. 꼭 그렇게 할게요.

해설 | 남자가 여자에게 아파트에 사는지 물은 후, 아파트에서 작은 화재가 있었지만 심각해지기 전에 불을 껐다고 하는 것으로 보아 정답은 ④ '소방관 — 시민'이다.

어휘 | luckily [lʌ́kili] 부 다행히 put out 끄다 electrical [iléktrikəl] 형 전기의

15 제안한 일 고르기

정답 ②

W Alex, can I borrow your cellphone for a minute?
M Sure. Here you go.
W Thank you. *[Pause]* Why is your phone so slow?
M I have no idea. It got slow recently.
W Maybe your phone's storage space is full.
M What should I do then?
W Why don't you delete some of your videos? Those take up a lot of space.
M I'll check the photo album and decide which ones to delete.

여 Alex, 잠깐만 네 휴대폰을 빌릴 수 있을까?
남 물론이지. 여기 있어.
여 고마워. *[잠시 멈춤]* 네 휴대폰 왜 이렇게 느리니?
남 잘 모르겠는데. 최근에 느려졌어.
여 아마 네 휴대폰의 저장 공간이 꽉 찼을 거야.
남 내가 뭘 해야 할까 그럼?
여 영상 중 일부를 삭제하는 건 어때? 그게 공간을 많이 차지해.
남 사진첩을 확인하고 어떤 걸 삭제할지 결정할게.

해설 | 여자가 남자에게 휴대폰에 저장된 영상 중 일부를 삭제할 것을 제안했으므로 정답은 ② '영상 삭제하기'이다.

어휘 | recently [rí:sntli] 부 최근에 storage [stɔ́:ridʒ] 명 저장 delete [dilí:t] 동 삭제하다 take up 차지하다

16 이유 고르기

정답 ②

M Excuse me.
W Yes? Would you like some more water?
M No. I want to order more food, but I need to see a menu.
W Here's a menu for you. *[Pause]* Does anything look good?
M Hmm... Can you recommend the most popular dish at this restaurant?
W I recommend the beef steak.
M It looks tasty. I'll have one of those.
W Alright.

남 실례합니다.
여 네? 물을 좀 더 드릴까요?
남 아니요. 음식을 더 주문하고 싶은데, 메뉴를 봐야 해서요.
여 여기 메뉴판이 있습니다. *[잠시 멈춤]* 맛있어 보이는 게 있으신가요?
남 흠... 이 식당에서 가장 인기 있는 요리를 추천해주시겠어요?
여 소고기 스테이크를 추천해 드릴게요.
남 맛있어 보이네요. 그걸로 하나 주세요.
여 알겠습니다.

해설 | 남자가 여자를 부른 후 음식을 더 주문하고 싶다고 했으므로 정답은 ② '추가 주문을 하려고'이다.
어휘 | recommend [rèkəménd] 동 추천하다 dish [diʃ] 명 요리; 접시 tasty [téisti] 형 맛있는

17 그림 상황에 적절한 대화 고르기

정답 ④

① W We should go to the restroom before the movie starts.
M That's a good idea.
② W Do you have any water left?
M Yeah. The water bottle is in my backpack.
③ W Did you bring your swimming cap?
M Oops. I forgot.
④ W This view from the top of the mountain is incredible.
M Yes. The town looks like a toy.
⑤ W Oh, it's raining! I don't have an umbrella.
M It's okay. Let's go wait under that tree.

① 여 우리 영화가 시작하기 전에 화장실에 가야 해.
남 좋은 생각이야.
② 여 남은 물이 좀 있니?
남 응. 내 배낭 안에 물병이 있어.
③ 여 수영모 가져왔니?
남 이런. 잊어버렸어.
④ 여 산 정상에서 보는 경치가 정말 엄청나다.
남 응. 마을이 장난감처럼 보여.
⑤ 여 오, 비가 와! 나 우산 없는데.
남 괜찮아. 저 나무 아래에서 기다리자.

해설 | 남자와 여자가 산 정상에서 아래를 바라보고 있고, 남자가 손가락으로 마을을 가리키고 있는 상황이므로 정답은 ④이다.
어휘 | restroom [réstru:m] 명 화장실 incredible [inkrédəbl] 형 엄청난, 믿어지지 않는

18 언급하지 않은 내용 고르기

정답 ⑤

W Jack, what are you doing?
M I'm buying tickets for the Robot Olympics. It's a robot competition.
W What do the robots do?
M The events involve activities like walking up stairs or folding laundry.
W Where is it held?
M This year, it will take place in our city at the Seattle Stadium.
W I might go then. Is it happening soon?
M It will be held on June 16th.
W Great. I'll buy a ticket as well.

여 Jack, 뭐 하고 있니?
남 Robot Olympics 표를 사는 중이야. 그건 로봇 대회야.
여 로봇이 뭘 하는데?
남 그 행사에는 계단 오르기나 빨래 개기 같은 종목이 포함돼 있어.
여 어디에서 열리니?
남 올해는, 우리 도시의 시애틀 경기장에서 열릴 거야.
여 그럼 나도 가봐야겠다. 곧 열리는 거니?
남 6월 16일에 열릴 예정이야.
여 좋아. 나도 표를 사야겠다.

해설 | ① 이름(Robot Olympics), ② 종목(계단 오르기, 빨래 개기), ③ 장소(시애틀 경기장), ④ 날짜(6월 16일)에 대해 언급했으므로 정답은 ⑤ '참가비'이다.
어휘 | involve [inválv] 동 포함되다, 관련되다 laundry [lɔ́:ndri] 명 빨래 take place 열리다, 일어나다

19 적절한 응답 고르기

정답 ③

W The garden is so beautiful, Phil.
M Thank you. I enjoy gardening in my free time.
W I think it is a good hobby.
M But I have a problem now.
W What is it?
M Some plants in my garden are turning brown.
W Perhaps they need water. Try watering them every morning.
M Okay. I'll try not to forget it.

여 정원이 정말 아름답다, Phil.
남 고마워. 난 여가 시간에 원예를 즐겨.
여 그건 좋은 취미라고 생각해.
남 그런데 요즘 문제가 있어.
여 뭔데?
남 내 정원의 식물 몇 개가 갈색으로 변하고 있어.
여 어쩌면 물이 필요한 걸지도 몰라. 매일 아침 물을 줘 봐.
남 알겠어. 잊어버리지 않도록 노력할게.

해설 | 남자에게 매일 아침 식물에 물을 줄 것을 충고하고 있으므로 정답은 충고를 수락하는 ③ 'Okay. I'll try not to forget it.'이다.

선택지 해석

① 우린 남아프리카에서 한 달을 보냈어. ② 그건 토마토 모종이야. ③ 알겠어. 잊어버리지 않도록 노력할게. ④ 아침에 그것들을 심을게.
⑤ 집 안으로 옮겨 둘게.

어휘 | hobby [hábi] 명 취미 water [wɔ́:tər] 명 물 동 물을 주다

20 적절한 응답 고르기

정답 ④

[Telephone rings.]
M Hello, may I help you?
W Yes. My cat is sick.
M Okay. What's wrong with your cat?
W She's sleeping a lot and doesn't eat much.
M When did she start acting this way?
W She has acted strangely for two days.
M I think it's best that you bring her to the hospital.
W Okay. When can I come by?
M How about around 3 in the afternoon?

[전화기가 울린다.]
남 안녕하세요, 도와드릴까요?
여 네. 제 고양이가 아파요.
남 그렇군요. 고양이가 무엇이 문제인가요?
여 잠을 많이 자고 많이 먹지를 않아요.
남 언제부터 그렇게 행동하기 시작했습니까?
여 이틀 동안 이상하게 행동했어요.
남 제 생각에 고양이를 병원으로 데려오시는 게 가장 좋을 것 같군요.
여 알겠습니다. 언제 들르면 될까요?
남 오후 3시쯤은 어떠세요?

해설 | 여자가 언제 들르면 되는지 묻고 있으므로 정답은 방문 시간을 언급하는 ④ 'How about around 3 in the afternoon?'이다.

선택지 해석

① 죄송하지만, 지금은 문을 닫았어요. ② 그는 병원에 갔어요. ③ 고양이와 더 자주 놀아줘야 해요. ④ 오후 3시쯤은 어떠세요?
⑤ 네. 사무실은 모퉁이 근처에 있어요.

어휘 | act [ækt] 동 행동하다 strangely [stréindʒli] 부 이상하게 come by 들르다

22회 고난도 모의고사

| 문제 pp.196-197

1	⑤	2	③	3	③	4	⑤	5	⑤	6	④	7	⑤	8	④	9	④	10	②
11	③	12	②	13	③	14	①	15	④	16	④	17	③	18	③	19	①	20	③

1 날씨 고르기

정답 ⑤

W Good morning, everyone! It's a beautiful Saturday with bright sunshine and clear skies. But light rain will start falling in the afternoon, and it will continue until tomorrow morning. It'll be partly cloudy on Sunday afternoon, but the clouds will disappear by next week. So, enjoy the sun on Monday.

여 안녕하세요, 여러분! 밝은 햇살과 맑은 하늘이 있는 아름다운 토요일입니다. 다만 오후부터 약한 비가 내리기 시작해, 내일 오전까지 이어지겠습니다. 일요일 오후에는 일부 흐리겠으나 다음 주까지는 구름이 사라지겠습니다. 그러니, 월요일에는 태양을 즐기세요.

해설 | 여자는 오늘이 토요일이라고 했고, 다음 날인 일요일 오후에는 부분적으로 흐리다고 했으므로 정답은 ⑤이다.
어휘 | disappear [dìsəpíər] 동 사라지다

2 알맞은 그림 고르기

정답 ③

M Mom, are you looking for something? W Yeah. I can't find my wedding ring. M Let me help you find it. What does it look like? W It has one round diamond in the middle. M Does it have four small pearls? W No. That's my grandmother's ring. M How about this one? W That one looks similar, but the one I'm looking for is thicker. M Oh, I think I found it.	남 엄마, 뭐 찾으시는 거 있으세요? 여 응. 내 결혼반지를 못 찾겠어. 남 제가 찾는 걸 도와 드릴게요. 어떻게 생겼어요? 여 가운데에 둥근 다이아몬드가 하나 있어. 남 작은 진주 네 개가 있나요? 여 아니. 그건 내 할머니의 반지란다. 남 이것은 어때요? 여 비슷하게 생겼지만, 내가 찾고 있는 것이 더 두껍단다. 남 오, 제가 찾은 것 같아요.

해설 | 여자가 찾는 반지는 가운데에 둥근 다이아몬드가 하나 있고, 두껍다고 했으므로 정답은 ③이다.
어휘 | round [raund] 형 둥근 pearl [pəːrl] 명 진주 similar [símələr] 형 비슷한

3 심정 고르기

정답 ③

M Can I talk to you for a second, Hanna? Did you hand in your homework today? W I couldn't, sir. My dog, Trevor, ate my homework. M This is the third time this week you have missed an assignment. W I know. But there was nothing I could do. M You promised to do your homework this time. W I'm sorry. M I expected you to keep your promise, but you let me down again.	남 잠깐 얘기 좀 할 수 있을까, 한나야? 오늘 숙제 제출했니? 여 할 수 없었어요, 선생님. 제 강아지 Trevor가 제 숙제를 먹었어요. 남 이번 주에 숙제를 놓친 것이 이번이 세 번째구나. 여 알아요. 하지만 제가 할 수 있는 게 아무것도 없었어요. 남 이번엔 숙제를 하기로 약속했잖니. 여 죄송해요. 남 네가 약속을 지킬 줄 알았는데, 또 나를 실망시키는구나.

해설 | 남자는 여자가 약속을 지킬 줄 알았는데, 또 실망시켰다고 했으므로 정답은 ③ 'disappointed'이다.
선택지 해석
① 수줍은 ② 당황한 ③ 실망한 ④ 긴장한 ⑤ 기쁜
어휘 | for a second 잠깐 hand in 제출하다 promise [prámis] 동 약속하다 명 약속 let down 실망시키다

4 한 일 고르기

정답 ⑤

W Jake, did you sign up for the bowling tournament? M Yes, I did. Did you register for it too? W Not yet. I'll do it tomorrow. M I'm looking forward to the tournament since it's my first time competing. W I'm sure we'll have lots of fun whether we win or lose. M But I hope we win. I've practiced a lot lately. W I watched the video of last year's competition. You should watch it. M Good idea. That will be very helpful.	여 Jake, 너 볼링 대회 신청했니? 남 응, 했어. 너도 등록했니? 여 아직. 내일 할 거야. 남 나는 처음 출전하는 경기라서 대회가 기대돼. 여 우리가 이기든 지든 분명 엄청 재미있을 거야. 남 하지만 나는 우리가 이기면 좋겠어. 최근에 연습을 많이 했거든. 여 나는 작년 대회 영상을 봤어. 그걸 봐야 해. 남 좋은 생각이야. 정말 도움이 될 거야.

해설 | 여자가 작년 대회 영상을 봤다고 말하면서 남자에게도 볼 것을 권했으므로 정답은 ⑤ '작년 경기 영상 보기'이다.
어휘 | sign up for ~을 신청하다 tournament [túərnəmənt] 명 대회, 경기 compete [kəmpíːt] 동 출전하다; 경쟁하다

5 장소 고르기

정답 ⑤

W It's such a beautiful day today.
M It really is. Let's go for a swim!
W Okay. But we can't go too far.
M Why not?
W The lifeguards said that we cannot swim farther than that rock.
M That's fine. Hey, do you have any sunscreen?
W Yes. It's here. I should put some on too. I feel like I'm starting to burn.

여 오늘 정말 아름다운 날이야.
남 정말 그렇네. 수영하러 가자!
여 좋아. 하지만 너무 멀리 가면 안 돼.
남 왜 안돼?
여 구조대원이 저 바위보다 더 멀리 수영할 수 없다고 했어.
남 알겠어. 잠깐, 너 자외선 차단제 있니?
여 응. 여기 있어. 나도 발라야겠다. 나는 타기 시작한 것 같아.

해설 | 남자가 수영하러 가자고 하자, 여자가 구조대원이 저 바위보다 더 멀리 수영할 수 없다고 했다는 말을 하는 것으로 보아 정답은 ⑤ '바닷가'이다.

어휘 | far [fa:r] 부 멀리 lifeguard [láifgà:rd] 명 구조대원 sunscreen [sʌ́nskri:n] 명 자외선 차단제 burn [bə:rn] 동 타다

6 의도 고르기

정답 ④

W Why do you have the long face, Kevin?
M I didn't win the gold medal. It's so disappointing.
W You can't win every race.
M I prepared so much for it. I wanted to break my record.
W Did something happen? I'm sure you still did well.
M I got really nervous.
W That's alright. You'll do better next time.

여 왜 우울한 얼굴을 하고 있니, Kevin?
남 내가 금메달을 따지 못했어. 너무 실망스러워.
여 모든 경주에서 이길 수는 없어.
남 나 그걸 위해 매우 많이 준비했어. 내 기록을 깨고 싶었거든.
여 무슨 일이 있었니? 나는 그래도 네가 잘했다고 확신해.
남 엄청나게 긴장했어.
여 괜찮아. 다음번에는 더 잘할 거야.

해설 | 남자가 경주에서 금메달을 따지 못해서 실망스럽다는 말을 하자 여자가 괜찮다며 다음번에는 더 잘할 거라는 말을 했으므로 정답은 ④ '격려'이다.

어휘 | long face 우울한 얼굴 disappointing [dìsəpɔ́intiŋ] 형 실망스러운 prepare [pripέər] 동 준비하다 break a record 기록을 깨다, 경신하다

7 특정 정보 고르기

정답 ⑤

M Honey, I'm home! I stopped by the supermarket, and bought flour and some fruits.
W Thanks! Did you buy any apples? I can bake an apple pie for dessert.
M They only had green apples, so I didn't get any.
W How about bananas and blueberries then?
M Sorry, but they were already sold out. But I got kiwis. They were on sale.
W Shawn, you know I have allergies to kiwis!
M Oops. I forgot.

남 여보, 나 왔어! 슈퍼마켓에 들러서 밀가루와 과일을 샀어.
여 고마워! 사과는 샀어? 내가 후식으로 애플파이를 구울 수 있는데.
남 초록 사과만 있어서, 사지 않았어.
여 그럼 바나나와 블루베리는?
남 미안하지만, 그것들은 이미 다 팔렸었어. 그래도 내가 키위는 샀어. 그것들이 할인 중이었거든.
여 Shawn, 내가 키위 알레르기가 있다는 거 알잖아!
남 아차. 잊어버렸어.

해설 | 남자가 키위를 샀다고 했으므로 정답은 ⑤ '키위'이다.

어휘 | stop by 들르다 on sale 할인 중인 allergy [ǽlərdʒi] 명 알레르기

8 할 일 고르기

정답 ④

W David, do you want to try this Spam musubi?
M What is Spam musubi?
W It's a Hawaiian food made with Spam, rice, and dried seaweed.
M Sounds delicious. I like eating Spam with rice.
W You should definitely try this then.
M Do you have an extra fork?
W Actually, you can eat it with your hands. Why don't you go wash your hands?
M Okay. I'll do that now.

여 David, 이 스팸 무스비 먹어볼래?
남 스팸 무스비가 뭐야?
여 스팸, 밥, 그리고 김으로 만든 하와이 음식이야.
남 맛있겠다. 나는 스팸을 밥이랑 같이 먹는 걸 좋아해.
여 이거 반드시 먹어봐야 해 그럼.
남 여분의 포크 있니?
여 사실, 손으로 먹어도 돼. 가서 손을 씻는 게 어때?
남 알았어. 지금 그렇게 할게.

해설 | 여자가 가서 손을 씻는 게 어떠냐고 묻자 남자가 알겠다며 지금 그러겠다고 했으므로 정답은 ④ '손 씻기'이다.

어휘 | seaweed [sìwíd] 명 김 extra [ékstrə] 형 여분의; 추가의

9 언급하지 않은 내용 고르기

정답 ④

M Hey, Sojin. Have you said hi to the new student?
W Her name is Jamie, right?
M I think so. Do you know where she is from?
W I heard that she came from Canada.
M Then, does she speak French too?
W Yeah. I don't remember her hobbies, though.
M I'll ask her when I introduce myself. I hope she likes taekwondo.
W I agree. It would be nice to invite her to our taekwondo club.

남 안녕, 소진아. 새로 온 학생에게 인사했니?
여 그녀의 이름은 Jamie야, 맞지?
남 그런 것 같아. 그녀가 어디 출신인지 아니?
여 캐나다에서 왔다고 들었어.
남 그럼, 프랑스어도 하니?
여 응. 하지만 그녀의 취미는 기억나지 않아.
남 내 소개를 할 때 물어볼게. 그녀가 태권도를 좋아했으면 좋겠다.
여 나도 동의해. 그녀를 우리 태권도 동아리에 초대하면 좋을 거야.

해설 | ① 이름(Jamie), ② 출신 국가(캐나다), ③ 언어(프랑스어), ⑤ 취미(기억나지 않음)에 대해 언급했으므로 정답은 ④ '가족 수'이다.

어휘 | say hi 인사하다 introduce [ìntrədjú:s] 동 소개하다 agree [əgrí:] 동 동의하다

10 주제 고르기

정답 ②

M Now, here's some information about our Dog Day event. It is open to anyone who has a dog. The event will be held at the Blair Dog Park at the corner of Durant Street. There will be fun activities like games and photo booths. We'll also provide treats for our furry friends. It's a free event, but we will ask for donations from participants. And this will be used to rescue dogs in danger.

남 이제, 애견의 날 행사에 대한 몇 가지 정보입니다. 이 행사는 반려견이 있는 누구에게나 열려 있습니다. 행사는 듀랜트 가의 모퉁이에 있는 블레어 애견 공원에서 열릴 예정입니다. 게임과 포토 부스 같은 재미있는 활동들이 있을 것입니다. 털북숭이 친구들을 위한 간식 또한 제공할 것입니다. 이것은 무료 이벤트지만, 저희는 참가자분들에게 기부금을 요청할 것입니다. 그리고 이것은 위험에 처한 개들을 구조하는 데 사용될 것입니다.

해설 | 남자가 애견의 날 행사에 대해 말하고 있으므로 정답은 ② '행사 정보 안내'이다.

어휘 | treat [tri:t] 명 간식 donation [dounéiʃən] 명 기부금; 기부 participant [pa:rtísəpənt] 명 참가자 rescue [réskju:] 동 구조하다 in danger 위험에 처한

11 일치하지 않는 내용 고르기

정답 ③

M Hello. This is LiveTour.com. How may I help you?
W Hi, I'd like information about the online tour of London.
M Sure. That tour is held every Saturday from 7 to 8 p.m.
W What's the cost?
M There's no charge. Any other questions?
W Are we able to talk to the guide during the tour?
M Of course. There's an online chat room.
W Okay. Can the tour accommodate large groups?
M Yes. But you must call our office first.

남 안녕하세요. LiveTour.com입니다. 어떻게 도와드릴까요?
여 안녕하세요, 런던 온라인 투어에 대한 정보를 알고 싶어요.
남 물론이죠. 그 투어는 매주 토요일 오후 7시부터 8시까지 열립니다.
여 비용이 얼마나 드나요?
남 무료입니다. 또 다른 궁금한 사항이 있으신가요?
여 관광하는 동안 가이드와 이야기를 나눌 수 있나요?
남 물론이죠. 온라인 채팅방이 있어요.
여 그렇군요. 그 투어는 큰 단체들을 수용할 수 있나요?
남 네. 하지만 먼저 저희 사무실로 전화하셔야 합니다.

해설 | 여자가 관광하는 동안 가이드와 이야기를 나눌 수 있는지 묻자 남자가 온라인 채팅방이 있다고 했으므로 정답은 ③ '가이드와 통화할 수 있다.'이다.

어휘 | charge [tʃa:rdʒ] 명 요금 accommodate [əká:mədeit] 동 수용하다

12 목적 고르기

정답 ②

W	Welcome. What can I help you with?	여	어서 오세요. 무엇을 도와드릴까요?
M	Do you have the new 4-Star Tablet PC?	남	새로 나온 4-Star 태블릿 PC 있나요?
W	We're sold out.	여	매진됐어요.
M	I see. When will the tablets be available again?	남	그렇군요. 태블릿은 언제 다시 구할 수 있나요?
W	Let me check. *[Typing sound]* On Thursday.	여	확인해 보겠습니다. *[타자 치는 소리]* 목요일이요.
M	In that case, can I buy one in advance? I will come pick it up.	남	그렇다면, 미리 하나 살 수 있을까요? 찾으러 올게요.
W	You can. Which color do you want?	여	그러셔도 됩니다. 무슨 색을 원하세요?
M	I'd like the red one.	남	빨간색이 좋겠어요.
W	That will be 500 dollars.	여	500달러입니다.

해설 | 남자가 새로 나온 4-Star 태블릿 PC가 있는지를 물은 후 미리 살 수 있는지 물어본 것으로 보아 정답은 ② '태블릿 PC를 선구매하기 위해서'이다.

어휘 | sold out 매진된 available [əvéiləbl] 형 구할 수 있는, 이용할 수 있는 in advance 미리, 사전에

13 숫자 정보 고르기

정답 ③

M	Diana, what are you planning to order for the year-end class party?	남	Diana, 연말 학급 파티 때 뭘 주문할 계획이니?
W	I still haven't decided yet. Maybe some pizza?	여	아직 결정하지 못했어. 아마 피자?
M	Hmm... It might get cold. How about donuts?	남	흠... 식을지도 몰라. 도넛은 어때?
W	Great idea. They would be easier to eat in class.	여	좋은 생각이야. 교실에서 먹기가 더 쉬울 거야.
M	How many donuts will we need?	남	도넛이 몇 개나 필요할까?
W	There are 24 students in our class. A box includes six donuts, so we need four boxes.	여	우리 반에는 24명의 학생이 있잖아. 한 박스에 도넛이 여섯 개 포함되니까, 네 박스가 필요해.
M	We also have to get one for our homeroom teacher, Mr. Scout.	남	우리 담임 선생님인 Scout 선생님 것도 하나 사야 해.
W	Oh, we'll have to buy one more box then.	여	오, 그럼 한 박스 더 사야겠네.

해설 | 여자가 네 박스가 필요하다고 했고, 남자가 선생님 것도 한 박스 더 사야 한다고 했으므로 정답은 ③ '5박스'이다.

어휘 | include [inklúːd] 동 포함하다

14 관계 고르기

정답 ①

W	Hello, Mr. Nicoles. I'll show you our living room first.	여	안녕하세요, Nicoles씨. 일단 저희 거실부터 보여드릴게요.
M	Okay. Which color do you want to paint the wall?	남	알겠습니다. 어떤 색으로 벽을 칠하고 싶으세요?
W	I'd like a light yellow paint.	여	연한 노란색 페인트가 좋겠어요.
M	And do you want the walls to match the ceiling?	남	그리고 벽을 천장에 맞추길 원하세요?
W	No. The ceiling should be white.	여	아니요. 천장은 하얀색이어야 해요.
M	Okay. I'll start painting the wall next Tuesday.	남	알겠습니다. 다음 주 화요일에 벽에 페인트칠을 시작할게요.
W	Should we move the furniture out of the living room?	여	거실 밖으로 가구들을 옮겨야 할까요?
M	Yes. I'd appreciate it.	남	네. 그래 주시면 감사하겠습니다.

해설 | 여자가 남자에게 거실을 보여주고, 남자가 벽을 어떤 색으로 칠하기를 원하는지를 묻고 있는 것으로 보아 정답은 ① '인테리어 디자이너 — 고객'이다.

어휘 | ceiling [síːliŋ] 명 천장 furniture [fə́ːrnitʃər] 명 가구

15 부탁·요청한 일 고르기

정답 ④

W Matt, what are you doing this Saturday?
M I'm going to rest at home. I've been too busy lately. Why?
W I'm working at the senior center, and we're having a table tennis tournament this week.
M That sounds interesting.
W I was wondering if you could volunteer and help me prepare for the event.
M Why not? I can ask my friends to help out if you need more volunteers.
W That would be great!

여 Matt, 이번 토요일에 뭐 할 거야?
남 난 집에서 쉴 거야. 요즘 너무 바빴어. 왜?
여 나는 노인 복지관에서 일하고 있는데, 이번 주에 우리는 탁구 대회를 열어.
남 그거 재미있겠는데.
여 네가 자원해서 내가 행사를 준비하는 것을 도와줄 수 있을까 해서.
남 왜 안 되겠어? 만약 봉사자가 더 필요하면 내 친구들에게 도와달라고 물어 볼 수 있어.
여 그럼 정말 좋지!

해설 | 여자가 남자에게 자원해서 자신이 행사 준비하는 것을 도와줄 수 있으면 한다고 부탁했으므로 정답은 ④ '봉사활동 하기'이다.

어휘 | senior center 노인 복지관 tournament [túərnəmənt] 명 대회 help out 도와주다

16 이유 고르기

정답 ④

W Andy, didn't you watch this movie before?
M Yeah, I did. This is about the seventh time.
W What? Why have you watched that movie so much? There are lots of other good movies.
M At first, I watched it for my English homework.
W And did it become your favorite?
M I fell in love with the actress. Her acting is incredible.
W Wow. I should watch it sometime.
M I think I have memorized her lines now.

여 Andy, 너 이 영화 전에 보지 않았니?
남 응, 봤어. 이번이 대략 일곱 번째야.
여 뭐? 그 영화를 왜 그렇게 많이 봤어? 다른 좋은 영화들도 많이 있잖아.
남 처음에는, 영어 숙제 때문에 봤어.
여 그리고서는 네가 가장 좋아하는 영화가 됐니?
남 여배우와 사랑에 빠졌어. 그녀의 연기는 정말 엄청나.
여 우와. 나도 언제 한번 봐야겠다.
남 난 이제 그녀의 대사를 외운 것 같아.

해설 | 남자는 영화 속 여배우와 사랑에 빠졌고, 그녀의 연기는 정말 대단하다고 말했으므로 정답은 ④ '배우의 연기가 훌륭해서'이다.

어휘 | fall in love with ~와 사랑에 빠지다 incredible [inkrédəbl] 형 엄청난 memorize [méməraiz] 동 외다; ~을 암기하다 line [lain] 명 대사; 선

17 그림 상황에 적절한 대화 고르기

정답 ③

① W Did you enjoy your dinner?
M Yes, thank you. Can you get me the bill?
② W Would you like your coffee for here?
M I'd like it to go please.
③ W I'd like to exchange a shirt I bought last week.
M I see. Do you have a receipt?
④ W What time does the bank open?
M At 9 o'clock, but it is closed today.
⑤ W How do you want to have your hair cut?
M Short, please. I also want to dye my hair brown.

① 여 저녁 맛있게 드셨나요?
남 네, 감사합니다. 계산서를 가져다주시겠어요?
② 여 커피는 여기에서 드시겠습니까?
남 포장해 주세요.
③ 여 지난주에 산 셔츠를 교환하고 싶어요.
남 그렇군요. 영수증을 가지고 계신가요?
④ 여 은행은 몇 시에 문을 여나요?
남 9시인데, 오늘은 문을 닫았어요.
⑤ 여 머리를 어떻게 잘라드릴까요?
남 짧게 해 주세요. 갈색으로 염색도 하고 싶어요.

해설 | 지난주에 산 셔츠를 교환하고 싶다고 했고, 남자가 영수증을 가지고 있는지 물어보는 상황이므로 정답은 ③이다.

어휘 | bill [bil] 명 계산서 exchange [ikstʃéindʒ] 동 교환하다 receipt [risíːt] 명 영수증 dye [dai] 동 염색하다

18 언급하지 않은 내용 고르기

정답 ③

W Would you like to escape from your daily life? Visit us at the Bancroft Resort! We just opened on March 27th. We have more than 100 rooms that come in five different types. We offer various kinds of foods and beverages at our restaurant on the 20th floor. You can also enjoy the scenery around our hotel from the rooftop swimming pool. To make a reservation, call 555-2356 or visit our website at www.BancroftResort.com.

여 일상생활에서 벗어나고 싶나요? 밴크로프트 리조트를 방문하세요! 저희는 3월 27일에 막 문을 열었습니다. 5가지 다른 유형의 객실을 100개 이상 보유하고 있습니다. 20층에 있는 저희 레스토랑에서는 다양한 종류의 음식과 음료를 제공하고 있습니다. 옥상 수영장에서는 호텔 주변의 풍경도 감상하실 수 있습니다. 예약을 하시려면, 555-2356으로 전화하시거나 저희 웹사이트 www.BancroftResort.com을 방문하십시오.

해설 | ① 개업일(3월 27일), ② 객실 수(100개 이상), ④ 시설(레스토랑, 옥상 수영장), ⑤ 예약 방법(전화, 웹사이트 방문)에 대해 언급했으므로 정답은 ③ '위치'이다.

어휘 | escape [iskéip] 동 벗어나다; 탈출하다 daily life 일상생활 beverage [bévəridʒ] 명 음료 scenery [síːnəri] 명 풍경

19 적절한 응답 고르기

정답 ①

M Excuse me. Can you tell me the time?
W Sure. It's almost noon.
M Thanks. My friend took a bus from Busan at 8 o'clock. The bus will arrive at 12, right?
W Actually, the bus was delayed.
M Oh, no. Really?
W Yes. There was a big car accident on the highway.
M That's terrible! Was it serious?
W Luckily, no one was hurt. But the bus got stuck in traffic.
M Then, what time is the bus arriving?
W It'll be here around 2 p.m.

남 실례합니다. 지금 몇 시인지 말씀해주실 수 있나요?
여 물론이죠. 정오가 다 되어 가요.
남 감사합니다. 제 친구가 부산에서 8시에 버스를 탔거든요. 버스는 12시에 도착하죠, 그렇죠?
여 사실, 그 버스는 연착됐어요.
남 오, 이런. 정말요?
여 네. 고속도로에 큰 교통사고가 있었어요.
남 끔찍하네요! 심각했나요?
여 다행히도, 아무도 다치지 않았어요. 하지만 버스가 교통체증에 갇혔어요.
남 그럼, 버스가 몇 시에 도착하나요?
여 오후 2시쯤에 올 거예요.

해설 | 남자가 버스가 몇 시에 도착하는지 묻고 있으므로 정답은 시간을 알려주는 ① 'It'll be here around 2 p.m.'이다.

선택지 해석

① 오후 2시쯤에 올 거예요. ② 더 이상 자리가 없어요. ③ 일찍 오셨네요. ④ 네. 한 시간 후에 착륙할 예정이에요.
⑤ 그런 끔찍한 소식을 듣게 되어 정말 유감이에요.

어휘 | noon [nuːn] 명 정오 car accident 교통사고 highway [háiwei] 명 고속도로 stuck [stʌk] 형 갇힌

20 적절한 응답 고르기

정답 ③

W Hey, Sam. You look worried. What's up?
M I got my medical test results.
W Is there a problem?
M Yeah. I'm a bit overweight.
W Do you have to go on a diet?
M No. But I should eat more vegetables. Also, I need to exercise every day.
W What's your plan?
M I don't know. I don't like to run or swim. What else can I do for exercise?
W I recommend walking.

여 안녕, Sam. 걱정이 있어 보이네. 무슨 일이야?
남 내 종합 검진 결과가 나왔거든.
여 문제가 있니?
남 응. 나 조금 과체중이야.
여 다이어트를 해야 하니?
남 아니. 하지만 채소를 더 먹어야 해. 매일 운동도 해야 해.
여 너의 계획은 뭐야?
남 나도 몰라. 나는 달리거나 수영하는 것을 좋아하지 않아. 그 밖에 운동으로 무엇을 할 수 있을까?
여 나는 걷는 것을 추천해.

해설 | 남자가 그 밖에 운동으로 무엇을 할 수 있을지 물었으므로 정답은 운동의 종류를 말하는 ③ 'I recommend walking.'이다.

선택지 해석

① 응. 체육관에 등록할 계획이야. ② 당근은 몸에 좋아. ③ 나는 걷는 것을 추천해. ④ 수영하는 것은 좋은 선택인 것 같아.
⑤ 걱정하지 마. 그는 곧 좋아질 거야.

어휘 | medical test 종합 검진 overweight [oùvərwéit] 형 과체중의

23회 고난도 모의고사

| 문제 pp.204-205

1	①	2	②	3	②	4	③	5	①	6	④	7	②	8	⑤	9	③	10	①
11	④	12	②	13	④	14	④	15	②	16	⑤	17	④	18	④	19	①	20	⑤

1 날씨 고르기

정답 ①

W Hello, everyone. Here's the global weather forecast. In Moscow, thunder and lightning are expected. New York is going to be foggy, so drivers should be careful. The temperature in Berlin will drop below zero, and a snowstorm is expected. Please wear warm clothes and stay inside. Thank you.

여 안녕하십니까, 여러분. 세계 일기 예보입니다. 모스크바에는 천둥과 번개가 예상됩니다. 뉴욕은 안개가 끼겠으니, 운전자분들은 주의하십시오. 베를린의 온도는 영하로 떨어질 예정이며, 눈보라가 예상됩니다. 따뜻한 옷을 입으시고 실내에 머무르시기 바랍니다. 감사합니다.

해설 | 베를린에는 눈보라가 예상된다고 했으므로 정답은 ①이다.

어휘 | global [glóubəl] 형 세계의, 세계적인 thunder [θʌ́ndər] 명 천둥

2 알맞은 그림 고르기

정답 ②

M Mindy, what are you cooking?
W I'm making some chocolates for my friends, Dad.
M The fish-shaped ones are very impressive.
W Thank you, Dad. I also made seashell-shaped chocolates.
M They look delicious. Are you going to put them in boxes?
W Yes. I'll put three fish-shaped chocolates and one seashell-shaped chocolate in each box.

남 Mindy, 뭘 요리하는 중이니?
여 제 친구들에게 줄 초콜릿을 만들고 있어요, 아빠.
남 물고기 모양의 초콜릿들이 매우 인상적이구나.
여 고마워요, 아빠. 조개 모양의 초콜릿도 만들었어요.
남 맛있어 보이는구나. 이것들을 상자에 담을 거니?
여 네. 각 상자에 물고기 모양 초콜릿 3개와 조개 모양 초콜릿 1개를 담을 거예요.

해설 | 여자가 각 상자에 물고기 모양 초콜릿 3개와 조개 모양 초콜릿 1개를 담을 것이라고 했으므로 정답은 ②이다.

어휘 | seashell [síːʃel] 명 조개

3 의도 고르기

정답 ②

W John, you look cheerful.
M Mom, I heard about an international art fair in Thailand this summer. I'd really like to go.
W Who do you want to go with?
M I was planning to go by myself.
W You're too young to travel abroad alone.
M Don't worry. I'll call you every day.
W Well, I don't think I can give you permission to do that.
M Please, Mom. The fair sounds incredible.

여 John, 기분이 좋아 보이는구나.
남 엄마, 올여름에 태국에서 열릴 국제 미술 박람회에 대해 들었는데요. 저 정말 가고 싶어요.
여 누구와 가고 싶은데?
남 혼자서 가는 걸 계획 중이었어요.
여 혼자 해외여행을 하기에 너는 너무 어리단다.
남 걱정하지 마세요. 매일 전화할게요.
여 글쎄, 나는 네가 그렇게 하도록 허락할 수 없을 것 같구나.
남 제발요, 엄마. 박람회가 굉장할 거 같아요.

해설 | 여자가 남자에게 혼자 해외여행을 하기에 너무 어리다며 허락할 수 없을 것 같다고 하자, 남자가 박람회가 굉장할 것 같다고 하며 다시 한번 부탁했으므로 정답은 ② '설득'이다.

어휘 | cheerful [tʃíərfəl] 형 기분 좋은, 쾌활한 by oneself 혼자서, 홀로 abroad [əbrɔ́ːd] 부 해외로 permission [pərmíʃən] 명 허락, 허가
incredible [inkrédəbl] 형 굉장한

4 한 일 고르기

정답 ③

W	Neil, what did you do last weekend?	여	Neil, 너는 지난 주말에 뭐 했니?
M	I visited a temple with my parents. What about you, Bella?	남	부모님과 절에 방문했어. 너는 어땠어, Bella?
W	I made candles at home.	여	나는 집에서 양초를 만들었어.
M	What a fun thing to do! Was it hard?	남	재미있는 일 했네! 어려웠어?
W	No. It was easy even though it was my first attempt.	여	아니. 첫 시도였는데도 불구하고 쉬웠어.
M	Great! Do your candles smell nice?	남	잘됐네! 네 양초는 향이 좋니?
W	Yeah. I put a drop of aroma oil in them.	여	응. 아로마 오일을 한 방울 넣었거든.

해설 | 여자가 지난 주말에 집에서 양초를 만들었다고 했고, 아로마 오일을 넣어서 향이 좋다고 했으므로 정답은 ③ '향초 만들기'이다.

어휘 | temple [témpl] 명 절 candle [kǽndl] 명 양초 attempt [ətémpt] 명 시도 동 시도하다

5 장소 고르기

정답 ①

W	Hello. Can I see your passport, please?	여	안녕하세요. 여권을 보여주시겠어요?
M	Sure. Here you go.	남	물론이죠. 여기 있어요.
W	*[Typing sound]* Here's your ticket to New York. The plane takes off at 3 p.m.	여	*[타자 치는 소리]* 여기 뉴욕행 표입니다. 비행기는 오후 3시에 이륙할 거예요.
M	Thank you. And I'd like to check luggage.	남	감사합니다. 그리고 제 수화물을 체크인하고 싶은데요.
W	Okay. How many suitcases do you have?	여	알겠습니다. 여행 가방이 몇 개나 되세요?
M	I have two.	남	두 개요.
W	Please place them on the scale one at a time.	여	그것들을 한 번에 하나씩 저울 위에 놓아주세요.

해설 | 여자가 남자에게 여권을 보여달라고 한 후 표를 건네주며 비행기의 이륙 시간을 말해주는 것으로 보아 정답은 ① '공항'이다.

어휘 | passport [pǽspɔːrt] 명 여권 take off 이륙하다 luggage [lʌ́gidʒ] 명 수화물, 여행 가방 place [pleis] 동 놓다, 두다 명 곳, 장소 scale [skeil] 명 저울

6 일치하지 않는 내용 고르기

정답 ④

M	Jenna, I bought this cake from the bakery on Park Street.	남	Jenna, 내가 파크 가에 있는 제과점에서 이 케이크를 샀어.
W	I didn't know that there's a bakery nearby.	여	근처에 제과점이 있는 줄 몰랐어.
M	Well, it opened last month.	남	음, 그곳은 지난달에 개업했어.
W	Are they expensive?	여	비싸니?
M	No. The bakery has very reasonable prices.	남	아니. 그 제과점은 가격이 매우 합리적이야.
W	I will visit it tomorrow afternoon.	여	내일 오후에 거기 방문해봐야겠다.
M	You should get there at least an hour before it opens. Can you make it at 8 a.m.?	남	적어도 문 열기 한 시간 전에는 도착해야 해. 오전 8시에 맞춰 갈 수 있겠어?
W	I can. But why? Do many people line up at the store?	여	갈 수 있어. 그런데 왜? 많은 사람이 가게에서 줄을 서니?
M	Yes, they do!	남	응, 그래!

해설 | 남자가 제과점이 문을 열기 적어도 한 시간 전에는 가야 한다면서 오전 8시에 갈 것을 제안했으므로 정답은 ④ '오전 8시부터 운영한다.'이다.

어휘 | reasonable [ríːzənəbl] 형 합리적인 line up 줄을 서다

7 할 일 고르기

정답 ②

M	Carla, do you run much these days?	남	Carla, 요즘에도 달리기를 많이 하니?
W	No. I don't like to run in the summer.	여	아니. 난 여름에 달리는 건 안 좋아해.
M	You can go running early in the morning. It will be cooler then.	남	아침 일찍 달리러 갈 수 있잖아. 그때는 더 시원할 거야.
W	I feel too tired when I wake up early.	여	일찍 일어나면 너무 피곤해.
M	Oh, you could join a gym.	남	오, 체육관에 등록하면 되겠다.
W	There isn't one near my house.	여	집 근처에 체육관이 없어.
M	What about buying a running machine?	남	러닝머신을 사는 건 어때?
W	That would be more convenient. I should order one now.	여	그건 좀 더 편리할 것 같네. 지금 주문해야겠어.

해설 | 남자가 여자에게 러닝머신 사는 것을 제안하자 여자가 지금 주문해야겠다고 했으므로 정답은 ② '기구 구매하기'이다.
어휘 | convenient [kənvíːnjənt] 형 편리한

8 할 일 고르기

정답 ⑤

M What's wrong, Silvia? You seem frustrated.
W I ordered a table, and it just arrived. But the color looks different from what I expected.
M Did the company make a mistake?
W No. But the color looked much brighter online.
M I see. Why don't you paint the table another color?
W That's actually not a bad idea.
M You can order the paint on the Internet.
W I'll do that now. I hope there's a nice blue paint.

남 무슨 일이야, Silvia? 불만스러워 보이네.
여 내가 식탁을 주문했는데, 막 도착했거든. 그런데 내가 기대했던 거랑 색상이 다르게 보여.
남 회사에서 실수한 거야?
여 아니. 그런데 온라인으로는 색상이 훨씬 밝아 보였어.
남 그렇구나. 식탁을 다른 색상으로 칠해보는 건 어때?
여 그거 나쁘지 않은 생각이네.
남 인터넷으로 페인트를 주문할 수 있어.
여 지금 해야겠다. 근사한 푸른색 페인트가 있으면 좋겠어.

해설 | 남자가 식탁을 칠할 페인트를 인터넷으로 주문할 것을 제안하자 여자가 지금 해야겠다고 했으므로 정답은 ⑤ '페인트 주문하기'이다.
어휘 | frustrated [frʌ́streitid] 형 불만스러워하는, 낙담한 company [kʌ́mpəni] 명 회사 bright [brait] 형 밝은

9 언급하지 않은 내용 고르기

정답 ③

M Wendy, have you heard about the new car from Fast Motors?
W Yes. Wasn't it released yesterday?
M Yeah. I really want to see it in person.
W Same here. It must be very efficient since it's an electric car.
M You have a point. If you could buy it, which color would you want?
W Hmm... The dark green one seems like the best.
M I agree. Why don't we go to a motor show to see the car soon?
W Sounds awesome!

남 Wendy, 너 Fast Motors에서 나온 신형 차에 대해 들었니?
여 응. 어제 출시되지 않았어?
남 맞아. 난 정말 그걸 직접 보고 싶어.
여 나도 마찬가지야. 그건 전기차라서 매우 효율적일 것이 틀림없어.
남 일리가 있어. 만약 네가 그걸 살 수 있다면, 어떤 색으로 하고 싶어?
여 흠... 암녹색 차가 가장 좋아 보여.
남 나도 동의해. 조만간 모터쇼에 차를 보러 가는 게 어때?
여 멋질 것 같아!

해설 | ① 제조사(Fast Motors), ② 출시일(어제), ④ 연료(전기), ⑤ 색상(암녹색)에 대해 언급했으므로 정답은 ③ '가격'이다.
어휘 | release [rilíːs] 동 출시하다, 발표하다 in person 직접 efficient [ifíʃənt] 형 효율적인; 유능한 agree [əgríː] 동 동의하다 awesome [ɔ́ːsəm] 형 멋진

10 주제 고르기

정답 ①

M Good evening, students. I'm your science teacher, Hojin Park. You should follow these rules in the lab for your safety. First, always follow my directions. Second, do not smell, taste, or touch the chemicals we use. Lastly, clean the experiment tables and tools after you are done. Wash your hands and arms with soap after removing your gloves.

남 안녕하십니까, 학생 여러분. 저는 여러분의 과학 선생님인 박호진입니다. 여러분은 안전을 위해 실험실의 다음 규칙들을 따라야 합니다. 먼저, 항상 제 지시를 따라주세요. 둘째로, 우리가 사용하는 화학 약품의 냄새를 맡거나, 맛을 보거나, 만지지 말아 주세요. 마지막으로, 모두 끝난 후에는 실험대와 도구를 청소해주세요. 장갑을 벗은 뒤에는 비누로 손과 팔을 씻어주세요.

해설 | 남자가 학생들에게 안전을 위해 실험실에서 따라야 할 규칙들을 설명하고 있으므로 정답은 ① '과학실 이용 수칙'이다.
어휘 | lab [læb] 명 실험실 directions [dirékʃənz] 명 지시 (direction [dirékʃən] 명 방향) chemical [kémikəl] 명 화학 약품, 화학 제품
remove [rimúːv] 동 벗다; 제거하다

11 일치하지 않는 내용 고르기

정답 ④

W Dad, can I go to the Mud Festival with my friends? It's held on August 22nd.
M Okay. Don't you need a ticket for it?
W Yes. But I can buy one online.
M How much does it cost? Is it expensive?
W No. It's only 10 dollars.
M Alright. What will you do there?
W I heard we'll be able to make pottery with clay.
M That sounds fun. Is there anything else to do?
W There will be a traditional music performance too.

여 아빠, 친구들과 Mud Festival에 가도 돼요? 8월 22일에 열려요.
남 그래. 표가 필요하지 않니?
여 필요해요. 그런데 온라인으로 살 수 있어요.
남 가격이 얼마니? 비싸니?
여 아니요. 겨우 10달러예요.
남 그렇구나. 거기에서 뭘 할 거니?
여 점토로 도자기를 만들 수 있다고 들었어요.
남 재미있을 것 같구나. 그 외에도 할 수 있는 것이 있니?
여 전통 음악 공연도 있을 거예요.

해설 | 여자가 축제에서 점토로 도자기를 만들 수 있다고 했으므로 정답은 ④ '진흙 성 쌓기 체험을 할 수 있다.'이다.
어휘 | pottery [pάtəri] 명 도자기 traditional [trədíʃənəl] 형 전통의 performance [pərfɔ́:rməns] 명 공연

12 목적 고르기

정답 ②

[Telephone rings.]
W You've reached Star Hair Salon.
M Hi. I need a haircut. How much would that cost?
W The price would be 35 dollars in total.
M That's a little more expensive than I expected.
W We offer a 5% discount for first-time customers. Would you like to make an appointment?
M Hmm... I need to think about it.
W Sure. We are open until 9 p.m., so you can call us before then.
M Thanks.

[전화기가 울린다.]
여 Star Hair Salon입니다.
남 안녕하세요. 제가 이발을 해야 하는데요. 얼마가 들까요?
여 가격은 총 35달러일 겁니다.
남 제가 예상했던 것보다 약간 더 비싸네요.
여 첫 방문 고객님들에게는 5% 할인을 제공하고 있어요. 예약하시겠어요?
남 흠... 생각을 해봐야겠어요.
여 그럼요. 오후 9시까지는 열려 있으니 그 전에 전화 주시면 돼요.
남 감사합니다.

해설 | 남자가 이발하는 데 비용이 얼마가 드는지 물었으므로 정답은 ② '가격을 확인하기 위해서'이다.
어휘 | customer [kʌ́stəmər] 명 고객, 손님 appointment [əpɔ́:intmənt] 명 예약, 약속; 임명

13 금액 정보 고르기

정답 ④

M Hello, welcome to Moon Sandwich. May I take your order?
W Yes, please. I'd like one regular sandwich and one sparkling water.
M Which meat do you want in your sandwich, beef or pork?
W I'll have beef. How much is it?
M The sandwich is 15 dollars and the drink is 6 dollars, so they are 21 dollars in total.
W Here's 25 dollars.
M Here's your change. Your sandwich and drink will be ready in a minute.
W Alright. Thank you.

남 안녕하세요, Moon Sandwich에 오신 걸 환영합니다. 주문하시겠어요?
여 네. 일반 샌드위치 하나와 탄산수 하나 주세요.
남 샌드위치에 소고기와 돼지고기 중 어떤 고기를 원하시나요?
여 소고기로 주세요. 얼마인가요?
남 샌드위치는 15달러고 음료는 6달러이니, 총 21달러입니다.
여 여기 25달러가 있어요.
남 여기 잔돈이 있습니다. 샌드위치와 음료는 금방 준비될 겁니다.
여 알겠습니다. 감사합니다.

해설 | 남자가 총 21달러라고 하자 여자가 25달러를 냈으므로 정답은 ④ '$ 4'이다.
어휘 | sparkling water 탄산수 pork [pɔ:rk] 명 돼지고기 in a minute 금방

14 관계 고르기

정답 ④

M	Hi. I need some new food for my dog.	남	안녕하세요. 저희 개를 위한 새 사료가 좀 필요해요.
W	This section has all our dog food. How big is your dog?	여	개 사료는 전부 이 구역에 있어요. 개가 얼마나 큰가요?
M	She's very small. She weighs about five kilograms.	남	매우 작아요. 5킬로그램 정도 나가요.
W	Alright. I recommend this one for small dogs.	여	알겠습니다. 이 소형견용 사료를 추천해 드릴게요.
M	Great. I'll take it. I'm also looking for some toys.	남	좋아요. 그걸로 살게요. 장난감도 좀 찾고 있는데요.
W	You can find toys in the next section.	여	장난감은 옆 구역에서 보실 수 있어요.
M	Thank you for your help.	남	도와주셔서 감사합니다.

해설 | 남자가 사료가 필요하다고 하자 여자가 사료가 있는 구역을 안내해주고 있는 것으로 보아 정답은 ④ '동물용품점 직원 — 손님'이다.

어휘 | weigh [wei] 동 (무게가) 나가다

15 부탁·요청한 일 고르기

정답 ②

W	Woosik, how was your trip to San Francisco?	여	우식아, 샌프란시스코 여행은 어땠어?
M	I had a great time.	남	정말 좋은 시간을 보냈어.
W	What did you do there?	여	거기서 뭐 했어?
M	I visited the Golden Gate Bridge, and I took many photos.	남	난 금문교를 방문했는데, 사진을 많이 찍었어.
W	Can I see them?	여	그것들을 볼 수 있을까?
M	Sure. Here's the album.	남	물론이지. 앨범 여기 있어.
W	Oh, wow. Could you send me this photo?	여	오, 우와. 이 사진 나한테 보내줄 수 있어?
M	Of course. What are you going to do with it?	남	당연하지. 그걸로 뭘 하려고?
W	I want to set this as my phone's wall paper.	여	내 휴대폰 배경 화면으로 설정해놓고 싶어.

해설 | 여자가 남자에게 여행 사진을 보내달라고 부탁했으므로 정답은 ② '사진 보내주기'이다.

어휘 | set [set] 동 설정하다; 놓다, 두다 wall paper 배경 화면; 벽지

16 이유 고르기

정답 ⑤

M	Ashley, didn't you say that you're going to a concert today?	남	Ashley, 오늘 콘서트에 간다고 하지 않았니?
W	Yeah. But something came up, and now I can't go.	여	맞아. 그런데 일이 생겨서 못 가게 됐어.
M	What happened?	남	무슨 일인데?
W	I have to attend a club meeting this afternoon.	여	오늘 오후에 동아리 모임에 참석해야 하거든.
M	Can't you miss it?	남	그거 빠질 수 없어?
W	No, I can't. I'm the president of the club, and we have to discuss important things today.	여	응, 못해. 내가 동아리 회장인데다가, 오늘 중요한 것들을 논의해야 해.
M	Then, can I go to the concert instead? The tickets are sold out now.	남	그러면, 내가 대신 콘서트 가도 될까? 표가 이제 매진됐거든.
W	Sure. I'll give you the ticket.	여	물론이지. 네게 표를 줄게.

해설 | 여자가 빠질 수 없는 동아리 모임에 참석해야 해서 콘서트에 갈 수 없게 됐다고 했으므로 정답은 ⑤ '동아리 모임이 있어서'이다.

어휘 | attend [əténd] 동 참석하다 discuss [diskʌ́s] 동 논의하다 sold out 매진된

17 그림 상황에 적절한 대화 고르기

정답 ④

① M Did you get my text message?
W No. My phone ran out of battery.
② M Are we on the right street?
W Yes. We just need to turn right here.
③ M Why are you so sad, Anna?
W I got a bad grade on my math test.
④ M Oh, no. We just missed the bus.
W It's okay. I'll call a taxi for us.
⑤ M Do you need anything from the convenience store?
W I would love a bag of chips, please.

① 남 내 문자 메시지 받았니?
여 아니. 휴대폰 배터리가 다 됐어.
② 남 우리 맞는 길에 있는 거니?
여 응. 여기서 우회전만 하면 돼.
③ 남 왜 그렇게 슬퍼하는 거야, Anna?
여 수학 시험에서 안 좋은 성적을 받았어.
④ 남 오, 이런. 우리 막 버스를 놓쳤어.
여 괜찮아. 내가 택시를 부를게.
⑤ 남 편의점에서 뭐 필요한 거 있어?
여 감자 칩 한 봉지 부탁할게.

해설 | 놓친 버스를 보고 남자는 곤혹스러워하고 있고 여자가 택시를 부르겠다고 하는 상황이므로 정답은 ④이다.

어휘 | run out of 다 되다, ~을 다 써버리다 grade [greid] 명 성적; 등급 miss [mis] 동 놓치다 convenience store 편의점

18 언급하지 않은 내용 고르기

정답 ④

W Good morning, I'm Molly Ashwood. I'll be your guide to a full-day bus trip on the San Marino City Tour. We'll be leaving in five minutes, at 8:30. Our tour begins with a visit to the San Marino City Museum. Lunch will be provided at 12:30 at a local restaurant near the Marino Beach Park. Then, we'll travel to popular spots in the city. Please watch your belongings carefully during the trip.

여 좋은 아침입니다, 저는 Molly Ashwood입니다. 제가 여러분의 San Marino City Tour의 일일 버스 여행 안내원이 될 것입니다. 저희는 5분 후인 8시 30분에 출발할 예정입니다. 저희 투어는 산마리노 시립 박물관을 방문하는 것으로 시작합니다. 점심은 12시 30분에 마리노 해변 공원 근처의 지역 식당에서 제공될 것입니다. 그리고서 저희는 도시의 관광 명소들을 여행할 것입니다. 여행 동안 소지품을 잘 확인해주십시오.

해설 | ① 가이드 이름(Molly Ashwood), ② 시작 시간(8시 30분), ③ 교통편(버스), ⑤ 방문 예정지(산마리노 시립 박물관, 마리노 해변 공원 근처의 식당, 도시의 관광 명소들)에 대해 언급했으므로 정답은 ④ '투어 비용'이다.

어휘 | provide [prəváid] 동 제공하다 local [lóukəl] 형 지역의 popular spot 관광 명소, 인기 장소 belonging [bilɔ́:ŋiŋ] 명 소지품

19 적절한 응답 고르기

정답 ①

M Can I volunteer at the hospital, Mom?
W Sure, Dongwon. When will you volunteer there?
M I'll go every Saturday. I start this weekend.
W That sounds good. Do you want me to drive you to the hospital?
M No, thank you. I can take the bus with my friend.
W Oh, okay. Who will volunteer with you?
M Chanwoo is going with me.

남 병원에서 자원봉사를 해도 될까요, 엄마?
여 물론이지, 동원아. 거기서 언제 자원봉사를 할 거니?
남 토요일마다 갈 거예요. 이번 주말에 시작해요.
여 좋구나. 내가 병원까지 데려다줄까?
남 아니요, 괜찮아요. 친구와 버스를 타고 가면 돼요.
여 오, 그렇구나. 누가 함께 자원봉사를 할 거니?
남 찬우가 저랑 갈 거예요.

해설 | 여자가 남자에게 누구와 함께 자원봉사를 할 것인지 묻고 있으므로 정답은 함께 갈 사람을 언급하는 ① 'Chanwoo is going with me.'이다.

선택지 해석

① 찬우가 저랑 갈 거예요. ② 네. 내일 시작해요. ③ 선생님과 함께 방문했어요. ④ 환자들이 도움이 필요해요. ⑤ 거기는 아동 병원이에요.

어휘 | volunteer [vὰləntíər] 동 자원봉사 하다 명 지원자 patient [péiʃənt] 명 환자

20 적절한 응답 고르기

정답 ⑤

M Hi, Ms. Kimmel. Do you have a minute? I have a question about the English homework.
W Do you mean the homework due next Monday?
M Yes. I was sick for a couple days, so I need more time to work on it.
W That's fine. When can you have it done?
M Is Wednesday okay?

남 안녕하세요, Kimmel 선생님. 잠깐 시간 있으세요? 영어 숙제에 대해서 질문이 있어요.
여 다음 주 월요일 예정인 숙제를 말하는 거니?
남 네. 제가 며칠 동안 아파서 숙제를 할 시간이 좀 더 필요해요.
여 그래도 괜찮단다. 언제까지 할 수 있겠니?
남 수요일은 괜찮을까요?

해설 | 여자가 언제까지 숙제를 할 수 있을지 묻고 있으므로 정답은 가능한 요일을 언급하는 ⑤ 'Is Wednesday okay?'이다.

선택지 해석

① 몸이 안 좋아요. ② 숙제를 검토해봐. ③ 집중을 못 하겠어요. ④ 마감일이 지났어. ⑤ 수요일은 괜찮을까요?

어휘 | due [djuː] 형 예정인 deadline [dèdlaín] 명 마감일

24회 고난도 모의고사

| 문제 pp.212-213

1	①	2	⑤	3	②	4	③	5	②	6	④	7	④	8	②	9	④	10	⑤
11	⑤	12	②	13	③	14	⑤	15	①	16	④	17	②	18	④	19	①	20	①

1 날씨 고르기

정답 ①

W Good evening. This is the Friday night weather report. We're getting a few raindrops right now. The rain will continue all night, and it'll start pouring in the morning. Thunderstorms are expected tomorrow evening, so stay indoors and pay attention to the news alerts. You won't be seeing clear skies during the weekend, and it will likely be a humid summer.

여 안녕하십니까. 금요일 밤 일기예보입니다. 현재 빗방울이 약간씩 떨어지고 있습니다. 밤새 비가 이어질 예정이며, 아침부터는 퍼붓기 시작하겠습니다. 내일 저녁에는 뇌우가 예상되니 실내에 머무르며 뉴스 경보에 주의를 기울이시기 바랍니다. 주말 동안에는 맑은 하늘이 보이지 않겠고, 습한 여름이 될 것 같습니다.

해설 | 금요일 밤 일기예보라고 한 후에 내일 저녁에는 뇌우가 예상된다고 했으므로 정답은 ①이다.

어휘 | raindrop [réindràp] 명 빗방울 pour [pɔ́ːr] 동 퍼붓다; 붓다 indoors [indɔ́ːrz] 부 실내에서 alert [əlɔ́ːrt] 명 경보, 경계 humid [hjúːmid] 형 습한

2 알맞은 그림 고르기

정답 ⑤

M Honey, what are we getting our son for Christmas?
W I was thinking about buying a new bicycle.
M What's wrong with the one he has?
W It has three wheels. He is too old for that.
M Right. The old bike has a basket in the front. Will he need one for the new one too?
W I don't think he will need it. But we should install a bell on the handle.
M That's a good idea. Let's order it online.

남 여보, 크리스마스에 우리 아들에게 뭘 줄까?
여 새 자전거를 사줄까 생각 중이었어.
남 그가 가지고 있는 것에 무슨 문제가 있어?
여 그건 바퀴가 세 개야. 그는 그것을 타기엔 너무 컸어.
남 그렇군. 그 오래된 자전거는 앞에 바구니가 있어. 새것에도 하나가 필요할까?
여 필요 없을 것 같아. 하지만 우린 손잡이에 종을 설치해야 해.
남 좋은 생각이야. 인터넷으로 주문하자.

해설 | 여자는 바퀴가 세 개인 것을 타기에는 아들이 너무 컸다고 한 후, 바구니는 필요하지 않지만 손잡이에 종을 설치해야 한다고 했으므로 정답은 ⑤이다.

어휘 | wheel [hwiːl] 명 바퀴 install [instɔ́ːl] 동 설치하다 order [ɔ́ːrdər] 명 주문하다

3 의도 고르기

정답 ②

[Cellphone rings.]
M Hey, Kate. Where are you?
W I'm almost there!
M How long will it take? We'll be late for the movie.
W About 30 minutes?
M Excuse me?
W I'm so sorry, Jack. I had a lot to take care of.
M You promised to be on time. And if you are on your way, why is it so quiet?
W Uh... I haven't left my apartment yet.
M Oh, Kate... You are late every time!

[휴대폰이 울린다.]
남 안녕, Kate. 어디 있어?
여 거의 다 왔어!
남 얼마나 걸려? 우리 영화 시간에 늦겠어.
여 30분 정도?
남 뭐라고?
여 정말 미안해, Jack. 해야 할 일이 많았어.
남 너 시간을 잘 지키기로 약속했잖아. 그리고 만약 오고 있다면, 왜 이렇게 조용한 거야?
여 어... 나 아직 아파트를 나가지 않았어.
남 오, Kate... 넌 매번 늦잖아!

해설 | 약속에 늦은 여자가 아직 아파트를 나가지 않았다는 이야기를 하자, 남자는 여자가 매번 늦었다고 말했으므로 정답은 ② '비난'이다.

어휘 | be on time 시간을 잘 지키다 leave [liːv] 동 나가다; 떠나다

4 한 일 고르기

정답 ③

M Hi, Jiyoon. Did you have fun at the beach yesterday?
W Yeah. The weather was warm and sunny. And the waves were perfect for surfing.
M I'm so jealous. I wanted to go with you.
W How did you do on your test today?
M Well, I did my best.
W Are you expecting a good result?
M I missed going surfing to study for the exam, so I hope I get a perfect score.

남 안녕, 지윤아. 어제 해변에서 재미있게 놀았니?
여 응. 날씨가 따뜻하고 화창했어. 그리고 파도는 서핑하기에 완벽했어.
남 너무 부럽다. 나도 너와 함께 가고 싶었어.
여 오늘 시험은 어떻게 봤어?
남 음, 나는 최선을 다했어.
여 좋은 결과를 기대하고 있니?
남 시험공부를 위해 서핑하러 가지 못했으니, 만점을 받았으면 좋겠어.

해설 | 남자가 어제 해변에서 재미있게 놀았는지 물은 후에 시험공부를 위해 서핑하러 가지 못했다고 했으므로 정답은 ③ '공부하기'이다.

어휘 | wave [weiv] 명 파도 jealous [dʒéləs] 형 부러워하는; 질투하는 result [rizʌ́lt] 명 결과

5 장소 고르기

정답 ②

W Can we take a break? I need some water.
M Of course. We'll record again in 10 minutes.
W How did my voice sound? Was the song okay?
M You sounded good, but you should sing more slowly.
W So you think it was too fast?
M It was a little fast. But overall, the song sounds great.

여 잠시 쉬어도 될까요? 물을 좀 마셔야겠어요.
남 물론이죠. 10분 후에 다시 녹음하겠습니다.
여 제 목소리는 어떻게 들렸나요? 노래는 괜찮았어요?
남 좋았는데, 좀 더 천천히 불러야 해요.
여 그래서, 너무 빨랐다고 생각하세요?
남 아주 조금 빨랐어요. 그렇지만 전반적으로, 노래는 너무 좋아요.

해설 | 10분 후에 다시 녹음을 하겠다는 말을 하는 것으로 보아 정답은 ② '녹음실'이다.

어휘 | take a break 잠시 쉬다, 휴식을 취하다 record [rikɔ́ːrd] 동 녹음하다 overall [óuvərɔ̀ːl] 부 전반적으로

6 일치하지 않는 내용 고르기

정답 ④

M That's a wonderful painting, Vicky.
W I know, right?
M The people in the painting look really interesting.
W Yeah. This is my favorite painting from the 1930s.
M Whose painting is it?
W Pablo Picasso painted it.
M I see. Do you know the name of the painting?
W It's *Guernica*. Picasso painted it to show the world the tragedy of war.
M Oh, that's why he only used dark colors.
W That's right.

남 정말 멋진 그림이야, Vicky.
여 맞아, 그렇지?
남 그림에 있는 사람들이 정말 흥미롭게 생겼어.
여 응. 이건 내가 가장 좋아하는 1930년대의 그림이야.
남 누구의 그림이니?
여 파블로 피카소가 그렸어.
남 그렇구나. 그림의 제목을 아니?
여 이건 <게르니카>야. 피카소는 세상에 전쟁의 비극을 보여주기 위해 이것을 그렸어.
남 오, 그래서 그가 어두운색들만 사용했구나.
여 맞아.

해설 | 여자가 피카소는 세상에 전쟁의 비극을 보여주기 위해 이것을 그렸다고 했으므로 정답은 ④ '평화를 상징하고 있다.'이다.

어휘 | tragedy [trǽdʒədi] 명 비극

7 특정 정보 고르기

정답 ④

W Did you find any clothes that you liked?
M I think so. I tried on a few things.
W Do you want to buy that green sweater? I loved the color.
M It was nice, but it was too fancy.
W You're so picky!
M Maybe. But I found two shirts I want to get. A gray one and a blue one.
W Are you going to get them?
M Yes. Did you buy something?
W I just picked up some socks.

여 마음에 드는 옷을 찾았니?
남 그런 것 같아. 몇 가지를 입어 봤어.
여 저 초록색 스웨터 사고 싶어? 나는 색이 너무 좋았어.
남 그건 괜찮은데, 너무 화려했어.
여 너 정말 까다롭구나!
남 아마도. 하지만 사고 싶은 셔츠 두 벌을 찾았어. 회색 하나와 파란색 하나야.
여 그것들 살 거니?
남 응. 너는 뭐 샀니?
여 나는 그냥 양말을 좀 샀어.

해설 | 남자는 사고 싶은 셔츠 두 벌을 찾았다고 했고, 여자가 살 건지 물어보자 그렇다고 했으므로 정답은 ④ '셔츠'이다.

어휘 | fancy [fǽnsi] 형 화려한, 장식이 많은 picky [píki] 형 까다로운

8 할 일 고르기

정답 ②

W May I help you, sir?
M Yes. I want to buy the new T Watch 3. It looked so cool on the TV advertisement.
W We have them over here.
M There are so many designs.
W You can also change the watch straps easily.
M Do you have the larger version? This one seems a bit small for my wrist.
W You can only order them now. We don't have any left in stock.
M Alright. How do I order it?
W Please fill this form with your information.

여 도와드릴까요, 손님?
남 네. 저는 새로운 T Watch 3을 사고 싶어요. TV 광고에서 너무 멋있어 보였어요.
여 그것들은 이쪽에 있습니다.
남 디자인이 정말 많네요.
여 시곗줄도 쉽게 바꿀 수 있습니다.
남 더 큰 버전이 있나요? 이건 제 손목에는 좀 작은 것 같아요.
여 지금은 주문만 가능합니다. 재고가 하나도 없어서요.
남 알겠습니다. 어떻게 주문하나요?
여 이 양식에 정보를 기재해 주세요.

해설 | 여자가 양식에 정보를 기재하라고 했으므로 정답은 ② '서류 작성하기'이다.

어휘 | advertisement [ædvərtáizmənt] 명 광고 wrist [rist] 명 손목 stock [stak] 명 재고

9 언급하지 않은 내용 고르기

정답 ④

[Telephone rings.]

W Hello. Beverly Grill.

M Hi, I'd like to make a reservation at your restaurant. It's for my son's birthday party.

W On what date?

M His birthday is November 3rd. Do you have a private room available?

W We do. How many guests will be coming?

M There will be 20 people.

W Okay. Anything else?

M And can I make a special request? Can you serve chocolate cake with candles for dessert?

W Sure. We can do that. I'll just need your name and phone number.

[전화기가 울린다.]

여 안녕하세요. Beverly Grill입니다.

남 안녕하세요, 식당에 예약을 하고 싶은데요. 제 아들 생일 파티를 위한 거예요.

여 며칠이죠?

남 그의 생일은 11월 3일이에요. 이용할 수 있는 개인실이 있나요?

여 있습니다. 손님이 몇 명이나 올 예정이신가요?

남 스무 명이요.

여 알겠습니다. 또 다른 건 없으신가요?

남 그리고 특별 요청을 드려도 될까요? 후식으로 초콜릿케이크와 초를 함께 제공해주실 수 있나요?

여 물론입니다. 그렇게 해 드릴 수 있어요. 성함과 전화번호만 알려주세요.

해설 | ① 예약 목적(아들 생일 파티), ② 이용 날짜(11월 3일), ③ 예약 인원 수(20명), ⑤ 특별 요청사항(초콜릿케이크와 초를 함께 제공)에 대해 언급했으므로 정답은 ④ '예약 시간'이다.

어휘 | private room 개인실 available [əvéiləbl] 형 이용 가능한 serve [səːrv] 동 제공하다; 복무하다

10 주제 고르기

정답 ⑤

M Hello, everyone. Today, let's talk about ways to save water at home. First, turn the water off when you brush your teeth. You don't need to run the water while you are brushing your teeth. Second, take showers quicker. You can save 12 liters of water by spending one minute less in the shower. Lastly, when you wash the dishes, fill up the sink with water first and do the dishes in it.

남 안녕하세요, 여러분. 오늘은 집에서 물을 절약하는 방법에 대해 이야기해 보겠습니다. 먼저, 이를 닦을 때는 물을 잠그세요. 여러분은 이를 닦는 동안 물을 흐르게 둘 필요가 없습니다. 두 번째로, 샤워를 더 빠르게 하세요. 여러분은 샤워를 1분 더 적게 함으로써 12리터의 물을 절약할 수 있습니다. 마지막으로, 설거지를 할 때는, 먼저 개수대를 물로 채우고 거기서 설거지하세요.

해설 | 남자가 집에서 물을 절약하는 방법을 말하고 있으므로 정답은 ⑤ '물 절약 방법'이다.

어휘 | brush one's teeth 이를 닦다 fill [fil] 동 채우다

11 일치하지 않는 내용 고르기

정답 ⑤

W Hey, Sam. What are you doing this weekend?

M I'm going to an amusement park in Seoul on Saturday.

W That sounds great! What will you do there?

M There are three big roller coasters and bumper cars. I'll ride all of them.

W It must be a big park. Will it be crowded?

M I think so, but I am going early. It opens at 9.

W That's a good idea. How much is the entrance fee?

M It's 40 dollars.

여 안녕, Sam. 이번 주말에 뭐 하니?

남 나는 토요일에 서울에 있는 놀이공원에 갈 거야.

여 좋겠다! 거기에서 뭐 할 거야?

남 거기엔 대형 롤러코스터 세 개와 범퍼카가 있어. 난 그것들을 모두 다 탈 거야.

여 큰 놀이공원이겠구나. 사람들로 붐빌까?

남 그럴 것 같지만 난 일찍 갈 거야. 9시에 개장하거든.

여 그거 좋은 생각이다. 입장료는 얼마니?

남 40달러야.

해설 | 여자가 입장료가 얼마인지 묻자 남자가 40달러라고 했으므로 정답은 ⑤ '입장료가 14달러이다.'이다.

어휘 | amusement park 놀이공원 crowded [kráudid] 형 (사람들로) 붐비는 entrance fee 입장료

12 목적 고르기

정답 ②

W Brian, what are you doing here?
M Oh, hi Tina. I just finished taking my violin lesson. Are you signing up for a lesson at this academy?
W Actually, I'm here to meet my sister. We are going shopping together after her lesson.
M Your sister goes here? She might be in the same class.
W She's in the beginner class. She just started last month. Oh, there she is.
M Well, it was nice to see you!

여 Brian, 여기서 뭐 해?
남 오, 안녕 Tina. 나는 막 바이올린 수업을 마쳤어. 이 학원 수업을 신청할 거니?
여 사실, 나는 여기에 여동생을 만나러 왔어. 그녀의 수업이 끝난 후에 함께 쇼핑을 갈 거거든.
남 여동생이 여기 다녀? 같은 반일 수도 있겠다.
여 그녀는 초급반에 있어. 그녀는 지난달에 막 시작했어. 오, 여동생이 저기 있다.
남 음, 만나서 반가웠어!

해설 | 여자가 여동생을 만나러 왔다고 했으므로 정답은 ② '여동생을 만나기 위해서'이다.
어휘 | sign up for ~을 신청하다

13 시간 정보 고르기

정답 ③

W Jerry, are you going to the library today? It's 2 o'clock now.
M Yes, Mom. I promised to meet Jason at 2:30.
W You should hurry then. He doesn't like to wait.
M I know. Can you pick me up later?
W Well, how long will you be there?
M We just need to review for a quiz. I'll be done studying in an hour.
W Okay. I'll come get you.

여 Jerry, 너 오늘 도서관에 가니? 지금 2시야.
남 네, 엄마. Jason과 2시 30분에 만나기로 약속했어요.
여 그럼 서둘러야겠다. 그는 기다리는 걸 싫어하잖니.
남 맞아요. 이따가 데리러 오실 수 있어요?
여 글쎄, 거기에 얼마나 오래 있을 거니?
남 시험을 위해 복습만 하면 돼요. 한 시간 후면 끝날 거예요.
여 좋아. 그때 데리러 갈게.

해설 | 남자가 Jason과 2시 30분에 만나기로 약속했다고 한 후, 한 시간 후면 끝날 거라고 했으므로 정답은 ③ '3:30 p.m.'이다.
어휘 | hurry [hə́:ri] 동 서두르다 review [rivjú:] 동 복습하다 명 평가

14 관계 고르기

정답 ⑤

M Can I help you?
W I'd like to buy one ticket from New York to Seoul.
M When are you flying out?
W On September 1st, and I'll return on September 13th.
M Would you like economy or business class?
W Economy. Oh, can I bring two suitcases?
M Yes. An extra fee will be charged for more than two bags.
W Alright.
M Let me check the available flights.

남 도와드릴까요?
여 뉴욕에서 서울까지 가는 표를 한 장 사고 싶은데요.
남 언제 출국하시나요?
여 9월 1일이고, 9월 13일에 돌아올 거예요.
남 이코노미석과 비즈니스석 중 무엇으로 하시겠습니까?
여 이코노미요. 오, 여행 가방을 두 개 가져갈 수 있나요?
남 네. 두 개 이상의 가방에는 추가 요금이 부가됩니다.
여 알겠습니다.
남 가능한 항공편을 확인해 보겠습니다.

해설 | 여자가 남자에게 뉴욕에서 서울까지 가는 비행기 표를 사고 있는 것으로 보아 정답은 ⑤ '항공사 직원 — 승객'이다.
어휘 | fee [fi:] 명 요금

15 부탁·요청한 일 고르기

정답 ①

M Irene, is this the video that you shot yesterday?
W Yeah. I still need to edit it.
M Can I help you with anything?
W You know how to upload a video, right?
M Sure. I can do that.
W Will you post video number 32 on the blog?
M Okay. *[Pause]* I got it. I uploaded video 33.
W Oh, no! I'm not done editing that one yet!

남 Irene, 이게 네가 어제 찍은 비디오니?
여 응. 아직 편집해야 돼.
남 뭐 좀 도와줄까?
여 영상 올리는 법은 알지, 그렇지?
남 물론이지. 그건 할 수 있어.
여 32번 영상을 블로그에 올려줄래?
남 그래. *[잠시 멈춤]* 알겠어. 33번 영상 올렸어.
여 오, 이런! 그건 아직 편집을 끝내지 않았어!

해설 | 여자가 남자에게 32번 동영상을 블로그에 올려달라고 부탁했으므로 정답은 ① '영상 올리기'이다.

어휘 | shoot [ʃuːt] 동 찍다; 쏘다 still [stil] 부 아직 edit [édit] 동 편집하다 post [poust] 동 (웹사이트에 정보·사진을) 올리다

16 이유 고르기

정답 ④

W I heard you are quitting the soccer team, Jared.
M Yeah. Tomorrow is my last day on the team.
W Is it because you fought with your teammate, Mason?
M No. That's not a problem anymore. We're good friends again.
W Then, why are you quitting the team?
M I decided to join the school newspaper this year.
W Really? Why can't you do both of them?
M Well, I want to focus on writing articles.

여 네가 축구팀을 그만둔다고 들었어, Jared.
남 응. 내일이 팀에서의 마지막 날이야.
여 팀 동료인 Mason과 싸워서 그런 거야?
남 아니. 그건 더 이상 문제가 아니야. 우리는 다시 좋은 친구가 되었거든.
여 그럼 왜 팀을 그만두는 거야?
남 올해 학교 신문사에 들어가기로 결정했거든.
여 정말? 왜 둘 다 하면 안 돼?
남 음, 기사를 쓰는 데 집중하고 싶거든.

해설 | 남자는 올해 학교 신문사에 들어가기로 결정했다고 말했으므로 정답은 ④ '다른 동아리에 가입하려고'이다.

어휘 | quit [kwit] 동 그만두다 decide [disáid] 동 결정하다 focus on 집중하다 article [áːrtikl] 명 기사

17 그림 상황에 적절한 대화 고르기

정답 ②

① M Can you recommend a restaurant?
W There's a great one on Main Street.
② M Excuse me. Are these your glasses?
W Oh, thank you. I guess I left them at our table.
③ M Should we clean the house today?
W Yes. Let's take the dog for a walk first.
④ M The neighbors invited us over for dinner tomorrow.
W That's nice. We should bring some dessert.
⑤ M Can you tell me where the swimming pool is?
W It's on the roof of the hotel.

① 남 식당을 추천해 줄 수 있니?
여 메인 가에 좋은 곳이 하나 있어.
② 남 실례합니다. 이것은 손님 안경인가요?
여 오, 고마워요. 우리 테이블에 두고 왔었나 보네요.
③ 남 우리 오늘 집 청소를 해야 할까?
여 응. 먼저 개를 산책시키자.
④ 남 이웃들이 내일 저녁 식사에 우리를 초대했어.
여 친절하다. 우리는 디저트를 좀 가져가야겠다.
⑤ 남 수영장이 어디에 있는지 알려줄 수 있나요?
여 호텔 옥상에 있습니다.

해설 | 남자가 여자의 안경인지를 묻고 있고, 여자가 테이블에 두고 왔던 것 같다고 하는 상황이므로 정답은 ②이다.

어휘 | neighbor [néibər] 명 이웃

18 언급하지 않은 내용 고르기

정답 ④

W Welcome to Pasadena Art Theater. I'd like to tell you about our newest play, *The Family Tree*. Some great actors will star in the play, and it will be held in the Grand Hall. Shows will begin on Friday, March 29th. Tickets will go on sale next week. You can get the ticket on our website. We would love to see you there!

여 패서디나 예술 극장에 오신 걸 환영합니다. 여러분에게 저희의 가장 최신 연극 <The Family Tree>에 대해 말씀드리고 싶습니다. 몇몇 훌륭한 배우들이 연극의 주연을 맡을 예정이며, 그랜드홀에서 상연될 것입니다. 공연은 3월 29일 금요일부터 시작됩니다. 표는 다음 주부터 판매될 예정입니다. 표는 저희 웹사이트에서 구매하실 수 있습니다. 극장에서 뵙기를 바랍니다!

해설 | ① 장소(패서디나 예술 극장의 그랜드홀), ② 제목(<The Family Tree>), ③ 시작 날짜(3월 29일 금요일), ⑤ 예매 방법(극장의 웹사이트에서 구매)에 대해 언급했으므로 정답은 ④ '공연 시간'이다.

어휘 | star [sta:r] 동 주연을 맡다

19 적절한 응답 고르기

정답 ①

W Brian, you look very sad. What's the problem?
M I didn't get a role in the school musical.
W Cheer up! You can audition for the next one.
M Yes. But I have to wait a while for the next musical.
W Well, you can audition for the school choir instead.
M What types of singers does the choir need?
W Basses and boy sopranos.

여 Brian, 너 매우 슬퍼 보여. 뭐가 문제니?
남 학교 뮤지컬에서 배역을 맡지 못했어.
여 힘내! 다음 오디션을 보면 돼.
남 맞아. 하지만 다음 뮤지컬은 한동안 기다려야 해.
여 음, 대신 학교 합창단의 오디션을 볼 수 있잖아.
남 합창단에는 어떤 유형의 가수가 필요하니?
여 베이스와 소년 소프라노야.

해설 | 남자가 합창단에는 어떤 유형의 가수가 필요한지 묻고 있으므로 정답은 필요한 유형의 가수를 알려주는 ① 'Basses and boy sopranos.'이다.

선택지 해석

① 베이스와 소년 소프라노야. ② 이 노래는 아름다워. ③ 너는 오디션에 지원해야 해. ④ 새 감독이 선출되었어. ⑤ 너 연습 많이 했구나.

어휘 | role [roul] 명 배역; 역할 Cheer up! 힘내! choir [kwaiər] 명 합창단 director [diréktər] 명 감독

20 적절한 응답 고르기

정답 ①

W Michael, you look upset. Are you okay?
M Not really. I got into a fight with Chris.
W What happened between you two?
M I made a joke, and it hurt his feelings. But I didn't mean to be rude.
W Well, in my opinion, you should apologize to him.
M You're right. Thanks for the advice.
W That's what friends are for.

여 Michael, 기분이 언짢아 보이네. 괜찮아?
남 아니, 별로. Chris와 다퉜어.
여 둘 사이에 무슨 일이 있었던 거야?
남 내가 농담을 했는데, 그의 기분을 상하게 했어. 하지만 무례하게 굴 생각은 없었어.
여 음, 내 생각에는, 네가 그에게 사과해야 할 것 같아.
남 네 말이 맞아. 조언해줘서 고마워.
여 친구 좋다는 게 뭐야.

해설 | 남자가 여자에게 조언해줘서 고맙다는 말을 하고 있으므로 정답은 고마움에 답하는 ① 'That's what friends are for.'이다.

선택지 해석

① 친구 좋다는 게 뭐야. ② 제발 용서해줘. ③ 그건 사실이 아니야. ④ 그들은 그것에 대해 아까 이야기했어. ⑤ 그녀는 내 말을 오해했어.

어휘 | get into a fight 싸우다 feeling [fí:liŋ] 명 기분 rude [ru:d] 형 무례한 in one's opinion ~의 의견으로는 apologize [əpálədʒàiz] 동 사과하다

MEMO

영어듣기 만점을 위한 완벽한 실전 대비서

해커스 중학영어듣기 모의고사 24회

| 해커스 중고등 교재 MAP | 나에게 맞는 교재 선택!

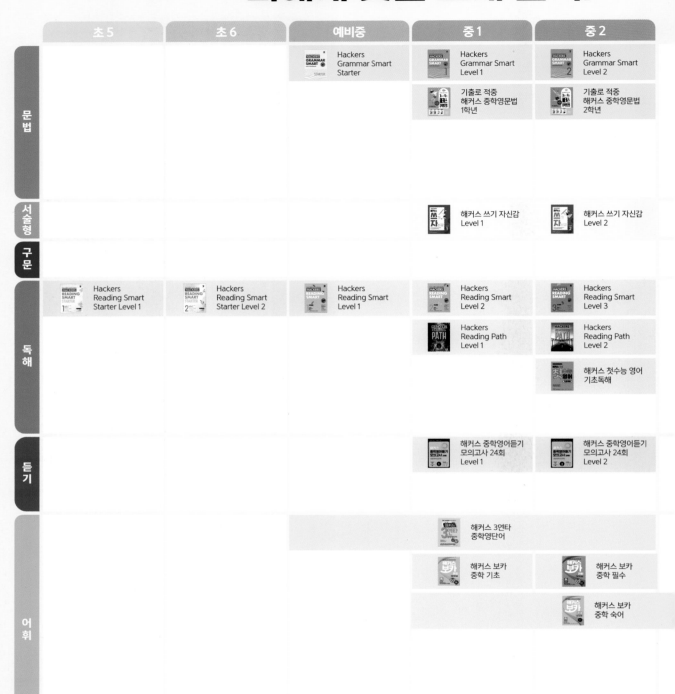

	초 5	초 6	예비중	중 1	중 2
문법			Hackers Grammar Smart Starter	Hackers Grammar Smart Level 1	Hackers Grammar Smart Level 2
문법				기출로 적중 해커스 중학영문법 1학년	기출로 적중 해커스 중학영문법 2학년
서술형				해커스 쓰기 자신감 Level 1	해커스 쓰기 자신감 Level 2
구문					
독해	Hackers Reading Smart Starter Level 1	Hackers Reading Smart Starter Level 2	Hackers Reading Smart Level 1	Hackers Reading Smart Level 2	Hackers Reading Smart Level 3
독해				Hackers Reading Path Level 1	Hackers Reading Path Level 2
독해					해커스 첫수능 영어 기초독해
듣기				해커스 중학영어듣기 모의고사 24회 Level 1	해커스 중학영어듣기 모의고사 24회 Level 2
어휘			해커스 3연타 중학영단어 (예비중~중 2)		
어휘				해커스 보카 중학 기초	해커스 보카 중학 필수
어휘				해커스 보카 중학 숙어 (중 1~중 2)	

토플

READING	LISTENING	VOCA
HACKERS APEX READING for the TOEFL iBT Basic/Intermediate/Advanced/Expert	HACKERS APEX LISTENING for the TOEFL iBT Basic/Intermediate/Advanced/Expert	HACKERS APEX VOCA for the TOEFL iBT HACKERS VOCABULARY